This publication is an essential navigation tool and practical application guide for construction lawyers, consultants, employers and contractors. Dr Donald Charrett as editor and his impressive team of expert contributors commendably achieved the aim of expertly identifying and lucidly explaining and illustrating the applicable laws that may impact on the operation of FIDIC contracts in Africa and the Middle East, the execution of the works and the determination of disputes arising therefrom.

Tjaart van der Walt, *Senior Counsel of the Maisels Group of Advocates in Sandton, FCIArb, FAArb, Construction ADR Practitioner and Vice-chair of the Association of Arbitrators (Southern Africa)*

The management of a construction contract is the management of risk. This book is essential reading for any contractor or consultant wanting to work or working in the African or Middle East regions, to understand the commercial and legal risks that might be encountered, finding some appropriate risk responses and where additional information can be sourced.

Ian Massey, *CEng, FICE, MSAICE, Director MDA Consulting (Pty) Ltd, FIDIC Presidents List Adjudicator*

This is another valuable book in the series that FIDIC users in the international community must have at hand. The introduction chapter at the start of this book helpfully covers some of the most pertinent, current issues such as key construction law principles, lex constructionis and COVID-19-related matters. The practical insight in this book gives readers a penetrative understanding of international construction contracts in our modern world, and good guidance on the effective use of FIDIC contracts.

Yvonne Foo, *Partner, Harry Elias Partnership*

A crucial compendium written by some of the most knowledgeable FIDIC practitioners. Practical and focused on regions that are often undeservedly overlooked, this book is a game-changer and sure to become an indispensable resource for anyone who aspires to excel in contract administration and legal aspects of the construction sector.

Aarta Alkarimi, *FCIArb, Founding Partner, Chrysalis LLP*

An important book that is sure to be welcomed by construction practitioners in Africa and the Middle East which superbly addresses important aspects of local law in the context of the FIDIC suite of contracts and in which the expertise of the chapter authors and editor shines through. Recommended!

Adrian Cole, *FZ LLE, Independent Arbitrator and Mediator*

FIDIC CONTRACTS IN AFRICA AND THE MIDDLE EAST

FIDIC contracts are the most widely used contracts for international construction around the world and are used in many different jurisdictions, both common law and civil law. For any construction project, the General Conditions of Contract published by FIDIC need to be supplemented by Particular Conditions that specify the specific requirements of that project.

FIDIC Contracts in Africa and the Middle East: A Practical Guide to Application provides readers with detailed guidance and resources for the preparation of the Particular Conditions that will comply with the requirements of the laws that apply to the site where the work is carried out, and for the governing law of the contract, for a number of the jurisdictions in which FIDIC contracts are or can be used. This book closely follows the format of *The International Application of FIDIC Contracts*. Each jurisdiction features an outline of its construction industry and information on the impact of COVID-19 on both the execution and operation of construction contracts.

This book is essential reading for construction professionals, lawyers and students of construction law.

Dr Donald Charrett is a barrister, arbitrator, mediator, expert and dispute board member practising in technology, engineering and construction (TEC) disputes. He is a member of the FIDIC President's List of Adjudicators and a Fellow of the Chartered Institute of Arbitrators. He was named Best Construction Law Practitioner, Australia 2016 by *Business Worldwide Magazine*. His legal publications include articles on expert evidence, FIDIC contracts, dispute boards, dispute avoidance and resolution, contract risk, forensic engineering, contractual lessons from past projects, design and construct contracts, quantum meruit and solidary liability.

PRACTICAL LEGAL GUIDES FOR CONSTRUCTION AND TECHNOLOGY PROJECTS

Series Editor: Donald Charrett

The books in this series provide lawyers and construction professionals with the relevant knowledge, resources and practical guidance to understand the contemporary construction industry and the law necessary to achieve successful outcomes for construction projects. The topics covered include front-end issues such as project procurement, the production, negotiation and administration of contracts, and the avoidance of disputes, as well as backend issues such as taking part in, managing or resolving disputes. The series aims to keep abreast of the technologies that have increasing impact in changing traditional ways of working, contracting and resolving disputes.

FIDIC CONTRACTS IN ASIA PACIFIC
A Practical Guide to Application
Donald Charrett

CONTRACTS FOR CONSTRUCTION AND ENGINEERING PROJECTS
Second Edition
Donald Charrett

CONTRACTS FOR INFRASTRUCTURE PROJECTS
An International Guide to Application
Philip Loots and Donald Charrett

FIDIC CONTRACTS IN EUROPE
A Practical Guide to Application
Donald Charrett

FIDIC CONTRACTS IN THE AMERICAS
A Practical Guide to Application
Donald Charrett

FIDIC CONTRACTS IN AFRICA AND THE MIDDLE EAST
A Practical Guide to Application
Donald Charrett

For more information, please visit: www.routledge.com/Practical-Legal-Guides-for-Construction-and-Technology-Projects/book-series/PLGCTP

FIDIC CONTRACTS IN AFRICA AND THE MIDDLE EAST

A PRACTICAL GUIDE TO APPLICATION

EDITED BY DONALD CHARRETT

informa law
from Routledge

Cover image: Donald Charrett

First published 2024
by Informa Law from Routledge
4 Park Square, Milton Park, Abingdon, Oxon OX14 4RN

and by Informa Law from Routledge
605 Third Avenue, New York, NY 10158

Informa Law from Routledge is an imprint of the Taylor & Francis Group, an informa business

British Library Cataloguing-in-Publication Data
A catalogue record for this book is available from the British Library

ISBN: 9781032074399 (hbk)
ISBN: 9781032074405 (pbk)
ISBN: 9781003206910 (ebk)

DOI: 10.4324/9781003206910

Typeset in Times New Roman
by Deanta Global Publishing Services, Chennai, India

This book is dedicated with grateful thanks to my wife, Jeyami, without whose continuing understanding of and tolerance for the time consuming demands entailed by my writing activities, this book would not have been possible.

CONTENTS

FIGURES

TABLES

ABOUT THE EDITOR

Dr Donald Charrett BE(Hons), LLB(Hons), MConstLaw, PhD, ProfCertArb, Dip International Arbitration, FIEAust, FCIArb

Dr Charrett is a barrister, arbitrator, mediator, expert and dispute board member practising in technology, engineering and construction (TEC) disputes. Prior to joining the Victorian Bar, he worked as a solicitor at a large Australian law firm. His construction law briefs have included litigation, mediation, expert determination, facilitation of experts' conferences, arbitration and membership of dispute boards. He is a Fellow of the Chartered Institute of Arbitrators and a member of the FIDIC President's List of Adjudicators. He was named Best Construction Law Practitioner, Australia 2016 by *Business Worldwide Magazine*. In 2019, 2020 and 2021, Who's Who Legal included him on their list of *Thought Leaders: Construction*, saying 'Donald Charrett is looked on with enormous favour by sources for his vast experience in construction and engineering disputes' and 'Donald is an excellent and knowledgeable lawyer'.

Prior to becoming a lawyer, he worked as an engineer for over 30 years, including 12 years as a director of a consulting engineering firm. Dr Charrett's engineering experience included computer applications, structural design, managing engineering projects, acting as an expert witness and management roles in contract negotiation and administration, insurance, international joint ventures and corporate restructuring. From 2012 to 2014 he was the non-executive chairman of the consulting engineering company AMOG.

Dr Charrett has published widely on legal and engineering subjects and has presented conference papers, workshops and training courses in Australia and internationally. He is a Senior Fellow at the University of Melbourne, teaching a Master of Construction Law subject on international construction law.

His legal publications include articles on expert evidence, FIDIC contracts, dispute boards, dispute avoidance and resolution, contract risk, forensic engineering, contractual lessons from past projects, design and construct contracts, *quantum meruit*, solidary liability, construction insurance, professional indemnity insurance and reinsurance. He is the author of *Contracts for Construction and Engineering Projects*; a joint author of *Contracts for Infrastructure Projects: An International Guide*, *The Application of Contracts in Developing Oil and Gas Projects* and *Practical Guide to Engineering and Construction Contracts*; and the editor of *FIDIC Contracts in the Americas*, *FIDIC Contracts in Europe*, *FIDIC Contracts in Asia Pacific*, *The International Application of FIDIC Contracts: A Practical Guide* and *Global Challenges, Shared Solutions*.

TABLE OF CASES

Australia

Akai Pty Ltd v. People's Insurance Co Limited [1996] HCA 39; (1996) 188 CLR 418............. 10
Attorney-General of Botswana v. Aussie Diamond Products Pty Ltd (No 3) [2010] WASC 14 10
Bonython v. the Commonwealth of Australia (1950) 81 CLR 486; [1951] AC 201 10
Garsec v. His Majesty the Sultan of Brunei [2008] NSWCA 211 9–10
John Pfeiffer v. Rogerson (2000) 203 CLR 503 10
Mendelsohn-Zeller Inc v. T&C Providores Pty Ltd [1981] NSWLR 366 10
Nelson v. Nelson [1995] HCA 25; (1995) 184 CLR 538 8

Kenya

Euromec International Limited v. Shandong Taikai Power Engineering Company Limited (Civil Case E527 of 2020) [2021] KEHC 93 (KLR) (Commercial and Tax).....................218
Mahan Limited v. Villa Care Limited [2021] eKLR 230
Mahan Limited v. Villa Care ML HC Misc. Civil App. No. 216 of 2018 [2019] eKLR 222
Ministry of Environment and Forestry v. Kiarigi Building Contractors & another [2020] eKLR.. 221, 222
Narok County Government v. Prime Tech Engineering Ltd [2017] eKLR 220, 222
Omar Gorhan v. Municipal Council of Malindi (Council Government of Kilifi) v. Overlook Management Kenya Ltd [2020] eKLR 220
Republic v. Director General of Kenya National Highways Authority (DG) & 3 others Ex-parte Dhanjal Brothers Limited [2018] eKLR 222
William Odhiambo Ramogi & 3 others v. Attorney General & 4 others; Muslims for Human Rights & 2 others (Interested Parties) [2020] eKLR... 222

Malaysia

Ooi Boon Long v. Citibank NA [1984] 1 M.L.J. 222 (Malaysian Privy Council)........................ 7

Nigeria

Acmel Nigeria Limited v. FBN Plc (2014) LPELR-22444 (CA), 14–15, 26.............................. 259
Adamen Publishers (Nig.) Ltd v. Abhulimen (2016) 6 NWLR (pt. 1509) 431 (CA)................ 278
Adetula v. Akinyosoye (2017) 16 NWLR (pt. 1592) 492 CA.. 268
African Natural Resources & Mines Ltd v. SS Minerals Resources Ltd (2021) LPELR-55151(CA) 261
AG Lagos State v. AG Federation & Ors. (2003) LPELR-620(SC), 187–189.......................... 245
Ahmadu Bello University v. VTLS Inc. (2020) LPELR-52142 (CA), 12–18 256
Alkamawa v. Bello (1998) 8 NWLR (pt. 561) 173; (1998) 6 SCNJ 127 236
Arfo Construction Co. Ltd. v. Minister of Works & Anor (2018) LPELR-46711(CA)............. 258
Aribisala Properties Ltd. v. Adepoju (2015) LPELR-25589(CA), 33 258
Asaka v. Raminkura (2015) All FWLR (pt. 787) 774 (CA) 262
Atolagbe v. Awuni (1997) 9 NWLR (pt. 522) 536 SC... 268, 269, 277
Barde v. Honourable Minister of Health & Ors (2017) LPELR-42998(CA), 17–18................. 265

Beaumont Resources Limited & Anor v. DWC Drilling Limited (2017) LPELR-42814 (CA), 49–50 255
Bill & Brothers Ltd & Ors v. Dantata & Sawoe Construction Co. (Nig) Ltd & Ors (2015) LPELR- 24770(CA), 10–12 257
Confidence Insurance Ltd v. Trustees of O.S.C.E (1999) 2 NWLR (pt. 591) 373 (CA) 279
Corona Schiffah R. MBH & Co. v. Emespo J. Continental Ltd (2002) NWLR (pt. 753) 205 CA 268–269
Damac Star Properties LLC v. Profitel Limited & Anor (2020) LPELR-50699 (CA), 44–52 255
Doleman & Sons v. Ossett Corporation (1912) 3 K.B. (C.A.) 257 279
Dyson Tech. Ltd. v. Nulec Ind. Plc. & Registrar General of Trademarks (2017) LPELR-50572(CA), 10–11 265
Egbe v. Adefarasin (1985) 1 NWLR (pt. 3) 549 268
Esso Petroleum and Production Nigeria Ltd & SNEPCO v. NNPC (Unreported) Appeal No CA/A/507/2012 265
Famfa Oil Ltd v. AG Federation & Anor (2007) LPELR-9023(CA) 261
FGN & Ors v. Zebra Energy Ltd. (2002) LPELR-3172(SC), 18 258
Fugro Subsea LLC v. Petrolog Limited (2021) LPELR-53133 (CA), 67–74 256
Hasting v. Nigerian Railway Corporation (1964) Lagos High Court Reports 135 279
Hull Blyth (Nig) Limited v. Jetmove Publishing Limited (2018) LPELR-44115 (CA), 8–25 256
Kano State Government & Anor v. A.S.J. Global Links (Nig.) Ltd (2017) LPELR-46215(CA) 246
Kano State Urban Development Board (K.S.U.D.B.) v. Fanz Construction Ltd (1990) LPELR-1659(SC) 279
KSUDB v. Fanz Construction Ltd (1990) 4 NWLR (pt. 142) 1, 32–33 (SC) 264
Lagos State Water Corporation v. Sakamort Construction (Nig) Ltd (2011) 12 NWLR (pt. 1262) 569 .... 257, 270
Lignes Aeriennes Congolaises v. Air Atlantic (Nig.) Limited (2005) LPELR-5808 (CA), 29–37 256
Majekodunmi & Anor v. National Bank of Nigeria Ltd. (1978) LPELR-1825(SC), 11 258
Mekwunye v. Imoukhuede (2019) LPELR-48996(SC) 246
Nasir v. Civil Service Commission, Kano (2007) 5 NWLR (pt. 1190) 253 SC 268
Niger Progress Ltd v. North East Line Corporation (1989) 3 NWLR (pt. 107) 68 (SC) 279
Nika Fishing Co. Limited v. Lavina Corporation (2008) LPELR-2035 (SC), 16–23 255
Obembe v. Wemabod Estates Ltd (1977) LPELR-2161(SC) 279
Onward Enterprises Ltd v. MV 'Matrix' (2010) 2 NWLR (pt. 1179) 530 (CA) 279
Owners of the MV 'Arabella' v. Nigerian Agricultural Insurance Cooperation (2008) 11 NWLR (pt. 1097) 182 268
Oyewumi v. Ogunesan (1990) LPELR-2880(SC) 46 236
R.C. Omeaku & Sons Ltd v. Rainbownet Ltd (2014) 6 NWLR (pt. 1401) 516 .... 257, 270
Sacoil 281 (Nig) Ltd & Anor v. Transnational Corporation of Nigeria Plc (2020) LPELR-49761(CA) 45–61 246
Shell Nigeria Exploration and Production Nigeria Ltd v. Federal Inland Revenue Service (Unreported) Appeal No CA/A/208/2012 265
Sino-Afric Agriculture & Ind Company Ltd & Ors v. Ministry of Finance Incorporation & Anor (2013) LPELR-22370(CA) 27–30 246
Sonnar (Nig) Limited & Anor v. Partnenreedri M.S Nordwind & Anor (1987) LPELR-3494 (SC), 31 .... 255, 256
Travelport Global Distribution Systems BV v. Bellview Airlines Ltd (2012) WL 3925856 (SDNY Sept. 10, 2012) 246
United World Ltd Inc. v. Mobile Telecommunications Services Ltd (1998) 10 NWLR (pt. 568) 106 (CA) 264
West London Diary Society Ltd. v. Abbot (1881) 44 L.T. 376 279
Yinusa v. Adesubokan (1971) All NLR 227 236

Phillippines

Lambert v. Fox 26 Phil 588 [Philippines] 8

South Africa

ABSA Bank Ltd v. Fouche 2003(1) SA 176 (SCA) 307
Bank v. Grusd (1939) TPD 286 304
Barkhuizen v. Napier (2007) (5) SA 323 (CC) 303, 304
Basil Read (Pty) Ltd v. Regent Devco (Pty) Ltd (unreported) 313
Beadica 231 CC and Others v. Trustees, Oregon Trust and Others 2020 (5) SA 247 (CC) 305
Bon Quelle (Edms) Bpk v. Munisipaliteit van Otavi (1989) (1) SA 508 (A) 306
Brisley v. Drotsky 2002(4) SA 1 (SCA) 304
Conradie v. Rossouw (1919) AD 279 303
Cool Ideas 1186 CC v. Hubbard and Another 2014 (4) SA 474 (CC) 289
Dalinga Beleggings (Pty) Ltd v. Antina (Pty) Ltd 1977(2) SA 56 (A) 316
Deloitte Haskins & Sells v. Bowthorpe Hellerman Deutsch 1991(1) SA 525 (A) 316
Ellerine Brothers (Pty) Ltd v. McCarthy Ltd 2014(4) SA 22 (SCA) 309
Evins v. Shield Insurance Co Ltd 1980(2) SA 814 (A) 316
Freeman NO and another v. Eskom Holdings Ltd [2010] JOL 25357 (GSJ) 313
Goldblatt v. Freemantle (1920) AD 123 303
Group Five Construction (Pty) Ltd v. Minister of Water Affairs and Forestry (3916/05) [2010] ZAGPPHC36 316
Jigger Properties CC v. Maynard NO and others (2017) (4) SA 569 (KZP) 306
McCarthy Retail Ltd v. Shortdistance Carriers CC (2010) (3) SA 482 (SCA) 306
National Home Builders Registration Council and Another v. Xantha Properties 18 (Pty) Ltd 2019 (5) SA 424 (SCA) 289
Nino Bonino v. De Lange (1906) TS 120 306
Novartis SA (Pty) Ltd and Another v. Maphil Trading (Pty) Ltd (2016) (1) SA 518 (SCA) 303
Peters, Flamman & Co v. Kokstad Municipality 1919 AD 427 300
Pretorius and Another v. Natal South Sea Investment Trust Ltd (under Judicial Management) 1965(3) SA 410 (W) 307
QwaQwa Regeringsdiens v. Martin Harris & Seuns OVS (Edms) Bpk 2000(3) SA 339 (SCA) 355 316
Secure Electronics v. The City of Cape Town [2017] ZAWCHC 95 316
Smith v. Mouton 1977(3) SA 9 (W) 316
Stefanutti Stocks (Pty) Ltd v. S8 Property (Pty) Ltd [2013] ZAGPJHC 388 313
Stocks and Stocks (Cape) (Pty) Ltd v. Gordon and others NNO 1993(1) SA 156 (T) 313
Telecordia Technologies Inc v. Telkom SA Ltd 2007(3) SA 266 (SCA) 313
Thomas Construction (Pty) Ltd (in liquidation) v. Grafton Furniture Manufacturers (Pty) Ltd 1988(2) SA 546 (A) 563 G 316
Thoroughbred Breeders' Association v. Price Waterhouse 2001(4) SA 551 (A) 316
Trollip v. Jordaan 1961(1) SA 238 (A) 307
Tubular Holdings (Pty) Ltd v. DBT Technologies (Pty) Ltd 2014(1) SA 244 (GSJ) 313
United Building Society v. Smookler's Trustees and Golambick's Trustee (1906) TS 623 306
Walker v. Syfront NO 1911 AD 141 309
Wells v. South African Aluminite Company 1927 AD 69 307
Wilma Petru Kooij v. Middleground Trading 251 CC and Another (1249/18) [2020] ZASCA 45 299, 300

United Kingdom

Bremer Handelgesellschaft mbH v. Vanden Avenne Izegem nv [1978] 2 Lloyd's Rep. 113 420
Fiona Trust & Holding Corp v. Privalov [2007] UKHL 40; [2007] All ER 951 26
Insaat Ve Sanayi AS v. OOO Insurance Company (Enka Insaat) [2020] UKSC 38 59
Power Curber International Ltd v. National Bank of Kuwait [1981] 1 WLR 1233 10
Printing and Numeral Registering Co. v. Sampson (1875) L. R. 19 Eq., 462 7
Vita Food Products Inc v. Unus Shipping Co Ltd [1939] AC 277 10

United States

A.J. Richard & Sons, Inc. v. Forest City Ratner Cos., LLC [2019] N.Y. Slip Op. 30215(U) (Sup. Ct. Kings County 28 January 2019) 221

Zambia

African Alliance Pioneer Master Fund v. Vehicle Appeal No. 21 of 2011 403
Jonathan Van Blerk v. The Attorney General and others SCZ/8/03/2020 [2021] ZMSC 31 385
Kalusha Bwalya v. Chadore Properties & Another Appeal No. 222 of 2013 417
Patel v. Patel [1985] Zambia Law Reports 220 (SC) 406
Pre-Secure Limited v. Union Bank Zambia Limited and Ikakumari Girishi Desai – Appeal No. 13/2003 417
PT Pedrusahaan Gas Negara (Persero) TBK v. CRW Joint Operation 409
Richard Mandona v. Total Energy Appeal No. 82 of 2019 386
Stanbic Bank PLC v. Savenda Management Services Limited (Appeal 16 of 2017) (Ruling) [2017] ZMCA 112 385
Zambia National Holdings Limited and United National Independence Party (UNIP) v. The Attorney General SCZ Judgment No. 3 of 1994 384

TABLE OF LEGISLATION

CONTRIBUTORS

Mr João Rocha de Almeida (Angola) graduated in Law in 2008 from the Catholic University of Porto, Portugal. João completed a master's degree in Administrative Law in 2011, from the Law School of the University of Porto. Also in 2011, João completed a post-graduate course in Public Procurement at the Catholic University of Porto.

João first began practising law in 2008 and joined Eversheds Sutherland FCB in 2014, where he is currently a Principal Associate, focusing primarily on practice areas within the Public, Administrative and Environmental Law Department and the Real Estate, Property and Construction Department.

João is an experienced litigation lawyer who regularly participates in arbitrations and public law disputes. He has been deeply involved in a wide variety of matters and has been advising and acting on behalf of contractors' disputes pertaining to both public and private construction contracts, including disputes related to sport infrastructure, hotels, water dams, underground stations and railway lines. João has assisted several clients with projects in Angola, including in some of the most relevant sectors of the Angolan economy such as construction, oil and gas, energy, mining and industry.

Contact details: jrochadealmeida@eversheds-sutherland.net

Mr James Banda (Zambia) is the current (2022 to 2023) Chair of the Chartered Institute of Arbitrators Zambia Branch. James is the past President of the Law Association of Zambia (LAZ) and past President of the SADC Lawyers Association. He is also a former council member of the International Bar Association. He holds a Master of Laws degree (Construction and Dispute Resolution) and a Bachelor of Laws degree. He is an advocate of all the Superior Courts in Zambia. He is a Fellow of the Chartered Institute of Arbitrators (FCIARB). James also serves as a Commissioner of the Small Claims Court in Zambia and is a member of the Disputes Resolution Board Foundation (DRBF), the Society of Construction Law (SCL) and the Federation of Consulting Engineers (FIDIC).

James has held several appointments as an arbitrator, mediator and legal expert on various large-scale domestic and international commercial disputes. His practice involves advising and representing parties in domestic and international arbitrations, adjudications and court proceedings. His clients include international and local employers, contractors and consultants on engineering, construction, energy, mining and information technology projects.

Contact details: james.banda@amwlegal.com

Mr Johan Beyers (South Africa, Zambia) practices as an advocate of the High Court at the Cape Town and Johannesburg Bars and is a member of Maisels Group in Johannesburg, South Africa. In addition, he is also admitted in the Kingdom of Lesotho.

He has held chambers as an advocate in South Africa for more than 29 years, specialising in domestic and international arbitrations involving construction, engineering, energy, mining, information technology and commercial disputes. He has held appointments as acting High Court judge, appeal arbitrator, arbitrator, adjudicator and legal expert. He is a Fellow of both the Chartered Institute of Arbitrators and the Malaysian Institute of Arbitrators.

His practice involves advising and representing parties in domestic and international arbitrations, adjudications and court proceedings. His clients include international and South African employers, contractors and consultants on engineering, construction, energy, mining and information technology projects in many African countries, the Middle East, the United Kingdom and South America.

Johan holds BA(Law) and LLB degrees from the University of Stellenbosch, South Africa, as well as an MSc degree in Construction Law and Dispute Resolution from King's College London, UK, in respect whereof he was the recipient of the Arbitration Club Philip Raner Prize.

He is a chapter author in Charrett (ed), *The International Application of FIDIC Contracts: A Practical Guide* (2019), a co-founder and the current chairperson of the Society of Construction Law for Africa (2013–2022) and the Cape Bar's representative on the construction committee of the Arbitration Foundation of South Africa.

Contact details: beyers@law.co.za

Mr Miguel Lorena Brito (Angola) graduated in Law in 1996 from the Catholic University in Lisbon, Portugal. In 2008 Miguel completed a post-graduate course on Public Contracts Law at the Lisbon University Law School.

Miguel has been practising Law as an attorney for almost 25 years, dedicating a significant part of his work to public procurement and public contracts, construction, real estate, urban planning and the environment. Having joined the firm in 2002, Miguel has been a Partner at Eversheds Sutherland FCB since 2007. Miguel has vast experience in the construction sector, being a regular participant in arbitration procedures related to the execution of public and private construction contracts. Some of his work highlights in recent years include advising and acting on behalf of Portuguese and foreign contractors in disputes pertaining to relevant infrastructure contracts (including a waste management plant, a football stadium, an underground tunnel, a water dam, public schools and hotels).

Miguel has extensive experience in assisting clients in projects and disputes in Angola. He has advised numerous clients in the context of public tenders in Angola and also in negotiating the terms for construction contracts governed by Angolan law.

Miguel is also the author of several articles for national and international publications in the areas of his expertise, addressing in particular public procurement and public contracts.

Contact details: mlorenabrito@eversheds-sutherland.net

Ms Aslı Budak (Türkiye) is a leader in Hergüner Biken Özeke Attorney Partnership's Projects and Infrastructure practice group. Aslı is known for her record of success in conducting complicated and extensive negotiations between all project stakeholders, including regulatory authorities and private counterparties. Her extensive experience in long-term, multiparty transactions and her inimitable approach towards garnering cooperation from all transaction parties, including local governmental authorities, by promoting common benefits is an indispensable asset, particularly in long-term infrastructure and project finance projects. Her extensive experience in the industry, her reputation for diligence and her deft personal touch make her a highly sought-after arbitrator in disputes related to the industry. Aslı represents financial institutions and project companies, and her practice focuses primarily on large-scale infrastructure development projects such as bridges, tunnels, roads, airports and electricity generation facilities. Some of her most significant work includes representing the project company developing the first tunnel linking Europe with Asia as well as the second-longest suspension bridge in the world.

Contact details: abudak@herguner.av.tr

Mr Jamie Calvy (UAE) is a Senior Associate in the Global Projects Disputes Practice at Freshfields Bruckhaus Deringer LLP. Jamie specialises in resolving disputes in the construction, infrastructure, engineering and energy sectors. He has experience with all major forms of international construction contracts and has represented clients in international arbitrations, mediations, dispute boards, adjudications, expert determinations and litigation before the courts of England and Wales.

Jamie is a Member of the Chartered Institute of Arbitrators (MCIArb) and is admitted as a solicitor in England and Wales.

Contact details: Jamie.Calvy@freshfields.com

Dr Belachew Asteray Demiss (Ethiopia) earned his PhD (2018) in Civil Engineering (Construction Engineering and Management Stream) from Pan African University and Jomo Kenyatta University of Agriculture and Technology, Department of Civil Engineering, Nairobi, Kenya. He earned his MSc (2011) in Civil Engineering (Construction Management) and BSc (2006) in Construction Technology from Adama University Ethiopia. Currently, he is an Assistant Professor in the Civil Engineering Department, College of Architecture and Civil Engineering, Addis Ababa Science and Technology University (AASTU). He also serves as an associate dean for research and technology transfer in the Construction Quality and Technology Center of Excellence at AASTU. He has been a Lecturer and Construction Director at Mizan-Tepi University (MTU) for more than seven years. He has participated in different professional services as a contract engineer, resident engineer, project manager and construction director in different construction projects in Ethiopia. Belachew has extensive expertise and experience in construction project management, construction law, construction contract administration, construction economics, procurement management and advanced construction materials. He has more than 13 years of teaching, research and consulting experience in Ethiopia and has published in peer-reviewed journals and conference proceedings. Belachew is a Member of the Ethiopian Construction Technology and Management Professionals Association (ECOTMPA) and is admitted as a Professional Engineer by the Ethiopian Construction Regulatory Authority.

Contact details: belachewasteray@gmail.com or belachew.asteray@aastu.edu.et

Mr Levent Irmak (Türkiye) is a civil engineer with 30 years of experience and has an MSc degree in Construction Management from Northeastern University in Boston, USA complemented with further education in construction law and arbitration at Robert Gordon University in the UK. He is both a FIDIC Certified Adjudicator and FIDIC Certified Trainer and is listed in the FIDIC President's list of Approved Adjudicators. He has been appointed as a Dispute Board (both single and three-member and as chairperson) in various projects such as wastewater treatment plants, railways and depot, roads, power plants and transmission lines. He has served as tribunal- and party-appointed expert witness in international arbitration cases (ICC, AFSA and others) involving multi-use real estate developments, industrial plants, wastewater treatment plants and hospitals on the matters of defects, damages and quantum. He advises contractors, employers, engineering and law firms in contracts, claims and dispute resolution and his experience extends over 25 countries in Europe, the Middle East, Africa, Asia and North and South America. He is the past President of the Dispute Resolution Board Foundation (DRBF) Region-2 and a member of the Board of Directors of ATCEA (Association of Turkish Consulting Engineers and Architects), FIDIC, EFCA and ISTAC (Istanbul Arbitration Center) Construction Committee and currently serves as Chair of DRBF Region-2 Mentoring Committee and Managing Director of MC2 MODERN International.

Contact details: levent@mc2modern.com

Mr Abba Usman Jaafar (Nigeria) is a public procurement expert with in-depth experience in all phases of procurement and contract management of goods, works and services including procurement and fiduciary policies, use of country procurement systems, mentoring, training and capacity building. He has over 25 years of experience in working with international donors' procurement and contract procedures – four years as Programme Manager of the UNDP-assisted Fourth Country programme for the environment in Jigawa State, Nigeria; six years as Procurement Officer for the World Bank–funded Hadejia Urban Upgrading project for Jigawa State; three years as Procurement Officer of the Delegation of European Union for Nigeria and ECOWAS; and 11 years as Principal Procurement Officer of the African Development Bank.

He started his work experience with the Kano State civil service in Nigeria as a sanitary engineer and was involved in the implementation of Kano urban stormwater drainage, sewerage and refuse management masterplan. He headed the Kano flood control, sewage treatment plants, industrial effluent and urban refuse management. In 1992, he was transferred to the newly created Jigawa State where he was involved in the supervision of the construction of 1,000 housing units at Dutse. He rose to the position of Director of Environment and was in charge of urban drainage and flood control, urban forestry and environmental sanitation.

Abba holds Bachelor of Science in Building and LLB degrees from Ahmadu Bello University, Zaria, Nigeria, and a Master's in Banking and Finance from Bayero University, Kano, Nigeria. He also holds a Master of Science in Urban Engineering from Loughborough University, UK, and a Master's degree in Public Procurement Management from ITC/ILO and University of Turin, Italy. He is a Chevening Scholar and belongs to some professional organisations.

Contact details: abba.jaafar@gmail.com

Ms Samantha Lord Hill (UAE) is Counsel in the international arbitration practice at Freshfields Bruckhaus Deringer LLP. Samantha focuses her practice on commercial and construction disputes arising out of global projects. She has advised and represented clients in international arbitrations under many of the major arbitration rules and also sits as an arbitrator.

Samantha is a Member of the Chartered Institute of Arbitrators, London, the Global Advisory Board of the International Centre for Dispute Resolution, Young and International, the International Bar Association, Arbitral Women and the Editorial Board of the Center for International Investment and Commercial Arbitration Pakistan. She is admitted as a barrister and solicitor of the Supreme Court of Western Australia and the High Court of Australia and is registered as a Foreign Legal Consultant in California and a Foreign Practitioner in both Dubai and Singapore.

Contact details: Samantha.LordHill@Freshfields.com

Mr Zenawi Mehari Limenih (Ethiopia) is a Lecturer at the University of Gondar, Institute of Technology, Department of Construction Technology and Management, one of the oldest higher institutions in Ethiopia located at Gondar, Amhara. He joined the university in May 2018 as an assistant lecturer and now is a full-time lecturer holding a Master of Science degree. He is widely involved in different research and community services in the university. Formerly he was a site engineer at a private construction contracting company for one and half years, and is now a licensed professional engineer. He is building information modelling (BIM) project management and BIM architecture certified by the Autodesk company in collaboration with the Construction Management Institute (CMI). Zenawi graduated with a Bachelor of Science degree in Construction Technology and Management in June 2017 from Jig-Jiga University, Jig-Jiga, Somali, Ethiopia. He also holds a Master of Science degree in Civil Engineering (construction technology and management) from Addis Ababa Science and Technology University, Addis Ababa, Ethiopia.

Contact: oduu329@gmail.com or zenawi.mehari@uog.edu.et

Mr Husni Madi (Jordan), BEng, PgDip Law, FCIArb, FCA, FCT, PMP, PMI-SP, is a FIDIC International Certified Trainer (FCT), as well as Founder and CEO of Shura Construction Management, a consultancy firm providing contract solutions for the construction industry. Husni is a Civil Engineer qualified in law (PgDip, LLM 2023) with over 25 years of experience, a delay analysis specialist and an accredited Professional in Scheduling (PMI-SP) and Project Management (PMP). He is a member of several multi-million USD international and domestic arbitration tribunals being an FCIArb, and DABs being a FIDIC Certified Adjudicator (FCA) listed on FIDIC President's List of Approved Dispute Adjudicators. Husni is the DRBF Country Representative for Jordan. He is also listed on FIDIC's List of Mediators.

Presently, he is serving as Chairman of FIDIC Task Groups 15 and 15B, establishing FIDIC's Golden Principles. He was a friendly reviewer of the Red, Yellow and Silver 2017 2nd Editions and the Emerald Book. Additionally, he is the official translator of the FIDIC 2017 suite into Arabic. Husni is a member of the Certification Board of FIDIC Credentialing Ltd (FCL) and a visiting lecturer at Leuphana University (Luneburg, Germany) teaching contract law, construction law and dispute resolution for a post-graduate programme.

Husni is Vice Chair of the influential FIDIC Contracts Committee and winner of FIDIC's Trainer(s) or Adjudicator(s) of the Year Award.

Contact details: husni@shuracm.com

Mr Firas Malhas (Jordan) is a Partner at International Business Legal Associates (IBLAW). He is licensed by the Jordan Bar Association to represent clients before all courts of Jordan and arbitration tribunals. He has extensive experience in corporate and commercial matters, where he advises clients on a wide range of corporate matters including mergers and acquisitions, joint ventures, licensing and general corporate matters. Firas advises private companies and sovereign states companies on infrastructure projects and real estate development including joint development agreements, development and management agreements, BOT contracts, other related construction and development contracts. Firas is advising the Aqaba Development Corporation, the investment arm of the Aqaba Special Economic Zone Authority, on several aspects of law that are related to the infrastructure and superstructure projects in the Aqaba Special Ecomania Zone, Jordan. Firas also advised Hikma Pharmaceuticals Plc, the multinational pharmaceuticals group, on its acquisition of the Arab Pharmaceutical Manufacturing Company (APM) for a total cash consideration of $163.6 million, and he was the leading legal member in the said acquisition.

Firas received an LLM from the University of Birmingham, UK, in 2010 and an LLB from the University of Jordan in 1993.

Contact details: fmalhas@iblaw.com.jo

Dr Waleed El Nemr (Egypt), PhD, LLM, MSc, BSc, FCIARB, has 25 years of experience in contracts and claims management, encompassing positions in various international project management firms such as Bechtel, Fluor Daniel and Hill International. He has also assumed several roles during dispute resolution proceedings in construction projects, acting as arbitrator, expert adjudicator, expert appointed by the tribunal, expert appointed by an arbitration party, arbitrator and dispute adjudication board (DAB) member. He is MENA Regional Director of the Dispute Resolution Board Foundation (DRBF), MENA Regional Director of the Association for the Advancement of Cost Engineering (AACE) International and Vice President of the Chartered Institute of Arbitrators (CIARB) – Egypt Branch. He is the author of numerous papers and a speaker in numerous conferences, seminars and webinars on the topic of construction contracts and claims. He is currently the Contracts Director of Hill International's North Africa branch, based in Egypt, and an Adjunct Assistant Professor at the American University in Cairo in the construction engineering department.

Contact: welnemr@gmail.com

Mr Barasa Ongeti (Kenya) holds a BSc in Civil and Structural Engineering and is currently pursuing an MSc in Construction Engineering Management at the University of East London, UK. Barasa is accredited by FIDIC Credentialing Limited (FCL) as a FIDIC Certified Contracts Manager. He is engaged as the Contracts Manager for Raxio Group, a premier data centre construction company with its footprint across Africa. Prior to joining Raxio, Barasa was in the consultancy space for over seven years as a Contract Administrator at Peter Cheyney and Associates, a highly reputed contracts specialist firm based in Kenya.

During this period he worked on several construction projects in East Africa, West Africa and Indonesia where he gained valuable experience in handling construction contract claims, income protection and dispute resolution. Barasa has been involved in projects of varying nature governed by the FIDIC Red Book, Yellow Book, Silver Book and Pink Book.

Contact details: ongetib@gmail.com

Ms Erin Miller Rankin (UAE) leads the Global Projects Disputes Practice at Freshfields Bruckhaus Deringer LLP. Erin works with a team of specialist practitioners supporting clients on major capital projects, with a particular focus on emerging markets. She has specific expertise of complex international arbitration in the oil and gas, power, mining and transportation sectors.

Erin is a co-editor and contributing author of *Dealing with Delay and Disruption on Construction Projects* (2020).

Contact details: Erin.MillerRankin@Freshfields.com

Mr Yusuf Sulayman (Nigeria), Esq., LLM, is a policy consultant, researcher and a law teacher with the University of Abuja, Nigeria. Until starting his PhD programme at the University of Portsmouth, UK, Yusuf was staff adviser to the Law Students Association, University of Abuja. He also served as the program coordinator for the Centre for Security and Legal Studies of the University of Abuja. He is currently a member of the Africa CDC Technical Working Group (West Africa RCC) working on the sub-region's Legal Frameworks for Biosafety and Biosecurity as well as Diseases Prevention and Control. He is also a volunteer legal consultant for One Community Inc USA and the Managing Attorney at Sulayman Attorneys, Abuja, Nigeria.

Yusuf has research interests in international law, public law, human rights, social development, governance and policy in which areas he has made academic contributions in books and journals.

Contact details: yusulayman@gmail.com or yusuf.sulayman@port.ac.uk

Mr Michael Uche Ukponu (Nigeria), LLM, MCIArb, obtained his LLB (Hons) degree from Madonna University, Okija, Nigeria, in 2012 and was called to the Nigerian Bar in 2013. Since then, he has been in active legal practice in diverse areas of law. He is currently a Senior Associate Counsel at the Law Partners (Barristers and Solicitors), a full services law firm with offices in Abuja and Kano. Michael specialises in 'E3' – energy, extractives and environmental law in Nigeria – and has authored legal articles and book chapters in these areas that have been published by globally renowned journals and book publishers. He also has an extended interest in construction-related issues as they tend to interplay with E3 issues.

It was on the strength of his passion for sustainable development in the renewable energy, natural resources and environment sectors that Michael was granted the Australia Awards Scholarship by the Australian Government through the Department of Foreign Affairs and Trade (DFAT) to undertake a Master of Energy and Resources Law (LLM) programme at the University of Melbourne, Australia.

Michael is also a recipient of the Melbourne Research Scholarship 2021/2022, a prestigious scholarship towards undertaking a PhD in Environmental Law at the University of

Melbourne. He is a member of notable international professional associations, including the Chartered Institute of Arbitrators, UK (Australian and Nigerian branches) and the Environment Institute of Australia and New Zealand. He pastimes making music, watching/playing soccer games and discussing political issues.

Contact details: ucheukponu@yahoo.com

Dr Mohamed Abdel Wahab (Egypt) is a Professor of International Arbitration, Private International Law and English Contract Law at Cairo University, Egypt; Founding Partner and Head of International Arbitration, Construction and Energy Groups at Zulficar and Partners Law Firm, Egypt; ICCA Treasurer and Member of the Governing Board; Dean of the Africa Arbitration Academy; Chair of the International Expert Committee of the Permanent Forum for China Construction Law; Vice-Chair of the ICC Governing Body for Dispute Resolution Services; Co-Chair of the IBA Arab Regional Forum; Vice-Chair of the Advisory Committee of the CRCICA; Member of the CIMAC Court of Arbitration; Member of the Advisory Board of the MIAC; Member of the LACIAC Court of Arbitration; Member of the Board of Trustees of the CIArb; and Member of the Court of PCA. He has served as arbitrator, legal expert and counsel in more than 245 cases, involving parties from Africa, Asia, Canada, Europe, the Middle East and the United States. He received the *LAW Magazine* 2017 Best Legal Practitioner Award, the 2018 ASA International Arbitration Advocacy Prize, the 2019 AYA Hall-of-Fame African Arbitrator Award and the 2020–2021 Client Choice International Awards. He is listed in *Who's Who Global Elite Thought Leaders: International Arbitration* (2021 and 2022) and selected among the Legal500 Africa Powerlist (2021). *Who's Who Legal: Construction* (2022) says: 'Peers and clients say: "Mohamed is an all time great of construction arbitration"', and *Who's Who Legal Construction* (2019) says: 'Mohamed Abdel Wahab is highlighted as "a leading heavyweight construction law specialist whose analytical skills are second to none"'.

Contact details: MSW@zulficarpartners.com

ACKNOWLEDGEMENTS

FIDIC Contracts in Africa and the Middle East: A Practical Guide to Application was inspired by the success of the book *The International Application of FIDIC Contracts: A Practical Guide*, published by Routledge in 2020. One of the reviewers of that book opined: 'In time and if its contents were allowed to spread to other jurisdictions in which FIDIC contracts are commonly used, it will develop into a vital encyclopaedia for all those tasked with the production, amendment and finalisation of a FIDIC construction contract.'[1]

The first outcome of that challenge was the publication of *FIDIC Contracts in Asia Pacific: A Practical Guide to Application* in late 2021, followed by *FIDIC Contracts in Europe: A Practical Guide to Application* in late 2022 and *FIDIC Contracts in the Americas: A Practical Guide to Application* in 2023. This book is the fourth in the series, comprising chapters on a number of the major jurisdictions in Africa and the Middle East. The contents covered in each jurisdiction chapter in *FIDIC Contracts in Africa and the Middle East* follow the original format of *The International Application of FIDIC Contracts* but have also been expanded to include a section on the construction industry and sections on the impacts of COVID-19 on the execution of construction projects and the operation of construction contracts.

This book has the ambitious aim of addressing the specific legal requirements of the applicable construction law in a number of jurisdictions in Africa and the Middle East. Each of these jurisdictions has its own particular legal landscape that impacts the application of FIDIC (and other) construction contracts. Articulating the breadth and complexity of construction law in each of these jurisdictions required the skill and knowledge of expert local construction law practitioners. The chapter authors and their profiles and affiliations are identified in the Contributors section. Each of those profiles demonstrates a deep well of legal and practical experience in local construction law in general and the requirements of FIDIC contracts in particular. The authors are all eminent professionals who have had to fit the writing for their chapters into their busy schedules, in circumstances where normal professional life in every country was severely impacted by the ravages of COVID-19 and the new ways of working it entailed. I am very grateful to each of them for their commitment and hard work. The exigencies of busy professional lives and the COVID-19 pandemic have inevitably delayed chapter delivery times, and the book has taken longer to complete than originally planned.

1 Nick Longley, 'Book Review: The International Application of FIDIC Contracts: A Practical Guide' (2020) 1 *International Construction Law Review* 96, 98.

The authors of the jurisdiction chapters closely followed a template that I provided; accordingly, any deficiencies in the scope of topics covered by the jurisdiction chapters are my responsibility, not those of the chapter authors. To state the obvious, this book could not have been written without the skill and expertise of the authors of the jurisdiction chapters.

I also sincerely thank Sir Robert Akenhead of Atkin Chambers for writing the Foreword.

In addition to those named above, I acknowledge and thank the many colleagues I have met at international FIDIC conferences and training courses who have contributed to my knowledge and interest in the international application of FIDIC contracts.

I also thank Terry Clague, Guy Loft and Amelia Bashford of Routledge, who have been unfailingly encouraging and helpful in publishing this book. Deanta Global have done an excellent job of the difficult task of copyediting the manuscript and ensuring consistency of style and presentation, for which I am most grateful.

FOREWORD

International developers, contractors, sub-contractors, suppliers and consultants operate in numerous countries throughout the world. Projects are often funded internationally, for instance by the World Bank, on major infrastructure such as roads, dams, hospitals, mains water and power. This is particularly so in Africa and the Middle East, which represent a massive market for specialist engineering and construction services and expertise of all types. FIDIC or FIDIC-based contracts are often used.

The laws of the countries in these areas of the globe are diverse, stemming from common and civil law origins, as well as Islamic legal principles, Roman-Dutch law and the Napoleonic Code. This book, however, demonstrates that, whilst there are numerous similarities between the laws of the different countries examined in relation to construction projects, there are differences and important divergences that the prudent would be well advised to be aware of.

A 'Practical Guide' is what this book is. It is an ambitious and well-researched book which addresses specific legal requirements of the relevant construction law in nine jurisdictions in various African and Middle Eastern jurisdictions by reference to the FIDIC contracts commonly used for engineering projects in those countries. They cover North, East, South, Central and West Africa (Egypt, Ethiopia, Kenya, South Africa, Zambia and Nigeria) and the Middle East (Türkiye, Jordan and the United Arab Emirates).

The helpful introductory chapters from the Editor, Dr Donald Charrett, who is extremely well known and respected in this field, address the legal setting of construction contracts in the context of legal systems, contract law, freedom of contract, the need for parties to observe the contract terms and the proper law of the contract, particularly in the FIDIC context. The FIDIC Golden Rules are considered in some detail.

The book moves on to the major contributions by experts for each of the countries whose law and practice in the area of construction law are examined. The authors are from different backgrounds with lawyers and other construction and procurement-related specialists contributing. They each consider the enforceability of standard FIDIC clauses in their country, for instance in Egypt where liquidated damages may be unenforceable in certain situations.

Other interesting topics are considered for the different jurisdictions such as the applicability of good faith, the relevant legislation and the need for Particular Conditions to accommodate the law of the specific country. One practical issue covered is the impact of COVID on construction contracts, particularly the consequences of lockdowns and other restrictions on construction projects; this would be applicable if this re-emerges as a major problem or if other epidemics break out either internationally or in the country in question. There are useful sections in the jurisdiction chapters on the construction industry and related constraints and risks.

I would commend this book for two principal reasons. The first is as a practical book for those becoming involved in projects in any one or more of the nine diverse countries addressed; that is, practical in the countries concerned to know what the legal, statutory and industrial environment is in order to assess the risks and how to overcome them. The second reason is the usefulness of a comparative legal analysis not just between the laws of the nine countries but also the often fundamental differences between their civil and common law systems.

For parties involved or likely to be involved in projects in any one or more of the nine countries, whether from the Employers', the Contractors' or the consultants' perspective, this book should be more than sufficient to alert them not just to the likely issues to be encountered but also as to the solutions.

Sir Robert Akenhead
Atkin Chambers, London

CHAPTER 1

Introduction

Dr Donald Charrett

CONTENTS

DOI: 10.4324/9781003206910-1

1.1 Construction contracts

1.1.1 Overview

Construction contracts can be defined in various ways. The following definition is used for the purposes of this book:

> any contract where one person [this includes a corporation] agrees for valuable consideration to carry out construction works, which may include building or engineering works, for another.[1]

A contract for design does not involve 'construction' as such, and for the purposes of this book is not considered to be a construction contract. A design and construct contract includes design, but it also involves construction and therefore falls within the definition adopted here. Moreover, a subcontract in which a Subcontractor undertakes construction work for a Contractor is a species of construction contract and may be 'back-to-back' with the Head Contract between the Employer and the Contractor.[2]

In this book, the **Contract** means the construction contract being referred to. In general terms, the parties to a construction contract are the **Employer** for whom the work is done and the **Contractor** who carries out the work. In the case of a subcontract, the Contractor under the **Head Contract** functions as the Employer, and the Subcontractor functions as the Contractor.

Construction contracts have a number of specific features that give them some unique characteristics that distinguish them from other commercial contracts. The following issues arise by operation of law or because of specific terms that are incorporated in most construction contracts, or because of the nature of construction work. The unique distinguishing features of construction law can be conveniently considered under the following headings that address issues generally relevant to all construction projects.

Scope

- The subject matter of the contract relates to construction of a unique facility that will be affixed to the land at a specific location over a specific period of time.
- The constructed facility becomes part of the real property of the landowner when attached.
- The required design, scope, time, cost and quality requirements of the Works and the finished project are usually defined by extensive and complex technical documentation.
- The Employer (generally) has the right to increase or decrease the originally agreed scope of work by the issue of Variations, and the Contractor is obliged to carry out or omit the varied work.
- The execution of the construction work and/or the performance of the Contract may be supervised by an 'independent' Engineer who is not a party to the Contract.
- The Contract may be an entire contract.

1 Stephen Furst and the Hon Sir Vivian Ramsey, *Keating on Construction Contracts* (Sweet & Maxwell, 8th ed, 2006) 1.

2 Capitalised terms not specifically defined in this book are defined in the relevant FIDIC Conditions of Contract. The Glossary contains definitions of terms specifically defined in this book.

- There are many different types of construction contract: e.g. construct only, design and construct, engineer procure and construct (**EPC**), engineer procure and construction management (**EPCM**).

Risk

- There are many risks in a construction project – known knowns, known unknowns and unknown unknowns.
- Ground conditions are never completely known, including geotechnical conditions, groundwater, contamination or heritage items.
- Weather conditions can have a significant impact on construction activities and delay completion.
- Freedom of contract may be constrained, e.g. *Security of Payment* legislation that mandates payment obligations and makes some provisions illegal, such as pay-when-paid clauses.
- Many aspects of a construction project are subject to Government laws and regulations.
- There are usually a series of independent and interrelated contracts between a number of different parties: e.g. Employer/designer, Employer/Engineer, Employer/Contractor/DAAB or DAB Member, Employer/Contractor, Contractor/Subcontractor, Subcontractor/sub-Subcontractor Employer/Insurer, Contractor/Insurer.
- Construction activities are potentially dangerous, e.g. heavy machinery, working at heights, confined spaces, etc.
- Construction involves significant environmental impacts: noise, dust, smells, vibration, nuisance, water run-off, sediment and erosion.
- Construction may adversely impact adjacent property.
- Insurance of the works is usually mandatory and is a significant risk transfer mechanism.
- Insolvency of parties to interrelated contracts may impact performance.

Time

- The time for contractual performance may extend over a number of years, including a period after completion of construction (and when the Employer is in possession of the Site) during which the Contractor is liable to rectify defects.
- There are usually significant financial consequences for late contract completion.

Cost

- The contract sum and cashflow are typically substantial – cash flow is the life-blood of construction.
- The Contractor is usually required to provide security for its performance.

Quality

- A construction contract may involve the assumption of obligations that are very long-term, e.g. maintenance or liability for defects arising many years after construction was completed.

- Construction works apparently completed in accordance with contractual requirements may contain latent defects which only manifest themselves many years after construction was completed.

Disputes

- Disputes are common and frequently involve complex technical issues and large volumes of documents.

Every construction contract is unique: the Site is a unique location in the Country, constructed by a particular Contractor for a particular Employer over a particular period of time for a specific purpose.

1.1.2 Legal systems

There are a number of 'families' or systems of law, the most widespread being the systems considered in this book: common law and civil law. Other legal systems include Shari'a law and socialist law.

Common law is the body of law developed by judges from around the 11th century in England and later exported to its various colonies such as Canada, the USA, Australia, Ghana, Kenya, Nigeria, South Africa and Zambia. The basic principle is that earlier judicial decisions, usually of the higher courts, made in a similar case should be followed in subsequent cases. The principle that precedents should be respected is known as ***stare decisis*** and although it has never been legislated, courts regard it as binding. However, superior courts can decide that a previous case was wrongly decided and modify the law accordingly. In addition to the law made by judges in decided cases, common law is also based on statutes, which judges interpret by discerning the intention of Parliament and apply accordingly.

Civil law is a system of law in which the laws are codified in a large number of general rules and principals. Pejovic describes civil law in the following terms:

> Civil law has its origin in Roman law, as codified in the Corpus Iuris Civilis of Justinian. Under this influence, in the ensuing period the civil law has been developed in Continental Europe and in many other parts of the world. The main feature of civil law is that it is contained in civil codes, which are described as a 'systematic, authoritative, and guiding statute of broad coverage, breathing the spirit of reform and marking a new start in the legal life of an entire nation'. Most civil codes were adopted in the nineteenth and twentieth centuries: French Code Civil, 1804, Austrian Bürgerliches Gesetzbuch, 1811, German Bürgerliches Gesetzbuch, 1896, Japanese Minpo, 1896, Swiss Zivilgesetzbuch, 1907, Italian Codice Civile, 1942. Between these codes there are some important differences, and they are often grouped in the Romanic and the Germanic families. Even though the civil codes of different countries are not homogenous, there are certain features of all civil codes which bind them together and 'sets them apart from those who practice under different systems'.
>
> Civil law is largely classified and structured and contains a great number of general rules and principles, often lacking details. One of the basic characteristics of the civil law is that the courts main task is to apply and interpret the law contained in a code, or a statute to case facts. The assumption is that the code regulates all cases that could occur in practice, and when certain cases are not regulated by the code, the courts should apply some of the general principles used to fill the gaps.[3]

3 Casalev Pejovic, 'Civil Law and Common Law: Two Different Paths Leading to the Same Goal' (2001) 32(3) *Victoria University of Wellington Law Review* 817. www.victoria.ac.nz/__data/assets/pdf_file/0008/830780/Pejovic (accessed 12 November 2021).

Notwithstanding the differences between common law and civil law systems and the differences between jurisdictions within either of these systems, construction contracts can be executed in the knowledge that, notwithstanding local law differences, there are appropriate methods of dispute resolution, broad agreement on what constitutes a just outcome in most situations and international norms that ensure remedies can be realised.

The differences between the common law and civil law have become much fewer in recent years:

- The volume of legislation in common law countries has increased substantially over recent decades. Increasingly, more of the law is explicitly stated in legislation, which either codifies or amends the previous common law or forms new 'social legislation' which achieves legislatively desirable social outcomes not addressed by the common law, e.g. the *Human Rights Act 1998* (UK), which incorporates the rights and freedoms of the *European Convention on Human Rights* into British law, and the *Housing Grants, Construction and Regeneration Act 1996* (UK), which introduced a statutory right to adjudication of construction disputes.
- Because the answer to a legal issue may not be found in the *Codes* (which may not have been updated recently), the courts in civil law countries are relying to a much greater extent than previously on the precedential value of court judgments on a similar issue, e.g. in a book on FIDIC contracts, the authors list a significant number of cases from the French and German civil law jurisdictions, as well as cases from various common law jurisdictions.[4]

1.1.3 Contract law

Contract law around the world is based on the two fundamental principles of freedom of contract and *pacta sunt servanda*. These principles are universal in jurisdictions subject to the rule of law, the necessary precondition for the exercise of the parties' autonomy and the enforcement of their rights and obligations. Freedom of contract sets the 'ground rules' which govern the parties' rights to enter into the contract of their choice. *Pacta sunt servanda* governs the performance of a contract after it has been entered into. These two principles of law apply to the entry into, execution and termination of contracts.

1.1.4 Freedom of contract

Freedom of contract is the ability of legal persons to enter into a binding agreement to do anything, providing it is not contrary to the law or public policy (and in some jurisdictions, morals). Subject to these qualifications, courts generally uphold freedom of contract, even if one of the parties has accepted risks that it cannot manage or insure for.

4 Axel-Volkmar Jaeger and Götz-Sebastian Hök, *FIDIC – A Guide for Practitioners* (Springer, 2010) xix–xxx.

This freedom to contract about anything has a long history in English common law. Well over 100 years ago, Sir George Jessell MR stated that freedom of contract was the paramount public policy in English common law:

> if there is one thing which more than another public policy requires it is that men of full age and competent understanding shall have the utmost liberty of contracting, and that their contracts when entered into freely and voluntarily shall be held sacred and shall be enforced by courts of justice.[5]

India is a common law country, but for over 100 years it has had a detailed statute that effectively constitutes a default contract code. The *Contracts Act 1972* (India) provides for freedom of contract in the following terms:

> 10 All agreements are contracts if they are made by the free consent of parties competent to contract, for a lawful consideration and with a lawful object, and are not hereby expressly declared to be void. Nothing herein contained shall affect any law in force in India and not hereby expressly repealed by which any contract is required to be made in writing or in the presence of witnesses, or any law relating to the registration of documents.

Malaysia is also a common law country with a *Contracts Act*. The *Contracts Act 1950* (Malaysia) enshrines freedom of contract in statute in the following terms:

> s1(2) Nothing herein contained shall affect any written law or any usage or custom of trade, or any incident of any contract, not inconsistent with this Act.
> 10. (1) All agreements are contracts if they are made by the free consent of parties competent to contract, for a lawful consideration and with a lawful object, and are not hereby expressly declared to be void.
> (2) Nothing herein contained shall affect any law by which any contract is required to be made in writing or in the presence of witnesses, or any law relating to the registration of documents.
> s24. The consideration or object of an agreement is lawful, unless–
> (a) it is forbidden by a law;
> (b) it is of such a nature that, if permitted, it would defeat any law;
> (c) it is fraudulent;
> (d) it involves or implies injury to the person or property of another; or
> (e) the court regards it as immoral, or opposed to public policy.

In each of the above cases, the consideration or object of an agreement is said to be unlawful. Every agreement of which the object or consideration is unlawful is void.

However, the very freedom of contract provided in the *Contracts Act 1950* (Malaysia) gives the parties the freedom to derogate from its provisions. In *Ooi Boon Long v Citibank NA*[6] Lord Brightman held that s1(2) of the *Contracts Act 1950*

> does not say that the contracting parties are unable by agreement to vary the legal consequences spelt out by the Act. Section 1 (2) has no effect on the freedom of contracting parties to decide upon what terms they desire to contract.

Therefore, if parties desire to oust the application of a certain provision of the *Contracts Act 1950*, their intention should be made clear expressly.

Freedom of contract is also a fundamental principle under civil law systems, e.g.

5 *Printing and Numeral Registering Co. v Sampson* (1875) L. R. 19 Eq., 462, 465 per Sir George Jessel MR.
6 [1984] 1 M.L.J. 222 (Malaysian Privy Council).

> In this jurisdiction [Philippines] contracts are enforced as they are read, and parties who are competent to contract may make such agreements within the limitations of the law and public policy as they desire, and the courts will enforce them according to their terms.[7]

In this case the principle is enshrined in statute – Article 1306 of the *Civil Code of the Philippines* states:

> The contracting parties may establish such stipulations, clauses, terms and conditions as they may deem convenient, provided they are not contrary to law, morals, good customs, public order or public policy.

Public policy is largely concerned with the potential for manifest unfairness or injustice in a given situation. Thus, the courts may disregard or refuse to give effect to contractual obligations which, whilst not directly contrary to any express or implied statutory prohibition, nevertheless contravene 'the policy of the law' as discerned from a consideration of the scope and purpose of the particular statute.[8]

Public policy has a very powerful reach in civil law systems. In the European community, most of whose member states have civil law legal systems, parties have similar freedom of contract to that applying under common law systems and are free to choose (within certain limits) the law which is to apply to their contract. *Regulation (EC) number 593/2008* of the European Parliament (***Rome I***) provides in Article 3.1 that 'A contract shall be governed by the law chosen by the parties'. However, it also provides in Article 21 that:

> The application of a provision of the law of any country specified by this Regulation may be refused only if such application is manifestly incompatible with the public policy (*ordre public*) of the forum.

The universal application of freedom of contract is reinforced by its statement in principles that may be regarded as private codifications or restatements of international contract law (modern statements of the *lex mercatoria*):

> *UNIDROIT Principles of International Commercial Contracts 2016:*[9]
>
> 1.1 The parties are free to enter into a contract and to determine its content.
>
> *Trans-Lex Principles:*[10]
>
> IV.1.1 The parties are free to enter into contracts and to determine their contents (principle of party autonomy).

Thus, one of the consequences of freedom of contract is that, subject to the applicable mandatory law and public policy, parties generally have the freedom to make an explicit

7 *Lambert v Fox* 26 Phil 588 [Philippines], cited in Edgardo L Paras, *Civil Code of the Philippines Annotated Volume Four* (14th ed, 2000) 332.

8 *Nelson v Nelson* [1995] HCA 25; (1995) 184 CLR 538, 552, 611.

9 The UNIDROIT Principles and their application to construction contracts are discussed in: Donald Charrett, *Contracts for Construction and Engineering Projects* (2nd ed, Informa Law from Routledge, 2022) Chapter 36.

10 www.trans-lex.org/principles/of-transnational-law- (accessed 30 October 2020).

choice of the proper or governing law of their contract, irrespective of the laws of the Country.

Governments legislate to restrain freedom of contract in various ways, including:

- Illegality/unenforceability of certain contractual terms.
- Implying terms into all contracts of a particular type.
- Creating statutory rights that coexist with contractual rights.
- Mandating the way in which a court or tribunal is to settle disputes or determine contractual rights.

1.1.5 Pacta sunt servanda

The obverse of the principle of freedom of contract is articulated by the doctrine of ***pacta sunt servanda***, a Latin phrase which means that agreements are to be kept. It is a fundamental principle of international law that the provisions of treaties concluded properly are to be observed. The principle means that once parties have exercised their freedom to enter into a contract, they have the legal rights and obligations they have agreed to, and these will be enforced by a court or an arbitrator. Thus, for instance, if the contracting parties have agreed that any disputes will be settled by arbitration, the courts will generally stay any court proceedings commenced in breach of the agreement to arbitrate on the principle that the parties should be kept to their agreement.

Article 1.3 (Binding character of contract) of the *UNIDROIT Principles of International Commercial Contracts 2016* gives effect to the principal of *pacta sunt servanda* in the following terms:

> A contract validly entered into is binding upon the parties. It can only be modified or terminated in accordance with its terms or by agreement or as otherwise provided in these Principles.

The universal nature of this principle has been stated as: 'All the world's legal systems focus on the sanctity of contracts, and damages as the remedy for breach of contract'.[11] The consequences are rather reassuring in the context of construction law:

> the principle of *pacta sunt servanda* ... is universal to all legal systems. This means that the vast majority of construction disputes are fought and won or lost primarily over the wording of the contract (and alleged facts).[12]

Thus, the contract language will generally govern the parties' rights most of the time.

1.1.6 Proper law of the contract

One important aspect of freedom of contract is that parties are generally free to choose the law that governs their contractual relations, known as the **governing law of the contract** or the **proper law of the contract**. In *Garsec v His Majesty the Sultan of Brunei* [2008]

---

11 Robert Knutson (ed), *FIDIC An Analysis of International Construction Contracts* (Wolters Kluwer, 2005) xiv.

12 *Ibid.* xvi.

NSWCA 211 [128], Campbell JA noted an Australian court's analysis of the factors to be considered if the parties have not made an explicit choice of the proper law:

> An important feature of the proper law of an international contract is that, subject to questions of public policy and bona fides, the parties are free to choose what the proper law will be: *Vita Food Products Inc v. Unus Shipping Co Ltd* [1939] AC 277. If, on construing the contract, the court is unable to conclude that the parties intended that contract to be governed by reference to a particular system of law, the court identifies a proper law by ascertaining the system of law with which the transaction has its closest and most real connection: *Bonython v Commonwealth of Australia* [1951] AC 201; *Akai Pty Ltd v. People's Insurance Co Limited* [1996] HCA 39; 91996) 188 CLR 418 at 440-1. But whether the proper law is ascertained from the intention of the parties, or under the *Bonython* test, makes no difference to those aspects of the contract – which might, on some accounts of the law, extend to its formation, validity, interpretation, and the rights and obligations of the parties under it – that are decided in accordance with the proper law of the contract. Other systems of law besides that of the forum and the proper law can sometimes come to bear upon the contract – as when its performance is illegal under the law of the place where it is to be performed. However it can be seen that one of the purposes of recognising a proper law of contract is to allow the parties to have freedom of choice about the system of law that will govern their relations, to the extent that other systems of law do not impose themselves upon the formation, performance or enforcement of the contract. That purpose is also advanced by applying the substantive/procedural distinction articulated in *John Pfeiffer v. Rogerson* (2000) 203 CLR 503 to litigation concerning international contracts.

In *Attorney-General of Botswana v Aussie Diamond Products Pty Ltd (No 3)* [2010] WASC 14, in dealing with the factors relevant to the ascertainment of the proper law of the contract In Australia, Murphy J noted in paragraphs 207 and 208:

> In my view, the law of Western Australia is the system of law with which the contract is most directly connected, and hence is the proper law of the contract: see *Bonython v. the Commonwealth of Australia* (1950) 81 CLR 486, 498: *Akai Pty Ltd v. The People's Insurance Co Ltd* (1996) 188 CLR 418, 434. The following features are relevant. The offer, in the quotation dated 13 May 2003, and all subsequent contractual communications, was in English. The consideration provided by the Department was in Australian dollars. It was to be paid by a confirming bank in Australia upon the presentation of documents. The goods were to be supplied from Australia and c.i.f obligations were to be undertaken by the defendant in Australia. Although commissioning was to occur in Botswana, that fact alone does not outweigh the other considerations to which I have referred, which point to the law of the contract being the law of Western Australia.
>
> Whilst the question of the proper law is, in each case, dependent on the particular nature and terms of the contract and its surrounding circumstances, the conclusion which I have reached here derives some support, I think, from *Mendelsohn-Zeller Inc v T&C Providores Pty Ltd* [1981] NSWLR 366 and *Power Curber International Ltd v. National Bank of Kuwait* [1981] 1 WLR 1233 and the factors considered relevant in those cases.

Where the parties have not made an explicit choice of the governing law of the contract, and there is more than one legal jurisdiction whose laws govern the Contract, there is a conflict of laws. A judge or arbitrator adjudicating a dispute must determine the governing law of the contract by the appropriate conflict of laws rules. The application of conflict of laws rules may involve a complicated interaction between the facts of the case and the procedural law and substantive law of different legal jurisdictions, where there is no unanimity of conflict of laws rules.

In this writer's view, it is highly desirable to make an explicit choice of the governing law of the contract in the Contract Data, to avoid the possibility of subsequent dispute over what it is. As noted in section 1.5.1, the default position in the FIDIC rainbow suite of contracts is that the law of the Country will be the governing law of the contract, excluding any conflict of law rules.

1.1.7 International construction contracts

The main focus of the book is on international contracts. An **international construction contract** is a contract for the provision of goods and services in which:

(a) The parties to the Contract have, at the time of the conclusion of their agreement, their places of business in different legal jurisdictions, or
(b) One of the following places is situated outside the legal jurisdiction in which the parties have their places of business:
    (i) The Site, or
    (ii) Any place where a substantial part of the obligations for the Works is to be performed.

Although building work is a species of construction, domestic building work is outside the scope of this book, and accordingly there is no reference to any legislation or other provisions that regulate domestic building contracts or work in any jurisdiction.

1.2 *Lex constructionis*[13]

1.2.1 What is it?

The use of FIDIC contracts across jurisdictions is of particular interest in considering the extent to which there is a 'common law of construction contracts' or a '*lex constructionis*', despite the differences in legal systems and jurisdictions. The book by Jaeger and Hök[14] is especially valuable for its commentary on different philosophical approaches to drafting international contracts, and how the FIDIC contracts are applied in civil law jurisdictions. The book edited by Knutson[15] contains chapters on the use of FIDIC contracts in 13 different countries – four common law,[16] eight civil law[17] and one Shari'a.[18] The commentaries in Knutson's book clearly underscore the differences between legal jurisdictions in the use of FIDIC contracts, leading one to question whether there could be any such concept as *lex constructionis*.

However, notwithstanding the common law genesis of FIDIC contracts, and the significant differences in a number of legal theories, the following observation from the perspective of German law suggests there may be substantive common ground:

13 This topic is discussed in more detail in: Donald Charrett, '*Lex constructionis* – or My Country's Rules?' [2021] *International Construction Law Review* 61; and Donald Charrett, *Contracts for Construction and Engineering Projects* (2nd ed, Informa Law from Routledge, 2022) Chapter 35.

14 Axel-Volkmar Jaeger and Götz-Sebastian Hök, *FIDIC – A Guide for Practitioners* (Springer, 2010).

15 Robert Knutson (ed), *FIDIC: An Analysis of International Construction Contracts* (Kluwer Law International, 2005).

16 England, India, Malaysia and the USA.

17 Brazil, Egypt, France, Germany, Japan, Netherlands, Sweden and Switzerland.

18 Saudi Arabia.

> The legal background of the 'Werkvertrag' as contained in the German Civil Code does not lead to a completely different structure of a construction contract compared to the FIDIC-new series model forms, however some features of the FIDIC-new series, which stem from English construction law, are either unknown (eg the Engineer) or differently regulated (eg provisional and final acceptance of the works) in German construction law. Apart from these two major differences both the structure and the system of a construction contract of CONS [red book] and P & DB [yellow book] seem to lead to both in similar legal principles and sometimes even the same results (eg *force majeure*, risk and responsibility, damages and compensation.[19]

Perhaps the clearest pointer to what there is of a *lex constructionis* is the following statement on the fundamental importance of the words of the contract itself, vindicating the twin principles of freedom of contract and *pacta sunt servanda*:

> Finally, deep in the night, with no one else around, most lawyers in their heart of hearts will admit – the Contract usually decides the issues, despite what the law is.[20]

1.2.2 Promotion of best practice for successful projects

It is suggested that *lex constructionis* can promote best practice for successful projects in which the contracting parties' legitimate expectations can be realised. In this writer's view, those legitimate expectations are typically along the following lines:

Employer

- Completion of the project on time, for the Contract Price and to the agreed standard of quality.
- Timely and adequate communication from the Contractor of any departures from the original scope of Works, the materialisation of risks and any claims.

Contractor

- Prompt payment of all amounts due under the Contract.
- Freedom to carry out the construction in accordance with the Contract without hindrance by the Employer.
- Timely and adequate communication from the Employer of the materialisation of any risks, communication of instructions and assessment of claims.

It is submitted that the principles proposed here, if followed, would fulfill those expectations. The proposed principles have been formulated taking into account the unique features of construction projects and construction contracts discussed earlier, the Abrahamson principles of balanced risk allocation,[21] the FIDIC General Conditions in the rainbow suite, the FIDIC Golden Principles[22] and 'social obligations' owed to third

19 Wolfgang Rosener and Gerhard Dorner, 'Germany' in Robert Knutson (ed), *FIDIC: An Analysis of International Construction Contracts* (Kluwer Law International, 2005) 87, 125.

20 Robert Knutson (ed), *FIDIC: An Analysis of International Construction Contracts* (Kluwer Law International, 2005) xix.

21 Max W Abrahamson, 'Risk Management' (1983) *International Construction Law Review* 241, 244.

22 See Chapter 2.

parties. They are also influenced by Molyneaux's paper on this topic in which he formulated a 'modest Mosaic ten' principles.[23]

One of the criticisms that could be directed to the proposed (or any) principles of *lex constructionis* is that they cannot cover all situations, nor can they necessarily be applied in their entirety in many situations. The following discussion of principles in the context of *lex mercatoria* is equally applicable to the proposed principles of *lex constructionis*:

> General principles do not necessarily have pre-set conditions for application. Instead they merely constitute 'rules of optimal application' which means that they may be complied with in varying degrees. The required degree of compliance depends not only on the actual but also on the legal options open to the target group. Application of general principles therefore requires a substantial process of weighing up contradictory principles and rules. General principles are therefore always subject to a continual discussion about the effectiveness and scope.[24] (citations omitted)

1.2.3 Proposed principles of lex constructionis

Overarching principles

1. Pacta sunt servanda.
2. ***Rebus sic stantibus*** – doctrines or rules relating to changed conditions.
3. The parties must act in accordance with good faith and fair dealing in construction contracts.

Scope

4. The contract defines, in writing, the original scope of Works and the known conditions at the Site.
5. The Employer has the right to instruct Variations consistent with the original scope of the Contract, and the Contractor has the obligation to carry out all such Variations.
6. Construction Works must be carried out so as to protect the health and safety of workers.
7. Construction Works must not adversely affect the environment or the interests of third parties.
8. Subject to any contractual requirements, the Contractor selects the methods and timing of the Works.

Risk

9. Each risk is allocated to the Party best able to manage and control it and the consequences if it eventuates, or to the Party who will derive any benefit or suffer the least consequences if the risk eventuates.
10. A Party is not allocated risks that it cannot insure for or has insufficient financial resources to bear.

23 Charles Molineaux, 'Moving toward a construction *lex mercatoria* A *lex constructionis*' (1997) 1 *JIntArb* 55.

24 Klaus Peter Berger, *The Creeping Codification of the New Lex Mercatoria,* (Wolters Kluwer The Netherlands, 2010), 201.

11. The Contractor is responsible for the Works whilst it is in possession of the Site.

Time

12. The parties have a reasonable time to perform their obligations and exercise their rights.
13. The Contractor provides the Employer with prompt and adequate notice of any unexpected conditions that affect its performance, the occurrence of any risk events and any Claims.
14. The Employer provides the Contractor with prompt and adequate notice of the occurrence of any risk events that affect the Contractor, instructions and responses to Claims.
15. The Contractor is liable to pay damages if it does not complete the Works by the contractually agreed date.

Cost

16. The Employer has adequate financial resources to complete the Contract.
17. The Contractor provides security for its performance.
18. The Employer pays the Contractor its contractual entitlements promptly.

Quality

19. The Contractor either rectifies defects in its Works or pays damages to reinstate the Works to the contractually specified quality.

Disputes

20. Unresolved disputes are finally determined by arbitration.

1.2.4 Discussion

Space does not permit a detailed exposition of each of the aforementioned principles. Some would probably be accepted as implied terms that go without saying. Others may be more controversial.

The overarching principles are contained in statements of the *lex mercatoria*, such as the UNIDROIT Principles. In this writer's view they are important for the successful execution of construction projects that frequently take place over a long time and involve changed circumstances. In particular, the requirements of honesty, fairness and reasonableness inherent in the good faith principle will necessarily be relied upon to resolve amicably (where possible) many of the expected and unexpected issues that can arise during the execution of a construction contract.

The principles on scope acknowledge the complexity of construction projects, the possibility that the scope may need to change and that the Works impact on third parties and the environment. Risks are inherent in any construction project, and their appropriate allocation is often critical to achieving a successful project.[25]

25 For a discussion of the consequences of inappropriately allocating risk, see: Japan International Cooperation Agency, 'Check List for One Sided Contracts' (2011), 1 www.jica.go.jp/english/our_work/types_of_assistance/oda_loans/oda_op_info/guide/c8h0vm0000aoeprl-att/guide02.pdf (accessed 4 April 2022).

The principles related to time reiterate the requirement of reasonableness and emphasise the importance of adequate and timely communication from Contractor to Employer and vice versa. Damages for late completion are appropriate to compensate the Employer for its inability to make commercial use of the constructed facility from the agreed date.

Certainty and promptness of payment are usually of great importance to the Contractor and may be critical to its solvency. The requirement for a Contractor to rectify or pay for defect rectification is merely a construction-specific implementation of *pacta sunt servanda.*

The near universal implementation of the *New York Convention*, the norms of international arbitration and the finality and enforcement of awards are the basis for arbitration to generally be the most appropriate method for resolving international construction disputes. However, litigation in the international commercial courts recently established in a number of jurisdictions may provide a viable alternative to arbitration for some international construction disputes.[26]

1.3 FIDIC contracts

1.3.1 Overview

The Fédération Internationale des Ingénieurs-Conseils (**FIDIC**) (known by its English name of the International Federation of Consulting Engineers) publishes standard form Conditions of Contract that are used in many countries and are probably the most widely used international construction contracts in the world. Although they have a common law pedigree, they are intended to be used in any legal jurisdiction whether common law, civil law or any other type of law.

FIDIC publishes the standard forms of construction contract between Employer and Contractor shown in Table 1.1.[27]

The various editions of the FIDIC Conditions of Contract for contracts between Employer and Contractor are tabulated in Table 1.4 in the Annexure to this chapter.

In March 2021 FIDIC announced that the Contracts Committee would set up task groups to develop three new FIDIC contract forms: Public Private Partnerships (**PPP** or **3Ps**), Engineering, Procurement and Construction Management (EPCM) and alliancing.

FIDIC publishes the following standard forms of subcontract between Contractor and Subcontractor:[28]

- Conditions of Subcontract for Work of Civil Engineering Construction – First Edition 1994
- Conditions of Subcontract for Construction – First Edition 2011
- Conditions of Subcontract for Plant and Design (Yellow Book 1999) – First Edition 2019.

26 International commercial courts, including the enforcement of international court judgments, are discussed in Philip Loots and Donald Charrett, *Contracts for Infrastructure Projects: An International Guide to Application* (Informa Law from Routledge, 2022) ¶28.13.2.

27 These FIDIC contracts were listed on the FIDIC website (www.fidic.org/bookshop) on 4 November 2020.

28 These FIDIC contracts were listed on the FIDIC website (www.fidic.org/bookshop) on 24 February 2022.

Table 1.1 FIDIC Conditions of Contract for contracts between Employer and Contractor

1977 Red Book	Conditions of Contract for Works of Civil Engineering Construction – Third Edition 1977
1987 Red Book	Conditions of Contract for Works of Civil Engineering Construction Fourth Edition 1987
1987 Yellow Book	Conditions of Contract for Electrical and Mechanical Works – Third Edition 1987
1995 Orange Book	Conditions of Contract for Design-Build and Turnkey – First Edition 1995
1999 Red Book	Conditions of Contract for Construction – First Edition 1999
1999 Yellow Book	Conditions of Contract for Plant and Design-Build – First Edition 1999
1999 Silver Book	Conditions of Contract for EPC/Turnkey Projects – First Edition 1999
2017 Red Book	Conditions of Contract for Construction – Second Edition 2017 This document has been amended by: Amendments Issue No 1 – December 2018, Amendments Issue No 2 – June 2019, Amendments Issue No 3 – November 2022[a] These amendments have been incorporated in the Construction Contract 2nd Ed (2017 Red Book, Reprinted 2022 with amendments)
2017 Yellow Book	Conditions of Contract for Plant and Design-Build – Second Edition 2017 This document has been amended by: Amendments Issue No 1 – December 2018, Amendments Issue No 2 – June 2019, Amendments Issue No 3 – November 2022[b] These amendments have been incorporated in the Plant and Design-Build Contract 2nd Ed (2017 Yellow Book Reprinted 2022 with amendments)
2017 Silver Book	Conditions of Contract for EPC/Turnkey Projects – Second Edition 2017 This document has been amended by: Amendments Issue No 1 – December 2018, Amendments Issue No 2 – June 2019, Amendments Issue No 3 – November 2022[c] These amendments have been incorporated in the EPC/Turnkey Contract 2nd Ed (2017 Silver Book Reprinted 2022 with amendments)
Green Book	Short Form of Contract – First Edition 1999, Second Edition 2021
Pink Book	Conditions of Contract for Construction – Multilateral Development Bank Harmonised Edition for Building and Engineering Works Designed by the Employer – Version 1: 2005, Version 2: March 2005, Version 3: 2010
Gold Book	Conditions of Contract for Design, Build and Operate Projects – First Edition, 2008
Blue-Green Book	Form of Contract for Dredging and Reclamation Works – First Edition 2006, Second Edition 2016
Emerald Book	Conditions of Contract for Underground Works First Edition 2019

[a] https://fidic.org/sites/default/files/bean_files/2017%20FIDIC%20Red%20-seperated%20errata.pdf (accessed 20 May 2023).

[b] https://fidic.org/sites/default/files/bean_files/2017%20FIDIC%20Yellow%20-%20seperated%20errata.pdf (accessed 20 May 2023).

[c] https://fidic.org/sites/default/files/bean_files/2017%20FIDIC%20Silver%20-%20seperated%20errrata.pdf (accessed 20 May 2023).

The **Red Book**,[29] **Yellow Book**[30] and **Silver Book**[31] (as well as the Pink Book) are commonly referred to as the **rainbow suite**. The focus of this book is mainly on the rainbow suite, and sub-clause references refer to the Second Edition 2017 Red, Yellow and Silver Books unless otherwise noted. However, the principles outlined are generally applicable to all the FIDIC standard form contracts.

A number of guides to the use of FIDIC contracts are listed in section 1.10.5.

The FIDIC rainbow suite standard forms generally comprise:

- Acknowledgements.
- Notes.
- General Conditions.
- Guidance for the Preparation of Particular Conditions.
- Annexes: Forms of Securities.
- Forms of Letter of Tender, Letter of Acceptance, Contract Agreement and Dispute Adjudication/Avoidance Agreement.

The Acknowledgements list the numerous groups and individuals that contribute to the rigorous process of developing, reviewing, refining and approval of FIDIC standard form contracts. These contributors include the Contracts Committee that drafts the documents, the Task Groups that provide input to the Contracts Committee, special advisors and friendly reviewers. The large number of individuals involved from many countries with extensive contract, construction, engineering and legal skills highlights FIDIC's comprehensive process of drafting contracts that acknowledge the importance of the many stakeholders and their endeavours to produce balanced contracts that represent best international practice.

1.3.2 MDB use of FIDIC contracts

A number of multilateral development banks (**MDBs**) use FIDIC General Conditions in their Standard Bidding Documents (**SBD**s). MDBs that have embraced FIDIC General Conditions include the World Bank, Asian Development Bank, Black Sea Trade and Development Bank, European Bank for Reconstruction and Development, Caribbean Development Bank and the Inter-American Development Bank.

The use of FIDIC General Conditions by MDBs in their SBDs lead to the promulgation of the Pink Book in 2005. This was based on the 1999 Red Book, with the addition of a number of provisions required by MDBs to further their development goals of enhancing living standards and to protect the MDBs' interests in probity and proper use of loan funds. In particular the Pink Book contains the following additional 12 sub-clauses in the Red Book clause 6 Staff and Labour:

6.12 Foreign personnel

29 References to the Red Book without a year preface refer to the 1999 Red Book and the 2017 Red Book.

30 References to the Yellow Book without a year preface refer to the 1999 Yellow Book and the 2017 Yellow Book.

31 References to the Silver Book without a year preface refer to the 1999 Silver Book and the 2017 Silver Book.

6.13 Supply of foodstuffs
6.14 Supply of water
6.15 Measures against insect and pest nuisance
6.16 Alcoholic liquor and drugs
6.17 Arms and ammunition
6.18 Festivals and religious customs
6.19 Funeral arrangements
6.20 Forced labour
6.21 Child labour
6.22 Employee records of workers
6.23 Workers' organisations

These 'social provisions' in the Pink Book provide protections for labour, local communities and the environment that may not be adequately covered by legislation in less developed countries. The Pink Book also contains draconian MDB-specific provisions on the consequences of corrupt or fraudulent practices by the Contractor or any of its employees.[32]

The extensive international input into the drafting of FIDIC General Conditions and its acceptance as an appropriate contract for international contracts is evidenced by the World Bank's implementation of the 2017 Red Book in its 2019 Standard Procurement Document.[33] The Particular Conditions of Contract in the World Bank Standard Procurement Document does not change the balanced risk/reward allocation in the General Conditions, and mainly comprises 'social provisions' such as those outlined for the Pink Book.

Japan International Cooperation Agency (JICA) is one of the world's largest bilateral aid agencies supporting socioeconomic development in developing countries in different regions of the world. It is in charge of administering Japan's Official Development Assistance and uses FIDIC General Conditions in some of its SBDs. JICA's rationale for its strong support of FIDIC contracts and its continued use of the Pink Book is explained elsewhere.[34]

1.3.3 FIDIC Contract documents

A 'FIDIC Contract' comprises a number of documents that are to be taken as mutually explanatory of one another, in the order of precedence in the event of inconsistency between them shown in Table 1.2.[35]

32 Sub-clause 15.6.

33 http://pubdocs.worldbank.org/en/865231562944956956/SPD-Request-for-Bids-WORKS-after-prequalification.docx (accessed 28 August 2020).

34 Takashi Ito and Michino Yamaguchi, 'JICA's Perspectives on the use of FIDIC Contracts' in Donald Charrett (ed), *The Application of FIDIC Contracts in Asia Pacific A Practical Guide to Application* (Informa Law from Routledge, 2022) Chapter 5.

35 Rainbow suite sub-clause 1.5.

Table 1.2 Order of precedence of Contract documents in the FIDIC rainbow suite

	2017 Red Book	2017 Yellow Book	2017 Silver Book
(a)	The Contract Agreement	The Contract Agreement	The Contract Agreement
(b)	The Letter of Acceptance	The Letter of Acceptance	The Particular Conditions Part A – Contract Data
(c)	The Letter of Tender	The Letter of Tender	The Particular Conditions Part B – Special Provisions
(d)	The Particular Conditions Part A – Contract Data	The Particular Conditions Part A – Contract Data	The General Conditions
(e)	The Particular Conditions Part B – Special Provisions	The Particular Conditions Part B – Special Provisions	The Employer's Requirements
(f)	The General Conditions	The General Conditions	The Schedules
(g)	The Specification	The Employer's Requirements	The Tender
(h)	The drawings	The Schedules	The JV Undertaking (if the Contractor is a JV)
(i)	The Schedules	The Contractor's Proposal	Any other documents forming part of the Contract
(j)	The JV Undertaking (if the Contractor is a JV)	The JV Undertaking (if the Contractor is a JV)	
(k)	Any other documents forming part of the Contract	Any other documents forming part of the Contract	

1.3.4 Contract Agreement

The Contract Agreement form is a two-page pro forma document that requires the essential details of the Contract to be filled in, and formally executed by the Parties. As this document is the highest in priority of the Contract documents, it is essential that it be accurate and comprehensive, and executed in accordance with the governing law of the contract. Appropriate legal advice should be sought to ensure that the resulting Contract complies with all of the relevant legal requirements. Particular jurisdictions may require specific formalities for the Contract to be legally binding, such as payment of stamp duty. Specific jurisdiction requirements are discussed in the later Chapters.

1.3.5 Particular Conditions

The list of Contract documents in Table 1.2 highlights that the Particular Conditions (those Conditions of Contract that are specific to the unique Contract) comprise two parts:

- Part A – Contract Data.
- Part B – Special Provisions.

1.3.6 Particular Conditions Part A – Contract Data

The Contract Data, as its name implies, contains the data that is required to define all the unique characteristics of the particular Contract, e.g. the Parties, the Site, the

Time for Completion, the governing law of the contract, Contract Price, liability, securities, Defects Notification Period, etc. It is pro forma, consisting of five pages of items referring to sub-clauses of the General Conditions which require insertion of data by the Employer (before calling Tenders), or the Contractor (in its Tender). The Annexure to Chapter 3 shows the Contract Data in the 2017 Yellow Book, annotated with default provisions.

1.3.7 Particular Conditions Part B – Special Provisions

Special Provisions necessary for the particular requirements of the Works may comprise either modifications to the General Conditions or additional provisions. Such modifications may be necessary or desirable:

- To comply or align with applicable law.
- For the specific requirements of the Site or the Works.
- For the Employer's preferences.

Each of these topics is dealt with in more detail in the following.

1.3.8 General Conditions

The General Conditions as printed are FIDIC copyright and accordingly cannot legally be reproduced or amended without FIDIC permission. In particular, this includes scanning to produce a soft copy that is then modified. As noted earlier, whilst the FIDIC General Conditions have been drafted to be applicable to a wide range of international construction contracts in various jurisdictions, the unique requirements of a particular Contract may mean that the FIDIC General Conditions require modification. The use of a single Conditions of Contract document incorporating both Particular Conditions and General Conditions is discussed in section 3.5.

1.4 The FIDIC Golden Principles

The Guidance for the Preparation of Particular Conditions in the Emerald Book contains the following recommendation:

> FIDIC strongly recommends that the Employer, the Contractor and all drafters of the Special Provisions take all due regard of the five FIDIC Golden Principles:
>
> GP1: The duties, rights, obligations, roles and responsibilities of all the Contract Participants must be generally as implied in the General Conditions, and appropriate to the requirements of the project.
> GP2: The Particular Conditions must be drafted clearly and unambiguously.
> GP3: The Particular Conditions must not change the balance of risk/reward allocation provided for in the General Conditions.
> GP4: All time periods specified in the Contract for Contract Participants to perform their obligations must be of reasonable duration.
> GP5: Unless there is a conflict with the governing law of the Contract, all formal disputes must be referred to a Dispute Avoidance/Adjudication Board (or a Dispute Adjudication

Board, if applicable) for a provisionally binding decision as a condition precedent to arbitration.[36]

These FIDIC golden principles are described and explained in the publication FIDIC's Golden Principles (http://http://fidic.org/bookshop), and are necessary to ensure that modifications to the General Conditions:

- are limited to those necessary for the particular features of the Site and the project, and necessary to comply with the applicable law;
- do not change the essential fair and balanced character of a FIDIC contract; and
- the Contract remains recognisable as a FIDIC contract.[37]

A more detailed explanation of the Golden Principles is in Chapter 2. That chapter includes some general guidance on preparing Particular Conditions to comply with the Golden Principles. The overarching justification for the Golden Principles is to enable a contract to be recognised as a 'FIDIC Contract' that complies with widely accepted international norms and promotes best practice in contract execution and administration.

For another view on the FIDIC Golden Principles, see the article in *Construction Law International* by Graeme Christie.[38]

1.5 Applicable laws

Applicable laws can be mandatory or non-mandatory:

- **Mandatory law** is based on public policy, and as it cannot be excluded by the parties, it will prevail over any Conditions of Contract.
- **Non-mandatory law** will apply to the extent that the parties have not agreed otherwise.

Distinguishing between mandatory and non-mandatory law can generally only be determined by construction of the relevant law itself.

Irrespective of the wording of the Conditions of Contract and notwithstanding freedom of contract, if the General Conditions are incompatible with mandatory law, mandatory law will apply. Applicable mandatory law that may be inconsistent with the General Conditions could be, *inter alia*, Laws relating to the execution of work at the Site or any other location and/or the governing law of the contract.

As Site personnel and Contract Administrators may not be familiar with all of the applicable law, in this writer's view it is desirable that Special Provisions are included in the Particular Conditions Part B that articulate all the changes to the General Conditions that are necessary to comply with mandatory law. As discussed further in section 3.1, it may

36 Since publication of the 2017 editions of the rainbow suite, GP5 has been amended as follows: '*Unless there is a conflict with the governing law of the Contract*, all formal disputes must be referred to a Dispute Avoidance/Adjudication Board (or a Dispute Adjudication Board, if applicable) for a provisionally binding decision as a condition precedent to arbitration' (emphasis added).

37 Emerald Book Guidance for the Preparation of Particular Conditions, 8. The 2017 Red Book, 2017 Yellow Book and the 2017 Silver Book contain a similar recommendation.

38 Graeme Christie, 'The Golden Principles – FIDIC's Shiny Christmas Present' (2018) 13.2 *Construction Law International* 10.

also be desirable for Particular Conditions to incorporate provisions that are not incompatible with the General Conditions but refer to issues within the scope of the mandatory law that are not referred to in the General Conditions. Such Particular Conditions will ensure that the Conditions of Contract are an accurate and comprehensive contract management manual that can safely be followed.

Each of the jurisdiction Chapters 4–13 addresses Special Provisions both necessary for consistency with mandatory law and desirable to articulate issues within the scope of the mandatory law which are not referred to in the General Conditions.

1.5.1 Laws

The 2017 Yellow Book has the following relevant provisions referring to Laws:

1.1 Definitions

1.1.49 '**Laws**' means all national (or state or provincial) legislation, statutes, acts, decrees, rules, ordinances, orders, treaties, international law and other laws, and regulations and by-laws of any legally constituted public authority.

1.13 Compliance with Laws:

The Contractor and the Employer shall, in performing the Contract, comply with all applicable Laws. ...

The definition of laws includes laws of the Country as well as the governing law of the contract. Compliance with Laws is referred to in a number of other subclauses in the Yellow Book:

3.5 Engineer's Instructions

... If ... the Contractor considers that the instruction: ...

(b) does not comply with applicable Laws ...

The Contractor shall immediately ... give a Notice to the Engineer with reasons.

4.8 Health and Safety Obligations

The Contractor shall:

(a) comply with all applicable health and safety regulations and Laws; ...

The Contractor shall ... maintain records and make reports (in compliance with the applicable health and safety regulations and Laws) concerning the health and safety of persons and any damage to property.

4.10 Use of Site Data

... the Contractor shall be deemed ... to have been satisfied before submitting the Tender as to all matters relevant to the execution of the Works, including:

(d) the Laws, procedures and labour practices of the Country; ...

4.18 Protection of the Environment

... The Contractor shall ensure that emissions, surface discharges, effluent and any other pollutants from the Contractor's activities shall exceed neither the values indicated in the Employer's Requirements nor those prescribed by applicable Laws.

5.1 General Design Obligations

The Contractor shall carry out, and be responsible for, the design of the Works. Design shall be prepared by designers who: ...

(c) are qualified and entitled under applicable Laws to design the Works. ...

5.3 Contractor's Undertaking

The Contractor undertakes that the design, the Contractor's Documents, the execution of the Works and the completed Works will be in accordance with:

(a) the Laws of the Country; ...

5.4 Technical Standards and Regulations

The Contractor's Documents, the execution of the Works and the completed Works (including defects remedied by the Contractor) shall comply with the Country's technical standards, building, construction and environmental Laws, Laws applicable to the product being produced from the Works, and other standards specified in the Employer's Requirements, applicable to the Works, or defined by applicable Laws. ...

6.2 Rates of Wages and Conditions of Labour

The Contractor shall pay rates of wages, and observe conditions of labour, which comply with all applicable Laws ...

6.4 Labour Laws

The Contractor shall comply with all the relevant labour Laws applicable to the Contractor's Personnel, including Laws relating to their employment (including wages and working hours), health, safety, welfare, immigration and emigration, and shall allow them all their legal rights.

The Contractor shall require the Contractor's Personnel to obey all applicable Laws, including those concerning health and safety at work.

7.4 Testing by the Contractor

... The Contractor shall provide all apparatus, assistance, documents and other information, temporary supplies of electricity and water, equipment, fuel, consumables, instruments, labour, materials, and suitably qualified, experienced and competent staff, as are necessary to carry out the specified tests efficiently and properly. All apparatus, equipment and instruments shall be calibrated in accordance with the standards specified in the Employer's Requirements or defined by applicable Laws and, if requested by the Engineer, the Contractor shall submit calibration certificates before carrying out testing. ...

7.7 Ownership of Plant and Materials

Each item of Plant and Materials shall, to the extent consistent with the mandatory requirements of the Laws of the Country, become the property of the Employer at whichever is the earlier of the following times, free from liens and other encumbrances: ...

11.11 Clearance of Site

... If the Contractor fails to comply with sub-paragraphs (a), (b) and/or (c) above within 28 days after the issue of the Performance Certificate, the Employer may sell (to the extent permitted by applicable Laws) or otherwise dispose of any remaining items and/or may reinstate and clean the Site (as may be necessary) at the Contractor's cost. ...

15.2 Termination for Contractor's Default

15.2.1 Notice

> The Employer shall be entitled to give a Notice … to the Contractor of the Employer's intention to terminate the Contract or, in the case of sub-paragraph (f), (g) or (h) below a Notice of termination, if the Contractor: …
>
> (g) becomes bankrupt or insolvent; goes into liquidation, administration, reorganisation, winding-up or dissolution; becomes subject to the appointment of a liquidator, receiver, administrator, manager or trustee; enters into a composition or arrangement with the Contractor's creditors; or any act is done or any event occurs which is analogous to or has a similar effect to any of these acts or events under applicable Laws; …
>
> **16.2 Termination by Contractor**
>
> 16.2.1 Notice
>
> The Contractor shall be entitled to give a Notice … to the Employer of the Contractor's intention to terminate the Contract or, in the case of sub-paragraph (g)(ii), (h), (i) or (j) below, a Notice of termination, if:
>
> (i) the Employer becomes bankrupt or insolvent; goes into liquidation, administration, reorganisation, winding-up or dissolution; becomes subject to the appointment of a liquidator, receiver, administrator, manager or trustee; enters into a composition or arrangement with the Employer's creditors; or any act is done or any event occurs which is analogous to or has a similar effect to any of these acts or events under applicable Laws; or …
>
> **19.2 Insurance to be provided by the Contractor**
>
> 19.2.6 Other insurances required by Laws and by local practice
>
> The Contractor shall provide all other insurance as required by the Laws of the countries where (any part of) the Works are being carried out, at the Contractor's own cost.

These provisions refer explicitly or implicitly to the Laws of the Country where the Site is located, with the exception of sub-clauses 5.1 (General Design Obligations) and 19.2 (Insurance to be Provided by the Contractor) where the relevant Works may be executed in a country other than the Country where the Site is located.

1.5.2 Governing law of the contract

The 2017 Yellow Book refers to the governing law of the contract as follows:

> **1.4 Law and Language**
>
> The Contract shall be governed by the law of the country (or other jurisdiction) stated in the Contract Data (if not stated, the law of the Country), excluding any conflict of law rules.

The governing law is referred to in the following additional sub-clauses of the Yellow Book:

> **1.16 Contract Termination**
>
> Subject to any mandatory requirements under the governing law of the contract, termination of the Contract under any Sub-Clause of these Conditions shall require no action of whatsoever kind by either Party other than as stated in the Sub-Clause.
>
> **18.6 Release from Performance under the Law**

In addition to any other provision of this Clause, if any event arises outside the control of the Parties (including, but not limited to, an Exceptional Event) which: (a) makes it impossible or unlawful for either Party or both Parties to fulfil their contractual obligations; or (b) under the law governing the Contract, entitles the Parties to be released from further performance of the Contract, ...

21.2 Failure to Appoint DAAB Member(s)

... Thereafter, the Parties and the member(s) so appointed shall be deemed to have signed and be bound by a DAAB Agreement under which: ... (ii) the law governing the DAAB Agreement shall be the governing law of the contract defined in Sub- Clause 1.4 *[Law and Language]*.

The governing law is referred to in the following sub-clauses of the Appendix General Conditions of Dispute Avoidance/Adjudication Agreement:

10 Resignation and Termination

10.9 Subject to any mandatory requirements under the governing law of the DAA's Agreement, termination of the DAA Agreement under this Clause shall require no action of whatsoever kind by the Parties or the DAAB Member (as the case may be) other than as stated in this clause.

1.5.3 Intersection of local laws with the governing law of the contract

The following are a few examples of issues in which the governing law may be inconsistent with applicable and mandatory Laws of the Country:

- Decennial liability and liability generally for the total or partial collapse of structures.[39]
- Use of liens.[40]
- Local procurement.[41]
- Adjudication of disputes.[42]
- Termination for reorganisation.[43]

These issues are covered in more detail in Chapter 3.

1.5.4 Laws with extra-territorial reach

In addition to obligations that arise under the governing law of the contract, or the Laws applicable to the Site and the Country, there may be laws applying to legal persons in particular jurisdictions that apply irrespective of the jurisdiction of the Site or Country. For example, no matter what jurisdiction they are operating in, anti-trust/corruption laws

39 E.g. see section 15.5.1.2.
40 E.g. see section 13.5.1.3.
41 E.g. see sections 12.8.1 and 13.8.1.
42 E.g. see section 9.11.
43 E.g. see Thiago Fernandes Moreira and Caio Gabra, 'Brazil' in Donald Charrett (ed), *FIDIC Contracts in the Americas: A Practical Guide to Application* (Informa Law from Routledge, 2024) 127.

apply to US companies, and human rights laws apply to European companies. Not only does the *Bribery Act 2010* (UK) apply to the UK and UK companies, but the UK courts have jurisdiction if an offence is committed by someone with a close connection with the UK, or by a corporation which does business in the UK, regardless of where the alleged offence was carried out.

1.5.5 Laws applicable to the execution of a construction project

Applicable Laws relevant to the execution of a construction project may include:

- The law governing the parties' capacity to enter into a contract.
- The governing or proper law of the contract.
- Laws relating to the Site where the Works are carried out (referred to in the FIDIC General Conditions as discussed in section 1.5.1) (***lex loci rei sitae***).
- The law relating to the disposition of property (***in rem* claims**).
- Procedural law that applies to any court proceedings, including the coercive power of the court in support of arbitration proceedings (**law of the forum** or ***lex fori***).
- Laws applying to a corporation which does business in a country (e.g. the *Bribery Act 2010* [UK]).

1.5.6 Laws applicable to arbitration of a dispute

The following laws may apply to arbitration of a dispute arising from a construction project:

- The law governing the parties' capacity to enter into an arbitration agreement.
- The law governing the substance of the dispute, generally the governing law of the contract.
- The law governing the arbitration agreement and the performance of that agreement.
- The law governing the existence and operation of the arbitral tribunal (***lex arbitrii***, sometimes referred to as the **curial law**), generally the law of the 'seat' of arbitration.
- The law (or laws) governing the recognition and enforcement of an arbitral award.

The arbitration agreement is usually incorporated in the Contract but is treated for legal purposes as a separate and independent agreement for the purpose of determining its validity or enforceability. This **doctrine of separability** is a generally recognised principle of the law of international arbitration.[44] It is specifically recognised in the *UNCITRAL Model Law*,[45] the basis of the arbitration law in 118 jurisdictions and 85 States.[46] In pro-

44 E.g. *Fiona Trust & Holding Corp v Privalov* [2007] UKHL 40; [2007] All ER 951.

45 **UNCITRAL** is the United Nations Commission on International Trade Law.

46 https://uncitral.un.org/en/texts/arbitration/modellaw/commercial_arbitration/status (accessed 19 November 2021).

viding the arbitral tribunal competence to rule on its own jurisdiction, Article 16(1) of the *UNCITRAL Model Law* provides:

> The arbitral tribunal may rule on its own jurisdiction, including any objections with respect to the existence or validity of the arbitration agreement. For that purpose, an arbitration clause which forms part of a contract shall be treated as an agreement independent of the other terms of the contract. A decision by the arbitral tribunal that the contract is null and void shall not entail *ipso jure* the invalidity of the arbitration clause.

The doctrine of separability raises the possibility that the governing law of the contract may not be the same as the governing law of the arbitration agreement, i.e. the law governing the existence and performance of the arbitration agreement. This issue is discussed further in section 3.2.3.

1.6 COVID-19

1.6.1 Government responses to COVID-19

The worldwide advent of the COVID-19 pandemic in 2020 and 2021 had tragic impacts on the lives of many people and resulted in enormous disruption to the economic fabric of countries around the world. Governments responded with legislation that implemented unprecedented policies in containment and border closure, economic assistance and health measures. The Blavatnik School of Government at the University of Oxford collected data from 186 countries and regions on the measures governments took to respond to the pandemic, and presented their findings in the Coronavirus Government Response Tracker (**Response Tracker**). The dataset in the Response Tracker contains 23 indicators organised into four groups:

- **Containment and closure policies** (indicators C1–C8) record information on containment and closure policies, such as school closures and restrictions in movement.
- **Economic policies** (indicators E1–E4) record economic policies, such as income support to citizens or provision of foreign aid.
- **Health system policies** (indicators H1–H8) record health system policies such as the COVID-19 testing regime, emergency investments into healthcare and most recently, vaccination policies.
- **Vaccine policies** (indicators V1–3) record vaccination policies: a country's prioritisation list, eligible groups, and the cost of vaccination to the individual. [47]

In addition to the 23 individual policy indicators, the Response Tracker calculates several indices to give an overall impression of government activity. The **stringency index** provides a single index combining all of the eight containment and closure policies, thereby

47 Thomas Hale et al. 'Oxford COVID-19 Government Response Tracker' (2020) *Blavatnik School of Government* www.bsg.ox.ac.uk/research/research-projects/coronavirus-government-response-tracker#data (accessed 22 November 2021).

providing one comparative measure of the impact of the pandemic on economic life.[48] The eight containment and closure policies recorded numerical measures for the following:

- C1 – closings of schools and universities.
- C2 – closing of workplaces.
- C3 – cancelling public events.
- C4 – limits on gatherings.
- C5 – closing of public transport.
- C6 – orders to 'shelter in place' and otherwise confine to the home.
- C7 – restrictions on internal movement between cities/regions.
- C8 – restrictions on international travel for foreign travelers.[49]

These indices have been plotted for some of the countries covered in this book for the period 1 January 2020 to 4 November 2021 in the following three figures for clarity – Figure 1.1 (Angola, Egypt, Ethiopia and Zambia), Figure 1.2 (Kenya, Nigeria and South Africa) and Figure 1.3 (Jordan, Türkiye and the UAE).

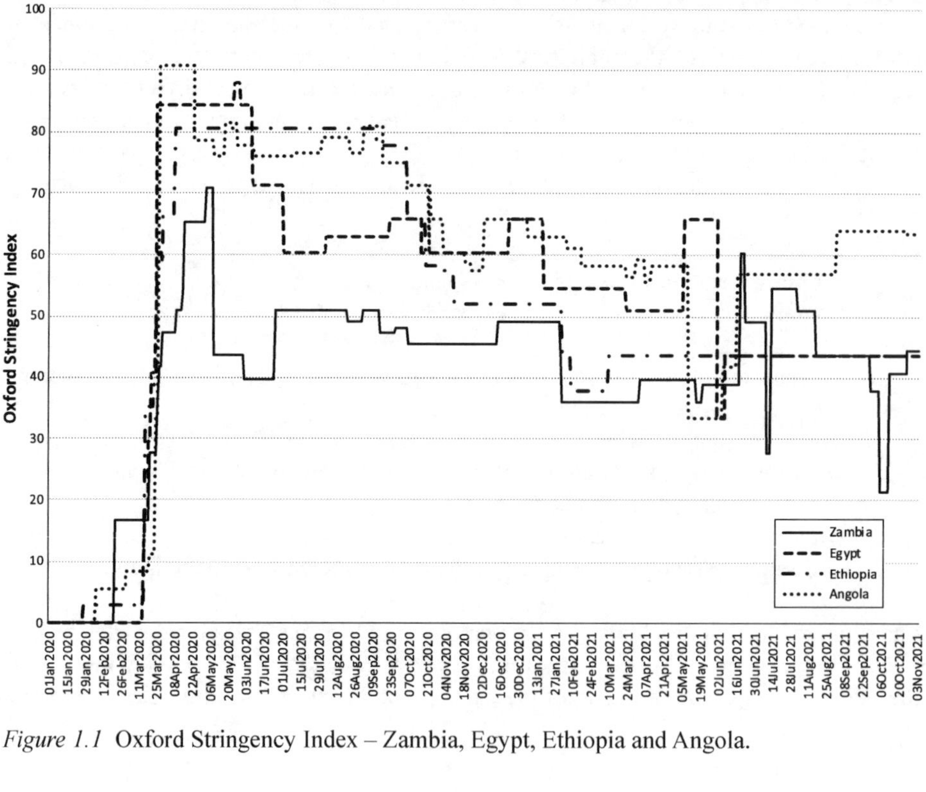

Figure 1.1 Oxford Stringency Index – Zambia, Egypt, Ethiopia and Angola.

48 https://github.com/OxCGRT/covid-policy-tracker/blob/master/documentation/index_methodology.md (accessed 23 November 2021).

49 https://github.com/OxCGRT/covid-policy-tracker/blob/master/documentation/codebook.md (accessed 24 February 2022).

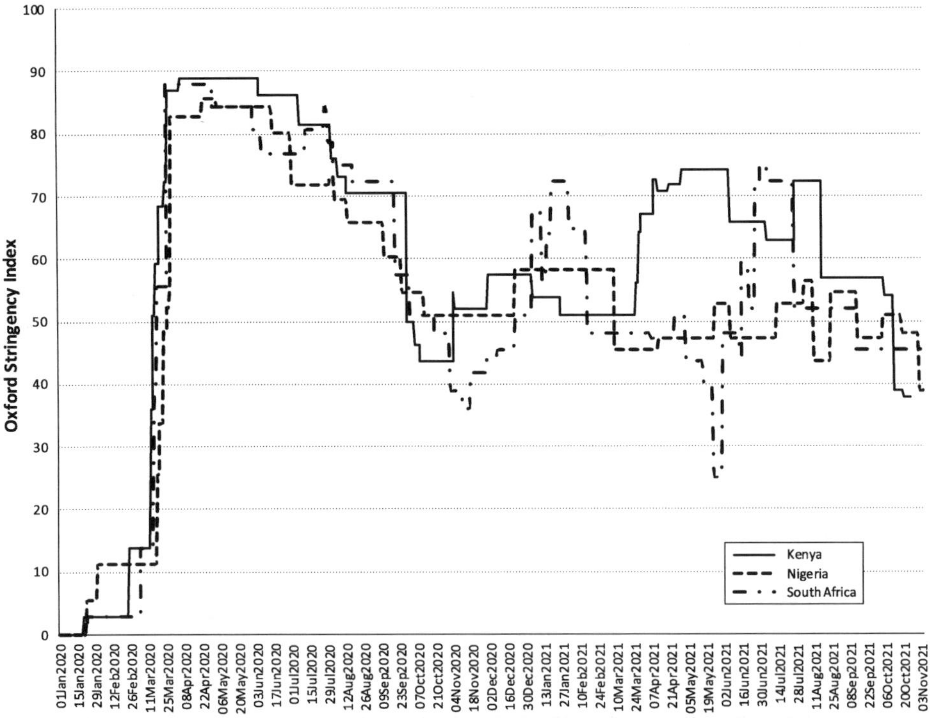

Figure 1.2 Oxford Stringency Index – Kenya, Nigeria and South Africa.

These figures show how rapidly most governments reacted quickly and strongly to the pandemic in February or March 2020. Countries were able to gradually reduce the level of stringency over the following months, however further waves in 2020 and 2021 required the reintroduction of greater stringency. The maximum stringency recorded for the 10 countries in March–June 2020 was typically between 80 and 90, with a maximum of 100. Few countries had reduced their level of stringency to below 40 by November 2021, indicating the persistent impact of significant government containment measures.

1.6.2 The impact of COVID-19 on construction

The closure of borders, shutdown of businesses, restrictions on movement, physical distancing, wearing masks and new health and safety protocols all impacted construction projects, resulting in increased costs and delays. Such impacts have inevitably resulted in claims for time and cost under construction contracts. Some of those claims will no doubt be rejected and result in disputes.

FIDIC responded rapidly to the COVID-19 challenges by running a series of webinars addressing some of the issues that may arise under FIDIC contracts. FIDIC also provided resources to assist contracting parties, including the 'FIDIC COVID-19 Guidance

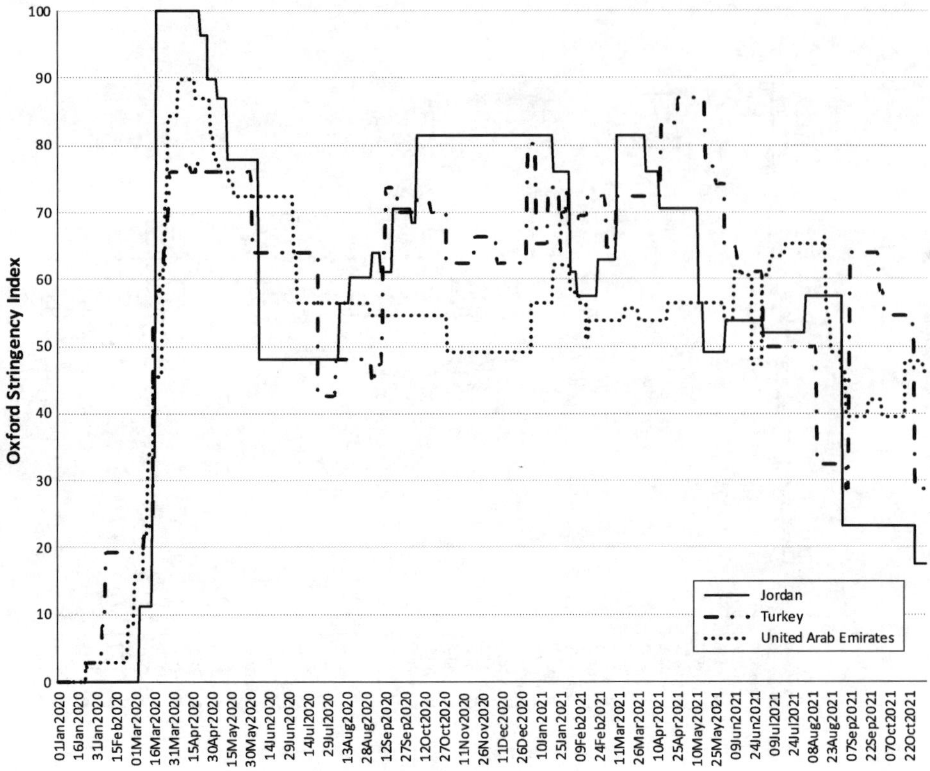

Figure 1.3 Oxford Stringency Index – Jordan, Türkiye and the UAE.

Memorandum to Users of FIDIC Standard Forms of Works Contract', prepared by the Contracts Committee.[50] This Guidance Memorandum is discussed in section 1.6.6.

The unprecedented array of legislation to deal with the health and economic impacts of COVID-19 significantly constrained freedom of contract in many situations, not least of which were those laws and regulations that impacted construction projects and construction contracts. The legislative interventions that are relevant to construction were measures that constrained:

- The execution of construction projects.
- The operation of construction contracts.
- Resolution of disputes arising out of COVID-19.

In some jurisdictions, the impacts were a result of legislation specifically addressing the construction industry, and others were part of more general government actions to

50 https://fidic.org/sites/default/files/COVID%2019%20Guidance%20Memorandum%20-%20PDF.pdf (accessed 4 April 2022).

control the spread of COVID-19 or to provide economic support. The following are some examples of the COVID-19-specific measures introduced in various jurisdictions. Each individual jurisdiction chapter following provides details of the measures adopted in that jurisdiction.

1.6.3 Execution of construction projects impacted by COVID-19

Restrictions on travel – some countries and regions closed their borders to non-residents.

Shut down of construction sites – some countries shut down construction sites after the onset of infection, others only permitted essential services to operate during certain periods.

Constraints on working on construction sites – the operation of some construction projects was significantly restricted by limiting the number of personnel on construction sites.

Increased hours of working – some jurisdictions permitted construction sites to operate on weekends and public holidays irrespective of what consents might otherwise allow.

Physical distancing was the primary method of protection mandated in many countries, requiring all persons outside their homes (and including construction sites) to be separated by a distance of 1.0, 1.5, 1.8 or 2 metres.

Additional OHS precautions – many jurisdictions required additional health precautions to be implemented, e.g. wearing face masks outside the home or temperature checks prior to entering workplaces.

Stringent cleaning protocols were required, including frequent hand washing and sanitising by regularly and frequently disinfecting contact surfaces in an endeavour to prevent infection and deep cleaning of premises where infection had occurred.

Enhanced documentation of employees such as mandatory daily declarations and updating by employers of work permits in the construction sector on stay-home notices, or enhanced record keeping to ensure that persons who had been in close contact with an infected person could be identified, advised and tested.

Isolation of infected personnel – personnel diagnosed with COVID-19 were required to isolate from others, typically for a period of 14 days.

Quarantine – many countries required incoming travellers to be quarantined for 14 days. Some countries required particular areas of high risk to be quarantined from outside contact.

Labour laws – some constraints on the employment of labour were temporarily put in abeyance, such as the introduction of flexible work schedules to use unused working hours to offset overtime hours or the reduction of workhours and/or workdays per week, and rotation of workers and forced leave were permitted.

Labour payments – some countries introduced new requirements to protect the income of infected persons, such as payment of the salary of a documented infected worker, or payment of full wages to a worker categorised as a suspected COVID-19 infection during the quarantine/isolation period.

1.6.4 Operation of construction contracts

Governments in various jurisdictions passed specific laws in respect of the impacts of COVID-19 on general commercial activities, such as financial compensation for reduced turnover, deferment of taxes and charges and insolvency provisions. Several of the jurisdictions covered in this book passed COVID-specific legislation that impacted the operation of construction contracts; e.g. in South Africa, *Regulations* prohibited the performance by service providers of their contractual obligations for the duration of the period of the lockdown,[51] and the UAE issued a *Decree* classifying the outbreak of COVID-19 as an 'exceptional economic circumstance' which provided for less rigid bankruptcy limitations.[52]

The provisions of the general law on the operation of a construction contract that may be engaged by the impact of COVID-19 include *force majeure*, *vis major,* hardship, frustration and impossibility. The operation of any of these doctrines in any specific case will depend on the wording of the contract and the governing law of the contract.

In common law jurisdictions, *force majeure* is entirely a creature of contract and will only apply if the factual circumstances of the COVID-19 impact fall within the contractual definition. Some *Civil Codes* have *force majeure* provisions that may provide for an extension of time for delays as a result of COVID-19 or additional compensation; e.g. the UAE *Civil Code* provisions may also apply in the event of hardship arising from substantial increases in cost arising from unforeseen circumstances.[53]

In the event that the impact of COVID-19 makes the performance of the Contract impossible, the common law doctrine of frustration may apply. Impossibility of performance is a similar doctrine under *Civil Codes*, e.g. the UAE.[54]

As discussed by several authors in the jurisdiction chapters to follow, the contractual consequences of the impact of COVID-19 are uncharted waters with little guidance from existing case law. Negotiation between Employer and Contractor in good faith (an integral aspect of *Civil Codes*) will generally be the most desirable means of resolving the most appropriate contractual outcome. Section 1.6.6 discusses the type of claims that may arise under FIDIC contracts.

1.6.5 Economic measures

In addition to the measures outlined already that directly impact the execution of construction projects and the operation of construction contracts, governments provided financial assistance to individuals and businesses that indirectly assisted the construction industry.

1.6.6 Claims arising from COVID-19 under FIDIC contracts

Construction projects were significantly delayed, postponed or terminated as a result of COVID-19; those that continued were subject to increased costs as a result of the health measures required to keep workers safe – stringent cleaning and disinfection, physical distancing

51 See section 13.3.2.
52 See section 15.3.2.
53 See section 15.3.2.
54 See section 15.3.2.

and increased use of personal protective equipment (**PPE**) among other economic impacts. Contractors will inevitably seek costs and EOTs and a substantial number of claims can therefore be expected. At the time of writing (June 2022), the COVID-19 pandemic is far from over, and there is already anecdotal evidence of claims on many construction projects.

Early in the pandemic (April 2020) FIDIC issued the 'FIDIC COVID-19 Guidance Memorandum to Users of FIDIC Standard Forms of Works Contract'.[55] That Memorandum contains an outline of the provisions in FIDIC's standard forms of contract for works relevant to likely scenarios arising as a consequence of COVID-19:

> FIDIC's core purpose of drafting this Guidance Memorandum is to help Parties to a FIDIC contract to consider mutually satisfactory solutions and avoid disputes arising between them. COVID-19 pandemic is a unique broad scale and extraordinary event which should be recognized as such.

The Guidance Memorandum does not refer to any specific legal system or jurisdiction and cautions that the legal interpretation of the contract will depend upon matters such as the precise wording of the various documents in the Contract and the governing law. The Memorandum takes the approach of outlining a number of possible scenarios and suggests likely relevant responses by reference to relevant provisions of FIDIC contracts.

FIDIC's list of scenarios identifies the following circumstances that are expected to give rise to claims unique to the impact of COVID-19: [56]

1. The local authorities/government do not promulgate any new piece of legislation or regulation banning construction activity or works on Site. However, the Contractor is facing difficulties in mobilizing personnel, who fear for their safety, and in obtaining Goods due to issues in the supply chain.
2. The Contractor is under the same circumstances as scenario No. 1 above. However, instead of facing difficulties in mobilizing personnel or obtaining Goods, the Contractor is suffering delays caused by the authorities (for example making repeated health and safety inspections on the Site).
3. The local authorities or government have promulgated changes to the Laws restricting construction activities and works on the Site. The Contractor is still able to proceed with the Works, however it is suffering delay and or incurring additional Cost as a result of those changes.
4. The local authorities/government have issued an order(s)/decree(s) preventing construction activities (including lockdown, curfew, inaccessible quarantined areas, etc), and execution of the Works on Site has now become impossible. Consequently, the Contractor and/or the Employer is prevented from performing obligations under the Contract.
5. Under scenario No. 4 above, can the Contractor subject this scenario to Clause 17 [*Risk and Responsibility/Care of the Works and Indemnities*]? Under Clause 17 the Contractor is entitled to a financial compensation in addition to an EOT, rather than only an EOT, when a natural Force Majeure or Exceptional Event occurs.
6. Under scenarios Nos. 1, 2, or 3, above, can the Employer or the Contractor resort to Clause 19 [*Force Majeure*], Clause 18 [*Exceptional Events*], or Clause

55 https://fidic.org/sites/default/files/COVID%2019%20Guidance%20Memorandum%20-%20PDF.pdf (accessed 4 April 2022).

56 *Ibid.*

18 [*Exceptional Risks*] (in the relevant FIDIC contract as the case may be), to address such scenarios?

7. There has been no change in Laws of the Country nor real impact on the availability of personnel or on the supply chain so far. However, the personnel of the Employer (including the Engineer or the Employer's Representative, as the case may be) are, as a precaution, working remotely and hence are most of the time away from Site. As a consequence, the Contractor suffers delay and/or incurred additional Cost due to slow decision making.

1.6.7 Dispute resolution

The spread of COVID-19 prompted government, judicial and other bodies around the globe to adopt measures responding to the need for greater flexibility and remote connectivity in the operation of courts and dispute resolution practice. The IBA documented the impact of COVID-19 on court operations and litigation practice in 37 countries.[57] The Chartered Institute of Arbitrators issued guidance for remote proceedings,[58] as did other arbitral institutions such as HKIAC[59] and AAA-ICDR.[60] The Dispute Resolution Board Foundation recognised the restrictions on in-person meetings during the pandemic and published best practice guidelines and a checklist for virtual Dispute Board proceedings.[61]

1.7 Impact of the applicable laws

In summary, the applicable law can impact the operation of a contract in various ways:

- The provisions of mandatory law will override any contractual provisions.
- A construction contract must be executed in accordance with the applicable Laws irrespective of the contract wording.
- Non-mandatory law may provide default options if they are not covered or explicitly derogated from by the specific terms of the Contract.

It is apparent that in any jurisdiction there is potentially a substantial number of laws that impact: the entry into, operation of and termination of a contract; the design and execution of the Works; and the resolution of any disputes that arise from or in connection with the Contract. Subject to the desirability of the Conditions of Contract comprising an accurate

57 'The Impact of COVID-19 on Court Operations and Litigation Practice' (June 2020), *International Bar Association* www.ibanet.org/Covid-19/Home.aspx (accessed 25 February 2021).

58 'Guidance Note on Remote Dispute Resolution Proceedings' (2020) *Chartered Institute of Arbitrators* www.ciarb.org/media/9013/remote-hearings-guidance-note_final_140420.pdf (accessed 23 November 2021).

59 'HKIAC Guidelines for Virtual Hearings' (2020) *HKIAC*.

60 'AAA-ICDR Virtual Hearing Guide for Arbitrators and Parties' (2020) *AAA-ICDR* https://go.adr.org/rs/294-SFS-516/images/AAA268_AAA%20Virtual%20Hearing%20Guide%20for%20Arbitrators%20and%20Parties.pdf (accessed 23 November 2021).

61 'Best Practice Guidelines for Virtual Dispute Board Proceedings' (2020) *Dispute Resolution Board Foundation* www.disputeboard.org/wp-content/uploads/2020/07/Best-Practice-Guidelines-for-Virtual-Dispute-Board-Proceedings-5-August-2020.pdf (accessed 23 November 2021); 'Checklist for Dispute Board Members in Preparation for Virtual Dispute Board Proceedings' (2020) *Dispute Resolution Board Foundation* www.disputeboard.org/wp-content/uploads/2020/07/DRBF-Checklist-for-Virtual-DB-Proceedings-5-August-2020.pdf (accessed 23 November 2021).

contract management manual, it is not the place of contract documents to constitute a complete definition of the parties' legal rights and obligations or a project management manual (nor would it be feasible). Accordingly, the Conditions of Contract, even in a well-written and comprehensive FIDIC Contract, can never identify all the applicable laws that may define the parties' rights and obligations in all circumstances.

Construction of any significant infrastructure or facility in the modern world is a complex undertaking in which the interests of many stakeholders must be considered, and a myriad of legal obligations complied with. Those involved at the 'coalface' of a construction project administering the Contract as Engineer, Employer or Contractor need to be generally aware of their legal obligations under the applicable Laws so that they can make the appropriate enquiries as to their specific obligations in particular circumstances. Complex or unusual situations will undoubtedly require input from competent construction lawyers experienced in the relevant jurisdiction.

However, except in exceptional circumstances, it is unlikely that such legal advice will be available on a day-to-day basis on the construction Site. The personnel administering the Contract may be engineers or other construction professionals with a general understanding of contract and other law, but they are unlikely to have the depth of knowledge of an experienced construction lawyer. The challenge for such Contract Administrators is to have sufficient knowledge of their obligations to know when and where to seek further information and advice on a specific issue. This problem may be particularly acute in a situation where the Contract Administrator is operating in a jurisdiction in which she/he is unfamiliar.

1.8 Country accessions to international conventions and agreements

Each of the countries considered in this book has acceded to certain international conventions and agreements and incorporated their principles into their domestic law. Table 1.3 identifies, for each country, whether they have a civil law or common law system and whether they have acceded to various international conventions, agreements or principles of relevance to construction law.

1.8.1 New York Convention

Perhaps the most important international convention for international users of FIDIC contracts is the *1958 New York Arbitration Convention on the Recognition and Enforcement of Foreign Arbitral Awards* (***New York Convention***). This convention ensures that commercial arbitration is an effective means of finally resolving international commercial disputes by means of an award that can be enforced by a court judgment in any state that is a party to the *New York Convention*. It is significant that all the countries covered in this book are party to the *New York Convention*.

The *New York Convention* gives practical effect to the principle of *pacta sunt servanda* by providing a mechanism to hold parties to the consequences of the bargain they have made. If a dispute arises out of or in connection with a contract, the appointed arbitral tribunal will determine the appropriate remedy in light of the terms of the contract and the applicable law. Their award is final and binding, and not subject to appeal on findings of fact or law. A court in a Convention State can only set aside or refuse to enforce an award on very narrow jurisdictional grounds.

Table 1.3 Country accessions to international conventions and agreements

Country	**Civil or common law**	***New York Arbitration Convention on the Recognition and Enforcement of Foreign Arbitral Awards, 1958***[a]	***United Nations Convention on International Settlement Agreements Resulting from Mediation (2018) (the "Singapore Convention on Mediation")***[b]	***Hague Convention of 30 June 2005 on Choice of Court Agreements***[c]	***UNCITRAL Model Law on International Commercial Arbitration (1985 with amendments as adopted in 2006)***[d]	***United Nations Convention of Contracts for the International Sale of Goods (CISG)***[e]	**Member State of UNIDROIT**[f]	**WTO Agreement on Government Procurement**[g]	***UNCITRAL Model Law on Cross-Border Insolvency (1997)***[h]	**ICSID Member State**[i]
Angola	Civil law	YES								YES
Egypt	Civil law	YES			YES	YES	YES			YES
Ethiopia	Civil law	YES								Signature
Jordan	Civil law	YES	Signature		YES			Observer		YES
Kenya	Common law	YES			YES				YES	YES
Nigeria	Common law	YES	Signature		YES		YES			YES
South Africa	Mixed	YES			YES		YES		YES	
Türkiye	Civil law	YES	YES		YES	YES	YES	Observer		YES
UAE	Civil law	YES			YES					YES
UAE – ADGM	Common law				YES				YES	
UAE – DIFC	Common law				YES				YES	
Zambia	Common law	YES			YES	YES				YES

[a] www.newyorkconvention.org/countries (accessed 3 February 2023).
[b] https://uncitral.un.org/en/texts/mediation/conventions/international_settlement_agreements/status (accessed 6 June 2022).
[c] www.hcch.net/en/instruments/conventions/status-table/?cid=98 (accessed 6 June 2022).
[d] https://uncitral.un.org/en/texts/arbitration/modellaw/commercial_arbitration/status (accessed 6 June 2022).
[e] https://uncitral.un.org/en/texts/salegoods/conventions/sale_of_goods/cisg/status accessed 6 June 2022).
[f] www.unidroit.org/about-unidroit/membership (accessed 6 June 2022).
[g] www.wto.org/english/tratop_e/gproc_e/memobs_e.htm (accessed 6 June 2022).
[h] https://uncitral.un.org/en/texts/insolvency/modellaw/cross-border_insolvency/status (accessed 6 June 2022).
[i] https://icsid.worldbank.org/about/member-states/database-of-member-states (accessed 3 February 2023).

The *New York Convention* is perhaps the single most important agreement that facilitates international commercial commerce in general and international construction law in particular. International arbitration removes a dispute from the jurisdiction of the courts of either party's home jurisdiction that may be perceived as giving one of them an advantage. The arbitration award can be enforced by normal court processes in any jurisdiction that is party to the *New York Convention*, typically in a jurisdiction where the debtor has assets. It is therefore unsurprising that FIDIC General Conditions require international arbitration to finally settle any disputes that have not been avoided or resolved by the decision of a Dispute Avoidance/Adjudication Board or Dispute Adjudication Board.

1.8.2 WTO Agreement on Government Procurement

Purchases of goods and services by government agencies with public resources for public purposes are generally referred to as government/public procurement.

Achieving 'value for money' is a primary aim of most procurement regimes. Open, transparent and non-discriminatory procurement is generally considered to be the best tool to achieve this goal as it optimises competition among suppliers. The liberalisation of government procurement markets holds the potential to generate benefits both in terms of procurement efficiency and commercial interests. One of the ways the World Trade Organisation (**WTO**) promotes the liberalisation of government is through the Agreement on Government Agreement (**WTO GPA**).

The WTO describes the WTO GPA as follows:

> The GPA is a plurilateral agreement within the framework of the WTO, meaning that not all WTO members are parties to the Agreement. At present, the Agreement has 20 parties comprising 48 WTO members. 36 WTO members/observers participate in the GPA Committee as observers. Out of these, 12 members are in the process of acceding to the Agreement.
>
> The fundamental aim of the GPA is to mutually open government procurement markets among its parties. As a result of several rounds of negotiations, the GPA parties have opened procurement activities worth an estimated US$ 1.7 trillion annually to international competition (i.e. to suppliers from GPA parties offering goods, services or construction services).
>
> The GPA is composed mainly of two parts: the text of the Agreement and parties' market access schedules of commitments.
>
> The text of the Agreement establishes rules requiring that open, fair and transparent conditions of competition be ensured in government procurement. However, these rules do not automatically apply to all procurement activities of each party. Rather, the coverage schedules play a critical role in determining whether a procurement activity is covered by the Agreement or not. Only those procurement activities that are carried out by covered entities purchasing listed goods, services or construction services of a value exceeding specified threshold values are covered by the Agreement.[62]

None of the countries covered by this book have acceded to the WTO GPA, although two countries have Observer status.

1.8.3 ICSID Convention

ICSID is the International Centre for the Settlement of Investment Disputes:

> ICSID is the world's leading institution devoted to international investment dispute settlement. It has extensive experience in this field, having administered the majority of all international

62 www.wto.org/english/tratop_e/gproc_e/gp_gpa_e.htm (accessed 9 November 2020).

> investment cases. States have agreed on ICSID as a forum for investor-State dispute settlement in most international investment treaties and in numerous investment laws and contracts.[63]

ICSID publishes the *Convention on the Settlement of Investment Disputes between States and Nationals of Other States.*[64] The ***ICSID Convention*** is a treaty ratified by 155 Contracting States which, *inter alia*:

- Establishes ICSID's jurisdiction.
- Authorises conciliation.
- Authorises arbitration.
- Addresses replacement and disqualification of Conciliators and Arbitrators.
- Discusses the cost of proceedings.
- Deals with the place of proceedings.
- Provides for disputes between Contracting States.[65]

The significance of other individual conventions is discussed in the later chapters.

1.9 Aims of the book

One of the aims of this book is to identify, for a range of jurisdictions in Africa and the Middle East in which FIDIC contracts are or can be used, the applicable laws that may impact the operation of the Contract, the execution of the Works or the determination of disputes arising under or in connection with the Contract. It does not purport to provide guidance on FIDIC Contracts *per se*; there are a number of texts which provide an in-depth discussion of FIDIC Contracts, including general commentary on what modifications may be required for use in particular jurisdictions. The following section contains a list of references on FIDIC contracts.

This book is intended to be a sourcebook for a Contract Administrator or lawyer unfamiliar with the requirements for the Particular Conditions of a FIDIC Contract or operating with a FIDIC Contract in a jurisdiction they are unfamiliar with. It does not provide specific guidance on what Particular Conditions clauses might be necessary or desirable for any jurisdiction; such guidance would always need to be specific to the requirements of the particular project at the particular point in time and require input from a competent construction lawyer. It should also be noted that, although the laws identified are believed to be correct as of July 2022, legislation and case law are constantly changing, another reason why competent advice needs to be sought when necessary.

Chapter 2 provides further details of the FIDIC Golden Principles, which FIDIC recommend should be complied with in preparing Particular Conditions. Chapter 3 provides more specific details of what should be in the Particular Conditions, choosing the governing law of the contract and guidance on the preparation of Particular Conditions necessary or desirable for particular purposes, without attempting to address the differences between jurisdictions.

63 https://icsid.worldbank.org/about (accessed 14 February 2022).

64 https://icsid.worldbank.org/sites/default/files/ICSID%20Convention%20English.pdf (accessed 14 February 2022).

65 https://icsid.worldbank.org/resources/rules-and-regulations/convention/overview (accessed 14 February 2022).

Each of the remaining chapters in the book deals with a specific jurisdiction, prepared by one or more construction lawyers and/or engineers, experienced in the application of FIDIC contracts in that jurisdiction. Each of those jurisdiction-specific chapters provides a brief overview of the legal landscape and the construction industry, the impact of the COVID-19 pandemic on construction contracts and construction projects, a discussion of any Special Provisions required if the governing law is that jurisdiction, and a listing of the applicable law if the Site is in the jurisdiction. The chapters also identify issues that a court or arbitrator may construe differently than expected from the words of the Contract because of local law or custom.

1.10 References

1.10.1 Books on construction law

Andrew Burr (ed), *Delay and Disruption in Construction Contracts* (Informa Law from Routledge, 2016)

Anthony Edwards and Roger Gibson, *A Practical Guide to Disruption and Productivity Loss on Construction and Engineering Projects* (Wiley, 2015)

Arent van Wassenaer, *A Practical Guide to Successful Construction Projects* (Informa Law from Routledge, 2017)

Charles O'Neill, *Human Dynamics* (Contract Dynamics Sdn Bhd, 2014)

Charles O'Neill, *Global Construction Success* (Wiley Blackwell, 2019)

David Chappell, Michael Cowlin, and Michael Dunn *Building Law Encyclopedia* (Wiley-Blackwell, 2009)

David Mosey, *Early Contractor Involvement in Building Procurement* (Wiley-Blackwell, 2009)

David Mosey, *Collaborative Construction Procurement and Improved Value* (John Wiley & Sons, 2019)

Donald Charrett (ed), *Global Challenges Shared Solutions* (Society of Construction Law Australia, 2013)

Donald Charrett, *Contracts for Construction and Engineering Projects* (2nd edn, Informa Law from Routledge, 2022)

Edward W Merrow, *Industrial Megaprojects Concepts, Strategies and Practices for Success* (Wiley, 2011)

Furmston, *Powell-Smith and Furmston's Building Contract Case Book* (4th edn, Blackwell, 2006)

John Scriven and Nigel Pritchard, *EPC Contracts and Major Projects* (Sweet & Maxwell, 2011)

John Uff, *Construction law: Law and Practice Relating to the Construction Industry* (12th edn, Sweet & Maxwell/Thomson Reuters, 2017)

John R Cooke, *Architects, Engineers and the Law* (Federation Press, 2010)

Julian Bailey, *Construction Law, Costs and Contemporary Developments: Drawing the Threads Together: A Festschrift for Lord Justice Jackson* (Hart Publishing, 2018)

Julian Bailey, *Construction Law (Volumes 1–3)* (3rd edn, London Publishing Partnership, 2020)

Justin Sweet and Mark Schneier, *Legal Aspects of Architecture, Engineering and the Construction Process* (Cengage Learning, 2009)

Keith Pickavance, *Construction Law and Management* (Informa Law from Routledge, 2016)

Lukas Klee, *International Construction Contract Law* (2nd edn, John Wiley & Sons Inc, 2018).

Monika Chao-Duivis, *Studies in European Construction Law* (Den Haag: Instituut voor Bouwrecht, 2015)

Michael Sergeant and Max Wieliczko, *Construction Contract Variations* (Informa Law from Routledge, 2014)

Nicholas Dennys and Robert Clay, *Hudson's Building and Engineering Contracts* (14th edn, Sweet & Maxwell, 2020)
P. John Keane and Anthony F Caletka, *Delay Analysis in Construction Contracts* (Wiley-Blackwell, 2015)
Paul Reed QC, *Construction All Risks Insurance* (Sweet & Maxwell, 2016)
Peter Edwards, Michael Edwards, and Paulo Vaz Serra, *Managing Project Risks* (Wiley-Blackwell, 2019)
Philip Bryan, *Successful Delivery of Resources Projects* (Clayton Utz, 2013)
Phillip Greenham (ed), *The International Compendium of Construction Contracts* (Society of Construction Law Australia & De Gruyter, 2021)
Philip Loots and Donald Charrett, *The Application of Contracts in Developing Offshore Oil and Gas Contracts* (Informa Law from Routledge, 2019)
Philip Loots and Donald Charrett, *Contracts for Infrastructure Projects: An International Guide for Application* (Informa Law from Routledge, 2022)
Richard Moorwood, Deborah Scott, and Ian Pitcher, *Alliancing: A Participant's Guide: Real Life Experiences for Constructors, Desoigners, Facilitators and Clients* (Maunsell AECOM, 2008)
Robert Hogarth, Alexandra Anderson, and Simon Goldring (eds), *Insurance Law for the Construction Industry* (2nd edn, Oxford University Press, 2013)
Robert J Gemmell, *Quantification of Delay and Disruption in Construction and Engineering Projects* (2nd edn, Thomson Reuters, 2021)
Roger ter Haar QC and Camilla ter Haar, *Remedies in Construction Law* (2nd edn, Informa Law from Routledge, 2017)
Sarah Lupton, *Cornes and Lupton's Design Liability in the Construction Industry* (Wiley, 2013)
Simon Tolson, *Dictionary of Construction Terms* (Informa Law from Routledge, 2012)
Stephen Furst and Vivian Ramsey, *Keating on Construction Contracts* (11th edn, Sweet & Maxwell/ Thomson Reuters, 2020)
Tim Read, *International Comparative Legal Guide to Construction and Engineering Law 2015* (Ashurst, 2015)
Tom Kendrick, *Identifying and Managing Project Risk* (AMACOM, 2009)
Will Hughes, Ronan Champion, and John Murdoch, *Construction Contracts Law and Management* (5th edn, Routledge, 2015)

1.10.2 References on dispute resolution

Cyril Chern, *The Law of Construction Disputes* (3rd edn, Informa Law from Routledge, 2020)
Cyril Chern, *Chern on Dispute Boards* (4th edn, Informa Law from Routledge, 2021)
Darryl Royce, *Adjudication in Construction Law* (Informa Law from Routledge, 2016)
Dimitar Kondev, *Multi-Party and Multi-Contract Arbitration in the Construction Industry* (John Wiley & Sons Inc, 2017)
Dispute Resolution Board Foundation, *Dispute Board Manual* (Dispute Resolution Board Foundation, 2019)
James Pickavance, *A Practical Guide to Construction Adjudication* (Wiley, 2015)
Paula Gerber and Brennan Ong, *Best Practice in Construction Disputes* (Lexis Nexis Butterworths, 2013)
Rashda Rana and Michelle Sanson, *International Commercial Arbitration* (Lawbook Co, 2011)
Redfern & Hunter, *Law & Practice of International Commercial Arbitration* (6th edn, Thomson/ Sweet & Maxwell, 2014)
Renato Nazzini, *Transnational Construction Arbitration: Key Themes in the Resolution of Construction Disputes* (Informa Law from Routledge, 2017)

1.10.3 Books on FIDIC contracts – 2017 Editions

Corbett & Co, *FIDIC 2017 a Practical Legal Guide* (Corbett & Co International Construction Lawyers Ltd, 2020)
Donald Charrett (ed), *FIDIC Contracts in the Americas a Practical Guide to Application* (Informa Law from Routledge, 2024)[66]
Donald Charrett (ed), *FIDIC Contracts in Europe a Practical Guide to Application* (Informa Law from Routledge, 2023)[67]
Donald Charrett (ed), *FIDIC Contracts in Asia Pacific a Practical Guide to Application* (Informa Law from Routledge, 2022)[68]
Donald Charrett (ed), *The International Application of FIDIC Contracts a Practical Guide* (Informa Law from Routledge, 2020)[69]
Jakob B Sørensen, *FIDIC Silver Book – A companion to the 2017 EPC/Turnkey Contract* (Institution of Civil Engineers, 2019)
Jeremy Glover and Simon Hughes, *Understanding the FIDIC Red and Yellow Books: A Clause-by-Clause Commentary* (4th edn, Sweet & Maxwell, 2018)
Leo Grutters and Brian Barr, *FIDIC Red, Yellow and Silver Books: A Practical Guide to the 2017 Editions* (Sweet & Maxwell, 2018)
Nicholas Alexander Brown, *FIDIC 2017: A Definitive Guide to Claims and Disputes* (Thomas Telford Ltd, 2022)
William Godwin QC, *The 2017 FIDIC Contracts: The Second Editions of the Red, Yellow and Silver Books* (Wiley Blackwell, 2020)

1.10.4 Books on FIDIC contracts – 1999 Editions

A Hewitt, *The FIDIC Contracts: Obligations of the Parties* (Wiley, 2014)
Axel-Volkmar Jaeger and Götz-Sebastian Hök, *FIDIC – A Guide for Practitioners* (Springer, 2010)
Brian Totterdill, *FIDIC Users' Guide: A Practical Guide to the 1999 Red and Yellow Books* (Thomas Telford, 2006)
Ellis Baker, Ben Mellors, Scott Chalmers, and Anthony Lavers, *FIDIC Contracts: Law and Practice* (Informa Law, 2009)
Jeremy Glover and Simon Hughes, *Understanding the FIDIC Red Book: A Clause-by-Clause Commentary* (3rd edn, Sweet & Maxwell, 2011)
M Robinson, *A Contractor's Guide to the FIDIC Conditions of Contract* (Wiley Blackwell, 2013)
M Robinson, *An Employer's and Engineer's Guide to the FIDIC Conditions of Contract* (Wiley Blackwell, 2013)
Nael G Bunni, *The FIDIC Forms of Contract* (Blackwell, 2005)
Raveed Khalani and Mahdi Saadat Fard, *FIDIC Plant and Design-Build Forms of Contract Illustrated* (Wiley, 2015)
Robert Knutson (ed), *FIDIC An Analysis of International Contracts* (Kluwer Law International, 2005)

---

66 This book has chapters on the application of FIDIC contracts in 9 jurisdictions in North and South America.

67 This book has chapters on the application of FIDIC contracts in 16 jurisdictions in Europe.

68 This book has chapters on the application of FIDIC contracts in 16 jurisdictions in Asia Pacific and a chapter on the application of the Emerald Book for Underground Works.

69 This book has chapters on the application of FIDIC contracts in the following jurisdictions not included in this book: Australia, Brazil, China, Czech Republic, Fiji, France, Germany, Hong Kong, Italy, Malaysia, Papua New Guinea, Peru, Romania, Sri Lanka and Switzerland.

1.10.5 Guides on FIDIC contracts[70]

DBO (2008 Gold Book) Contract Guide 1st ed, 2011.

Design – Build and Turnkey Guide (1st ed. 1996). Guide to the Use of FIDIC Conditions of Contract for Design-Build and Turnkey. A clause-by-clause commentary on the provisions contained in Part 1 of the 1995 Orange Book.

Electrical and Mechanical Works Guide (1st ed, 1988). Guide to the Use of the FIDIC Conditions of Contract for Electrical and Mechanical Works 3rd ed. 1987 Yellow Book. Includes Yellow Book 3rd ed 1987 conditions.

FIDIC 4th – A Practical Legal Guide (1991). A commentary on the Red Book 4th ed, 1987 by E.C. Corbett.

FIDIC Contracts Guide to the Construction, Plant and Design-Build and EPC/Turnkey Contracts (1st Edition, 2000).

FIDIC Contracts Guide Supplement: MDB Harmonised Construction Contract (2006). Guide to the March 2006 release of the MDB Harmonised Construction Contract.

Red Book Guide (1st ed, 1989). Guide to the Use of FIDIC Conditions of Contract for Works of Civil Engineering Construction 4th ed, 1987 Red Book. Includes Red Book Conditions.

Standard Letters and Notices. For use with the FIDIC Conditions of Contract for Works of Civil Engineering Construction, 4th ed, 1987 Red Book.

The EIC Silver Book Guide, 2nd Edition, 2003. European International Contractors (EIC) Contractors Guide to the FIDIC Conditions of Contract for EPC/Turnkey Projects.

The New EIC Red Book Guide, 2001. European International Contractors (EIC) Contractors Guide to the FIDIC Conditions of Contract for Construction.

The New EIC Yellow Book Guide, 2003. European International Contractors (EIC) Contractors Guide to the FIDIC Conditions of Contract for Plant and Design-Build.

1.10.6 Internet resources

Construction and Engineering Laws and Regulations 2018 https://iclg.com/practice-areas/construction-and-engineering-law-laws-and-regulations (accessed 8 June 2022).

1.10.7 Case law

A list of cases and publicly available arbitration awards is available at: http://corbett.co.uk/wp-content/uploads/Table-of-FIDIC-Cases.pdf

70 'Contract advice' – www.fidic.org/bookshop (accessed 24 February 2022).

Annexure

Table 1.4 Editions of FIDIC Conditions of Contract for contracts between Employer and Contractor

Short Form of Contract (Green Book)	**Construction (Red Book)**	**Construction (MDB edition) (Pink Book)**	**Plant and Design Build (Yellow Book)**	**EPC/Turnkey (Silver Book)**	**Design, Build and Operate (Gold Book)**	**Underground Works (Emerald Book)**	**Dredging and Reclamation Works (Blue-Green Book)**
	First ed. 1957 Second ed. 1969 Third ed. 1977 Fourth ed. 1987 1992 Revised ed. 1996 DAB Supplement	2005 ed. 2006 Revised ed.	First ed. 1963 Second ed. 1980 Third ed. 1987	1995 Orange Book			
Short Form of Contract First ed. 1999	Conditions of Contract for Construction First ed. 1999	Conditions of Contract for Construction MDB Harmonised Edition 2010	Conditions of Contract for Plant and Design Build First ed. 1999	Conditions of Contract for EPC/ Turnkey Projects First ed. 1999	Conditions of Contract for Design, Build and Operate Projects First ed. 2008		Form of Contract for Dredging and Reclamation Works First ed. 2006
Short Form of Contract Second ed. 2021	Conditions of Contract for Construction Second ed. 2017		Conditions of Contract for Plant and Design Build Second ed. 2017	Conditions of Contract for EPC/ Turnkey Projects Second ed. 2017		Conditions of Contract for Underground Works First ed. 2019	Form of Contract for Dredging and Reclamation Works Second ed. 2016

CHAPTER 2

The FIDIC Golden Principles[1]

Dr Donald Charrett[2]

CONTENTS

1 This chapter was first published in (2018) *Construction Law International* 13(2) and is reproduced by kind permission of the International Bar Association, London, UK © International Bar Association.

2 Principal Drafter, FIDIC Working Group TG15.

DOI: 10.4324/9781003206910-2

2.1 Introduction

FIDIC publishes General Conditions of contract that are widely used for international construction contracts. They are intended to be used in any legal jurisdiction. FIDIC General Conditions are explicitly based on a fair and equitable risk allocation between Employer and Contractor and are widely recognised as striking an appropriate balance between the reasonable expectations of the contracting Parties.

Arguably, a contract recognised as a fair and balanced 'FIDIC contract' has real commercial value to both Employer and Contractor, both at the tendering stage and while the Works are being performed.

General Conditions prepared for use in a wide range of projects and jurisdictions inevitably require supplementation with Particular Conditions that address the particular requirements of the Site and the unique features of the specific project. Particular Conditions may also be necessary to amend the General Conditions to comply with mandatory law that applies to the Site or the legal jurisdiction.

Provided that such modifications are limited to those necessary for the particular features of the Site and the project and do not change the essential fair and balanced character of a FIDIC Contract, the contract is recognisable as a FIDIC contract.

The essential features of a FIDIC Contract that make the risk/reward allocation fair and balanced are referred to as the **FIDIC Golden Principles (GPs)**.

This chapter outlines the development of the GPs, the reasons for them and their application in drafting Particular Conditions.

2.2 Fair and balanced contracts

Contract risks refer to the chance that contractual objectives will not be fulfilled. The Contract defines who bears the liability for the contract risks. The form and terms of the Contract can increase or decrease those risks from the norm. Thus, use of the appropriate form and terms of a construction contract can play a major role in minimising the risk that the contractual objectives will not be fulfilled. Conversely, use of an inappropriate form or terms of a construction contract can significantly increase the risk that the contractual objectives will not be fulfilled.

Strictly, it is incorrect to refer to contracts as 'allocating' risk, as contracts allocate obligations and confer rights.[3] A risk, being the chance of an event happening, is not 'allocated' to either Party by the Contract. A risk event may exist separate from and independent of the obligations and rights of the Parties, or the risk event may be under the 'control' of one of the Parties. Whether or not one of the Parties has 'control' over a risk event, it is the obligations and rights arising as a consequence of the risk event happening that are 'allocated' by the Contract, and this is the commonly accepted usage of the term 'risk allocation'.

3 Report by NPWC/NBCC Joint Working Party, 'No Dispute Strategies for Improvement in the Australian Building and Construction Industry' (May 1990) 7.

Many standard form contracts are based on the explicitly stated principle of balanced or fair risk allocation, e.g., the Australian Standard 4000 series,[4] the US ConsensusDocs,[5] the UK New Engineering Contract,[6] contracts promoted by the European Engineering Industries Association,[7] the International Chamber of Commerce,[8] the Baltic and International Marine Council[9] and the UK offshore oil and gas industry.[10] The principle is also espoused by government procurement agencies in the UK,[11] Australia[12] and the USA.[13]

Many writers suggest that adherence to the principle of balanced risk allocation enhances the prospect of successful contracts, by encouraging contractual performance that minimises adverse outcomes and thereby reduces disputation.[14] In a survey of ten case studies of Australian projects to determine project-related factors critical to project success, Sidwell et al. found that equitable risk allocation was one of the top four factors found to be critical in explaining overall project performance and was the most significant factor related to the conditions of contract.[15]

'Non-standard' contract terms (in the sense of altering the 'normal' balanced risk allocation in standard form contracts) in either standard form contracts or bespoke contracts are usually put forward by one party to alter the risk allocation to be more favourable to it. As Employers generally put forward proposed conditions of contract with the tender documents, it is likely that non-standard terms in these contracts will involve the Contractor in accepting more risk than 'normal'.

The conditions of contract based on a standard form contract typically comprise General Conditions and Particular Conditions (or amendments to the General Conditions). The General Conditions are typically drafted by a committee representing a wide range of interests and represent a consensus of contract terms appropriate to many 'typical'

---

4 'Standard Conditions of Contract' (2001) 4 *BDPS News* 1, 4.

5 www.consensusdocs.org/FooterSection_About/FooterSection_WhyConsensusDocs (accessed 18 March 2018).

6 Brian Eggleston, *The New Engineering Contract: A Commentary* (Blackwell Publishing 1996) 7.

7 Orgalime Turnkey Contract for Industrial Works.

8 International Chamber of Commerce Model Turnkey Contract for Major Projects (2007). www.iccbooks.com/Product/ProductInfo.aspx?id=488 (accessed 18 March 2018).

9 www.bimco.org/about-us-and-our-members/about-us/our-history (accessed 18 March 2018).

10 Leading Oil and Gas Industry Competitiveness (LOGIC) www.logic-oil.com (accessed 18 March 2018).

11 HM Treasury, *The Green Book Appraisal and Evaluation in Central Government* http://greenbook.treasury.gov.uk/annex04.htm (accessed 26 August 2008): 'The governing principle is that risk should be allocated to whichever party from the public or private sector is best placed to manage it. The optimal allocation of risk, rather than maximising risk transfer, is the objective, and is vital to ensuring that the best solution is found.'

12 Department of Treasury and Finance Victorian Government, *Partnerships Victoria Updated Standard Commercial Principles* (2008) 99: 'Both the government and the private party should seek to ensure that cost and adequate risk transfer are balanced as far as possible to achieve the best value for money on a particular project.'

13 US Department of Transportation Federal Highway Administration, *Risk Assessment and Allocation for Highway Construction Management* (2006) § 6.1.1 www.international.fhwa.dot.gov/riskassess/risk_hcm06_06.cfm (accessed 26 August 2008): 'A fundamental tenet of risk management is to allocate the risks to the party best able to manage them. The party assuming the risk should be able to best evaluate, control, bear the risk of, and benefit from its assumption.'

14 NPWC/NBCC Joint Working Party, 'No Dispute Strategies for Improvement in the Australian Building and Construction Industry' (May 1990) 6–7; Sir Michael Latham, 'Constructing the Team' (July 1994) Final Report 37.

15 AC Sidwell, RJ Kennedy and APC Chan, 'Re-Engineering the Construction Delivery Process' (2002) *Construction Industry Institute Australia Report* 34.

projects and locations. However, these General Conditions cannot take account of the specific requirements of a particular project, or perhaps the requirements for a particular location. General Conditions typically require modification for the project.

Every project has unique circumstances, and there are many legitimate reasons for Particular Conditions that alter standard-form General Conditions to suit these circumstances. For example, provisions in the General Conditions may be inconsistent with the mandatory law of the Site.

Typically, there is no formal constraint on the extent of risk transfer to the Contractor via the Particular Conditions, other than the requirements of mandatory law. However, arguably, Particular Conditions that alter the fundamental balanced risk allocation in the General Conditions change the character of the contract so that it is no longer recognisable as a contract of the type understood by the name of the General Conditions.

The consequences of inappropriately allocating excessive risk to the Contractor can actually have the opposite effect to that desired, by increasing the Employer's risks. The Japan International Cooperation Agency (JICA) commissioned the Association of Japanese Consulting Engineers to prepare a 'Check List for One Sided Contracts' to be used for the preparation of reasonable bidding documents. JICA noted that if modifications for a particular project alter the originally contemplated risk distribution in a FIDIC Red Book Contract to a large extent and the risks allocated to the Contractor become excessively high, the following problems may occur:

- Higher bid price.
- Bid failure and disruption of project implementation.
- Non-participation in the bid by conscientious and capable contractors.
- Contract award to a bidder who failed to or was not capable of estimating the risks properly.
- Poor construction quality and delay to the progress of the work due to lack of risk contingency.
- Undermining the relationship of mutual trust and respect between the Employer and the Contractor.
- Repetition of groundless claims from the Contractor.
- Frequent disputes between the Employer and the Contractor.
- In an extreme case, termination of the contract.[16]

2.3 The FIDIC Golden Principles

The Golden Principles were developed by FIDIC Task Group 15 (**TG15**),[17] which reported to the FIDIC Contracts Committee. Consistent with FIDIC's structured approach to developing consensus documents, drafts of TG15's report were reviewed by the Contracts Committee and a number of friendly reviewers. As noted in Chapter 1, section 1.4, the Emerald Book and the Second Editions of the FIDIC Red, Yellow and Silver Books

16 Checklist for One Sided Contracts (Japan International Cooperation Agency 2011), 1.

17 The author was the Principal Drafter for TG15. The other members were Husni Madi (Jordan) – Team Leader, Axel Jaeger (Germany) and Dr Rafal Morek (Poland).

recommend that the drafters of Particular Conditions take all due regard to the Golden Principles.[18]

The Golden Principles have been articulated for Works Contracts and not Services Contracts. FIDIC has confined its attention to Particular Conditions (**PCs**) that change the General Conditions (**GCs**) to the extent that they do not comply with the GPs. It has not considered misuse of unamended GCs.

In order to promote understanding, the GPs have been formulated at a conceptual level to encapsulate the essence of a FIDIC contract. Each GP expresses a single readily understood and generally accepted concept. The GPs have been limited to the minimum number necessary for completeness. Except for GP5, the GPs are stated in broad terms, without reference to specific clauses of the GCs.

GPs function as constraints on modifications to the GCs made in the PCs. They cannot prevent the misapplication of existing unamended GCs. By definition, unamended GCs are an application of the GPs.

The following overarching considerations underpin the GPs:

- The terms of the contract are comprehensive and fair to both contracting Parties.
- The legitimate interests of both contracting Parties are appropriately considered and balanced. The legitimate interests of each Party include the right to enjoy the benefits of the contractual relationship generally recognised as implicit in the GCs. For example, the Employer's legitimate interests include the right to a facility constructed to the contractually specified quality, within the time and for the price in the Contract. The Contractor's legitimate interests include the right to execute the Works in the manner contracted for, within a reasonable time and for a commercial price paid on time.
- Best practice principles of fair and balanced risk allocation between the Employer and the Contractor are put into effect in accordance with the provisions of the GCs.
- No Party shall take undue advantage of its bargaining power.
- Payments to the Contractor or Subcontractor in accordance with the Contract are adequate to maintain its cash flow.
- The Employer obtains the best value for money.
- To the extent possible, co-operation and trust between the contracting Parties is promoted, and adversarial attitudes are to be discouraged and should be avoided.
- The contract provisions can be practically put into effect.
- Disputes are avoided to the extent achievable, minimised when they do arise, and resolved efficiently.

The Golden Principles are as follows:

GP1: The duties, rights, obligations, roles and responsibilities of all the Contract Participants must be generally as implied in the General Conditions, and appropriate to the requirements of the project.

18 Guidance for the Preparation of Particular Conditions, 8.

GP2: The Particular Conditions must be drafted clearly and unambiguously.

GP3: The Particular Conditions must not change the balance of risk/reward allocation provided for in the General Conditions.

GP4: All time periods specified in the Contract for Contract Participants to perform their obligations must be of reasonable duration.

GP5: Unless there is a conflict with the governing law of the Contract, all formal disputes must be referred to a Dispute Avoidance/Adjudication Board (or a Dispute Adjudication Board, if applicable) for a provisionally binding decision as a condition precedent to arbitration.

2.4 Reasons for Golden Principles

GP1: The duties, rights, obligations, roles and responsibilities of all the Contract Participants must be generally as implied in the General Conditions and appropriate to the requirements of the project.

As with most construction contracts, FIDIC Contracts refer to a number of other persons (such as the Engineer, DAAB/DAB and Subcontractors), in addition to the contracting Parties (Employer and Contractor). All the persons referred to in a FIDIC Contract (**Contract Participants**) have clearly defined roles, duties and obligations important to the efficient administration and proper functioning of the Contract. Concomitant with those roles are rights defined in the Contract.

The allocation of specific roles, duties and obligations to the various Contract Participants in FIDIC Contracts has evolved over a long period and has stood the test of time. Experience has shown that this allocation is consistent with widely accepted and understood international usage. Further, it is submitted that it provides the best opportunity for the Contract Participants to deliver a project that satisfies the Parties' reasonable performance expectations.

The delivery of a large construction project involves a complex interaction between all the Contract Participants. Each has its own roles, duties and obligations, which interface with the roles, duties and obligations of the other Contract Participants. The roles, duties and obligations defined in a FIDIC Contract have been determined to be those most appropriate to the efficient delivery of the contractual objectives and best suited to the skills and expertise normally expected of and exercised by the Contract Participants.

A FIDIC contract is based on the Employer and the Contractor undertaking their roles, duties and obligations and having their rights as implicit in the General Conditions. For the Employer this involves, for example, providing access to the Site at the time contracted for and paying the Contractor. For the Contractor it involves, for example, executing and completing the Works in accordance with the Contract and rectifying defects during the Defects Notification Period.

The roles, duties and obligations of other Contract Participants as defined in the GCs are equally important for efficiently delivering the contractual objectives (notwithstanding that, not being Parties, they are not bound by the terms of the Contract). Thus, for the Red, Pink and Yellow Books, this requires that an Engineer be appointed with appropriate authority, competence and resources to carry out the role and that they fulfil their duties and obligations as defined in the Contract. Further, the Engineer must exercise its contractual authority and make fair determinations in accordance with the Contract, taking due regard of all relevant circumstances. This means that it must not make determinations that only suit the Employer's interests without having due regard to the Contractor's rights under the Contract.

Similarly, for the Silver Book, the Employer's Representative must have appropriate authority to carry out the role and must carry out that role to enable the Contractor to enjoy its contractual rights.

GP2: The Particular Conditions must be drafted clearly and unambiguously.

FIDIC GCs undergo a comprehensive drafting and independent review process to ensure that they are clear and unambiguous. Clear and unambiguous drafting is fundamental to all Contract Participants understanding their roles and duties so they can fulfil their obligations and exercise their rights.

The conditions of a FIDIC Contract comprise the GCs and the PCs, which incorporate any additions or changes to the GCs. A 'FIDIC contract' will only be clearly and unambiguously drafted if the Particular Conditions are clearly and unambiguously drafted, and interface harmoniously with the GCs and the Appendix to Tender/Contract Data.

GP3: The Particular Conditions must not change the balance of risk/reward allocation provided for in the GCs.

Fair and balanced risk allocation is widely accepted as the most appropriate basis for drafting of construction contracts to minimise the prospects of disputes and enhance the likelihood of achieving successful project outcomes. It is a fundamental principle on which FIDIC contracts are based.

The **Abrahamson Principles**, well known to construction lawyers, are widely regarded as the basis of 'balanced' or 'fair' risk allocation.[19] These principles, as refined by Dr Nael Bunni, stipulate that risks should be allocated by considering:

- Which Party can best control the risk and the associated consequences?
- Which Party can best foresee the risk?
- Which Party can best bear the risk?
- Which Party ultimately most benefits or suffers when the risk eventuates? [20]

GP4: All time periods specified in the Contract for Contract Participants to perform their obligations must be of reasonable duration.

Time periods specified in the GCs have evolved as a consensus among the international construction community as an appropriate balance between the interests of a Contract

19 Max W Abrahamson, 'Risk Management' [1983] *International Construction Law Review* 241, 244.

20 Nael Bunni, 'The Four Criteria of Risk Allocation in Construction Contracts' (2009) 26 *International Construction Law Review* 4, 9.

Participant required to perform a duty and the interests of the Party whose rights are dependent on the execution of that duty. FIDIC considers they are reasonable time periods, sufficient to carry out the required duties, but without undue delay.

The consequences of reducing the time periods provided for in the GCs may result in a Contract Participant having insufficient time to perform their required duties properly or to exercise their rights. An earlier trigger of a time bar than is contemplated in the GCs is one potential consequence of reducing time periods.

Conversely, significantly extending those time periods may adversely affect the rights and entitlements of the Party for whose benefit the duties are being performed. For example, a longer period for issuing a Payment Certificate will result in the Contractor's cash flow being adversely affected.

In many provisions of the GCs, the Parties are invited to amend the 'default' time periods by agreement, using words such as 'unless otherwise agreed'. Such time periods are recognised as being determined by negotiation if appropriate, whilst providing a default option considered to be a reasonable time period.

GP5: Unless there is a conflict with the governing law of the Contract, all formal disputes must be referred to a Dispute Avoidance/Adjudication Board (or a Dispute Adjudication Board, if applicable) for a provisionally binding decision as a condition precedent to arbitration.

The Dispute Avoidance/Adjudication Board (**DAAB**) in the 2017 Red, Yellow and Silver Books, the Dispute Adjudication Board (**DAB**) in the 1999 Red Book and the Dispute Board (**DB**) in the 2010 Pink Book have evolved as important entities to help the Parties avoid disputes and as a procedure for resolving disputes (at least provisionally) at much lower cost and in much less time than required for arbitration. The DAAB/DAB procedure provides an independent third party that assists in maintaining appropriate communication between the contracting Parties and promotes early resolution of disputes to enable the project to proceed without unnecessary disruption. The 1999 Yellow Book and the 1999 Silver Book provide for an '*ad hoc*' DAB, implemented when a dispute has arisen. A DAAB or DAB resolves the conflicts of interest that formerly occurred, where the Engineer (engaged and paid by the Employer) not only certified the Contractor's entitlements under the Contract but also had the authority to resolve disputes.

If one of the Parties is not satisfied with a DAAB/DAB decision, it can issue a Notice of Dissatisfaction and trigger the arbitration process. However, arbitration can be delayed until the project is complete, helping to prevent project personnel from becoming distracted. In the meantime, the Parties have a decision that provides a provisional resolution of the dispute.

FIDIC considers the availability of an independent and impartial DAAB/DAB to (provisionally) resolve disputes fundamental to a fair and balanced contract. A DAAB/DAB can resolve disputes in real time and thereby enable the Parties to plan their future activities based on the reasoned decision of experienced, independent and impartial persons who are familiar with the execution of projects and administration of construction contracts.

2.5 Guidance for drafting contract documents for consistency with the Golden Principles

Minor additions or grammatical changes to the wording of a GC sub-clause that do not alter the intent are not a breach of the GPs. However, such cosmetic changes should only be made for good reasons.

In the PCs, changes to the GCs required to comply with local law are consistent with GC sub-clause 1.13 and are necessary and appropriate for the Contract to express the Parties' legal and contractual obligations properly. Such changes do not constitute a breach of the GPs.

One of the following terms in a GC generally indicates that it may be amended by the PCs without being in conflict with the GPs:

- 'or as otherwise agreed'
- 'except as otherwise agreed'
- 'unless otherwise agreed'
- 'unless otherwise agreed by both Parties'
- 'unless otherwise stated in the Particular Conditions'
- 'except as otherwise stated in these Conditions' or
- 'unless otherwise stated in the Contract' (however, this is ambiguous as it does not necessarily refer to the Particular Conditions)

It is important that the technical documents do not redefine the duties, rights, obligations, roles or responsibilities of any Contract Participants in a manner that is inconsistent with the GCs as modified by the PCs. For example, the Engineer has a clearly defined role in the Red and Yellow Books to make determinations as required by the Contract, after consulting both Parties. It would be a breach of GP1 for a Contract to require the Engineer to seek approval from the Employer before issuing any determination under sub-clause 3.5 (1999 editions) or sub-clause 3.7 (2017 editions).

The requirements of the project include the Laws applicable to execution of the Works, as well as the applicable Laws relevant to the rights and obligations of the Contract Participants. Changes in the PCs to make the Contract compliant with the relevant legal regimes are appropriate and necessary, and not in conflict with GP1.

Compliance with GP2 requires, amongst other things, that each of the documents comprising the Contract provide a cohesive and comprehensive whole, without overlap or inconsistencies. The contents of each Contract document should be confined to its scope as generally understood. The appropriate document to amend the GCs is the PCs; the 'contractual' issues detailed in the GCs should not be amended in other documents such as the Employer's Requirements or the Specification.

The content of 'technical' documents such as the Employer's Requirements, drawings or Specifications should be confined to technical issues, consistent with the provisions of the GCs as modified by the PCs.

GP3 is a fundamental principle that should be considered in any PC amendment to the GCs. The yardstick to apply in drafting any provision that amends the roles, duties or obligations as defined in the GCs is to enquire whether risks are being allocated to the

Party that is in the best position to control them and bear the consequences of a potential risk becoming a reality. If so, the amendment is compliant with GP3.

There are two alternative considerations involved in complying with GP4 in respect of providing the Contract Participants with a reasonable time to perform their obligations and exercise their rights:

- 'Fixed' timeframes (i.e., those that are not qualified by a phrase such as 'unless the parties agree otherwise') should not be significantly changed from their value in the GCs.
- 'Default' timeframes (i.e., those that are qualified by a phrase such as 'unless the parties agree otherwise') when amended should not provide unreasonably short or unreasonably long timeframes. A timeframe would be unreasonably short if it did not provide sufficient time for the Contract Participant to perform its duties properly or exercise its rights; a time frame would be unreasonably long if it significantly affects a Party's enjoyment of its rights, such as the Contractor's right to suspend or terminate the Works.

GP5 requires that the Contract provide for a DAAB or DAB to give a provisionally binding decision on any formal dispute, as a condition precedent to referring a dispute to arbitration. Compliance with GP5 (and GP1) entails retention of the GC clauses referring to the role and operation of the DAAB/DAB and not significantly changing its role, duties, obligations and rights as defined in the GCs.

2.6 Conclusion

FIDIC's initiative in promoting the recognition and application of the GPs is intended to encourage the use of FIDIC GCs as they have always been intended: fair and balanced risk/reward allocation, clear definition of scope, duties, roles, rights and responsibilities and contract documents that constitute a contract management manual for best practice international project execution.

The use of the GPs is endorsed in the 2017 Editions of the Red, Yellow and Silver Books and the Emerald Book in the following terms:

> FIDIC strongly recommends that the Employer, the Contractor and all drafters of the Special Provisions take all due regard of the five FIDIC Golden Principles.[21]

21 Guidance for the Preparation of Particular Conditions, 8.

CHAPTER 3

Preparation of Particular Conditions

Dr Donald Charrett

CONTENTS

DOI: 10.4324/9781003206910-3

3.1 What should be in the Particular Conditions?

As noted in section 1.3.5, the Particular Conditions in the 2017 rainbow suite comprise Part A – Contract Data and Part B – Special Provisions.

3.1.1 Particular Conditions Part A – Contract Data

The Contract Data provides the specific information referred to in the General Conditions required to define the unique characteristics of the particular Contract. Most of this information will be provided by the Employer to define its requirements in the Tender documents, including the time and cost parameters of the Contract, certain risk allocation parameters and a number of contract administration matters. The 'legal' data required is confined to the governing law of the contract; if this is not specified, the governing law of the contract will be the law of the Country. Certain parts of the Contract Data may be provided by the Contractor in its Tender.

Not all of the data items will require completion, as some refer to options in the General Conditions that may not be applicable, e.g. the data for the proportions of local and foreign currency (sub-clause 14.15(a)(i)) does not need to be completed if payment is to be made in one currency only. Many of the data items have default provisions specified in the relevant sub-clause that will apply if the item is not completed in the Contract Data. The Annexure to this chapter comprises the Contract Data from the 2017 Yellow Book, annotated with the default provisions in the General Conditions.

If data is not provided for some items, the data may be provided by the applicable law, e.g. if the number of days for the Time for Completion is not defined for sub-clause 1.1.86, the law would generally imply that the time period be reasonable.

It is strongly recommended that, to avoid ambiguity, all the items in the Contract Data be filled in, with the project-specific data, reference to the default in the sub-clause if that is appropriate or Not Applicable if the sub-clause provision does not apply. This will materially assist in the subsequent administration of the Contract by providing all the relevant information in one location.

3.1.2 Particular Conditions Part B – Special Provisions

Particular Conditions Part B – Special Provisions is the contract document where any changes or additions to the General Conditions are documented. All references in the following sections to Particular Conditions refer to Part B – Special Provisions in the 2017 rainbow suite.

Special Provisions necessary for the particular requirements of the Works may comprise either modifications to the General Conditions or additional provisions that supplement the General Conditions. Such modifications may be necessary or desirable so that:

- The Contract wording is consistent with applicable law.
- The Contract wording draws attention to relevant applicable law that must be complied with.
- Specific requirements for the Site or the Works are documented.
- The Employer's preferences are defined.

As noted in the table of contract document hierarchy in Table 1.2, the Particular Conditions have precedence over the General Conditions in the event of any ambiguity. Thus, any Special Provisions that modify the General Conditions supersede the relevant parts of the General Conditions.

For clarity, the Special Provisions should comply with the following:

- A Special Provision modification to a sub-clause of the General Conditions should use the same sub-clause numbering as in the General Conditions.
- Additional Special Provisions should use sub-clause numbers that are not used in the General Conditions.
- Special Provisions may provide additional provisions to the General Conditions or may change provisions in the General Conditions.

Skilled legal advice is required to determine whether the contractual provisions of the General Conditions are incompatible with the applicable mandatory law and to make the necessary amendments in the Special Provisions. Legal review should also determine whether it is appropriate to add Special Provisions to modify non-mandatory law that would otherwise apply. The following chapters provide guidance on the applicable law in a range of jurisdictions where FIDIC contracts are or can be used.

3.2 Governing law

3.2.1 Governing law of the contract

The principle of freedom of contract means that subject to any mandatory law, the Parties are free to choose the governing law of their Contract, even if this is in a different jurisdiction to where the work is carried out or to the domicile of the contracting Parties. This principle of party autonomy in selecting the governing law of a contract is widely recognised. For example, the following articles of the *2015 Principles on Choice of Law in International Commercial Contracts*[1] of the Hague Conference on Private International Law (**Hague Principles**) provide:

> **Article 2 Freedom of choice**
>
> 1. A contract is governed by the law chosen by the parties.
>
> […]
>
> 4. No connections required between the law chosen and the parties for their transaction.
>
> **Article 3 Rules of law**
>
> The law chosen by the parties may be rules of law that are generally accepted on an international, supranational or regional level as a neutral and balanced set of rules, unless the law of the forum provides otherwise.
>
> Article 11 Overriding mandatory rules and public policy (ordre public)
>
> 1. These Principles shall not prevent a court from applying overriding mandatory provisions of the law of the forum which apply irrespective of the law chosen by the parties.

1 https://assets.hcch.net/docs/5da3ed47-f54d-4c43-aaef-5eafc7c1f2a1.pdf (accessed 23 February 2021).

2. The law of the forum determines when a court may or must apply or take into account overriding mandatory provisions of another law.
3. A court may exclude application of a provision of the law chosen by the parties only if and to the extent that the result of such application would be manifestly incompatible with fundamental notions of public policy (*ordre public*) of the forum.
4. The law of the forum determines when a court may or must apply or take into account the public policy (*ordre public*) of a State the law of which would be applicable in the absence of a choice of law.
5. These Principles shall not prevent an arbitral tribunal from applying or taking into account public policy (*ordre public*), or from applying or taking into account overriding mandatory provisions of a law other than the law chosen by the parties, if the arbitral tribunal is required or entitled to do so.

The nature of the Hague Principles is as follows:

> **I.8** As their title suggests, the Principles do not constitute a formally binding instrument such as a Convention that States are obliged to directly apply or incorporate into their domestic law. Nor is this instrument a model law that States are encouraged to enact. Rather, it is a non-binding set of principles, which the Hague Conference encourages States to incorporate into their domestic choice of law regimes in a manner appropriate for the circumstances of each State. In this way, the Principles can guide the reform of domestic law on choice of law and operate alongside existing instruments on the subject (see Rome I Regulation and Mexico City Convention both of which embrace and apply the concept of party autonomy).[2]

The Hague Principles have so far only been implemented in legislation in Paraguay[3] and Uruguay.[4] However, a number of arbitration centres either have incorporated the Principles into their own institutional rules or are advertising or facilitating their use in other ways compatible with the Hague Principles. For example, in respect of the Council for National and International Commercial Arbitration in India (**CNICA**):

- The CNICA Arbitration Rules are consistent with the Hague Principles.
- The CNICA Arbitration Rules allow parties to select the applicable law (Article 2).
- Tribunals constituted under the CNICA Arbitration Rules respect the law chosen by the parties.
- Parties are free to select a non-state law under the CNICA Arbitration Rules (Article 3).
- Tribunals constituted under the CNICA Arbitration Rules respect the parties' choice of a non-state law (Article 3).[5]

The law of the forum (or *lex fori* as it is sometimes known) is the law of the place in which court or arbitral proceedings are conducted. Thus, under the Hague Principles and more generally, if the Parties have not selected the governing law of the contract, it will be determined by a judge in the jurisdiction where legal proceedings are initiated, or by an arbitral tribunal. Due to differences in conflicts of law rules, the outcome may be unpredictable.

2 www.hcch.net/en/instruments/conventions/full-text/?cid=135 (accessed 23 February 2021).

3 *Paraguayan Law 5393 of 2015* regarding the applicable law to international contracts, https://assets.hcch.net/upload/contractslaw_py.pdf (accessed 23 February 2021).

4 www.diputados.gub.uy/wp-content/uploads/2020/11/00130.pdf (accessed 23 February 2021).

5 https://assets.hcch.net/docs/b9627fbb-eac1-4aae-a23c-ef059e24849e.pdf (accessed 8 June 2022).

It should be noted that the Hague Principles do not require the rules of law to be laws of a country. The UNIDROIT Principles of International Commercial Contracts would be regarded as 'an international neutral and balanced set of rules'. Such anational rules of law are also permitted by the *European Contracts Convention* (***Rome I***)[6] and the *Inter-American Convention on the Law Applicable to International Contracts.*[7]

3.2.2 Choosing the governing law of the contract

As noted in the Annexure to this chapter, if the Parties do not nominate the governing law of the contract in the Contract Data for sub-clause 1.4 in the 2017 rainbow suite, the default position in the General Conditions is that the governing law of the contract will be the law of the Country.

Issues to consider in choosing the governing law if it is not to be the law of the Country include:

- Are there any legal constraints on selecting the governing law in the Country or the domiciles of the contracting Parties?[8]
- Is the proposed law well known?
- Is legal advice on the proposed law readily available?
- Is the proposed law familiar to the contracting Parties, the DAAB/DAB and arbitrators?
- Is the governing law predictable?
- Are there any potential inconsistencies with the Laws of the Country?
- What is the extent of modification of FIDIC General Conditions necessary for consistency with the governing law?
- What are the preferences of the contracting Parties?
- What is the availability of reference materials (e.g. books, legislation, case law) in the language for communication?

3.2.3 The law governing the agreement to arbitrate

In respect of sub-clause 21.6 Arbitration, the Notes on the Preparation of Special Provisions in the 2017 rainbow suite recommend careful selection of the place or '**seat**' of arbitration in a jurisdiction other than the Country:

> For major projects tendered internationally, it is desirable that the place of arbitration be situated in a country other than that of the Employer or Contractor. This country should have a modern and liberal arbitration law and should have ratified a bilateral or multilateral convention (such as the *1958 New York Convention on the Recognition and Enforcement of Foreign Arbitral Awards*), or both, that would facilitate the enforcement of an arbitral award in the states of the Parties.

---

6 *Regulation (EC) No 593/2008* of the European Parliament and of the Council of 17 June 2008 on the law applicable to contractual obligations.

7 www.oas.org/juridico/english/treaties/b-56.html (accessed 8 June 2022).

8 For example, Article 869 of the *Colombian Commercial Code* states that Contracts that are performed in Colombia will be governed by Colombian Law.

The consequence of nominating the seat of arbitration is the selection of that jurisdiction's law as the *lex arbitrii* – the law governing the arbitration process. The intent of FIDIC's recommendation is to ensure that neither Party will have a 'home country' advantage in the dispute resolution process.

As discussed in section 1.5.6, the law governing the arbitration process (*lex arbitrii*) is not necessarily the same as the governing law of the contract, or the law governing the agreement to arbitrate. Where the governing law of the contract is different to the *lex arbitrii*, there may be a question of what the governing law of the arbitration is, that is, the law governing the validity and scope of the arbitration agreement. Where the Parties have not made an explicit choice of the governing law of the contract, there are arguments (and case law) in support of the law governing the arbitration agreement being either the governing law of the contract or the *lex arbitrii*.

The finely balanced arguments for either possibility were canvassed in the case of *Enka Insaat Ve Sanayi AS v OOO Insurance Company (Enka Insaat)*.[9] In this case, the central issue concerned which system of national law governed the validity and scope of the arbitration agreement when the governing law of the contract containing it differed from the law of the seat of the arbitration. The Parties had not made an explicit choice of the governing law of the contract but had selected London as the seat of arbitration. The majority (Lord Hamblen and Lord Leggatt, Lord Kerr agreeing) applied English common law rules for resolving conflicts of laws and held that in the absence of the parties' choice, the law applicable to the arbitration agreement is the system of law with which the arbitration agreement is most closely connected. Where the parties have chosen a seat of arbitration, the governing law of the arbitration agreement will generally be the law of the seat, even if this differs from the governing law of the contract.[10] In dissent, Lord Burrows (with whom Lord Sales agreed) held that the 'main contract' approach should be preferred to the 'seat' approach in determining the governing law of the arbitration agreement.

Where the Parties have made a choice of governing law of the contract, the majorities' summary in *Enka Insaat* noted that under English law:

> iv) Where the law applicable to the arbitration agreement is not specified, a choice of governing law for the contract will generally apply to an arbitration agreement which forms part of the contract.
>
> v) The choice of a different country as the seat of the arbitration is not, without more, sufficient to negate an inference that a choice of law to govern the contract was intended to apply to the arbitration agreement. [11]

As the FIDIC Conditions of Contract specify the governing law of the contract either by explicit nomination or in default as the law of the Country, the issue of a different law governing the agreement to arbitrate is probably unlikely to arise except in unusual circumstances.

9 [2020] UKSC 38.
10 *Ibid.* [170].
11 *Ibid.*

3.3 Special Provisions for consistency with applicable law

Irrespective of the wording of the Conditions of Contract, mandatory law will always apply, and the Parties are required to comply with it both as a matter of law and to comply with the Contract. Such mandatory law may comprise either

(a) Provisions that are incompatible with the General Conditions, or
(b) Provisions that are not incompatible with the General Conditions, but the General Conditions do not refer to the issue within the scope of the mandatory law.

In the case of (a), it is highly desirable that Special Provisions are written to modify the General Conditions and make them consistent with the mandatory law. In addition, it is also desirable to prepare Special Provisions to incorporate mandatory law provisions of type (b), to draw attention to these obligations in a document that (hopefully) is used as a contract management manual.

Special Provisions that incorporate mandatory law of type (a) will ensure that the contract wording is accurate and not misleading; Special Provisions that incorporate mandatory law of type (b) will significantly enhance the usefulness of the Conditions of Contract as a comprehensive contract management manual.

As discussed in section 1.5, statute law may be either mandatory or non-mandatory. If a law is not mandatory, contracting Parties may choose not to follow it by incorporating specific terms in the Contract. However, unless there are such contract terms 'otherwise' the law will apply as a default option, whether or not the Parties are aware of it. In the circumstances where the Parties do not wish to apply the default law, Special Provisions will be necessary to define the contractual alternative.

Thus, the General Conditions may require modification, or it may be desirable to modify them where the governing law of the contract is that of a particular jurisdiction. The following are some examples of issues where it may be necessary or desirable to prepare Special Provisions that align the Conditions of Contract with the provisions of the governing law:

- Changed conditions:
  - Laws of economic disequilibrium, e.g. France, former French colonies and Türkiye.
  - Rules about commercial impracticability, e.g. USA.
- Limitation period for liability, e.g. Brazil.
- Delay damages (liquidated damages)/proof of loss:
  - May be lowered if the actual damage is less in a civil law jurisdiction, e.g. Switzerland.
  - May be nullified if it is not a genuine pre-estimate of loss in a common law jurisdiction, e.g. Australia, England.
- Termination, e.g. Australia, Brazil, France.
- *Force majeure*, e.g. China, the Philippines, Indonesia, United Arab Emirates.
- Obligation to complete with a certain result, e.g. Peru.
- Subcontractors, e.g. China, France.
- Provisions relating to the extinguishing of liability will not apply in jurisdictions which do not allow contractual waiver of liability in the case of gross negligence or fraud, e.g. California.

- Disputes relating to non-contractual claims may not be arbitrable, e.g. fraud in Pakistan.
- Rights of 'set off', 'abatement' or similar rights that are inconsistent with the payment provisions in the General Conditions, e.g. under the common law, a right of set-off is difficult to exclude by contract language.
- Valuation of Variations, e.g. France.
- Burdensome obligations on the Contractor in the EPC Silver Book are unlikely to be upheld in France and Francophone and other countries of French civil law tradition.
- The responsibility of Contractors to implement Variations instructed by the Employer, e.g. Germany.
- The corresponding duty of Employers to pay for Variations, e.g. Brazil, Italy.
- Principles relating to the obligations to produce a result versus the obligation to apply the means, e.g. Peru.
- Good faith, e.g. Brazil, Peru.
- Time bars may not be allowed under the governing law as a breach of good faith in civil law jurisdictions, e.g. Peru, United Arab Emirates.
- Legislation dealing with unfair contract conditions, e.g. Germany, the Netherlands, Sweden, England, France.
- Allocation of ground risk, e.g. Brazil, Germany.

Each of the following chapters of this book provides guidance on the application of FIDIC contracts in a particular jurisdiction and addresses the foregoing issues where they are relevant to the jurisdiction.

3.4 Guidance for the preparation of Particular Conditions

The 'Guidance for the Preparation of Particular Conditions' in the 2017 rainbow suite contains detailed Notes on the preparation of Special Provisions in the section titled 'Particular Conditions Part B – Special Provisions'. The Introduction to this section includes a strong recommendation 'that the Employer, the Contractor and all drafters of the Special Provisions take all due regard of the five FIDIC Golden Principles' enumerated in bold (see section 1.4). The FIDIC Golden Principles are listed and discussed in detail in Chapter 2.

Some direct warnings on amending sub-clauses then follow:

> Before incorporating any new or changed sub-clauses, the wording must be carefully checked to ensure that it is wholly suitable for the particular circumstances. Unless it is considered suitable, example wording should be amended before use.
>
> Where any amendments or additions are made to the General Conditions, great care must be taken to ensure that the wording does not unintentionally alter the meaning of other clauses in the Conditions of Contract, does not inadvertently change the obligations assigned to the Parties or the balance of risks shared between them and/or does not create any new ambiguity or misunderstanding in the rest of the Contract documents.

The 'Notes on the Preparation of Special Provisions' are prefaced with the following caution prior to providing detailed suggestions for specific clauses:

> It is very important that all Employers (and all drafters of the Special Provisions) work with their professional advisers to review specific terminology in the General Conditions for compliance and consistency with accepted practice in the legal jurisdiction they are operating in.
>
> [...]

The following references and examples show some of the Sub-Clauses in the General Conditions which may need amending to suit the needs of the project or the requirements of the Employer. The selected Sub-Clauses and the example wording are included as examples only. They also include, as an aide memoire, references to other documents such as the Specification and/or Drawings and the Contract Data, where particular issues may need to be addressed.

The selected Sub-Clauses do not necessarily require changing and the example wording may not suit the needs of a particular project or Employer. It is the responsibility of the drafter of the Special Provisions to ensure that the selection of the Sub-Clauses and the choice of wording is appropriate to the project concerned.

Furthermore, there may be other Sub-Clauses, not mentioned below, which need to be amended. Great care must be taken when amending the wording of Sub-Clauses from the General Conditions, or adding new provisions, to ensure that the balance of obligations and rights of the Parties are not unintentionally compromised.

The following sections identify four distinct types of modifications that may be required to the clauses in the General Conditions, as identified in the 2017 rainbow suite:

- Special Provisions necessary or desirable for consistency with the governing law of the contract.
- Special Provisions necessary or desirable for consistency with applicable laws.
- Special Provisions necessary or desirable for the Project requirements.
- Special Provisions necessary or desirable for the Employer's preferences.

The following sections are intended as a brief introduction to some of the more common and well-recognised General Conditions clauses that may require modification. Although extracted from the Notes in the 2017 rainbow suite, they are not intended to provide detailed guidance, nor to suggest specific wording for particular sub-clauses – those are covered in considerable detail in the FIDIC rainbow suite.

The following tables do not provide any indication of which modifications may be necessary or desirable for a particular jurisdiction – those are covered in the following chapters, each of which addresses the requirements of a particular jurisdiction.

3.4.1 Special Provisions necessary or desirable for consistency with the governing law of the contract

Some of the following Special Provisions are also included in the table in section 3.4.2, as the Laws in the Country may be applicable in some circumstances.

Yellow Book sub-clause	**Special Provision**	**Page**[1]
1.1.XX[2] Additional Definitions	Add definition of Gross Negligence	15
1.6 Contract Agreement	Contract Agreement: if entry into a formal Contract Agreement is mandatory, delete the words 'unless they agree otherwise'.	15
4.2 Performance Security	The provisions in sub-clause 4.2 in respect of Performance Securities may have to be amended to comply with applicable law.	22

Yellow Book sub-clause	Special Provision	Page[1]
8.XX Additional sub-clause for Concurrent Delay	Add a Special Provision 8.XX to define the rules and procedures applicable to concurrent delay under the governing law of the contract.	35
11.10 Unfulfilled Obligations	It may be necessary to review the effect of sub-clause 11.10 in relation to the period of liability imposed by the applicable law, and in particular, the second paragraph may require amending.	36
15.2 Termination for Contractor's Default	Sub-clause 15.2 may require amendment for consistency with the governing law of the contract.	47
15.5 Termination for Employer's Convenience	Amend the wording of sub-clause 15.5 if it is not permissible under the governing law of the contract for the Employer to terminate the Contract for convenience.	48
16.2 Termination by Contractor	Amend the wording of sub-clause 16.2 if the General Condition provision for termination by the Contractor is not compatible with the governing law of the contract.	48

[1] Page numbers are the page numbers in the Guidance for the Preparation of Particular Conditions in the 2017 Yellow Book.

[2] XX denotes a new number distinct from the numbering in the General Conditions. See section 3.1.2.

3.4.2 Special Provisions necessary or desirable for consistency with applicable laws

The following Special Provisions generally refer to applicable laws of the Site and in the Country.

Yellow Book sub-clause	Special Provision	Page[1]
1.6 Contract Agreement	Contract Agreement: if entry into a formal Contract Agreement is mandatory, delete the word 'unless they agree otherwise'.	15
1.13 Compliance with Laws	Add a Special Provision in sub-clause 1.13 in respect of the Goods for a plant contract.	16
3.5 Engineer's Instructions	Amend sub-clause 3.5 if the applicable law prevents the Contractor from complying with any Engineer's instruction that may have an adverse effect on the health and safety of the Contractor's Personnel.	21
4.2 Performance Security	The provisions in sub-clause 4.2 in respect of Performance Securities may have to be amended to comply with applicable law.	22
4.16 Transport of Goods	Add a Special Provision to sub-clause 4.16 if the Contractor is required to obtain permission prior to the delivery of Goods to the Site.	25
5.2.2 Contractor's Documents – Review by Engineer	Amend sub-clause 5.2.2 if there is a requirement under the applicable law for the mandatory review/checking of certain elements of design (by an authorised professional or other legally recognised individual) and/or verification that such design is in accordance with the applicable law before such design can be implemented in the Works.	29

Yellow Book sub-clause	Special Provision	Page[1]
6.3 Recruitment of Persons	Amend or delete sub-clause 6.3 if the relevant labour Laws applicable to the Contractor's Personnel and/or the Employer's Personnel do not permit any restriction on the right of any worker to seek other positions.	30
11.10 Unfulfilled Obligations	It may be necessary to review the effect of sub-clause 11.10 in relation to the period of liability imposed by the applicable law, and in particular, the second paragraph may require amending.	36
14.1 The Contract Price 14.XX Additional sub-clause for Import Duties	Amend sub-clause 14.1 and add an additional sub-clause 14.XX if the Contractor is not required to pay import duties on Goods imported by the Contractor into the Country.	40
14.1 The Contract Price 14.XX Additional sub-clause for Expatriate Staff Income Tax	Amend sub-clause 14.1 and add an additional sub-clause 14.XX if expatriate staff are exempted from paying local income tax.	40

[1] Page numbers are the page numbers in the Guidance for the Preparation of Particular Conditions in the 2017 Yellow Book.

3.4.3 Special Provisions necessary or desirable for the project requirements

Yellow Book sub-clause	Special Provision	Page[1]
1.1 Definitions	Amend definitions of Country and Local Currency and add new definitions.	14
Various	Consider increasing the timescales for Notices in the General Conditions if Notices are only to be given in paper format by post. The following sub-clauses in the Yellow Book provide for specific periods of time for submitting a Notice: 1.9; 3.4; 3.5; 3.7.3; 3.7.4; 3.7.5; 4.2.2; 4.3; 4.4; 4.5.1; (4.7.2); 4.9.1; 4.12.2; 4.16; 4.17; 5.2.2; 6.12; 7.5; 8.1; 8.3; 8.12; 9.1; 9.2; 10.1; 10.3; 11.6; 11.7; 11.9; 12.1; 15.2.2; 16.1; 16.2.1; 16.2.2; 17.3; 18.2; 20.2.1; 20.2.2; 20.2.4; 21.4.4. The following sub-clauses in the Yellow Book Dispute Adjudication Agreement provide for specific periods of time for submitting a Notice: 2.2; 9.1. Rule 10 in the Yellow Book DAAB Procedural Rules provides for specific periods of time for submitting a Notice.	15
1.5(g) Priority of Documents	If the Employer's Requirements are to comprise a number of documents, consider amending sub-clause 1.5(g) by adding an order of precedence for the various documents in the Employer's Requirements.	15
1.14 Joint and Several Liability	Add Special Provisions in sub-clause 1.14 if the Contractor is a Joint Venture.	16

Yellow Book sub-clause	Special Provision	Page[1]
2.1 Right of Access to the Site	Amendments to sub-clause 2.1 if right of access to, and possession of, the Site cannot be granted by the Employer in the normal way.	18
3.4 Delegation by the Engineer	Amendments to sub-clause 3.4 if it is anticipated that the Engineer's Assistants may not all be fluent in the language for communication are defined in 1.4.	20
3.5 Engineer's Instructions	Add a Special Provision to sub-clause 3.5 to allow for the giving of oral instructions by the Engineer.	21
4.2.1 Performance Security – Contractor's Obligations	If the sample forms for Performance Securities are not used, consider adding to sub-clause 4.2.1 a Special Provision to reduce the amount of the Performance Security following issue of the Taking-Over Certificate for the whole of the Works.	22
4.3 Contractor's Representative	Add Special Provisions to sub-clause 4.3 if it is necessary to stipulate that the Contractor's Representative shall be qualified, experienced and competent in a particular engineering discipline in relation to the Works, be fluent in a particular language other than the language for communications or is not required to be fluent in the language for communications.	22
4.8 Health and Safety Obligations	Amend sub-clause 4.8 if the Contractor is sharing occupation of the Site with others.	24
4.21 Security of the Site **4.22** Contractor's Operations on Site	Amend sub-clauses 4.21 and 4.22 if the Contractor is sharing occupation of the Site with others.	26
6.8 Contractor's Superintendence	Amend sub-clause 6.8 if it is permissible that the Contractor's superintending staff are not all fluent in the language for communications.	30
6.8 Contractor's Superintendence	Add a Special Provision to sub-clause 6.8 if it is necessary to stipulate that the Contractor's superintending staff shall be fluent in a particular language.	31
6.12 Key Personnel	Add a Special Provision to sub-clause 6.12 if it is permissible that all Key Personnel are not fluent in the language for communications.	31
6.XX Additional sub-clauses for circumstances of the Site	It may be necessary, appropriate and/or desirable to include additional Special Provisions to clause 6 to take account of the circumstances and locality of the Site: Foreign personnel Supply of foodstuffs Supply of water Measures against insect and pest nuisance Alcoholic liquor or drugs Arms and ammunition Festivals and religious customs Funeral arrangements Forced labour Child labour Employment records of workers Workers organisations Non-discrimination and equal opportunity	

Yellow Book sub-clause	Special Provision	Page[1]
8.3(a)–(k) Programme	For less complex projects, consider simplifying the requirements for the Contractor's programme in sub-clause 8.3(a)–(k).	34

[1] Page numbers are the page numbers in the Guidance for the Preparation of Particular Conditions in the 2017 Yellow Book.

3.4.4 Special Provisions necessary or desirable for the Employer's preferences

Yellow Book sub-clause	Special Provision	Page
1.5 Priority of Documents	Amend sub-clause 1.5 if no order of precedence of documents is to be prescribed in the Contract. In the event of an ambiguity or discrepancy, the priority will be determined by the governing law of the contract.	15
1.10 Employer's Use of Contractor's Documents	Special Provisions to sub-clause 1.10 may be required if all rights to particular items of e.g. computer software are to be assigned to the Employer.	15
1.15 Limitation of Liability	Replace sub-clause 1.15 if it is required that the limitation of each Party's liability to the other Party is to include certain 'indirect or consequential loss or damage' and is also to take into account liabilities to be insured under clause 19.	16
2.6 Employer-Supplied Materials and Employer's Equipment	Add Special Provisions to sub-clause 2.6 if Employer Supplied Materials or Employer's Equipment are listed in the Employer's Requirements.	18
3.2 Engineer's Duties and Authority	Any requirements for the Engineer to obtain the Employer's consent should be added to sub-clause 3.2.	20
4.4 Subcontractors	Add a Special Provision to sub-clause 4.4 if it is appropriate or desirable to encourage the Contractor to employ local subcontractors.	23
4.4 Subcontractors	Delete the last three paragraphs of sub-clause 4.4 if no consent by the Engineer to Subcontractors is required.	23
4.4 Subcontractors	Amend sub-clause 4.4 if the Engineer's consent is required for the suppliers of certain Materials or subcontracts should provide for assignment of the subcontractor to the Employer pursuant to sub-clause 15.2 or after the expiry of the DNP.	23
4.4 Subcontractors	Amend sub-clause 4.4 if it is anticipated that a Subcontractor that is not a Nominated Subcontractor is to be instructed under sub-clause 13.3.	24
4.12 Unforeseeable Physical Conditions	If the risk of Unforeseeable physical conditions is to be shared between the Parties, amend sub-clause 4.12.	25
4.17 Contractor's Equipment	Add a Special Provision to sub-clause 4.17 if vesting of the Contractor's Equipment to the Employer is required (and consistent with the Laws of the Country).	26
4.XX Additional sub-clause for completion of certain parts of the Works	Add a Special Provision 4.XX if the Employer wishes to have certain parts of the Works completed within certain times but does not wish to take over such parts when completed (Milestones).	27

Yellow Book sub-clause	Special Provision	Page
14.4 Schedule of Payments	Amend sub-clause 14.4 if certain payments to the Contractor to be made on completion of each Milestone.	28
7.7 Ownership of Plant and Materials	Add a Special Provision to sub-clause 7.7 if the Contractor is to provide high-value items of Plant and/or Materials.	33
7.XX Additional sub-clause for financing institution rules	Add a Special Provision 7.XX if the Contract is being financed by an institution whose rules or policies require a restriction on the use of its funds.	34
8.1 Commencement of Works	Amend sub-clause 8.1 if the Commencement Date is not to be within 42 days after the Contractor receives the letter of Acceptance.	
8.XX Additional sub-clause for early completion incentives	Add a Special Provision 8.XX if the Contract provides incentives for early completion.	35
9.1 Contractor's Obligations	Amend sub-clause 9.1 if the product produced by the Tests on Completion is to be retained by the Contractor and not the Employer.	36
11.3 Extension of Defects Notification Period	Amend the period of two years in sub-clause 11.3 if the Employer requires a longer or shorter period.	36
11.XX Additional sub-clause for new or innovative technology	Add a Special Provision 11.XX if the Works comprise new or innovative technology in the Country and the Employer requires its permanent operating personnel to be given supervisory assistance in the operation and maintenance of the Plant during the DNP.	37
12.1 Procedure for Tests after Completion	Amend sub-clause 12.1 if the provisions for Tests after Completion are to be different to those in the General Conditions.	37
13.2 Value Engineering	Add Special Provisions for sharing of the benefit, costs and/or delay between the Parties applying to a Value Engineering Variation instructed by the Engineer.	
13.7 Adjustments for Changes in Cost	Amend sub-clause 13.7 if it would be unreasonable for the Contractor to bear the risk of escalating costs due to inflation.	38
14.XX Additional sub-clauses for exceptions to payment provisions	Add Special Provisions 14.XX to cover any exceptions to the provisions in sub-clause 14.1 and if sub-clause 14.1(a) (lump sum) is not to apply.	40
14.2 Advance Payment	Amend sub-clause 14.2 if the Employer wishes to provide the advance payment in instalments.	42
14.XX Additional sub-clause for interim payments	Add a Special Provision 14.XX if interim payments are to be paid other than on the basis of a Schedule of Payments.	43
14.XX Additional sub-clause for simple measurement for interim valuations	If the Works consist of only a few different types of operations, a simple measurement type of approach for interim valuations may be detailed in a Special Provision 14.XX.	44
14.8 Delayed Payment	Amend sub-clause 14.8 if payment is to be on the basis of the Contractor's actual financing Costs.	45
14.XX Additional sub-clause for guarantee instead of Retention Money	Add a Special Provision 14.XX if part of the Retention Money is to be released and substituted by an appropriate guarantee.	45

Yellow Book sub-clause	Special Provision	Page
14.15 Currencies of Payment	Replace sub-clause 14.15 if all payments are to be made in Local Currency.	45
14.XX Additional sub-clause for requirements of financing entities	Add Special Provisions 14.XX to cover the requirements of financing entities such as aid agencies, development banks, export credit agencies or other international financing institutions.	46
14.XX Additional sub-clause for Contractor finance	Add a Special Provision 14.XX for Contractor finance.	47
15.XX Additional sub-clause for Employer-Supplied Materials	A Special Provision 15.XX may be appropriate if the Employer has made available any Employer-Supplied Materials and/or Employer's Equipment.	47
16.3 Contractor's Obligations after Termination	Amendment of sub-clause 16.3 may be desirable if the Employer has made available any Employer Supplied Materials and/or Employer's Equipment.	48
17.XX Additional sub-clause for Contractor's use of Employer's facilities	Add a Special Provision 17.XX if the Contractor is to be allowed to use and/or occupy any of the Employer's facilities and/or accommodation temporarily during the Contract.	49
19 Insurance	Amend sub-clause 19 if the Employer wishes to change the insurance provisions in the General Conditions.	49
20.1 Claims	Consider replacing the words 'within a reasonable time' in the last paragraph of sub-clause 20.1 with a specified time period.	50
1.1.22 Definition of DAAB 1.1.23 Definition of DAAB Agreement **21.1** Constitution of the DAAB **21.3** Avoidance of Disputes **21.4** Obtaining DAAB's Decision	Amendments to sub-clauses 1.1.22, 1.1.23, 21.1 and 21.4 and deletion of sub-clause 21.3 will be required if an ad-hoc Dispute Adjudication Board (DAB) is to be appointed instead of a DAAB.	52
21.5 Amicable Settlement	A longer period than 28 days may be desirable under sub-clause 21.5 to give the Parties an opportunity to arrive at an amicable settlement procedure.	53
Various	If Building Information Modelling (BIM) is to be adopted, a number of sub-clauses need to be thoroughly reviewed when drafting the Special Provisions.	58

3.5 Format of Conditions of Contract

As noted earlier, there are a number of legitimate reasons why the General Conditions may need to be modified and/or supplemented by Special Provisions.

In an endeavour to discourage users from changing the General Conditions excessively, FIDIC currently insists on the use of the General Conditions in their original form, irrespective of the extent to which Particular Conditions might change them.

Before a Contract has been entered into, a tenderer needs to assess the Conditions of Contract to determine, amongst other things, the risks that are to be undertaken by the Contractor. A tenderer familiar with FIDIC General Conditions needs to assess, in particular, those Particular Conditions that alter the risk allocation under the General Conditions. From the practical perspective of assessing how far a Contract deviates from a 'FIDIC contract', a redlined markup of the FIDIC General Conditions is the most user-friendly. It avoids a reviewer spending any time assessing unaltered sub-clauses, and it draws specific attention to those sub-clauses that have been altered and the specific way in which they have been altered. This is not necessarily straightforward if the alterations are in a separate Particular Conditions document, as this requires a close comparison of the corresponding General Conditions sub-clauses.

However, once a contract has been executed, for the purpose of complying with and administering the Contract, users generally prefer a single 'clean' document of the Conditions of Contract that incorporates the General Conditions, plus the Particular Conditions, Contract Data, the General Conditions of the Dispute Adjudication Agreement, the Dispute Adjudication Agreement and the Procedural Rules all using the FIDIC sub-clause numbering.

Under current arrangements, users can obtain the benefits of a single Conditions of Contract document by negotiating a licence for an electronic copy with FIDIC. This avoids the inconvenience of referring to a separate Particular Conditions document in addition to the General Conditions to understand the Contract Conditions.

Under existing arrangements, FIDIC may negotiate an electronic licence on an exceptional basis as follows:

- FIDIC provides a soft copy of the General Conditions.
- The licensee may alter the text of the General Conditions.
- The final issued version of the Contract must append a markup of the amended FIDIC General Conditions that identifies the changes by redlining.
- The amended General Conditions may only be used for a single Project.
- **The resulting Contract will no longer be a 'FIDIC contract' and must not be represented as one.**

Thus, those preparing Conditions of Contract must weigh up the cost and convenience of having a single user-friendly document (and a redlined version showing changes to the General Conditions), with the traditional approach of having a separate document for Particular Conditions that must be read in conjunction with the printed General Conditions to understand the Conditions of Contract.

3.6 References

- Conditions of Contract for Construction (2nd edn, 2017) Guidance Notes for the Preparation of Particular Conditions.
- Conditions of Contract for Plant and Design-Build (2nd edn, 2017) Guidance Notes for the Preparation of Particular Conditions.
- Conditions of Contract for EPC/Turnkey Projects (2nd edn, 2017) Guidance Notes for the Preparation of Particular Conditions.

Annexure

Table 3.1 Contract Data in 2017 Yellow Book, annotated with default provisions

Sub-clause	Data to be given	Default data
1.1.20	Where the Contract allows for Cost Plus Profit, percentage profit to be added to the Cost:	5%
1.1.27	Defects Notification Period (DNP):	One year
1.1.30	Employer's name and address:	
1.1.35	Engineer's name and address:	
1.1.86	Time for Completion:	
1.3(a)(ii)	Agreed methods of electronic transmission:	System(s) acceptable to the Engineer
1.3(d)	Address of Employer for communications:	
1.3(d)	Address of Engineer for communications:	
1.3(d)	Address of Contractor for communications:	
1.4	Contract shall be governed by the law of:	The law of the Country.
1.4	Ruling language:	The language of these Conditions.
1.4	Language for communications:	The ruling language of the Contract.
1.8	Number of additional paper copies of Contractor's Documents:	0
1.9	Period for notification of errors, faults or other defects in the Employer's Requirements:	42 days
1.15	Total liability of the Contractor to the Employer under or in connection with the Contract:	The Accepted Contract Amount.
2.1	After receiving the Letter of Acceptance, the Contractor shall be given right of access to all or part of the Site within:	Within such times as may be required to enable the Contractor to proceed in accordance with the Programme or, if there is no Programme at that time, the initial programme submitted under Clause 8.3 (Program).
2.4	Employer's financial arrangements:	
4.2	Performance Security (as percentages of the Accepted Contract Amount in Currencies): Percent: Currency: Percent: Currency:	Sub-clause 4.2 does not apply.

(*Continued*)

Table 3.1 (Continued)

Sub-clause	Data to be given	Default data
4.4(a)	Maximum allowable accumulated value of work subcontracted (as a percentage of the Accepted Contract Amount):	The whole of the Works.
4.4(b)	Parts of the Works for which subcontracting is not permitted:	
4.7.2	Period for notification of errors in the items of reference:	28 days.
4.19	Period of payment for temporary utilities:	Each month.
4.20	Number of additional paper copies of progress reports:	0
6.5	Normal working hours on the Site:	
8.3	Number of additional paper copies of programmes:	0
8.8	Delay Damages payable for each day of delay:	
8.8	Maximum amount of Delay Damages:	No limit.
13.4(b)(ii)	Percentage rate to be applied to Provisional Sums for overhead charges and profit:	
14.2	Total amount of Advance Payment (as a percentage of Accepted Contract Amount):	Sub-clause 14.2 does not apply.
14.2	Currency or currencies of Advance Payment:	
14.2.3	Percentage deductions for the repayment of the Advance Payment:	25%
14.3	Period of payment:	After the end of each month.
14.3(b)	Number of additional paper copies of Statements:	0
14.3(iii)	Percentage of retention:	
14.3(iii)	Limit of Retention Money (as a percentage of Accepted Contract Amount):	
14.5(b)(i)	Plant and Materials for payment when shipped:	
14.5(c)(i)	Plant and Materials for payment when delivered to the Site:	
14.6.2	Minimum amount of Interim Payment Certificate (IPC):	
14.7(a)	Period for payment of Advance Payment to the Contractor:	21 days

(*Continued*)

Table 3.1 (Continued)

Sub-clause	Data to be given	Default data
14.7(b)(i)	Period for the Employer to make interim payments to the Contractor under sub-clause 14.6 (Interim Payment):	56 days
14.7(b)(ii)	Period for the Employer to make final payment to the Contractor under sub-clause 14.13 (Final Payment):	28 days
14.7(c)	Period for the Employer to make final payment to the Contractor:	56 days
14.8	Financing charges for delayed payment (percentage points above the average bank short–term lending rate as referred to under sub-paragraph (a))	3% above benchmark specified in sub-clause 14.8.
14.11.1(b)	Number of additional paper copies of draft Final Statement:	0
14.15	Currencies for payment of Contract Price:	
14.15(a)(i)	Proportions or amounts of Local and Foreign Currencies are: Local: Foreign:	
1415(c)	Currencies and proportions for payment of Delay Damages:	
14.15(g)	Rates of exchange	Those prevailing on the Base Date.
17.2(d)	Forces of nature, the risks of which are allocated to the Contractor:	
19.1	Permitted deductible limits: Insurance required for the Works: Insurance required for Goods: Insurance required for liability for breach of professional duty: Insurance required against liability for fitness for purpose (if any is required): Insurance required for injury to persons and damage to property: Insurance required for injury to employees: Other insurances required by Laws and by local practice:	
19.2(1)(b)	Additional amount to be insured (as a percentage of the replacement value, if less or more than 15%):	

(*Continued*)

Table 3.1 (Continued)

Sub-clause	Data to be given	Default data
19.2(1)(iv)	List of Exceptional Risks which shall not be excluded from the insurance cover for the Works:	
19.2.2	Extent of insurance required for Goods:	
19.2.3(a)	Amount of insurance required for liability for breach of professional duty:	The amount agreed with the Employer.
19.2.3(b)	Insurance required against liability for fitness for purpose:	No insurance required against liability for fitness for purpose.
19.2.3	Period of insurance required for liability for breach of professional duty:	
19.2.4	Amount of insurance required for injury to persons and damage to property:	The amount agreed with the Employer.
19.2.6	Other insurances required by Laws and by local practice (give details):	
21.1	Time for appointment of DAAB:	28 days.
21.1	The DAAB shall comprise:	Three members.
21.1	List of proposed members of DAAB: - Proposed by Employer: - Proposed by Contractor:	
21.2	Appointing entity (official) for DAAB members:	

CHAPTER 4

Applying FIDIC Contracts in Angola

Miguel Lorena Brito and João Rocha de Almeida

CONTENTS

 DOI: 10.4324/9781003206910-4

4.1 Outline of Angola's legal environment

4.1.1 The constitutional structure of Angola

The *Constitution of the Republic of Angola* (***CRA***) currently in force was enacted in September 2008 and came into force on 5 February 2010 upon being published in the official gazette (*Diário da República*). The *CRA* is structured around certain basic principles such as the rule of law and separation of state powers between the legislative, executive and judicial independent branches.

The Angolan parliament (*Assembleia Nacional*) is the primary legislative body, with full legislative powers within the limits of the *Constitution*. The Parliament is also responsible for the approval of the yearly state budget (*Orçamento de Estado*) and holds powers to conduct inquiries.

The President of the Republic acts as the head of the executive power but also holds legislative power over a broad range of issues. The President is also the commander-in-chief of the Angolan armed forces. The election of the President takes place in the context of the election of the members of the parliament. Political parties running for parliament submit a list of candidates. The head of the list of the most voted party is appointed President of the Republic.

Traditionally, Angolan Presidents hold broad executive and legislative powers. In addition to enacting laws (using their own legislative powers and also in the context of authorisations granted by the Parliament), it is quite common for Angolan Presidents to regulate certain relevant issues by way of *Presidential Decrees*, which are not subject to validation by the *Assembleia Nacional*.

The judicial branch comprises several different types of courts, including:

- A Constitutional Court to rule on specific matters related to constitutional conformity, among others, of draft laws, laws and their interpretation and application by the other Courts.
- Common Courts with jurisdiction over all sorts of disputes (e.g., civil, criminal, employment).
- Military courts with jurisdiction over disputes involving the armed forces.
- A Court of Auditors with a wide range of powers, mostly pertaining to assessing the legality and conformity of public expenditure.

The *Angolan Constitution* foresees that Administrative Courts can be created to rule on administrative, tax and customs disputes. In broad terms, the administrative jurisdiction would rule on disputes pertaining to relations between individuals or companies and public bodies. However, to this date, the administrative jurisdiction has not been created and, as a result, this sort of public law falls within the jurisdiction of the *Administrative, Tax and Customs* Chambers of the Common Courts.

In addition to the aforementioned State courts, contracting parties may also refer their disputes to arbitration, pursuant to the *Law on Voluntary Arbitration* (*Law nr. 16/03, of 25 July*).

The Angolan territory is divided at a regional level (*Províncias*), each governed by a Regional Governor (*Governador Provincial*) appointed by the President of the Republic. Regions are further divided into Municipalities. The regional and municipal public bodies are an important part of the Angolan state machine. The regional and municipal bodies do not hold legislative powers but are entitled to approve certain administrative regulations that might be relevant, among many other areas, for construction licensing. The municipalities are, in general, the relevant authority for the approval of private building projects and for issuing construction permits.

4.1.2 The legal system in Angola

The Angolan legal system is based on civil law, heavily influenced by the Portuguese civil law. When Angola became independent in 1974, Angolan authorities did not revoke the most relevant pieces of legislation in force, as was the case of the *Civil Code* (1966), or the *Civil Procedural Code* (1966), which are still in force (with minor amendments). Many new laws and regulations have been enacted since 1974 to regulate all sorts of matters, in particular regarding foreign investment, oil and gas and mining activities. Many statutes on more general matters (such as administrative procedure or public procurement) are also influenced by Portuguese law.

Portuguese is the official language of Angola, and therefore all laws are published in the Portuguese language.

As mentioned, the *Civil Code* is one of the most relevant legal statutes in force in Angola, outlining all the major principles and rules applicable to, among others, ownership, contracts and all types of relations between private parties. Private contractual law is subject to the basic principle of private autonomy according to which contracting parties may agree on the terms and conditions that rule their relations, unless otherwise foreseen in mandatory law. As a result of this principle, the *Civil Code* sets two different types of rules: (1) default rules that shall apply whenever the parties have not ruled otherwise and (2) mandatory provisions which shall apply irrespective of the parties' wishes. One section of the *Civil Code* is dedicated to certain typical contracts (including, among others, construction contracts). This section contains mostly default rules which parties may set aside, but also a number of mandatory rules, as addressed later.

The Angolan legal system comprises an entirely different set of public law rules applicable to relations between individuals and public entities, notably state entities such as central government bodies, regional governments and local municipalities. This includes a *Public Contracts Law* (***PCL***)[1] which provides, firstly, a very detailed public procurement legal regime, with a complex set of rules to determine the perimeter of the awarding entities and contracts that are subject to the *Code* and the governing rules of several pre-contractual awarding procedures. The *PCL* also provides the legal framework applicable to public contracts in general entered into between public and private entities, as well as to typical public contracts (including public works construction contracts). Unlike the default regime set forth in the *Civil Code*, the legal provisions of the *PCL* are mostly mandatory and contracting parties are not free to set them aside.

Angola's legal system includes several legal statutes relevant to foreign entities that wish to perform their activities in the country, which rule on private investment and local content, among others. In this regard, the provisions of the *Angolan Private Investment*

1 Approved by *Law 41/20, of 23 December.*

Law[2] (***APIL***) in force are important for foreign investors who wish to benefit from the rights foreseen in this legal statute, including, in particular, the right to repatriate funds (such as profits and dividends originated by operations in Angola). There is also a *Local Content Law*[3] related to the provision of services and supply of goods and equipment to the oil industry that encourages (and, in certain circumstances, requires) oil companies operating in Angola to hire local entities. This is discussed further in section 4.2.8.

Disputes pertaining to the relations between private and public entities are subject to the jurisdiction of a special Chamber of the Common Courts, as mentioned earlier. This is relevant to disputes pertaining to public construction agreements among others.

A relevant feature of the Angolan legal system is that the *Constitution* acknowledges the authority of traditional entities rooted in tribal social structures. This is notably the case of the *Sobas*, respected elder citizens of a given village, who, according to local tradition, exercise relevant powers such as the power to settle certain disputes between members of their villages.

4.1.3 The court system in Angola

As mentioned earlier, the jurisdiction of the Common Courts covers most disputes between private entities and between private entities and public bodies. As such, in theory, disputes pertaining to the validity, performance or interpretation of construction contracts – i.e., the disputes that typically arise in the context of construction contracts – should fall within the jurisdiction of the Common Courts, irrespective of whether the contract in question is a public construction contract or a private construction contract.

The jurisdiction of the Common Courts comprises (1) local courts (*Tribunais de Comarca*), (2) courts of appeal (*Tribunais da Relação*) and (3) a Supreme Court. In a certain very limited number of cases, appeals may also be submitted to the Constitutional Court.

Arbitration is also an option for dispute resolution in construction contracts and is a usual feature of contracts involving foreign companies, investors or financing entities. Arbitration has been increasingly adopted in construction agreements involving local parties. This is a result of the many challenges of litigating before the State Courts, of which we would highlight long delays in issuing decisions and the difficulty of dealing with highly complex technical issues that may arise in the context of disputes pertaining to more sophisticated construction contracts.

The *Law on Voluntary Arbitration*[4] (***LAV***) sets the legal framework applicable to arbitration in Angola. The first main principle regarding arbitration is that it is voluntary, meaning that, as a general principle, parties may not be forced to submit a dispute to arbitration. It is therefore common for parties to add arbitration clauses to construction agreements whenever it is their intention to submit future disputes in the context of such agreements to arbitration. However, it should be noted that in the context of public construction agreements, the *PCL* allows for awarding entities to specify in the tender documents that any

2 *Law 10/18, of 26 June.*
3 Approved by *Presidential Decree 271/20, of 20 October.*
4 *Law 16/03, of 25 July.*

disputes arising from a specific agreement shall be referred to arbitration and, by doing so, effectively impose arbitration on the Contractor.

Pursuant to the *LAV*, parties may refer their disputes to arbitral tribunals (1) within arbitration centres or (2) specifically created to adjudicate a specific dispute (*ad hoc*). For public construction contracts, the default option is to refer disputes to existing arbitration centres. Exceptionally, a dispute may be referred to an *ad hoc* tribunal only when (1) the dispute pertains to very complex technical or legal issues, (2) the economic value of the dispute is very high, and (3) submitting the dispute to an existing arbitration centre would either cause delays in the decision or increase the costs to be borne by the public entity.

The fact that a dispute has been referred to arbitration does not prevent parties from obtaining interim injunctions (among others, when a claimant seeks temporary relief or intends to have a decision suspended until a ruling is issued by the arbitral tribunal). In such cases, parties are free to choose whether they wish to submit the request to the arbitral tribunal or to State Courts.

As a general rule, the *LAV* sets forth that the tribunal shall consist of one single arbitrator (fairly uncommon) or an odd number of arbitrators, usually three. It is usual for the claimant to appoint one arbitrator in the notice for arbitration and the defendant to appoint a second one within 30 days. The claimant may request State Courts to appoint the second arbitrator whenever the defendant fails to do so within the 30-day deadline. Both appointees shall then agree on a third arbitrator.

Unless the parties have already agreed on the rules that shall govern the proceedings, the arbitral tribunal is in general free to set the procedural rules and how to conduct the proceedings, provided that a number of basic mandatory principles are complied with throughout the proceedings (e.g., parties shall be treated equally and shall be heard prior to decisions being adopted). The *PCL* sets out that arbitration procedures pertaining to public construction agreements shall be subject to a simplified procedure that shall comply with the following basic rules: (1) the claimant may submit a claim and the defendant may submit its defence, (2) each party may only offer two witnesses to depose on each relevant fact and (3) discussion between the parties shall be in writing.

The arbitral tribunal in principle has the authority to resolve the dispute and issue all the decisions required for this purpose. However, for certain specific situations, the parties may ask State Courts to rule on specific issues such as the impeachment of arbitrators and obtaining evidence in possession of the counterparty/third parties, among others.

Parties are allowed to waive their right to appeal from the arbitral decision but are prevented from waiving the right to submit to State Courts a claim for the annulment of the arbitral decision (which may only be based on very specific grounds, e.g., violations of the basic principles of arbitration, or the decision exceeding the scope of arbitration or the claim).

4.2 The construction industry in Angola

4.2.1 Overview

Construction is a regulated activity in Angola, where, in order to perform construction works, contractors are required to hold either: (1) a title of registration (*título de registo*) enabling them to perform works up to Kwanza (**AOA**) 35,000,000 (US$67,655) or (2) a contractor's permit (*alvará*) to perform any works exceeding this threshold. Titles of registration and contractor's permits of classes 1 (works up to AOA 45,000,000/US$87,030) and 2 (works up to AOA 75,000,000/US$145,050) are issued by local (municipal) authorities. Contractor's permits of classes 3 (works up to AOA 100,000,000/US$193,400) and 4 (works up to AOA 250,000,000/US$483,500) are issued by Provincial Governments (regional entities). All remaining permits (from class 5, corresponding to works up to AOA 550,000,000/US$1,063,700 and above) are issued by the Institute for the Regulation of Construction and Public Works (*Instituto Regulador da Construção Civil e Obras Públicas* [**IRCCOP**]). According to the information made available by IRCCOP,[5] as of January 2023, 5,318 companies held titles of registration or contractor's permits, although 54.4% of those titles and permits have expired. While the vast majority of the titles and permits were granted to local companies (4,616), 268 Portuguese companies have successfully obtained permits, as well as 220 Chinese contractors.

While a slight majority (56%) of the contractors hold permits up to class 5 (allowing them to perform works up to AOA 550,000,000/US$1,063,700), there are 339 listed contractors (both national and international) with the top-class permit (class 10) qualified to perform works above AOA 5,000,000,000 (US$9,670,000).

4.2.2 Licensing requirements for contractors

To operate in Angola, contractors are required to register and hold a title of registration or a contractor's permit issued by the relevant authority (either local authorities, provincial governments or the IRCCOP, depending on the type of registration/permit and the relevant class) that is adequate to the nature, type and value of works they intend to perform. Breach of such legal obligation constitutes an administrative offence and may lead to the application of fines by the relevant authorities.

Registration and permit requirements for contractors performing public or private construction works in Angola are currently ruled by the *Regulation on the Activities of Construction and Public Works, Projects and Works Supervision* (*Regulamento sobre o Exercício das Actividades de Construção Civil e Obras Públicas, Projectos de Obras e de Fiscalização de Obras*) approved by *Presidential Decree no. 146/20, of 27 May*. Such requirements depend on several factors, the first of which is the public/private nature of the works to be performed under the permit. The legal requirements to obtain a permit to perform public works include technical capacity (having the staff with the required qualifications in view of the category and value of works the applicant wishes to perform), economic and financial capacity (meeting certain sales turnover and equity criteria) and holding adequate insurance.

Contractors' permits are classified according to predetermined classes which define the maximum value of works or services that the contractor can perform under such permit. There are currently ten classes that vary from class 1 corresponding to works up to AOA 45,000,000 (US$86,985) to class 10, pertaining to works valued above AOA 5,000,000,000 (US$9,665,000). The technical and financial requirements mentioned above (when applicable) vary in view of the classes of the permit.

5 Available at https://ircop.gov.ao/instituicao/estatistica/.

Pursuant to the *PCL*, a contractor must hold a permit covering the types of works detailed in the tender specifications and the class corresponding to the full amount of the bid in order to participate in a tender for public works contracts.

It should be noted that Angolan law does not specify whether the foregoing requirements apply (1) only to the entities that actually perform the works, or (2) to all entities that enter into the construction agreements as contractors irrespective of the fact that they perform the works directly or assign it to subcontractors. This topic can be relevant in case foreign operators wish to enter into construction agreements in Angola as main contractors and assign the works to local subcontractors holding the required permits (e.g., local affiliates of a foreign contractor). In our view, the concept of '*construction subcontracting*' provided by Angolan law refers to the relationship established between a construction company holding a permit (the head Contractor) and a third party holding some permit (subcontractor), therefore assuming that both parties in a construction subcontract – including the head Contractor – are licensed construction companies. Therefore, the general rule is that any entity that enters into a construction contract in the capacity of a contractor should hold a valid contractor's permit issued by the relevant authority, even if such entity plans to assign the construction services to a licensed subcontractor.

4.2.3 Foreign investment

The construction sector in Angola is open to foreign players wishing to tender for and to execute construction contracts in the country, subject to mandatory requirements applicable to any foreign companies wanting to operate in Angola.

Notwithstanding the fact that the incorporation of an Angolan company by a foreign investor is not subject to prior approval by any authority, pursuant to the *APIL*, both (1) incorporation of a company and (2) setting up a branch are deemed as private investment operations, meaning that, in order to benefit from the rights set forth in the *APIL*, the foreign investor is required to submit a Private Investment Project (**PIP**) to the Foreign Investment Regulator (**AIPEX**).

The rights set forth in the *APIL* for foreign investors include the following:

- Right to repatriate funds (including profits and dividends).
- Right to tax incentives.
- Right to obtain at least two privileged visas.

Upon submitting a PIP to AIPEX, the foreign investor undertakes a minimum investment commitment, covering the amount deemed reasonable by AIPEX for the investor to set up its business unit, including all initial costs necessary for the local company/branch to start its operations.

The APIL foresees three different investment regimes for investors to opt between in view of the specific features of the investment envisaged: (1) prior declaration, (2) special regime and (3) contractual regime. This approval for foreign investors has consistently evolved towards a simpler procedure in the last decade but remains still a very relevant aspect to be considered by investors seeking to invest in Angola.

4.2.4 Professional qualifications

Pursuant to *Presidential Decree no. 146/20, of 27 May*, only qualified professionals may engage in activities such as project design and project supervision. Such professionals (like architects or engineers) who wish to act as project designers, site managers or supervision managers in Angola must comply with several legal requirements, including mandatory registration with the corresponding professional association, and hold adequate qualifications to provide architecture and engineering services.

4.2.5 Private construction contracts

Both the private and public sectors are important for the construction activity in Angola. However, these two sectors have different legal environments and frameworks with specific rulings and requirements that need to be taken into consideration when entering into a private or a public construction agreement.

Private construction contracts are subject to civil law (mainly provided by the *Civil Code*) and parties are, in general, free to set the terms and conditions that rule their relations, unless otherwise foreseen in mandatory law (refer to section 4.1.2).

The *Civil Code* contains a specific section on construction contracts, which provides a relatively simple framework for these contracts (in regard to acceptance of the works, defects' liability and warranty among others). In addition, construction contracts are also subject to general contract law also provided for in the *Civil Code*, as well as to other specific laws and regulations on matters such as, for example, licensing, health and safety, waste management, immigration and others.

The *PCL* currently in force contains a detailed set of provisions governing all relevant aspects of public works contracts. This includes specific rules and time bars on additional works, variations, claims, payment and other topics.

The fact that the PCL sets such a detailed framework applicable to public works contracts is likely the reason why FIDIC model contracts are not usually used in public works contracts. By contrast, it is much easier to apply standard forms (such as FIDIC) in the context of private construction contracts, where parties are mostly free to agree on the terms and conditions applicable, as detailed here.

4.2.6 Public sector procurement and public contracts

4.2.6.1 Public procurement

As a general rule, construction contracts entered into by public entities must be awarded under the rules of the *PCL*. There are several rules to determine whether a specific contract is or is not subject to the procurement provisions of the *PCL*, mostly related to the nature of the awarding entity (e.g., central or local government and other public bodies) and the value of the contract. However, in certain cases, other criteria may also apply (e.g., certain classified contracts may not be subject to such rules).

Awarding entities include, among others, central government, local government bodies (*Governos Provinciais*), municipalities and public institutes and public sector companies, as well as other entities engaged in public affairs and benefiting from Angolan state budget funds.

Public procurement is not restricted to a specific governmental body in charge of all public purchases. On the contrary, it is quite usual for each Contracting Authority to set up and conduct its own public procurement procedures. The National Service for Public Procurement (*Serviço Nacional de Contratação Pública* [**SNCP**]) is the governmental body created for the purpose of supervising public procurement and assisting the authorities in implementing public procurement procedures.

The SNCP was originally[6] established as the *Office for Public Procurement* (*Gabinete de Contratação Pública*). Operating under the name SNCP since 2015,[7] this service is responsible for supporting the central government bodies in establishing public procurement procedures and policies. In addition to supervising and auditing public procurement procedures launched by public awarding entities, the SNCP also publishes templates for relevant documents to be used by awarding entities, such as tender rules, tender specifications and model agreements, among others.

The *PCL* provides different awarding procedures, including open, restricted or negotiated procedures. The most frequent types of awarding procedures are the public tender (open to all operators and in which only the proposals, and not the bidders, are evaluated), the tender subject to invitation (open to operators invited to take part in the tender), the pre-qualification limited tender (open to all operators but in which only bidders that qualify in a first phase are able to submit their proposals) and the simplified award (restricted to operators invited by the awarding entity).

The *PCL* also sets the criteria to determine which sort of procedure may be promoted by the awarding entities to award a certain contract depending on its maximum expected price, which varies according to the nature of the contract (e.g., public works, provision of services or supply contract). The law also provides several material criteria (other than the price of the contract, such as, for example, extreme urgency) to determine which sort of procedure may be used for the award of certain contracts.

Under the *PCL*, open procedures such as the public tender and pre-qualification tender shall be advertised in the Official Gazette (*Diário da República*), as well as in a major local newspaper and in the Public Procurement Portal.[8] The Public Procurement Portal, operated by the SNCP, is also used for the registration of tenderers wishing to engage in tenders (including limited tenders), simplified awards and others. In the case of emergency awards, the *PCL* sets out that a report on the procurement procedure is to be published in the Public Procurement Portal within 15 days of the awarding decision. The Public Procurement Portal serves the purpose of advertising sensitive issues such as amendments to the scope of ongoing public contracts and listing private contractors that have a history of contract breaches, among others.

4.2.6.2 Audit Court

Public construction contracts (among other public contracts) awarded by the President or by any entities using powers delegated by the President with a price higher than AOA 11,000,000,000[9] (US$21,274,000) only become effective upon being granted a prior clearance by the Audit Court. When awarded by central governmental bodies, regional governments, local municipalities or public institutes or others, prior clearance is only required for contracts with a price above AOA 700,000,000 (US$1,353,800).

6 Pursuant to now revoked *Presidential Decree 298/10, of 3 December.*

7 By way of *Presidential Decree 162/15, of 19 August.*

8 https://compraspublicas.minfin.gov.ao/.

9 This threshold is updated yearly by way of the *State Budget Law.*

The prior clearance of the Audit Court conditions the effectiveness of the contracts which are subject to this procedure, and therefore parties are prevented from executing the agreement until the clearance is granted.

In this procedure, the Audit Court assesses not only whether the public expenditure in question is covered by proper budget provision, but also whether the contract was adequately awarded under the applicable procurement rules. When clearance is refused, the contract in question becomes ineffective. The financial managers of the awarding entity and the Contractor shall be held liable for refunding all amounts paid under any agreement not cleared by the Audit Court, in addition to also facing criminal and disciplinary sanctions.

The clearance is tacitly granted if, within 30 days of the request having been submitted to the Audit Court, no decision has been issued and no additional information has been requested from the awarding entity or the Contractor.

4.2.6.3 Terms and conditions of public construction contracts

As mentioned in section 4.1.2, the *PCL* specifies not only public procurement (detailing the rules that govern several pre-contractual awarding procedures) but also the legal framework applicable to public contracts in general, as well as to typical public contracts such as construction agreements pertaining to public works.

This framework addresses the main contractual matters pertaining to the execution of a public construction contract, such as payment conditions, advanced payments, performance bond, suspension and supervision of works, modification of contract and variations, assignment of contract and subcontracting, acceptance and delivery of the works, defects liability period, breach of contract, penalties and termination.

Unlike the default regime set forth in the *Civil Code*, the legal provisions of the *PCL* that apply to public construction contracts are mostly mandatory and cannot be set aside by the parties. Therefore, when bidding in a public awarding procedure and entering into a public construction contract, contractors should be aware that the main contractual provisions to which the contract shall be subject are already provided by law (the *PCL*) and cannot be amended by the parties.

In addition to the *PCL* rules, it is also necessary to consider the contractual specifications approved by the awarding entity as part of the tender regulations (together with the technical specifications). These specifications usually detail and implement the rules of the *PCL* (in particular, those open rules of the *PCL* that allow the tender provisions to detail or provide differently) and set the terms and conditions of the contract to be awarded. Bidders are usually prevented from submitting alternative contractual provisions with their proposals (e.g., shorter defects liability period, different termination events or limitation of liability provisions) at the risk of having their proposals excluded from the tender procedure. Even though public awarding procedures may include a negotiation phase after the bid is presented and before the contract is executed by the parties, the general rule is that only the terms offered in the bid – and not the terms and conditions set in advance by the awarding entity – are subject to negotiation.

As a result of this, in public construction contracts, there is less space for the application of FIDIC conditions of contract since the main terms and conditions are previously defined in the *PCL* and in the contractual specifications of each tender.

As outlined in the following, some of the mandatory provisions of the *PCL* that apply to public construction contracts may conflict with FIDIC's General Conditions of Contract.

4.2.7 Insurance requirements

Under the *General Labour Law,*[10] employer's liability insurance is mandatory for contractors to perform all sorts of construction works. However, such a mandatory requirement does not apply whenever the contractor qualifies as a small company (fewer than ten workers and annual turnover of less than the equivalent in AOA of US$250,000) or a micro company (fewer than 100 workers and annual turnover of less than the equivalent of US$3,000,000 in AOA). Such insurance must cover the risks of professional illness and personal injury of construction workers. Failure to comply with this obligation is deemed an administrative offence, punishable by a fine.[11]

While not mandatory, it has become common practice for Employers to demand that Contractors enter into contractors' all risk insurance policies to cover risks arising from performance of the Works. Provisions in such regard are common in both private and public construction contracts. In certain instances, notably in less sophisticated contracts, it is common for Employers to accept insurance policies with a limited scope, such as insurance against damages caused to third parties (e.g., owners of neighbour buildings, bystanders) as a consequence of performance of the Works by the Contractor or its personnel.

4.2.8 Local content requirements in the oil and gas sector

Angolan Local Content Law (***LCL***) approved by *Presidential Decree no. 271/20 of 20 October* defines a number of local content requirements applicable to companies in the oil and gas sector, including both oil companies (acting as business partners of the National Concessionaire Angolan Agency for Petroleum, Gas and Biofuels [**ANPG**]), but also any companies operating as service providers for the oil sector.

Pursuant to the *LCL*, ANPG organised the goods and services typically purchased by oil companies for their operations into three different categories/regimes, subject to different rules.[12]

Regime	**Comment**
Exclusivity	Activities which may only be carried out by companies 100% held by Angolan nationals
Preferential	Activities that must preferentially be performed or supplied by Angolan Companies (irrespectively of the nationality of their shareholders). Notwithstanding, Angolan companies 100% held by Angolan nationals have preference in case of equal footing in terms of quality, technical capacity, price and delivery time; foreign companies may also be hired in certain circumstances.
Competition	All remaining activities (i.e., any activities that do not fall under the Exclusivity or the Preference regimes) may be performed by either Angolan or foreign entities. However, in equal circumstances, Angolan companies have preference.

10 *Law 7/15, of 15 June.*

11 Pursuant to *Presidential Decree 154/16, of 5 August.*

12 The relevant lists are available at ANPG's website: https://anpg.co.ao/conteudo-local-lista-de-bens-e-servicos/.

Certain engineering services (including design and project management), activities related to seismic data gathering, drilling and construction services fall within the preferential regime, and therefore must preferentially be performed or supplied by Angolan Companies.

The LCL also sets regulatory requirements applicable to service providers (including contractors) who intend to render services to oil and gas sector companies. Among other requirements, such contractors must be registered online and certified by ANPG, prior to entering into a contract with oil sector companies. Upon incorporation, the branch/subsidiary should submit its application on ANPG's official website along with a number of mandatory documents and information. Violation of the rules in the *LCL* is deemed a transgression and may lead to the application of fines.

4.2.9 Common forms of contract

The use of standard forms of contract is not uncommon in Angola, namely in the oil and gas sector. However, such standard forms are rare in the context of public sector construction contracts, as such contracts are subject to the specific and detailed framework under the *PCL* (as discussed in section 4.2.6.3). As such, standard forms are mostly used in private sector contracts, usually as a requirement from foreign investors or financing entities. International employers (such as oil and gas companies and other multinational companies) resort to model contracts on a more regular basis, FIDIC being the most used for construction in Angola.

The law does not provide for a standard form for public works contracts in Angola. The award procedure and performance of public contracts are subject to the extensive and detailed provisions set in the *PCC*. Such rules apply to all agreements entered into by public sector entities and are mostly mandatory. Among other issues, the *PCL* covers most matters that are usually addressed by standard contract forms, such as risk allocation, additional works, penalties for delays, bonds, liability for defects and defects liability period, among others.

4.2.10 Dispute resolution

Disputes pertaining to the interpretation or performance of construction agreements may be referred to State Courts. However, in recent years arbitration became an option for dispute resolution of private construction contracts, in particular for high-value contracts.

Private operators (including both Employers and Contractors) usually rely on *ad hoc* tribunals. However, as detailed in section 4.1.3, the Angolan *PCL* favours the use of arbitration centres. Several arbitration centres have recently been created in Angola. We would highlight the *Centro de Resolução Extrajudicial de Litígios* (**CREL**), established by *Executive Decree nr. 230/14, of 27 June*, as being the most widely accepted when the seat of arbitration is Angola. The CREL Arbitration Rules were enacted in 2017, by way of *Executive Decree 290/17, of 11 May.*

Angolan law also allows other alternative dispute resolution mechanisms such as meditation or conciliation, although the use of these alternative mechanisms is not widespread.

There are no mandatory adjudication processes for disputes related to construction agreements currently in effect in Angola.

In private construction agreements, parties are free to set whichever adjudication processes they see fit. Adjudication procedures are often used when parties agree on standard contract forms such as FIDIC or NEC4 or in the AIEN[13] model contracts, often used in the oil and gas sector.

More recently, and under the influence of such international contract forms, in particular the FIDIC Conditions of Contract, some construction contracts have provided for Dispute Boards, with the purpose of having disputes between the parties swiftly resolved during the execution of the contract and avoiding litigation in more costly and lengthy arbitration or judicial procedures. Although Dispute Boards still have no significant tradition in Angola, it should be expected that they will become a more frequent mechanism in the future.

It is not unusual for high-priced construction contracts entered into with foreign investors to refer disputes to international arbitration. In such cases, it is important to note that pursuant to Angolan Law, decisions by foreign State Courts/arbitral tribunals shall only be enforceable if properly revised and confirmed by the Angolan Supreme Court.

Because of Angola's accession to the *New York Convention on the Recognition and Enforcement of Foreign Arbitral Awards* (finalised through the deposit of the Angolan instrument of accession on 6 March 2017), arbitral awards issued outside of the Angolan territory (provided that they are in the territory of a contracting state) may be enforced once the requirements foreseen in Article IV of the *New York Convention* are met and provided that none of the causes for rejection in Article V applies.

The procedure for revision and confirmation by the Angolan Supreme Court is detailed in the *Angolan Civil Procedure Code.*

As noted earlier, in view of Angola's accession to the *New York Convention*, a request for confirmation and enforcement of an award by a foreign arbitral tribunal may only be rejected in the situations set forth in Article V of the *Convention*, i.e., in short, if the party against whom the confirmation and enforcement are sought provides evidence of the following circumstances:

(a) The arbitration agreement is not valid.
(b) The Defendant was not given proper notice of the appointment of the arbitrator, the arbitration proceedings, or the possibility of presenting its defence.
(c) The award is beyond the scope of the agreement that sets the terms of the submission to arbitration.
(d) The composition of the tribunal was not in accordance with the agreement by the parties or the law of the country in which the arbitration took place.
(e) The award is not yet binding for the parties according to the law of the state where the arbitration took place.

Additionally, pursuant to paragraph 2 of Article V, the confirmation and enforcement may be rejected in view of the following causes:

(a) The subject matter of the difference is not capable of settlement by arbitration under the laws of Angola.

13 Association of International Energy Negotiators, formerly the Association of International Petroleum Negotiators (AIPN).

(b) The recognition or enforcement of the award would be contrary to the public policy of Angola.

An assessment of the possibility of a rejection based on the aforegiven grounds may only be made in view of the actual content of the award.

Accession by Angola to the *New York Convention* is widely regarded as a very relevant milestone in Angola's relationship with foreign investors.

4.2.11 Current challenges

The construction sector plays a significant role in the Angolan economy. Nevertheless, in recent years the sector has faced relevant challenges. According to the information made available by the National Institute for Statistics (*Instituto Nacional de Estatística*[14]) (**INE**), in 2021 the construction sector accounted for 6.2% of the Angolan GDP. In the first nine months of 2022, construction's share in the GDP varied from 6.2% in Q1 to 3.3% in Q2 and lastly 6.6% in Q3. However, this seems to be a decrease in relation to the previous years. In fact, in 2019 and 2020, construction accounted for 10.7% and 8.2% of GDP respectively. It should be noted that despite certain efforts by the Angolan Government to diversify the economy, the Angolan economy remains largely dependent on natural resources, notably on the oil and gas sector.

Even though in the last few years public spending on infrastructure was not at the level of previous years, public infrastructure still accounts for a significant part of the Angolan construction market, as does the oil and gas sector.

As in the rest of the world, Angola has been facing very significant increases in the price of raw materials since 2020. Factors such as the COVID pandemic and the subsequent worldwide supply chain disruption contributed decisively to the price escalation. According to the information made available by the National Institute for Statistics, by November 2022 the price of aluminium had increased by 13.4% in comparison with November 2021. Likewise, in the same period, the price of concrete increased by 15.9%. By November 2022, the price of glass products was up by 16%. This caused – and is likely to continue to cause – a significant increase in construction prices which may produce additional pressure on ongoing construction contracts.

4.3 The impact of COVID-19 in Angola

4.3.1 The impact of COVID-19 on the execution of construction projects in Angola

On 11 March 2020, the World Health Organization (**WHO**) declared the disease COVID-19 an international pandemic. Subsequently, several exceptional measures were approved in Angola with the aim of preventing the general spread of the virus, measures that affected and imposed restrictions on various economic and commercial activities.

As a result of the pandemic, Angola declared a nationwide state of emergency by way of *Presidential Decree nr. 81/20, of 25 March*, which immediately authorised the public authorities to impose a set of measures to prevent and combat the pandemic, including restrictions on the free movement of people. In May 2020, a Public Calamity Situation

14 Available at www.ine.gov.ao/inicio/estatisticas (accessed 3 February 2023).

was declared by means of *Presidential Decree nr. 142/20, of 25 May,* which lasted for almost two years, up until *Presidential Decree nr. 112/22, of 16 May* ended the sSituation.

Several laws and regulations were enacted during the Public Calamity Situation, with the purpose of establishing measures to combat the spread of the virus. Among several others, such measures included mandatory confinement of certain persons, the obligation to adopt telework when possible, closure of several facilities and establishments, closures and restrictions on the functioning of public services and the need to comply with individual protection recommendations issued by health authorities (social distancing and use of masks, among others). Both the COVID-19 pandemic and the combat measures adopted by public authorities produced an impact on economic activity in general and on the execution of many contracts, including construction contracts.

In addition to the effects of the pandemic itself, economic activity was also affected by the many exceptional measures enacted by public authorities with the aim of preventing the general spread of the disease.

Regarding the construction sector, *Presidential Decree nr. 142/20, of 25 May* clarified that public works deemed "*strategic, priority or urgent*" would be allowed to proceed from 26 May 2020 onwards, while the remaining works (including private ongoing works) could be resumed from 8 June 2020. As such, the construction sector was only directly affected by operation restrictions for a short period of a few months. However, other more general restrictions also affected the sector, including, for instance, rules on lay-off limitations which remained in effect for the duration of the Public Calamity Situation. Additionally, the pandemic also caused limitations on the international movement of workers (namely high-skilled workers). Limitations on international transportation, including the disruption of construction material supply chains, caused severe shortages of construction materials which affected the ability of Angolan Contractors to timely perform ongoing works.

The various legal mechanisms available (such as the case of *force majeure* or the unforeseen and abnormal change in circumstances) require the application of concepts that, despite being known and discussed for a long time, are still of indeterminate nature and a cause for uncertainty. In this sense, Angolan Courts will have a decisive role in the final shaping of the response of the Angolan legal system to the pandemic and its impact on contracts (including in the construction sector). This is an issue to follow up on in the next few years.

From a legal and contractual perspective, those disturbing events (the pandemic and the combat measures adopted by the public authorities) may constitute – in general and in a very high-level approach – causes of exoneration of the contracting parties' liability arising from delays or breach of contract, as well as a cause of modification of the contract and, ultimately, grounds for restoring the financial balance of the contract or for the award of financial compensation to the private contracting parties.

4.3.2 The impact of COVID-19 on the operation of construction contracts in Angola

In construction contracts, the parties benefit from the general mechanisms provided by law/contract, such as *force majeure* and frustration addressed earlier. As such, in certain circumstances, parties (in particular Contractors) may hold that the pandemic constitutes a *force majeure* or a frustration event that prevented the timely completion of certain obligations. Subject to the particulars of the case, these mechanisms have been used to justify or entitle the suspension of the contract, the temporary (or even permanent) relief of the contractual tasks affected by the pandemic and, in general, exoneration from the consequences of the non-performance of the contract (such as penalties or liquidated damages for delay).

The pandemic is not, in general, a cause for the financial rebalance of public contracts. However, if certain requirements are met, the pandemic may constitute a cause for modification of the contract or for awarding a financial compensation to the Contractor based on abnormal and unforeseeable events. It should, however, be noted that the modification of public contracts and the payment of compensations for unforeseeable events is subject to strict limits and requirements.

The concept of *force majeure* is addressed in Angolan law and has been detailed by academics and courts. Although parties are free to agree on which events shall be deemed *force majeure* and its consequences (and these clauses are very common in construction contracts), the common understanding is that it refers to natural or third-party events not controlled by the parties that prevent them (or one of them) from performing their tasks. In such cases, the affected party is usually released (normally just temporarily) from the obligations affected by the *force majeure* event and by the consequences of the delay (in particular, for the purpose of the application of penalties). Towards the final stage of the Public Calamity Situation, a change in parties' approach to COVID-19 implications became clear as parties increasingly agreed on excluding minor COVID-19 implications from the concept of *force majeure* in construction contracts. Since then, the trend seems to be that limitations caused by COVID-19 shall only qualify as *force majeure* events if and to the extent that such limitations (1) have been determined by a legislative or administrative act and (2) consist of actual restrictions, such as mandatory confinements restrictions on international travel.

Angolan law also includes the concept of frustration (impossibility), applicable to situations in which, due to events not caused by the parties, their obligations become impossible to meet (temporarily or permanently, partially or totally). These concepts apply, in general, to both private and public construction contracts.

Under Angolan law, a contract becoming uneconomic is not necessarily related to *force majeure* events and does not, *per se*, constitute grounds for suspension, compensation or termination. If such loss of financial balance is a result of abnormal and unforeseeable events, the Contractor may be entitled to a rebalance of the contract (which may or not involve financial compensation) if such event (1) exceeds the risks that are usual for the type of agreement in question and (2) causes a situation where it is unreasonable to demand that the Contractor upholds its obligations as initially foreseen in the agreement.

4.4 Angolan governing law of the contract

4.4.1 Constraints on the governing law of a construction contract

Pursuant to the *Civil Code*, contracting parties may freely choose the law applicable to contracts, including construction contracts. However, certain limitations apply to this general principle. The choice of governing law must correspond to a serious interest by the parties or be in connection with a feature of the contract (e.g., the fact that one of the parties is located in the country). Another relevant limitation is that a choice of governing law will not apply to the extent that it would cause a violation of the principle of international *ordre public* of Angola.

Also, it should be noted that even when a contract is governed by a foreign law, the latter shall not apply outside the relation between the contracting parties. In this regard, it should be assumed that Angolan law shall apply, in general, to the contractual relations between a contractor and its local suppliers or subcontractors or to the contracting parties' civil liability towards third parties. Similarly, the choice of governing law does not in any way limit application of the mandatory Angolan provisions to works performed in Angola. This includes certain provisions pertaining to warranty period, health and safety and the parties' liability, among many others.

In the context of public contracts, this is a very relevant limitation, given that public construction contracts are subject to the provisions of the *PCL*. This public law regime is quite detailed and provides mandatory rules on many matters addressed by FIDIC model agreements, such as risk allocation, Variations, parties' claims, causes for termination, works measurement and acceptance, defects liability and dispute resolution, among many others. As a result, parties are left with little freedom to set contractual terms and conditions and elect foreign governing law.

4.4.2 Formal requirements for a construction contract

Pursuant to Angolan law, agreements in general become legally binding when an offer by one of the parties is accepted by the other. The general rule under the *Civil Code* is that parties are generally free to decide whether they wish to enter into agreements in writing. This rule applies to construction agreements governed by the *Civil Code*, meaning that written form is, in general, not mandatory. Nevertheless, written form is the rule in the relevant construction agreements, in particular in the agreements executed by international owners and/or international contractors.

On the contrary, written form is a mandatory requirement for public construction contracts. As a general rule, under the *PCL*, written form is required for all public contracts (including supply agreements, services agreements, construction agreements and others), with certain exceptions. In the case of public works contracts, the exception is for agreements valued below AOA 36,000,000 (US$69,624), and therefore written form is required for all construction agreements valued above such threshold entered into with public awarding entities. In certain cases (e.g., for national security reasons) the awarding entity may exempt the agreement from such requirement. Whenever (1) written form is not required or (2) the awarding entity decides on waiving the requirement for written form, the relevant provisions in the tender specifications and the awarded bid shall govern the construction contract. The *PCL* also sets forth that public construction contracts must mention: (1) full identification of the parties and their representatives, (2) the awarding decision and the decision that approved the draft agreement, (3) scope of the works, (4) price, (5) time schedule for completion and (6) details on the performance bond provided by the Contractor. Failure to include such specific items causes the contract to be deemed null and void.

Before execution of a public works contract, the Contractor must submit to the awarding entity its qualification documents (e.g., criminal records and tax and social security clearance certificates) and the performance bond.

4.5 What Special Provisions in the Particular Conditions are necessary for consistency with applicable laws in Angola?

4.5.1 FIDIC General Conditions are incompatible or inconsistent with governing law of the contract

The following issues are noted as incompatibilities between FIDIC General Conditions and the laws of Angola as the governing law of the contract.

4.5.1.1 Defects notification period

Angolan law sets mandatory warranty periods for works performed under both private and public construction agreements. During the mandatory warranty period, the Contractor is liable for performing all necessary works to remedy existing defects. Failure to remedy any defects shall entitle the Employer to hire a third party to execute such works at the cost of the original Contractor.

The mandatory warranty period for private construction agreements is of either two or five years from completion depending on the type of the works.[15] The defects notification period is of one year upon detection, within which the Employer must inform the Contractor of any defects found.

For public construction agreements, the *PCL* sets forth (1) a general principle under which the warranty period is to be set forth by the awarding entity in the tender specifications, and (2) a default three-year period applicable whenever the tender specifications do not provide otherwise. Employers in public construction agreements may issue a defects notification to the Contractor up to the final acceptance of the Works (at the end of the warranty period).

To comply with the legal provisions that set mandatory warranty periods for both private and public construction contracts, the provision in the Red Book sub-clause 11.3 should be amended.

4.5.1.2 Allocation of ground risk

As a general principle, under Angolan law, the risk of unforeseen ground conditions falls on the Employer. Nevertheless, this risk may be assigned to the Contractor in the construction agreement. As such, in the context of private construction contracts, the provisions in Red Book sub-clauses 4.10 and 4.12 are generally admissible under Angolan law.

For public construction contracts, however, the *PCL* sets specific risk allocation rules. Depending on the particulars of the case, ground risk may be addressed as (1) an abnormal and unforeseeable event, or as (2) an error or omission of the project. Whenever the ground condition was indeed unforeseeable, the Contractor may be entitled to claim a modification of the contract to set an extension of time (EOT) and a price adjustment.

Unfavourable ground conditions may also be addressed as an error or omission of the project and (if that is the case) be subject to the following main rules:

---

15 The five-year warranty applies to the construction of buildings and other long duration immovable assets.

(i) The Contractor shall bear the costs of additional works to remedy such errors/omissions whenever he was responsible for the implementation project.

(ii) Likewise, the Employer shall bear such costs whenever the Contractor was provided with a project by either the Employer or a designer engaged by the Employer.

(iii) The Contractor shall bear 50% of the costs of additional works to remedy errors/omissions whenever:

(a) The Contractor should have detected such errors/omissions in the tender phase but failed to do so; as well as

(b) The Contractor failed to detect any errors and omissions within 30 days of the date in which, as a result of the works being performed, such errors and omissions could have been detected by the Contractor.

4.5.1.3 Priority of documents

Red Book sub-clause 1.5 sets forth that in case of discrepancy between the documents forming the Contract, the priority shall be in accordance with the sequence therein. Article 108 of the *PCL* contains a similar rule with the same purpose (setting the priority between relevant contractual documents in case of discrepancy) but sets a very different order of priority, as detailed in the following.

Order	**Red Book sub-clause 1.4**	**Order**	**Article 108 of *PCL***
1	Contract Agreement	1	Clarifications and amendments to the Tender Specifications by the Contracting Authority (Employer)
2	Letter of Acceptance	2	Tender Specifications
3	Letter of Tender	3	Contractor's bid
4	Particular Conditions A – Contract Data	4	Clarification provided by the Contractor in respect to its bid
5	Particular Conditions B – Special Provisions	5	Contract Agreement
6	General Conditions		
7	Specification		
8	Drawings		
9	Schedules		
10	JV Undertaking		
11	Any other document forming the contract		

The priority rule set forth in Article 108 of the *PCL* is mandatory for public construction contracts and cannot be set aside by the parties. As such, the priority rule set forth in Red Book sub-clause 1.4 is not consistent with Angolan law in the context of public construction contracts.

4.5.1.4 Contractor's claims – time bar

Pursuant to Red Book sub-clause 20.2, parties must submit a notice of claim within 28 days from the time when such party became aware – or should have become aware

– of an event or circumstance that gave rise to a claim. A fully detailed claim may be submitted within 84 days of such event, or by whatever deadline the Engineer deems appropriate (Red Book sub-clause 20.2.4). When the Contractor is the claiming party, failure to comply with such deadline shall prevent the Contractor from obtaining relief (EOT, additional payment or compensation). However, for public construction contracts, the *PCL* sets mandatory deadlines for the Contractor to submit to the Employer claims based on compensation events, which are usually ten days (for claims arising from events recorded in official documents).

In addition, it should also be noted that the *Administrative Judicial Procedural Code*[16] sets a 45-day deadline for the Contractor to challenge in court certain decisions of the Employer (which may include the Employer's rejection of certain claims by the Contractor). Failure by the Contractor to submit the dispute to court within this timeframe (when applicable) will render the Employer's decision final and binding.

4.5.2 FIDIC General Conditions are incompatible or inconsistent with the law of the Site/Country

The following issue is an incompatibility between FIDIC General Conditions and the laws of Angola as the law of the Site.

4.5.2.1 Subcontractors

For public construction contracts, the *PCL* sets forth that the tender specifications may set a limit to the percentage of the Works that may be assigned to Subcontractors. Such limitation, when applicable, shall therefore be replicated in the Contract Data for the purposes of Red Book sub-clause 5.1 (a).

It should also be noted that Contractors may only subcontract work to entities that hold the mandatory permits for performing the works in the scope of the subcontract. See section 4.2.2.

4.5.3 FIDIC General Conditions are incompatible or inconsistent with the relevant laws on dispute determination in Angola

There are no Special Provisions required for consistency with the relevant laws on dispute resolution in Angola.

4.6 What Special Provisions in the Particular Conditions are desirable for consistency with applicable laws in Angola?

4.6.1 Labour

A working visa is required for foreign workers to be allowed to work in Angola.[17] Consent by the Ministry of Public Administration, Employment and Social Security is required for the issuance of a foreign citizen work visa or residence permit.

16 Approved by *Law 33/22, of 1 September.*

17 Refer to the *Labour Law*, the *Presidential Decree 43/17, of 6 March*, and *Law 13/19, of 23 May.*

In order to qualify to obtain such a visa, applicants must comply with a number of requirements, including presenting criminal good standing certificates and evidencing that they hold the necessary qualifications to perform the tasks within the scope of the employment contract.

Although the foreign and non-resident employment regime currently in effect states that the working visa is valid for the entire duration of the employment agreement, in practical terms, the authorities advise that the initial duration of the contracts entered into with foreign employees cannot exceed 36 months.

In view of the foregoing, we believe it to be advisable to clearly set out in construction contracts that the Contractor will be liable for ensuring full compliance with the relevant laws regarding the use of foreign workers and that the Contractor shall keep the Employer safe from any liability in such regard. The same principle applies in relation to agreements entered into between a Contractor and its Subcontractors.

4.6.2 Environment

Pursuant to *Presidential Decree nr. 190/12, of 24 August*, and *Executive Decree nr. 17/13, of 22 January*, the Contractor bears responsibility for dealing with construction waste, including debris resulting from demolition works. As a general rule, construction debris is deemed non-hazardous material. In such cases, the Contractor is under the obligation of segregating the waste in accordance with the type of materials therein. However, certain waste containing specific materials (e.g., asbestos, mercury or others) is deemed hazardous and additional requirements apply to Contractors dealing with such waste. Pursuant to *Executive Decree nr. 17/13, of 22 January*, the Employer may also be held liable for compliance with waste management rules; however, such liability may be assigned by way of contract.

Irrespective of the specific type of waste, Contractors are required to submit a waste management plan to the relevant authorities.

Failure to comply with waste management obligations is deemed an administrative offence and punishable with a fine. Pursuant to the Angolan *Penal Code*, in certain extreme cases, causing pollution may also be deemed a criminal offence.

4.6.3 Employer's sale of Contractor's Equipment, surplus material, wreckage and Temporary Works

Pursuant to the *Civil Code*, a sale is null and void whenever the seller is not the owner of the goods sold to the buyer. As such, the Employer may not sell any equipment belonging to the Contractor. However, if the Contractor fails to clear the site upon completion, the Employer is allowed to dispose of any equipment left by the Contractor and shall be entitled to compensation for any costs incurred in connection with such disposal and with the cleaning of the Site. Any surplus material left on the Site shall, in principle, belong to the Employer, who shall be free to dispose of it. While not essential, Special Provisions setting forth that any surplus material on site becomes the property of the Employer are advisable so that Red Book sub-clause 11.8 may apply.

4.7 Summary of applicable legislation for Angola governing law of the contract

4.7.1 Entry into a construction contract

Contracts generally	*Civil Code Public Contracts Law*
Construction contracts	*Civil Code Public Contracts Law*

4.7.2 Operation of a construction contract

Force majeure	*Civil Code Public Contracts Law*
Hardship	*Civil Code Public Contracts Law*
Guarantees under forms of Security (Tender Security, Demand Guarantee, Surety Bond, Advance Payment Guarantee, Retention Money Guarantee, Payment Guarantee by Employer)	*Civil Code Public Contracts Law*

4.7.3 Termination of a construction contract

Frustration	*Civil Code Public Contracts Law*
Bankruptcy, insolvency, liquidation	*Law 13/21, of 10 May*

4.7.4 Dispute resolution

Limitation periods	*Civil Code Public Contracts Law*
Liability	*Civil Code Public Contracts Law*
Arbitration	*Law nr. 16/03, of 25 July* *Executive Decree nr. 290/17, of 11 May* *Public Contracts Law* *Administrative Judicial Procedural Code*

4.8 Summary of applicable legislation if the Site/Country is in Angola

4.8.1 Operation of a construction contract

Registration and administration of professionals – Engineers, Architects	*Decree nr. 39-E/92, of 28 August* *Decree nr. 54/04, of 17 August*
Registration/licensing of Contractors and subcontractors	*Presidential Decree no. 146/20, of 27 May*
Subcontractors	*Civil Code* *Public Contracts Law*
Use of liens/assignment of debts	*Civil Code* *Public Contracts Law*
Labour	*Labour Code* *Presidential Decree nr. 43/17, of 6 March* *Law 13/19, of 23 May*
Design/moral rights	*Law 15/14, of 31 July* *Presidential Decree nr. 239/19, of 29 July*
Copyright	*Law 15/14, of 31 July* *Presidential Decree nr. 239/19, of 29 July*

Planning	*Law nr. 3/04, of 25 June* *Law nr. 9/04, of 9 November* *Decree nr. 2/06, of 23 January* *Presidential Decree nr. 201/17, of 5 September*
Work affecting adjacent property to the Site	*Civil Code*
Heritage	*Law nr. 2032, of 25 November*
Health and Safety	*Executive Decree nr. 128/04, of 23 November* *Decree nr. 31/94, of 5 August* *Legislative Act 3281, of 18 July*
Environment	*Executive Decree nr. 17/13, of 22 January* *Presidential Decree nr. 190/12, of 24 August*
Public procurement	*Public Contracts Law*
Building and construction permits, execution of construction work, standard of construction work	*Decree nr. 13/07, of 26 February* *Decree nr. 80/06, of 30 October*
Insurance	*Labour Code*
Statutory rights that coexist with contractual rights	*Civil Code* *Public Contracts Law*
Liability for defective work	*Civil Code* *Public Contracts Law*
Liability for nuisance	*Civil Code*

4.8.2 Termination of a construction contract

Bankruptcy, insolvency, liquidation	*Law 13/21, of 10 May*
Decennial liability and liability generally for the total or partial collapse of structures	*Civil Code* *Public Contracts Law*

4.8.3 Dispute resolution

Limitation periods	*Civil Code (for private contracts)* *Public Contracts Law (for public contracts)*

4.9 Summary of applicable legislation if the 'seat' of the dispute determination is Angola

Dispute resolution	*Law nr. 16/03, of 25 July* *Executive Decree nr. 290/17, of 11 May*
Limitation periods	*Civil Code* *Public Contracts Law* *Administrative Courts Procedural Code*
Arbitration	*Law nr. 16/03, of 25 July* *Executive Decree nr. 290/17, of 11 May*

4.10 Additional references for Angola

4.10.1 Internet

4.10.1.1 Legislation
www.legis-palop.org

4.10.1.2 Court decisions

https://jurisprudencia.tribunalconstitucional.ao/
https://tribunalsupremo.ao/Categoia/jurisprudencia/acordaos/

4.10.1.3 Other

ANPG – https://anpg.co.ao/
INE – www.ine.gov.ao/inicio/estatisticas
IRCOP – https://ircop.gov.ao/
SNPC – https://compraspublicas.minfin.gov.ao/ComprasPublicas/

CHAPTER 5

Applying FIDIC Contracts in Egypt

Dr Mohamed S Abdel Wahab and Dr Waleed El Nemr

CONTENTS

DOI: 10.4324/9781003206910-5

5.1 Outline of Egypt's legal environment

5.1.1 The constitutional structure of Egypt

After two revolutions and two repealed constitutions (*the 1971 and 2012 Constitutions*) and a number of constitutional declarations, Egypt adopted the new *2014 Constitution* and amended this in two public referenda in 2014 and 2019 respectively.[1]

The *Egyptian Constitution* is Egypt's supreme legal instrument, which prevails over all laws and binds all public and private entities.[2] Most importantly, the Egyptian Supreme Constitutional Court has the power to review the constitutionality of the legislative instruments issued by the parliament.[3] Constitutional rules and principles are equally important in both private and public sector dealings. In fact, it is not uncommon to see Egyptian high courts relying on constitutional principles directly to uphold or overrule decisions of lower courts.[4] In addition, the administration, in concluding some administrative contracts, is bound by some constitutional constraints.[5]

5.1.2 The legal system in Egypt

The Egyptian legal system is a civil law system and is mainly built on the combination of Islamic (*Shariah*) law and the *Napoleonic Code*. In contracts, generally, the most important legislation is the *Egyptian Civil Code of 1948* (the ***ECC***).

In addition to the rules normally applicable to contracts and other civil law matters, the Egyptian legal system also recognises a specific set of laws applicable to transactions/actions involving the State (or any of its institutions, subsidiaries or state-owned enterprises) acting as a sovereign power (administrative law matters).[6]

The *ECC* also provides that 'provisions of laws govern all matters to which these provisions apply in letter or spirit'.[7] Dr Al Sanhoury explains that 'it has to be noted that the meaning intended by the provision is not only exclusive to its wording but may also extend by way of connotation/implication [*Dalalah*] to another meaning'.[8] For instance, the principle that no party may benefit from its own wrongdoing and the principle of estoppel are not expressed in the *ECC*; however, this does not negate their inclusion as overarching general principles of law in Egypt.[9]

1 MS Abdel Wahab, 'UPDATE: An Overview of the Egyptian Legal System and Legal Research' (2019) www.nyulawglobal.org/globalex/Egypt1.html (accessed on 22 June 2022).

2 RA Selim, *Egyptian Constitutional Encyclopedia* (1st ed, 2011), 1.

3 Constitutional Court, Case No. 86 for 22 JY, hearing session dated 14 May 2022; Article 25 of the *Supreme Constitutional Court's Law No. 48 of the Year 1979*.

4 Cassation, Challenge No. 3036 for 85 JY, hearing session dated 1 December 2020; also see Cassation Challenge No. 86 for 702 JY, hearing session dated 7 March 2017.

5 Article 127 of the *Egyptian Constitution for 2014*.

6 Abdel Wahab, 'UPDATE: An Overview of the Egyptian Legal System and Legal Research', above, n1.

7 Article 1(1) *ECC*.

8 A Al Sanhouryand A Abosteet, *The Principles of Law or the Introduction to the Study of Law* (Committee of Authorship, Translation and Publication, 1950) 241; S Tanagho, *The General Theory of Law* (Monsha'at Al Ma'aref, 1986) 759.

9 MS Abdel Wahab, 'The Egyptian Court of Cassation Sets Standards and Affirms Arbitration-Friendly Principles and Trends in a Ground-Breaking Judgment' (2020) http://arbitrationblog.kluwerarbitration.com/2020/12/22/the-egyptian-court-of-cassation-sets-standards-and-affirms-arbitration-friendly-principles-and-trends-in-a-ground-breaking-judgment/; Egyptian Court of Cassation, Challenge No. 18309 of JY 89, hearing session dated 27 October 2020.

In case of the absence of a legislative principle, whether expressly or impliedly, the *ECC* provides that courts or tribunals may resort to other secondary sources such as custom, Islamic *Shariah* and principles of natural law and justice.[10]

More specifically, in commercial transactions,[11] Egyptian law provides in case no agreement exists between the parties, the provisions of the *Egyptian Commercial Law No. 17 for 1999* (***Commercial Law***) and other laws related to commercial matters shall apply, then the rules of trade usage and customs, then the provisions of the *ECC* shall apply.

It should be noted that Egyptian law, like most legal systems, upholds the principle of party autonomy to the extent it does not contravene mandatory Egyptian law rules. Thus, parties to a contract are free to agree on an applicable law, and their agreement will normally be upheld by courts insofar as their agreement does not violate public policy considerations or fundamental mandatory norms.

Finally, despite the non-existence of an established system of legally (*de jure*) binding *stare decisis* in Egypt, Egyptian court decisions applying the *ECC* and interpreting contracts do have persuasive authority.[12] Arguably, in administrative matters, there appears to be a system of precedents when it comes to applying and abiding by the decisions issued by the Unification of Principles Committee of the Egyptian *Conseil d' Etat* (whenever it exercises its power to issue a principle resolving a contradiction between the principles established by the Supreme Administrative Courts' decisions in a given issue).[13] In addition, the Egyptian Constitutional Court's interpretation of a law is binding on all courts.[14]

5.1.3 The court system in Egypt

Besides the standalone Egyptian Constitutional Court referred to earlier,[15] Egypt has a dual judicial system: (i) administrative courts (headed by the Supreme Administrative Court with the lower courts being the Court of Administrative Adjudication and Administrative Courts) having exclusive jurisdiction as to administrative matters,[16] and (ii) general courts (headed by the Egyptian Court of Cassation with the lower courts being Economic Courts, Courts of Appeal and Courts of First Instance and District Courts) having exclusive jurisdiction over civil and criminal matters.

Besides the binding interpretations of the Egyptian Constitutional Court and the principles issued by the Unification of Principles Committee of the *Conseil d' Etat* in relation to administrative matters mentioned earlier,[17] the Egyptian Court of Cassation decisions also have persuasive authority upon lower courts as a natural result of its function to review

---

10 Article 1(2) *ECC*.

11 Article 2 of the *Egyptian Commercial law No. 17 For 1999*.

12 Abdel Wahab, 'UPDATE: An Overview of the Egyptian Legal System and Legal Research', above, n1.

13 Article 54 of the *Law No. 136 for 1984*.

14 Article 25 of the *Supreme Constitutional Court's Law No.48 of the Year 1979*.

15 See *supra*, 5.1.1. By virtue of Article 25 of the *Supreme Constitutional Court's Law No. 48 of the Year 1979*, the court is empowered to: (i) determine the constitutionality of laws and regulations; (ii) decide on jurisdiction disputes between judicial bodies or authorities of judicial competence; (iii) decide on the disputes that might take place as a result of enforcing two final contradictory rulings issued by two different judicial entities; and (iv) interpret the laws issued by the Legislative Authority and the decrees issued by the Head of the State in case of any divergence with respect to their implementation.

16 *State Council Law No. 47 For 1972*.

17 See section 6.1.2.

the decisions of the lower courts and provide exclusive and uniform interpretation and application of the law.[18]

Notably, the Egyptian Court of Cassation's review of the lower courts' decisions is limited to issues of law and not fact; however, the Egyptian Court of Cassation also has original and appellate jurisdiction to review merits in exceptional matters.[19]

Likewise, the Egyptian Supreme Administrative Court's decisions have persuasive authority as to the interpretation and application of administrative law issues in light of its authority to review the decisions of the lower courts.

With respect to the international jurisdiction of Egyptian courts, parties may be subjected to Egyptian courts regarding an international commercial dispute involving a foreign element on the basis of any of the following criteria:[20]

- Cases in which the defendant is Egyptian, unless the dispute pertains to immovables located in a foreign state.
- Cases in which the defendant, despite being a foreign national, is either domiciled or resident in Egypt, unless the dispute pertains to immovables located in a foreign State.
- Cases involving property (movables or immovables) located in Egypt even though the defendant is a foreign national who is not domiciled or resident in Egypt.
- Cases pertaining to an obligation created, performed or required to have been performed in Egypt.
- Cases pertaining to a bankruptcy or insolvency declared in Egypt.
- Cases in which the defendant voluntarily submits to the jurisdiction of Egyptian courts (full effect to the principle of party autonomy).
- Claims, counterclaims, defences, incidental questions and other issues that are closely connected to cases filed before Egyptian courts.
- Cases involving interim and provisional measures to be executed in Egypt.

In addition, Egypt recognises and upholds alternative dispute resolution methods that could either take away jurisdiction from state courts (be it administrative or general) or render cases that would have been otherwise admissible before state courts inadmissible (especially in cases involving an international element). In this respect, the most common and effective alternative dispute resolution method for construction contracts in Egypt is arbitration, which is regulated under the *Egyptian Arbitration Law No 27 for 1994*. Agreeing to an arbitration clause renders cases inadmissible before state courts.[21]

It is noteworthy that the Egyptian Court of Cassation has acknowledged that arbitration has become the normal dispute resolution process when it comes to international commercial disputes such as mega construction projects, which usually consist of a myriad of commercial transactions that transcend the borders of any single state. In this respect, the

18 Article 248 of the *Civil and Commercial Procedures Code (Law No.13 of 1968)*.

19 To decide on cases that arise from a judge's action, to decide cases where a final judgment is issued in violation of another judgement that has *res judicata*, etc. www.cc.gov.eg/?page_id=292 (accessed on 22 June 2022).

20 Abdel Wahab, 'UPDATE: An Overview of the Egyptian Legal System and Legal Research', above, n1.

21 Article 13 of the *Egyptian Arbitration Law*.

Court ruled in 2022 that 'Arbitration has practically become the general rule in resolving international commercial disputes'.[22]

5.2 The construction industry in Egypt

5.2.1 Overview

The Egypt construction market is a key player in the country's overall economic growth and is reported to reflect solid growth in recent years, despite recent events on the international scene that caused economies to decline. A survey conducted in 2021[23] demonstrated that the Egyptian construction market is estimated to grow at a compound annual growth rate (**CAGR**) of approximately 6% during the forecast period of 2020 to 2025. The survey records that the Egyptian construction market performed strongly in 2019 (contributing to 6.2% of Egypt's GDP) and is steadily expected to grow further. The attributed factors to this growth are expanding government investments towards construction and infrastructure. In recent years, the Egyptian government has placed a strong emphasis on construction and infrastructure as key drivers of financial stability and urban growth. This emphasis played a pivotal role in Egypt's construction industry weathering the storm of the COVID pandemic. Although investments from the private sector declined notably, the government's investment in roads and bridges (a noticeable fact evidenced by everyone living in the country) caused the construction industry to rebound in the third and fourth quarters of 2020 and contributed to the projected steady growth of the industry.[24]

5.2.2 Structure

There are several construction contracting companies in Egypt that are considered among the top in the industry and whose work volume stretches outside the boundaries of the country. Among these contractors is Orascom Construction, which was established in 1950, and which has projects in Egypt, Africa, the Middle East and the United States of America. Operations include infrastructure, industrial and commercial sectors. Revenues generated by the end of 2020 are reported to be US$ 3.4 billion, including a 50% share in the Belgian construction company, BESIX.[25] Another large contracting company is Hassan Allam Construction, with 80 years of experience in the industry and projects encompassing building, industrial, oil and gas, airports and building technologies among other disciplines.[26] A third large contracting company with an outreach surpassing just Egypt is Rowad Modern Engineering (RME), which was established in 1998 and has extensive project experience in industrial, infrastructure, commercial, reinforced earth systems and heritage restoration. Projects encompass Egypt and Africa.[27]

The aforementioned contractors are a few among many large-size contractors in Egypt with a portfolio of projects inside and outside Egypt. A comprehensive list of key players

22 Egyptian Court of Cassation, Challenge No. 8199 for 80 JY, Hearing Session dated 22 March 2022.

23 www.mordorintelligence.com/industry-reports/egypt-construction-market (accessed 10 June 2022).

24 https://finance.yahoo.com/news/egypt-construction-industry-market-size-142200685.html?guccounter=1&guce_referrer=aHR0cHM6Ly93d3cuZ29vZ%E2%80%A6 (accessed 10 June 2022).

25 https://orascom.com/ (accessed 11 June 2022).

26 www.hassanallam.com (accessed 11 June 2022).

27 https://rowad-rme.com (accessed 11 June 2022)

in the Egyptian construction industry, in terms of contractors, consultants, real estate developers and others, can be accessed in the Business.com directory.[28]

A statistical analysis of the extent of subcontracting in Egypt could not be accessed by the authors; however, it is the authors' experience from working 25 years in the Egyptian construction industry that subcontracting is very common. There are subcontractors in a wide range of disciplines within the industry, including steel, electromechanical works, woodwork, aluminium and foundry glass, among others. A list of these companies can be accessed in the Business.com directory referred to earlier. Due to the extensive use of subcontractors in the industry, it is perhaps not surprising that another experience of the authors is that subcontractor claims in times of economic turbulence caused by exceptional events, such as the COVID pandemic of 2019–2021 or the flotation of the Egyptian Pound by the Central Bank of Egypt in November 2016, are the most prevalent type of claims presented by main contractors. Another noteworthy remark about subcontracting in Egypt is that, perhaps due to its prevalence in the industry since the early twentieth century, there is an article in the *Egyptian Civil Code* dedicated to subcontractor claims against Contractors for lack of payment, which gives a subcontractor the right to claim these amounts from the Employer.[29]

There are a number of international construction companies in Egypt, although the number seems to be decreasing throughout the past three decades. International contracting companies that currently have a strong presence in Egypt include Al Marasem Development,[30] the Arabian Construction Company[31] and the Consolidated Contractors Company.[32] Aside from the Belgian company BESIX, of which Orascom Construction owns 50% as mentioned earlier, there is also the China State Construction Engineering Corporation,[33] which recently gained a solid presence in Egypt with its awarded contracts in the New Administrative Capital Project.[34]

5.2.3 Licensing/registration

In 1992, the Egyptian government promulgated a law[35] to establish the Egyptian Federation for Construction and Building Contractors (the **Federation**), for the purpose of managing and regulating the contracting industry in Egypt. Any contracting company undertaking construction work in Egypt, whether local or foreign, must be registered by the Federation.[36] The Federation divides contractors into several classes; the highest is

28 www.egypt-business.com/company/katalog/Construction (accessed 11 June 2022).

29 *Egyptian Civil Code*, Article 662. This article is also prevalent in several MENA countries due to the fact that the Egyptian Civil Code formed the basis for such laws.

30 https://almarasemdevelopment.com (founded in Saudi Arabia).

31 https://accgroup.com (founded in the United Arab Emirates).

32 www.ccc.net (founded in Beirut).

33 https://english.cscec.com/ (accessed 5 August 2022).

34 In 2015, CSEC was awarded the construction of buildings that would house government ministries and agencies as well as the President's office. The following year, the company was awarded the Central Business District, which spans 1.9 million square metres in area, and which includes a 385.5 m tall tower, the tallest in Africa (https://constructionreviewonline.com/project-timelines/egypts-new-administrative-capital-project-timeline-and-what-you-need-to-know (accessed 11 June 2022).

35 *Law 102 for the year 1992.*

36 Article 8 of the *Executive Regulation of Law No. 104 of 1992* states that: 'Any person engaged in construction, buildings, public works, land reclamation, installation, marine construction and any other works of

the first class while the lowest is the seventh class in some specialties. Those classes are formed based on the composition of the technical and administrative body, capital and turnover permitted for the company.

Aside from being the country's entity that registers contractors, the Federation is also a key player in the major events that affect the construction industry. For example, when the Central Bank of Egypt decided to float the Egyptian Pound in November 2016, the Federation took the initiative to suggest to the government mechanisms for compensating contractors[37] and thereafter issued statements that contractors would be awarded time extensions.[38] It is worthy of note that on 9 July 2017, the government issued *Law 84* (known as the *Compensation Law*) to compensate contractors due to the consequences of the flotation, and that the Federation was on the committee that was tasked to set out the criteria, conditions and percentages for compensation.[39]

5.2.4 Labour relations

Labour relations are regulated by the *Labour Law* as well as certain complementary *decrees*.[40] In relation to labour working in construction, the following can be highlighted as a non-exhaustive sample:[41]

- Working hours are eight hours per day, 48 hours per week, in the case of a six-day work week. The employee may work additional hours if required.[42]
- Foreign employees are not permitted to work in Egypt without a residency and a work permit.
- Foreign technical experts must have two Egyptian employees as assistants.
- According to the *Companies Law*, only 10% of the employees in a company can be foreigners with salaries that do not exceed 20% of the total salaries.
- Labour strikes are permissible through labour unions, subject to being approved by two-thirds of the Board of Directors of the concerned labour union organisation. Strikes in vital government establishments are not permissible.
- An Employees' Union is required for companies hiring more than 50 employees.
- In case of injury in the workplace, employees are covered by social insurance.
- An employer is required to protect employees from hazardous material, chemicals, machinery, infections, noise and sound pollution in the workplace and to equip the workplace with fire protection and first aid.

---

the same nature, whether natural or juristic person, whatever legal system he may be subject to, shall apply for membership of the federation.'

37 https://invest-gate.me/news/contractors-federation-suggest-resolutions-to-economic-challenges-in-construction/ (accessed 12 June 2022).

38 www.egypttoday.com/Article/3/12019/Contractors-to-be-paid-compensation-'in-days'-Federation (accessed 12 June 2022).

39 https://riad-riad.com/law-compensation-contractors-governmental-projects/ (accessed 14 June 2022).

40 *Law 47 for the year 1978*, *Law 48 for the year 1978*, *Law 203 for the year 1991* and *Law 12 for the year 2003*.

41 The following are general provisions affecting labour but reference here is made to construction in terms of applicable concepts, namely working hours, foreign companies, labour strikes, labour unions, insurance and safety standards.

42 In the authors' experience, these hours are usually used in the Particular Conditions of the 1999 FIDIC contract (sub-clause 6.5).

5.2.5 Safety culture

Safety culture in the Egyptian construction industry is not one of the industry's strengths. From both authors' many years of experience in the industry, safety was not (and still is not) a priority unless enforced by an international entity.[43] This fact is corroborated by research that compared the safety approaches in construction projects in the United States and in Egypt.[44] The results revealed that the safety programs of large-size American contractors were more formal than those applied by large-size contractors in Egypt. Few Egyptian contractors provided safety orientation to their workers or kept records of accidents by projects. Other research linked work injuries in construction projects to substance (cannabis) abuse among rural workers in particular and recommended drug testing to control such risk.[45]

5.2.6 Modular construction using factory-fabricated components

Although not currently popular in Egypt, modular construction is slowly gaining ground. A recent article refers to three modular construction companies in Egypt[46] and anticipates that with the anticipated growth of the construction industry during the coming decade, there could be an increasing demand.[47] This expected demand increase is attributable, in part, to the introduction of new cities such as the Al Alamein and the New Administrative Capital as well as increasing projects in the transport and energy sectors. There are also signs that the use of modular construction can extend beyond the housing and real estate sectors, as evidenced by the use of modular construction in water projects conducted by the government. Modular construction using prefabricated building systems has been recently advocated as a means to develop the construction industry in Egypt and consequently develop the national economy.[48] Specifically, the study refers to the New Capital City, expansion of the Suez Canal, infrastructure development and the construction of new housing settlements as large-scale plans that render the enhancement of the construction industry's performance a must. In respect of modular construction, the study calls on contractors to use advanced construction methods and on architects to use prefabricated buildings in large settlements.

43 This can be in the form of an international contractor entering into a joint venture with a local contractor, or an international lender such as the World Bank, JICA or others.

44 Ragaa Hanna and Amr Hassanein, 'Safety Performance in the Egyptian Construction Industry' (2008) 134 *ASCE Journal of Construction Engineering and Management* 451.

45 AH El-Gilany, M E-Helaly et al., 'Risk Factors for Non-Fatal Occupational Injuries among Construction Workers: A Case-Control Study' (2018) 34 *Toxicology and Industrial Health* 83.

46 Arabian Construction House, Qubix and Hilti Egypt.

47 https://enterprise.press/hardhats/prefab-and-modular-construction-are-making-their-way-to-egyptian-building-sites/ (accessed 20 June 2022).

48 Eman MO Mokhtar, 'A Vision on Future Development of Building and Construction Industry in Egypt' (2020) 59 *Egyptian Society of Engineers* 17–20.

5.2.7 Technology/innovation/BIM

Although building information modelling (BIM) is used in Egypt, its use is not prevalent. A recent study[49] on the extent of utilisation of BIM in the Egyptian construction industry, which used an online survey to solicit the views of 120 contracting companies and ten consultancy firms, concluded that the majority of construction practitioners know little or nothing about BIM.[50] Other notable conclusions were that major barriers to BIM application in Egypt are lack of client demand, cost of BIM systems and lack of company experience. It was also concluded that the government does not support the use of BIM in public projects. These results accord with a master's thesis that aimed at understanding the implementation of BIM in Egypt for sustainable construction. This highlighted among its conclusions that, although there is a slow rate of implementation of BIM in Egypt, there are promising initiatives from universities and private entities. Yet, the research notes the lack of BIM use by the government and calls on the government to expand the use of BIM to achieve sustainability in the construction industry.[51] Other research points out that, although there is good potential for the use of BIM in Egypt, there is doubt as to whether its use would spread due to the lack of knowledge among practitioners about it and because of the existence of some risks that can become obstacles to its implementation.[52]

5.2.8 Government/private sector procurement

Prior to 2018, the procurement for public projects was regulated by *Law 89 for the year 1998* (also known as the *Tenders Law*). The law consisted of numerous regulations and procedures that govern tenders in Egyptian public construction projects as well as providing guidance regarding certain terms and conditions used in such projects. *Law 89* is currently superseded by *Law 182 for the year 2018* (also known as the *Law for Contracts Executed by Government Entities*), which also provides tender procedures and contract conditions. It is the second author's opinion from his experience in the construction industry that some of these contractual conditions, which are commonly used in both public and private contracts, generated (and still generate) controversy in their application. Further elaboration on this point is made later in this chapter.

There are no standard procurement procedures for private projects, although those of the administrative law mentioned earlier are commonly used for guidance. Although as mentioned in the following, FIDIC is by far the most commonly used standard form of international contract used in Egypt for decades, it is the authors' opinion from their experience in Egypt that FIDIC's Procurement Procedures Guide[53] is of limited to no use.

49 AH Elyamany, 'Current practices of building information modelling in Egypt' (2016) 6 *International Journal of Engineering Management and Economics* 59–71.

50 This conclusion was deduced from a 17.2% response rate of the practitioners to whom the survey was sent.

51 Amira Mohamed, 'The implementation of building information modelling (BIM) towards sustainable construction industry in Egypt The pre-construction phase', Master's Thesis, American University in Cairo. AUC Knowledge Fountain.

52 Mohamed Elmikawi, Ahmed Elessawy et al., 'Building Information Modelling (BIM) in the Egyptian Construction Industry' (2017) 39 *Al-Azhar University Civil Engineering Research Magazine (CERM)* 12–21.

53 https://fidic.org/books/fidic-procurement-procedures-guide-1st-ed-2011 (accessed 25 June 2022).

5.2.9 Insurance requirements

There is no explicit requirement for insurance in *Law 182*, although there is a requirement that the Contractor take all measures to avoid injuries, fatal accidents to workers or any other person and damage to public property or that of individuals.[54] The situation is different in the *Egyptian Civil Code*, which governs private projects, as there is a notable section within the code dedicated to insurance. The section defines insurance[55] and then delves into general principles, including life insurance[56] and insurance against fire,[57] which led commentators to opine that, in a construction context, a Contractor is obligated to provide insurance against injury or death to workers and third parties (life insurance) and against fire.[58]

However, in a practical sense, insurance provisions in construction, whether undertaken by Contractors or Employers, are very common in all types of construction contracts within the country, whether public or private.

5.2.10 Common forms of contract

It is suggested that there is no common form of contract for public projects, although the terms and conditions provided in *Law 182* are frequently used. FIDIC contracts are arguably the most commonly used form of construction contract in the Egyptian private sector for over three decades. In 1994 it was reported that the FIDIC form of contract was the most used international standard form of civil engineering contract in the Arab Middle Eastern countries and that the FIDIC form of contract has been widely used in a considerable number of important projects in Egypt, particularly in all projects financed by the World Bank and USAID (United States Aid for International Development), both of which fund a large number of infrastructure projects in Egypt.[59] Nearly three decades after that report, the popularity of the FIDIC contract in Egypt never waned, as its use has been prevalent in many of Egypt's major projects throughout the years, including the Grand Egyptian Museum, Cairo Airport Terminals 3 and 2, New National Cancer Institute Phase 1 – 500500 Hospital, Magdy Yaacoub Hospital Package 1, Hurghada International Airport and New Giza University – Phase 1, among many others.

The importance of FIDIC in Egypt is further highlighted by the conferences FIDIC hosts in Egypt and which are attended by professionals from Egypt and the Middle East, such as the conference hosted by FIDIC and the International Chamber of Commerce (ICC) in April 2005, titled 'International Construction Contracts and Dispute Resolution', which attracted 130 participants from more than 26 countries.[60] In January 2011 FIDIC collaborated with the Cairo Regional Centre for International Commercial Arbitration (**CRCICA**) and the Egyptian Society for Consulting Engineers (**ESCONE**) to hold a

54 Article 105 of *Law 182's Executive Regulations.*

55 Article 747 of the *Egyptian Civil Code.*

56 Articles 754 to 775 of the *Egyptian Civil Code.*

57 Articles 766 to 770 of the *Egyptian Civil Code.*

58 Merhem Luther Girgis, *Idarat 'Uqud Al Tashyeed* [*Management of Construction Contracts*] (1st ed Dar Al Nahda Al 'arabiyya, 2021) 124.

59 H Sarie El-Din, 'Operation of FIDIC civil engineering conditions in Egypt and other Arab Middle Eastern countries' (1994) 28 *The International Lawyer* 951–972.

60 S Hanafi, 'International construction contracts and dispute resolution: An Egyptian perspective' (2005) 22 *The International Construction Law Review* 443–452.

conference at the CRCICA to discuss the latest developments in FIDIC contracts. The conference included 19 speakers, three of whom were key FIDIC representatives and the rest of whom were prominent speakers on construction disputes in Egypt and the Middle East, including Jordan, Libya, Syria and Saudi Arabia. The conference was attended by numerous representatives from Egypt and the Middle East. In April 2016, the FIDIC–CRCICA–ESCONE collaboration resulted in another conference that was well-attended. Throughout 2016 to 2019, the Egypt branch of the Society of Construction Law (SCL), in collaboration with the ICC, conducted annual conferences that addressed numerous demanding issues in construction law within the construction industry.

Another indicator of the strong presence of FIDIC in Egypt, resulting in the common use of its forms throughout the years, is the research about FIDIC that emanates from that country. In 2011 a PhD thesis compared the FIDIC 1987 Red Book provisions pertaining to risk to those of Egyptian civil law.[61] In 2017, another PhD thesis compared the enforceability of time bar clauses (particularly that in sub-clause 20.1 of the FIDIC 1999 Red Book) in the English and Egyptian legal jurisdictions.[62] In 2018, a book was published that addressed the application of FIDIC in civil law jurisdictions, predominantly citing case law from the Egyptian jurisdiction.[63] Aside from the academic research, numerous articles on the application of FIDIC in Egypt had been published throughout the last three decades. Before the publication of the 1999 editions, there had been several articles that compared the *Egyptian Civil Code* provisions with the FIDIC 1987 contract.[64] Shortly after the publication and commercial use of the 1999 editions, books were published that compared the FIDIC contracts to Egyptian law.[65] Other international journal articles provided a detailed analysis of the FIDIC 1999 contracts vis-a-vis the *ECC*[66] while others addressed popular construction law concepts, such as the 'prevention principle' and 'time at large', and compared them to the Egyptian law position.[67] Others simply highlighted key concepts in Egyptian law and compared these to the FIDIC contract.[68]

---

61 TH Hamed, *Ahkam al makhater fi 'oqood muqawalat al bina' wal tashyeed: dirasa muqarana bayn al qanoon al madani al misry wa shoroot 'aqd al FIDIC [Risk Provisions in Building and Construction Contracts, A Comparative Study between the Egyptian Civil Code and the FIDIC Conditions of Contract]* (2011) PhD thesis, Cairo University, Giza.

62 W El Nemr, 'The Enforceability of Time Bar Clauses in Construction Contracts: A Comparative Analysis between the Egyptian Civil Code and the English and Welsh Common Law Jurisdictions' (2017) PhD thesis, University of Salford, School of Built Environment.

63 S Fawzy, T Hamed, M Abdel Wahab and I El-adawy, *Practicing FIDIC in Civil Law Jurisdictions – Application of Time and Additional Payment Provisions* (1st ed Lambert Academic Publishing, 2018).

64 A El-Shalakany, 'The application of the FIDIC civil engineering conditions of contract in a Civil Code system country: a comparison of legal concepts 409 and solutions' (1989) V6 *The International Construction Law Review* 266–281; H Sarie El-Din, 'Operation of FIDIC civil engineering conditions in Egypt and other Arab Middle Eastern countries' (1994) 28 *The International Lawyer* 951–972.

65 MM Badran, *'Aqd al insha'at fel qanoon al masry: dirasa fel mushkelat al 'amaleyya li 'uqud al ettihad al dawly lel muhandeseen al istishareyyeen [The construction contract under the Egyptian law: a study of the practical problems of the contracts of the International Federation of Consulting Engineers]* (1st ed, Dar Al Nahda, 2001); B Atalla, 'Egypt' in R Knutsen (ed), *FIDIC: An Analysis of International Construction Contracts* (Kluwer Law International, 2005) 21–35.

66 JAD Nassar, 'Claims, disputes and arbitration under the Red Book and the New Red Book (Part 1)' (2009) 25 *Construction Law Journal* 405–443.

67 Fawzi, El-Adawy and Hamed, 'Contracting in a Global World: Application of the 'Time at Large' Principle' (2015) 7 *Journal of Legal Affairs and Dispute Resolution in Engineering and Construction* 1–7.

68 Helmi, Qodsi, Serag and Shafik, 'Application of FIDIC Contracts under the Egyptian Civil Code' (2017) 8 *Journal of Legal Affairs and Dispute Resolution in Engineering and Construction* 1–9.

5.2.11 Dispute resolution

Arbitration is arguably the most common form of dispute resolution of construction disputes in Egypt, although there is a notable number of Employers who prefer litigation. The Cairo Regional Centre for International Commercial Arbitration (CRCICA) is one of the major arbitration centres in the country and in the region. CRCICA was put into full commercial operation in 1983[69] while adopting the arbitration rules of the United Nations Commission on International Trade Law (UNCITRAL) of 1976. The rules were then amended in 1998, 2000, 2002 and 2007.[70] The Centre also published rules of mediation in 2011 and of Dispute Boards in 2021. Despite the publication of mediation and Dispute Board rules, the practice of arbitration in construction as a form of ADR by far exceeds the practice of mediation and Dispute Boards. It is the authors' experience that Dispute Boards are predominantly used in internationally funded projects that use the FIDIC form of contract, which in turn requires the use of Dispute Boards to resolve disputes. It is suggested that the Egyptian market generally does not favour the use of Dispute Boards as a means of dispute resolution in construction projects.

5.2.12 Current challenges

There are four distinct challenges that struck the Egyptian construction industry in the past six years:

- *The 2016 inflation.* Throughout the majority of 2016, Egypt went through economic turbulence, which affected the construction industry. According to a World Bank report issued during the first quarter of that year,[71] the turbulent economy in the first quarter of 2016 was due to foreign exchange shortages. The report concluded that the economy was expected to decline further throughout the year before rebounding again and that the Central Bank of Egypt (**CBE**) had recently started tightening monetary policy to curb inflation, especially in light of the recent exchange rate depreciation. The report was correct regarding the continued hit to the economy, except that matters went from bad to worse in November 2016.
- *The flotation of the Egyptian Pound in 2016.* The peak of the economic turbulence that shook the construction market was when the CBE decided to float the Egyptian Pound to meet demands from the International Monetary Fund (**IMF**) for a US$ 12b loan over a three-year period. The Egyptian Pound went from 9 to the US$ up to 13 overnight. The economic crisis that ensued, which was described as the 'worst economic crisis in decades',[72] caused construction Contractors to present claims due to increased prices and inability to continue under current financial conditions. This caused the government to promulgate a law in July

69 The Centre was put into temporary operation from 1979 to 1983.

70 https://crcica.org/Arbitration_rules.aspx (accessed 9 July 2022)

71 www.worldbank.org/en/country/egypt/publication/economic-outlook-spring-2016 (accessed 10 July 2022).

72 www.theguardian.com/world/2016/nov/03/egypt-devalues-currency-meet-imf-demands-loan (accessed 10 July 2022).

2017 (the *Compensation Law*) in an attempt to compensate Contractors working in the public sector.

- *COVID.* Like the rest of the world, the Egyptian economy and its construction industry were greatly affected by the COVID crisis in 2020 and 2021. Elaboration on this point is made in the next section.
- *Further Egyptian Pound devaluation in March 2022.* On 21 March 2022, as a reaction to the Russian war on Ukraine, the Egyptian government devalued the Egyptian pound by nearly 14%. As in the situation of the 2016 devaluation, construction prices soared and claims from Contractors mounted.

The foregoing events caused the propagation of claims and disputes throughout the construction industry. At the time of writing this chapter, the effect of the fourth factor is still felt strongly throughout the industry.

5.3 The impact of COVID-19 in Egypt

5.3.1 The impact of COVID-19 on the execution of construction projects in Egypt

The Egyptian government responded to the threat of COVID-19 on 19 March 2020, when all flights were suspended, public areas (including schools, restaurants and universities) were closed and a curfew until the end of March 2020 was enforced from 7 pm until 6 am. Restrictions were gradually loosened throughout the following two months so that, on 11 June 2020, it was announced that the curfew would start from 8 pm until 4 am and travel would be permissible for certain governorates in the country. Public areas were still not accessible. Restrictions were gradually loosened, as vaccinations were available and processed throughout 2021 and reported cases started to reduce notably.

The effect on construction can be summarised as follows:

- The restriction on flights directly affected the importing of materials into the country, which in turn caused delays and additional costs.
- The curfews imposed by the government disrupted progress on many sites and resulted in notable issuance of delay notices by Contractors.
- The restrictions on wearing masks and social distancing measures (including the reduction of labour working in a certain area) led to reduced productivity.
- According to the experience of the authors, there were several instances when work on several sites was shut down due to the infection of several labourers and/or personnel with the virus.
- Travel was of course restricted for a while, which led to the increased use of online meeting platforms.

Although the foregoing may seem like negative impacts on the construction industry, there were some distinct advantages. Perhaps the most apparent is the flood of knowledge that has become available to everyone at the ease of their fingertips. Before COVID-19, seminars or conferences required registration fees and travel expenses that were considered expensive for most young practitioners. However, during COVID-19, webinars focusing on construction law topics worldwide, and from prominent institutions, became accessible to all. One clear example is FIDIC's COVID-19 series of webinars,[73] which were frequently held and discussed numerous topics in the industry pertaining to FIDIC and the pandemic. Another key advantage relates to the last point on the list, which is the increased use of online meeting platforms, such as Zoom and Microsoft Teams. It is suggested that the use of such platforms for conducting business greatly facilitated communication within a company (particularly an international company of which Egypt is a branch) and outside of it.

5.3.2 The impact of COVID-19 on the operation of construction contracts in Egypt

In the authors' experience, COVID-19 has had little impact on the operation of construction contracts in Egypt. There was no specific legislation or edicts that changed the 'normal' operation of construction contracts. However, the Egyptian legislator enacted some general health and safety regulations that might have had an impact on the performance of a construction contract.[74] While as mentioned earlier the FIDIC contract is arguably the most commonly used form in Egypt, the contract users in Egypt predominantly relied on the existing clauses to assert or respond to a claim related to COVID-19. The most commonly used clauses in the FIDIC 1999 Red Book,[75] for instance, were the following:

- *Sub-clauses 19.1 and 19.2.* The event of COVID-19 was frequently referred to as a *force majeure* event under clause 19. It is observed that, while users commonly referred to the description of *force majeure* in sub-clause 19.1,[76] a few of these users gave attention to the condition that such an event 'prevented' the party's performance of its obligations under the contract.[77] Clearly, the majority of the time, COVID-19's impact on construction activities did not 'prevent' performance, but rather 'impacted' the ongoing performance.
- *Sub-clause 13.7.* This change in legislation clause was a common reference for COVID-19's impact on construction activities, as it pertains to the government-imposed curfews and restricted travel.
- *Sub-clause 8.4/sub-clause 20.1.* To a lesser extent than the two previous clauses, the users referred to the general claims procedures. It is interesting to note that sub-clause 8.4 contains a direct reference to 'epidemics' as a justification for an extension of time,[78] but this reference was not commonly used in claims experienced by the second author.

Notwithstanding the foregoing observation regarding the use of the FIDIC 1999 contract in relation to COVID-19 claims, there were certain impacts of COVID-19 on the operation

73 https://fidic.org/events/other-fidic-events/fidic-covid-19-webinar-series-2021 (accessed 11 July 2022).

74 See section 6.9.

75 As of mid-2022, the FIDIC 2017 contract is not commonly used in Egypt.

76 Namely that it is an event (a) beyond a party's control, (b) which such party could not reasonably have provided against before entering into the Contract, (c) which, having arisen, such party could not reasonably have avoided or overcome and (d) which is not substantially attributable to the other party.

77 The word 'prevented' is used throughout sub-clauses 19.4 and 19.6.

78 Sub-paragraph (d) refers to: 'Unforeseeable shortages in the availability of personnel or Goods caused by *epidemic* or governmental actions', which in many ways seems to fit very well the condition of COVID-19.

of construction contracts in Egypt concluded after March 2020, which can be summarised as follows:

- There were provisions in *ad-hoc* contracts, predominantly for public or semi-public entities, that explicitly excluded COVID-19 from the list of excusable delay events.[79]
- Particular Conditions were introduced to the FIDIC 1999 forms to limit the excusability and compensability of COVID-19 as a delay event.

Hence, it is suggested that the general trend in Egypt was for Employers to place the risk on the Contractor in relation to COVID-19, as opposed to the Employers' sharing the risk with Contractors. Ultimately, this led Contractors to assert claims using certain mandatory provisions of the law, in lieu of the contract.[80] Be that as it may, as part of their pre-contractual review, Contractors should carefully consider whether such concepts as *force majeure* and *imprévision* are subject to mandatory or non-mandatory regulation under the potentially applicable *lex causae*, so that their choices and drafting are informed by legal considerations.[81]

For instance, under Egyptian law, parties may agree to regulate the ramifications of *force majeure* differently by allocating the risk of impossibility among themselves as they deem fit. However, unlike *force majeure*, *imprévision* is generally subject to an overriding mandatory legislative regulation that does not allow the parties to a contract to derogate from such mandatory regulation by agreement.[82] In this respect, Article 658(4) of the *ECC*, which exclusively applies to 'lump sum' construction contracts (not re-measured contracts such as the standard FIDIC forms), states that

> if the economic equilibrium between the obligations of the employer and the contractor collapses, due to exceptional events of general character, which were unforeseen at the time of contracting, causing the basis for the monetary valuation of the contract to fizzle, the Court may order an increase in payment to the contractor or the rescission of the contract.

Article 658/4 of the *ECC* is a special application of the general principle enshrined in Article 147/2 of the *ECC*. They share the same conditions of application, yet the court or arbitral tribunal is not entitled to rescind the contract under Article 147/2, but can so order under Article 658/4 of the *ECC* in the specific context of lump sum construction contracts.[83]

In administrative disputes and based on the facts of each case, even if COVID-19 is deemed neither a *force majeure* nor an *imprévision* event, a Contractor might still be granted remedy based on the theory of *fait du prince*. This is triggered if an act or measure, whether public or private (targeting only the opposing contracting party), is issued or

79 This was particularly the case at the end of 2020, and throughout 2021, when COVID-19 was a foreseeable event and part of the usual course of business.

80 For example, Articles 142-2 and 658 of the *ECC* which refer to exceptional circumstances.

81 MS Abdel Wahab, 'Dispute Prevention, Management and Resolution in Times of Crisis Between Tradition and Innovation: The COVID-19 Catalytic Crisis', in M Scherer, N Bassiri et al. (eds), *International Arbitration and the COVID-19 Revolution* (Kluwer Law International, 2020) 1–26.

82 MS Abdel Wahab, 'Construction Arbitration in the MENA Region' (19 October 2021) *Global Arbitration Review*, https://globalarbitrationreview.com/guide/the-guide-construction-arbitration/fourth-edition/article/construction-arbitration-in-the-mena-region (accessed 1 August 2022).

83 *Ibid.*

undertaken by a contracting public authority without fault or breach on its part, and results in increasing the contractual burden of the Contractor in an administrative contract. In such a case, the theory of *fait du prince* would oblige the contracting authority to compensate the Contractor for the damage sustained (loss suffered).[84]

Another noteworthy comment related to the impact of COVID-19 on construction contracts in Egypt is that, in April 2020, FIDIC issued the 'FIDIC COVID-19 Guidance Memorandum to Users of FIDIC Standard Forms of Contract'.[85] This provides guidance in respect of likely scenarios arising out of COVID-19 to contracting parties in finding mutually satisfactory solutions and avoiding disputes arising between them. Although this guidance document is directly relevant to COVID-19 claims, and although FIDIC is arguably the most common form of contract used for decades in Egypt, it is opined that FIDIC users in the Egyptian construction industry did not give this document the attention it deserved when asserting or responding to claims associated with COVID-19.

Finally, being a contract in which performance is normally stretched over time, parties to a construction contract are encouraged to consider whether a contract review mechanism ought to be set in place to ensure that their contractual bargain is not short-lived and survives on a long-term basis.[86]

5.4 Egyptian governing law of the contract

Egyptian law can govern a construction contract in a number of ways as set out below. Egyptian law will also normally govern the interpretation of the contract if it is the law governing the contract.[87]

5.4.1 Party autonomy and the choice of Egyptian law

Universally, party autonomy allows the parties to freely choose the governing law of the contract (be it Egyptian law or any other state or non-state law).[88] The FIDIC Golden Principles also invite the parties to introduce changes to the GC of the FIDIC Contract if 'they are appropriate and necessary to ensure that the Contract terms are expressed consistently with the way they would be construed by an arbitral tribunal'.[89] However, while exercising party autonomy, parties are discouraged (unless circumstances suggest otherwise) from complicating matters by agreeing to (1) a *tronc commun* clause where Parties

84 Supreme Administrative Court Challenges Nos. 1562 of JY 10 and 67 of judicial year 11, hearing session dated 11 May 1968. Cassation Challenge No. 4424 of JY 61, hearing session dated 15 November 1997.

85 Available free at https://fidic.org/sites/default/files/COVID%2019%20Guidance%20Memorandum%20-%20PDF.pdf (accessed 12 July 2022).

86 MS Abdel Wahab, above, n81.

87 G Conrdero-Moss, *Boilerplate Clauses, International Commercial Contracts and the Applicable Law* (Cambridge University Press 2011) 182.

88 Egyptian Court of Cassation, Challenge No. 10305 for 83 JY, Hearing session dated 17 November 2021; Ernst Rabel, *The Conflict of Laws: A Comparative Study*, Vol. 2 (2nd edn, University of Michigan Law School, 1960) 378; FIDIC, 'The FIDIC Golden Principles' 13, https://fidic.org/sites/default/files/_golden_principles_1_12.pdf (accessed 1 August 2022).

89 FIDIC, 'The FIDIC Golden Principles' 13, https://fidic.org/sites/default/files/_golden_principles_1_12.pdf (accessed on 22 June 2022); I Amr El-Hoteiby, *Common conditions of construction contracts in Egypt*, thesis dissertation (2016), AUC Knowledge Foundation, Under the Supervision of Dr O Hosny and Dr A Waly 20–21. https://fount.aucegypt.edu/cgi/viewcontent.cgi?article=1390&context=etds (accessed 1 August 2022).

agree to apply principles which are common to both Egyptian law and another state law, or to (2) a dual clause where Parties agree to apply a state law as long as it doesn't contradict with Egyptian law.

There are some constraints to party autonomy as to the choice of law, as discussed later in some detail.[90]

5.4.2 Conflict of law rules and Egyptian law as the lex causae

In the unfortunate event that the Parties fail to choose the governing law of a construction contract, Egyptian law might still govern a construction contract according to the applicable conflict of law rules.

Generally, conflict of law rules, in the absence of a choice of law clause, are (i) the presumed or implied intention of the Parties, (ii) the ***lex loci contractus*** or the law of the place where the contract is made,[91] (iii) the ***lex loci solutionis*** or the 'most effective' law[92] or the law of the place of performance,[93] (iv) the domicile and nationality of the parties,[94] (v) the law most favourable to the contract,[95] (vi) the law with the most characteristic connection[96] or (vii) the '*No Rule*' approach.[97]

Practically, a conflict of law rule leading to Egyptian law would vary depending on the procedural rules applicable to the dispute as clarified in the following.

5.4.3 Conflict of law rules in institutional arbitration

If the parties subject their dispute to institutional rules that provide for conflict of law rules, an arbitral tribunal might choose Egyptian law as the governing law in the following scenarios:[98]

- Article 21 of the ICC (International Chamber of Commerce) Rules, Article 22.3 of the LCIA (London Court of International Arbitration) Rules and Article 36 of the HKIAC (Hong Kong International Arbitration Centre) Rules provide that the arbitral tribunal shall apply the law chosen by the parties, or, if no choice was made, the 'rules of law' that it deems appropriate while taking into account the contract and trade usage. In this respect, albeit a system of law and not 'rules of law', Egyptian law might be applicable by virtue of the trade usage between the parties who might be proven to have had a usage to apply Egyptian law in all their previous and similar course of dealing. In addition, the tribunal might apply the general principles of Egyptian law as applicable rules of law, which are

90 See section 5.4.3.

91 E Rabel, *The Conflict of Laws: A Comparative Study* Vol 2 (2nd edn, University of Michigan Law School, 1960) 432, 448.

92 *Ibid.* 442.

93 *Ibid.* 465.

94 *Ibid.* 475.

95 *Ibid.* 476.

96 *Ibid.* 444.

97 *Ibid.*

98 GB Born, 'Choice of Substantive Law in International Arbitration' in Gary B Born (ed), *International Commercial Arbitration* (3rd ed, Kluwer Law International, 2021) 2817–3000.

generally derived from the maxims and jurisprudential principles of *Shariah* and civil law.

- Similarly, in case of the absence of the parties' agreement, Article 22 of the SCC (Stockholm Chamber of Commerce) Rules and 31 of the SIAC (Singapore International Arbitration Centre) Rules provide that, the Tribunal shall apply the 'most appropriate' law or rules of law, and Article 35 of the SCAI (Swiss Arbitration Centre) Rules provides that the arbitral tribunal shall apply the rules of law with which the dispute has 'the closest connection'. It is noted that, unlike the ICC, LCIA and HKIAC, under these institutional rules, arbitral tribunals might equally apply a system of law as well as rules of law to the dispute.
- Taking a different approach, Article 33 of the CRCICA Rules provides that the tribunal shall apply the law determined by the conflict of laws rules that it considers applicable. As such, a tribunal under the CRCICA Rules, applying one of the conflict of law rules mentioned earlier, might find Egyptian law as the governing law. In so doing, the tribunal is also expected to take account of the contract and the trade usage.

5.4.4 Conflict of law rules in *ad hoc* arbitrations

If the parties have subjected their dispute to *ad hoc* arbitration where the applicable rules are the UNCITRAL Rules or any other country relying on the *UNCITRAL Model Arbitration Law*, the tribunal would determine the governing law on the basis of the conflict of laws rules which it considers applicable.[99]

In addition, if the procedural rules applicable are the rules of a seat of arbitration such as Egypt, then the law that the tribunal considers most closely connected to the dispute will govern the dispute.[100] Another example is if the *lex arbitri* is the *English Arbitration Act 1996* or any similar *Act*, unless agreed otherwise by the parties, Egyptian law might be applicable if the conflict of laws rules considered by the tribunal lead to Egyptian law.[101]

5.4.5 Conflict of law rules in the lex fori

If the parties have not subjected their dispute to arbitration and Egypt is the *lex fori*, then, relying on Articles 19–28 of the *ECC*, the judge may find Egyptian law to be the governing law. Generally, unless otherwise expressly or implicitly agreed by the parties, Article 19 of the *ECC* provides that

- Contractual obligations are governed by the law of the domicile when such domicile is common to the contracting parties.
- In the absence of a common domicile, the contract will be governed by the law of the place where the contract was concluded.
- However, contracts relating to immovable property are exclusively governed by the law of the place in which the immovable is situated.

99 Article 33 of the UNCITRAL Rules. and Article 28 of the *UNCITRAL Model Law*.
100 Article 39 of the *Egyptian Arbitration Law No. 27 for 1994*.
101 Article 46 of the *English Arbitration Act of 1996*.

It is to be noted as well that, according to Egyptian law, these provisions only apply when no provisions to the contrary are included in a special law or in an *International Convention* in force in Egypt.[102]

5.4.6 Constraints on the governing law of a construction contract

As seen earlier, Egyptian law can be the law governing a construction contract in a number of ways either through the parties' agreement or by virtue of the applicable procedural rules. However, the authors observe that some constraints might render (i) Egyptian law applicable despite the parties' agreement to choose a different applicable law, or (ii) render the nominated applicable Egyptian law inapplicable.

In general, there are some restrictive rules to party autonomy as to the choice of governing law. These are (i) imperative rules, which are rules of *ordre public* and ***lois de police*** or overriding mandatory norms,[103] (ii) ***fraude à la loi*** or fraudulent evasion of the law of a certain state by the choice of the law of another state or what was sometimes referred to as '*contracts without foreign elements*'[104] or (iii) the requirement of a substantial connection between the law chosen by the parties and the contract.[105]

As such, an arbitral tribunal, being careful to produce an award that would be enforceable in Egypt, might find itself compelled to apply Egyptian law in the following cases:[106]

- If the construction project subject of the construction contract is connected to an immovable property located in Egypt, Egyptian law would *exclusively* govern the said contract even with respect to the personal rights arising therefrom as per Article 19 of the *ECC*, which applies as the *lex situs* to immovable properties.[107]
- If there were a transfer of technology provisions in a construction contract, Egyptian law would be mandatorily applicable as per Article 87 of the *Commercial Law No. 17 for 1999*,[108] which might create a situation of legal ***dépeçage*** where the law governing the transfer of technology provisions is distinct from those applicable to the rest of the contract.
- If an issue is regarded as an issue of public policy under Egyptian law (e.g. decennial liability, punitive damages, exemption of liability as to *force majeure* and

102 Article 23 of the *ECC*.

103 E Rabel, *The Conflict of Laws*, above, n91, 394.

104 *Ibid.* 400.

105 *Ibid.* 402.

106 Abdel Wahab, 'UPDATE: An Overview of the Egyptian Legal System and Legal Research'.

107 Egyptian Court of Cassation, Challenge No. 8714, for JY 66, hearing session dated 14 March 1999; Hani Sarie Eldein, 'Operation of FIDIC Civil Engineering Conditions in Egypt and Other Arab Middle Eastern Countries' (1994) 28, *The International Lawyer* 4, 957, https://core.ac.uk/download/pdf/216911992.pdf (accessed on 22 June 2022).

108 CR Ternieden, T Badawy and S Abd El-Shahid, 'Arbitrability and Choice of Law in Transfer of Technology Agreements Under Egyptian Law' (2017) *Journal of International Arbitration* http://shahidlaw.com/wp-content/uploads/2017/02/JOIA-340104.pdf (accessed on 22 June 2022). See also MS Abdel Wahab, 'The Law Applicable to Technology Transfer Contracts and Egyptian Conflict of Laws: A Triumph of Nationalism over Internationalism?' (2010) 12 *Yearbook of Private International Law*.

usury) and the application of the foreign law would result in a different outcome than that prescribed by Egyptian law, then Egyptian law would apply.[109]

5.4.7 Formal requirements for a construction contract

In private international law rules, the prevailing approach is that conflict of law rules as to the form of the contract are drafted in a way that favours the validity of the contract.[110] Under Egyptian law, the form of a contract is governed by either the law of the country in which the contracts are concluded, the law governing the merits or the law of the parties' common domicile or nationality.[111]

Generally, construction contracts have no formal requirements under Egyptian law.[112] They can be validly concluded whether orally or in a written format. Nevertheless, a distinction has to be made between governmental projects subject to Egyptian administrative law and Egyptian private-sector projects subject to private law.

Under Egyptian law, an administrative contract is a contract where:[113]

- One of the parties is a public entity.
- Its subject matter relates to a public utility.
- It includes clauses that are unusual in civil law.

In this respect, Article 127 of the *Egyptian Constitution for 2014* seems to impose a formal requirement for some administrative contracts (i.e. the approval of the parliament). Also, the *Tenders and Bids Law No. 182 for 2018* stipulates that the normal contracting method for administrative contracts is through the procedures stipulated therein. Moreover, according to the *Decree No. 2592 of 2020*, all governmental entities and state-owned companies shall not conclude any contract with a foreign investor or agree to arbitrate without first referring the matter to the Higher Authority for Studying and Opining on International Arbitration Cases.[114]

However, arguably and subject to the facts of each case, the lack of those formal requirements might not affect the validity of the construction contract in light of the recent Egyptian court practice. In this respect, in the context of arbitration agreements, it has been ruled that a state entity cannot avoid an arbitration agreement relying solely on the lack of a minister's approval because it would be, in that case, contrary to good faith for

109 Article 28 of the *ECC*; H Sarie Eldein, 'Operation of FIDIC Civil Engineering Conditions in Egypt and Other Arab Middle Eastern Countries' (1994) V28 *The International Lawyer* 4, 964.

110 E Rabel, *The Conflict of Laws*, above, n91, 489.

111 Article 20 of the *ECC*.

112 A Al Sanhoury, *Al Wasit in the Explanation of the Civil Code* Vol. 1, Part 1 (Dar El Sherouk, 2021) 125–128.

113 S Al-Tammawy, *Principles of Administrative Law* (Dar Alfikr Alaraby, 2007) 942–943; H Sarie Eldein, 'Operation of FIDIC Civil Engineering Conditions in Egypt and Other Arab Middle Eastern Countries' (1994) 28 *The International Lawyer* 4, 954.

114 F Salah, 'Egypt – New Approval Required for Government Contracts and Arbitration Agreements' (26 December 2020), https://riad-riad.com/egypt-new-approval-required-government-contracts-and-arbitration-agreements/ (accessed on 22 June 2022). The constitutional validity of such requirement might be called into question being a requirement imposed by a decree issued by the administration itself, but not by a legislative provision.

the administration ('who has the most authority and sovereignty') to rely on the actions of its own bodies to avoid agreements.[115]

In the same vein, the general rule in Egypt is that 'the administration does not have to follow the tenders or bids contracting methods unless where the law states so'.[116] In this respect, Article 7 of the *Tenders and Bids Law No. 182 for 2018* imposes the tender method as to construction contracts, but may, exceptionally, apply other methods.[117] In all cases, the Contractor party usually has no say in the administration's choice of the contracting method, which also militates against an interpretation that would lead to the invalidity of the contract based on failure to follow the correct method prescribed by the law.

5.5 What Special Provisions in the Particular Conditions are necessary for consistency with applicable laws in Egypt?

5.5.1 FIDIC General Conditions are incompatible or inconsistent with Egyptian governing law of the contract

There are certain provisions in the FIDIC 1999 rainbow suite which may be inconsistent with or contradictory to Egyptian law. Such provisions include the following.

5.5.1.1 Time bar clauses and statute of limitations

One of the most popular clauses in the FIDIC 1999 rainbow suite of contracts is the time bar provision in sub-clause 20.1, precluding the Contractor from entitlement to cost or time if a notice of claim is not served after 28 days from the time when the Contractor knew, or should have known, of the event giving rise to the claim. A common view among legal practitioners is that, under Egyptian Law,[118] agreeing to limit the period during which compensation could be claimed may be characterised as a limitation of liability clause. Limitation of liability clauses are permissible as per Article 217 of the *ECC*. This seems to be the correct characterisation of the issue; however, other practitioners seem to characterise the issue as an agreement to amend the statutory limitation period of the claim. This latter view is not shared by the authors, though it is not uncommon in the MENA region to try and argue that time bar clauses are unenforceable because they conflict with the mandatory limitation periods in the law. This position emanates from Article 388 of the *ECC*, which states:

> It is neither permissible to waive the right [to invoke] the statutory limitations before acquiring same, **nor to agree on a limitation period other than that fixed by law**. (emphasis added)

In clarifying the rationale, the Egyptian Court of Cassation provides that 'it is impermissible to leave the issue of deciding the durations of limitation periods to individuals' wills and thus the legislator has prohibited <u>every</u> consensual amendment to the duration

115 Court of Appeal, Challenge No. 87 for JY 133, hearing session dated 8 March 2017.

116 S Al-Tammawy, *Principles of Administrative Law* (Dar Alfikr Alaraby, 2007) 955.

117 A Al-Boushy, 'Methods of Concluding Administrative Contracts in Compliance With the Provisions of Law No. 182 of 2018 Governing Contracts Concluded by Public Authorities' (2021) 2(1) *The IJARLG* 58 https://ijarlg.journals.ekb.eg/article_200556_6c45e521878da2578a765524de3f7b01.pdf (accessed on 22 June 2022).

118 This view applies to most MENA Arab countries as well, as the majority of these countries contain similar provisions in their respective laws.

of limitation periods as fixed by the law'.[119] Relying on Article 388 of the *ECC*, some practitioners are of the view that the FIDIC time bar is a 'limitation period other than that fixed by law' because the sub-clause may extinguish the Contractor's right to claim if the 28-day notice period is not complied with. It is therefore beneficial to demonstrate some of the literature produced on this topic prior to analysing the matter from a legal perspective.

Sakr[120] discusses turnkey contracting under the ICC Model Turnkey Contract for Major Projects (the Model Contract) and examines provisions in the Model Contract that may be rendered invalid or unenforceable in the Arab legal systems. He refers to Article 388 of the *ECC* and, in respect of the 28-day notice period in sub-clause 20.1 of the FIDIC 1999 contract, states:

> the limitations contained in this clause should be held invalid under the laws of the Arab countries, because they modify the period of limitation provided for in the laws of those countries. This solution seems to prevail under the laws of Egypt (which is the main source of inspiration of the law of the GCC countries).

Sakr's rationale for this is not explained in the article but it can be deduced that sub-clause 20.1 may be interpreted to have reduced the limitation period of contractual liability as fixed by the law from 15 years (in civil matters) or seven years (in commercial matters) to only 28 days. Therefore, by the plain words of Article 388, such 'reduction' may be considered null and void.

The year following the publication of Sakr's article, in the FIDIC Middle East Contract Users' Conference in Abu Dhabi, El Haggan[121] made a presentation on time limitations in the FIDIC Yellow Book and made reference to the two principles in the Arab *Civil Codes* mentioned by Sakr, namely the *Civil Code* limitations and the preclusion periods. As in Sakr's article, El Haggan states that the *Civil Code* limitation periods cannot be modified by contracting parties as a matter of public policy, while preclusion periods may be modified. He mentions that some commentators conclude that the time bar in sub-clause 20.1 of the FIDIC 1999 Red Book is considered invalid due to the notion that it violates the *Civil Code* limitation period within the Arab countries and expresses his disagreement. He clarifies that the *Civil Code* limitation is not a matter of public policy and that sub-clause 20.1 does not attempt to reduce the *Civil Code* limitation period. Rather, he clarifies, the time bar under sub-clause 20.1 can be categorised as a preclusion period and, therefore, is enforceable under the Arab *Civil Codes*. He concludes the section of his presentation on time limitations with the observation that many arbitrators choose to ignore the agreement of the parties and hold the time bar unenforceable, thereby creating a dangerous precedent due to the parties' uncertainty in evaluating their position when referring disputes to arbitration.

On the assumption that the time bar is a condition precedent or an agreed preclusion period, an Employer ought not to be surprised with a finding against it despite the Contractor's non-compliance with the express notice requirement in light of the prevailing contractual and legal considerations. Similarly, a Contractor may choose to not refer

119 Cassation Challenge No. 524 for 35 JY, dated 3 February 1970.

120 M Sakr, 'Turnkey Contracting under the ICC Model Contract for Major Projects: A Middle Eastern Law Perspective' (2009) 26 *The International Construction Law Review* 146–160.

121 S El-Haggan, 'FIDIC Yellow Book: 1. Fitness for Purpose 2. Time Limits 3. Unforeseeable physical conditions', in *FIDIC and IBC Legal. The FIDIC Middle East Contract Users' Conference* (Abu Dhabi, 24–25 February 2010).

certain disputes to arbitration in light of the assumption that its entitlement has been time-barred by the express provisions in sub-clause 20.1 only to find that, in similar cases, arbitrators considered that the express time bar provision has been overridden and evaluated the submitted disputes in light of the facts, circumstances and governing legal principles in the specific case.

In the FIDIC Middle East Contract Users Conference of 2016, Attia and Joshi[122] argued that the FIDIC time bar is unenforceable under UAE law due to its conflict with the mandatory limitation periods under the law. Attia states there are two possible defences for a Contractor against the time bar in the FIDIC contract. One of these defences is a jurisdictional defence, taking into account that the statutory time bars under Article 487.1 of the *UAE Civil Code* are mandatory and that the ten-year time limit in the code shall apply to (commercial) construction contracts. The equivalent to the ten-year period in the *UAE Civil Code* is Article 388 of the *ECC*. Attia clarified in his presentation that the FIDIC time bar will not be upheld under UAE law and that, according to his experience, there were two instances where arbitration proceedings upheld the statutory provisions against the FIDIC time bar in sub-clause 20.1.

The following year at the same conference, Witt[123] took a different viewpoint and clarified that:

> There is a substantive difference between a contractual provision which seeks to prevent the Contractor from commencing any proceeding before the expiry of a statutory limitation period (which clearly offends the code provisions), and a contractual provision which does not seek to bar any such proceeding being commenced, but provides that there shall be no entitlement to an EOT or further remuneration (see Sub-Clause 20.1) or similar relief in any such proceeding.

This topic was given centre attention in the doctoral research that compared the Egyptian and English legal jurisdictions in terms of the enforceability of time bar clauses. On the matter of the FIDIC time bar clause being considered a limitation period under the *ECC*, El Nemr (2017)[124] offers two viewpoints: first, although there are two types of time limitations under the *ECC* that may bar a right of action (namely, prescription/limitation periods and preclusion periods), the FIDIC time bar clause can be considered to be in conflict with both and therefore, pursuant to *ECC* Article 388, can be unenforceable. Second, there is the viewpoint (which is endorsed by the research) that the FIDIC time bar is enforceable under Egyptian law because it is a contractual agreement pertaining to a waiver of right or a limitation of liability that does not prevent either contracting party from commencing legal action within the limitation periods set in the law.

Abdel Wahab, El-adawy, Fawzy and Hamed[125] address the application of FIDIC in civil law jurisdictions, focusing on Egyptian civil law as the prime example of civil law jurisdictions. In terms of the enforceability of time bar clauses in Egypt, they opine that the

122 F Attia and C Joshi, 'Practical techniques for dealing with modified contracts', in *FIDIC and IBC Lega:. The FIDIC Middle East Contract Users' Conference* (Dubai, 16–17 February 2016).

123 J Witt, 'Time bars and their enforceability in Arab Middle East Civil Code Jurisdictions', in *FIDIC and KNect365 FIDIC Middle East Contract Users' Conference* (Abu Dhabi, 14–15 February 2017).

124 W El Nemr, 'The Enforceability of Time Bar Clauses in Construction Contracts: A Comparative Analysis between the Egyptian Civil Code and the English and Welsh Common Law Jurisdictions' (2017) PhD thesis, University of Salford, School of Built Environment.

125 S Fawzy, T Hamed, M Abdel Wahab and I El-adawy, 'Practicing FIDIC in Civil Law Jurisdictions – Application of Time and Additional Payment Provisions' (1st ed, Lambert Academic Publishing, 2018).

FIDIC time bar is enforceable, as it does not contradict a mandatory provision in the law. They cite examples in the *ECC* to conclude that Egyptian law acknowledges and enforces contracting parties' agreement that a right would be waived if a party does not provide a notice within a certain period. They suggest that, in order for damages to be compensable under Egyptian law, a notice must be served pursuant to *ECC* Article 216. They mention, however, that there are legal principles in Egyptian civil law, which may counter the enforceability of time bar clauses, including good faith, abuse of a right, unjust enrichment and estoppel. Thus, it can be reasonably deduced – by their reference that time bar clauses do not conflict with 'a mandatory provision in the law' – that the argument that *ECC* Article 388 cannot be reconciled with the FIDIC time bar clause is untenable and should be excluded.[126]

Therefore, in the authors' view, no Special Provision in the Particular Conditions is required in relation to the time-bar provisions.

5.5.1.2 Excess quantities in a remeasured contract affecting the Contract Price

It is commonly known in the construction industry that a remeasured or unit price contract is one in which the Contractor is paid for the actual quantities of work executed. The quantities in the bills of quantities (BOQ) are approximate and do not reflect the actual quantities to complete the work. Therefore, if the designer underestimates the quantities, or produces an erroneous design that results in quantities significantly exceeding those in the BOQ, thereby increasing the Contract Price, it is generally accepted that the Contractor would be compensated according to the actual quantities executed. This is reflected in the FIDIC 1999 Red Book in sub-clause 12.2 (Method of Measurement), which states:

> Except as otherwise stated in the Contract and notwithstanding local practice: (a) measurement shall be made of the net actual quantity of each item of the Permanent Works.

As straightforward as this internationally accepted principle seems, Egyptian law tackles the situation differently. *ECC* Article 657 states the following regarding remeasured contracts:

1. When a contract is concluded in accordance with an estimate drawn up on a unit price basis and it becomes apparent, during the course of the work, that it will be necessary, in order to complete the works according to the agreed design, to considerably exceed the estimated price, the contractor is bound to notify the employer thereof forthwith and to inform him/her of the anticipated value of the increase in price; if he/she fails to do so he/she forfeits his/her right to recover the expenses incurred in excess of the estimate.
2. When the estimated excess in the price for the execution of the design is considerable, the employer may rescind the contract and stop performance, provided that he/she does so without delay and pays the contractor the value of the works done by him/her, estimated in accordance with the terms of the contract, without being liable to compensate the contractor for the profit he would have realized had he/she completed the works.

126 *Ibid.*

The conflict between the FIDIC contract and Egyptian law here lies in the responsibility being thrust on the Contractor to immediately notify the Employer if the Contract Price is anticipated to significantly increase due to an underestimate by the designer of the quantities in the BOQ. There is no such requirement under the FIDIC contract. The Contractor's responsibility for design-related matters is limited to the extent of the Contractor's design scope. This is reflected in sub-clause 4.1 (Contractor's General Obligations), which states:

> If the Contract specifies that the Contractor shall design any part of the Permanent Works, then unless otherwise stated in the Particular Conditions:
>
> [...]
>
> (c) the Contractor shall be responsible for this part and it shall, when the Works are completed, be fit for such purposes for which the part is intended as are specified in the Contract.

A reading of sub-clauses 4.1 and 12.2 therefore can result in the understanding that, since the Contractor is not responsible for design and since the excess quantities in the BOQ were not attributable to the Contractor, the Contractor would in any case, and in particular due to the nature of a remeasured contract, be entitled to be paid this excess amount without an obligation to notify the Engineer or Employer of this excess quantities' impact on the Contract Price. An argument can be made, however, that the 2017 Second Edition of the FIDIC Red Book imposes an obligation on the Contractor to notify the Engineer of any probable increase in the quantities, which can result in a notable increase in the Contract Price. This is through the newly introduced sub-clause 8.4 ([*Advance Warning*]), which states:

> Each Party shall advise the other and the Engineer, and the Engineer shall advise the Parties, in advance of any known or probable future events or circumstances which may:
>
> [...]
>
> (c) increase the Contract Price.

In this case, the obligation is not put squarely on the Contractor, as in the case of Egyptian law, but rather, the obligation extends equally to the Employer and Engineer, if any of them is aware of any event or circumstance that may affect the Contract Price. Hence, if prior to commencing a construction tendering process, the Employer is aware that there are faults in the design that may result in the BOQ being inaccurate, it can be argued that the Employer or Engineer is obligated to notify the Contractor accordingly or, as a minimum, the Contractor would not be held responsible to provide an advance warning due to the Employer and/or Engineer's prior knowledge and awareness.

It must be noted that, while the plain words of *ECC* Article 657 may appear harsh and contradictory to FIDIC and to the internationally accepted norms of the definition of a remeasured contract, there is case law[127] that suggests that there is no need for a notice if the Employer knew or foresaw the increase in quantities. The court's ruling included the following rationale:

127 Cassation Challenge No. 1164 for 48 JY, dated 12 March 1984.

> the rationale of the legislator in respect of the notice is to not surprise the employer of an increase in the determined BOQ that the employer did not expect and did not take into account. As such, if he/she knew about the said increase or expected it at the time of contract conclusion, there would be no need to serve the said notification ... In light of the contract dated 28/3/1966 ... and the parties' agreement that the quantities (in the BOQ) are subject to increase, decrease or omission, this demonstrates that the employer expected an increase in the quantities in the BOQ during construction ... therefore if the appellant requires the notice from the appellee as a condition to the entitlement of the excess quantities, then the appellant has erred in the application of the law and its interpretation.

Notwithstanding this ruling, the plain words of the law – and even the words of the ruling – can give the impression that the notice is not required so as to not surprise the Employer with something the Employer had not taken into account. So, if an Employer is aware that the Contract Price may increase (say, to 5% of the Contract Price) due to its remeasured nature and possibly due to imperfections in the design, but the Employer did not expect a *significant* increase (say, 30%), it can be argued from the letter of the law and this case that *ECC* Article 657 stands. The Contractor, in that case, can still be under an obligation to notify of the significant quantity increase although in a typical remeasured contract the Contractor is always entitled to the excess quantities, regardless of the increase.

In his doctoral research that compares risk provisions in the *ECC* and in the FIDIC 1987 Red Book, Hamed,[128] comments on *ECC* Article 657 and categorises an increase in the Contract Price into four categories: (a) change in the design due to a defect therein, (b) increase in the scope of work or in the contracted quantities due to inaccuracies within the BOQ, (c) increase in the scope of work or in the contracted quantities due to a Contractor's default and (d) change in the design due to unforeseen and unavoidable physical conditions. Recognising that these four categories are encompassed in the wording of *ECC* Article 657, he advocates that the provisions of the article be implemented for factors that are within the Contractor's control, such as that of a defective design (factor a) or a change in the design (factor d). Hamed does not recommend that the natural increase in quantities in the BOQ due to a design defect (factor b) would be considered in the implementation of *ECC* Article 657.

In his research about the enforceability of time bar clauses in Egypt in comparison to that in England and Wales and using the FIDIC 1999 Red Book as the key time bar clause example, El Nemr (2017)[129] sheds light on *ECC* Article 657 as an example of a time bar provision within the Egyptian law, which supports the argument that time bar clauses are in general enforceable under Egyptian law. On the matter of the article and its relation to the nature of a remeasured contract, El Nemr refers to the Court of Cassation case highlighted earlier to suggest that the court's reasoning deviates from the industry understanding of a remeasured contract because it does not distinguish between an Employer's expectation of a normal increase in the quantities and an unanticipated substantial increase. He further refers to the work of Professor Al Sanhoury, the key drafter

128 TH Hamed, *Ahkam al makhater fi 'oqood muqawalat al bina' wal tashyeed: dirasa muqarana bayn al qanoon al madani al misry wa shoroot 'aqd al FIDIC [Risk Provisions in Building and Construction Contracts, A Comparative Study between the Egyptian Civil Code and the FIDIC Conditions of Contract]* (2011) PhD thesis, Cairo University, Giza.

129 W El Nemr, 'The Enforceability of Time Bar Clauses in Construction Contracts: A Comparative Analysis between the Egyptian Civil Code and the English and Welsh Common Law Jurisdictions' (2017) PhD thesis, University of Salford, School of Built Environment.

of the *ECC*, to suggest that the nature of a remeasured contract was well understood while the *ECC* was under preparation and that such understanding entails that a mere expectation that there can be an increase in the Contract Price cannot be equated to an expectation of a substantial increase.

In respect of the question as to whether any Special Provision is recommended to align the FIDIC contract with the *ECC*, it is suggested that the FIDIC contract is not the one that needs alignment. Rather, the authors agree with Hamed that it is the *ECC* provision (Article 657) that needs to be adjusted so that it is aligned with the construction industry norms. The topic of the adjustments necessary to align the *ECC* with FIDIC in respect of remeasured construction contracts is extensive and falls outside the scope of this chapter. In any event, and until the *ECC* provision is amended, it may be prudent for the parties to a remeasured contract to include an express contractual provision in their Special Conditions to define what constitutes 'normal' and 'substantial' increases and what their ramifications are for the parties' contract.

5.5.1.3 Quantities exceeding 25% in administrative contracts

A related topic to the previous is that of quantities exceeding 25% in administrative contracts. The FIDIC 1999 Red Book does not contain a ceiling for quantities in any item in the BOQ. However, the contract does contain four factors that, if achieved for any item in the BOQ, can result in the contracting parties negotiating a new rate for that specific BOQ item. These factors are listed in sub-clause 12.3 of the FIDIC 1999 Red Book as follows:

a) The measured quantity of the item is changed by more than 10% from the quantity of this item in the BOQ.
b) This change in quantity multiplied by its rate exceeds 0.01% of the Contract Price at award (the Accepted Contract Amount).
c) This change in quantity changes the cost per unit quantity of this item by more than 1%.
d) This item is not specified in the Contract as a 'fixed rate item'.

There is a common misconception in Egypt that FIDIC contracts contain a provision that quantities for any item in the BOQ cannot exceed 25%. This misconception, however, stems from the administrative law governing public contracts, not from FIDIC. It is therefore beneficial to shed light on such provision from the latest administrative law, namely *Law 182 for the year 2018* (*Law 182*). The law consists of the base provisions and the *Executive Regulations*, which expand on the base provisions. The pertinent references in *Law 182* regarding the 25% ceiling are the following:

> Article 46 of the *Law 182* Base Provisions:
> If, after entry into the contract, circumstances arose that necessitated the adjustment of the contracted volume, the administrative authority may adjust its contracts with an increase or a decrease so as to not exceed 25% of the quantities of each item in construction contracts, and so as to not exceed 15% of the quantities of each item in the other contracts of the same conditions, specifications and prices, provided that the tender documents include such a provision.
>
> It is mandatory for the adjustment of the contract to take place that approval by the relevant authority or council of ministers be obtained, as the case may be, the availability of the necessary financial approvals, the change is issued throughout the contract duration, the priority of the contractor's tender is not affected and that the original contract duration is adjusted if necessary in accordance with the extent of the increase or decrease.

Article 96 of the *Executive Regulations*:
[...] If during execution circumstances arose that necessitated the adjustment of the contract, an adjustment shall be made so to not exceed 25% of the quantities of each item in construction contracts, and so as to not exceed 15% of the quantities of each item in the other contracts [of the same conditions, specifications and prices,] provided that the tender documents include such a provision and that the appropriate duration or time schedule is adjusted as the case may be regarding the supply or execution and in accordance with the extent of the adjustment, subject that the contracting department shall take into account the following:

1. The existence of a necessity and supporting reasons for such adjustments;
2. The obtainment of approval from the relevant authority or from the council of ministers – as the case may be – on the adjustment;
3. The adjustments are on the items of the original contract at the same conditions, specifications and contracted prices;
4. Preparation of an amendment to the contract, incorporating these adjustments;
5. Obtaining permission from the finance unit for the item adjustment
6. The adjustment must be within the contract duration and must not be within the defects notification period.
7. The adjustment must not affect the contractor's ranking in the tender

The contracting department must record these adjustments and supporting documentation and preserve these documents in the project file. The final contract price shall be subsequently published on the public contracting gateway.
An examination of the above provisions in respect of FIDIC and Egyptian administrative law demonstrates that there is simplicity in approach under the FIDIC contract when certain factors combined (including an increase in the quantity of a BOQ item) are satisfied. Simply, according to FIDIC, a new rate for that item can be negotiated between the contracting parties. However, the situation is different and more complex under Egyptian law. This merits a few observations as set out next.

1. There seems to be an element of uncertainty in the opening provisions of the law, whether in the base provision or in the *Executive Regulation*. The triggering event is when there is an increase or decrease in the *contract*, however, the 25% limitation applies to the quantities of a *BOQ item*. Due to the novelty of the *Egyptian Tenders and Auctions Law of 2018*, there is no established judicial trend on this issue. The question thus remains whether judgments rendered under the old *Egyptian Tenders and Auctions Law No. 89 for 1998* can be of assistance in this respect. Nevertheless, it should be noted that the wording of *Law 89* and that of *Law 182* are different, so judgments rendered under the old law ought to be approached with great caution and may not necessarily guide the interpretation of the provisions of *Law 182*. That said, it should be noted that 'Contract Price' and 'BOQ item quantities' are two separate matters. For example, it is very possible, and not uncommon, that the actual earthworks quantities exceed those in the BOQ by 50% without affecting the Contract Price.
2. There seem to be logistical complications in the application of *Law 182* that are not proportional to the all too frequent situation of an increase in an item in the BOQ by more than 25%. The law refers to entry by the parties into a contract amendment, to required permissions by government authorities, to possible

extensions of time and to there being compelling justifications for the adjustment, among others. From a practical standpoint, if the quantities of a wall plastering item in the BOQ increase by 75%, would such an event warrant an amendment? Would it warrant a time extension? Would it really need approval from a government authority to proceed? It can be reasonable to assume that such measures can be applicable if the Contract Price as a whole exceeds a certain percentage. That would align with *ECC* Article 657 discussed earlier. However, the plain words of the law reflect an impracticality of application, as a literal application would entail the entry into tens, and possibly hundreds of amendments (including time extensions), for every quantity increase beyond the 25% limit.

3. *Law 182* explicitly states that its provisions apply only to items that are present in the BOQ, which begs the question: what about items that are not in the BOQ, but which are deemed necessary by a Variation? This observation can result in the 25% limit not being applicable to such items. The significance here is that work items not listed in the BOQ but that are necessary for the execution of the work are very common on all projects. The FIDIC 1999 Red Book addresses this matter in sub-clause 12.3 as follows:

> For each item of work, the appropriate rate or price for the item shall be the rate or price specified for such item in the Contract or, if there is no such item, specified for similar work. However, a new rate or price shall be appropriate for an item of work if … [the four factors listed above are listed herein] … Each new rate or price shall be derived from any relevant rates or prices in the Contract, with reasonable adjustments to take account of the matters described in sub-paragraph (a) and/or (b), as applicable. If no rates or prices are relevant for the derivation of a new rate or price, it shall be derived from the reasonable Cost of executing the work, together with reasonable profit, taking account of any other relevant matters.

The most probable interpretation in light of *Law 182*'s silence on items of work that are not in the BOQ is that they could be treated as those items that exceed 25% (i.e. a new contract will have to be agreed with the other party regarding those items).[130] However, this is not expressly stated in *Law 182*, so other interpretations are possible. That said, another possible interpretation is that there is no limit to excess quantities regarding these items. Such an interpretation would accord with the FIDIC 1999 Red Book, as there is no limitation in the FIDIC contracts based solely on the quantities increase of a BOQ item. However, the FIDIC contract is clear regarding the processing of a new BOQ item, as it would be first compared to any similar item in the BOQ and, if there are no similar items, the new item would be calculated by calculating the cost of the item then adding the overheads and profit (overheads being included under the Cost definition in FIDIC). *Law 182* does not offer much guidance and greater detail regarding items of work not in the BOQ (contrary to its predecessor, *Law 89*).

4. Another notable distinction between the FIDIC contract and *Law 182* in terms of the excess quantities limit is the condition in the law that the priority of the Contractor's ranking in the tender process must be maintained. This is a notable

130 See Administrative Challenge No. 3828 for 54 JY (23 January 2018), where it was held, under the old *Tenders and Auctions Law No. 89/1998*, that amounts exceeding 25% are subject to the parties' agreement on a new contract.

factor, as it begs the question as to what would be the consequence if, due to unforeseeable Variations and quantity increases, the Contractor's ranking did change? Under the old *Law 89*, the prevailing judicial trend was to subtract from the value of the additional works the amounts exceeding the value that would otherwise not maintain the ranking of the Contractor in the tendering process.[131] Nonetheless, there is a notable lack of clarity regarding the matter of priority of tenders in the law, which is beyond the scope of this chapter. Suffice it to conclude that there is no such limitation in the FIDIC contract. After a contract is awarded, there is no consequence to any increase in the BOQ quantities, unless such an increase is coupled with the fulfilment of the three remaining factors, which in turn leads to the negotiation of a new rate for that item.

In conclusion on this point, the key distinction between the FIDIC 1999 Red Book and *Law 182* in terms of the limit to quantity increases is that, in the former, there is no clear consequence to any significant increase in quantities. The only consequence mentioned is the negotiation of the new rate, although that would not depend on the item quantity increase alone. In the latter, a limit of 25% is placed on the quantities of any BOQ item but numerous conflicting information, impracticalities and questions arise, which leads to uncertainty. It is noteworthy to conclude that, since *Law 182* is fairly recent, there is no sufficient body of judgments available to ascertain any notable judicial trend to deal with this uncertainty. It may be the case that administrative courts will continue to draw parallels and inferences from the old *Law 89*, but as mentioned earlier, courts need to be cautious given the clearly different wording in both laws.

See section 5.6.3 for suggested Special Provisions to align the FIDIC contract with *Law 182*.

5.5.1.4 Liquidated damages

Sub-clause 8.7 of the FIDIC 1999 Red Book addresses the situation when liquidated damages would be applied by an Employer on a Contractor. The sub-clause starts:

> If the Contractor fails to comply with Sub-Clause 8.2 [Time for Completion], the Contractor shall subject to Sub-Clause 2.5 [Employer's Claims] pay delay damages to the Employer for this default.

It is apparent from this sub-clause's opening statement that the ultimate cause for applying liquidated damages is the Contractor's non-achievement of the contract completion date. There is a condition on the Employer to apply damages, which is the compliance of the Employer claims procedure in sub-clause 2.5, which in turn requires a notice and supporting details. The sub-clause also states that:

> These delay damages shall be the only damages due from the Contractor for such default, other than in the event of termination under Sub-Clause 15.2 [Termination by Employer] prior to completion of the Works.

There are significant contrasts between FIDIC and Egyptian law in respect of the application of liquidated damages. These are elaborated upon briefly after highlighting the below provisions from the Egyptian law, both civil code and administrative:

131 Administrative Challenge No. 18724 for 51 JY (26 January 2010).

ECC Article 216

The judge may reduce the amount of damages or may refuse to award any damages if the creditor, by his/her own fault, has contributed to the cause of, or increased, the loss.

ECC Article 218

Damages, subject to an agreement to the contrary, are not due unless the debtor has been served.

ECC Article 224

1. Damages fixed by agreement are not due, if the debtor establishes that the creditor has not suffered any loss.
2. The judge may reduce the amount of these damages, if the debtor establishes that the amount fixed was grossly exaggerated or that the principal obligation has been partially performed.

Any agreement contrary to the provisions of the two preceding paragraphs is void.

Law 182 Article 48

[...] Application by the administrative authority of liquidated damages on the contractor because of delay shall not prejudice the authority's right to recover from the contractor all damages borne by the authority due to the delay.

Several contrasts and similarities between the FIDIC contract, the *ECC*, and *Law 182* become apparent, namely:

1. If the Contractor delays the contract completion date but proves that the Employer has not suffered any loss, liquidated damages should not be applied.
2. In terms of procedure, a Contractor should (as a general rule) be notified by the Employer. This represents a commonality between FIDIC and Egyptian law, since in both the Contractor must be notified that damages will be applied. The Egyptian law on this point allows the parties to agree otherwise. Thus, the procedures for Employer's claims under sub-clause 2.5 would be applicable.
3. If the Contractor can prove that the amount of damages is grossly exaggerated, then the liquidated damages can be reduced by the judge or arbitrator. No such provision is present in the FIDIC contracts, although it is generally established in common law jurisdictions that the liquidated damages in the contract should be a genuine estimate of the damages the Employer is expected to bear.
4. If the Contractor had completed a portion of the Works at the time the liquidated damages are applied, then the value of these works should be removed from the amount on which the liquidated damages are applied.
5. If the Employer contributed to the delay, then that shall be taken into account by the judge and the liquidated damages shall be reduced by the Employer's contribution.
6. In administrative contracts, if the actual loss suffered exceeded the liquidated damages amount in the contract, the administrative authority would still be entitled to full reparation for the losses sustained. This is another difference between FIDIC and the administrative law position enshrined in *Law 182*. While the FIDIC's principle is that 'These delay damages shall be the only damages due from the Contractor for such default', Article 48 of *Law 182* expressly provides,

in pertinent part, that 'payment of the penalty for delay shall not prejudice the administrative authority's right to seek full compensation for all the harm resulting from the delay'.

An examination of the above points demonstrates that, while there are points of commonality between FIDIC and Egyptian law, there are notable differences. Although not explicitly mentioned in sub-clause 8.7, the concepts of the liquidated damages being a genuine estimate of the damage and the concept of concurrent delay resulting in an adverse effect on the liability and quantum of damages, are among the common principles. Similarly, procedural matters such as the Contractor being notified prior to the application of the damages are another commonality.[132]

However, a notable difference is that under Egyptian law, even though the Contractor may be in delay, the Employer's ability to apply liquidated damages is contingent upon the existence of a legal presumption that the Employer suffered loss; hence, if the Contractor was able to refute the said presumption in part or in whole, the Employer may be entitled to less or no liquidated damages.[133] This principle under the *ECC* may not be easily reconciled with the concept of delay *penalties*, which are agreed-upon damages at the time of signing the Contract that are due to the Employer by the mere fact of the Contractor's delay. The concept of delay penalties finds application in Egyptian administrative law cases but is prohibited under the FIDIC 1987 contract.[134]

Additionally, in Egyptian administrative contracts governed by Egyptian law, the amount of damages recovered from the Contractor may generally exceed the liquidated damages in the contract as already expressed in Article 48 of *Law 182*. This is not entirely consistent with FIDIC, which mandates that (as a general rule, though subject to some exceptions) the liquidated damages are the Employer's sole remedy for the delay of a project. Nonetheless, similar to the FIDIC, in private contracts under the *ECC*, liquidated damages work as a limitation of liability clause. For instance, an employer cannot claim damages for delay in excess of the amount stipulated in a liquidated damages clause unless gross fault or fraud is established and attributed to the Contractor.[135]

See section 5.6.4 for suggested Special Provisions to align the FIDIC contract with *Law 182* for public contracts. No Special Provision is required for consistency with the *ECC* for private contracts.

5.5.1.5 Engineer's Determination

In respect of the Engineer's determination, it can be concluded that the procedure under the 1999 editions does not seem to be inconsistent or in conflict with Egyptian law. However, the neutral role the Engineer plays in the 2017 editions in determining a Claim is questionable in the Egyptian construction industry, from a practical and sometimes legal standpoint. Sub-clause 20.2 of the FIDIC 2017 Red Book details the Claims procedure that would be applied by the Contractor and Employer. It is observed that the Parties are

132 E.g. Cassation Challenge No. 6363 of JY 88, hearing session dated 19 January 2019 and Cassation Challenge No. 7359 of JY 63, hearing session dated 30 May 2002.

133 E.g. Cassation Challenge No. 5302 of JY 86, hearing session dated 27 February 2018, Cassation Challenge No. 11215 of JY 75, hearing session dated 3 November 2014 and *Article 224/1 of the ECC*.

134 Cassation Challenge No. 34642 for 59 JY. Dated 28 July 2020; Cassation Challenge No. 253 for 29 JY. Dated 6 February 1964.

135 Article 225 of the *ECC*.

equally obligated to provide the required Notices and detailed particulars to the Engineer. Instead of addressing the Parties as 'Contractor' and 'Employer' in the 1999 edition, with the Contractor's claims procedures set out in sub-clause 20.1 and the Employer's claim procedures set out in sub-clause 2.5, the only references in sub-clause 20.2 of the 2017 editions is 'the claiming Party' and 'the other party'. This, in turn, places on the Employer the burden of having a contracts/claims department to handle the role that the Engineer used to handle in the 1999 edition. Alternatively, the Employer can hire a claims consultant to take on the role of preparing the Employer's claims. Hence, the Employer would in effect be employing the Engineer and a claims consultant to properly accomplish the Claims administration tasks in sub-clause 20.2. It is suggested that this claims procedure is not aligned with current practices in Egypt, where Employers always prefer to avoid incurring an additional financial burden. It is the authors' opinion from their experience in the Egyptian construction industry that, hitherto, most Employers prefer the setup in the 1987 edition, where the Engineer acts as the quasi-adjudicator and there is no Dispute Board in place.

5.5.2 FIDIC General Conditions are incompatible or inconsistent with the law of the Site/Country

In private international law, contracts related to an immovable property are generally governed by the law of the place in which the immovable property is situated. Being a contract that is most likely related to an immovable, Egyptian law would impose itself as the governing law if the construction project is situated in Egypt.[136] However, given that this conflict of law rule is a procedural rule under Egyptian law, its application is conditional upon Egyptian law being the applicable law procedurally as well. This could be Egyptian law if Egypt is the seat of arbitration, the place where enforcement is sought, or if Egyptian law is the applicable procedural law by the parties' agreement.

As such, Egyptian law would normally govern construction contracts concerning immovable properties if the project is taking place in Egypt. Hence, given that the project is in Egypt and the construction contract is related to an immovable, it is not possible for contracting parties to agree on a governing law that is different from Egyptian law. Accordingly, the conflicts and inconsistencies between the FIDIC 1999 contract and Egyptian law that were highlighted in the previous section are applicable to this section.

However, despite the mandated applicability of Egyptian law in the said specific scenario, the parties' agreement as to any FIDIC 1999 issue, which the parties could derogate from by way of agreement, would still prevail over Egyptian non-mandatory laws. In other words, party autonomy remains sacred under Egyptian law; all that is prohibited is agreeing to a different governing law when the contract is related to an immovable property situated in Egypt. Only where the FIDIC 1999 contract that is related to an immovable property is silent on a certain issue would Egyptian law govern the issue, irrespective of whether it was a mandatory or a non-mandatory rule.

136 *Article 19 of the ECC.*

5.5.3 FIDIC General Conditions are incompatible or inconsistent with the relevant laws on dispute determination in Egypt

Dispute determination under the FIDIC contracts (1999 and 2017) follows several steps. The first is a determination by the Engineer,[137] followed by a decision by the Dispute Adjudication Board (DAB)/Dispute Avoidance/Adjudication Board (DAAB),[138] followed by amicable settlement, then arbitration.[139] The first three are creatures of the contract, hence the following legal principle under Egyptian law applies:

> *ECC* Article 147
> The contract makes the law of the parties. It can be revoked or altered only by mutual consent of the parties or for reasons provided for by law.

In respect of Dispute Boards, the extent to which a Dispute Board's decision is binding and enforceable either on its own or before a court or a tribunal is questionable due to the lack of Egyptian court decisions on the issue. This is the case despite the legal maxim mentioned earlier about the contract forming the law of the parties, and despite the contracting parties' agreement in the FIDIC contract that the decision of a Dispute Board is binding in case a notice of dissatisfaction (NOD) is issued within the specified time frame, and that the decision is final and binding if the NOD is not issued within the specified timeframe.

At face value, this may seem contradictory, since the law supports freedom of contract, yet questions the bindingness or enforceability of a decision rendered by a contractually formed Dispute Board. However, this is only a façade contradiction because, lexically, there is a distinction between the consequences of a contract (which is generating an obligation), the consequences of an obligation (which is the commitment to perform it),[140] and the consequences of resolving a dispute (which differs based on whether the party seeking performance may be granted an *exequatur* or not). In this respect, when an obligation is in dispute, the law does not grant any dispute resolution method (whether contractually agreed or even legally imposed) the ability to be enforceable or, in other words, be granted an ***exequatur*** (i.e. the ability to enforce an obligation through state authorities). In other words, for a decision to be enforceable, it must be a decision that may be granted an *exequatur*. Therefore, unless confirmed by a decision of a tribunal or a court, whose decisions may be granted an *exequatur*, a binding obligation does not *ipso facto* mean that a party has the right in enforceability even if an agreed method of dispute resolution (other than arbitration or litigation) decides in that party's favour.

However, this does not undermine the binding nature of the parties' agreement to refer their dispute to Dispute Boards or the subsequent binding nature of the Dispute Board's decision upon the parties, irrespective of its enforceability, as per the parties' agreement and the facts of the case. All that remains is obtaining a decision/document, which the law may grant an *exequatur*. An arbitral award or a final court decision may usually be granted an *exequatur*. Nonetheless, the Dispute Board's decision will not acquire *res judicata* before an arbitral tribunal or a court, and therefore, the issue would still be up to the arbitral tribunal or the court to decide on the binding effect or persuasiveness of a Dispute

137 Sub-clause 3.5 in the FIDIC 1999 contracts, 3.7 in 2017.

138 Sub-clause 20.4 in the 1999 edition; sub-clause 21.4 in the 2017 edition (DAB is termed as DAAB – Dispute Avoidance/Adjudication Board).

139 Sub-clause 20.6 in the 1999 edition; sub-clause 21.6 in the 2017 edition.

140 A Al Sanhoury, *Al Wasit in the Explanation of the Civil Code*, Volume 2 (2010) 689.

Board's decision, which is a fact-sensitive issue that would largely depend on the parties' agreement, the applicable law and the arbitral tribunal's jurisdiction.

In respect of arbitration, the FIDIC contract, whether the 1999 or 2017 edition, does not conflict with the relevant Egyptian law, i.e. *Arbitration Law No. 27 for the year 1994*. The FIDIC wording leaves to the contracting parties' discretion the rules of arbitration they prefer but recommends the Rules of Arbitration of the International Chamber of Commerce. From the authors' experience, this sub-clause in the Egyptian construction industry is sometimes altered, for certain projects, in the Particular Conditions so that the applicable rules are those of the Cairo Regional Centre for International Commercial Arbitration (CRCICA).

5.6 What Special Provisions in the Particular Conditions are desirable for consistency with applicable laws in Egypt?

In light of the discussion under section 5.5.3, the following provisions in the Particular Conditions are desirable for consistency with the laws of Egypt.

5.6.1 The good faith provision

Both the *ECC* and *Law 182* require good faith in all contract matters.[141] Due to the vagueness as to what good faith actually entails, and due to the potential conflict this concept may have with the provisions of the FIDIC contract, it is desirable that the Particular Conditions are drafted to introduce an express obligation on the contracting parties to act in good faith. Although the FIDIC 1999 editions do not include any express provisions of good faith, it can be argued that the 2017 edition introduced a semi-good faith provision with the advance warning obligation being put on the Employer, Engineer and Contractor equally.[142] However, to make the FIDIC contract consistent with Egyptian law, it is suggested that there should be a clear obligation on the parties and the Engineer to act in good faith. It is also suggested that, in order to avoid ambiguity as much as possible, the principle of good faith should be defined or be expressed in examples, as is the case in FIDIC 2017 sub-clauses 8.5 (extensions of time), 13.1 (Variations) and 19.1 (exceptional circumstances).

5.6.2 Time bar clauses

As highlighted in section 5.5.3, the authors do not agree with the view that the FIDIC time bar clause contravenes the statutory limitation period. Therefore, it is opined that the FIDIC clauses do not need any adjustment in this regard. It is observed, however, that the FIDIC 2017 edition reduced the effect of the waiver of rights if a Claim notice is not issued within the stipulated 28-day period. Examples of such reduced effect include the validity of the Claim Notice if the Engineer fails to give notice within 14 days of receiving the late Claim Notice,[143] the leeway given to the claiming Party to provide justifications for the

141 Article 148 of the ECC *and* Article 170 of the *Law 182 of the Executive Regulations.*
142 Sub-clause 8.4.
143 Sub-clause 20.2.2.

Engineer's consideration as to why the Claim Notice is late,[144] and the leeway given to the claiming party to justify lateness of the contractual or legal basis for a fully detailed Claim for the Engineer's consideration.[145] Interestingly, in respect of consistency with Egyptian law, the FIDIC 2017 edition lists factors that the Engineer can consider to justify a late Claim Notice.[146] This reduced influence has been recently referred to as a possible 'civil law influence' on the FIDIC 2017 contract.[147]

5.6.3 Adjustment of quantities in public contracts

The FIDIC contracts, 1999 and 2017 editions, are inconsistent with *Law 182* in respect of the adjustment in quantities provision, as noted in section 5.5.1.3. Although the majority of these inconsistencies are in relation to impracticalities within the law (i.e. it is the law that needs to be corrected), there are amendments that can be made in the FIDIC contract so that the law and contract are aligned. For instance, sub-clause 12.3 can be amended in the Particular Conditions so that it refers to the 25% limit in *Law 182*, except that it would exclude the practical obstacles referred to in section 5.5.1.3 and include in clear terms the consequence of exceeding the limit (which is critically absent in the law, as discussed). In all cases, it is suggested that the concept of priority of tenders should be eliminated in its entirety from the law and the contract.

5.6.4 Liquidated damages

Several issues have been highlighted in section 5.5.3 in respect of liquidated damages in administrative contracts, which all would require to be addressed in the Particular Conditions, in order to make FIDIC and Egyptian law consistent in this topic. Significantly, the concept of liquidated damages being tied to whether the Employer suffered any loss and the concept of the agreed-upon ceiling of liquidated damages being adjusted (increased) to the actual harm borne by the government entity represent a real challenge in terms of amendments to the FIDIC form of contract.

5.7 Applicable legislation for Egyptian governing law of the contract

Given that Egyptian law is applicable to a construction contract in the scenarios clarified earlier (especially when the construction project is in Egypt),[148] some legislation will be of particular application as to the conclusion, performance, operation and termination of the contract as well as to the resolution of the disputes arising therefrom as clarified in the following.[149]

144 Sub-clause 20.2.2.

145 Sub-clause 20.2.4.

146 Sub-clause 20.2.5. It is suggested that these factors reflect the overriding obligation of good faith.

147 W El Nemr, 'The role of good faith as a challenge to the implementation of the claim procedures under the FIDIC Red Book 2017 edition in Egypt' (2018) 13 *Construction Law International* 16–21.

148 See section 6.4.

149 See section 5.8.

5.7.1 Applicable legislation as to contracts involving the administration

Most notably, if the administration or a public entity or enterprise is a party to the construction contract, some particular provisions (mainly the provisions of the *Tenders and Bids Law No. 182 of 2018* and the principles set by the Supreme Administrative Court) will find application together with the generally applicable *ECC* provisions governing contracts in general or the contracts of works specifically.

5.7.2 Procedural vs substantive issues and the governing law

It is also noted that the determination of whether an issue is procedural or substantive (e.g. presumptions and limitation periods) will impact the applicability of the provisions of the following identified Egyptian legislation[150] if it is not also the law governing the procedures.

5.7.3 Judicial decisions and general principles of law

The legislation applicable to a construction contract cannot be exclusively determined beforehand and might vary from one contract to another, and the matter shall be considered on a case-by-case basis. In addition, applicable legislation is not understood to exclusively govern a construction contract, but shall always be considered hand in hand with the applicable judicial decisions and general principles of law as elucidated by Egyptian judiciary and doctrine as clarified in the following.[151]

5.7.4 Impact of COVID-19 on the applicable legislation

Albeit not a legislative principle in its own right, events like the COVID-19 pandemic serve as a reminder that normal rules of legitimacy are bound to be interpreted and applied differently in exceptional circumstances. Some insights as to how COVID-19 would impact the application of Egyptian law were discussed earlier,[152] and others are discussed in the following.[153]

5.8 Summary of applicable legislation for Egyptian governing law of the contract

The general considerations clarified earlier shall be taken into account while considering the following.[154] In addition, the authors note that events such as the COVID-19 pandemic may as well have an impact on the operation of construction contracts if characterised as a *force majeure*, an exceptional circumstance or where special laws are issued specifically

150 See section 5.8.
151 See section 5.13.
152 See section 5.3.2.
153 See sections 5.8, 5.9 and 5.10.
154 See section 5.7.

to govern the operation of contracts (especially administrative contracts) in light of the pandemic as detailed earlier.[155]

5.8.1 Entry into a construction contract

Contracts generally	Articles 89–152 of the *ECC*
Constructioncontracts	Articles 646–667 of the *ECC* *Tenders and Bids Law No. 182 for 2018*

5.8.2 Operation of a construction contract

Force majeure	Articles 165 and 247 of the *ECC*
Hardship	Article 147 (2) of the *ECC*
Guarantees under forms of Security (Tender Security, Demand Guarantee, Surety Bond, Advance Payment Guarantee, Retention Money Guarantee, Payment Guarantee by Employer)	Articles 22, 40, 44 and 74 of the *Tenders and Bids Law No. 182 for 2018*

5.8.3 Termination of a construction contract

Frustration	Article 664 of the *ECC*
Bankruptcy, insolvency, liquidation	Article 666 of the *ECC* Article 50 of the *Tenders and Bids Law No. 182 for 2018*
5.8.4 Dispute resolution	
Limitation periods	Article 68 of the *Commercial Law* Articles 374–388 of the *ECC*
Liability	Article 176 of the *ECC*
Adjudication	*Egyptian Civil Procedures Law No. 13 for 1968 and State Council Law No. 47 for 1972*
Arbitration	Articles 71 and 87 of the *Egyptian Trade Law* *Egyptian Arbitration law No. 27 for 1994*

5.9 Applicable legislation if the Site/Country is in Egypt

It is worth noting that some temporary legislation might impact a construction contract in Egypt. For instance, due to the COVID-19 pandemic, the Egyptian legislator enacted some health and safety regulations;[156] these might have an impact (as long as they remain applicable) on the speed and efficiency of the construction and shall be taken into consideration.

155 See section 5.3.2; MS Abdel Wahab, 'Petroleum Concessions in Egypt: A Recipe for Disputes?' (2020) V7 *BCDR International Arbitration Review* 1, 73–108.

156 E.g. *Presidential Decrees No. 1165 for 2021, and. 3012 for 2021*, etc.

5.10 Summary of applicable legislation if the Site/Country is in Egypt

5.10.1 Operation of a construction contract

Registration and administration of professionals	*Egyptian Engineering Syndicate Law No. 66 for 1974*
Registration/licensing of Contractors and subcontractors	*Egyptian Federation for Construction and Building Contractors Law No. 104 for 1992*
Subcontractors	Article 56 of the *Executive Regulation No. 692 for 2019* Articles 661–662 of the *ECC*
Use of liens/assignment of debts	Articles 78 and 92 of the *Tenders and Bids Law No. 182 for 2018* Articles 315–322 of the *ECC*
Labour	*Egyptian Labour Law No. 12 for 2003*
Design/moral rights, Copyright and the product being produced from the Work	*Egyptian Intellectual Property Rights Law No. 82 for 2002*
Planning	*The Unified Building Law No. 119 for 2008*
Work affecting adjacent property to the Site	*The Unified Building Law No. 119 for 2008* Article 806 to 804 of the *ECC*
Heritage	*Protection of Antiques Law No. 117 for 1983* *Law No. 44 for 2006*
Environment, health and safety	*Environment Law No. 4 for 1994* *Labour Law No. 12 for 2003*
Public procurement	*Tenders and Bids Law No. 182 for 2018*
Building and construction permits, execution of construction work, standard of construction work	*The Unified Building Law No. 119 for 2008*
Insurance	Articles 747–771 of the *ECC*
Liability for defective work	Articles 647–654 of the *ECC*

5.10.2 Termination of a construction contract

Bankruptcy, insolvency, liquidation	Articles 50–51 of the *Tenders and Bids Law No. 182 for 2018* *Bankruptcy Law No. 11 for 2018* Articles 235–245 of the *ECC*
Decennial liability and liability generally for the total or partial collapse of structures	Article 651 of the *ECC*

5.10.3 Dispute resolution

Limitation periods	Article 68 of the *Commercial Law* Articles 374–388 of the *ECC*

5.11 Applicable legislation if the 'seat' of the dispute determination is Egypt

It is noted that COVID-19 has been seen to affect how proceedings are conducted in Egypt. For instance, in arbitration, very recently the Egyptian Court of Appeal upheld the Tribunal's right to conduct virtual hearings.[157]

157 MS Abdel Wahab and NK Abdel Rahim, 'Parties Not Indicated, Court of Appeal of Cairo, Case No. 43 of JY 138, 26 April 2022' (2022) A contribution by the ITA Board of Reporters (Kluwer Law International).

5.12 Summary of applicable legislation if the 'seat' of the dispute determination is Egypt

Dispute resolution	Articles 71 and 87 of the *Commercial Law* *Egyptian Arbitration law No. 27 for 1994* *Egyptian Civil Procedures Law No. 13 for 1968*
Limitation periods	Article 68 of the *Commercial Law* Articles 374–388 of the *ECC*
Adjudication	*Civil Procedures Law No. 13 for 1968* *State Council Law No. 47 For 1972*
Arbitration	*Arbitration law No. 27 for 1994* *Decree No. 2592 of 2020*

5.13 Issues that a court or arbitrator may construe differently than expected from the words of the Contract because of local law or custom

Besides the issues highlighted as to concepts such as liquidated damages and time limits/bars,[158] some considerations come to mind when speaking of possible contractual interpretation issues under Egyptian law. Whether it is the FIDIC 1999 contract or any other contract, some Egyptian law principles may alter or warrant a different interpretation of contractual clauses on a case-by-case basis.

Generally, there are common rules of interpretation under Egyptian law that apply to all contracts and shall be considered whenever Egyptian law is the governing law, such as:

- Insofar as ambiguity does not taint a contract, no deviation, by way of interpretation, from the intended meaning of the clear terms of the contract is warranted, noting that this applies in accordance with the expressed intention of the parties.[159]
- Even if the wording of a contractual term is clear on its face, the nature of the contract or the circumstances of its conclusion may reveal that the said term's intended meaning differs from the words used. In such an event, courts and tribunals must discern the parties' common intention through the rules of interpretation.[160]
- There is a rebuttable presumption that the expressed intention of the parties is identical to their unequivocal intention.[161]
- A tribunal or court applying Egyptian law may apply the *ejusdem generis* principle of interpretation and deviate from the literal meaning of texts in view of the

158 See sections 5.5.1.1 and 5.5.1.4.

159 MS Abdel Wahab, 'Construction Arbitration in the MENA Region' (2021) *Global Arbitration Review*, https://globalarbitrationreview.com/guide/the-guide-construction-arbitration/fourth-edition/article/construction-arbitration-in-the-mena-region (accessed 2 August 2022); Cassation, Challenge No. 498 of JY 4, hearing session dated 29 June 1963.

160 MS Abdel Wahab, 'Construction Arbitration in the MENA Region'(2021) *Global Arbitration Review*, https://globalarbitrationreview.com/guide/the-guide-construction-arbitration/fourth-edition/article/construction-arbitration-in-the-mena-region (accessed 2 August 2022); Cassation Challenge No. 1735 of JY 80, hearing session dated 10 July 2012.

161 Abdel Wahab, 'Construction Arbitration in the MENA Region' above, n160; A Al Sanhoury, *Al Wasit in the Explanation of the Civil Code*, Vol. 1 (Dar El Sherouk, 2010) 504–550.

wider context of the contractual terms.[162] By virtue of this rule, tribunals may in principle look into the negotiation phase to discern the parties' intention.

- Furthermore, interpretation of construction contracts should be consistent with commercial common sense and business efficacy.[163]
- Ambiguity may, as a general rule, be interpreted in favour of the debtor as per the applicable principles of interpretation.[164]

Nonetheless, on one hand, a tribunal shall always be aware of the intrinsic differences, under Egyptian law, between civil and administrative contracts, which result in different interpretations and applications to contractual clauses. For instance, there are contractual terms implied in administrative contracts, irrespective of the parties' agreement, such as the public employer's power to unilaterally (within certain limits) amend or vary the scope of work, dissolve or rescind the contract, or increase the quantities within certain limits.[165] In addition, there are some doctrines that may alter the way an administrative contract is expected to be applied (as opposed to private contracts) such as the theory of *le fait du prince* and *théorie des sujétions imprévues*.[166]

On the other hand, if the contract is not administrative, then the Employer party (or Contractor in a Subcontractor relationship) does not have the right to invoke or imply any administrative law concepts that are exclusive to administrative contracts, even if that party is an administrative body. It is also uncommon to see parties in a private law relationship granting the other party any of the powers of the administration as is normally the case in an administrative contract.

5.14 General principles, theories and doctrines that impact the application of contractual clauses in Egypt

There are some general civil law principles, theories and doctrines that can equally affect the expected application of contractual clauses under both private and administrative construction contracts in Egypt. These concepts mainly apply to militate against absurd or prejudicial interpretation.[167] These concepts include good faith, implied terms, suspensive conditions, abuse of right, estoppel, prohibition of taking advantage of one's own wrongdoings, the duty of mitigation, exceptional circumstances (*imprévision*), *force majeure*, notices for breach, contractual liability, decennial liability, ***exceptio non adempleti contractus***,[168] limitation and exclusion of liability, unjust enrichment claims and revocation of contracts (nullity, termination, rescission).

162 Cassation, Challenge No. 169 of JY 37, hearing session dated 7 May 1974.

163 *Article 150 of the ECC*.

164 Abdel Wahab, 'Construction Arbitration in the MENA Region' above, n160.

165 H Sarie Eldein, 'Operation of FIDIC Civil Engineering Conditions in Egypt and Other Arab Middle Eastern Countries' (1994) 28 *The International Lawyer* 4, 955.

166 **Sujétions imprévues** are technical difficulties of an unforeseeable nature and of sufficient magnitude to affect fundamentally the Contractor's performance.

167 Abdel Wahab, 'Construction Arbitration in the MENA Region' above, n160.

168 The exceptional withholding of contractual performance.

CHAPTER 6

Applying FIDIC Contracts in Ethiopia

Belachew Asteray Demiss and Zenawi Mehari Limenih

CONTENTS

DOI: 10.4324/9781003206910-6

6.1 Outline of the Ethiopia legal environment

6.1.1 The constitutional structure of Ethiopia

Ethiopia, officially the Federal Democratic Republic of Ethiopia (**FDRE**), located in the horn of Africa, is a rugged, land-locked country. It is a place of ancient civilisation, with archaeological artefacts dating back over three million years. Lalibela, with its rock-hewn Orthodox Tewahido Christian churches from the 12th to 13th centuries CE, is one of its most important sites. Ethiopia is an uncolonised country as it defeated the Italian army at the battle of Adwa with the help of King Menelik II.

Ethiopia has had four constitutions in its history.

King Haile Selassie introduced the *1931 Constitution*, the first written Ethiopian constitution in the country's 3,000-year history, as a compact between himself and the Ethiopian people.

In November 1955, Emperor Haile Selassie issued a revised *Constitution* for the Ethiopian Empire. This *Constitution*, like its predecessor from 1931, was driven by concerns about world opinion. Such views were especially relevant at a period when other neighbouring African governments were fast progressing under European colonial influence, and Ethiopia was pursuing international recognition for Eritrea, which had an elected parliament and a more contemporary administration since 1952.

The Derg suspended the *Constitution* in *Proclamation No. 1*, which was issued three days after Emperor Haile Selassie was ousted, on 15 September 1974. In 1974, a suggested modification to the *1955 Constitution* was released, but it had no legal impact and was quickly forgotten in the Ethiopian revolution.

The People's Democratic Republic of Ethiopia *Constitution*, often known as the *1987 Constitution of Ethiopia*, was Ethiopia's third constitution, and it took effect on 22 February 1987, following a referendum held on 1 February 1987. Its adoption marked the beginning of Ethiopia's People's Democratic Republic (**PDRE**).

The Federal Democratic Republic of Ethiopia's *Constitution*, often known as the *Ethiopian Constitution of 1995*,[1] is the country's supreme law. The Constituent Assembly, which was elected in June 1994, drafted the *Constitution*, which took effect on 21 August 1995. The Ethiopian Transitional Government adopted it in December 1994, and it went into effect after the general election in May–June 1995. The *Constitution* consists of 106 articles in 11 chapters. Articles 1–7 in Chapter 1 cover broad issues such as state nomenclature, territorial jurisdiction and the Ethiopian flag, while Articles 8–12 in Chapter 2 cover sovereignty, the supremacy of the *Constitution*, democratic rights, separation of state and church and government responsibility. Chapter 3 covers fundamental rights and freedoms, Chapters 4–6 establish a Federal Government comprised of nine ethnically diverse regions ruled by a parliament comprised of two chambers: the House of Peoples' Representatives and the House of Federation. Chapters 7 and 8 establish a parliamentary system with a primarily ceremonial President as head of state and an executive council led by a Prime Minister. Chapter 9 covers the power and structure of the courts. National policy and objectives are covered in Chapter 10 whilst miscellaneous provisions are in Chapter 11.

1 https://ethiopianembassy.be/wp-content/uploads/Constitution-of-the-FDRE.pdf (accessed 30 May 2023).

The concepts of Ethiopian government had been codified in the *Kebra Nagast* (which presented the concept that the Emperor of Ethiopia's legitimacy was based on its asserted descent from King Solomon of ancient Israel) and the *Fetha Nagast* (a legal code used in Ethiopia at least as early as 1450 to define the rights and responsibilities of the monarch and subjects, as defined by the Ethiopian Orthodox Tewahedo Cult) until the adoption of the first of these *Constitutions.*

6.1.2 The legal system in Ethiopia

Ethiopia's legal system is primarily based on civil law. The common law system, on the other hand, is distinguished by its case law system. The Ethiopian legal system obviously belongs in the civil law system with its codes and predefined rules with the judge seeking the legislator's intention and the historical backdrop of the legislation to interpret the law.

In the civil law system, there have been many efforts to exhaustively lay down pre-established rules to regulate subsequent behaviours. Thus, codes have been outstanding manifestations of the civil law tradition's belief in human prescience to establish the rules and apply them to future cases.

The Ethiopian legal system has federal and state legislative organs which are clearly separated from the judiciary through the doctrine of the independence of the judiciary and exclusive legislative power in all federal/state matters. The legislative field in the Ethiopian legal system is definitely overcrowded for the recent use of the precedent system, even if it is accepted that judicial law-making is tenable. However, in a legal system where nearly every area is covered by legislation and has implemented several codes since the 1950s, and where the judges are trained to interpret the legislation by seeking the intentions of the legislature, it takes much more than a single provision in a proclamation to depart, or even to deviate, from such a well-established system.

The Ethiopian legal system with its full-time legislatures both at the federal and regional levels and the resultant myriad number of codes and piecemeal legislation requires the intervention of the legislator to amend, repeal or make new law; this definitely takes time to deliver. On the other hand, the case law system with a judiciary that covertly adjusts the rules in tandem with social exigencies under the pretext of interpretation injects flexibility into the legal system. As the legislature has been the sole lawmaker in the Ethiopian legal system, the advent of the precedent system may obviate the lengthy law-making process to bring law in line with practical necessities. In the common law tradition, case law has in-built systems, overruling and distinguishing, to manipulate the common law to develop law in particular areas without waiting for the action of the legislature.

The Ethiopian legal system is a codified system of law. There are five main codes:

(1) *Civil Code of 1960*
(2) *Criminal Code of 1960*
(3) *Civil Procedures Code of 1965*
(4) *Criminal Procedures Code of 1965*
(5) *Commercial Code of 1960, then 2021/22*

6.1.3 The court system in Ethiopia

Ethiopia has a dual judicial system with two parallel court structures: the federal courts and the state courts with their own independent structures and administrations. Judicial powers, both at federal and state levels, are vested in the courts. The *FDRE Constitution* states that supreme federal judicial authority is vested in the Federal Supreme Court and empowers the House of People's Representatives (**HPR**) to decide by a two-thirds majority vote to establish subordinate federal courts, as it deems necessary, nationwide or in some parts of the country.

The Federal Supreme Court that sits in Addis Ababa is the main court with national jurisdiction. Federal courts at any level may hold circuit hearings at any place within the State or 'area designated for its jurisdiction' if deemed 'necessary for the efficient rendering of justice'.[2] Each High Court has a civil, criminal and labour division with a presiding judge and two other judges in each division.

The Federal Supreme Court includes a Cassation Division with the power to review and overturn decisions containing fundamental errors of law issued by lower federal courts, the Supreme Court itself in its regular division and State Supreme Courts. In addition, judicial decisions of the Cassation Division of the Federal Supreme Court on the interpretation of laws are binding on federal as well as state courts.

The *Federal Courts Proclamation* allocates subject-matter jurisdiction to federal courts on the basis of three principles: laws, parties and places. It stipulates that federal courts shall have jurisdiction over, first, 'cases arising under the *Constitution*, federal laws and international treaties', and second, 'over parties specified in federal laws'. Article 3(3) of the *Federal Courts Proclamation* states that federal courts shall have judicial power in places specified in the *FDRE Constitution* or in federal laws.

Federal courts have civil jurisdiction over 'cases in which a Federal Government organ is a party; suits between persons permanently residing in different regions; cases involving the liability of federal officials or employees in connection with their official responsibilities or duties'. According to Article 5 of the same *Proclamation*, federal courts also have jurisdiction over cases in which a foreign national is a party; suits involving matters of nationality; suits relating to business organisations registered or formed under the jurisdiction of Federal Government organs; suits regarding negotiable instruments; suits relating to patent, literary and artistic-ownership rights; and suits regarding insurance policies and application for *habeas corpus*.

In several spheres of social activity, the *FDRE Constitution* provides the framework for the autonomous legality of non-state or unofficial laws such as customary and religious laws. Article 34(5) of the *FDRE Constitution* states:

> This *Constitution* shall not preclude the adjudication of disputes relating to personal and family laws in accordance with religious or customary laws, with the consent of the parties to the dispute. Particulars shall be determined by law.

Article 78(5) states:

> Pursuant to sub-Article (5) of Article 34, the House of Peoples' Representatives and State Councils can establish or give official recognition to religious and customary courts. Religious and customary courts that had state recognition and functioned prior to the adoption of

2 *Civil Code of the Empire of Ethiopia Proclamation No. 165 of 1960.*

the *Constitution* shall be organized on the basis of recognition accorded to them by this *Constitution.*

Despite their constitutional status, customary courts are not formed by law. They are merely recognised by law, not implemented. Tradition and local norms give these courts their authority. These courts originated from ancient elder councils, which have no legal status but do have moral authority and are still commonly used as major decision-makers in Ethiopia's rural communities. The Shemagelle in Amhara, the Bayito and Abo Gereb in Tigray and the Luba Basa in Oromia are just a few of the traditional courts. Shemagelle is a widely practised and known dispute resolution method parallel to the modern court system in Amhara and Ethiopia.

Furthermore, the parties have complete autonomy in deciding whether to pursue a disagreement in conventional courts or in one of those non-official venues.

The Courts of the Federal Government and Regional states are:

(1) First Instance Courts
(2) High courts
(3) Supreme Courts

6.2 The construction industry in Ethiopia

6.2.1 Overview

The Ethiopian construction industry is characterised by a large number of micro-entrepreneurs, the majority of whom operate in the country's informal economy. Ethiopia's formal construction sector comprises local and international firms.

In real terms, the Ethiopian construction industry is predicted to rise by 4.7% in 2022, up from 3.1% in 2021. Despite the outbreak of the COVID-19 pandemic, construction activities were mostly unaffected. Although the government declared a state of emergency in early April 2020 in response to the pandemic, construction activities were urged to continue during the crisis, which aided industry output growth in 2020.

The Ethiopian Council of Ministers agreed on a budget for the financial year (FY) 2020/2021 of about ETB476 billion (US$13.7 billion) in June 2020 (the FY runs from 8 July 2020 to 7 July 2021). The government set aside ETB160.3 billion (US$4.6 billion) for capital spending, up 22.7% from the previous fiscal year's allocation of ETB130.7 billion (US$4.5 billion). Although the construction industry is expected to develop in 2022, the unpredictable political environment produced by the conflict between Ethiopia's Federal Government and an armed rebel group in the Tigray area which started in November 2020 could pose a downside risk. Investor confidence could be harmed as a result, damaging the economy and the construction industry.

Between 2022 and 2025, the industry is predicted to increase at an annual rate of 8.3%, thanks to investments in transportation, electricity, tourism, manufacturing and industrial park developments. By 2025, the country wants to be an African light manufacturing centre and a lower-middle-income economy. It intends to raise the number of functioning industrial parks in the country from five in 2018 to 30 by 2025 in order to achieve this. The government announced its ten-year economic growth strategy in June 2020, with a focus on agriculture, tourism, manufacturing, information and communication technology

(**ICT**) and mining. The government's focus on enhancing the ease of doing business in the country would also help the construction industry grow in the long run.

6.2.2 Structure

The Ethiopian construction industry is open to all competitive and legal construction firms; Chinese, Turkish, Japanese and Italian construction firms are mostly involved. There is therefore a high level of expertise in the Ethiopian construction market itself, even if major projects are dominated by a few local market players.

The construction industry (supply side) is still fiercely competitive, with a plethora of sophisticated companies. As a result, labour costs and margins for contractors remain low, forcing general contractors to reduce their own Ethiopian workforce in favour of working with international contractors. Decisions have been made at both the national and international levels to combat social dumping and unfair competition, and specific actions are being implemented by the industry.

According to the Ministry of Urban Development, Housing and Construction, Ethiopia has about 140 Grade 1 Contractors (general contractor, building contractor and special contractor) registered and actively participating in the construction industry. Furthermore, professional general contractors continue to export their know-how and seek employment in places with higher profit margins, such as Africa and the Middle East.

Subcontracting in the Ethiopian construction industry is well established. Most of the time national contractors are involved as a subcontractor when a foreign contractor wins the tender.

Article 14 of the Ethiopian Public Procurement Agency (**PPA**) Standard Conditions of Construction Contract 2011 (**PPA 2011**) regulates subcontracting in all contracts. It states that a subcontract shall be valid only if it is a written agreement by which the Contractor entrusts the performance of a part of the Contract to a third party. In the event the Contractor requires subcontracting of the works to Subcontractors that are not included in the Contract, the Contractor shall obtain the prior written approval and clearance of the Public Body for all Subcontractors. The work to be subcontracted and the identity of the Subcontractors shall be notified to the Public Body. Within 15 days of receiving the notification, the Public Body shall notify the Contractor of its decision, citing reasons if it withholds such authorisation, in accordance with the terms of General Condition of Contract Clause 10. Any subcontract terms must be subject to and comply with the provisions of this contract. Subcontractors must satisfy the eligibility criteria applicable to the award of the contract and must not be in any of the situations excluding them from participating in the contract. Subject to the General Condition of Contract Clause 66, the Public Body shall have no contractual relations with the Subcontractors.[3]

6.2.3 Licensing/registration

Before any contractors, architects or engineers undertake any construction work in Ethiopia, they need to be licensed and registered. Licensing and registration regulations may differ from one country to the next or from one legal system to the next.

3 Public Procurement Agency (PPA) 2011 Standard Conditions of Construction Contract.

The current rationale for contractor licensing in Ethiopia is to verify that project applicants have the required capacity and capability. This need is addressed through the prequalification process for each offer for contracts in other countries and for multilateral donor initiatives. This necessitates knowledge of the contractor's present status and historical performance. The current procedure for registration and issuance of graded licenses relies on ownership of relevant equipment and number of skilled or educated labourers. These license and registration standards are unrelated to past performance or the contractor's (architect's, engineer's or consultant's) ability to lease or hire equipment, making it difficult for contractors with strong technical and financial backgrounds to enter new markets.

Construction Certification and Registration Directive No. 648/2021 clearly states the preconditions to obtain any certificate and license, issued by the Federal Democratic Republic of Ethiopia Ministry of Urban Development and Construction. Those are:

1. Any natural or juridical person who satisfies the requirements specified in the *Directives* may file an application with the Ministry of Urban Development and Construction to be registered and to have their name entered in the Registrar.
2. The application of contractors and construction professionals shall be submitted by filing two forms prepared for this subject only.
3. All construction professionals and contractors desiring to carry out activities related to construction works are required to register with the Ministry in accordance with the *Directive*. No company or professional may carry out any construction without getting a certificate of competence from the Ministry.
4. All foreign construction companies and their professionals who may undertake any activity related to construction works in the country are to be registered by the Ministry.
5. All foreign contractors who wish to take part in national competitive bidding (**NCB**) shall be registered as a contractor of only class I for all categories, and they should not participate in national competitive bidding below class I.
6. Every person whose name is entered in the register shall keep the Department promptly informed of any change in the particulars listed in his/her application and the Department shall amend the Register accordingly.
7. An applicant shall submit photocopies of their authenticated degrees and work experience which needs to be pertinent to the field of practice applied for.
8. Foreign professionals or professionals with experience from foreign countries should submit documents authenticated by appropriate bodies.
9. Professionals with foreign educational qualifications must provide an Ethiopian higher education system equivalent credential certifying it is recognised by an authorised organisation.
10. Foreign professionals who wish to be registered should supply evidence of both work and residence permits.

As per the *Directive*, any local or foreign construction worker, professional or organisation must have a certificate of competency or certificate of registration.

Professionals registered under this *Directive* shall have the following categories according to their types of profession:

a) Technician (Technician I, Technician II)
b) Associate Engineer (Engineering Aide III, Engineering Aide IV)
c) Professional (Graduate professional, professional and practising professional)

Contractors can register under the following categories by following all the legal procedures and by fulfilling the relevant requirements: General Contractor, Building Contractor, Road Contractor and Special Contractor (including pre-tensioning, post-tensioning, landscaping, foundation work, construction completion, site maintenance, road safety signs, aluminium door and window assembly, painting and decoration work, wood and metal work and plumbing and sanitation work).

Consultants can register under the following categories: Building Consultant, Consultant Architect, Engineering Consultant (including structural, highway and bridge, geotechnical engineering, electrical and electromechanical and sanitary engineering firms), Construction Management Consultant, Urban Planning Work Consultant and Special Consultant (including asset valuation, interior design and decoration, landscaping, construction audit, etc.).

6.2.4 Labour relations

Ethiopia has issued *Labour Proclamation No. 1156/2019* and is also a member of the International Labour Organization (**ILO**) which endeavours to maintain the rights and responsibilities of labour.

The Ethiopian *Labour Proclamation No. 1156/2019* states that it is essential to ensure that worker–employer relations must be governed by basic principles of rights and obligations with a view to enabling workers and employers to secure durable industrial peace, sustainable productivity and competitiveness through cooperative engagement towards the all round development of the country.

The Ethiopian *Labour Proclamation* has 12 parts, more than 14 chapters and includes more than 25 sections. It details employment relationships, wages, hours of work, working and non-working days, leave, working conditions of women and young workers, occupational health and safety and working environment, collective relations, labour disputes, priority of claims and enforcement of labour law. It also contains administrative measures and miscellaneous provisions.

A contractor shall comply with all the relevant labour laws applicable to the contractor's personnel, including laws relating to their employment (including wages and working hours), health, safety, welfare, immigration and emigration, and shall allow them all their legal rights.

The Ethiopian *Labour Proclamation No. 1156/2019* demands a cooperative relationship between employer and labour. However, union membership is not currently common, nor are strikes. Although the *Proclamation* states all the rules and regulations related to labour and employer, most employers fail to comply with the directives.

6.2.5 Safety culture

Construction projects are dynamic in nature and the changing characteristics make them prone to accidents and health problems. Hence a lack of safety may result in serious consequences.

Occupational safety is well defined and stated in Ethiopian *Labour Proclamation No. 1156/2019*. Part seven of the *Proclamation* refers to the preventative measures to avoid accidents and defines the obligation of stakeholders (Employers, Contractors, Consultants and statutory bodies). The *Proclamation* declares that all the stakeholders must obey the safety-related issues stated in the *Proclamation*. As a minimum, the Contractor must provide health and safety equipment such as personal protective equipment (PPE), e.g., safety shoes, helmets, safety glasses and reflective jackets.

In reality, most of the contractors do not apply the rules and regulations stated by the *Labour Proclamation* and consequently, many workers become injured or die due to a lack of adequate health and safety procedures. In particular, many contractors do not respect their personnel, do not provide any PPE, do not pay wages and salaries timeously, do not provide any insurance coverage and compel workers to work even in risky areas.

Safety problems on Ethiopian construction sites arise due to falling objects, use of hazardous substances, electrical hazards, plant rollovers (e.g., cranes, trucks, excavators, rollers, etc.), work in confined spaces and lack of PPE.

6.2.6 Modular construction using factory-fabricated components

Many modern construction projects in Ethiopia are predominantly made of reinforced concrete. It is common in Ethiopia to build all the structural elements using in-situ methods of construction, where concrete is mixed both on-site and at the batching plant and poured using both manual labour and concrete pumps.

Precast construction methods are now also applicable and practised in Ethiopia. The first and only precast production company in Ethiopia, the Prefabricated Building Parts Production Enterprise (**PBPPE**), was established in 1987 with the help of the then-socialist country of Yugoslavia. The Ethiopian construction sector was still in its infancy at the time, with only a few modern structures, mostly made of prefabricated pieces, being built in Addis Ababa. PBPPE has not made much progress as an organisation in its more than 27 years of existence. It still uses the same old batching plant, crane system and even moulds that were installed when it first opened those many years ago. Additionally, it has fixed specifications for every single component of building construction, due to lack of moulds. Because PBPPE does not have slabs spanning greater than 4.20 metres in each (x or y) direction, if one designed a building with slabs spanning 6 metres, as is the case in many building designs in Ethiopia, the project would have to be erected in-situ (not prefabricated). Neither does the plant have column sections greater than 0.30 m by 0.30 m, or shear wall heights exceeding 2.62 m, among several other restrictions.

PBPPE has three main departments: Construction, Production and Logistics.

It is well known that the precast method is better in quality and utilisation of resources and saves time over the in-situ construction method. It is also known that certain types of structures are better suited to the precast method of construction. In the National Precast Concrete Association (**NPCA**) standard quality control manual used in the United States to evaluate precast plants and give accreditations, the Ethiopian PBPPE precast plant received a lower score than the passing level. This was due to its oldness and the lower attention of the government to modern construction.

6.2.7 Technology/innovation/BIM

Ethiopia is undergoing a major and fast transformation in the subject of building construction. The country is now building grand projects in areas such as housing, higher education, health buildings and many more. This fast-building construction industry faces many challenges, one of these challenges being the gap in building design process management basically caused by incomplete design and less integrated design management. International practice has moved from the conventional to the integrated design modality, with the latest intervention of building information modelling (BIM).

There have been a few attempts at BIM in Ethiopia, even though it is in its infant stage. The Ethiopian Construction Management Institute is taking the responsibility to adopt BIM in the Ethiopian construction industry. The Institute is preparing codes for the successful implementation of BIM and preparing different conferences to create awareness for different construction stakeholders. The Ethiopian Construction Management Institute is an authorised BIM training centre. It has signed an agreement with the Autodesk company to provide BIM training and to certify in collaboration with Autodesk university lecturers and other concerned stakeholders.

BIM's popularity has recently exploded in the public construction industry in other countries. However, in low-income nations like Ethiopia, it is not generally practised or adopted.

Studies show that the following are barriers to successful BIM implementation in the Ethiopian construction industry. Those BIM implementation barriers comprise four principal components: legal and contractual, process, cultural and organisational and government-related barriers. The main legal and contractual-related barriers are lack of a standard form of contract for BIM adoption, lack of BIM Regulations and Standards, inclusion of BIM protocols in contracts and lack of insurance applicable to BIM implementation. The complexity of BIM software, BIM model ownership rights and poor collaboration among major parties are the main process-related adoption barriers to BIM. The cultural and organisational-related barriers are BIM misunderstanding, lack of awareness, lack of trained professionals and resistance to change. Governmental-related barriers are insufficient IT infrastructure, poor government support and lack of BIM research and courses in universities.[4]

However, a new educational curriculum has been devised and BIM included as one course for Bachelor of Science students under the Department of Construction Technology and Management in all Ethiopian universities. In addition, currently in the capital city of Ethiopia (Addis Ababa) construction projects are carried out using BIM, and many studies are also conducted in different higher institutions.

6.2.8 Government/private sector procurement

6.2.8.1 Government procurement

Ethiopia has modernised its public procurement laws. The newly enacted Ethiopian *Federal Government Procurement and Property Administration Proclamation No.*

4 Solomon Belay, James Goedert, Asregdew Woldesenbet and Saed Rokooei, 'Enhancing BIM implementation in the Ethiopian public construction sector: An empirical study' (2021) V8.1 *Cogent Engineering* Taylor and Francis Online: www.tandfonline.com/doi/full/10.1080/23311916.2021.1886476 (accessed 9 December 2022).

649/2009 attempts to consolidate the end-to-end processes involving public procurement and property administration.

With the proclamation of the *Civil Code* in 1960,[5] Ethiopia received the French procedure of allocation of contracts by tender which formed part of the administrative contract law in Ethiopia. The *Civil Code* provisions did not require the use of the procedure; rather, it was set out for use by the administrative bodies whenever required by other pertinent laws or whenever they decided to use it. It is submitted that Ethiopia did not have the tradition to guide the administrative authorities and, thus, it was important to 'establish a framework for administrative action'.[6] Thus, the *Civil Code* rules on administrative contracts[7] contain a significant number of provisions on procurement contract formation and contract administration.

The next major step towards regulating administrative actions was taken by better elaborating the procurement processes in the *Federal Financial Administration Proclamation No. 57/1996* and the *Council of Ministers Financial Administration Regulation No. 17/1997.*

The enactment of the *Federal Financial Administration Proclamation No. 57/1996* dedicated some of its provisions[8] to the regulation of, albeit insufficiently, public procurement proceedings. Similarly, some of the provisions of the *Council of Ministers Financial Administration Regulation No. 17/1997* also deal with public procurement proceedings.[9] The Ministry of Finance and Economic Development also issued *Directive No. 1/1998* enunciating detailed working rules and procedures for the implementation of the aforementioned *Proclamation* and *Regulation.*

The *Federal Public Procurement Proclamation No. 430/2005* (the *2005 Proclamation*) was a watershed moment in Ethiopian public procurement law, bringing it up to date and aligning it with worldwide standards.[10]

In September 2009, the Federal Government enacted the *Federal Procurement and Property Administration Proclamation No. 649/2009* (the *2009 Proclamation*)[11] and the *Federal Financial Administration Proclamation No. 648/2009.22*. With regard to procurement, the latter is relevant as it attempts to further consolidate the role of the internal auditing system and establishes detailed rules on the modalities of financing and effecting payments in the procurement of goods, construction works and services. The new *2009 Proclamation* (which entered into force as of 9 September 2009) entirely repealed the previous *2005 Proclamation* and all other laws, regulations, directives or practices that do not accord with it.

Thus, with the recent issuance of the *Federal Procurement Directives* which entered into force as of 8 June 2010, Ethiopia can be considered as one of the African countries which has successfully modernised its procurement laws.

5 *Civil Code of the Empire of Ethiopia Proclamation No. 165 of 1960.*

6 *Civil Code of the Empire of Ethiopia Proclamation No. 165 of 1960.*

7 Articles 3131–3306 of the *Civil Code.*

8 Articless 54–57 of *Federal Financial Administration Proclamation No. 57/96.*

9 *Council of Ministers Financial Administration Regulation No. 17/1997.*

10 In drafting the law, the drafters relied heavily on the *UNCITRAL Model Law on Procurement of Goods, Construction and Services with Guide to Enactment* (1994).

11 The Federal Government *Procurement and Property Administration Proclamation No. 649/2009, Federal Negarit Gazeta*, Year 15, No. 60, 9 September 2009; this *2009 Proclamation* is comprehensive in style, as it tries to cover the procurement process end to end: i.e., procurement planning, contract formation, contract administration, property administration and finally disposal.

All *Regulations*, *Proclamations* and *Directives* stated here are currently in practice without any amendment, but the concerned body has the right to amend them when it is necessary. They supplement each other without any violation.

Goods, works and services can be procured by any governmental department to which a budget (usually an itemised budget) is appropriated. Thus, all ministries, commissions, authorities, agencies and public enterprises (at federal, state and city levels) carry out procurement of goods, services or works within the ambit of their budget. The federal procurement system is by and large run and/or monitored by a variety of institutions, entities or persons.

The procurement process follows certain phases. These phases normally run through:

1) Procurement planning
2) Contract formation, and
3) Contract administration phases

Ethiopia is a member of the Common Market for Eastern and Southern Africa (**COMESA**) free trade area. Due mainly to the direct and indirect pressure by some of the multilateral development banks (particularly the World Bank Group) to modernise its financial administration and public procurement systems, Ethiopia commenced the reform of its procurement laws earlier than the COMESA Public Procurement Project in 2002. This involved Ethiopia designing its procurement laws based mainly on the *UNCITRAL Model Law on Procurement of Goods, Construction and Services (1994)* and, to some extent, international best practice. Thus, in Ethiopia, the COMESA Public Procurement Project assisted a process of public procurement reform which had already substantially matured in its draft form and the use of the *UNCITRAL Model Law* cannot be seen as a direct result of COMESA's influence. However, the Project ensured that the reform benefited from COMESA's work on best practices and did not contradict COMESA's public procurement objectives.

The procurement methods used in Ethiopia are adapted from the *1994 UNCITRAL Model Law on Procurement of Goods, Construction and Services* to achieve the stated procurement objectives in Ethiopia.

Open tendering, restricted tendering, request for quotation, request for proposal, two-stage tendering, direct or single-source procurement, and special allowed procurement are the several types of tendering used in Ethiopia. The Ethiopian procurement system is based on the principles of value for money, non-discrimination, transparency, accountability and assisting national procedures and micro and small-sized enterprises.

6.2.8.2 Private procurement

Private procurement in Ethiopia is carried out by using the *Ethiopian Federal Government Procurement and Property Administration Proclamation No. 649/2009* as a guideline to procure works, goods and services. No constraint is applied or observed in private procurement. The procurement in private firms is generally based on tendering and the tenderer with the lowest price will become the winner of the tender. However, the law states that tenders in construction projects with a price 20% below or above the engineering estimation will be disqualified/rejected.

6.2.9 Insurance requirements

It is generally understood that insurance in the Ethiopian construction industry is taken out for the following reasons: compulsion by legislation, requirement by the contract, self-protection and requirement by the financer. The responsible authority for licensing construction firms in Ethiopia does not consider insurance as a criterion for issuing a license. This being the case, construction firms, both consulting and contracting are not fully aware of insurance and they do not want to purchase policies unless they are forced by legislation or contract conditions.

The government make insurance a mandatory criterion for issuing a license (as referred to in section 6.2.3). The local Building and Transport Construction Design Authority conditions of contract require contractors to buy relevant insurance policies after proper risk assessments have been made. However, the general practice in the Ethiopian construction industry is far from this. Most of the contractual agreements between stakeholders do not require adequate insurance coverage. Consultants are liable for any damage that could arise due to their failure in design work, and accordingly, they should be insured or indemnified by insurance should a claim arise against their work for breach of professional duty.

In the Ethiopian context, Contractors are required to at least have a performance bond. Though it normally only lasts a year, a contractor's performance bond serves to protect the Employer by ensuring that its construction is completed in compliance with the contract's terms.

Since most Employers do not have proper knowledge about insurance, they do not ask for adequate insurance coverage from the construction firms they select for their project.

The major parties in the construction industry, i.e., clients, consultants, contractors, concerned local and Federal Government authorities, lawmakers, financers, etc. share responsibility for the non-existence of appropriate insurance guidelines in the construction sector of Ethiopia.

Generally, it is clear that there is a need for suitable insurance policies for the Ethiopian construction industry to satisfy the Employer's interest, to achieve the required quality and standard, to provide safety for the workers and for proper utilisation of national resources.

6.2.10 Common forms of contract

FIDIC contracts are commonly employed in the Ethiopian construction industry, especially for foreign contractors.

But, for national competitive bidders, it is mandatory to use and abide by the PPA 2011 Standard Conditions of Contract. However, based on the interest of the bidders they can also use their own Special Conditions of contract by modifying some articles in the Standard Conditions of contract. PPA 2011 has two parts, one for national competitive bidders (NCB) and one for international competitive bidders (ICB).

The Ethiopian contract forms require the following documents, which must be organised in a hierarchical order: the contract agreement, the letter of acceptance, the tender, the Conditions of Contract Part I (General Conditions), Conditions of Contract Part II (Special Conditions), the specifications, the drawings and the priced bill of quantities. The hierarchy is to maintain procedural workflow and if there is a conflict between documents, the document which occurs at the top will govern – that is, the sequence of the documents arranged in the contract governs one over the other.

The only Standard Conditions of contract in Ethiopia are PPA 2011 and MoWUD 1994.

In the Ethiopian construction industry, the following types of construction contracts are used, as listed in the *Federal Government Public Procurement Directive June 2010*, PPA 2011 and the FIDIC Red Book.

- Lump sum contract: When the project or Tender price is determined and quoted as a total sum of money without individual ratings to execute the whole of the Works and/or services according to the drawings and specifications, it is called a lump sum contract.
- Bill of quantities contract: When the project or Tender price is determined and quoted from unit rates assigned to a detailed bill of quantities, it is called a bill of quantities contract. The bill of quantities includes short description specifications or work, units of measurement, quantities and columns for pricing the unit rate and its total amounts.
- Cost plus fixed fee contract: When projects are fast-tracked and required to be completed expeditiously and where it is difficult to estimate the project cost before the project commences, expenses called costs will be recorded and a fixed amount which is agreed upon by the contracting parties will be added as payment to the Contractor. A contract that stipulates reimbursement of cost together with an additional fixed fee is called a cost plus fixed fee contract.
- Cost plus percentage of cost contract: This type of contract is similar to the cost plus fixed fee contract but its fee is made variable using a percentage of the cost which is intended to cover the overhead and profit costs of the Contractor.
- Labour contract: When the Employer is responsible for the provision of major resources such as materials and Equipment other than labour, small tools and their management, it is called a labour contract.
- Hybrid contract: Hybrid contracts are contracts that incorporate two or more contract types. This form of contract is tailored to fit the unique requirements of specific types of work.
- Special contract: As the term suggests, special arrangements are required in particular circumstances such as the usage of specialities, urgency, additional nature and continuation of services or works, distance and smallness of projects and so on. These include a packaged contract, continuing/supplementary contract, running contract and subcontract.

  The Contract Price is often per unit rate of goods, services or works where the payment is based on actual goods delivered and/or services rendered and/or works executed. Contract Prices can in some instances be fixed specifically for services.
- Subcontract: This type of contract is made when specialised works are involved in the project package or if the Employer envisaged other tangible as well as intangible benefits by using such a contract type.

6.2.11 Dispute resolution

Construction is plagued, perhaps more than any other industry, with disputes due to the inherent conflict of interest between the buyers of construction services (i.e., the owner or Employer) and the sellers of the services (i.e., the Contractor).

The Ministry of Work and Urban Development (**MoWUD**) Standard Conditions of Contract for Construction of Civil Work Projects 1994 (**MoWUD 1994**) states that a dispute shall be referred to and settled by the Engineer who shall within a period of 90 days after being requested by either party to do so give written notice of his decision to the Employer and the Contractor. According to MoWUD 1994 clause 1 (c), the Engineer is the natural or judicial person designated as Engineer in writing by MoWUD. This is applicable for contracts entered into under either PPA 2011 or MoWUD 1994 conditions.

Disputes mainly from contractors are presented to the Ministry of Infrastructure, Design and Construction Supervision Office. This is applied to MoWUD 1994. MoI's experts evaluate the evidence according to the rules, contract and practice that is applied appropriately in the dispute, propose the likely outcomes of the case, and give their final decision. The process is rather similar to adjudication in certain projects and conciliation in others. It is not a formal arbitration ruling and award. Further, when a Contractor enters into a contract agreement with public authorities for public works, their contract is an administrative contract according to Article 3132 of the *Civil Code*. This implies that the contract is non-arbitral according to the *Civil Procedure Code* Article 315 (2). Thus, in reality, there is no arbitration clause in MoWUD 1994. Thus, it implies that the parties have agreed based on their contract that the decision of the MoI's Engineer or the Minister is binding on them.

The Ethiopian Road Authority (**ERA**) Standard Specification deals with the settlement of disputes mainly for road construction projects. This has five sections in successive steps in settling disputes, commencing with the Engineer, who shall respond within 120 days, and his/her recommendation shall be final and binding. If the Engineer fails to make a recommendation within the prescribed period of 120 days or if either party is dissatisfied with his recommendation, either party may, within 150 days of the original request to the Engineer, refer the dispute to the General Manager of Highways. The General Manager shall decide the matter within 30 days, furnishing each party with a copy of his decision. The decision of the General Manager of Highways shall be final and conclusive and binding on both parties unless, within 30 days of receipt of such decision, the Contractor presents notice to the General Manager of Highways of its intention to submit the dispute to arbitration. In the event the Contractor presents notice of its intention to submit the dispute to arbitration, the General Manager of Highways shall refer the matter to the Imperial Highway Authority (**IHA**) Board of Commissioners who shall hear the parties, review the record, hear witness if need be and attempt to bring the parties to agreement. Failing such agreement, the IHA Board of Commissioners shall within a reasonable time render a written decision. Such decision shall be final and conclusive unless within 30 days by notice to the General Manager of Highways, the Contractor appeals to arbitration. Arbitration shall be in Addis Ababa under the Rules of Arbitral Submission (Articles 3325–3346) of the *Civil Code*. Both parties shall have the right of appeal to the High Court of Ethiopia against such award.

The PPA Standard Conditions of Contract 2011 has an arbitration option. PPA 2011 clause 26.6 states that 'only those public bodies that are allowed by law to proceed to arbitration can do so'.

Generally, the Ethiopian construction industry adopts both amicable dispute resolution methods (negotiation, mediation and conciliation) and judgmental dispute resolution methods (adjudication, arbitration and litigation). Negotiation and mediation are the most widely used methods of dispute resolution preferred by Ethiopian contractors.

6.2.12 Current challenges

The Ethiopian construction industry, like that in most developing countries, faces many challenges that impede its development. The Ethiopian construction industry has passed through different periods facing challenges associated with the political ideologies and perception of governments towards the industry.

The problems of the construction industry are broad-based and multidimensional. The nature of the problems is context-specific, and the requirements for improvement vary in different periods. Improvement in the construction industry needs identification of the challenges, setting objective indicators and continual performance measurement and improvement practice at the industry level.

The major challenges in Ethiopian construction are the completion of projects beyond their completion time; in construction industry development policy implementation and corruption due to the government's role; weak capacity of contractors and consultants due to resource-related variables; lack of collaboration and professionalism due to the nature of the industry; and a lack of benchmarking construction industry development practice due to the industry's limited vision for development.

Challenges in the construction industry are interrelated. For example, the low level of professionalism is associated with the capacity of firms which results in poor performance and leads to unethical practices and a poor image of the industry. Unethical practices create an unhealthy business environment which affects the relationships of stakeholders.

Overcoming challenges in the industry needs the concerted effort of the stakeholders. It primarily needs the commitment of the government as it is the biggest client, promoter and regulator of the industry. The major emphasis should be on the implementation of policy and regulations. Benchmarking performance is important for the sustainable development of the industry.

Industry organisations also have to improve their competitiveness by adopting best management practices which will help them to build and maintain their reputation in the industry.

6.2.13 Unique features of the construction industry in Ethiopia

Ethiopia's construction sector is one of the most robust in Africa, having unique features and challenges. The main unique features observed in the Ethiopian construction industry are as follows.

Labour intensiveness: The construction industry in developed countries is far different from that in developing countries. In Ethiopia, most construction works are still carried out using labour because of the cheap cost of labourers and the low practicability of technologies. That is why most construction projects are finished beyond their completion time.

Participation of both local and international firms: Ethiopian construction law has a framework for different firms to be involved in the construction industry, so it allows any eligible, qualified and competent local or international construction firm.

Lack of health and safety: Until it adopts international health and safety laws there is a shortfall in health and safety performance.

Practice of both national and international norms: The Ethiopian construction industry adopts international norms, frameworks, methods and principles. For instance, FIDIC is applicable in different contracts. Further, national norms are widely practised such as those of the Public Procurement Agency (PPA), the *Civil Code* and the Ethiopian Construction Practice Norm (**ECPN**) which is promulgated by the Ministry of Urban Development, Housing and Construction (**MUDHCo**).

The updating and building of new infrastructure links, residential developments and so on are of considerable interest to the Ethiopian Government. Indeed, the nation's Second Growth and Transformation Plan (GTP II) prioritises the development of these areas.

According to studies, construction workers are more prone to diseases, traumatic injuries and fatalities than those in any other field. Poor equipment and workstation design, a lack of personal protective equipment and inadequate worker training all contribute to poor occupational health and safety in Ethiopia. Despite the statistical case for emphasising the problem, it remains neglected by employers and authorities who are mandated to enforce workers' rights

Currently, the construction industry is upgrading and enhancing its methods of construction, adopting new technologies and innovations, enforcing legal frameworks and training different professionals to eliminate the gaps observed.

6.3 The impact of COVID-19 in Ethiopia

6.3.1 The impact of COVID-19 on the execution of construction projects in Ethiopia

The major negative impacts of the COVID-19 pandemic on the execution of construction projects were:

- Time and cost overruns
- Delays in delivery of materials and machinery
- Increased idle hours of labour and machinery
- Loss of productivity
- Escalation of material prices
- Cash flow shortage
- Additional costs due to new health and safety requirements and PPE
- Increased overhead cost
- Global supply chain disruption
- Foreign currency
- Shortage of material to support ongoing projects
- Extensions of time
- Disruption of planning and scheduling
- Workforce shortage
- The uncertainty of survival
- Increase of unemployment
- Income reduction

However, the COVID-19 pandemic also had positive impacts and presented opportunities such as:

- Improving health and safety agendas
- Planning for unforeseen circumstances

- Ability to secure loans at a low-interest rate
- Improving existing systems (work redesign)
- Using virtual alternatives

Although the Ethiopian construction industry was highly affected by the pandemic, the Ethiopian government did not show any willingness to strengthen the sector. The government allowed Contractors to carry out their work if they provided personal protective equipment for their employees and maintained a two-metre social distance between employees.

6.3.2 The impact of COVID-19 on the operation of construction contracts in Ethiopia

Ethiopia announced a State of Emergency in *Proclamation 3/2020*.[12] The *Proclamation* did not specifically refer to the construction industry but implemented several rules aimed to implement the suspension of rights and measures to be taken to counter and mitigate the humanitarian, social, economic and political damage that could be caused by COVID-19. The *Proclamation 3/2020* also provided that any suspension of construction works due to the coronavirus pandemic was strictly prohibited but it advised that employees must wear face masks and hand gloves and maintain physical distance. This was due to the construction sector being a large employer; if the construction works were suspended, most of the labourers wouldn't have any guaranteed income for their food and accommodation.

6.4 Ethiopian governing law of the contract

6.4.1 Constraints on the governing law of a construction contract

The Contract, its meaning and interpretation and relations between the Parties are governed by and interpreted in accordance with the laws of Ethiopia, unless otherwise stated in Special Conditions of Contract which are formulated and amended based on the interests of the contracting parties. The jurisdiction allows the governing law of both a private and public contract to be a jurisdiction other than Ethiopia. Generally, there is no constraint for the choice of the governing law for any construction contract; it is based on the interest of the contracting bodies both in public and private contracts.

6.4.2 Formal requirements for a construction contract

Contract means the binding agreement entered into between the Client (Employer) and the Contractor, comprising Contract Documents referred to therein, including all attachments, appendices and documents incorporated by reference therein. The construction contract, in principle, is only binding between the Employer and the Contractor.

According to Article 1678 (Elements or requirements of formal construction contract) of the *Civil Code*:

12 *State of Emergency Proclamation Enacted to Counter and Control the Spread of COVID-19 and Mitigate Its Impact Proclamation No. 3/2020.*

No valid contract shall exist unless:

I The parties are capable of contracting and give their consent sustainable at law.
II The object of the contract is sufficiently defined and is possible and lawful.
III The contract is made in the form prescribed by law, if any.

The forms are templates prepared by the concerned government legal body to be practised by both private and governmental contracts and can be translated and written in any language in which all the stakeholders can read, hear and understand. The contracting parties must be present in person in a justice office and sign a written agreement and must pay a fee for the office of the Department of Justice.

The fundamental elements of contract also must be fulfilled for the contract to be valid. Those fundamentals are:

- Capacity of the contracting parties
- Consent of the contracting parties
- Object of the contract
- Form of contract, if any

For contracts, the Standard Bidding Document for national competitive bidders states that a Bidder will be debarred from participation in public procurement for a specified period of time if at any time it is determined that the Bidder has engaged in corrupt, fraudulent, collusive, coercive or obstructive practices in competing for or in executing a contract.

It is the Government of the Federal Democratic Republic of Ethiopia's policy to require that Public Bodies, as well as bidders/suppliers, observe the highest standards of ethics during the procurement and execution of contracts. In pursuance of this policy, the Ethiopian Government represented by the Public Procurement and Property Administration Agency (PPA) requires that Public Bodies shall include in bidding documents provisions against corrupt practices.

Avoidance of any taxes, duties and levies is strictly prohibited and unless otherwise specified in the Special Conditions of Contract, the Contractor shall bear and make all payments imposed on the Contractor by all municipal, state or national government authorities, both within and outside the Federal Democratic Republic of Ethiopia, in connection with the Works to be carried out under the Contract.

The currency for the bid and payment for those inputs to the works which the Bidder expects to provide from within Ethiopia shall be quoted in Ethiopian Birr, unless otherwise specified in the Bid Data Sheet (**BDS**).

6.5 What Special Provisions in the Particular Conditions are necessary for consistency with applicable laws in Ethiopia?

6.5.1 FIDIC General Conditions are incompatible or inconsistent with Ethiopian governing law of the contract

The following sections identify provisions of Ethiopian mandatory law for both private and public contracts that are inconsistent with FIDIC provisions, necessitating Special

Provisions in the Particular Conditions. PPA 2011 is mandatory for national competitive bidders to enter into a contract either with private or public firms.

6.5.1.1 Variations

The FIDIC 2017 Red Book states that a Variation may be initiated by the Engineer at any time before the issue of the Taking Over Certificate for the Works. However, the PPA 2011 Standard Conditions of Construction Contract provides that the Engineer shall have power to order any modification to any part of the works necessary for the proper completion and/or functioning of the works. Such modifications may include additions, omissions, substitutions, changes in quality, quantity, form, character, kind, position, dimension, level or line and changes in the specified sequence, method or timing of execution of the works. No order for a modification shall have the effect of invalidating the contract, but the financial effect, if any, of all such modifications shall be valued in accordance with PPA 2011 Standard Conditions of Contract clauses 15.5 and 15.7.

6.5.1.2 Engineers' duty and authority

FIDIC clause 3.1 states that the Employer shall appoint the Engineer who shall carry out the duties assigned to him/her in the Contract. The Engineer's staff shall include suitably qualified engineers and other professionals who are competent to carry out these duties. The Engineer shall have no authority to amend the Contract. The Engineer may exercise the authority attributable to the Engineer as specified in or necessarily to be implied from the Contract. If the Engineer is required to obtain the approval of the Employer before exercising a specified authority, the requirements shall be as stated in the Particular Conditions. The Employer undertakes not to impose further constraints on the Engineer's authority, except as agreed with the Contractor. However, whenever the Engineer exercises a specified authority for which the Employer's approval is required, then (for the purposes of the Contract) the Employer shall be deemed to have given approval.

The PPA 2011 Standard Conditions of Construction Contract clauses 12.1 and 12.2 state that except where otherwise specifically stated and subject to any restriction in the Special Conditions of Contract (**SCC**), any action required or permitted to be taken and any document required or permitted to be executed under this Contract by the Public Body or the Contractor may be taken or executed by the Engineer named in the SCC. Except as expressly stated in the SCC, the Engineer shall not have authority to relieve the Contractor of any of its obligations under the Contract. Any notice, information or communication given to or made by an Engineer shall be deemed to have been given or made by the Public Body.

6.5.1.3 Delay damages

The PPA 2011 Standard Conditions of Construction Contract sub-clause 78.1 states that if the Contractor fails to complete the works within the time period(s) specified in the Contract the Public Body shall, without formal notice and without prejudice to its other remedies under the Contract, be entitled to liquidated damages for every day or part thereof which shall elapse between the end of the period specified for implementation of tasks or extended Intended Completion Date under General Condition of Contract (**GCC**) clause 72 and the actual date of completion, at the rate and up to the maximum amount specified in GCC clause 27. If the works have been the subject of partial acceptance in accordance with GCC clause 86, the liquidated damages specified in GCC clause 27 may be reduced in the proportion which the value of the accepted part bears to the value of the whole of the works.

6.5.1.4 Force majeure

PPA 2011 sub-clause 18.1 states that *force majeure* shall mean an event or events which are beyond the reasonable control of the Contractor, and which makes the Contractor's performance of its obligations hereunder impossible or so impractical as reasonably to be considered impossible in the circumstances, and includes:

(a) An official prohibition preventing the performance of a contract
(b) A natural catastrophe such as an earthquake, fire, explosion, storm, floods or other adverse weather conditions
(c) International or civil war
(d) Other instances of *force majeure* identified as such by the *Civil Code*

6.5.2 FIDIC General Conditions are incompatible or inconsistent with the law of the Site/Country

No Special Provisions are necessary to amend the FIDIC General Conditions for consistency with the law if the Site is in Ethiopia.

6.5.3 FIDIC General Conditions are incompatible or inconsistent with the relevant laws on dispute determination in Ethiopia

6.5.3.1 Dispute settlement

The PPA 2011 clause 26 refers to dispute settlement raised by different parties. The dispute settlement methods widely implemented in the Ethiopian construction industry are broadly classified as amicable and non-amicable. Amicable includes negotiation, mediation and conciliation. Non amicable includes arbitration, litigation and adjudication.

Dispute Boards are not used in Ethiopia because most of the contracting parties prefer litigation as a dispute resolution method.

6.6 Summary of applicable legislation for Ethiopian governing law of the contract

6.6.1 Entry into a construction contract

Contracts generally	*Civil Code of the Empire of Ethiopia Proclamation No. 165 of 1960* Article 1675
Public Construction contracts	MOWUD Standard Conditions of Contract for Construction of Civil Work Projects December 1994 clause 9 PPA Standard Conditions of Construction Contract 2011 section B

6.6.2 Operation of a construction contract

Force majeure	*Civil Code of the Empire of Ethiopia Proclamation No. 165 of 1960* Article 1792 PPA Standard Conditions of Construction Contract 2011 clause 18
Hardship	Not applicable in Ethiopia under the current law
Guarantees under forms of Security (Tender Security, Demand Guarantee, Surety Bond, Advance Payment Guarantee, Retention Money Guarantee, Payment Guarantee by Employer)	*Civil Code of the Empire of Ethiopia Proclamation No. 165 of 1960* Articles 1851 (A), 1920, 3160 (1) and 173 (2) PPA Standard Conditions of Construction Contract 2011 clause 21.2 (L)

6.6.3 Termination of a construction contract

Bankruptcy, insolvency, liquidation	*Civil Code* Article 2582 PPA Standard Conditions of Construction Contract 2011 clause 21.2 (C)

6.6.4 Dispute resolution

Limitation periods	*Civil Code of the Empire of Ethiopia Proclamation No. 165 of 1960* Article 3334 (1) PPA Standard Conditions of Construction Contract 2011 sub-clause 26.5
Liability	PPA Standard Conditions of Construction Contract 2011 clauses 27, 39
Arbitration	*Civil Code of the Empire of Ethiopia Proclamation No. 165 of 1960* Article 723 (1) PPA Standard Conditions of Construction Contract 2011 sub-clause 26.6

6.7 Summary of applicable legislation if the Site/Country is in Ethiopia

6.7.1 Operation of a construction contract

Registration and administration of professionals – Engineers, Architects, Quantity Surveyors, Certifiers, Building Surveyors, Surveyors	*Construction Certification and Registration Directive No. 648/2021*
Registration/licensing of Contractors and subcontractors	*Construction Certification and Registration Directive No. 648/2021*
Subcontractors	*Construction Certification and Registration Directive No. 648/2021*

Labour	*Federal Democratic Republic of Ethiopia Constitution* *Civil Code of the Empire of Ethiopia Proclamation No. 165 of 1960* *Labour Proclamation No. 1156/2019* PPA Standard Conditions of Construction Contract 2011
Design/moral rights	*Civil Code of the Empire of Ethiopia Proclamation No. 165 of 1960*
Copyright	*Federal Democratic Republic of Ethiopia Constitution* *Civil Code of the Empire of Ethiopia Proclamation No. 165 of 1960*
First Nation people's land rights	*Federal Democratic Republic of Ethiopia Constitution* *Civil Code of the Empire of Ethiopia Proclamation No. 165 of 1960*
Heritage	*Federal Democratic Republic of Ethiopia Constitution* *Classification of Cultural Heritages in National and Region Cultural Heritages Proclamation No. 839/2014*
Environment	*Environmental Pollution Control Proclamation No. 300/2002*
Local procurement	*Federal Government Procurement and Property Administration Proclamation No. 649/2009*
Public procurement	*Federal Procurement and Property Administration Proclamation No. 649/2009*
Building and construction permits, execution of construction work, standard of construction work	*Ethiopian Building Proclamation No. 624/2009* Ethiopian Construction Practice Norm ECPN-MUDHCo No 26/2015
Health and safety	*National Building Proclamation No. 624/2005* *Labour Proclamation No. 1156/2019* *Occupational Health and Safety Directive 2008* PPA Standard Conditions of Construction Contract 2011
Calibration of testing apparatus, equipment and instruments	*Ethiopian Standard Agency Council of Ministers Regulation No. 193/2010* *Quality and Standards Authority of Ethiopia Establishment Proclamation No. 413/2004*
Ownership of Plant and Materials	*Construction Certification and Registration Directive No. 648/2021*
Employer's sale of Contractor's Equipment, surplus material, wreckage and Temporary Works Insurance	*Construction Certification and Registration Directive No. 648/2021* PPA Standard Conditions of Construction Contract 2011
Statutory rights that coexist with contractual rights	PPA Standard Conditions of Construction Contract 2011
Liability for defective work	PPA Standard Conditions of Construction Contract 2011

6.8 Summary of applicable legislation if the 'seat' of the dispute determination is Ethiopia

Dispute resolution	*Civil Code of the Empire of Ethiopia Proclamation No. 165 of 1960* PPA Standard Conditions of Construction Contract 2011
Limitation periods	*Civil Code of the Empire of Ethiopia Proclamation No. 165 of 1960* Article 3334 (1) PPA Standard Conditions of Construction Contract 2011 sub-clause 26.5
Arbitration	*Civil Code of the Empire of Ethiopia Proclamation No. 165 of 1960* Article 723 (1) PPA Standard Conditions of Construction Contract 2011 clause 26, sub-clause 26.6

6.9 Issues that a court or arbitrator may construe differently than expected from the words of the Contract because of local law or custom

6.9.1 Capacity and form

The capacity to dispose of a right without consideration shall be required for the submission to arbitration of a dispute concerning such right. The arbitral submission shall be drawn up in the form required by law for disposing without consideration of the right to which it relates.[13]

6.9.2 Good faith

The Ethiopian law requirements of good faith of the parties to a contract agreement applies to the construction of contract terms; frequently the principle of reasonable interpretation is not formulated explicitly but is applied in the guise of good faith. In particular, Notices and Notice periods and the application and execution of time-bar clauses will not be as stringent, literal and rigorous as under common law. Instead, they will be restrained by the good faith legal standard that applies to civil law. In situations governed by Ethiopian law, the precise application of the FIDIC suite's time-bar provisions – frequently found in various common law jurisdictions – will not be made without first considering reasonableness and good faith.

6.9.3 Consent

Consent is the declared will of the individual to enter into a contract. It reflects the willingness of the parties to enter into a legally binding relation. Consent of the intended contracting parties decomposes into offer and acceptance.[14] A contract shall depend on

13 *Civil Code of the Empire of Ethiopia* Article 3326.
14 *Civil Code of the Empire of Ethiopia* Article 1679.

the consent of the parties who defined the object of their undertaking and agree to be bound thereby. This shows the contracting parties are not intended to sign any agreement forcefully or without their willingness. Further, a contract shall be completed where the contracting parties have expressed their agreement thereto.

6.9.4 Object of Contract

The object of the contract shall be freely determined by the contracting parties subject to restrictions and prohibitions as are provided by law. The object of a contract is the outcome of the obligations of the contracting parties in the construction contract, the obligations of the Employer and of the Contractor. The obligations of the contracting parties can be divided into two broad terms: promises and considerations.[15] The obligations are given for each contracting party to do or not to do something. Considerations are the preconditions to be fulfilled by each contracting party in order to be bound by a contract agreement.

6.10 Additional references for Ethiopia

6.10.1 Books

Biruk Seyoum Tafesse, 'Challenges of lower grade contractors in Addis Ababa' (October 2019) Independent project submitted to the School of Graduate Studies in partial fulfilment of the requirements for the degree of Master of Engineering in Civil Engineering (Construction Technology and Management). http://etd.aau.edu.et/bitstream/handle/123456789/21886/Biruk%20Seyoum.pdf?sequence=1&isAllowed=y

Million Bayou Taddesse, 'Building Information Modelling (BIM) Project Implementation Assessment: The Case of Ethiopian Construction Works Corporation' (2020) Thesis submitted to St Mary's University School of Graduate Studies in partial fulfilment of the requirements for MBA in Project Management. http://repository.smuc.edu.et/bitstream/123456789/5827/1/BIM%20implementation%20assessement.pdf

Tecle Hagos Bahta, *The Regulatory Framework for Public Procurement in Ethiopia* (Cambridge University Press, 2017). https://doi.org/10.1017/CBO9781139236058.005

6.10.2 Journal articles

Aberra Bekele, 'Alternative Dispute Resolution Methods in Construction Industry: An Assessment of Ethiopian Situation' (2005). http://etd.aau.edu.et/handle/123456789/506

Abebe Dinku, 'Insurance Requirements and Practices of Ethiopia's Construction Sector' (2000) V17 *Zede Journal*. www.ajol.info/index.php/zj/article/view/124064

Alem Tesfahunegn, 'Construction in Ethiopia' (2018) *Building Design Enterprise, Ethiopia*. www.humanitarianlibrary.org/resource/construction-ethiopia-0

Assefa Ayana, 'Investigation on the Impact of Covid-19 Pandemic in Public Building Construction in Bahir Dar City, Ethiopia' (Bahir Dar University, 2021).

Elias Defalgn Debelo, 'Comparisons between FIDIC (1999) and Ethiopian PPA (2011) Conditions of Contract in Terms of Time' (2022) 10.5 *Global Scientific Journals*. www.researchgate.net/publication/360609595_Comparisons_between_FIDIC_1999_and_Ethiopian_PPA_2011_Conditions_of_Contract_in_terms_of_Time

15 *Civil Code of the Empire of Ethiopia* Article 1711.

Fuad Jemal, 'Comparisons between MDB FIDIC (2010) and PPA (2011) Condition of Contract and Applicable Law Special Emphasis to Delay and Disruption Claim' (11 February 2019) *Construction Contracts and Business Law.* www.academia.edu/40254315/Comparisons_between_MDB_FIDIC_2010_and_PPA_2011_condition_of_contract_and_applicable_law_special_emphasis_to_delay_and_disruption_claim
Tadesse Ayalew Zelele, 'Assessment on Performance and Challenges of Ethiopian Construction Industry' (January 2016). www.researchgate.net/publication/315516093_Assessment_on_Performance_and_Challenges_of_Ethiopian_Construction_Industry
Wendy Dereje Tula, 'An Independent Project on Comparison between FIDIC and PPA Condition of Contracts for the Selected Clauses' (5 May 2017). https://nadre.ethernet.edu.et/record/2376

6.10.3 Internet

https://en.wikipedia.org/wiki/Constitutions_of_Ethiopia#:~:text=Ethiopia%20has%20had%20four%20constitutions,1987%20Constitution%20of%20Ethiopia
https://en.wikipedia.org/wiki/Ethiopia
www.nyulawglobal.org/globalex/Ethiopia1.html#federalcourts
https://constructionproxy.com/
www.nyulawglobal.org/globalex/Ethiopia1.html#:~:text=1.1.-,Structure%20and%20Jurisdiction,are%20vested%20in%20the%20courts
www.trans-lex.org/604600/_/ethiopian-civil-code/

CHAPTER 7

Applying FIDIC Contracts in Jordan

Husni Madi and Firas Malhas

CONTENTS

 DOI: 10.4324/9781003206910-7

7.1 Outline of the Jordanian legal environment

7.1.1 The constitutional structure of Jordan

Jordan is a constitutional monarchy state that gained its independence on 25 May 1946. Jordan was transformed from an Emirate to a Kingdom and it is now named as the Hashemite Kingdom of Jordan. The first *Constitution* of the Hashemite Kingdom of Jordan was enacted in 1947 and it was repealed by the current *Constitution of the Hashemite Kingdom of Jordan of 1952.*

The *Constitution of 1952* has been subject to several amendments, the most important of which is the one made in 2011, after the so-called 'Arab Spring', where one-third of the *Constitution* was amended. The amended *Constitution of 2011*, among other things, has introduced the Constitutional Court to enhance the rule of law and legal transparency.[1] The current *Constitution* includes ten Chapters with 131 Articles.

It is worth mentioning that the *Constitution* contains a range of human rights principles, which are reorganised, protected and guaranteed by the *Constitution* such as personal freedom, work and education, freedom of expression, freedom of scientific research and literary, technical, cultural and sports excellence. In addition, the *Jordanian Constitution* provides for the protection of private property, which cannot be expropriated except for public benefit. The right of fair compensation is enshrined in Article 11 of the *Constitution*, which provides that 'No property of any person or any part thereof may be expropriated except for purposes of public utility and in consideration of a just compensation, as may be prescribed by law'.

7.1.2 The legal system in Jordan

In Jordan, the legislation is the primary source of law and the *Constitution* is on top of the legislation. While the *Constitution* is considered '*supreme and superior* over all other legislations',[2] the *Civil Law*, which was issued in 1976 and came into force on 1 January 1977, is considered the main cornerstone of the Jordanian legal system.[3]

The *Civil Law 1976* 'repealed large parts of the nineteenth century Ottoman Majalla',[4] whereby Article 1448 of the *Civil Law 1976* provides that: 'Whatever contradicts with the provisions of this law shall be repealed from the Al-Majallah al-Ahkam al-Adaliyyah'.[5]

According to Article 2 of the *Civil Law 1976*, the judge shall apply the sources of jurisdiction in the order stipulated in the *Civil Law*, the first of which is the law in general including the law enacted by the Parliament and the regulations and instructions issued pursuant thereto. If the judge did not find anything in the first source, then the judge will apply the provisions of Islamic jurisprudence as the second source. The third source to

1 Shams Al Din Al-Hajjaji, 'Jordanian Constitutional Court: Toward a Democratic, Effective and Accessible' (2017) IV *Indonesian Journal of International & Comparative Law* 269–277.

2 Judgment 6/2017 issued by the Constitutional Court, published in the Official Gazette No. 5484 dated 3 October 2017.

3 The *Civil Law*, published in the Official Gazette No. 2645 dated 1 August 1976.

4 Lynn Welchman, *Beyond the Code: Muslim Family Law and the Shari'a Judiciary in the Palestinian West Bank* (1st ed, Kluwer Law International, 2000) 72.

5 Al-Majallah al-Ahkam al-Adaliyyah is the *Civil Code* of the Ottoman Empire for the year 1876 and it was applied in Jordan until the issuance of the *Jordanian Civil Law* in the year 1976.

be followed is the legal precedents, and if the judge 'finds nothing in the above-stated sources, it is expected to use the general principles of justice'.[6]

In the context of international treaties and conventions, the principle of supremacy of the international conventions and treaties is well-established by the Jordanian courts. The Court of Cassation, the highest court in Jordan, has adopted this principle and confirmed that 'international treaties and conventions take precedence over local laws and have priority in application when they conflict with the said laws',[7] provided that the said treaties and conventions do not contradict with provisions of the *Constitution*. The aforesaid principle was reaffirmed by the Constitutional Court in 2020 in its interpretational decision number 1 for the year 2020, where it confirmed that 'international treaties have binding force among their parties, and the States are under the obligation to respect the same as long as the said treaties remain in force and as long as these treaties have been concluded and ratified' and therefore 'it is not permissible to issue a law that completely contradicts the obligations imposed on the parties to an international treaty'.[8]

7.1.3 The court system in Jordan

Under the *Constitution*, the ordinary courts have jurisdiction 'over all persons in all matters, civil and criminal, including cases brought by or against the Government'.[9] The *Constitution* identifies three categories of courts: the civil courts, religious courts and special courts.[10] Generally speaking, the ordinary courts consist of the Magistrate Courts, the First Instance Courts, the Courts of Appeal and the Court of Cassation. These are in addition to the administrative courts, namely the Primary Administrative Court and the High Administrative Court.

As for the special courts, they include, among others, the military courts which are considered part of this category and have jurisdiction over matters related to national security crimes and military personnel. Also, the taxation courts are part of these special courts, and they have jurisdiction over taxation cases and disputes. As for civil issues, statuses such as marriage, divorce, inheritance and child custody are matters that fall under the religious courts.

7.2 The construction industry in Jordan

7.2.1 Overview

The construction industry in Jordan is one of the major and oldest sectors of the economy. This sector is heavily regulated where the consulting engineers, architects and designers operate under the umbrella of the Engineering Offices Commission (**EOC**),

6 Philip Dew, Jonathan Wallace and Anthony Shoult, *Doing Business with Jordan* (1st ed, GMB Publishing Ltd, 2004) 275.

7 The decisions issued by the Civil Cassation Court 4309/2003 dated 22 April 2004, 847/2001 dated 8 January 2001 and 818/2003 dated 9 June 2003.

8 Interpretational Decision Number 1 for the year 2020 issued by the Constitutional Court, published in the Official Gazette No. 5640, page 2153 dated 3 May 2020.

9 Article 102 of the *Jordanian Constitution*.

10 Article 99 of the *Jordanian Constitution*.

and the contractors' operations are regulated by the Jordanian Construction Contractors Association (**JCCA**).

The law prohibits contractors from performing engineering consultancy and design works, and similarly, consulting engineers, architects and designers are prohibited by law from performing construction works. Therefore, Contractors under the Yellow Book, Silver Book, Gold Book or Emerald Book will have to employ licensed consulting engineers/designers as Subcontractors in order to perform the design under those FIDIC forms of contract.

The construction sector is one of the major contributing sectors to the economy in Jordan. For example, in the year 2021, there were 8,201 projects awarded to contractors in the value of 1,024.30 million JOD[11] (US$ 1,444.73 million),[12] and the total certified built-up area for the same year was 11,518,211 m^2.[13] Moreover, this sector is a major employer of the workforce in Jordan, where in the year 2021 there were 3,195 registered contractors,[14] and there were 8,115 professionals employed by 1,295 engineering consultancy firms.[15]

7.2.2 Structure

The construction industry in Jordan is driven by the market's demand for building and civil engineering works. This has had a direct influence on the nature and distribution of the engineering disciplines offered by both consultants/designers and contractors; 49.4% of the 1,295 engineering consultancy firms registered in the year 2021 were civil engineering firms, 33.4% were architectural firms and 15.5% were electro-mechanical engineering firms.[16]

Similarly, the preceding is also reflected in the type of projects awarded to contractors. The total value of projects of US$ 1,444.73 million awarded in 2021 was distributed as follows: 66.57% building works, 9.80% electro-mechanical works, 7.60% water and wastewater, 4.71% roads and highways and 11.41% other types of works.[17]

The majority of investments, and by extension construction projects, are concentrated in the capital of Jordan, Amman. It follows, therefore, that out of the 8,201 projects with a value of 1,024.30 million JOD (US$ 1,444.73 million) awarded in 2021, 4,862 projects with a value of 484 million JOD (US$ 682.66 million) were in Amman.[18]

Consequently, this requires that the majority of consultants and contractors be based in Amman; 74.8% of engineering consultancy firms[19] and 56.51% of contractors are based in Amman.[20] Naturally, nearly all of the foreign consultants and contractors operating in Jordan have their local branches registered in Amman.

11 Jordanian Dinar.
12 Jordanian Construction Contractors Association (JCCA), *Annual Report 2021* (JCCA 2022).
13 Engineering Offices Commission (EOC), *Annual Report 2021* (EOC 2022).
14 Above, n12.
15 Above, n13.
16 *Ibid.*
17 Above, n12.
18 *Ibid.*
19 Above, n13.
20 Jordanian Construction Contractors Association (JCCA), *Annual Report 2020* (JCCA 2021).

7.2.3 Licensing/registration

Under the *Construction Contractors Law 1987* as amended,[21] construction contracting works in Jordan may be executed only by Jordanian contractors. Non-Jordanian contractors may access the Jordanian market and execute projects of a specialised nature requiring foreign expertise. The specialised nature of the project is determined by an official specialised technical committee (**Technical Committee**), which is chaired by the Minister of Public Works and Housing and the membership of the Secretary General of the Ministry of Public Works and Housing, the Director of the Government Tenders Department, the President of the Jordanian Engineers Association, the President of the Jordanian Construction Contractors Association (JCCA) and a representative of the department related to the project.

The non-Jordanian contractors who are awarded a project must cooperate with Jordanian contractor(s). This cooperation may take the form of a partnership or joint venture subject to the prior approval of the JCCA and the Council of Ministers, based on the recommendations of the Technical Committee.

In accordance with the *Construction Contractors Law 1987*, it is not permissible for any natural or legal person, whether Jordanian or non-Jordanian, to engage in construction contracting business in Jordan unless it is registered with the JCCA.

Non-Jordanian contractors, after being awarded construction works, have to register a branch, known as an 'operating foreign company'. This branch will be registered with the Companies Control Department at the Ministry of Industry and Trade, and after that, it has to be licensed by the JCCA.

Usually, the joint venture concluded between the non-Jordanian contractor and the Jordanian firm needs to be notarised by a competent Notary Public. In the event that the project will be executed in the Aqaba Special Economic Zone, the joint venture must be registered with the Aqaba Special Economic Zone Authority as a 'registered enterprise' in order to benefit from the exemptions and privileges furnished in the zone such as the custom duties exemption, the 5% income tax on the net income of any project and the 7% sales tax.

Under the applicable regulations and instructions issued pursuant to the *Aqaba Special Economic Zone Law 2000*,[22] the joint venture must provide the following documents in order to be registered as a 'registered enterprise' in the Aqaba Special Economic Zone: (a) a copy of the joint venture agreement, provided that it is notarised by a Notary Public and duly translated into the Arabic language; (b) a document showing the authorised signatory on behalf of the joint venture; (c) the registration certificate for the parties of the joint venture, proving that the parties are registered with the Aqaba Special Economic Zone Authority.

As for foreign consulting engineering firms, they are not allowed to provide any consulting engineering services unless they register with the Engineering Offices Commission (EOC) and the Jordan Engineers Association. Also, they have to associate themselves

21 The *Construction Contractors Law*, published in the Official Gazette No. 3468 date 1 April 1987, came into force on 1 May 1987 and was amended in 2014 by virtue of the *Law Number 4 for the year 2014*, published in the Official Gazette number 5268 dated 2 February 2014.

22 The *Aqaba Special Economic Zone Law*, published in the Official Gazette No. 4453 date 31 August 2000, came into force on 31 August 2000 and was amended several times, the last of which was in 2022 by virtue of the *Law Number 14 for the year 2022*, published in the Official Gazette No. 5799 dated 16 June 2022.

with a Jordanian engineering firm(s), and they have to obtain the approval of the EOC and the Jordan Engineers Association in respect of their association with the Jordanian engineering firm.

7.2.4 Labour relations

The employer–employee relationship is governed mainly by the *Labour Law Number 8 for the year 1996* as amended.[23] The *Labour Law 1996* defines the 'employee' as 'every person, male or female, who performs a work against salary and is a subordinate to the Employer and at his service. This covers the juveniles and those under probation or rehabilitation'. The key elements of the employer–employee relationship lie in subordination, supervision and salary. When these elements exist in a relationship, the relationship will fall under the umbrella of *Labour Law*.

Under Article 4 of the *Social Security Law 2014*,[24] all employees who are subject to the *Labor Law* shall be covered by the provisions of the *Social Security Law 2014* regardless of their nationality, contract duration or form and nature of salary. The employer is under the obligation to enrol his/her employees with the Social Security Corporation when his/her relation with the employees is 'regular'. The relation is deemed 'regular' when (i) the employee is retained on a daily basis and works over 16 days a month (a day is calculated based on eight-hour working shifts); (ii) the employee is retained on an hourly/per item/delivery basis who work over 16 days a month (regardless of the number of hours they work/items they produce/deliveries they make each day); or (iii) the employee receives a monthly salary, irrespective of the number of days he/she works, with the exception of the first month of employment, given that he/she works for over 16 days a month.

In the context of construction contracts, there is an important article in the *Labour Law 1996* which enables employees to initiate cases against the Employer, the Contractor and the Subcontractor, as the case may be. Article 15 (e) of the *Labour Law 1996* provides that:

> e. 1. The employees of the contractor, who work in the execution of a contracting work, may institute a lawsuit directly against the owner of the project to claim their entitlements from the contractor within the limits of entitlements due to the contractor from the owner of the project at the time of instituting the lawsuit.
> 2. The employees of the sub-contractor may institute a lawsuit directly against each of the principal contractor and the owner of the project within the limits of entitlements due on the owner of the project to the principal contractor and due on the principle contractor for the subcontractor at the time of instituting the lawsuit.
> 3. The employees mentioned in the previous two paragraphs may collect their rights by concession over the amounts due for the account of the principal contractor or the sub-contractor, and to collect their rights pari passu with the percentage of each one's right.

The courts set out certain qualifications in respect of accepting these types of cases if initiated by the employee, whereby the employee should establish the existence of amounts

23 The *Labour Law*, published in the Official Gazette No. 4113 dated 15 April 1996, came into force on 14 June 1996 and was amended several times, the last of which was in 2019 by virtue of the *Law Number 14 for the year 2019*, published in the Official Gazette No. 5573 dated 16 May 2019.

24 The *Social Security Law*, published in the Official Gazette No. 5267 dated 29 January 2014, came into force on 28 February 2014 and was amended several times, the last of which was in 2019 by virtue of the *Law Number 24 for the year 2019*, published in the Official Gazette No. 5599 dated 1 October 2019.

due on the owner of the project or the Contractor, as the case may be. The Court of Cassation concluded in several cases that

> whereas [the employee] did not provide any evidence to prove the amounts owed to the sub-contractor towards the original contractor at the time of filing the lawsuit … then the conclusion reached by the [Court of Appeal] by dismissing the lawsuit initiated against the original contractor is legally correct.[25]

The same principle was reaffirmed in another decision issued by the Court of Cassation whereby it concluded that:

> whereas, according to the provisions of Article (15/H/1), the original contractor has no amounts due from the project owner at the time of filing the lawsuit then the claim made by the employee against the original contractor is not based on a legal proper ground.[26]

Generally speaking, the *Labour Law 1996* sets out the rights and obligations of the employer and the employee including sick leave, annual leave, maternity leave and paternity leave. It also identifies the working hours, overtime, as well as the events where the employer can terminate the employment contract without compensation. Under the *Labour Law 1996*, any condition in a contract or agreement under which the employee waives any of his/her rights given to him/her by the *Labour Law* shall be deemed invalid.

The termination of unlimited period employment contracts by the employer for reasons other than those stipulated in the law, including Article 28 of the *Labour Law 1996*, enables the employee to claim compensation of half a month's salary for every year of work, with a two months' salary being the minimum compensation.[27]

7.2.5 Safety culture

Safety and occupational health are dealt with in more than one law in Jordan. The *Constitution* paved the way for establishing the main principles to protect the health of employees,[28] and then the *Labour Law 1996* established the main obligations of the employers to protect their employees from dangers and diseases arising from performing the work. In addition to these laws, the *Public Health Law 2008*[29] empowered the Ministry of Health to monitor the occupational health environment of employees in order to safeguard the safety and health of employees in the workplace. In addition, the *Social Security Law 2014* created the umbrella for compensating employees who are injured during their work, starting from obliging the employer to enrol their employees under the social security scheme up until the mechanism of compensating the employee in case of injury or death.

In addition to the local laws, the relevant international treaties and conventions dealing with safety and occupatioal health are recognised in Jordan. This includes the *Convention on Safety and Health in Construction No. 167 for the year 1988*, which focuses on the

25 The decisions issued by the Civil Cassation Court 5168/2020 dated 24 December 2020.

26 The decisions issued by the Civil Cassation Court 4647/2020 dated 1 December 2020.

27 Article (25) of the *Jordanian Labour Law 1996*.

28 Article 23 of the *Constitution*.

29 The *Public Health Law*, published in the Official Gazette No. 4924 dated 17 August 2008, came into force on 17 August 2008.

'development and implementation of laws or regulations that ensure the safety and health of construction workers'.[30]

The Ministry of Labour periodically issues occupational safety and health procedures including safety-related issues in the construction sector. These procedures usually include safety procedures to avoid major risks on construction sites as well as safe access to sites; providing tools to prevent work risks such as gloves, clothes, shoes and glasses (personal protective equipment, i.e. PPE) and guiding and training employees on how to use and maintain the tools; safety procedures for working at heights and using scaffolds and ladders, in addition to other dangerous tools and equipment. This is in addition to keeping records by the employer to register accidents and injuries as well as reporting them to the competent authorities.

7.2.6 Modular construction using factory-fabricated components

While modular construction, or what is commonly known in Jordan as pre-cast concrete construction, is not alien to the Jordanian construction industry, it is rarely used in residential or commercial building projects. The main use of modular construction is in bridge projects, marine works and industrial and heavy civil works projects.

7.2.7 Technology/innovation/BIM

Intellectual property rights are protected by several laws in Jordan such as the *Copyright Law 1992*,[31] *Industrial Designs Law 2000*,[32] *Patents Law 1999*,[33] *Trademarks Law 1952*[34] and *Trade Secrets and Unfair Competition Law 2000*,[35] as well as the *Labour Law 1996*.

Article 3 of the *Copyright Law 1992*, as amended, establishes the protection of innovative works in arts and sciences, regardless of the type of these works, their importance or the purpose of their production. This protection includes illustrative pictures, maps, designs, plans and three-dimensional works related to geography and surface maps of the earth, as well as computer programmes, whether in the source or machine languages.

The protection furnished by the *Copyright Law 1992* includes enabling the author to initiate criminal or civil actions before the competent courts to protect his/her rights. The infringing party may be subject to criminal penalties in the form of imprisonment for a period not less than three months and not more than three years and a fine not less than 1,000 Jordanian Dinars (US$ 1,410) and not more than 3,000 Jordanian Dinars (US$ 4,230).

30 Jordan Labour Watch Phenix Centre for Economic and Informatics Studies in cooperation with Friedrich Ebert-Stiftung, 'Occupational Health and Safety in Jordan' (August 2011). www.labor-watch.net/uploads/en_labor-watch.net_635434224369543274.pdf (accessed 25 August 2022).

31 The *Copyright and Neighbouring Rights Protection Law*, published in the Official Gazette No. 3821 dated 16 April 1992, came into force on 16 April 1992.

32 The *Industrial Designs Law*, published in the Official Gazette No. 4423 dated 2 April 2000, came into force on 2 April 2000.

33 The *Patents Law* published in the Official Gazette No. 4389 dated 1 November 1999.

34 The *Trademarks Law* published in the Official Gazette No. 1110 dated 1 June 1952.

35 The *Trade Secrets and Unfair Competition Law*, published in the Official Gazette No. 4423 dated 2 April 2000, came into force on 2 April 2000.

In addition to the foregoing, under Article 20 of the *Labour Law 1996* and Article 6 of the *Copyright Law 1992*, the intellectual property rights that are invented by the employee are vested in the employer, provided that the work was invented during his/her work with the employer and it was related to the employer's business or if the employee utilised or used the employer's data, tools or material in respect thereto.

While BIM is used sporadically in major private sector projects, there are no national BIM protocols or guidelines, as the implementation of BIM is not mandatory by law.

7.2.8 Government/private sector procurement

The *Public–Private Partnership Projects Law* for the year 2020 came into force on 2 May 2020, repealing the *Public–Private Partnership Law* for the year 2014.[36] The *Public–Private Partnership Projects Law 2020* was introduced by the Government in order to stimulate and attract investments and to increase economic growth through projects that are aimed to help revitalise the national economy.

The main aims introduced by the *Public–Private Partnership Projects Law 2020* include the construction, rehabilitation, operation, maintenance, management and development of public infrastructure and public utilities. This is in addition to the provision of public services and providing financing for government projects, along with benefiting from the private sector's expertise and technical and technological knowledge in the construction and management of Public–Private Partnership Projects.

A National Register was created in accordance with the *Public–Private Partnership Projects Law 2020*, under which public investment projects were identified. The projects are published on the website of the PPP Unit[37] and investors are able to obtain the necessary information regarding these projects. The law enables the private sector to submit a direct proposal for any PPP Project in order to be listed in the Register and its execution in accordance with the due process established under the *Public–Private Partnership Projects Law 2020* and the associated *Regulations*.

In accordance with the *Public–Private Partnership (PPP) Regulation for the year 2021*,[38] a PPP Project will pass through several phases, progressing from the selection phase up to the execution phase. The *Public–Private Partnership Projects Law 2020* and the associated *Regulations* identify the preparation of the projects and their tendering process.

The *Public–Private Partnership Projects Law 2020* provides the general legal framework that should be applied in order to execute PPP Projects. It also sets out the roles, duties and responsibilities of all the stakeholders involved in PPP Projects.

7.2.9 Insurance requirements

Insurance in Jordan is governed generally by the *Insurance Regulatory Law No. (12) of 2021*. There are no legal stipulations in respect of who, as between the Employer and the Contractor, shall affect and maintain insurance in construction projects.

36 The Public–Private Partnership Projects Law published in the Official Gazette No. 1972 dated 2/4/2020.

37 https://pppu.gov.jo/ (accessed 18 October 2022).

38 The Public–Private Partnership Projects Law No. 23/2021 published in the Official Gazette No. 5721 dated 1 June 2021.

Nevertheless, it is usually the Contractor who is responsible for effecting and maintaining insurance, typically by obtaining Construction All Risks insurance (**CAR insurance**), sometimes referred to as Contractors' All Risks insurance. Normally, CAR insurance includes coverage for the Works and the Contractor's Equipment, against injury to persons and damage to property (third-party insurance), and for the Contractor's Personnel.

Professional Indemnity insurance (**PI insurance**) is available in Jordan at reasonable prices for designers and 'professionals' to be obtained on a voluntary basis, as there are no legal obligations upon designers and 'professionals' to obtain such insurance.

It is worth noting that, unlike many jurisdictions which mandate a decennial liability, there is no obligation under the law for the Contractor to take out and maintain a decennial liability insurance, which remains uncommon in Jordan and can only be obtained at unreasonably high prices.

7.2.10 Common forms of contract

The FIDIC forms of contract have been, and still are, the most dominant form of contract used in the construction industry in Jordan. In 1996 the Ministry of Public Works and Housing (**MPWH**) issued the first edition of the Contract Agreement Book for Construction Projects,[39] a local form of contract heavily based on the FIDIC Red Book 1987.

In 2004, the MPWH issued its first edition of the Contract Agreement Book for Construction Projects which is closely based on the FIDIC Book Red Book 1999.[40] Since 2004, subsequent editions of the Contract Agreement Book were released, and the current edition is the 2013 Second Reprint with Amendments to the 2010 Edition.[41]

While the use of the Contract Agreement Book is only mandatory in governmental and public sector projects, the private sector followed suit voluntarily in using the Contract Agreement Book. Today, the Contract Agreement Book is by far the most predominant form of construction contract in Jordan.

In 2007, the MPWH released its first and current edition of the Short Contract Agreement[42] for simple and uncomplicated projects, which is closely based on the FIDIC Green Book 1999. Nevertheless, it did not meet the same success as that of the Contract Agreement Book, even within the public sector.

Notwithstanding the preceding, the FIDIC forms of contract are still used in the construction industry in Jordan, particularly for international projects. The most widely used form of contract is the FIDIC Red Book 1999, followed by sporadic uses of the Yellow Book 1999, and the Silver Book 1999.

There is talk about using the Gold Book on new future water projects; however, it appears that the Gold Book will not be properly used as the operation period will be significantly shorter than the recommended 20 years.

---

39 The Ministry of Public Works and Housing of Jordan (MPWH), *Contract Agreement Book for Construction Projects* (1st ed, MPWH, 1996).

40 The Ministry of Public Works and Housing of Jordan (MPWH), *Contract Agreement Book for Construction Projects* (1st ed, MPWH, 2004).

41 The Ministry of Public Works and Housing of Jordan (MPWH), *Contract Agreement Book for Construction Projects* (2nd ed, MPWH, 2013).

42 The Ministry of Public Works and Housing of Jordan (MPWH), *Short Contract Agreement* (1st ed MPWH, 2007).

Recently, a growing interest in the 2017 rainbow suite has been noticed. Nevertheless, this interest is more directed towards training on this new suite rather than adopting the suite for projects in the near future.

7.2.11 Dispute resolution

7.2.11.1 DAAB/DAB

In accordance with Jordanian laws, Dispute Avoidance/Adjudication Boards (DAAB) under the FIDIC 2017 rainbow suite, or Dispute Adjudication Boards (DAB) under the FIDIC 1999 rainbow suite, are not considered an arbitration tribunal and the decisions issued by the DAAB/DAB by their nature are not arbitration awards. The DAAB/DAB is considered to be a form of alternative dispute resolution such as mediation or conciliation. Hence, the parties to the contract may choose whether or not to incorporate a DAAB/DAB clause in their contract, since it is not obligatory.

The DAAB/DAB FIDIC sub-clauses were argued before the Jordanian courts in the context of when the parties fail to refer a dispute to the DAAB/DAB as agreed in the Contract; this renders the referral to arbitration as premature, and accordingly, it would not be possible to proceed with arbitration procedures. The Court of Cassation held in its decision number 964/2012 that: ‘after referring to the tendering offer, we find that it is included in one of its paragraphs the formation of the Dispute Adjudication Board, the method of appointing its members, the duration of their appointment, … etc.’. The court added that:

> from the foregoing, it is clear that resorting to arbitration, including the appointment of an arbitrator, shall not take place until after a resolution is issued by the Dispute Adjudication Board, if the said Board does exist, and if it was not possible to reach to an amicable settlement between the Parties.

The court concluded that no evidence was presented in the lawsuit showing that there was ‘a decision issued by the Dispute Adjudication Board regarding the dispute, or that this Board has not been formed … to that effect, the request of the applicant to appoint an arbitrator is premature’, and it was not possible to proceed with arbitration.

Despite the foregoing, the Court of Cassation has reversed this position in its decision number 1416/2019, in which it concluded that

> it is clear that [the agreement] included clauses in respect of the procedures for resolving the disputes, whether it was by means of amicable settlement or through the Dispute Adjudication Board; the said agreement has imposed an obligations on the parties in this regard, and whereas nothing was introduced in this [lawsuit] indicating that any of the parties had submitted a request to form the Dispute Resolution Board, or that either of them has resorted to an attempt to resolve the dispute through amicable settlement, therefore the commencement of arbitration procedures, which shall begin with the appointment of an arbitrator or arbitrators do comply with the provisions of the law.

Accordingly, a dispute that has not been referred to a DAAB/DAB may be referred to arbitration and the parties can proceed with the arbitration.

7.2.11.2 Jordanian courts/arbitration clauses

Generally speaking, in the event that any agreement between the parties includes an arbitration clause, such clause will be binding upon them. In a case where any party initiates any claim related to the arbitration agreement before the Jordanian courts, they will dismiss the claim based on the existence of an arbitration agreement between the parties.

In Jordan, arbitration is regulated under the *Arbitration Law No. 31* for the year 2001 as amended.[43] This law 'is based on the UNCITRAL Model Law, and is therefore considered to be the closest equivalent to the *Model Law*, although it contains some amendments in its provisions, in order to comply with Jordanian legislation'.[44] It is well established by the Jordanian courts that the disputes arising from a construction contract are arbitrable if it contains an arbitration clause. Under the *Arbitration Law 2001*, the parties can choose the rules that govern their dispute including the application of the rules of any arbitration centre in Jordan or abroad such as the International Chamber of Commerce (**ICC**), the London Court of International Arbitration (**LCIA**) and the International Centre for Dispute Resolution (**ICDR**).

In respect of the construction projects related to ministries, official institutions and government departments including the companies that are wholly owned by the Government, these projects are subject to the *Government Procurement Regulation for the year 2022*.[45] Under this *Regulation*, it is allowed to agree on referring a dispute to alternative dispute resolution such as negotiation, the appointment of conciliators or mediators or the appointment of a DAB.

In terms of dispute resolution mechanism, the *Government Procurement Regulation 2022* sets a general rule that Jordanian courts shall have jurisdiction to hear any dispute arising from a contractual relationship. However, under the *Regulation*, it is allowed for the contracting parties to agree on arbitration as a dispute resolution mechanism instead of the Jordanian courts. As per the *Government Procurement Regulation 2022*, the language of arbitration must be in principle Arabic, yet the contracting parties may agree otherwise.

Procuring entities that are subject to the *Government Procurement Regulation 2022* such as ministries, official institutions and government departments, including the companies that are wholly owned by the Government, must obtain the approval of the Council of Ministers when selecting international arbitration as a dispute resolution mechanism in their contracts. Also, they should seek the approval of the Council of Ministers if an international arbitration body is used as a body for settling the dispute arising from such a contract. In any event, the contract must include the procedural mechanism for selecting the arbitrators and the place of arbitration.

7.2.11.3 Enforcement of foreign judgments in Jordan

Judgments that are issued by foreign courts as well as foreign awards that are issued by foreign arbitration panels can be executed and enforced in Jordan in accordance with the *Foreign Judgments Enforcement Law No. (8) for the year 1952*.[46] 'Foreign Judgment' is defined by this law as:

43 The *Arbitration Law No. 31/2001* published in the Official Gazette No. 4496 dated 16 July 2001, amended as per the *Law No. 41/2018*, published in the Official Gazette No. 5551 dated 27 December 2018.

44 Al-Dhahir, Ahmad Khaldoun, 'The new Jordanian Arbitration Act 2001 and the contribution of the model law to its development' (2005). www.proquest.com/openview/4b880439e7d2bd5f6ea8a0bbd64d61b9/1?pq-origsite=gscholar&cbl=2026366&diss=y (accessed 25 August 2022).

45 The *Government Procurement Regulation No. 8/2022* published in the Official Gazette No. 5769 dated 16 January 2022.

46 The *Foreign Judgments Enforcement Law No. 8/1952* published in the Official Gazette No. 1100 dated 16 February 1952.

> every judgment issued by a court outside the Hashemite Kingdom of Jordan (including the religious courts); and related to a civil procedure and require the payment of a certain sum of money, or the delivery or transfer of title of a movable property, or settlement of account. It includes the arbitration award issued by arbitrators in arbitration proceedings, provided that this award, under the applicable law of the country where the arbitration took place, is enforceable as a judgment in the said country.

In principle, foreign judgments may be enforced in Jordan by filing a lawsuit for its enforcement before the competent court of first instance. Article 7(1) of the *Foreign Judgments Enforcement Law 1952* identifies the events where the court may announce the dismissal of the lawsuit and accordingly refuse the enforcement of the foreign judgment subject matter of the lawsuit. These events are: (a) if the court which issued the judgment had no jurisdiction; (b) if the judgment-debtor had not carried out his/her business within the jurisdiction of the court which issued the judgment, or if he/she was not residing within its jurisdiction and did not voluntarily appear before the court and did not submit to its jurisdiction; (c) if the judgment-debtor was not served with a notice to attend by the court which issued the judgment and did not appear before the court although he/she was residing or carrying out his/her business within its jurisdiction; (d) if the judgment has been obtained by fraud; (e) if the judgment-debtor established to the satisfaction of the court that the judgment has not yet become final; or (f) if the judgment was given on a cause of action which will not be entertained by Jordanian courts because either it is contradictory to public order (public policy) or public morality.

Article 7(2) of the *Foreign Judgments Enforcement Law 1952* adopted the notion of reciprocal treatment in the enforcement of foreign judgments, whereby the Jordanian competent court may refuse the enforcement in the event that the judgment is issued by a non-Jordanian court that does not allow the enforcement of judgments given by the Courts of the Hashemite Kingdom of Jordan.

The court precedents in Jordan indicate that foreign judgments can be enforced in Jordan as long as they comply with all the conditions required under the *Foreign Judgments Enforcement Law 1952.*

7.2.11.4 New York Convention

Jordan is a contracting party to *New York Convention.* Accordingly, Jordan is committed to recognising and enforcing arbitration awards as defined in the *Convention.*

In principle, foreign arbitration awards can be enforced in Jordan, provided that they are enforceable in the country in which they were issued in accordance with the laws of that country. Under the *New York Convention*, the enforcement of foreign awards may be rejected in case:

a. The parties to the arbitration agreement lack capacity;
b. The arbitration agreement is invalid under the law to which the parties agreed or the law of the location where the award was rendered;
c. The respondent was not given proper notice of the appointment of the arbitrator or of the arbitration proceedings, or was otherwise unable to present his/her case and was unable to exercise his/her right of defence;
d. The award exceeds the limits of the arbitration agreement;

e. The composition of the arbitral authority or the arbitral procedures was not in accordance with the agreement of the parties, or, in the absence of such agreement, was not in accordance with the laws of the country where the arbitration took place; or
f. The award has not yet become binding on the parties or has been set aside or suspended by a competent authority of the country in which, or under the laws of which, that award was made.

Furthermore, the *New York Convention* lists other reasons for the denial of recognition and enforcement of foreign awards by the competent authority in the country where recognition and enforcement are sought. These reasons include:

- The subject matter of the dispute is not capable of settlement by arbitration under the law of that country; or
- The recognition or enforcement of the award would be contrary to the public policy of that country.

The court precedents in Jordan indicate that foreign arbitration awards can be enforced in Jordan as long as they comply with all the conditions required under the *New York Convention* as well as the *Foreign Judgments Enforcement Law 1952*.

It is worth mentioning that the Jordanian courts tend to scrutinise if the foreign arbitration award is considered binding and final. In the event that the court is convinced that the award has not yet become binding on the parties under the laws of the country in which that award was issued, then the court may dismiss the application to enforce the award and, accordingly, refuse its enforcement.

In 2000, the Jordanian courts rejected the enforcement of an arbitration award based on the fact that the award was not final and binding on the parties. In this case, the Jordanian court argued that the French civil procedures had recognised the arbitration award, but this award could not be executed unless it was vested with *exequatur*. And whereas the award which was presented to the Jordanian courts was not presented to the courts of France for this purpose, the Jordanian court concluded that this award could not be enforced in Jordan.

In the context of the reciprocity requirements under Article 7(2) of the *Foreign Judgments Enforcement Law 1952*, it is noteworthy that it was argued before the Jordanian courts whether the courts should apply this point while scrutinising the arbitration award when considering enforcement. In 1991 the court concluded that international conventions prevail over local law and they have preference in their application, and as Jordan has subscribed to the *New York Convention* without any reservation concerning the reciprocal treatment in the enforcement of international arbitration awards, then the reciprocity principle required under the *Foreign Judgments Enforcement Law* will not apply, especially when the country where recognition and enforcement are sought and the country where the award is issued are parties to the *New York Convention*.

It should be noted that Jordan is party to the *ICSID Convention* and the vast majority of the bilateral investment treaties signed by Jordan provide for access to international arbitration.[47] These international instruments provide foreign investors with direct access

47 OECD, 'OECD Investment Policy Reviews: Jordan 2013' (2003).

to a form of international dispute settlement. In addition, foreign investors will not be restricted to Jordanian courts to settle their disputes.

7.2.12 Unique features of the construction industry in Jordan

One of the main unique features of the construction industry in Jordan is that the Contractor executing the project must be a registered and classified contractor. In addition to this unique feature, the execution of construction works in Jordan must be performed in principle by Jordanian contractors. The only exception is the execution of projects of a specialised nature requiring foreign expertise as elaborated in section 7.2.3.

The consequences of not complying with the above requirements will result in the annulment of the agreement concluded with the Contractor. Article 8 of the *Construction Contractors Law 1987* obliges official bodies such as ministries, governmental departments, public official institutions, local authorities, municipalities as well as public shareholding companies and any other entity to contract with a registered and classified contractor, and any engagement with a contractor, without being registered and classified under the applicable law, will entail annulment of this engagement.

Furthermore, if the execution of construction works is performed by a non-Jordanian contractor, the engagement may be subject to annulment if the non-Jordanian contractor is not authorised and approved by the competent Jordanian authorities.[48]

Another unique feature of the construction industry in Jordan is that engineering firms and companies including their employees (who are members of the Jordan Engineers Association) are not allowed to engage in contracting works including maintenance, operation, manufacturing or participation therein. This is in addition to not engaging in trade in materials and equipment related to the aforesaid works.[49]

7.3 The impact of COVID-19 in Jordan

7.3.1 The impact of COVID-19 on the execution of construction projects in Jordan

7.3.1.1 General overview – COVID-19-related measures

In March 2020 and in light of the global developments related to the outbreak of COVID-19 all over the world, the Government of Jordan took several decisions and measures in order to reduce the risk(s) associated with the outbreak of the virus on public health.

The King enacted a *Royal Decree* under which the *Defence Law No. (13) of 1992* came into force and effect in Jordan as of 17 March 2020.

The *Royal Decree* states the following:

> In view of the emergency conditions the Hashemite Kingdom of Jordan is going through, and because of the World Health Organization's announcement of the spread of the Coronavirus

48 Article 16(a)(1) of the *Construction Contracting Law 1987* provides that: 'It is not permissible to execute construction contracting works in the Kingdom except by Jordanian contractors, under penalty of nullity of the construction contract and the procedures related thereto, with the exception of projects of a specialised nature where non-Jordanian contractors are allowed to participate in the execution thereof with Jordanian contractors through participation or joint venture upon the approval of the Council of Ministers that should be based on the recommendation of the Technical Committee stipulated in paragraph b of this Article'.

49 Article 23 of the Jordan Engineers Association and Article 16 of *Engineering Offices Commission Regulation*.

> epidemic, and to counter this epidemic at the national level and protect public safety throughout the Kingdom, the Cabinet decided, in accordance with the provisions of Article (124) of the Constitution and paragraphs (a) and (f) of Article (2) of the Defence Law No. (13) of 1992, to proclaiming the implementation of the Defence Law No. (13) of 1992 throughout the Hashemite Kingdom of Jordan from the date of the issuance of the Royal Decree.

The operation of the *Defence Law 1992* encompasses all geographic areas in Jordan. Consequently, and based on the *Defence Law 1992*, the Prime Minister issued several defence orders setting certain measures all over the country in order to be able to deal with the circumstances. For example, defence orders were issued related to (i) imposing a curfew and lockdown, (ii) suspending the effectiveness of certain provisions of the *Companies Law 1997* related to the meetings of the Board of Directors and General Assemblies and (iii) organising the employer–employee relationship and suspending certain provisions of the *Labour Law 1996*.

On 17 March 2020, the Council of Ministers issued a decision under which it considered all public and private sectors, including courts and execution departments, under vacation/public holiday. The duration of this public holiday was renewed by the Prime Minister until the end of May 2020.

On 20 March 2020 the *Defence Order No. (2)* in connection with imposing a curfew and lockdown was issued by the Prime Minister (***Def. Ord. #2***). This defence order provides that:

> Based on the provisions of Paragraph (a) of Article (4) of the Defence Law No. (13) of 1992 - Given the emergency conditions in our region and the world as a whole, and to prevent the spread of epidemics, I decide to issue the following defence order:
>
> 1. It is prohibited for people to move or to violate curfew in all regions of the Kingdom, starting from seven in the morning on Saturday, 21 March 2020 until further notice.
> 2. All shops in all regions of the Kingdom will be closed. On Tuesday morning, corresponding to 24 March 2020, specific times will be announced that allow citizens to fulfil their necessary needs and with the mechanism that will be announced at the time.
> 3. The restrictions exclude persons authorized by the Prime Minister and the Minister of Defence whose nature of their work requires the maintenance of public facilities.
> 4. As for the emergency medical cases, citizens must inform the General Security / Civil Defence to take the necessary measures to protect their health and safety as per the rules.
> 5. Anyone who violates the provisions of this defence order and the circulations issued by the Prime Minister and the Minister of Defence pursuant to it, shall be punished by immediate detention for a period not exceeding one year.

On 8 April 2020, the *Defence Order No. (6)*, in connection with the employer–employee relationship, was issued by the Prime Minister (***Def. Ord. #6***). This *Defence Order* provides that:

> Since the main goal of the curfew is to protect the lives and health of Jordanians, and in pursuing the appropriate efforts in taking the necessary measures to reduce the negative economic impacts on operators and companies of the private sector companies as well as the employees thereto, and in order to enable the economy to recover after the end of the current crisis, while studying the possibility of gradually allowing the opening of the economic sectors and to resume their work in accordance with the public health and safety measures and taking into consideration the national priorities, I decided to issue the following defence order:

First: A – All workers in private sector institutions and establishments or any other entity subject to the Labour Law shall be entitled to receive their wages for the period from March 18 to March 31; as for the workers in the sectors excluded from the public holiday announced by the Council of Ministers shall not be entitled to overtime pay, unless they are assigned to work overtime in accordance with the provisions of Article (59) of Labour Law No. (8) for the year 1996.

[...]

Second: A – The sectors, institutions, or establishments of the private sector or any other entity subject to the Labour Law that will be authorized to resume their work should obtain approval from the Minister of Industry, Trade and Supply, the Minister of Labour and the Minister of Health and the relevant competent minister collectively.

[...]

Third: To facilitate the mechanisms of work 'remotely' in whole or in part and to enable the economic sectors in these circumstances to resume their work and production, I decided the following:

A – Private sector establishments and any other entity subject to the Labour Law shall resume their work 'remotely' in whole or in part.

[...]

Fourth: As of 1 April 2020, the wages of workers in private sector establishments and institutions and in any other entity that is subject to the Labour Law are determined as follows:

A – Workers who perform their work in the workplace shall be entitled to full wages, yet it is permissible to agree, subject to the consent of the worker, to reduce his/her wage, provided that the amount of the reduction does not exceed 30% of the wage and that this option is not used unless the reduction includes the salaries of the high management of the institution.

B – Workers who perform their work 'full time' remotely at the institutions and establishments authorized to work, or at institutions included under the public holiday decision, or at institutions not authorized to work shall be entitled to receive their full salaries. Also, the workers who perform their work 'part-time' remotely at the authorized establishments and institutions, or those included under the public holiday decision and not authorized to work shall be entitled to receive their wages according to the actual working hours, provided that it is not less than the minimum amount per hour, or according to the wages stipulated in Paragraph (e) of this Article, whichever is higher.

[...]

E – The employers of the establishments and institutions authorized to work 'part-time' with regard to workers who are not authorized to work, or institutions included under the public holiday decision and are not authorized to work shall have the right to submit a request to the Minister of Labour to allow them to pay at least 50% of the value of the ordinary wage for these workers, provided that amount paid to the employee is not less than the limit of minimum wages.

F – The standards and conditions according to which employers are allowed to pay no less than 50% of the amount of the original wage shall be determined according to instructions issued by the Minister of Labour for this purpose.

Fifth: The employer of institution or an establishment of the private sector and any other entity subject to the Labour Law and authorized to work, or those included under the public holiday decision and not authorized to work, and who is unable to pay wages as mentioned in article (fourth) above shall be entitled to submit a request to a joint committee formed by the Ministers of Industry, Trade, and Supply and Labour, in order to completely stop the work at his institution or establishment, and to suspend the employment contracts of all workers. The employer must not take any action in this regard except after obtaining the approval of that committee and must attach to the request a statement showing the names of workers, the forms of their contracts, duration, working hours and the amount of their wages according to what is registered at the Social Security Corporation (SSC). The issuance of the decision approving the stoppage shall result in the following:

A– The employer whose work was completely stopped in his establishment shall not be permitted to perform any work or any activity during the stoppage period.

B – The contractual relationship between the employer and the worker shall not be interrupted during the stoppage period, but the employer is not obligated to pay the wages of the workers during this period.

C – The stoppage period is not considered as part of the period of the employment contract.

D – All financial and contractual obligations incurred by the employer remain valid during the stoppage period, except for the wages of the workers.

E – The employer of establishments and institutions at the private sector or any entity subject to the Labour Law shall not benefit from any economic protection programs for the private sector from the date of stoppage.

F – A sign of ceasing the disposal of movable and immovable property owned by the establishment shall be made on the same during the stoppage period by a decision of the committee.

Eighth: A – The employer may not exert pressure on the worker to force him to resign or to end his service or discharge him except in accordance with the provisions of paragraphs (c) and (d) of Article (21) and paragraphs (a, g, h, i) of Article (28) of Labour Law No. (8) of 1996.

B – For the purposes of implementing paragraph (a) of this item, Article (23) and the provisions of paragraphs (b, c, d, e, and f) of Article (28) of Labour Law No. (8) of 1996 shall be suspended and the Minister of Labour shall be authorized to take measures and procedures necessary to implement paragraph (e) thereof.

C – Every employer who has forced any worker to resign, or ends his service, or discharged him from work in cases other than those stipulated in Paragraph (A) of this item and during the period between March 18 and until the date of the issuance of Defence Order No. (6) for the year 2020, shall be obliged to return them back to work within a week of the date of issuing this order in Official Gazette.

Eleventh: A – Any person who violates any of the procedures for obtaining the approval referred to in item (2) of this defence order shall be punished by closing the violating establishment for a period of 60 days.

B – Anyone who violates any other provision of this defence order and the circulations issued by the Prime Minister or the ministers charged therewith pursuant thereto shall be punished with imprisonment for a period of three years and a fine of JOD3,000.

C – The penalties stipulated in this defence order do not prevent the worker from claiming his labour rights in accordance with the provisions of Labour Law No. (8) for the year 1996.

7.3.1.2 The impact of COVID-19 in numbers

COVID-19 had its toll on the construction industry in Jordan. For example, the total certified built-up area dropped from 8,196,912 m^2 in 2019[50] to 8,099,855 m^2 in 2020.[51] In 2021,

50 Engineering Offices Commission (EOC), *Annual Report 2019* (EOC 2020).

51 Engineering Offices Commission (EOC), *Annual Report 2020* (EOC 2021).

the total certified built-up area was 11,518,211 m^2,[52] which is around the normal average such as the 10,562,977 m^2 of 2018.[53]

Similarly, the total value of awarded projects has dropped from 1,035.30 million JOD (US$ 1,460.24 million) in 2019[54] to 831.8 million JOD (US$ 1,1170.22 million) in 2020.[55] In 2021, the total value of awarded projects of 1,024.30 million JOD (US$ 1,444.73 million)[56] has somewhat returned to its pre-COVID-19 range.

7.3.2 The impact of COVID-19 on the operation of construction contracts in Jordan

7.3.2.1 Defence Law 1992 and Civil Law 1976

The *Defence Law 1992* which came into effect on 17 March 2020 states the following:

> Article (2). Cases of applying this law:
>
> A. If an event occurs that calls for the defence of the homeland in the event of an emergency threatening national security or public safety in all parts of the Kingdom or in a region thereof due to a war, or a situation threatening to occur, or the occurrence of internal disturbances or armed strife, public disasters, or the spread of a pest or epidemic The implementation of this law shall be announced with a Royal Decree issued upon the decision of the Council of Ministers.
> B. Royal Decree will include a statement of the case for which it was decided to implement this law and the region in which it is applied and the date of its implementation.
> C. It is announced that this law will be suspended with a Royal Decree issued upon the decision of the Council of Ministers.
>
> Article (3). Take the necessary measures to ensure public safety:
>
> A. The application of this law is entrusted to the Prime Minister to take the necessary measures and procedures to ensure public safety and defend the Kingdom **without adhering to the provisions of the regular laws in force**. [emphasis added]
> B. The Prime Minister exercises his powers under written orders.
> C. The Prime Minister may delegate all or some of his powers to whomever he deems fit to do so in all parts of the Kingdom or in a specific region thereof, and with the conditions and restrictions that he appoints.
>
> Article (4). The Powers of the Prime Minister:
> The Prime Minister may exercise the following powers:
>
> A. Place restrictions on the freedom of persons to gather, move, and reside, and arrest and detain suspects or persons who are dangerous to national security and public order. [emphasis added]
> B. Entrusting any person with carrying out any work or performing any service within his ability.
> C. Searching people, places and vehicles without being bound by the provisions of any other law, and ordering the use of appropriate force in the event of a reluctance.

52 Engineering Offices Commission (EOC), *Annual Report 2021* (EOC 2022).
53 Engineering Offices Commission (EOC), *Annual Report 2018* (EOC 2019).
54 Jordanian Construction Contractors Association (JCCA), *Annual Report 2019* (JCCA 2020).
55 Jordanian Construction Contractors Association (JCCA), *Annual Report 2020* (JCCA 2021).
56 Jordanian Construction Contractors Association (JCCA), *Annual Report 2021* (JCCA 2022).

D. Setting possession of movable and immovable property, postponing the payment of debt and the outstanding obligations. [emphasis added]
E. Preventing, restricting or limiting the import, export or transfer of materials from one place to another, specifying dealing with them, prohibiting their concealment, destruction, purchase or barter, and setting their prices. In addition, these powers enable the seizure of any land, building, road, or water and energy source, the establishment of defence works upon or within them, the removal of any trees or installations within, and order it to be managed, exploited, and have its use regulated.
F. [...]Evacuating or isolating some areas and imposing curfews.
G. Determine the dates of opening and closing public stores, in whole or in part. [emphasis added]
H. Organizing and determining the means of transportation and transport between the different regions, closing any road, path, or stream of water or changing its direction and preventing traffic on it or regulating it.
I. Monitor messages, newspapers, publications, pamphlets, drawings, and all means of expression, propaganda and advertising before they are published, in addition to seizing and/or confiscating said materials, and closing places of their preparation.
J. Preventing taking pictures or making designs or maps for any specific place or thing that might benefit the enemy, preventing keeping near these places of any photographic devices or equipment used to take or produce pictures, make designs and maps, and preventing staying or presence in such places without a legitimate excuse.
K. Cancellation of licenses of firearms, ammunition, explosives, or explosive materials that are used in the manufacture of explosives, preventing their manufacture, sale, purchase, transfer, or their disposal, in addition to ordering their delivery and seizures, and closing their stores and storage facilities.
L. Preventing the manufacture, sale, purchase, or possession of telecommunications equipment and ordering their delivery and seizure.

> Article (10). Discontinuation of work in any text or legislation:
>
> The effect of any provision or legislation that contradicts any provision of this law and the orders issued pursuant thereto shall be suspended.
>
> Article (11). Inability to perform contracts and obligations due to this law:
>
> If it is impracticable to execute any contract or obligation due to the compliance with the provisions of this law or any order or mandate or instructions issued by virtue of it, or due to the compliance with the provisions thereof, then the person associated with the said contract shall not be considered in breach of its conditions, as the contract shall be considered suspended to the extent that the execution of the contract is impracticable. This shall be considered a defence in any claim initiated or filed against this person or in any procedures taken against him arising from his failure to execute the contract or the obligation.

Based on the *Defence Law 1992*, the Prime Minister of Jordan issued *Def. Ord. #2* and *Def. Ord. #6* as detailed above under section 7.3.1.1.

Article 205 of the *Civil Law 1976* states:

> If exceptional [extraordinary] general circumstances occur which could not have been expected [foreseen] and as a result of their occurrence, the implementation of the contractual obligation, although not impossible, became exhausting [burdensome] for the debtor so as to threaten him with a heavy loss, the court may, depending on the circumstances and after balancing the interests of the two parties, limit the burdensome obligation to the reasonable extent if justice so required. Every agreement to the contrary is void.

Article 247 of the *Civil Law 1976* states:

> In contracts binding on both parties, if a force majeure occurred and rendered the performance of the obligation impossible, the corresponding obligation shall lapse and the contract terminates on its own. If the impossibility is partial, the corresponding part to the impossible part lapses, and the same that applies to the partial impossibility applies to temporal impossibility in continuous contracts. In both of these cases, the creditor may terminate the contract on condition that the debtor is informed.

Article (261) of the *Civil Law 1976* states:

> If the person proves that the damage was caused by a foreign cause in which he has no hand, such as a heavenly pest, a sudden accident, force majeure, the act of others or the act of the aggrieved, he is not obligated to compensate unless the law or agreement stipulates otherwise.

It is clear from the foregoing provisions that the applicability of all of these instruments, *vis-à-vis* construction contracts, is to be decided on a case-by-case basis. In each case it depends on the facts of each 'event' and whether such event will qualify under the contract as being impracticable from being executed and, accordingly, the contract and obligation will be suspended (1) by virtue of Article 11 of the *Defence Law 1992*; (2) as being exhausting (burdensome) due to the occurrence of exceptional (extraordinary) general circumstances, which makes the execution of the contract exhausting (burdensome) (under Article 205 of the *Civil Law 1976*); or (3) as being impossible to be executed due to the occurrence of a *force majeure* event that rendered the performance of the obligation impossible and, accordingly, the contract will be terminated by itself (under Article 247 of the *Civil Law 1976*). Evidently, the COVID situation is unprecedented, leaving us with no case law available to provide guidance on this question.

Initially, the application of Jordanian laws will provide room to argue that the inability/impracticability of performance is attributed to the enforcement of *Defence Law 1992* as well as the *Defence Orders*, such as *Def. Ord. #2* and *Def. Ord. #6* as detailed earlier under section 7.3.1.1. This is in addition to making the argument based on the application of Article 205 and Article 247 of the *Civil Law 1976*. This is a preliminary view that will be subject to further revision in light of the relevant agreements/contracts.

To the best of our knowledge and until the date of writing this chapter, the Court of Cassation, the highest court in Jordan, did not issue a decision related to construction contracts in terms of the COVID-19 effect on such contracts. However, in its decision number 5158/2021 dated 26 October 2021, the Court of Cassation concluded that:

> whereas the period between 17 April 2020 to 1 May 2020 was a period of closure for all commercial shops, companies, public and private institutions in accordance with the defence orders, and, in addition, curfew was imposed, which made the execution of the contractual obligations of the [defendants] impossible due to the force majeure circumstance related to the COVID-19 pandemic, … and therefore the rent that is due during this period shall not be considered due because it was impossible to benefit from the property pursuant to the provision of Article 247 of the Civil Code and Article 11 of the Defence Law, therefore the application of the Court of Appeal of the provisions of Article 247 of the Civil Law is correct in this lawsuit.

7.4 Jordanian governing law of the contract

7.4.1 Constraints on the governing law of a construction contract

Construction contracts are considered to be civil contracts, and due to this nature, they are governed by the *Civil Law 1976* in general, and Articles 780 to 804 in particular.

Article 20 of the *Civil Law 1976* states that:

1. Contractual obligations shall be governed by the law of the State of the common domicile of the two contracting parties if they are of the same domicile, but if they are different the applicable law shall be that of the state in which the contract was made, unless otherwise agreed by the two contracting parties.
2. The law of the place where the immovable property is located shall be applicable to contracts made in respect of that property.

Under the *Civil Law 1976* and in respect of contractual obligations, the *Civil Law* permits the application of foreign law. However, for contracts dealing with immovable property, the choice of law is the *lex situs* whereby 'the law of the place where the immovable property is located shall be applicable to contracts made in respect of that property'.

In practice, construction contracts that are related to a site in Jordan and/or when one of its parties is the government or one of its agencies, the governing law of the contract will be Jordanian law.

It should be noted that in the event that the contract provides for a foreign governing law of the contract, the court may apply the foreign law, provided that the foreign law does not contradict the public order or morality in Jordan (Article 29 of the *Civil Law 1976*).

Under the *Government Procurement Regulation 2022* and in respect of construction projects related to ministries, official institutions and government departments including the companies that are wholly owned by the Government, the applicable governing law, as a general rule, must be Jordanian law. However, under the *Regulation*, the parties may agree otherwise in their contracts.

7.4.2 Formal requirements for a construction contract

The main formal requirements for contracts in general (not only construction) are generally encapsulated by the *Civil Law 1976*, particularly Articles 87 to 249.

As is the case with other general contracts, the main formal requirements for construction contracts include capacity, consent, subject matter and cause.

In respect of capacity: under the *Civil Law 1976*, every person with capacity has the right to enter into contracts. If this capacity is lost or limited by virtue of the law, then that person will not be entitled to enter into contracts. Article 116 of the *Civil Law 1976* provides that 'Every person has capacity to contract unless his capacity is lost or limited by virtue of the law'.

In respect of consent: Article 90 of the *Civil Law 1976* provides that 'The contract shall be concluded as soon as the offer is met with acceptance subject to the conditions which the law prescribes in addition thereto'. Yet, it should be noted that the consent may be affected by duress (Article 135 of the *Civil Law 1976*), deceit (Article 143 of the *Civil Law 1976*) and error (Article 151 of the *Civil Law 1976*). For example, if consent is given as a result of an act of violence or deceit, then this consent is not considered to be valid.

In respect of the subject matter and cause of the contract: generally speaking, there are two main conditions that need to be considered in this regard:

- The subject matter must be possible, otherwise the contract may be considered null and void. For example, a contract that is concluded by a lawyer filing an appeal in a lawsuit in which an appeal was previously filed falls under the umbrella of an impossible subject matter (Article 159 of the *Civil Law 1976*).
- In addition, the subject matter must be defined or can be defined in a manner in which the subject matter is clear and recognisable by the parties thereof, such as referring to its particular location or by the statement of its distinctive marks and its amount if it can be measured (Article 161 of the *Civil Law 1976*).
- Furthermore, Article (782) of the *Civil Law 1976*, in the context of construction contracts, created additional elements for this type of contract, in particular those including a description of the subject matter, its nature, its amount, method of performance, period of completion and the consideration.

7.5 What Special Provisions in the Particular Conditions are necessary for consistency with applicable laws in Jordan?

7.5.1 FIDIC General Conditions are incompatible or inconsistent with Jordanian governing law of the contract

7.5.1.1 Limitation/prescription periods

The statutory periods of limitation/prescription are governed by Articles 449 to 464 of the *Civil Law 1976*. These limitation/prescription periods are a matter of public policy, which the Parties cannot amend or contract out of as stipulated by Article 463(1) of the *Civil Law 1976* which provides, in part, that 'no agreement on a period different from that prescribed by the law to preclude the hearing of the case shall be permissible'.

Therefore, coupled with the principle of good faith, a Party and/or the Engineer (under the Red Book or the Yellow Book) may well face difficulties in arguing that the claiming Party's entitlements are lost and time-barred due to the fact that the claiming Party has failed to provide the requisite notice within the time prescribed under the Contract, e.g. the 28-day Notice of Claim under sub-clause 20.2.1 (Notice of Claim) of the 2017 rainbow suite (or sub-clause 20.1 [Contractor's Claims] under the 1999 rainbow suite).

In light of the preceding, there may well be a need to add a stipulation in the Special Provisions in the Particular Conditions that all of the time bars (the barring provisions) under the General Conditions are subject to the stipulations of Articles 449 to 464 of the *Civil Law 1976*.

7.5.1.2 Exemption from or limitation of liability for injurious/harmful acts

More often than not, this relates to the extinguishing or limitation of the Employer's liability for fraud, gross negligence, deliberate default or reckless misconduct by way of a contractual waiver.

Article 270 of the *Civil Law 1976* provides that 'Any condition for exemption from the liability resulting from the injurious/harmful act shall be void'. Given that Article 270 is a matter of public policy, sub-clause 1.15 (Limitation of Liability) of the 2017 rainbow suite (or sub-clause 17.6 [Limitation of Liability] of the 1999 rainbow suite) or sub-clause 14.14 (Cessation of Employer's Liability) cannot be amended in the Special Provisions to exclude or limit the Employer's liability for fraud, gross negligence, deliberate default or reckless misconduct.

In the same vein, it may be argued that sub-clause 14.14 (Cessation of Employer's Liability) is inapplicable under the *Civil Law 1976*, due to the fact that it is a barring provision which bars Claims by the Contractor (see sections 7.5.1.1 and 7.5.1.2). Nevertheless, this argument may well prove to be flawed as the operation of sub-clause 14.14 is in tandem with sub-clause 14.12 (Discharge), where in this discharge the Contractor confirms that the total of the Final Statement or the Partially Agreed Final Statement (as the case may be), represents the full and final settlement of all money due to the Contractor under or in connection with the Contract. Such discharge is upheld and enforceable under the *Civil Law 1976*.

7.5.1.3 Misrepresentation

The *Civil Law 1976* deals with the matter of misrepresentation under Articles 143 to 150. Article 143 defines misrepresentation as follows:

> Misrepresentation is when one of the two contracting parties deceives the other by means of trickery of word or deed which leads the other to consent to what he would not otherwise have consented to.

The consequences of misrepresentation can be found under Article 145 which states the following:

> If one of the contracting parties makes a misrepresentation to the other and it transpires that the contract was concluded with gross unfairness, the person so misled may cancel the contract.

This is a matter of public policy, which the Parties cannot contract out of. Therefore, it is essential that the Special Provisions under sub-clause 15.2 (Termination for Contractor's Default) of the 2017 rainbow suite (or sub-clause 15.2 [Termination by Employer] of the 1999 rainbow suite) and sub-clause 16.2 (Termination by Contractor) are amended to add misrepresentation as an additional ground for termination by the Employer or the Contractor, respectively.

7.5.2 FIDIC General Conditions are incompatible or inconsistent with the law of the Site/Country

7.5.2.1 Decennial liability and the Defects Notification Period

Article 788 of the *Jordanian Civil Code 1976* deals with decennial liability by stipulating the following:

> 1. If the contract for independent work shall be for the construction of a building the design of which is to be made by the engineer under whose supervision the contractor is to build, both of them shall be liable to compensate the employer for whatever happens during ten years from the total or partial collapse of the buildings they have constructed or the constructions they have built and for every defect which threatens the strength and safety of the building unless the contract provides for a longer period.

2. Liability for the said compensation shall subsist even if the defect or collapse results from a defect in the land itself or the employer's consent to the building of the defected constructions.
3. The period of the ten years shall commence on the date of the taking over of the work.

As can be noted, the decennial liability is distinct and different from the Defects Notification Period of clause 11 (Defects after Taking Over) of the 2017 rainbow suite (clause 11 [Defects Liability] of the 1999 rainbow suite). Under the decennial liability, the Contractor and the Engineer are jointly liable for a period of ten years from the date of taking over to compensate the Employer for any total or partial collapse of a building or construction and for any defect which threatens the stability or safety of the same.

As stipulated by Article 788(3), the said ten years shall commence from the date of taking over by the Employer, i.e. from the date stated in the Taking-Over Certificate which is now defined as the Date of Completion under the 2017 rainbow suite. The decennial liability extends to include those defects which were visible at the time of taking over, and even in the event that the Employer has given consent to the construction of the defective Works (Article 788[2]).

Decennial liability does not apply only to the total collapse of the Works, but also to partial collapse. In certain situations, it may well be difficult to decide whether the decennial liability is applicable if there was a very minor partial collapse which does not affect the safety and stability of the Works, which remains a question of circumstances, e.g. a collapse of the ceiling plastering, or a collapse of the rainwater drainage pipe extending from the parapet to the building's sidewalk.

Normally, regular and minor defects discovered during the Defects Notification Period or minor latent/hidden defects discovered after the expiry of the Defects Notification Period[57] are outside the scope of the decennial liability. Nevertheless, the moment such defects jeopardise the strength and safety of the Works, the decennial liability shall automatically apply (Article 788[2]).

Moreover, unlike the Defects Notification Period under the Contract, Article 788 does not expressly require the notification of the Contractor by the Employer (or the Engineer under the Red Book and the Yellow Book) promptly after the discovery of the defect,[58] nor does it expressly place an obligation on the Contractor to repair such defects;[59] however, such obligations may well be reasonably implied from Article 788.

It is worth noting that, unlike many jurisdictions which mandate a decennial liability, there is no obligation under the law for the Contractor to take out and maintain a decennial liability insurance, which insurance remains uncommon in Jordan and can only be obtained at unreasonably high prices.

The decennial liability is a matter of public policy, which the Parties cannot reduce or contract out of; they can only increase the period of ten years. As such, it may well be prudent to add a stipulation in the Special Provisions in the Particular Conditions that the decennial liability is separate and distinct from the Defects Notification Period, and that it

57 Covered by sub-clause 11.10 [*Unfulfilled Obligations*] of the 2017 and 1999 rainbow suites.

58 Cf. sub-clause 11.1 [*Completion of Outstanding Work and Remedying Defects*] of the 2017 and 1999 rainbow suites.

59 Cf. sub-clause 11.2 [*Cost of Remedying Defects*] of the 2017 and 1999 rainbow suites.

cannot be excluded from the limitation of liability clauses, e.g. sub-clause 1.15 [Limitation of Liability) of the 2017 rainbow suite, or sub-clause 17.6 (*Limitation of Liability*] of the 1999 rainbow suite. To the same extent, sub-clause 11.9 [*Performance Certificate*] may well be amended to expressly state that the decennial liability is excluded from the operation of sub-clause 11.9.

7.5.2.2 Delay Damages/penalties

Under sub-clause 8.8 [*Delay Damages*] of the 2017 rainbow suite (or sub-clause 8.7 [*Delay Damages*] of the 1999 rainbow suite) the Contractor shall be liable for Delay Damages for failure to comply with sub-clause 8.2 [*Time for Completion*], i.e. failure to complete the Works within the Time for Completion.

The *Civil Law 1976* deals with the matter of Delay Damages/penalties under Article 364 as follows:

1. The two contracting parties may in advance and subject to the provisions of the law limit the amount of damages by express provision in the contract or by a subsequent agreement.
2. And the Court may in all cases and on the application of either party amend that agreement to render the estimation equal to the damage and any contrary agreement shall be void.

As is the case under the majority of civil laws, penalties are allowed under the *Civil Law 1976*, and as such, Article 364 deals with the concept of Delay Damages and penalties, equally and interchangeably as between these two concepts.

As can be seen, the court (or an arbitrator), upon an application of either Party, can amend the amount of the Delay Damages so as they become equal to the actual damages suffered by the Employer. There is no restriction on the nature of this amendment, hence it can be in the positive or the negative.

This is a matter of public policy, which the Parties cannot contract out of. As such, it may well be prudent to add a stipulation in the Special Provisions in the Particular Conditions that the Delay Damages calculation is subject to the stipulations of Article 364.

7.5.2.3 Financing charges (interest)

Article 167(4) of the *Civil Procedures Law 1988* (as amended) stipulates that the maximum allowable interest rate shall be at the simple rate of 9% per annum. This Article is a matter of public policy, which the Parties cannot amend or contract out of. Therefore, a provision needs to be added in the Special Provisions in the Particular Conditions that all of the financing charges (interest rates) shall comply with Article 167(4). Such provision shall be added under sub-clause 11.4 [*Failure to Remedy Defects*] (under sub-paragraph [d] of the 2017 rainbow suite or sub-paragraph [c] of the 1999 rainbow suite) and sub-clause 14.8 [*Delayed Payment*].

7.5.2.4 Principles relating to measured (remeasured) contracts

Article 794 of the *Civil Law 1976* provides the following principles which address measured (remeasured) contracts:

1. If the contract for independent work shall be on a unit basis and according to a certain design for specified remuneration for every unit and it is discovered that the execution

of the design requires a high increase in costs the employer may after being notified of the increase release himself from the contract and pay the value of the work executed by the contractor in accordance with the terms of the contract or accept the contractor's proceeding with execution and be bound for the increase.

2. And if the increase shall not be high but noticeable and necessary for the execution of the design agreed upon the contractor shall notify the employer before continuing execution of the amount of the increase he expects in costs, and if he shall proceed with execution without notification he shall have no right to claim for the increase.

It is evident that the *Civil Law 1976* mandates serious consequences in the event of a high or noticeable increase in the cost of executing the Works, and/or the Contractor's failure to give the requisite Notice. These consequences manifest themselves in the form of the Employer's entitlement to terminate the Contract, or the Contractor's loss of his/her entitlement to such increase, respectively.

Therefore, it is imperative for the Special Provisions in the Particular Conditions of the Red Book to amend sub-clause 12.1 [*Works to be Measured*], sub-clause 12.3 [*Valuation of the Works*] of the 2017 Red Book (or sub-clause 12.3 [*Evaluation*] of the 1999 Red Book) and sub-clause 15.2 [*Termination for Contractor's Default*] of the 2017 Red Book (or sub-clause 15.2 [*Termination by Employer*] of the 1999 Red Book) so as to reflect the rights and obligations stipulated under Article 794 of the *Civil Law 1976*, as this Article is a matter of public policy.

7.5.2.5 Valuation of Variations

The *Civil Law 1976* does not specifically deal with the valuation of Variations. Nevertheless, Variations may well result in an increase in the Contract Price where Article 754 may come into play, whether it is a 'high increase in costs' (Article 794(1]) or an increase which is not high 'but noticeable and necessary for the execution of the design' (Article 794(1)). See section 7.5.1.7 for further explanation of Article 794.

Therefore, it is imperative for the Special Provisions in the Particular Conditions of the Red Book to amend sub-clause 12.3 [*Valuation of the Works*] of the 2017 Edition (or sub-clause 12.3 [*Evaluation*] of the 1999 Edition), which addresses the matter of valuation of Variations, so as to reflect the rights and obligations stipulated under Article 794 of the *Civil Law 1976*, as this Article is a matter of public policy. Similarly, the Special Provisions of the Yellow Book and the Silver Book should amend sub-clause 13.3 [*Variation Procedure*] which deals with the valuation of Variations.

7.5.3 FIDIC General Conditions are incompatible or inconsistent with the relevant laws on dispute determination in Jordan

There are no Special Provisions in the Particular Conditions which are required for consistency with Jordanian law in this regard. Nevertheless, sub-clause 21.6 [*Arbitration*], which calls for international arbitration under the ICC Rules of Arbitration, is usually amended for domestic contracts to stipulate that arbitration shall be domestic arbitration under the *Arbitration Law No. 31 for the year 2001* as amended. See section 7.2.11.

7.6 What Special Provisions in the Particular Conditions are desirable for consistency with applicable laws in Jordan?

7.6.1 Good faith

The *Jordanian Civil Law 1976*, as is the case with many civil law jurisdictions, is distinct from common law jurisdiction in that it contains an obligation to perform the contract in good faith.

Article 202 of the *Civil Law 1976* provides the following:

1. The contract shall be performed according to its provisions and in a manner consistent with the requirements of good faith.
2. And the contract shall not be limited to the obligation of the contracting party by its provisions but shall also include what the law, custom and the nature of the disposition attach thereto.

Article 202 places an obligation on the parties to perform the contract not only according to its express provisions, but also in a manner consistent with the requirements of good faith as implied by the 'law, custom and the nature of the disposition', e.g. the provision of information, and cooperation between the parties' personnel. In other words, the principle of good faith may well imply certain terms into the contract.

A good example of the application of the good faith principle relates to the operation of time bars, e.g. the 28-day Notice of Claim under sub-clause 20.2.1 [*Notice of Claim*] of the 2017 rainbow suite (or sub-clause 20.1 [*Contractor's Claims*] under the 1999 rainbow suite). The application of time bars under the *Civil Law 1976* will not be as literal and strict as that under common law, for such application is tempered by the principle of good faith.

While this obligation does not require any specific amendments in the Special Provisions in the Particular Conditions, being a matter of public policy, it may well be desirable, particularly in international contracts involving foreign contractors, to indicate that the Contract is governed by the principle of good faith under Article 202.

7.6.2 Health and safety (sub-clause 4.8)

There are occupational safety and health procedures including safety-related issues in the construction sector that are periodically issued by the Ministry of Labour under the relevant applicable legislation. This legislation and procedures need to be considered by Contractors when they operate in Jordan in order to make sure that they comply with the law. For further details, refer to section 7.2.4.

7.6.3 Design (sub-clauses 5.1, 5.2 and 5.3)

The law prohibits contractors from performing engineering consultancy and design works, and similarly, consulting engineers, architects and designers are prohibited by law from performing construction works. Therefore, Contractors under the Yellow Book, Silver Book, Gold Book or Emerald Book will have to employ licensed consulting engineers/designers as Subcontractors in order to perform the design under the FIDIC forms of contract. See section 7.2.1 for further details.

Moreover, the designer, whether he/she is the Engineer or only responsible for the design, is under the decennial liability in accordance with Articles 788 and 789 of the *Civil Law 1976*. See section 7.5.1.3 for further details.

7.6.4 Labour (sub-clauses 6.2 and 6.4)

The main principle in this regard is that the employees engaged in the project will be subject to the provisions of the *Labour Law 1996* and the *Social Security Law 2014*. The *Labour Law* enables the employees to initiate cases against the Employer, the Contractor and the Subcontractor, as the case may be. In addition, any termination of employment must be in compliance with the provisions of the *Labour Law 1996*, otherwise, the employer will be at risk of arbitrary dismissal compensation. For further details, refer to section 7.2.4.

7.6.5 Principles relating to lump sum contracts

Article 795 of the *Civil Law 1976* provides the mechanism for dealing with lump sum contracts as follows:

1. If the contract for independent work shall be signed on the basis of an agreed design for a lump sum the contractor shall not claim any increase in the remuneration required for the execution of that design.
2. And if an amendment or addition shall be made to the design with the employer's consent the agreement made with the contractor in respect of that amendment or addition shall be complied with.

As can be seen, the *Civil Law 1976* does not provide any special requirements for lump sum contracts. Nevertheless, it may well be prudent to add in the Special Provisions of a lump sum contract (an amended Red Book, the Yellow Book or the Silver Book) under sub-clause 14.1 [*The Contract Price*] that such sub-clause is governed by Article 795 of the *Civil Law 1976*.

7.6.6 Bankruptcy, insolvency, liquidation (sub-clauses 15.2 and 16.2)

The notions and principles addressed in sub-clause 15.2.1(g) and sub-clause 16.2.1(i) regarding insolvency matters are quite similar to the ones existing in the *Insolvency Law 2018*.[60] In some events, some of the terminologies used in the relevant clauses of FIDIC could be misinterpreted by the professional advisors; therefore, the parties could consider adopting the same terminologies used in the *Insolvency Law 2018* by stating them in the Special Provisions.

60 The *Insolvency Law Number 21 for the year 2018*, published in the Official Gazette number 5514, came into force on 12 November 2018.

7.7 Summary of applicable legislation for Jordanian governing law of the contract

Civil Law 1976
Insolvency Law 2018 (this law may be applied if one of the parties has assets or operations in Jordan)
Arbitration Law 2001 (this law may be applied if the parties select the said law as the law governing their arbitration)

7.7.1 Entry into a construction contract

Contracts generally	*Civil Law 1976*; Articles 87–249 and Articles 780–804
Construction contracts	*Civil Law 1976*; Articles 780–804

7.7.2 Operation of a construction contract

Force majeure	*Civil Law 1976*, Articles 205, 247 and 261
Hardship	*Civil Law 1976*; Article 205
Guarantees under forms of Security (Tender Security, Demand Guarantee, Surety Bond, Advance Payment Guarantee, Retention Money Guarantee, Payment Guarantee by Employer)	*Civil Law 1976*; Articles 780–804 and Articles 950–1017

7.7.3 Termination of a construction contract

Frustration	*Civil Law 1976*; Articles 780–804 and Articles 205, 247 and 261
Bankruptcy, insolvency, liquidation	*Insolvency Law 2018*

7.7.4 Dispute resolution

Limitation periods	*Civil Procedures Law for the year 1988* as amended; Articles 109, 170 *Civil Law*; Articles 449–464, 788, 791
Liability	*Civil Law 1976*; mainly Articles 246, 788 and 270
Mediation	*Mediation to Resolve Civil Disputes for the year 2006* as amended (if the parties choose this law as the procedural law of mediation)
Arbitration	*Arbitration Law for the year 2001* as amended (if the parties choose this law as the procedural law of arbitration)

7.8 Summary of applicable legislation if the Site/Country is in Jordan

7.8.1 Operation of a construction contract

Registration and administration of professionals – Engineers, Architects, Quantity Surveyors, Certifiers, Building Surveyors, Surveyors	*Construction Contractors Law 1987* *Aqaba Special Economic Zone Law 2000* *Government Procurement Regulation for the year 2022* *Companies Law 1997*

Registration/licensing of Contractors and subcontractors	*Construction Contractors Law 1987* *Aqaba Special Economic Zone Law 2000* *Government Procurement Regulation for the year 2022* *Companies Law 1997*
Subcontractors	*Civil Law 1976* *Government Procurement Regulation for the year 2022* *Construction Contractors Law 1987* *Aqaba Special Economic Zone Law 2000* *Labour Law 1996* *Social Security Law 2014*
Use of liens/assignment of debts	*Civil Law 1976*
Labour	*Labour Law 1996* *Social Security Law 2014*
Design/moral rights	*Civil Law 1976* *Labour Law 1996* *Copyright Law 1992* *Industrial Designs Law 2000* *Patents Law 1999* *Trademarks Law 1952* *Trade Secrets and Unfair Competition Law 2000*
Copyright	*Civil Law 1976* *Labour Law 1996* *Copyright Law 1992*
The product being produced from the Works	*Civil Law 1976* *Labour Law 1996*
Local procurement	*Civil Law 1976*
Public procurement	*Civil Law 1976* *Government Procurement Regulation for the year 2022*
Building and construction permits, execution of construction work, standard of construction work	*Civil Law 1976* *Construction Contractors Law 1987* *Aqaba Special Economic Zone Law 2000* *Government Procurement Regulation for the year 2022*
Health and safety	*Civil Law 1976* *Labour Law 1996* *Social Security Law 2014* *Public Health Law 2008*
Ownership of Plant and Materials	*Civil Law 1976*
Employer's sale of Contractor's Equipment, surplus material, wreckage and Temporary Works	*Civil Law 1976*
Insurance	*Insurance Regulatory Law No. (12) of 2021*
Liability for defective work	*Civil Law 1976*
Liability for nuisance	*Civil Law 1976*

7.8.2 Termination of a construction contract

Bankruptcy, insolvency, liquidation	*Insolvency law 2018*
Decennial liability and liability generally for the total or partial collapse of structures	*Civil Law 1976*

7.8.3 Dispute resolution

Mediation	*Mediation to Resolve Civil Disputes Law for the year 2006* as amended
Arbitration	*Arbitration Law 2001* as amended *Civil Procedures Law 1988* as amended
Limitation periods	*Civil Law 1976* *Civil Procedures Law 1988 as amended*

7.9 Summary of applicable legislation if the 'seat' of the dispute determination is Jordan

Dispute resolution	*Constitution of the Hashemite Kingdom of Jordan of 1952* as amended; Articles 101–103, 110 *Civil Law for the year 1976* *Civil Procedures Law for the year 1988* as amended
Limitation periods	*Civil Procedures Law for the year 1988* as amended; Articles 109, 170 *Civil Law*; Articles 449–464, 788, 791
Adjudication	*Constitution of the Hashemite Kingdom of Jordan of 1952* as amended; Articles 101–103, 110 *Civil Procedures Law for the year 1988* *Mediation to Resolve Civil Disputes for the year 2006* as amended *Arbitration Law for the year 2001* as amended *Government Procurement Regulation for the year 2022* *Construction Contractors Law for the year 1987* as amended
Arbitration	*Arbitration Law for the year 2001* as amended *Civil Procedures Law for the year 1988* as amended; Article 109 *Government Procurement Regulation for the year 2022* *ICSID Convention* *New York Convention*

7.10 Issues that a court or arbitrator may construe differently than expected from the words of the Contract because of local law or custom

7.10.1 Good faith

As explained in section 7.6.1, Article 202 places an obligation on the parties to perform the contract not only according to its express provisions, but also in a manner consistent with the requirements of good faith as implied by the 'law, custom and the nature of the disposition', e.g. the provision of information and cooperation between the parties' personnel. In other words, the principle of good faith may well imply certain terms into the contract.

7.10.2 Notice provisions and time bars

The application of time bars under the *Civil Law 1976* will not be as literal and strict as that under common law, for such application is tempered by the principle of good faith. See section 7.6.1 for further explanation.

Therefore, coupled with the statutory periods of limitation/prescription examined under section 7.5.1.1, a Party and/or the Engineer (under the Red Book or the Yellow Book) may well face difficulties in arguing that the claiming Party's entitlements are lost and time-barred due to the fact that the claiming Party has failed to provide the requisite notice within the time prescribed under the Contract, e.g. the 28-day Notice of Claim under sub-clause 20.2.1 [*Notice of Claim*] of the 2017 rainbow suite (or sub-clause 20.1 [*Contractor's Claims*] under the 1999 rainbow suite).

7.10.3 Financing charges (interest)

Article 167(4) of the *Civil Procedures Law 1988* (as amended) stipulates that the maximum allowable interest rate shall be at the simple rate of 9% per annum. This Article is a matter of public policy, which the Parties cannot amend or contract out of. Therefore, sub-clause 11.4 (Failure to Remedy Defects) (under sub-paragraph [d] of the 2017 rainbow suite, or sub-paragraph [c] of the 1999 rainbow suite) and sub-clause 14.8 [*Delayed Payment*] shall be interpreted accordingly. See section 7.5.2.3 for further explanation.

7.10.4 Delay Damages/penalties

As can be seen in section 7.5.2.2, this is a matter of public policy which the Parties cannot contract out of. As such, the Delay Damages calculation under sub-clause 8.8 [*Delay Damages*] of the 2017 rainbow suite (or sub-clause 8.7 [*Delay Damages*] of the 1999 rainbow suite) is subject to the stipulations of Article 364, where the court (or an arbitrator), upon an application of either Party, can amend the amount of the Delay Damages so they become equal to the actual damages suffered by the Employer.

7.10.5 Ownership of Plant and Materials (sub-clause 7.7)

Article 783 of the *Civil Law 1976* provides that:

1. If it is stipulated that the contractor shall provide all or part of the work material he shall supply it in accordance with the terms of the contract.
2. And if the employer shall be the party who shall provide the work material, the contractor shall take care of it, comply with technical requirements in his work and return its remainder to its owner and if a breach thereof is committed and it is demolished, impaired or lost he shall be liable.

Additionally, Article 784 of the *Civil Law 1976* provides that:

> The contractor shall provide at his expense the additional machinery and equipment he requires for the performance of the work unless the agreement or custom otherwise provides.

It is evident from the foregoing provisions of the *Civil Law 1976* that the issue of Plant and Materials needs to be considered while preparing the Contract since the law refers to the agreement of the parties in this regard. In other words, providing the Plant and Materials could be left to the Parties to agree upon in the Contract, where the Parties could agree that the Materials could be provided by the Contractor or the Employer as the case may be. If the Materials are provided by the Contractor, then he/she is under the obligation to provide them in accordance with the terms of the Contract. In the event that the Materials will be provided by the Employer, then the Contractor shall be under the obligation to take care of them, comply with the technical requirements in his/her work and return any surplus Materials to their owner, i.e. the Employer. However, if the Contractor fails to do so, then he/she will be held liable if the Materials are damaged, impaired, deteriorated or lost.

In respect of the equipment and machines, the *Civil Law 1976*, in principle, imposes an obligation on the Contractor to provide such equipment and machines. Yet, it is possible that the Parties may agree that the Employer will be providing the equipment and machines. In this latter event, the Contractor will be under the obligation to take care of it, comply with its technical requirements in his/her work and return it to the Employer. If the Contractor fails to do so, then he/she will be held liable if the equipment and machines are damaged, impaired, deteriorated or lost.

Noting that when the Plant and Materials will be provided by the Contractor, the Employer still has the right, contractually, to sell the items if the terms and conditions described in sub-clause 15.2 [*Termination for Contractor's Default*] of the 2017 rainbow suite (or sub-clause 15.2 [*Termination by Employer*] of the 1999 rainbow suite) are met. Nevertheless, it is advisable that the Employer obtains a court order before exercising this right.

7.10.6 Employer's sale of Contractor's Equipment, surplus material, wreckage and Temporary Works (sub-clause 11.11)

Sub-clause 15.2 [*Termination for Contractor's Default*] of the 2017 Edition (or sub-clause 15.2 [*Termination by Employer*] of the 1999 Edition) entitles the Employer, after termination under this sub-clause, to use any Goods and Contractor's Documents (and other design documents, if any) made by or on behalf of the Contractor to complete the Works, and that the Contractor's Equipment and Temporary Works (e.g. formwork, scaffolding, etc.) will be released to the Contractor at or near the Site after completion of the Works by the Employer or other entities, i.e. they will be withheld by the Employer on Site until such time. Moreover, if by this time the Contractor has failed to make a payment due to the Employer, these items may be sold (to the extent permitted by applicable Laws) by the Employer in order to recover this payment.

In accordance with the *Civil Law 1976* and as a matter of principle, a contract is binding on the parties and they are under the obligation to perform the contract according to its express provisions. The *Civil Law 1976* recognises the conditions stated in the contract signed between the parties and in the event that such condition is met, then this condition will have an effect and, accordingly, it can be implemented by the relevant party.

In the context of the right of the Employer to sell the items described in sub-clause 15.2 [*Termination for Contractor's Default*] of the 2017 rainbow suite (or sub-clause 15.2 [*Termination by Employer*] of the 1999 rainbow suite), the *Civil Law 1976*, namely under Articles 393, 400 and 401 thereof, gives full effect to this condition in the contract. Therefore, if the requirements stipulated in the relevant clauses of the Contract including the ones described in sub-clause 15.2 [*Termination for Contractor's Default*] of the 2017 rainbow suite (or sub-clause 15.2 [*Termination by Employer*] of the 1999 rainbow suite), then the Employer can exercise the right to sell the said items. However, in practice, it is recommended that the Employer obtain a court order to sell the items in order to avoid any risk that may be associated with the sale such as the risk of disposing of property that is owned by another person or any rights on the said item to the account of creditor(s) of the Contractor.

7.10.7 Finality of Engineer's or DAAB/DAB's decisions

In respect of the decisions issued by the DAAB/DAB, some of the jurisprudence and literature consider that such decisions are binding on the Parties unless a Notice of Dissatisfaction (NOD) is given during the period(s) agreed upon in the Contract, thus echoing what the

General Conditions state on this regard.[61] In the event that one of the Parties fails to give this NOD during the period(s) agreed upon in the Contract, then this will most likely be interpreted as consent to the DAAB/DAB decision. Most of the commentators see that the sub-clause dealing with the duration for giving the NOD is legal and does not contradict the law or the public order (public policy). In the view of these commentators, the specified period(s) are not statutory periods, thus the Parties may agree otherwise.

The foregoing argument is based mainly on the *Civil Law 1976*, which provides the following:

> The condition is a future obligation on the fulfillment of which legal effect subsists or terminates.[62]
>
> That which is subject to a condition shall become effective when the condition is fulfilled.[63]
>
> Effect shall be given to the condition to the extent possible.[64]

In one of the cases examined by the Court of Cassation, the Employer argued that the arbitral tribunal failed to exercise its duties and that the award issued by the arbitral tribunal was purely based on the decision issued by the DAB. The court decided that 'this argument does not constitute any ground to accept the annulment of the award' whereas, in the opinion of the Court 'the arbitral tribunal in its award has applied the provisions of the Jordanian Arbitration Law as agreed between the two parties to the case'.[65]

On the other hand, other commentators see that such sub-clauses could be interpreted as depriving the person of his/her constitutional right to refer a dispute to court or arbitration, especially if the sub-clause entails forgoing his/her right to refer a dispute to court or arbitration after the lapse of the agreed period. In their opinion, the mere fact that the DAAB/DAB decision was subject to a NOD by one of the Parties does not mean that the decision has become binding on the other Party if he/she fails to give a NOD during the period(s) agreed upon in the Contract.

Those commentators rely on the decision issued by the Court of Cassation in its decision number 1873/1998 in which the court stated the following:

> the right to resort to courts is a constitutional right that the litigants themselves do not have the right to preclude by means of an agreement under which any one of them will be prevented from resorting to the court in order to exercise his right of defence, the said agreement is contrary to public order [policy] and contradicts the provisions of the constitution.

In light of the preceding, a clear and final decision by the Court of Cassation on this controversial point is still to be seen, and the door is still open for debate. Therefore, it is recommended that the Parties do not rely on the contractual stipulations that an Engineer's determination becomes final and binding, and a DAAB/DAB decision becomes final and binding if the relevant NOD is not given within the prescribed time, thus precluding the Parties from pursuing the dispute any further.

61 Mohammad Eid Bundukji, 'Claims, Dispute Resolution and Arbitration According to the Standard Contracting Contract (FIDIC 99)' (Lecture in respect of Arbitration and Dispute Resolution Course, September 2004).

62 Article 393.

63 Article 400.

64 Article 401.

65 The decision issued by the Civil Cassation Court 169/2016 dated 3 April 2016.

CHAPTER 8

Applying FIDIC Contracts in Kenya

Barasa Ongeti

CONTENTS

 DOI: 10.4324/9781003206910-8

8.1 Outline of Kenya's legal environment

8.1.1 The constitutional structure of Kenya

The Republic of Kenya is a sovereign, multi-party democratic state. Kenya practices a devolved system of government, consisting of 47 counties each with a county assembly and county government for the provision of services.

Kenya's supreme law is the *Constitution of Kenya.* The *Constitution* asserts that all sovereign power belongs to the people and shall be exercised in accordance with the *Constitution.* The *Constitution of Kenya* has been in force since 2010, following a referendum. It was promulgated on 27 August 2010, replacing the previous constitution which had been in force since 1963 when Kenya attained independence.

The *Constitution of Kenya* consists of a Preamble which defines the foundational structure, 18 chapters and six schedules. The 18 chapters are divided into articles, which cover areas that the people of Kenya deemed to be important and needed to be recorded in a constitution. These chapters relate to matters such as the sovereignty of the people and the supremacy of the *Constitution,* the Republic, Citizenship, the *Bill of Rights,* land and environment, leadership and integrity. The chapters further go on to define the structure of government, public financial structures, and national security.

It is important, in the context of this book, to highlight that Chapter 4 of the *Constitution* dwells on the *Bill of Rights.* The *Bill of Rights* encompasses the so-called 'Three Generations of Rights', namely the (1) civil and political rights, (2) social, economic and cultural rights and (3) collective or solidarity rights.

Also significantly, Chapters 8, 9 and 10 define the governance structure of Kenya. Under these chapters, the principle of separation of powers is the underlying philosophy and Kenya is structured into three arms of government. Thus, the Government of Kenya comprises the Executive, the Legislature and the Judiciary. The roles of each arm are set out in the *Constitution,* and their independence from each other is emphasised.

8.1.1.1 The Executive

This arm consists of the President, the Deputy President, the Cabinet and other state offices. The President is the head of State and the Commander in Chief of the Defence forces. The President is mandated to exercise the executive authority of the Republic. The President is deputised by a Deputy, and together they are elected every five years following a national election. The President nominates up to 22 Cabinet Secretaries, who, along with the Attorney-General, the Deputy President and the President, form the Cabinet.

Cabinet Secretaries are individually and collectively accountable to the President in the exercise of their powers and the execution of their functions. They may also be summoned to appear before a Committee of Parliament to answer any question regarding a matter within their responsibility. The National Executive governing principles apply, with necessary variations, to the executive structures of the county governments.

The other state offices which make up the Executive comprise the office of the Attorney-General and the Office of the Director of Public Prosecutions

8.1.1.2 The Legislature

This consists of Parliament and the legislative assemblies in the county governments. Parliament comprises the Senate and the National Assembly.

The Senate has 47 members elected from each of the 47 counties, along with 16 nominated women representatives, two youth representatives and two representatives of people with disabilities. The Senate is the 'backbone of the counties', and it participates in the law-making function of Parliament by considering, debating and approving Bills concerning counties.

The members of the National Assembly are elected by a popular vote every five years in the general elections at the 290 constituencies. Besides the elective positions, there are 12 reserved slots for nominated members of parliament to represent special-interest groups such as youth, people with disabilities and workers. Further, there are 47 women, who are elected from each of the 47 counties to increase the representation of women in parliament. The National Assembly enacts legislation, represents the people of the constituencies and deliberates on the issues of concern to the public, as well as performs the role of oversight of the State.

Both the Senate and the National Assembly have a Speaker, who is an ex-officio member. Notably, neither of the two houses of parliament is designated the 'upper' chamber.

8.1.1.3 The Judiciary

This arm of government is made up of Courts and independent tribunals, which exercise judicial authority allocated to them by the people. The Judiciary consists of the judges of the superior courts, magistrates, other judicial officers and staff. The Chief Justice heads the Judiciary and is deputised by a Deputy Chief Justice. Under the *Constitution*, the office of the Chief Registrar of the Judiciary who is the chief administration and accounting officer is also established.

The independence of the Judiciary is a key facet of the *Constitution*, and it is covered under Article 160 of the *Constitution of Kenya*.

8.1.2 The legal system in Kenya

Section 3 of the *Judicature Act (Cap. 8)* Laws of Kenya encapsulates the legal system in Kenya by providing that the jurisdiction of all the courts in Kenya shall be exercised in conformity with:

a) The *Constitution of Kenya*, and subject thereto
b) All written laws (i.e., statutes or *Acts* of Parliament), and subject to those written laws
c) The substance of common law, and
d) The doctrines of equity amongst other statutes of general application.

Kenya is a former colony of the United Kingdom. Owing to this fact, the Kenyan legal system stems from the British common law system and borrows heavily from the British legal system. The *Constitution*, as the supreme law, ranks top in the hierarchy of laws followed by statutes which form the breadth of the legal system.

Statutes in Kenya are made in Parliament in line with the 'Westminster model' of operationalisation of a legislature. A bill is first introduced to Parliament and goes through the First Reading, the Second Reading, consideration by a parliamentary committee and a Third Reading. Thereafter, the head of State grants the bill Presidential Assent to the law, and it becomes an *Act* of Parliament. The date on which it comes into effect, known as its commencement, is often notified by the Cabinet Secretary responsible for the matters which the *Act* legislates.

One of the fundamental doctrines adopted from common law and used in the legal system in Kenya is the doctrine of precedent (*stare decisis*). A judgement or decision of a higher court is used as an authority in obtaining a decision for a subsequent case. Precedents are often recorded in a law report, published online by the National Council for Law Reporting (which goes by the brand name *Kenya Law*). *Kenya Law* is a semi-autonomous state corporation under the Judiciary of Kenya and was established by the *National Council for Law Reporting Act No. 11 of 1994*.

It is important, in the context of this book, to highlight that the *Constitution* under Article 2(5) explicitly provides that the general rules of international law shall form part of the law of Kenya. The import of this provision is to allow the application, in Kenya, of rules that have attained international customary acceptance and ratified treaties.

8.1.3 The court system in Kenya

Kenya's judicial authority is derived from the people and is exercised by courts and tribunals established under the *Constitution*. The court system comprises the superior courts and the subordinate courts.

The superior courts are the High Court, the Court of Appeal and the Supreme Court. These are established under the *Constitution*. Others are the Employment and Labour Relations Court (**ELRC**) and the Environmental and Land Court, specialised courts of equal status with the High Court anchored in the *Constitution* and established by specific legislation known as *Acts* of Parliament.

The subordinate courts are the Magistrates' Courts and the *Kadhis*' Courts (which deal specifically with matters of Muslim law relating to marriage, divorce or inheritance for persons who profess Islam as a religion), Courts-Martial and independent tribunals. The Magistrates' Courts and the *Kadhis'* Courts are all established under Article 169 of the *Constitution*. The jurisdiction, functions and powers of the subordinate courts are established by Parliament.

The Supreme Court is the highest court in Kenya and its decisions are binding on all courts subordinate to it. The Supreme Court is also bound by its own decisions, but it may overrule them and set them aside so they cease to have the force of precedent.

Likewise, decisions made in the Court of Appeal are binding on the High Court and the Magistrates Courts. Decisions made in the High Court create a binding precedent for the Magistrate's Courts.

Besides these main courts in the judicial structure, alternative dispute resolution (ADR) mechanisms including reconciliation, mediation, arbitration and traditional dispute resolution mechanisms are permitted under Article 159(2)(c).

Article 159(2)(c) of the *Constitution* states that:

> [A]lternative forms of dispute resolution including reconciliation, mediation, arbitration and traditional dispute resolution mechanisms shall be promoted.

Particularly, traditional dispute resolution mechanisms apply to the extent that they do not contravene the *Constitution* or any written law nor are they 'repugnant to justice and morality'. 'Traditional dispute resolution' in this sense is used to mean any of the cultural ways of justice that were historically exercised by the over 40 indigenous ethnic groups that make up Kenya.

The *Constitution of Kenya* emphasises the 'independence of the Judiciary'. This concept arises from historical instances in Kenya where the Judiciary was viewed as being heavily reliant on – or even under the control of – the Executive. During the constitutional reforms, the authors of the *Constitution* saw fit to explicitly separate the three arms of Government and emphasise the independence of the Judiciary.

8.2 The construction industry in Kenya

8.2.1 Overview

The infrastructure sector is a key driver of the Kenyan economy. There has been exponential growth in Kenya's population in recent years, from around 40.9 million people in 2009 to 47.6 million people in 2019, according to data from the Kenya National Bureau of Statistics.[1] With this population surge comes an increased demand for housing, telecommunications and commercial properties. These sectors of the construction industry are mainly covered by privately owned companies.

Major political and legal reforms occurred between 2007 and 2010 in Kenya. As a consequence, Kenya's construction industry has undergone steady growth, especially in public infrastructure, commercial buildings and housing. Successive governments from 2007 have continually invested heavily in the public infrastructure sector, especially in roads and highways, water supply, ports, airports and railroads.

From the foregoing, Kenya's construction industry may be seen as driven by (1) the government, whose mainstay is public infrastructure and (2) the private sector, whose mainstay is housing and commercial properties. The National Construction Authority (**NCA**) categorises construction companies in Kenya under three classes of works: (1) Water and Roads, classified under civil engineering works, (2) Building engineering works and (3) Mechanical and Electrical, classified as specialist engineering services.

As of 2022, there are five companies listed on the Nairobi Securities Exchange under Construction and Allied and four companies listed under Energy and Petroleum.

8.2.2 Structure

There are about 18,000 contractors legally listed in Kenya as of 2022.[2] Local contractors form about 50% of these. However, most local contractors lack the financial and technical capacity to undertake large-scale projects.

Historically, indigenous firms typically undertook infrastructure projects in Kenya. However, around 2007, following political and economic changes that occurred in that year, there arose an influx of foreign contractors. Kenya's construction landscape,

1 Kenya National Bureau of Statistics, *2019 Kenya Population and Housing Census: Volume 1, 2019*, 15.

2 This figure is obtained from a media news site directly quoting the Director of the NCA (www.capitalfm.co.ke/business/2015/11/nca-registers-18000-contractors/ [accessed 21 November 2022]). Although the NCA keeps a register of all registered contractors (https://nca.go.ke/search-registered-contractors/[(accessed 21 November 2022]), the figures on the website may not be not truly representative. The NCA register is a record of companies under all the construction categories. Thus, a single firm may be listed multiple times, appearing under each of the categories that it operates.

especially public infrastructure, is currently populated with foreign-owned firms. Mostly, these large contracting firms are from China, Japan, Spain, France, Germany, India and the UK.

8.2.3 Licensing and registration

8.2.3.1 Contractors and Subcontractors

Construction firms are required by law to register under the NCA. The legal mandate of the NCA is to regulate and streamline both local and foreign construction firms with operations in Kenya. The NCA keeps a register of all contractors, skilled labour and trades in the construction industry.[3]

Contractors may register under one of eight categories of Contractor Classes, which are named NCA 1, NCA 2 and so forth up to NCA 8. The categories are delineated as per the value of the works to be undertaken and the level of specialist skills required for such works.

A firm must be incorporated to be eligible for registration under any of these categories, as a limited liability company (**LLC**), a partnership or a sole proprietorship. At least one of the directors must have a technical qualification in a construction-related industry. The registration prerequisites for local firms and foreign firms are slightly different. Foreign contractors should only seek registration after the issuance of a letter of award and before signing the contract. For foreign contractors, the registration is only applicable to the project being undertaken.

Foreign firms operating in Kenya are required to sign a commitment stating that they shall transfer to local personnel all technical skills unavailable locally. Foreign contractors are only permitted to carry out works in class NCA 1, which is for works whose value is above KES 500 million (US$ 4.5 million).

If all the requisite requirements are met, the company is issued with a Certificate of Registration, commonly called an 'NCA Certificate'. The entire registration procedure and prerequisites are detailed on the NCA website.[4]

8.2.3.2 Engineers

Professionals in Kenya are registered by the various professional bodies that exist to govern their professions.

Professional Engineers are registered under the Engineers' Board of Kenya (**EBK**). The EBK is a corporate body established by law, under the *Engineers Act 43 of 2011.* The body is mandated to carry out the registration of engineers and engineering consulting firms as well as to regulate engineering professional services. Professionals may be registered as a consulting firm, a consulting engineer, a professional engineer, or a graduate engineer as the case may fit. Foreign engineers are registered on a temporary basis for the duration of any specific work for which he/she has been engaged as per s 23 of the *Engineers Act 2011.*

3 https://nca.go.ke/search-registered-contractors/ (accessed 4 May 2022).
4 National Construction Authority, www.nca.go.ke (accessed on 23 March 2022).

8.2.3.3 Architects and Quantity Surveyors

Architects and Quantity Surveyors are registered under the Board of Registration of Architects and Quantity Surveyors (**BORAQS**). The board is established under s 4 of the *Architects and Quantity Surveyors Act of 1934 (Cap. 525)* Laws of Kenya. The board is mandated to regulate the professions of architecture and quantity surveying through training, registration and enhancement of ethical practice.

Plans are underway to repeal the existing Cap. 525 and replace it with the *Architectural and Quantity Surveying Practitioners Bill, 2021.* The proposed bill is an apparent shift towards prevailing trends where the traditional architectural and quantity surveying fields have more specialised sub-sectors and allied practice fields. The proposed bill goes further to give consideration to landscape architects, interior designers, project managers and technicians as well as other paraprofessionals.

8.2.4 Labour relations

Labour relations in Kenya are entrenched in Article 41 of the *Constitution* and elaborated under the *Labour Relations Act of 2007*. The *Constitution* provides for core labour principles, such as the prohibition of inhuman treatment in Article 29 and the protection from slavery and forced labour in Article 30.

Other existing legal frameworks that relate to labour relations at the workplace and may be applicable to construction are the *Employment Act 2007*, the *Labour Institutions Act 2007* and the *Work Injury Benefits Act 2007*.

Positive labour relations in Kenya are fairly well-legislated and practised. Construction workers are legally protected in these statutes and they have the right to collective bargaining and formation of trade unions, as well as the right to strike, picket or engage in demonstrations within the limits of the law.

Workers may seek redress for grievances related to employment at the Employment and Labour Relations Court (ELRC), which is established under Article 162(2)(a) of the *Constitution of Kenya 2010*.

8.2.5 Safety culture

Kenya is a member of the International Labour Organization and has ratified and domesticated several *ILO-OSH Conventions* through the *Occupational Safety and Health Act, 2007* (colloquially known as *OSHA 2007*). Therefore, compliance with occupational health and safety regulations is a legal requirement with penalties for default. Besides *OSHA 2007*, other subsidiary statutes are applicable to construction and general workplace safety and public health.

In Kenya, the Directorate of Occupational Health and Safety Services (**DOSHS**) is mandated to ensure compliance with the provisions of *OSHA 2007*. All workplaces and construction sites are obliged to register under DOSHS within their administrative region (County or Sub-County).

The NCA and DOSHS regularly carry out inspections to verify adherence to construction site safety requirements.

Generally, the construction safety culture is not well-developed in Kenya. Due to limitations in technical and financial capacity, it is common to find construction workers without basic PPE and workplaces with no written safety manual or policy. However, within the larger construction firms and more so the international contractors, safety culture is promoted as a primary requirement for work. Foreign-owned construction companies with an emphasis on workplace safety may require additional effort in inculcating a safety culture among their site staff.

8.2.6 Modular construction using factory-fabricated components

Modular construction refers to a construction technique in which building components are constructed off-site and then delivered to site for installation at their ultimate location. Modular construction has not taken off in Kenya, with the exception of a few firms which engage in the production of prefabricated or expanded polystyrene (**EPS**) panels.

The National Housing Corporation (**NHC**) is undertaking a campaign to encourage the use of EPS panels in construction in an effort to boost the supply of affordable housing in the country.[5] The NHC is a state-operated organisation.

Other privately owned firms have entered this evolving market, and it remains to be seen if modular construction will be widespread and accepted in Kenya in the coming years.

8.2.7 Technology/innovation/BIM

The application of BIM in the construction industry in Kenya is lagging behind other countries. It should be noted that Kenya is a developing country, with only about 798,000 fixed data subscriptions as of 2021.[6] If this is an adequate measure of internet penetration, Kenya remains underserved in terms of access to reliable fixed data. Consequently, the use of digital and web-based technology as a reliable basis for decision-making, exchange of information and communication is not widespread.

While the benefits and awareness of BIM are clear to many players in the architecture, engineering and construction (**AEC**) industry, Kenya remains a late adopter of technology and innovation in construction.

With regard to the adoption of technology, there are small advances towards innovation and the adoption of new and sustainable building technology. A recent case in point is the construction of the first-ever 3D-printed house in central Kenya, which marked the pioneer deployment of 3D printing technology into the Kenyan construction market.

The Kenyan market is an open one and it is likely that more instances of technology and innovation including BIM will gradually be adopted in construction.

8.2.8 Government/private sector procurement

Prior to 2005, procurement in Kenya was largely regulated by circulars and regulations issued by the Ministry of Finance, the Ministry of Public Works and the Office of the President. Under these institutional arrangements, there was an increased likelihood of

5 National Housing Corporation, www.nhckenya.go.ke/eps (accessed 23 April 2022).

6 Communications Authority of Kenya, *Second Quarter Sector Statistics Report for the Financial Year 2021/2022, 2021*, 12.

the fairness and impartiality of the procurement process being undermined. Ultimately, it was found necessary to conduct reforms in the public procurement sector. These reforms came by way of restructuring the legislative framework that governs public procurement. This led to the introduction of the *Public Procurement and Disposal Act (PPDA) of 2005.*

Between 2005 and 2016, Government procurement in Kenya was administered under the *Public Procurement and Disposal Act (PPDA) of 2005* and the *Procurement Regulations of 2006*, both of which are legal instruments enacted by Parliament. These regulations establish a sound and comprehensive legal framework for public procurement with a clear hierarchical distinction. The *PPDA* clearly establishes the choice of procurement procedures, the invitation to tender rules and time bars, the structure and nature of tender, owners' requirements and technical specifications, criteria for evaluation and award of tenders, submission, receipt and opening of tenders as well as the complaints system for dissatisfied bidders. Further to these, the *PPDA* also has a section on international tendering.

In January 2016 the *Public Procurement and Asset Disposal Act No. 33* of 2015 (***PPADA Act***) was enacted, and this legislation superseded its predecessor, the *PPDA* of 2005. This measure transformed the role of the Public Procurement Oversight Authority (**PPOA**) by restructuring it and renaming it to the Public Procurement Regulatory Authority (**PPRA**). The body then assumed regulatory function and was now mandated to monitor, assess and review the public procurement and asset disposal system in line with the legal provisions and the (then relatively new) 2010 *Constitution.*

The foundational basis of the procurement law and the regulatory authority, Article 227 of the *Constitution* states that state organs or other public entities shall carry out their procurement of goods or services, in accordance with the principles of fairness, equity, transparency, competition and cost-effectiveness. As such, it can be said that the legal framework for government procurement in Kenya is robust.

Private sector procurement in Kenya is more liberal and is generally governed by the contract terms that the parties will rely on. In a loose sense, private procurement in Kenya is governed by the principle of freedom of contract. The procurement will be done and executed as per the words of the contract, and competent parties will make agreements within the ambit of the law.

8.2.9 Insurance requirements

In Kenya, matters relating to insurance are covered by the *Insurance Act Cap. 487 of 1985.* The ambit of the act is to 'amend and consolidate the Law relating to insurance, and to regulate the business of insurance and for connected purposes'.

The *Act* under its Third Schedule delineates several classes of general insurance. Amongst these and pertinent to construction, are Contractor's All Risk and Engineering Insurance which fall under the class of 'Engineering, Insurance including Contractor's Risks, Machinery Breakdown, Erection All Risks and Consequential Loss from Breakdown'. As such, insurance in construction and engineering is a requirement of law.

8.2.10 Common forms of contract

The choice of contracts may be directly linked to the commercial outcome of a project for both the Employer and the Contractor. In Kenya, several developers both in the public and private sectors have historically adopted standard forms of contracts for their projects. Standard form contracts are useful because of their familiarity, the relative ease of agreement upon the terms and, consequently, ease of adoption by the parties.

One of the more common forms of contract widely used in Kenya is the Agreement and Conditions for Contract for Building Works, popularly known as the 'JBC Contract 1999'. The JBC contract was developed by the Joint Building Council, a company sanctioned by the Architectural Association of Kenya (**AAK**) and the Kenya Association of Building and Civil Engineering Contractors.

The JBC 1999 Contract is structured into 45 clauses, which cover the extent of contractual matters such as obligations of the Parties, obligations of the Architect and the Quantity Surveyor, quality of works, payments, variations, progress and completion, termination and settlement of disputes. The JBC Contract 1999 is popular amongst developers of privately owned residential and commercial buildings.

The Institute of Quantity Surveyors of Kenya recently published the Agreement and Conditions for Contract for Small Construction Works 2020. It is a condensed, simple contract touted as being suitable for smaller projects of short duration and low value. This contract provides a range of options for dispute resolution.

With regard to public projects, state bodies usually adopt the standard construction contract agreement recommended by the PPRA. As mandated by law, the PPRA develops various standard forms of procurement which they refer to as **STD** (standard tender documents). The procedures and practices presented in these STD are intended to fulfil the requirements of the *Procurement Act* and best practices.

Pertinent to construction, the PPRA publishes the standard tender documents for:

- Procurement of Works (Building and Associated Civil Engineering Work)
- Procurement of Works (Roads and Water Bridges, etc.)
- Procurement of Small Works
- Procurement of Design and Build-Turnkey Contracts.

All these and others are available for free download from the PPRA website.[7]

For projects involving international bidding, FIDIC contracts are common. The so-called 'traditional contracting' is widespread in Kenya and this makes the FIDIC forms, especially the FIDIC Red Book, hugely popular. Other projects have adopted the design-and-build approach, and the FIDIC Yellow Book is applied. Government projects have for a number of years been funded by MDBs, and the procurement route for such projects has resulted in the adoption of the FIDIC MDB Harmonised edition, known as the Pink Book.

More recently, there has been a shift to Public–Private Partnership (**PPP**) arrangements, especially in energy and public infrastructure. Relevant legislation applicable to PPPs is the *Public Private Partnership Act, No. 15 of 2013* (*PPP Act*).

In PPP contracting, it is arguable that the most practical route is concessions, Build-Operate-Transfer (**BOT**), and Design-Build-Operate (**DBO**) schemes. Several projects in Kenya have been procured under the PPP framework even though the contract details are not easily available in the public domain. The 27-kilometre (16.7-mile) Nairobi Expressway project – commissioned in 2022 – is one such project. Others are the development of a

7 Public Procurement Regulatory Authority, www.ppra.go.ke (accessed 20 May 2023).

140 MW geothermal power plant at Olkaria (Olkaria VI) near central Kenya, the Nairobi-Nakuru-Mau Summit Highway Project and the Lamu Port Development Project. All these projects are valued above US$500 million.[8] It is likely that future large-scale infrastructure projects will increasingly adopt this arrangement. The FIDIC Gold Book and the Silver Book are well suited for the complexity of PPP transactions.

A cursory reference to case law records on the *Kenya Law* website indicates that a significant number of projects brought before the courts were governed by the 1999 editions of FIDIC, with an equally significant number being based on the 1987 editions. On an elementary level, this may be an indication that the uptake of the 2017 FIDIC editions in Kenya has been slow. Perhaps, this slow uptake may be attributed to mere resistance to change and the comfort of familiarity. Industry players remark that the 2017 editions of the Red, Silver and Yellow Books are more rigorous and procedural than their predecessors. It is possible then that most users of FIDIC prefer to retain the use of the older versions which they are more familiar with.

8.3 The impact of COVID-19 in Kenya

8.3.1 The impact of COVID-19 on the execution of construction projects in Kenya

In Kenya, like in the rest of the world, the global outbreak of COVID-19 impacted the movement of goods, personnel and equipment, more so for contractors engaged in international contracts. In response to the outbreak and as a measure of containment, various *Presidential Directives*, gazetted legislation and edicts, and judicial practice directives with legal bearing emanated from the authorities.

Consequently, the construction industry was impacted in some ways. These are highlighted in the following with links to the relevant edict or legislation.

8.3.1.1 Prohibition on construction

The measures to suppress COVID-19 were announced in the *Gazette* or on mass media by the Cabinet Secretary of the Ministry of Health, designating an area as an 'Infected Area'. Based on this declaration, the Cabinet Secretary may regulate the activities that may be carried out within the Infected Area. Such authority is drawn from the *Public Health Act Cap. 242 (Act No. 12 of 2012)*, which is existing legislation that pre-dates the COVID-19 pandemic.

During the initial stages of the pandemic, the Government of Kenya through the Ministry of Health published containment measures and regulations in the *Kenya Gazette Supplement Number 41 issued 6 April 2020.*[9] Under this gazettement was Legal Notice No. 50 which entailed the *Public Health (Covid-19 Restriction of Movement of Persons and Related Measures) Rules 2020.* The rules ran for an initial 21 days and were periodically extended or lifted by the authorities, depending on the prevailing situation.

Generally, the rules resulted in restricted movement and access to 'public places', which were defined to mean 'any outdoor, indoor, enclosed or partially enclosed area which is open to the public or any part of the public, or to which members of the public ordinarily

8 Kenya PPP Platform, pppunit.go.ke (accessed 4 May 2022).

9 Public Legal Information on Kenya's Response to Covid-19 | Kenya Law, http://kenyalaw.org/kenyalaw-blog/kenyas-response-to-covid-19/ (accessed 4 May 2022).

have access'. Flowing from this definition, it may be interpreted that such public places include construction sites.

However, sub-rule 4 (b) of these rules excluded the transportation of 'all types of lawful cargo and goods including construction material' upon the relevant party obtaining written permission. So, despite the restriction of movement of personnel, construction material could be delivered to infected areas within the restricted period.

8.3.1.2 Constraints on working hours on construction sites

A nationwide dusk-to-dawn curfew was implemented in March 2020 pursuant to a *Presidential Directive*, covering the entire territory of the Republic of Kenya. Initially, the curfew ran from 7:00 pm to 5:00 am, and these times varied based on the caseload as the disease progressed. The *Presidential Directives* on curfew were formalised in the *Public Order (State Curfew) Order, 2020* which was published under *Legal Notice No. 36* dated 25 March 2020.

Significantly, *Legal Notice No. 36* gave exemption to workers who perform 'essential services'. Some essential services which were exempted and could be directly linked to construction are services rendered by personnel from Kenya Ports Authority, Kenya Civil Aviation Authority, water service providers and Kenya Pipeline Company. These are state-owned and semi-autonomous organisations which ordinarily have construction projects running.

The State Curfew orders fall under the purview of *Public Order Cap. 56*, which is existing legislation that pre-dates the COVID-19 pandemic. The curfew was eventually lifted in October 2021.

8.3.1.3 Other health and safety measures

The Ministry of Health was responsible for issuing guidelines which posed constraints on employees, for example, the compulsory wearing of face masks in public areas. Other regulations and guidelines were also issued that impacted the normal operation of a construction site, such as physical distancing of at least 1.5 metres, frequent cleaning and disinfection, record keeping and preparation for a COVID-19 infection. These were contained in *Legal Notice No. 49* of 3 April 2020 and *Legal Notice No. 50* of 6 April 2020 which were published in the *Kenya Gazette*. They generally applied to all business premises and workers and were not specific to construction.

Construction sites were at liberty to implement measures compliant with the guidelines and legal edicts.

8.3.1.4 Constraints on travel

The President issued a *Directive* mandating the full lockdown of two areas in April 2020. The *Directive* ordered the cessation of all movement by road, rail or air in and out of (a) the Nairobi Metropolitan Area and (b) the counties of Kilifi, Kwale and Mombasa areas located on the Kenyan Coast. This *Directive* was issued cognisant that the majority of all cases of infection were concentrated within two areas: the coastal strip and the capital city, Nairobi.

The lockdown *Directive* was gazetted in *Legal Notice No. 51*, *Legal Notice No. 52*, *Legal Notice No. 53* and *Legal Notice No. 54*, which designated these four areas as Infected Areas. As such, the *Public Health (Covid-19 Restriction of Movement of Persons and*

Related Measures) Rules came into effect for these areas. In this sense, the two regions (Nairobi Metropolitan and the coastal area) were most impacted by COVID-19 legislation whose aim was to restrict the movement of personnel and goods.

Kenya's inbound and outbound travel policy is regulated by the Kenya Civil Aviation Authority (**KCAA**),[10] which publishes regulatory notices from time to time. For most of 2020 and 2021, passengers coming into Kenya required a valid COVID-19 negative PCR test certificate conducted within 96 hours prior to travel. Children below five years and flight crew were exempted from this requirement. All travellers were required to submit health information to a web-based platform before travel. Once the vaccine was rolled out, it became mandatory for all passengers to be vaccinated with at least two doses where applicable, prior to entry.

In the early stages of the pandemic, quarantine at government facilities was necessary for all inbound travellers. However, this was later lifted and inbound travellers only needed self-isolation for 14 days. Certain countries considered 'high-risk' were listed from time to time as compulsory quarantine and the list was updated from time to time on the KCAA website.[11]

These constraints specifically impacted construction sites whose personnel come from foreign countries. Kenya's construction landscape is diverse with consultants and contractors from different nationalities plying their trade. China, specifically, where the virus is said to have originated and was considered a high-risk area, has a significant number of construction staff engaged on different projects in Kenya. Others who were affected were personnel associated with MDB-funded projects by JICA, the World Bank, the African Development Bank and the Asian Development Bank by virtue of their presence in Kenya.

8.3.1.5 Financial support

Financial support from the Government largely came in the form of *Legal Notice No. 35* which was issued on March 2020, under the purview of the *Value Added Tax Act No. 35 of 2013*. By virtue of this *Legal Notice*, Value Added Tax (VAT) was reduced from the statutory 16% to 14% by amending paragraph (b) of s 5 (2) of the *Value Added Tax, 2013*. This reduction offered relief to businesses, including those engaged in construction.

Further legislative changes targeted at cushioning businesses were made on 18 March 2020 when the President assented to the *Tax Laws (Amendment) Bill, 2020* made by Parliament. The Bill targeted several tax-related laws in Kenya, including the *Income Tax Act (Cap. 470)*, the *Value Added Tax Act of 2013*, the *Excise Duty Act (2015)*, the *Tax Procedures Act (2015)*, the *Miscellaneous Levies and Fees Act (2016)* and the *Retirement Benefits Act (1997)*. Among the interventions were:

i) An increase in the threshold for turnover tax to KES 1,000,050 (US$8,600) so as to exclude small-scale business
ii) Lowering the rate for turnover tax from 3% to 1%
iii) Employees earning less than KES 28,000 (US$ 240) per month were granted a 100% relief on PAYE (Pay-As-You-Earn) tax. A reduction of PAYE from 30% to 25% was granted for those earning above this new threshold

10 Covid-19 Travel Requirements | Kenya Civil Aviation Authority, www.kcaa.or.ke (accessed 2 May 2022).

11 Covid-19 | Kenya Civil Aviation Authority, kcaa.or.ke (accessed 2 May 2022).

iv) Corporate Tax was revised to 25% and non-resident tax on dividends was adjusted from 10% to 15%.

Other changes included an overhaul of the Second Schedule to the *Income Tax Act*, which outlines various forms of capital deductions and allowances pertinent to construction. For example, the amendment included a reduction from 37.5% to 25% on the rate for heavy earth-moving equipment. The construction of hospital buildings and educational buildings was also affected by the deductions and allowances.

8.3.2 The impact of COVID-19 on the operation of construction contracts in Kenya

The Government of Kenya did not operationalise any legislation that changed the 'normal' operation of construction contracts. Likewise, there were no governmental interventions in the operation of construction contracts, such as the forced extension of time or provisions for hardship allowances as was the case in some countries. In essence, parties were left to resolve issues arising from the pandemic including financial compensation, termination of the contract, suspension of contractual obligations or extension of time based on existing contract provisions. In the case of FIDIC Contracts, the General Conditions are often heavily amended by the parties and the interpretation of such provisions would depend on the exact wording of the contract.

It has been postulated that the impact of COVID-19 could be construed as a *force majeure* event.[12] However, there is no statutory definition of *force majeure* in Kenyan Law and instead, the applicability of *force majeure* as a contractual relief for any party failing to meet its obligations due to the effects of the COVID-19 pandemic would depend upon the wording of the Contract as well the governing law of the contract. Parties who choose to invoke the *force majeure* clause in relation to COVID-19 must demonstrate that the threshold of *force majeure* as defined in the Contract was met.

Some construction contracts were impacted in instances where the venue of arbitration was outside of Kenya, especially as a result of travel restrictions in the place of arbitration. It is important to note that the distinction between 'place', 'seat' and 'venue' of arbitration is significant and could bring about differing interpretations by the parties. One instance is the case of *Euromec International Limited v Shandong Taikai Power Engineering Company Limited*,[13] where one of the issues that formed part of the suit was what test would be utilised by the courts to determine whether a chosen venue could be treated as the seat of arbitration. One party argued that arbitration in Hong Kong, the venue of arbitration, would be costly and difficult due to the ongoing pandemic. The other party argued that Hong Kong was only the seat of the venue, and arbitral pleadings could be conducted online. The court applied the bright-line test on the distinction between 'seat' and 'venue' of arbitration and ruled that it is possible to conduct arbitration hearings online, since 'online filing of pleadings and virtual hearing is cheap, convenient and effective'.

---

12 'FIDIC Covid-19 Guidance Memorandum to Users of FIDIC Standard Forms of Works Contracts', FIDIC, 2020.

13 *Euromec International Limited v Shandong Taikai Power Engineering Company Limited* (Civil Case E527 of 2020) [2021] KEHC 93 (KLR) (Commercial and Tax).

Court proceedings were particularly impacted following the enactment of the Electronic Case Management Practice Directions, 2020. The Practice Directions were given by the Chief Justice, on the grounds of authority conferred under Articles 159 (2) and 161 (2) (a) of the *Constitution 2010*, s 10 of the *Judicature Act* and s 81 (3) of the *Civil Procedure Act Cap. 5 of 1948*. Consequently, the proceedings of any matters related to construction contracts that were before the courts during this period had to be adjusted to comply with the Practice Directions.

In order to find a balance between keeping the judiciary systems running while safeguarding the health of judicial staff, the Chief Justice and the National Council on the Administration of Justice resolved to use technology in judicial proceedings, including e-filing and service of documents, use of real-time transcript devices, teleconferencing and use of computers in the courtroom.

The execution of civil orders and decrees and eviction orders made before 16 March 2020 were suspended in April 2020, pending the monitoring of how the pandemic progressed. Some cases were held and are still held in 'open court', in the open air with minimal staff and attendance. Where possible, some cases are heard electronically through teleconference.

8.4 Kenyan governing law of the contract

8.4.1 Constraints on the governing law of a construction contract

The law that creates and governs the contract is often referred to as the proper or governing law of the contract. This is the substantive law that the parties have chosen as that which will ascertain their legally enforceable rights and obligations.

Kenya's *Law of Contract Act (Cap. 23) No. 2 of 2002* governs the formation of all contracts, including construction contracts. The *Law of Contract Act* states that except for any written law being in force, the common law of England relating to contract, as modified by the doctrines of equity, shall extend and apply to Kenya.

Pursuant to this statute, the parties have the right to select the proper law of their contract. The proper law may be expressly or impliedly chosen by the parties, or in the absence of such law, it then becomes the system of law which has 'its closest and most real connection'.[14] In Kenya therefore, parties may choose a governing law and must imply or express it within their contract. In this regard, the FIDIC Conditions are in agreement with the law of Kenya, which, under sub-clause 1.4 (Law and Language) states that the governing law of the contract shall be the law of the country or other jurisdiction that the Parties may choose and state in the Contract Data. If such law is not stated, then the law of the Country is applicable.

Parallel to the *Law of Contract (Cap. 23) No. 2 of 2002*, construction works done in the public sector (government projects) are governed by the *Public Procurement and Asset Disposal Act, No. 33 of 2015*. So, whereas some aspects of the law of contracts are regarded as 'common construction law', the courts may construe such differently.

Unlike other jurisdictions like New Zealand or Ireland, Kenya does not have an explicit statute that is specific to construction contracts (besides the public procurement law). This

14 B. A. Marshall, 'Reconsidering the Proper Law of the Contract' (2012) 13 *Melbourne Journal of International Law* 1.

situation poses an immediate constraint on the governing law of construction contracts in Kenya, especially in the case of public procurement.

The following observation, as an example, highlights a position that may be taken by the courts in instances of construction law:

> The provisions of our statutes and the regulations made thereunder will take precedence in terms of the hierarchy of the laws to be administered by the courts as set out in section 3 of the Judicature Act (Cap. 8) of the Laws of Kenya. In other words, the substance of the common law and doctrines of equity cannot override the statutory provisions as contained in the Public Procurement and Disposal Act of 2005 and the regulations made thereunder. The doctrine of *quantum meruit* is a common law principle and for that reason it can also not override the provisions of the Public Procurement and Disposal Act of 2005 and the regulations made thereunder.[15]

In this ruling, the court leaned towards applying the public procurement law to override the common law principle drawn from the *Law of Contracts Act*.

In the case of public procurement, therefore, the governing law of the contract must always be the law of Kenya.

8.4.2 Formal requirements for a construction contract

In Kenya, construction contracts are governed by:

i) The Law of Contract Act (Cap. 23) No. 2 of 2002
ii) Legal precedents under case law, and
iii) Contracts in the public sector are governed by the particular statute controlling that sector. For instance, a public procurement works contract is governed by the *PPADA Act of 2015.*

Since the *Law of Contract Act (Cap. 23) No. 2 of 2002* is based on the common law of England relating to contracts, the basic principles of contract are required for a construction contract.[16] These basic principles are:

(i) An offer and acceptance
(ii) A consideration
(iii) Intention to be legally bound, and
(iv) The parties must have contractual capacity to enter into a contract.

As is the case with other common law jurisdictions, a contract may contain express terms and terms implied in law and by statute. In this regard, the provisions of FIDIC Contracts are compliant with Kenyan law, where in sub-clause 1.5 the priority of contract documents is listed. Among them are the letter of acceptance (acceptance), letter of tender (offer) and the intention to be legally bound (Contract Agreement).

Under s 3 of the *Law of Contract Act (Cap. 23) No. 2 of 2002*, certain contracts must be in writing. While oral contracts are generally valid, some subject matters such as the disposition of an interest in land fall under the class of contracts that need to be in writing.

15 *Narok County Government v Prime Tech Engineering Ltd* [2017] eKLR.

16 *Omar Gorhan v Municipal Council of Malindi (Council Government of Kilifi) v Overlook Management Kenya Ltd* [2020] eKLR.

The law does not mention construction contracts as contracts which must be in writing, therefore it is implicit that oral construction contracts are valid.

With regard to public procurement, s 129 of the *PPADA Act of 2015* requires the contract to be in writing. The contract must stipulate the time limit and the maximum amount that can be paid under the contract.

In some jurisdictions, the matter of whether a letter of intent is distinguished from a provisional contract or is legally binding has been the subject of some dispute.[17] Section 87(4) of the *PPADA Act of 2015* puts certainty to this matter by expressly providing that:

> For greater certainty, a notification under subsection (1) does not form a contract nor reduce the validity period for a tender or tender security.

The notification referenced under subsection (1) is a letter from the procuring entity notifying in writing the successful tenderer that its tender has been accepted.

8.5 What Special Provisions in the Particular Conditions are necessary for consistency with applicable laws in Kenya?

8.5.1 FIDIC General Conditions are incompatible or inconsistent with Kenyan governing law of the contract

In Kenya, the courts have historically leaned towards the principle of freedom of contract. The law does not intervene in contracts to rewrite contractual agreements; rather, it seeks to enforce the terms of the contract as they are worded. In essence, the general principle is that the court will rarely interpose itself between contracting parties unless the contract itself or the contract terms are illegal, outrightly unconscionable or manifestly against public policy.

The issue of public policy is a matter of subjectivity. Thus, even if contractual obligations are not directly opposed to any stated or implicit statutory obligation, the courts may decline to give effect to them if they violate 'the policy of the law' as established by the intention of the statute. It is no wonder that the matter of public policy has variously been labelled as one of 'fluid nature',[18] 'open-textured nature'[19] and 'inconsistent, unpredictable and variable'.[20] The courts have themselves declared it as 'a broad, infinite and malleable concept'.[21] Nevertheless, public policy remains a frequently cited defence for public authorities in construction contracts case law. Be that as it may, in *Constitutional Petition No. 159 of 2018*, the High Court of Kenya at Mombasa made a significant ruling on the doctrine of freedom of contract. In delivering the ruling, the judges held that:

---

17 *A.J. Richard & Sons, Inc. v Forest City Ratner Cos., LLC* [2019] N.Y. Slip Op. 30215(U) (Sup. Ct. Kings County 28 January 2019).

18 Allan A. Abwunza, 'Taxonomy of the Public Policy Defence in the Recognition and Enforcement of Arbitral Awards' (2018) 6(3) *Alternative Dispute Resolution* 261.

19 Andrew Tweeddale, 'Enforcing Arbitration Awards Contrary to Public Policy in England' (2000) *International Construction Law Review* 159.

20 Saber Habibisavadkouhi and Sadegh Habibisavadkouhi, 'The Position and Problem of Public Policy in Indian Arbitration and Conciliation Act 1996' (2014) 3(12) *Research Journal of Recent Sciences* 91, 92. www.isca.in/rjrs/archive/v3/i12/14.ISCA-RJRS-2013-1047.pdf (accessed 4 May 2022).

21 *Ministry of Environment and Forestry v Kiarigi Building Contractors & another* [2020] eKLR.

> [the] State has leeway to regulate and limit the freedom to contract by individuals in order to achieve other public interest objectives including the objective of achieving the social and economic rights of citizens. [22]

Thus, the doctrine of freedom of contract may be seen as being curtailed in cases of public procurement, where public policy comes into play. Since the *Constitution of Kenya* plainly envisages a directive role of the State in respecting, promoting and fulfilling the various enumerated fundamental rights of individuals and groups, any provisions of a contract should be in line with these rights. The state has leeway to intervene if it is deemed such intervention will safeguard public interest objectives.

Parties are at liberty to use the FIDIC General Conditions as is, as long as they both agree to the terms contained therein. However, care should be taken with certain areas that are potentially inconsistent or incompatible with the governing law of the contract if the *Public Procurement Act* applies (see section 8.5.2).

8.5.2 FIDIC General Conditions are incompatible or inconsistent with the law of the Site/Country

As mentioned in the previous section, Kenya is unlike some jurisdictions which have a specific construction contract law. Public infrastructure projects contracted under FIDIC Conditions of Contract would therefore be governed by the *PPADA Act of 2015* as the substantive law. As determined by the courts in *Narok County Government v Prime Tech Engineering Ltd*,[23] the public procurement law overrides the substance of common law. Contrastingly, and of significance, is the matter of *Judicial Review No. 47 of 2017* which avers that 'the law of contract which is the substantive law in this case, should be used to determine and settle any dispute'.[24]

It can be inferred that the courts consider the *Law of Contract Act* (which adopts the UK common law) as the substantive law for construction contracts generally, and the *PPADA Act of 2015* as the substantive law for construction contracts publicly procured. The *PPADA Act of 2015* self-imposes its superiority in s 5, which states that this *Act* shall prevail in case of any inconsistency between this *Act* and any other legislation or government notices or circulars.

By virtue of the *PPADA Act of 2015*, the following issues may require Special Provisions for publicly procured FIDIC Contracts in Kenya.

8.5.2.1 Variations and amendments

The *Public Procurement and Asset Disposal Regulations, 2020* make a distinction between variations and amendments. An amendment, according to the *Regulations*, is defined as an alteration to the terms of a contract, while a variation refers to a change in the price, time for completion or the requirements of a contract.

Section 139 of the *PPADA Act 2015* covers amendments and variations to contracts. It stipulates that a variation or amendment is only effective if it is approved in writing by the

---

22 *William Odhiambo Ramogi & 3 others v Attorney General & 4 others; Muslims for Human Rights & 2 others (Interested Parties)* [2020] eKLR.

23 [2017] eKLR.

24 *Republic v Director General of Kenya National Highways Authority (DG) & 3 others Ex-parte Dhanjal Brothers Limited* [2018] eKLR.

tendering authority within a procuring entity. The (1) extension of the contract period, (2) use of prime costs, (3) use of contingencies and (4) use of provisional sums are subject to the approval of an accounting officer in a procuring entity, upon the recommendation of an evaluation committee. In this context, the *Act* defines a 'procuring entity' as a public entity making a procurement or asset disposal to which the *Act* applies.

This provision makes it necessary to include a Special Provision in a FIDIC contract for consistency and compliance with the law. A Special Provision should be included to ensure that Variations and amendments to the Contract are approved in writing by the tender-awarding authority within the Employer's ranks for consistency with s 139 of the *PPADA Act 2015*.

8.5.2.2 Variation procedure

With reference to the 2017 FIDIC Red Book, sub-clause 13.1 (Right to Vary) assigns the duty of initiating a Variation to the Engineer. Sub-clause 13.3 (Variation Procedure) then goes on to state that the Engineer may determine an extension of time or adjustment to the Contract Price. This is in apparent conflict with s 139 of the *PPADA Act*.

It may be necessary to align the role of the Engineer under the Contract with the part of the 'accounting officer' of the procuring entity, with respect to Variations and amendments. The accounting officer may co-opt a technical department or professionals for contract administration as permitted by s 150 (2) and 151 (3) of the *PPADA Act*, to act as 'the Engineer' under the Contract. Sub-clause 3.2 (Engineer's Duties and Authority) states that the Engineer is deemed to act for the Employer. Whenever carrying out the duties specified or implied by the Contract, then the Engineer is known to be acting on behalf of the Employer. However, due to the technical nature of construction projects, it is unlikely in practice that the Employer's accounting officer would be the same person as the Engineer appointed to administer the Contract. The prudent thing, when drafting Special Provisions, would be to include the role of an (Employer's) accounting officer as a second layer of approval of Variations after the Engineer initiates and approves them under the Contract. Such a Special Provision should be included in the Particular Conditions.

8.5.2.3 Adjustments for changes in Cost

Sub-clause 13.7 (Adjustments for Changes in Cost) deals with what is habitually called in Kenyan local practice 'variation of price', 'price adjustment' or 'price escalation'. This sub-clause is only applicable if the Schedule(s) of cost indexation is included in the Contract. Contractors – and indeed project owners – who wish to protect themselves from the risks of fluctuation of costs of material, labour, fuel, construction equipment and other inputs should be keen to include the cost indices in the Schedules.

Care should be taken when drafting Special Provisions to make this sub-clause consistent with s 4 (a) of the *PPADA Act of 2015* which stipulates any variation of a contract shall only be considered after twelve months from the date of signing the contract. It further states that variations in price shall only be considered if the price variation is based on the prevailing consumer price index obtained from the Kenya National Bureau of Statistics or the monthly inflation rate issued by the Central Bank of Kenya.

As such, the source of indexes to be considered when preparing the cost indexation should be the Kenya National Bureau of Statistics and the inflation rate should be the local rate. This is not practical for projects paid in foreign currency, as is the case for most international contracts. Therefore, some form of mechanism for currency conversion will be necessary.

8.5.3 FIDIC General Conditions are incompatible or inconsistent with the relevant laws on dispute determination in Kenya

No Special Provisions are necessary for consistency with the relevant laws on dispute determination in Kenya.

8.6 What Special Provisions in the Particular Conditions are desirable for consistency with applicable laws in Kenya?

It may be desirable to align the Contract with local practices or to replace non-mandatory law. The FIDIC Conditions make repeated reference to 'applicable Laws' of the Site/Country in instances of design, environment, insurance and subcontracting among others. These subsequent laws and other laws of the Site/Country are constantly being changed, repealed and amended. Prior to making Special Provisions, the contract administrators should seek legal advice on the proper wording of Particular Conditions for compliance.

8.6.1.1 Labour

Labour in the construction industry is often the beneficiary of industrial court orders and collective bargaining agreements between trade unions and their employers. This is especially with regard to working hours, overtime, annual leave, housing and insurance. Thus, when drafting the Particular Conditions, care should be taken to align these aspects with the prevailing collective agreement that relates to the nature of the Works.

The Employment Act of 2007 provides for basic minimum conditions of employment under s 26. Under this section, the *Act* states that if any terms and conditions of a contract of service are regulated by any collective bargaining agreement, written law or any judgement award or Industrial Court order, the more favourable terms and conditions of service shall apply.

Sub-clause 6.5 of the FIDIC Conditions states that no work shall be carried out outside the normal working hours stated in the Contract Data. So, it may be desirable to align the contract with the requirements of the *Employment Act of Kenya 2007* and stipulate the working hours in the Contract Data.

8.6.1.2 Insurance

As explained in earlier sections of this Chapter, insurance is a requirement of the law as per the *Insurance Act Cap. 487 of 1985.*

The FIDIC Conditions of Contract for Construction (Red Book, 2017) requires that the Contractor takes out insurance for the Works, Goods, Professional Liability, Injury to employees, injury to persons and damage to property. The Red Book then goes on to stipulate that the Contractor shall provide 'other insurances required by Laws and by local practice'. These other requirements are to be detailed in the Contract Data, so it would be desirable for drafters of Contracts to elaborate on which additional insurances are required based on the nature of the project and in line with the *Insurance Act.*

8.6.1.3 Environmental Laws

The *Environmental Management and Co-ordination Act No. 8 of 1999*[25] is a law that obliges construction works to have several permits and licenses such as for trans-boundary movement of waste, sand harvesting sale and transportation, effluent discharge and waste management. Some of these are under the purview of the Contractor and others under the Employer during the lifecycle of contract execution. It is desirable that if it is required for the Contractor to apply for and/or comply with particular environmental permits, the relevant permits should be stated in the Specification or Employer's requirements together with the Contractor's obligations associated with each permit.

8.6.1.4 Subcontracting

The *National Construction Authority Act No. 41 of 2011* (***NCA Act***) s 18 (3) (d) provides that a foreign firm shall sub-contract not less than 30% of the works and carry out skills transfer to local firms. For consistency with sub-clause 5.1 (Sub-Contractors) of the Red Book 2017 or sub-clause 4.4 (Subcontractors) of the Yellow Book 2017, it may be desirable to add Particular Conditions to this effect, so that the Contract reflects local practice.

8.6.1.5 Arbitration

Kenya's judiciary system is receptive to ADR mechanisms including amicable settlement, arbitration and adjudication. In fact, this allowance for ADR is entrenched in the *Constitution* with the view of resolving and managing disputes without resorting to adversarial litigation. Therefore, the provisions of clause 21 of FIDIC Contracts relating to mechanisms of dispute resolution are not in conflict with any law of Kenya with regard to dispute determination.

As discussed in section 8.11, there are no necessary Special Provisions required for consistency with the applicable laws on dispute determination by arbitration.

With regard to the place of arbitration, sub-clause 21.6 (Arbitration) of the FIDIC General Conditions provides that any Dispute shall be finally settled by 'international arbitration'. In view of this, it is desirable for the Parties to consider the specific circumstances of the project to be consistent with s 3 of the *Act* on the place of arbitration.

The *Act* allows for both domestic arbitration and international arbitration. An arbitration is international if the Parties have their places of business in different states, the juridical seat of arbitration or a substantial part of the Contract is in more than one state. Domestic arbitration is where the agreement expressly provides or implies that arbitration shall be held in Kenya. If the Site is located in Kenya, the arbitration will be domestic since 'the place where a substantial part of the obligations of the commercial relationship is to be performed, or the place with which the subject-matter of the dispute is most closely connected, is Kenya' (s 3 [2] of the *Arbitration Act 1995*).

The *Arbitration Act 1995* gives the Parties liberty to select the place, number of arbitrators and language. As such, it is desirable for the Parties to make Special Provisions on:

(i) The place of arbitration, to be consistent with s 21
(ii) The number of arbitrators to be consistent with s 11, and
(iii) The language of arbitration, to be consistent with s 23 of the *Arbitration Act.*

25 National Environment Management Authority, www.nema.go.ke (accessed 29 February 2022).

The enforcement of arbitral awards is specified in s 36 of the *Act*. While domestic arbitral awards are recognised as binding, international awards shall be recognised pursuant to the *New York Convention* acceded to by Kenya in 1989.

If the Parties agree that arbitration shall be international, then it is desirable that they make Special Provisions to include explicit reference to the *New York Convention* or any other convention to which Kenya is a signatory.

8.6.1.6 Termination

Under the common law, each party has a right to terminate the contract when the other party fails to fulfil its material obligations. Since the *Law of Contract Act 23* adopts the common law of England, similar provisions apply.

For publicly procured construction projects, the procedures for termination ought to be laid out in the construction contract. By dint of s 153 (2) of the *PPADA Act, 2015*:

> A contract document shall specify the grounds on which the contract may be terminated and specify the procedures applicable on termination.

FIDIC forms of contract have an elaborate termination procedure contained in clauses 15 and 16, which is consistent with this legislation. There are no further detailed requirements under the *PPADA Act* for termination.

A conspicuously present ground for termination in the FIDIC contracts is the so-called 'termination for convenience' under sub-clause 15.5 (Termination for Employer's Convenience). A termination for convenience clause enables a party to a contract to bring to an end the future rights and obligations of a party without the need to establish that the other party is in default.

8.7 Applicable legislation for Kenya governing law of the contract

The section that follows gives a summary of applicable legislation for Kenya's governing law of the contract.

As explained in section 8.4.1, Kenya adopts the law of contract of the UK in its entirety through the *Law of Contracts Act Cap. 23*, along with the *Acts of Parliament* of the United Kingdom specified in the Schedule to the *Act*. Among the *Acts* adopted is the *Law Reform (Frustrated Contracts) Act, 1943* of the UK. The whole *Act* is adopted under s 2, 'provided that the reference in paragraph (c) of subsection (5) of section 2 to section 7 of the *Sale of Goods Act (Cap. 31)* shall be construed as a reference to section 9 of the *Sale of Goods Act (Cap. 31)*'.

8.8 Summary of applicable legislation for Kenya governing law of the contract

8.8.1 Entry into a construction contract

Contracts generally	*Law of Contract Act (Cap. 23) Act No. 43 of 1960*
Construction contracts	*Law of Contract Act (Cap. 23) Act No. 43 of 1960* *Public Procurement and Asset Disposal Act No. 33 of 2015* Case law and legal precedent

8.8.2 Operation of a construction contract	
Force majeure Guarantees under forms of Security (Tender Security, Demand Guarantee, Surety Bond, Advance Payment Guarantee, Retention Money Guarantee, Payment Guarantee by Employer)	*Law of Contract Act (Cap. 23) Act No. 43 of 1960* *Public Procurement and Asset Disposal Act No. 33 of 2015*
8.8.3 Termination of a construction contract	
Frustration	*The Law Reform (Frustrated Contracts) Act, 1943 (6 and 7 Geo. 6, c. 40)* (UK) – Pursuant to s 2 of the *Law of Contract Act (Cap. 23)* Laws of Kenya
Bankruptcy, insolvency, liquidation	*Insolvency Act No. 18 of 2015* *Companies and Insolvency Legislation (Consequential Amendments) Act No. 19 of 2015* *Bankruptcy Act (Cap. 53)*
8.8.4 Dispute resolution	
Limitation periods	*Arbitration Act No. 4 of 1995* *Limitation of Actions Act (Cap. 22) No. 7 of 2007*
Adjudication	*Civil Procedure Act (Cap. 21)* *Constitution of Kenya 2010* Article 159
Arbitration	*Arbitration Act No. 4 of 1995* *Civil Procedure Act (Cap. 21)*

8.9 Applicable legislation if the Site/Country is in Kenya

The section that follows gives a summary of applicable legislation if the Site is in Kenya.

The regulation of built-environment and construction professions is governed by professional bodies, which are established by law.

Architects are regulated by the Board of Architects and Quantity Surveyors (BORAQS), which is a body set up under the *Architects and Quantity Surveyors Act of 1934 (Cap. 525)*. However, *Cap. 525* commenced in 1934 and was last amended in 1978 and many players in the industry do not view it as an *Act* relevant to the present-day built environment. Plans are underway to overhaul the *Act* and replace it with the *Architectural and Quantity Surveying Practitioners Bill, 2021*.

Engineers are regulated by the Engineers Board of Kenya (EBK) which is a legal body set up under the *Engineers' Act 2011*. All engineers ought to be registered under the EBK and obtain a practising license under the relevant category. This extends to foreign engineers who are engaged in projects within Kenya. Registration details are contained on the Engineers' Board of Kenya website.[26] FIDIC General Conditions sub-clause 3.1 (the Engineer) stipulates that the Engineer shall be 'a professional engineer having suitable qualifications, experience and competence'. In this regard, the party appointed to act as the Engineer (whether a person or an institution) should demonstrate compliance with the *Engineers' Act 2011*.

26 https://ebk.go.ke (accessed 30 May 2022).

8.10 Summary of applicable legislation if the Site/Country is in Kenya

8.10.1 Operation of a construction contract

Registration and administration of professionals – Engineers, Architects, Quantity Surveyors, Surveyors	*Engineers Act No. 43 of 2011* *Architects and Quantity Surveyors Act (Cap. 525)* *Survey Act (Cap. 299)*
Registration/licensing of Contractors and subcontractors	*National Construction Authority Act. No. 41 of 2011*
Subcontractors	*National Construction Authority Act. No. 41 of 2011*
Use of liens / Assignment of debts	*Insolvency Act No. 18 of 2015*
Labour	*Constitution of Kenya, 2010* Article 73 (Prohibition of inhuman treatment); Article 74 (Slavery and forced labour); Article 80 (Freedom of Association) *Employment Act (Cap.226)* *Regulation of Wages and Conditions of Employment Act (Cap. 229)* *Trade Unions Act (Cap. 233)* *Trade Disputes Act (Cap. 234)* *Workmen's Compensation Act (Cap. 236)* *Factories Act (Cap. 514)*
Copyright	*Copyright Act No. 12 of 2012*
Planning	*Physical and Land Use Planning Act No. 13 of 2019*
Environment	*Environmental Management and Co-ordination Act (Cap. 387)*
Public procurement	*Constitution of Kenya*, Article 227 *Public Procurement and Asset Disposal Act No. 33 of 2015*
Building and construction permits, execution of construction work, standard of construction work	*National Construction Authority Act. No. 41 of 2011*
Health and safety	*Occupational Safety and Health (Cap. 514) Act No. 15 of 2007*
Insurance	*The Insurance Act (Cap. 487)*

8.10.2 Termination of a construction contract

Bankruptcy, insolvency, liquidation	*Insolvency Act No. 18 of 2017*

8.10.3 Dispute resolution

Dispute before a local board/Adjudication	*Civil Procedure Act (Cap. 21)* *Nairobi Centre for International Arbitration Act, No. 26 of 2013*
Limitation periods	*Limitation of Actions Act (Cap. 22)*

8.11 Applicable legislation if the 'seat' of the dispute determination is Kenya

The applicable law for arbitration as an alternative means of dispute resolution is the *Arbitration Act No. 4 of 1995*. The *Act* stipulates, among others, the legal provisions for the composition and jurisdiction of an arbitral tribunal, conduct of arbitral proceedings, recourse to the High Court against an arbitral award and recognition and enforcement of awards.

Article 159(2)(c) of the *Constitution of Kenya, 2010* promotes alternative dispute resolution. This Article sets out that:

> alternative forms of dispute resolution including reconciliation, mediation, arbitration and traditional dispute resolution mechanisms shall be promoted.

The foregoing provision is on the condition that such alternative forms of dispute resolution do not contravene the *Bill of Rights*, are not repugnant to justice and morality and are not inconsistent with the *Constitution* or any written law.

According to s 4 of the *Arbitration Act*, an arbitration agreement may be in the form of an arbitration clause in a contract or in the form of a separate agreement. FIDIC Conditions of Contract allow for arbitration in sub-clause 21.6 of the 2017 editions or sub-clause 20.6 of the 1999 editions, and the parties will be deemed to have agreed to these provisions unless otherwise modified in the Particular Conditions. In this sense, the FIDIC Contracts are consistent with the laws of Kenya on alternative dispute resolution.

Kenyan courts have been seen to promote arbitration by ordering a stay of any court proceedings to allow for arbitration proceedings to progress and conclude. Under s 6 (1) of the *Arbitration Act of 1995*, a court may stay proceedings and refer the parties to arbitration unless it finds:

(a) (T)hat the arbitration agreement is null and void, inoperative or incapable of being performed; or
(b) that there is not in fact any dispute between the parties with regard to the matters agreed to be referred to arbitration.

While the courts promote arbitration on the one hand, on the other hand, they are permitted by law to intervene before or during arbitral proceedings. Section 7(1) of the *Arbitration Act* reads:

> It is not incompatible with an arbitration agreement for a party to request from the High Court, before or during arbitral proceedings, an interim measure of protection and for the High Court to grant that measure.

The rationale is that the court has the mandate to support and assist the arbitral process. Thus, the court may grant any measure in as far as it aids the arbitral process and prevents any party from ultimately eluding arbitral awards or proceedings.

The limitation of the role and intervention of the courts in arbitration is provided in s 10 of the *Arbitration Act, 1995*, which reads that no court shall intervene in matters governed by the *Act*. The only recourse in the High Court against an arbitral award is given under s 35, which allows the court to set aside an arbitral award. The arbitral award may be set aside only in certain instances, including incapacitation of a party to the arbitration agreement, invalidity of the arbitration agreement, absence of proper notice on appointment or proceedings, issues with the composition of the tribunal or conflict with public policy.

As held in *Ministry of Environment and Forestry v Kiarigi Building Contractors & another*[27] and supported by referenced case law:

27 [2020] eKLR.

> The court, under section 35 of the Act, does not exercise appellate jurisdiction as the parties are entitled to reserve the same if they wish. As Tuiyott J., held in Mahan Limited v Villa Care ML HC Misc. Civil App. No. 216 of 2018 [2019] eKLR:
>
>> [9] It may well be that the conclusion reached by the Arbitrator is not sustainable in law yet by clause 13.2 (Dispute Resolution and Arbitration Clause) the parties made a covenant to each another that the decision of the Arbitrator would be final and binding on them. It must have been within the contemplation of the parties that the Arbitrator may sometimes get it wrong but they are happy to bind themselves to the risks involved in a final and binding clause and to live with the outcome absent the grounds in Section 35 of the Act.

The restriction of the courts' role in arbitration is so as to give effect to the polity of arbitration and to promote the efficiency of the arbitral process as a dispute resolution mechanism.

A controversial matter though is the right of appeal under the *Arbitration Law* in Kenya. Whereas the FIDIC General Conditions are explicit that disputes shall 'be finally settled by international arbitration', the law envisages the intervention of the courts under certain given parameters. The principle of finality is intended to facilitate efficient and expeditious settlement of disputes.

This position of finality has been supported by the Courts, as was the case in *Mahan Limited v Villa Care*[28] in which the court ruled, in part:

> there are matters or disputes whose appeal to this court is not automatic. There are matters which may require leave of the trial or even this court before instituting such an appeal. One of those matters is appeals to this court arising out of arbitration proceedings pursuant to section 35 of the Arbitration Act.

In this instance, the courts held that it may well be that the Arbitrator's award is not sustainable by law, yet the Parties, if they adopt the FIDIC General Conditions, will have agreed that the dispute shall be 'finally settled by international arbitration'.

Therefore, parties who resort to adopting the arbitration clause in the FIDIC General Conditions must be aware of the certain manners discussed above in which the intervention of the courts may be sought, and not merely to obtain a chance at reversing an arbitral award.

In a significant number of cases, FIDIC Contracts in Kenya are used for projects funded by multilateral development banks (MDBs) using the General Conditions in the FIDIC Contract for Multilateral Development Bank Harmonised Edition June 2010 (Pink Book). This stipulates that arbitration shall be international arbitration if the Contract is with a foreign Contractor. In the case of a domestic Contractor, arbitration proceedings are to be conducted in accordance with the laws of the Employer's country.

Under the Pink Book sub-clause 20.6 (Arbitration), the place of arbitration shall be the neutral location specified in the Contract Data. It is imperative that drafters of FIDIC Contracts using the Pink Book intended for use in Kenya select the place of arbitration and stipulate it in the Contract Data. For foreign Contractors, a neutral place would be desirable (neither the home country of the Contractor nor of the Employer, that is, Kenya).

Indeed, s 21 (Place of Arbitration) of the *Arbitration Act 1995* states that the parties are free to agree on the juridical seat of arbitration and the location of any hearing or meeting.

28 *Mahan Limited v Villa Care Limited* [2021] eKLR.

The 'juridical seat' or 'place' of arbitration does not necessarily mean where the hearings will be conducted, nor does it reflect the law governing the contract. As such, there are significant consequences on the selection of the seat of dispute determination.

If the seat of dispute determination is in Kenya, the applicable law remains the *Arbitration Act 1995*. This law adopted the 1985 *UNCITRAL Model Law* exactly, as a means to formulate the law in line with internationally accepted principles. However, it was later amended by the *Arbitration (Amendment) Act No. 11 2009* which introduced further clauses on arbitrator immunity, the general duty of parties, costs, interest, expenses and the effect of the award.

Kenya acceded to the *New York Convention on the Recognition and Enforcement of Foreign Arbitral Awards*, which is referenced in the *Act*. As such, the *Act* facilitates the enforcement of an arbitral award in the states of the Parties.

Kenya has a statute of limitations (the *Limitations of Actions Act*), which under s 34 provides for the application of the limitation law to arbitration. This statute contains no provision limiting the bringing of arbitration claims within a specified period. However, there is a limit of six years as the number of years that an action founded on contract and tort can be brought to the court.

Kenya is also in the process of developing an alternative dispute resolution law, currently known as the *Alternative Dispute Resolution Bill, 2021*. It is expected that this Bill, once enacted into law, will cover aspects of mediation, conciliation, adjudication and other aspects of alternative dispute resolution.

8.12 Summary of applicable legislation if the 'seat' of the dispute determination is Kenya

Dispute resolution	*Constitution of Kenya 2010*, Article 227 *Nairobi Centre for International Arbitration Act 2013* *Alternative Dispute Resolution Bill, 2021* (not enacted)
Limitation periods	Open to interpretation by the Courts
Adjudication	*Alternative Dispute Resolution Bill, 2021* (not enacted)
Arbitration	*Arbitration Act 1995*

8.13 Additional references for Kenya

8.13.1 Books

Kariuki Muigua, *Settling Disputes through Arbitration in Kenya* (3rd edn, Glenwood Publishers, 2017).

8.13.2 Journal articles

Allan Abwunza, Titus Kivaa, and Kariuki Muigua, 'Effectiveness of Arbitration in Contractual Disputes: Tension between Procedural Efficiency and Award Quality' (2019) 11 *Journal of Legal Affairs and Dispute Resolution in Engineering and Construction* 04519003. 10.1061/(ASCE)LA.1943-4170.0000290.

Kariuki Muigua, 'Overview of Arbitration and Mediation in Kenya' A Paper Presented at a Stakeholder's Forum on Establishment of Alternative Dispute Resolution (ADR) Mechanisms for Labour Relations in Kenya, Kenyatta International Conference Centre, Nairobi, on 4–6 May 2011.

Kariuki Muigua, 'Alternative Dispute Resolution and Article 159 of the Constitution', (2012) Legal Resource Foundation Trust, Programme for Judges and Magistrates Training. Lake Baringo Soi Lodge.

Kariuki, Francis and Ng'etich, Raphael, 'The Promotion of Alternative Dispute Resolution Mechanisms by the Judiciary in Kenya and its Impact on Party Autonomy' (2018) 6(2) *Alternative Dispute Resolution* 63–77, Available at SSRN: https://ssrn.com/abstract=3644361 (accessed 30 May 2022).

8.13.3 Internet

8.13.3.1 Legislation

Kenya Law, 2022. Laws of Kenya. [Online] Available at: http://kenyalaw.org (accessed 26 March 2022).

United Nations Commission on International Trade Law, 2006. International Commercial Arbitration. [Online] Available at: https://uncitral.un.org/en/texts/arbitration/modellaw/commercial_arbitration (accessed 11 March 2022).

8.13.3.2 Authorities and institutional websites

Architectural Association of Kenya, 2022. Objectives of AAK: Architectural Association of Kenya. [Online] Available at: https://aak.or.ke/objectives-of-aak/ (accessed 3 May 2022).

Association of Consulting Engineers of Kenya, 2022. About Us. [Online] Available at: https://acek.co.ke/ (accessed 3 May 2022).

Engineers' Board of Kenya, 2022. Downloads and Publications. [Online] Available at: https://ebk.go.ke/ (accessed 3 May 2022).

Institute of Quantity Surveyors of Kenya, 2022. About Us: Background Information. [Online] Available at: https://iqskenya.org/about-iqsk/background-information/ (accessed 3 May 2022).

Ministry of Transport, 2022. About Us. [Online] Available at: www.transport.go.ke/ (accessed 3 May 2022).

8.13.3.3 Court decisions

Kenya Law, 2022. Case Law. [Online] Available at: http://kenyalaw.org/caselaw/ (accessed 26 March 2022).

8.13.3.4 Other

International Labour Organization, 2022. National Labour Law Profile: Kenya. [Online] Available at: www.ilo.org/ifpdial/information-resources/national-labour-law-profiles/WCMS_158910/lang--en/index.htm (accessed 18 March 2022).

CHAPTER 9

Applying FIDIC Contracts in Nigeria

Abba Usman Jaafar, Michael Uche Ukponu and Yusuf Sulayman

CONTENTS

DOI: 10.4324/9781003206910-9

9.1 Outline of Nigeria's legal environment

Nigeria is a heterogeneous country with diverse climates, communities and cultures as well as rich human and natural resources. It is the most populous country and the largest economy in Africa. The country's legal setting, ranging from its governance to its judicial system, is uniquely structured to complement the nature of the Nigerian environment.

9.1.1 The constitutional structure of Nigeria

The *Constitution of the Federal Republic of Nigeria 1999 (as amended)* sets out for the country its existential foundation, federal structure and fundamental obligations. The Nigerian state and society are founded upon strong constitutional arrangements and all their affairs are strictly regulated by the letters and spirit of the *Constitution*. It is the *grundnorm* and its provisions are supreme and binding on all inhabitants, both persons and authorities.[1] Nigeria is a federation which practises a presidential system of government. Nigeria consists of 36 states and the Federal Capital Territory (**FCT**) as its federating units[2] and shares governmental responsibilities between the federal and state entities under the Exclusive and Concurrent Legislative Lists.[3] There is also a Local Government System comprising 774 Local Government/Area Councils[4] established by the *Constitution* as part of the federating units and having their constitutionally guaranteed functions.[5] Nigeria's *Constitution* is considered to be a rigid one because the constitutional amendment process is very strenuous and stringent.

In line with democratic ideals, the *Constitution* entrenches the doctrine of separation of powers to allow for adequate checks and balances across the legislative, executive and judicial arms of government. The executive functions of government are vested in the President and Governors – exercisable directly or through constituted cabinets,[6] the government's legislative functions are vested in the National Assembly[7] and the State Houses of Assembly,[8] and the judiciary is vested with the judicial powers of the country.[9] All through the governance cascade, the principle of federal character is to be respected in order to ensure that there is no predominance of persons from any given section of the country.[10] The obligation of the government across all levels of the federation involves the provision and promotion of good governance and the welfare of inhabitants. Beyond that, the government has the responsibility of directing its policy towards guaranteeing

1 *Constitution of the Federal Republic of Nigeria*, s 1(1) and (3).

2 *Constitution of the Federal Republic of Nigeria*, s 2(2).

3 *Constitution of the Federal Republic of Nigeria*, 2nd sch, pts I and II.

4 This is broken down into 768 Local Governments across the 36 States and 6 Area Councils in the FCT. See *Constitution of the Federal Republic of Nigeria*, s 3(6).

5 See *Constitution of the Federal Republic of Nigeria*, s 7. However, there are concerns that the constitutional powers of the Local Government authorities are frequently usurped by the State and Federal Governments in many respects.

6 *Constitution of the Federal Republic of Nigeria*, s 5(1) and (2).

7 Nigeria operates a bicameral legislature at the federal level. The National Assembly has both an Upper Chamber known as the Senate with 109 members and the Lower Chamber known as the House of Representatives with 360 members.

8 Legislation enacted by the National Assembly are referred to as '*Acts*', while legislation enacted by State Houses of Assembly are referred to as '*Laws*': *Constitution of the Federal Republic of Nigeria*, s 4(1) and (6).

9 *Constitution of the Federal Republic of Nigeria*, s 6.

10 *Constitution of the Federal Republic of Nigeria*, s 14(3) and (4).

order and security and entrenching a social order based on freedom, equality and national integration.[11]

9.1.2 The legal system in Nigeria

Nigeria, being a multifaceted society with a multitude of ethnic groups, languages and religions, is pluralistic. The legal system accommodates regional and religious diversities inherent in the country through applicable laws and the court system. This stems from the realisation of the necessity to encourage and provide adequate facilities for citizens to manifest and propagate their beliefs, including in practice and observance.

Nigeria's legal system is trichotomic. It operates the Western (English common law), traditional (customary law) and Shari'a (Islamic law) systems side by side. The English common law is the predominant body of law upon which the *Constitution*, legislation and judicial precedents are premised. Its doctrines regulate all matters except those peculiar to questions of Islamic personal law and customary practices in civil proceedings and are applicable in all the courts in the country except the Shari'a and Customary courts.

Customary law is that belonging to indigenous peoples of diverse communities or ethnic groups. It arises from practices that have obtained the force of law from long usage.[12] For rules of customary law to apply, they must be shown not to be incompatible with any written law or repugnant to natural justice, doctrines of equity and good conscience.[13] Customary law governs the questions of customs and traditions in civil proceedings and is applicable in the Customary Court of Appeal and other lower courts over which the Customary Court of Appeal exercises its supervisory and appellate jurisdiction.[14]

The practice of Shari'a in Nigeria dates back to the pre-colonial era and is currently recognised by the *Constitution*. There were existing legal systems in use by empires across the area now known as Nigeria, most notably the *Alkali* courts in the north. In the period between the advent of colonial rule in 1861 and the declaration of Protectorates in 1900, the British seized and consolidated their grip over existing administrative institutions and legal systems in line with the imperialist indirect rule policy and in order to reduce the cost of administration.[15] Shari'a applies to civil proceedings involving questions of Islamic personal law and is applicable in the Shari'a Court of Appeal established under the *Constitution* or the courts over which it exercises supervisory and appellate jurisdiction.[16] Shari'a can be sometimes confused with customary law because it has been so assimilated into the practice of the people of Northern Nigeria[17] that it now looks more like the custom of the region. Shari'a, which is a comprehensive system of law in written form, in itself is distinct and different from any customary law which is largely by oral tradition.[18] In order

11 *Constitution of the Federal Republic of Nigeria*, ch II.

12 *Evidence Act* 2011, s 258. See also *Oyewumi v Ogunesan* (1990) LPELR-2880(SC) 46.

13 This is referred to as the 'twin test'. See *Yinusa v Adesubokan* (1971) All NLR 227.

14 *Constitution of the Federal Republic of Nigeria*, ss 265, 267, 280 and 282.

15 HO Danmole, 'The Alkali Court in Ilorin Emirate During Colonial Rule' (1989) 18 *Transafrican Journal of History* 173.

16 *Constitution of the Federal Republic of Nigeria*, ss 260, 262, 275 and 277.

17 The Northern region consists of 19 states spread across three geo-political zones. The North West ('core' North) comprises Kano, Kaduna, Katsina, Jigawa, Sokoto, Kebbi and Zamfara States; the North East comprises Borno, Yobe, Adamawa, Bauchi, Taraba and Gombe States; and the North Central comprises Abuja (FCT), Nasarawa, Plateau, Benue, Kogi, Niger and Kwara States.

18 See *Alkamawa v Bello* (1998) 8 NWLR (pt. 561) 173; (1998) 6 SCNJ 127.

to guarantee fair hearing for the users of Shari'a and Customary courts, the membership of justices for the Court of Appeal and the Supreme Court – being courts of final determination – are constituted to accommodate persons learned in all applicable laws within the legal system, including English common law, customary law and Islamic law.[19]

9.1.3 The court system in Nigeria

The court system is complex owing to the pluralistic nature of the Nigerian society. It can be categorised based on the level of courts, region and subject matter of jurisdiction, and it follows a hierarchical structure that ensures decisions get to be tested from lower courts of first instance up to the Supreme Court which is the apex court. The *Constitution* provides for a comprehensive judicature wherein some of the courts are explicitly mentioned and called the superior courts of record.[20] The list of superior courts in ascending order is as follows: (i) Customary Courts of Appeal of FCT and the States, (ii) Shari'a Courts of Appeal of the FCT and the States, (iii) Federal High Court, High Courts of the FCT and the States and the National Industrial Court (courts of coordinate jurisdiction), (iv) Court of Appeal and (v) Supreme Court. The National Assembly and the Houses of Assembly of States are equally empowered to establish more courts in addition to the ones listed on the condition that those courts will be subordinate in jurisdiction to the superior courts of record.[21] This presupposes that any other court in the country not expressly mentioned in the *Constitution* shall be an inferior court by sheer nomenclature. These courts can either be federal or state courts.

The courts in Nigeria are either courts of general or special jurisdiction. The general courts are the regular courts established under the general section on judicature in the *Constitution*,[22] whereas the special courts are courts or tribunals established either by the *Constitution* or by powers conferred on the states or federal government to achieve specific purposes such as determination of elections (election petition tribunals), determination of code of conduct matters (code of conduct tribunal), special military trials (court-martial) and courts of inferior record such as magistrate courts, district courts, area courts, upper area courts, Shari'a courts, mobile environmental courts and juvenile matters (juvenile courts). In most cases, they are *ad hoc* courts set up only to achieve a time-specific resolution of special disputes and their appeals lie directly to the Court of Appeal. Both the general and special courts may have limited or unlimited jurisdictions to hear and determine matters of criminal and civil nature.

9.2 The construction industry in Nigeria

9.2.1 Overview

The organised Nigerian construction industry was formed in the early 1940s with a few foreign companies and grew rapidly after the country's independence in 1960. The 'oil boom' of the 1970s and the increasing demand for investment in infrastructure development to

19 *Constitution of the Federal Republic of Nigeria*, s 288.
20 *Constitution of the Federal Republic of Nigeria*, s 6 (3).
21 *Constitution of the Federal Republic of Nigeria*, s 6 (4)(a).
22 *Constitution of the Federal Republic of Nigeria*, s 6.

drive economic growth subsequently aided the speedy growth of the industry.[23] The construction sector has played an important role in the growth of the economy as it continues to attract capital expenditure largely from annual public appropriation. Its contribution to Nigeria's total real GDP was 3.19% and 8.74% to nominal GDP in the second quarter of 2021.[24] The sector grew by 44.26% in nominal terms (year on year) in Q1 of 2020, dropping –22.73% compared to the rate of 66.99% recorded in the same quarter of 2019.[25] Notwithstanding, the infrastructure deficit in Nigeria is still high and the available capital to close this deficit is inadequate.

Realising the need for adequate financing to address infrastructure gaps and development needs, the African Development Bank (**AfDB**) proposed an Infrastructure Action Plan (**IAP**) in 2013 to guide Nigeria towards securing adequate financing for infrastructure development in four critical sectors – transport, energy, water resources and information and communications technology.[26] Subsequently, in 2015, the Nigerian Integrated Infrastructure Masterplan estimated that a total investment of about ₦1.2 quadrillion (US$3.0 trillion) will be required over the next 30 years to build and maintain infrastructure in Nigeria.[27] The investment is expected to be sourced from public and private sectors. To this end, the federal government has been expending resources from its dwindling revenue on infrastructure, especially in the transport and energy sectors. The federal government established the Infrastructure Concession and Regulatory Commission (**ICRC**) to accelerate investment in national infrastructure through private sector funding by regulating Public Private Partnerships (**PPPs**). Also, the federal government set up the Nigeria Sovereign Investment Authority (**NSIA**) to manage an Infrastructure Fund to provide public finance for infrastructure development, primarily domestic infrastructure projects that meet targeted financial returns.[28] As part of the federal government's efforts to address Nigeria's huge road infrastructure gap and provide legal backing for the government to mobilise adequate funding for the construction of 'federal roads' all around the country through private sector finance, the National Assembly passed the *Federal Roads Bill* and the *National Roads Fund Bill* into law.[29] At the time of writing, both bills are awaiting the President's assent in order to give legal effect to their implementation.

The number of indigenous firms among the major construction industry players is not significant. Over the years, the Nigerian government has been encouraging the entry of indigenous firms in order to improve local content in construction works and services through policy and regulations.

23 National Bureau of Statistics, *Nigerian Construction Sector – Summary Report: 2010–2012*, 1–2 https://nigerianstat.gov.ng/elibrary/read/265 (accessed on 12 October 2021).

24 Nigerian Bureau of Statistics, *Nigerian Gross Domestic Product Report (Q1 2020)*, 20 www.nigerianstat.gov.ng/pdfuploads/GDP_Report_Q1_2020.pdf (accessed on 12 October 2021).

25 *Ibid.*

26 African Development Bank (AfDB), *An Infrastructure Action Plan for Nigeria: Closing the Infrastructure Gap and Accelerating Economic Transformation* (Summary Report, August 2013) www.afdb.org/fileadmin/uploads/afdb/Documents/Project-and-Operations/An_Infrastructure_Action_Plan_for_Nigeria_-_Closing_the_Infrastructure_Gap_and_Accelerating_Economic_Transformation.pdf (accessed on 27 November 2021).

27 The Presidency, Federal Republic of Nigeria, *National Integrated Infrastructure Master Plan 2015*, xi https://nesgroup.org/storage/app/public/policies/National-Intergrated-Infractructure-Master-Plan-2015-2043_compressed_1562697068.pdf (accessed on 12 October 2021).

28 https://nsia.com.ng/about-us/fund-mandates (accessed on 12 October 2021).

29 www.vanguardngr.com/2021/12/how-national-roads-fund-federal-roads-bills-ll-end-infrastructure-decay-in-nigeria-reps-deputy-minority-leader/ (accessed on 6 December 2021).

9.2.2 Structure

The Federation of Construction Industry (**FOCI**), founded in 1954, is the umbrella body and mouthpiece for construction companies in Nigeria. Its main activities are registration of members, representing members and promoting their interests, engaging the government in relevant policy issues and fostering labour relationships with construction workers' unions.[30] FOCI has a membership of 70 major contractors, dominated by foreign contractors. However, there are some major construction companies such as the Chinese construction companies that have been very active in the Nigerian construction industry but are not members of FOCI. The membership of subcontractors includes specialised and medium-sized firms.

Foreign companies intending to do business in Nigeria are required to obtain incorporation as a separate legal entity. Until so incorporated (or specifically exempted from incorporation), a foreign company shall not carry on business in Nigeria or exercise any of the powers of a registered company and shall not have a place of business or an address for service of documents or processes in Nigeria for any purpose other than the receipt of notices and other documents as part of matters preliminary to incorporation under the *Companies and Allied Matters Act*.[31]

9.2.3 Licensing/registration

The Bureau of Public Procurement (**BPP**) has the responsibility to maintain a national database of federal contractors and service providers and to prescribe classifications and categorisations for the contractors and service providers on the register.[32] To implement this requirement, in December 2014 the Federal Government directed that any federal contractor and service provider that is not registered in the national database of federal contractors and service providers will no longer be allowed to do business with the federal government.[33] State laws have similar provisions for the registration of different categories of contractors and service providers doing business with the State Governments.[34]

The Council for the Regulation of Engineering in Nigeria (**COREN**) is statutorily empowered to regulate the training of engineers in Nigerian educational institutions.[35] COREN also enforces the registration of all engineering personnel and consulting firms wishing to engage in the practice of engineering in Nigeria. COREN is also empowered with prosecutorial powers against any individual or firm that contravenes any provisions of the *Act*.[36] Other professionals in the construction industry are also regulated by similar

30 https://foci.org.ng/about/# (accessed on 12 October 2021).

31 *Companies and Allied Matters Act 2020*, s 78.

32 *Public Procurement Act 2007*, s 6(1)(f).

33 Federal Government Circular (Ref. No. SGF/50/S.52/II), 11 December 2014 www.bpp.gov.ng/wp-content/uploads/2019/01/Use-of-Standard-Bidding-Documents-and-adoption-of-its-General-Conditions-of-Contract-and-Specific-Conditions-of-Contract-in-Contract-Agreement-13th-January-2014.pdf (accessed on 15 October 2021).

34 At least 19 out of Nigeria's 36 States have enacted their respective procurement laws – Adamawa, Anambra, Bauchi, Bayelsa, Delta, Ebonyi, Edo, Ekiti, Enugu, Imo, Jigawa, Kaduna, Kebbi, Kwara, Lagos, Niger, Ondo, Osun, and Rivers: www.unodc.org/documents/corruption/WG-Prevention/Art_9_Public_procurement/Nigeria.pdf (accessed on 22 November 2021).

35 *Council for the Registration of Engineers (Establishment) (Amendment) Act 2018*.

36 *Council for the Registration of Engineers (Establishment) (Amendment) Act 2018*, s 18A(1)(a).

bodies such as the Architects Registration Council of Nigeria (**ARCON**) for architects; Surveyors Registration Council of Nigeria (**SRCN**) for surveyors; Council of Registered Builders of Nigeria (**CORBON**) for builders; Quantity Surveyors Registration Board of Nigeria (**QSRBN**) for Quantity Surveyors; etc. In addition, professional associations such as the Nigerian Society of Engineers (**NSE**), Nigerian Institute of Architects (**NIA**), Nigerian Institute of Building (**NIOB**) and Nigerian Institute of Quantity Surveyors (**NIQS**) pursue the interests of their respective members and organise regular conferences, seminars and training to improve professional capacity, standards and ethics.

The *Council for the Registration of Engineers (Establishment) (Amendment) Act 2018* empowers COREN with additional responsibilities of ensuring that all foreign engineering firms establish their design offices in Nigeria and granting compulsory attestation to expatriate quota applications for engineering practitioners affirming that there are no qualified and competent Nigerians for the job in question at the time of application.[37]

Other licenses and permits that are relevant to construction works and services in Nigeria are:[38]

(i) Building design approvals and development permits from the Federal Capital Territory or States' planning authorities
(ii) Construction of high-rise buildings/structures; communication masts; tower permits from the Nigerian Civil Aviation Authority
(iii) Environmental Impact Assessment Clearance and Compliance permit; relevant Fire, Health and Safety permits and licenses
(iv) Quarry lease for sourcing construction materials from the Federal Ministry of Mines, and
(v) Connection to electricity, water supply and sewerage from the FCT and States' utility regulatory agencies.

9.2.4 Labour relations

The Federal Government has the exclusive power to legislate on all issues relating to labour, including trade unions; industrial relations; conditions, safety and welfare of labour; industrial disputes; prescribing a national minimum wage for the Federation or any part thereof; and industrial arbitration.[39] The *Labour Act*[40] is the main legislation that governs employment under a contract of manual labour or clerical work in both private and public sectors. The *Act* requires employers to engage employees with written contracts and to provide for employees' rest hours, holidays, sick leave and maternity leave.[41] In 2021, the Federal Executive Council approved ten days' paternity leave for civil servants in the Public Service Rules.[42] The *Act* also makes it illegal to engage persons in forced labour, to pay wages other than money, to tamper with employees' right to join workers'

37 Section 1(1)(g).

38 www.dlapiperrealworld.com/law/index.html?t=construction&s=legal-framework&q=licences-and-permits&c=NG (accessed on 5 November 2021).

39 *Constitution of Federal Republic of Nigeria*, 2nd sch, pt 1, Exclusive Legislative List.

40 *Labour Act 1971*, LFN 2004.

41 *Labour Act*, ss 7(1)(g), 16, 17, 18 and 54.

42 www.youtube.com/watch?v=2nsmCXmkXow (accessed on 22 November 2021); https://guardian.ng/news/fec-approves-14-days-paternity-leave-for-public-servants/ (accessed on 7 December 2021).

unions and to make deductions from salaries without their consent.[43] The *Employees' Compensation Act*[44] provides for the payment of compensation to workmen for injuries suffered in the course of their employment. It mandates employers to remit 1% of their total monthly payroll to the National Social Insurance Trust Fund as part of the social insurance of workers across the various economic sectors.

9.2.5 Safety culture

The *Constitution* specifically mandates the government to direct its policy towards ensuring that the health, safety and welfare of all persons in employment are safeguarded and not endangered or compromised.[45] Currently, Nigeria has adopted three core occupational safety and health conventions, namely C155 – Occupational Safety and Health 1981; C032 – Protection against Accidents (Dockers) 1932; and C019 – Equality of Treatment (Accident Compensation) 1925.[46] In 2006, the Federal government developed the National Policy on Occupational Safety and Health to facilitate the improvement of occupational safety and health performance in all sectors of the economy and ensure harmonisation of the protection of workers' rights with regional and international standards.[47] However, due to the lack of National occupational safety and health (**OSH**) management systems, the country is guided by the International Labour Organization's Convention C155 – Occupational Safety and Health 2001.[48]

The main legislation on OSH is the *Factories Act*.[49] It provides protection for factory workers and other professionals exposed to occupational hazards and improves their working conditions. It also makes adequate provisions regarding the safety of workers and imposes penalties for any breach. Building on the safety provisions of the *Factories Act*, the *Lifting and Allied Work Equipment (Safety) Regulations* specifically expanded its coverage to include construction workers.[50] The *Factories Act* and the *Lifting and Allied Work Equipment (Safety) Regulations* are discussed further in section 9.3.1.3. At the time of writing (2021) there is a bill awaiting the assent of the President of Nigeria known as the *Labour, Safety, Health, and Welfare Bill* which seeks to repeal the *Factories Act*, and when passed into law, it will provide a comprehensive OSH legislation in Nigeria.[51]

9.2.6 Modular construction using factory-fabricated components

In recent years, modular construction has made its way into the mainstream construction conversation and it is being deployed for construction works ranging from hotels to office

---

43 *Constitution of the Federal Republic of Nigeria*, s 34(1)(c); *Labour Act*, s 73 (1).

44 *Employees' Compensation Act 2010.*

45 *Constitution of the Federal Republic of Nigeria*, s 17(3)(c).

46 International Labour Organization (ILO), *Nigeria Country Profile On Occupational Safety and Health* (Report, 2016) 10, www.ilo.org/wcmsp5/groups/public/---africa/---ro-abidjan/---ilo-abuja/documents/publication/wcms_552748.pdf (accessed on 18 October 2021).

47 *Ibid.* 10 and 21.

48 *Ibid.* 11.

49 *Factories Act*, Cap F1, LFN 2004.

50 Construction workers operate lifting equipment in the course of construction works. See *Lifting and Allied Work Equipment (Safety) Regulations 2018*, ss 1 and 2(1)(b) and (d).

51 www.dlapiperrealworld.com/law/index.html?t=construction&s=legal-framework&q=health-and-safety&c=NG (accessed on 5 November 2021).

buildings. As the construction industry continues to face a shortage of skilled workforce, rising costs and other uncertainties, resort is increasingly being made to modular construction as a way to improve safety, productivity, quality, cost, schedule and sustainability performance.[52] In Nigeria, construction works are still generally executed *in situ*. The technology of permanent modular construction is not available. Nevertheless, relocatable modular construction is applied for emergency shelters or for temporary spaces such as construction site offices, classroom blocks, health laboratories, canteens, etc.

However, professional associations are gradually introducing modular technology to their members. The NSE organises professional training on Building Information Modelling (BIM) using Civil 3D, Infraworks and BIM360.[53]

9.2.7 Procurement

9.2.7.1 Public procurement

Subsequent to the recommendation of the World Bank Country Procurement Assessment Report (**CPAR**)[54] and the need to reduce waste and achieve value for money in public expenditure, the *Public Procurement Act*[55] was signed in 2007 to regulate the conduct of government procurement and disposal of assets at the federal level. The *Act* was drafted based on the *UNCITRAL Model Law on the Procurement of Goods, Construction and Services 1994*.[56] Thereafter, the procurement regulatory institution, the Bureau of Public Procurement (**BPP**) was established. This triggered public procurement reforms in the country and several States have now promulgated their respective procurement laws similar to the federal legislation. The *Act* also provides for the establishment of a National Council of Public Procurement (**NCPP**) as an overall procurement policymaking body that regulates the functions of the BPP, including approving the monetary threshold for prior review.[57] The members of the NCPP are yet to be appointed by the President of Nigeria as required by s 1(4) of the *Public Procurement Act* (as of December 2021).

The BPP operates monetary thresholds for high-value contracts for service-wide applications approved by the President of Nigeria. Effective from 19 January 2022, the thresholds are as follows: Goods – ₦300 million (US$721,000); Works – ₦1,500 million (US$3 .6 million); and Services – ₦300 million (US$721,000),[58] and the award decisions require its prior review.[59] In accordance with the *Act*, the BPP is the sole authority to certify award decisions for high-value federal contracts and grant 'No Objection' certificates.[60] However, in practice, this power is subject to the approval of the Federal Executive Council (**FEC**).[61]

52 www.metalarchitecture.com/articles/deconstructing-modular-construction (accessed on 31 October 2021).

53 www.nse.org.ng/news-events/recent-news/costech-workshop (accessed on 31 October 2021).

54 https://openknowledge.worldbank.org/handle/10986/14333 (accessed on 22 November 2021).

55 *Public Procurement Act 2007.*

56 https://uncitral.un.org/en/texts/procurement/modellaw/procurement_of_goods_construction_and_services (accessed on 22 November 2021). The 1994 version of this UNCITRAL Model Law has been replaced by the 2011 version.

57 *Public Procurement Act*, s 2(a).

58 Federal Government Circular, Ref. No. PROC/OSGF/BPP/709/85 of 19 January 2022.

59 *Public Procurement Act*, ss 2(a), 6(a)–(b), 16(1)(a), 16(2)–(4), 17 and 19(h).

60 *Public Procurement Act*, s 6(1)(b) and (c).

61 Prior to the *Act*, the BPP's predecessor body, the Budget Monitoring and Price Intelligent Unit (BMPIU), sought FEC's approval for all high value contracts: Sope William-Elegbe, 'The Reform and Regulation of

In 2020, some provisions of the *Public Procurement Act* were amended through the *Finance Act.*[62] These amendments expanded the application of the Act to specifically include the Judiciary and National Assembly as procuring entities and others like the federal financial, security, educational and health institutions and Government-owned enterprises utilising public funds.[63] In addition, the amendments created three approving authorities for high-value contracts for the three arms of the government – the FEC, the National Assembly Tender's Board and the National Judicial Council Tender's Board.[64] The amendment also introduced e-procurement by stating that bids can be submitted in electronic format and signed electronically.[65] The *Finance Act* also raised the maximum amount of mobilisation fees for local contractors[66] from 15% to 30%.[67]

Furthermore, there is the Federal Competition and Consumer Protection Commission (**FCCPC**) established by virtue of Part II of the *Federal Competition and Consumer Protection Act 2018* (***FCCPA***). On a general note, under s 1(d) of the *FCCPA*, one of the relevant objectives of the FCCPC in relation to procurement is to prohibit restrictive or unfair business practices which prevent, restrict or distort competition or constitute an abuse of a dominant position of market power in Nigeria. Specifically, s 109 of the *FCCPA* prohibits bid-rigging in procurement and tender processes – a prohibited act that involves an agreement in which one or more Undertakings (bidders) agree not to submit a bid in response to a call for bids, or where two or more Undertakings submit bids in response to a call for bids based on an agreement among themselves to submit such bids.

9.2.7.2 Private procurement

There is no legal framework regulating the conduct of procurement activities in the private sector. Individual firms are guided by their respective corporate administrative procedures for procurement. The most common procedure seems to be to purchase from suppliers that already have records with the company or suppliers that are recommended

---

Public Procurement in Nigeria' (2012) V41(2) *Public Contract Law Review* 339, 345.

62 *Finance Act 2020*, explanatory memorandum, long title, ss 1 and 63–74.

63 *Finance Act*, ss 63 (Amendment of *Public Procurement Act*, s 15). This expanded coverage may require the re-composition of the NCPP to include representation of these two arms of the government. There are 1,004 procuring entities at the federal level, which is a major challenge for BPP's monitoring function with respect to ensuring that procurement transactions comply with relevant federal procurement laws.

64 *Finance Act*, s 64 (Amendment of *Public Procurement Act*, s 17). By this provision, high-value contract award decisions will go through BPP certification and approval of the respective authorities. It is likely that the subsequent approvals would be an endorsement of the 'No-Objection' certificates.

65 *Finance Act*, s 69 (Amendment of *Public Procurement Act*, s 27[1]). But this provision still fell short of the use of e-procurement by insisting on bids 'placed in a sealed envelope'.

66 The terms local, domestic and indigenous contractors seem to have different connotations in the procurement process. 'Contractor' also refers to 'Supplier' (*Public Procurement Act*, s 60) but the term 'local contractor' is not defined by the *Public Procurement Act*. By virtue of ss 78–84 and 788 of the *Companies and Allied Matters Act 2020*, a foreign entity (company or limited liability partnership) must be registered or incorporated as a separate legal entity in Nigeria to carry on business in Nigeria. Thus, where this is the case, they should ordinarily fall under the consideration of a domestic preference (see *Public Procurement Act*, ss 32(3)(g) and 34)); but to benefit from the 'margin of preference' (*Public Procurement Act*, s 49[2]) – the bar has been raised in the *Regulation* (see *Public Procurement Regulation for Goods and Works*, 2nd sch).

67 *Finance Act*, s 71 (Amendment of *Public Procurement Act*, s 35). The reason for this increase is unclear, especially at a period where the government is challenged by dwindling revenues and its inability to meet payments for executed works. In 2020, local contractors picketed the Federal Ministry of Finance Headquarters protesting delayed payment on executed works. www.premiumtimesng.com/business/411875-contractors-protest-delayed-payment-of-commissioned-projects.html (accessed on 22 October 2021).

by Trustees.[68] Large supply and works contracts are often procured by restrictive competition and negotiation. Parent companies of international firms often influence the selection process of contractors and suppliers.[69]

9.2.8 Insurance requirements

Most standard construction contracts require Contractors to provide insurance for the Works and Contractor's Equipment, for Contractor's personnel and against injury to persons and damage to property. These are often comprehensively covered by Contractor's All Risk insurance (**CAR insurance**). The insurance of Goods in transit is covered by the relevant Incoterms. Insurance companies also issue securities during the procurement and contracting phases of construction such as securities for bids, contract performance, advance payment and retention. Generally, Employers prefer bank guarantees to insurance bonds because they are easier to call in the event of a default.

9.2.9 Common forms of contract

The common forms of contracts in Nigeria are the modified versions of (i) the Institute of Civil Engineers (**ICE**) Conditions of Contract; (ii) the FIDIC Red Book 1999 (now 2017) for civil works; (iii) the FIDIC Yellow Book 1999 for mechanical and electrical works; and (iv) the Joint Contracts Tribunal (**JCT**) for Building Works. The FIDIC Silver Book 1999 is sometimes applied to EPC Turnkey projects. The ICE conditions of contract and the JCT conditions of contract have their origin of use in the colonial administration. They have been modified and used in the 'old' public works departments. Generally, these standard forms of contract are usually varied to suit the specific circumstances of the construction project such as the nature of the parties to the contract, as well as the nature, size and technicalities of the project.

Specifically, the BPP is responsible for preparing and updating Standard Bidding and Contract Documents for federal public contracts.[70] Some State Governments have established their respective procurement agencies with similar responsibilities.[71] The contract forms are part of the following standard bidding documents (as currently being revised) for goods, works and services available on the BPP website[72] and the editions for May 2011 are:

- Standard Bidding Documents – Goods, Works, National Shopping and Small Works
- Request for Proposals – Complex Assignment (Time-based and Lumpsum)
- Request for Proposals – Small Assignment (Time-based and Lumpsum)
- Request for Proposals – Individual Consultant.

68 World Bank, *Nigeria Country Procurement Assessment Report* (Vol. II, 30 June 2000) [72].
69 *Ibid.* [74].
70 *Public Procurement Act*, s 5(m); *Public Procurement Regulations for Goods and Works 2007*, s 29(m).
71 See n35.
72 www.bpp.gov.ng/all-downloads (accessed on 11 October 2021).

Procuring entities are mandated to use the standard bidding documents and any changes thereof to address specific contract requirements should be introduced in the specific instructions and the specific conditions of contract.[73] Some State Governments in Nigeria have adopted the federal standard bidding documents, although they are not obligated to do so.[74] Perhaps, this is due to the need to strengthen their procurement reforms and align with international best practice.

The current Conditions of Contract for Works are a modified version of the Conditions of Contract in the Harmonised Master Document for Procurement of Small Works prepared by the participating Multilateral Development Banks (**MDBs**) and international financing institutions. Despite the insistence by the federal government on the use of these conditions of contract, some specialised Federal Ministries, Department and Agencies use other forms of contracts to suit their specific requirements such as the Standard Conditions of Contract (Roads) 2016 prepared by the Federal Ministry of Works and Housing; the Abridged Standard Conditions of Contract for Design, Build and Installation prepared by the Federal Ministry of Power; and the Standard Form of Building Contracts in Nigeria 1990 prepared by the Nigerian Institute of Architects.

For donor-funded projects, MDBs and multilateral organisations require borrowers to use the contract forms in the Standard Bidding Documents for major works contracts, namely the FIDIC Pink Book 2010 and the Standard Bidding Document for Plant Design, Supply and Installation.[75]

9.2.10 Dispute resolution

Litigation is the most deployed means of settling disputes in Nigeria. However, recent times have witnessed an increasing trend of referrals to alternative dispute resolution (**ADR**) mechanisms for the settlement of construction and other commercial disputes. This increasing trend comes as a result of the backlog of court cases in Nigerian courts as it may take many years for a court to determine a case at any instance due to the slow pace of the trial system. ADR is gaining so much traction that various procedural rules of courts in Nigeria encourage referrals of litigation matters to settlement via ADR,[76] and some courts have established court-annexed ADR institutions known as Multi-Door Court Houses.[77]

In Nigeria, the common ADR mechanisms are arbitration, mediation, med-arb, conciliation, adjudication and negotiation (out-of-court settlements). While there are no federal

73 *Public Procurement Regulations for Goods and Works*, s 118. See also *Public Procurement Regulations for Consultancy Services 2007*, ss 72 and 73.

74 The States have the power to procure goods and services within their jurisdictions and constitutional limits. See *Constitution of the Federal Republic of Nigeria*, 2nd sch, pt II, Concurrent Legislative List. See also the *Constitution of the Federal Republic of Nigeria*, s 4(7)(a), (b) and (c) (s 4(7)(c)2 pertains to the 'Residual List' of powers of State Governments); *AG Lagos State v AG Federation & Ors.* (2003) LPELR-620(SC), 187–189.

75 This is based on the Model Form of International Contract for Process Plant Construction published by the Engineering Advancement Association of Japan (**ENAA**).

76 For example, see the *Federal High Court (Civil Procedure) Rules 2019*, or. 52; *High Court of the Federal Capital Territory, Abuja (Civil Procedure) Rules 2018*, or. 19; *High Court of Lagos State (Civil Procedure) Rules 2019*, or. 28.

77 For example: Abuja Multi-Door Court House (Uwais Dispute Resolution Centre); Lagos Multi-Door Court House; Rivers State Multi-Door Court House, etc.

laws governing adjudication, conciliation and negotiation, a referral to any of these ADR mechanisms based on the terms of the contract is applicable with the consent of the parties or by the interpretation of the courts. This means that adjudication through Dispute Boards, notably in FIDIC contracts, is also applicable based on the terms of the contract. This is to say that the entire process of adjudication such as the procedure for referral, appointment of an adjudicator and rules of procedure are entirely governed by the construction contract.

Arbitration is the most preferred ADR mechanism due to its advantages over others such as the confidentiality of the arbitral process and the finality, bindingness and enforceability of the arbitral award on the parties. Mediation and med-arb are also highly preferred within ADR circles.[78] As the courts continue to embrace and advance jurisprudence on arbitration, parties increasingly feel more comfortable with settling their disputes via arbitration and other ADR methods. Today, many commercial agreements, including construction contracts, contain arbitration clauses or agreements. A well-researched report by Templars on the arbitration space in Nigeria, which considered arbitration-related case law between 1990 and 2021, submitted that 20.7% of arbitration-related litigations at the Supreme Court of Nigeria (the apex court) related to construction contracts, second only to general commercial and undisclosed contracts which accounted for 59.7% of arbitration-related disputes.[79]

The relatively increasing liberal judicial approach to arbitration, as highlighted in this empirical report,[80] is reflected in the celebrated case of *Mekwunye v Imoukhuede*.[81] Pursuant to the contemporary disposition of the Nigerian judiciary towards achieving substantive justice over technicalities, and in a bid to improve Nigeria's global standing as an arbitration-friendly jurisdiction, the Supreme Court held *inter alia* that the arbitration agreement's reference to the 'President of the Chartered Institute of Arbitrators London, Nigeria Chapter' (non-existent/incorrect nomenclatures for an arbitral institution and its Chair position) instead of the 'Chairman of the Chartered Institute of Arbitrators UK, Nigerian Chapter' (the existent/correct nomenclatures for an arbitral institution and its Chair position) was a mere misnomer, a pathological clause which does not invalidate the arbitral agreement and consequent final award.[82] In reaching this decision, the foreign case of *Travelport Global Distribution Systems BV v Bellview Airlines Ltd*[83] was cited and relied upon as a persuasive authority in *Mekwunye v Imoukhuede*.

At the federal level, arbitration (as well as mediation) is governed by the *Arbitration and Mediation Act*,[84] while some States such as Lagos and Rivers States have enacted their own respective arbitration laws.[85] Where stated in the contract or specifically elected by the

78 Some States have enacted their respective mediation laws: *Lagos State Multi-Door Court Law 2007*; *Rivers State Multi-Door Court Law 2019*; *Abuja Multi-Door Court House Rules 2018*.

79 www.templars-law.com/wp-content/uploads/2021/10/TEMPLARS-ARBITRATION-REPORT-ON-NIGERIA-2021.pdf (accessed on 6 October 2021).

80 *Ibid*. 4.

81 (2019) LPELR-48996(SC).

82 (2019) LPELR-48996(SC) 75–76. See also *Sacoil 281 (Nig) Ltd & Anor v Transnational Corporation of Nigeria Plc* (2020) LPELR-49761(CA) 45–61; *Sino-Afric Agriculture & Ind Company Ltd & Ors v Ministry of Finance Incorporation & Anor* (2013) LPELR-22370(CA) 27–30; *Kano State Government & Anor v A.S.J. Global Links (Nig.) Ltd* (2017) LPELR-46215(CA).

83 (2012) WL 3925856 (SDNY Sept. 10, 2012).

84 *Arbitration and Mediation Act 2023*. This new Act repealed the *Arbitration and Conciliation Act 1988*, Cap A18, LFN 2004.

85 *Lagos State Arbitration Law 2009*; *Rivers State Arbitration Law 2019*.

parties, the arbitral process is also governed by the *Arbitration Rules* and the *Arbitration Proceedings Rules.*[86] The *Act*, the *Arbitration Rules*, and the *Arbitration Proceedings Rules* contain clear provisions for the entire arbitral process, including referral to arbitration; appointment and removal of arbitrators; emergency arbitration, pleadings; hearings, evidence (including expert witness), consolidation and concurrent hearings; preliminary orders and interim measures of protection; joinder of parties; third party funding; the option of an award review tribunal; enforcement of the arbitral award; and the extent of the court's intervention in the arbitral process.[87]

The final decision of an arbitration, the arbitral award, is binding, final and enforceable on the parties;[88] but could be set aside by the court on stringent grounds of legal incapacity of a party to the arbitration agreement; invalidity/illegality of the arbitration agreement; failure to properly notify a party of the arbitral proceedings or appointment of an arbitrator; an award delivered beyond the scope of the dispute submitted to arbitration; invalid/ illegal arbitral procedure or composition of the Arbitral Tribunal; unarbitrability of the dispute under Nigerian law; repugnance of the award to the public policy of Nigeria; in the case of an award by an Award Review Tribunal, the award is unsupportable having regards to the grounds for setting aside the award by the first instance Arbitral Tribunal; or, in the case of an arbitral award governed by a foreign law/court, the award is not yet binding under the foreign law or has been set aside or suspended by the foreign court.[89] It is not enough for any of these grounds to be proven by a party seeking the court to set aside the award. By virtue of Section 55(5) of the *Act*, it is a conjunctive requirement that the court is satisfied that any of the grounds have been proven and it caused substantial injustice to the applicant party.

There are two modes of arbitration – *ad hoc* arbitration and institutional arbitration. The former allows for the resolution of the dispute without recourse to an institution. Institutional arbitration, as the name implies, involves the resolution of disputes by the parties' referral to an arbitral or other specialised institution. For highly technical disputes such as construction disputes, the parties usually prefer arbitral institutions experienced in engineering and construction matters. The Chartered Institute of Arbitrators (**CIArb**), Nigerian Society of Engineers (**NSE**), Council for the Regulation of Engineering in Nigeria (**COREN**) and Council of Registered Builders of Nigeria (**CORBON**) are notable examples of arbitral and specialised institutions that may conduct institutional arbitration of construction disputes, subject to the agreement of the parties or appointment by the court. While the *Act* does not expressly provide for this categorisation, certain provisions can be implied in this regard, particularly those provisions that give parties the choice to determine the qualification of the arbitrator(s).[90]

---

86 *Arbitration Rules – First Schedule to the Arbitration and Mediation Act*, art 1; *Arbitration Proceedings Rules 2020 – Third Schedule to the Arbitration and Mediation Act.* By virtue of Rule 17 of the *Arbitration Proceedings Rules 2020*, the rules of the various courts regarding the courts' role and extent of intervention in the arbitral process are all superceded by the *Arbitration Proceedings Rules 2020.*

87 *Arbitration and Mediation Act*, ss 33, 6–13, 16–17, 36, 38–39 and 42–43, 19–29, 40, 61–62, 56, 57–58, 64 respectively. See also *Arbitration Rules*, arts 3, 7–14, 27, 20–22, 24, 17, 28–30, 32–33, 39, 26, 18–26, 34–38. With respect to the extent of the court's intervention in the arbitral process, see particularly *Arbitration Proceedings Rules 2020 – Third Schedule to the Arbitration and Mediation Act.*

88 *Arbitration and Mediation Act*, s 57; *Arbitration Rules*, art 42(2).

89 *Arbitration and Mediation Act*, ss 55, 56(8)–(9) and 58.

90 *Arbitration and Mediation Act*, ss 7(5)–(6) and 8(3).

The *Act* also governs international arbitrations in Nigeria where the substance/subject matter of the dispute is in Nigeria and/or the 'seat' of the arbitration is Nigeria.[91] However, subject to the implications of certain federal laws which are discussed in this chapter, the parties may elect for their arbitration to be governed by the legislation of another country, transnational laws/treaties/conventions or the arbitration rules of an arbitral institution, e.g. the CIArb Arbitration Rules, ICSID Arbitration Rules or ICC Rules of Arbitration.

As a signatory to the *New York Convention*, international arbitral awards delivered in signatory countries are generally enforceable in Nigeria and *vice versa*. The *New York Convention* has been ratified and domesticated as part of Nigeria's jurisprudence on arbitration.[92]

9.2.11 Current challenges

The challenges facing Nigeria's construction industry are similar to those in other developing countries. In particular, the construction industry in Nigeria faces challenges in:

- **Finance** – the initial payment to mobilise Contractors to Site is often delayed or inadequate. The Federal and State Governments are the major financiers of infrastructure projects.[93] The payment by the government for executed works is irregular and volatile,[94] and the interest on delayed payment clause is rarely applied. In public contracts, the actual release of funds to procuring entities does not match the budgetary appropriation, which constrains their financial obligations.[95] Consequently, the Contractor's working capital is often overstretched and the cost of borrowing is high. The exchange rate of the local currency dwindles constantly thereby increasing the cost of imported materials which exposes the project to the risk of the use of substandard local materials.
- **Security and social strife** – currently, the security situation in the country has worsened due to the activities of insurgents, bandits, sectarian agitators and, a few times, rogue state actors or state-sponsored non-state actors. Projects in remote locations are often either abandoned or executed at a high cost. Sometimes, inexperienced local contractors with knowledge of the areas where the construction works are taking place are subcontracted to complete such projects with low client supervision.
- **Planning and scoping** – inadequate planning and scoping of works lead to several changes being introduced by the Employer at the construction stage, thereby increasing the scope of the work and the Contractor's claims. Owing to cost and time overruns, project completion is extended or projects are abandoned.
- **Procurement** – the quality of the construction works to achieve value for money depends largely on the quality of the procurement of the Works and supervision contracts. Despite efforts to reform the procurement system, political interference

91 *Arbitration and Mediation Act*, ss 15 and 32.

92 *Convention on the Recognition and Enforcement of Foreign Arbitral Awards – Second Schedule to the Arbitration and Mediation Act*. See also *Arbitration and Mediation Act*, s 60.

93 AfDB, *supra* n26 8.

94 *Ibid.*

95 William-Elegbe, *supra* n61 366.

in the selection process is a major concern.[96] This often results in the selection of less qualified contractors and consultants and uncompetitive/excessively high contract prices.

9.2.12 Unique features of the construction industry in Nigeria

The Nigerian construction industry is one of the most vibrant in Africa and boasts some of the largest ongoing mega projects in the continent.[97] However, the industry is dominated by international companies – foreign firms and domestic firms with foreign parent companies. Over the years, the Government had encouraged the entry of indigenous firms to improve the local content in construction services without appreciable success. Indigenous local firms have only grown in size but are unable to compete with international firms. In the Nigerian construction market, 95% of all the construction firms are indigenous while the remaining 5% are foreign by origin.[98] Poor management and inadequate financing have been the main bane of their growth.

Foreign loans also encourage the participation of foreign contractors in Nigeria's construction industry. Some bilateral loans are 'tied'[99] – a condition that the borrower should utilise the loan to procure goods and services from the lender's country.[100] Multilateral Financing Institutions always insist on the application of their procurement procedures with strict qualification criteria, especially the 'average annual turn-over' requirement, which weeds out local contractors from the bidding process.

A peculiarity of the Nigerian construction industry is in its attitude towards the application of certain clauses of the construction contracts it considers 'punitive'. Most conditions of contract make provision for 'interest on delayed payment' for the Contractor. In some cases, this provision is a 'right' to be added to the subsequent payment without the Contractor making any claim. However, in practice, payments are often delayed and no interest is paid. The Contractors hardly raise issues about it, probably to sustain their good relationship with the Employer. In other cases, when contracts are not completed by the agreed date, the Employer rarely invokes the liquidated damages clause. By this, the completion date becomes 'time at large' and the Contractor is only obligated to complete the works within a reasonable time.

---

96 *Ibid.*

97 Ajaokuta-Kaduna-Kano (AKK) 614 km Long Natural Gas Pipeline (US$2.8 billion); the Green Light Mega Project identified public and private investments like the 1.6 km long Second Niger Bridge and 10.3 km Highway (US$1.1 billion); World Trade Centre, Abuja (US$1.0 billion); Centenary City, Abuja (US$180.6 billion); Eko Atlantic, Lagos ($6.0 billion); the Lagos-Calabar Coastal Railway Line (US$3.2 billion); the 38 km Fourth Mainland Bridge, Lagos (US$2.5 billion); Dangote Refinery Project (US$12 billion); etc. www.youtube .com/watch?v=5jFxxJSqHsY (accessed 13 October 2021).

98 PF Tunji-Olayeni, TO Mosaku, OI Fagbenle and LM Amusan, 'Project Management Competence of Indigenous Contractors in Nigeria' (2016) V1(1) *African Journal of Built Environment Research* 49.

99 OECD, *Untying Aid to the Least Developed Countries* (Policy Brief, 2001) 2 www.oecd.org/finance /2002959.pdf (accessed on 24 November 2021).

100 *Ibid.* 1.

9.3 The impact of COVID-19 in Nigeria

9.3.1 The impact of COVID-19 on the execution of construction projects in Nigeria

The first case of COVID-19 was confirmed by the Federal Ministry of Health on 27 February 2020 in Lagos, Nigeria.[101] In response to this development, on 29 March 2020, the President of Nigeria issued the *COVID-19 Regulations 2020*,[102] pursuant to the *Quarantine Act 1926*,[103] effectively restricting movements (otherwise known as a lockdown) in the Federal Capital Territory, Lagos and Ogun States for an initial period of 14 days[104] – which was ultimately extended to end on 5 May 2020. The *Regulations* also ratified the establishment and mandate of the Presidential Taskforce on COVID-19 for the coordination of the fight against the pandemic.[105] Some state governments equally issued their own *COVID-19 Regulations* to complement or extend that of the Federal Government.[106]

Among other pre-existing challenges, the COVID-19 pandemic negatively impacted various economic sectors, including the Nigerian construction industry.[107] This negative impact affected the execution and operation of construction projects on many fronts, particularly during the lockdown period. However, implementation of COVID-19 *Regulations* and protocols in the construction industry has been challenging owing to systemic and social impediments associated with a lack of prioritisation of public health matters in some economic sectors or by their stakeholders.[108] It is worth noting that the BPP released its Guidelines on COVID-19 wherein emergency procurement activities as part of the government's response to the pandemic were mandated to be executed under the Emergency Procurement Method rather than the usual Open Competitive Bidding Method.[109]

While the lockdown and the *COVID-19 Regulations* are now largely technically ineffective (as of December 2021), both the public and private sectors have continued to implement safety protocols, in addition to pre-existing applicable laws and regulations, to limit the spread of the virus. Also, due to the 'new normal' arising from the impact of the pandemic, many construction companies are deploying technology and virtual means to continue their construction activities while protecting themselves from contracting the virus.

101 https://ncdc.gov.ng/news/227/first-case-of-corona-virus-disease-confirmed-in-nigeria (accessed on 22 October 2021).

102 https://covid19.ncdc.gov.ng/media/archives/COVID-19_REGULATIONS_2020_20200330214102_KOhShnx.pdf (accessed on 22 October 2021).

103 *Quarantine Act 1926*, Cap Q2, LFN 2004, ss 2, 3 and 4.

104 *COVID-19 Regulations 2020*, s 1(1).

105 *COVID-19 Regulations 2020*, s 6.

106 For example, *Edo State Dangerous Infectious Diseases (Emergency Prevention) Regulations 2020*; *Lagos State Infectious Diseases (Emergency Prevention) Regulations 2020*; *Ebonyi State Infectious Diseases (Emergency Prevention) Regulations 2020*; etc.

107 IC Osuizugbo, 'Disruptions and Responses within Nigeria Construction Industry Amid COVID-19 Threat' (2020) V8(2) *Covenant Journal in Research & Built Environment* 37, 38.

108 Such impediments include poor attitude and culture of contractors and workers towards OSH and lack of effective implementation, monitoring and evaluation of adherence to OSH regulations and policies. On this point, see: PO Kukoyi et al., 'Managing the Risk and Challenges of COVID-19 on Construction Sites in Lagos, Nigeria' (2021) V20(1) *Journal of Engineering, Design and Technology* 1, 3.

109 Bureau of Public Procurement, *Guidelines on the Conduct of Public Procurement Activities by Ministries, Departments and Agencies as a Result of the COVID-19 Pandemic/Lockdown* (May 2020) www.bpp.gov.ng/wp-content/uploads/2020/05/BPP-Guideline-on-COVID-19-Procurements-1.pdf (accessed on 7 December 2021).

9.3.1.1 Prohibition on construction

Generally, the *COVID-19 Regulations* did not exempt construction workers from the implications of the restriction of movement,[110] hence construction sites in the FCT, Lagos and Ogun States were subject to the Federal Government COVID-19 restrictions. As of December 2021, many construction sites have resumed work, subject to safety protocols such as temperature checks, wearing of face masks, social distancing, restriction of entry for unauthorised visitors to site, washing of construction equipment and tools with soap, use of personal protective equipment (**PPE**), personal hygiene and the presence of a safety compliance officer to monitor adherence to COVID-19 protocols on site.[111]

9.3.1.2 Constraints on working on construction sites

For example, Nigeria's petroleum regulator known as the Department of Petroleum Resources (**DPR**),[112] released a Circular on 30 March 2020 directing oil and gas operators, contractors and service providers to ensure strict compliance with social distancing, curfews and lockdowns; limit the number of their workers at project/construction sites; and immediately withdraw non-essential staff from remote/offshore locations.[113] The Circular also directed the demobilisation of DPR personnel at these sites to one staff per rotation as well as the temporary suspension of staff rotation of operators, contractors and service providers where such staff rotations are for a period of fewer than 28 days, implying that a staff person is required to stay a minimum of 28 days at these locations per rotation.[114]

Notably, the Circular emphasised adherence to the provisions of DPR's *Guidelines and Procedure for Travel to Offshore/Swamp Location and Obtainment of Offshore Safety Permit 2019* in respect of health and hygiene protocols for travelling to offshore/swamp locations.[115] These protocols include body temperature checks, sanitisation of reusable PPE, sanitisation of location materials, sanitisation/washing of hands, medical assessment upon arrival at offshore/swamp locations, site medics to be clad with PPE and tools to respond to suspected infections.[116]

9.3.1.3 Changes to normal employment law

Prior to the pandemic, the *Factories Act*[117] was enacted to provide for the regulation of 'factory workers and a wider spectrum of workers and other professionals exposed to occupational hazards, but for whom no adequate provisions had been formerly made', as well as 'to make adequate provisions regarding the safety of workers to which the

110 *COVID-19 Regulations 2020*, s 6.

111 IC Osuizugbo, *above* n107, 45; see also FO Ezeokoli, MI Okongwu and DO Fadumo, 'Adaptability of COVID-19 Safety Guidelines in Building Construction Sites in Anambra State, Nigeria' (2020) V20(4) *Archives of Current Research International* 69, 72.

112 DPR is now defunct having being statutorily bifurcated into two separate regulatory agencies known as the Nigeria Midstream and Downstream Petroleum Regulatory Authority (**NMDPRA**) and Nigeria Upstream Petroleum Regulatory Commission (**NUPRC**) pursuant to the recently passed *Petroleum Industry Act 2021.*

113 DPR's circular of 30 March 2020 titled 'Re: Management of Covid-19 Outbreak' www.instagram.com/p/B-XuroehlIH/ (accessed on 11 November 2021). Note that the new official Instagram handle of the defunct DPR (@dprhotline) now Nigeria Upstream Petroleum Regulatory Commission (NUPRC) is @nuprc_ng.

114 *Ibid.*

115 *Guidelines and Procedure for Travel to Offshore/Swamp Location and Obtainment of Offshore Safety Permit 2019*, s 4.4.

116 *Ibid.*

117 *Factories Act No. 16 of 1987*, Cap F1, LFN 2004.

Act applies'.[118] In essence, while the short title of the *Act* might be misleading as being applicable only to factory workers, the *Act* also applies to construction workers when 'the wider spectrum of workers and other professionals exposed to occupational hazards' is put into consideration. The *Act* gives a wide definition of factories which implies the inclusion of construction sites;[119] refers to the word 'construction' at least 40 times; and expressly provides for the meaning of 'work of engineering construction' to include the construction of several types of infrastructure such as docks, harbours, inland navigation, tunnels, bridges, viaducts, waterworks, reservoirs, pipelines, sewers, etc.[120]

The impact of the COVID-19 pandemic on all categories of workers covered by the *Factories Act* and who are exposed to occupational hazards, including construction workers, brought the implementation of the pre-existing *Lifting and Allied Work Equipment (Safety) Regulations*[121] to the fore. This *Regulation* was issued by the Minister of Labour and Employment in 2018 pursuant to s 49 of the *Factories Act*. The *Regulations* make provision for the safety of persons – employers and employees – coming in contact with or involved with the design, construction, use, installation, alteration, maintenance, manufacture, repair, inspection or testing of lifting equipment, or other allied work equipment used in raising, lowering, pushing and pulling items or persons in a workplace or premises accessible to the general public.[122] Key among the provisions of the *Regulations* is the mandate to employers to ensure that a person who operates, manages, plans or supervises lifting operations is always provided with extant health and safety information.[123] The *Regulations* further mandate employers at sites where lifting and allied works take place to adhere to ISO Standards and Safety Codes of the International Labour Organization (**ILO**).[124] In 2020, the ILO issued the *Occupational Health and Safety Management – General Guidelines for Safe Working During the COVID-19 Pandemic*,[125] and by virtue of the *Regulations*, the ISO Standards and ILO Safety Codes are applicable to construction workers for the mitigation of COVID-19-associated occupational risks.[126]

9.3.2 The impact of COVID-19 on the operation of construction contracts in Nigeria

9.3.2.1 Force majeure provisions

In the pre-COVID-19 era, most commercial contracts generally did not (expressly) include pandemics or epidemics as incidents to qualify for *force majeure*. In its Circular of 30 March 2020, the DPR (now NUPRC) also declared a *force majeure* on forms of all

---

118 *Factories Act*, long title.

119 *Factories Act*, s 87.

120 *Factories Act*, s 88. See also *Labour Act*, ss 28(4), 67(b) and 91(1).

121 *Lifting and Allied Work Equipment (Safety) Regulations No. 3 of 2019*.

122 *Lifting and Allied Work Equipment (Safety) Regulations*, ss 1 and 2(1).

123 *Lifting and Allied Work Equipment (Safety) Regulations*, s 14(2).

124 *Lifting and Allied Work Equipment (Safety) Regulations*, s 3 (1).

125 ISO/PAS 45005:2020(en) www.iso.org/obp/ui/#iso:std:iso:pas:45005:ed-1:v1:en (accessed on 10 November 2021).

126 Applies to organisations and their employees have been operating throughout the pandemic; are resuming or planning to resume operations following full or partial closure; are re-occupying workplaces that have been fully or partially closed; or are new and planning to operate for the first time. See ISO/PAS 45005:2020(en), art 1.

oil and gas-related operations (which also affected construction contracts in the oil and gas sector) due to COVID-19.[127]

This declaration of *force majeure* by DPR remains controversial. While the DPR as a regulator has the general power to issue OSH-related circulars and directives, there are legal complexities associated with this *force majeure* declaration. As a result, any reliance on the *force majeure* circular by Contractors is potentially problematic to the extent that the Circular is regarded as legal authority to terminate or alter the terms of a construction contract in Nigeria's oil and gas sector, where the Contractor's claim of *force majeure* is without contractual basis.

It is trite that sovereign governments (or their regulatory agencies) sometimes make laws and regulations that could alter contracts – this appears to occur frequently in the oil and gas industry and there are usually contractual safeguards to manage the effects of such occurrences. DPR is a statutory agency of the Nigerian Government and a department within the Federal Ministry of Petroleum (its successors NUPRC and NMDPRA are stand-alone statutory agencies/regulators under the Ministry's supervision). Some legal experts argue that the Circular was intended by DPR to have the force of law as subsidiary legislation and the implementation of same could alter the terms of contracts.[128] Assuming this argument is tenable on the one hand, the Circular throws up legal questions of the privity of contract between contracting parties and the foisting of extra-contractual *force majeure* provisions into agreements between parties that neither contain *force majeure* clauses nor envisage global pandemics as incidents that qualify for the declaration of *force majeure*. Furthermore, this Circular is likely not legally binding on a party to a contract who does not fall under the regulatory purview of the DPR.[129]

On the other hand, it could be posited that in contracts where the government or its agency is a party to the agreement, a sovereign legislation or declaration of *force majeure* is most likely not to be perceived as illegal, whether or not the agreement contains *force majeure* clauses. But in the case of DPR, this declaration was made by the Director of DPR and not the Minister in charge of oil and gas matters. Under the repealed *Petroleum Act*, the Minister reserves the sole power to make orders and *Regulations*.[130] Under the newly enacted *Petroleum Industry Act*, the Minister, on the recommendation of NUPRC/NMDPRA, may suspend petroleum operations until arrangements to preserve life or property have been made to his/her satisfaction.[131] Either way, the involvement or input of the Minister in declaring *force majeure* and effectively suspending operations is a statutory requirement, the absence of which renders the declaration voidable.

127 See DPR's Circular dated 2 April 2020 titled 'Re: Management of COVID-19 Outbreak – Update 2' www.aelex.com/wp-content/uploads/2020/04/Department-of-Petroleum-Resources-Circular-on-COVID-19.pdf (accessed on 11 November 2021). See also DPR's post of 2 April 2020 on Instagram – www.instagram.com/p/B-eGU1Qh-xc/ (accessed on 11 November 2021).

128 www.gelias.com/images/Newsletter/DPR_Circular_Declaring_COVID-19_Pandemic_force_Majeure.pdf 2 (accessed on 11 November 2021); www.kusamotu.com/wp-content/uploads/2020/05/The-DPR%E2%80%99s-declaration-of-the-COVID-19-Pandemic-as-a-Force-Majeure-event-Issues-Arising-by-Racheal-Obong-1.pdf 2 (accessed on 11 November 2021).

129 *Ibid.*

130 *Petroleum Act 1967*, LFN 2004, s 12(1).

131 *Petroleum Industry Act No. 142 of 2021*, s 3(1)(k)(i).

9.3.2.2 Commencement or continuation of court or arbitration proceedings

In response to the *COVID-19 Regulations* issued by the Federal Government, the Office of the Honourable Chief Justice of Nigeria (**CJN**), through a Circular dated 23 March 2020 and addressed to all Heads of Courts, suspended all court sittings for an initial period of two weeks, effective 24 March 2020, except in matters that are 'urgent, essential or time bound according to extant laws'.[132] The suspension was further extended via another Circular dated 8 April 2020.[133]

Upon the relaxation of the lockdown by the federal government, the courts resumed sittings, subject to the provisions of the 'Guidelines for Court Sittings and Related Matters in the Covid-19 Period' issued by the National Judicial Council on 6 May 2020.[134] By the Guidelines, access to courtrooms is limited to one counsel per litigant who must maintain social distancing in their sitting arrangements. While the use of masks and sanitisers in the court premises are also mandated by the Guidelines, key among its provisions is the promotion of virtual hearings to avoid physical sittings by courts in courtrooms as much as possible during the COVID-19 period except for time-bound, extremely urgent and essential matters that may not be heard virtually or remotely by the Court.

Matters that are time bound, extremely urgent or essential were not clearly defined, leaving room for confusion and abuse, particularly with respect to disputes arising out of construction contracts. Some lawyers argue that matters where economic rights accrue only to an individual or a group of individuals and not the general public, such matters may not qualify as urgent or essential.[135] However, whether a construction-related dispute will be heard expeditiously as an urgent matter in the COVID-19 period will depend largely on regard to the circumstances of the dispute and the likely adverse consequences *in personam* or *in rem* of not hearing construction disputes as urgent.

During the lockdown, arbitral proceedings were largely suspended, especially in the aforementioned affected States. There were no new regulations or amendments (temporary or permanent) to the *Arbitration and Conciliation Act* to cater for the impacts of the COVID-19 pandemic.[136] However, various private stakeholder initiatives have been embarked upon to address the new normal influenced by the pandemic. There is an increased resort to technological tools and virtual proceedings by arbitral tribunals and parties, especially in urgent situations and where physical presence is difficult or impracticable. In April 2020, the Africa Arbitration Academy issued its Protocol on Virtual Hearings in Africa,[137] a 'context-specific and custom-made' guide for virtual arbitration

132 National Judicial Commission Circular (Ref No: NJC/CIR/HOC/II/631), 23 March 2020.

133 National Judicial Commission Circular (Ref No: NJC/CIR/HOC/II/656), 8 April 2020.

134 www.mondaq.com/nigeria/operational-impacts-and-strategy/941464/a-review-of-the-national-judicial-council-guidelines-for-court-sittings-and-related-matters-in-the-pandemic-period-part-one (accessed on 13 November 2021).

135 https://punuka.com/the-covid-19-directives-of-the-chief-justice-of-nigeria-and-state-of-the-judiciary/ (accessed on 13 November 2021).

136 The *Arbitration and Conciliation Act 1988* was the applicable arbitration law of Nigeria at the material time. This old Act has been repealed by the *Arbitration and Mediation Act 2023* which is now Nigeria's current arbitration law – *Arbitration and Mediation Act*, s 90. However, arbitral proceedings commenced before the enactment of the new Act are still governed by the old Act – *Arbitration and Mediation Act*, s 89.

137 www.africaarbitrationacademy.org/wp-content/uploads/2020/04/Africa-Arbitration-Academy-Protocol-on-Virtual-Hearings-in-Africa-2020.pdf (accessed on 7 November 2021).

hearings in Africa.[138] Although this protocol is relatively new and data on its application in arbitration is yet to be publicly available, its application protocol is likely to benefit parties to construction contracts which have substantial reliance on adjudication and arbitration to settle construction disputes, especially in contexts where there is an urgent need for the resolution of construction disputes.

9.4 Nigerian governing law of the contract

Generally, contracts in Nigeria are primarily governed by the common law and the various contract laws of the States. Both the Federal High Court and the High Courts of the States share original jurisdiction to entertain contractual disputes under ss 251, 257 and 272 of the *Constitution*. Except for a few exceptions,[139] there is no legislation mandating parties to a construction contract (including foreign construction companies) to adopt Nigerian law as the governing law of their contract. Generally, parties have the liberty to determine a governing law of their choice for their contracts, be it Nigerian law or foreign law. Nigerian courts generally enforce a foreign law where such law is stated to be the governing or proper law of the contract and determine the parties' dispute in accordance with the provisions of that foreign law to the extent of the jurisdiction of the court. There is a general principle in Nigeria's jurisprudence that it is the law chosen by the parties which will guide the Court in the determination of their rights in the absence of compelling circumstances such as misrepresentation, fraud or duress.[140]

9.4.1 Constraints on the governing law of a construction contract

Despite their peculiar technicalities, the terms and conditions of construction contracts, where they are clear and unambiguous, are generally interpreted literally as other commercial contracts. However, in the context of the parties' choice of law and forum, there are some exceptions which allow for the departure from the forum chosen by the parties and the enforceability of foreign law as the governing law of a contract. Even where the contract states a foreign law as the governing law, Nigerian courts are loath to apply a foreign law where doing so will be inimical to public policy or ultimately enforce an absurdity, fraud or illegality.[141] In *Sonnar (Nigeria) Limited v Partnenreedri M.S. Nordwind*,[142] the Supreme Court of Nigeria, sitting as a full court of seven judges, held that '[the] choice of the proper law by the parties is not considered by the Courts as conclusive'.[143] The Supreme Court further held that the choice of a foreign law by the parties (which in the instant case was German law) as the governing law of their contract will have to pass the

138 *Ibid.* 3. See also http://arbitrationblog.kluwerarbitration.com/2020/05/07/africa-arbitration-academy-takes-over-the-baton-on-thought-leadershiplaunches-virtual-hearing-protocol-in-africa-for-africa/?print=print (accessed on 7 November 2021).

139 Such as in cases related to admiralty (maritime) and aviation in Nigeria.

140 *Beaumont Resources Limited & Anor v DWC Drilling Limited* (2017) LPELR-42814 (CA), 49–50. See also: *Sonnar (Nig) Limited & Anor v Partnenreedri M.S Nordwind & Anor* (1987) LPELR-3494 (SC), 31; *Damac Star Properties LLC v Profitel Limited & Anor* (2020) LPELR-50699 (CA), 44–52; *Nika Fishing Co. Limited v Lavina Corporation* (2008) LPELR-2035 (SC), 16–23.

141 www.mondaq.com/nigeria/contracts-and-commercial-law/309168/enforcement-of-choice-of-foreign-law-and-jurisdiction-in-transaction-agreements? (accessed on 13 November 2021).

142 *Sonnar (Nig.) Limited & Anor v Partnenreedri M.S Nordwind & Anor* (1987) LPELR-3494 (SC).

143 *Ibid.* 37.

tests of genuineness, bona fides, legality and reasonableness before such foreign law can be applied by the court.[144] In essence, where a foreign law is expressly adopted by the parties as the governing law of their contract, such foreign law must bear some relationship to and must be connected to the realities of the entire contract.[145]

Another point to consider is that the Supreme Court of Nigeria may have been wary of an imminent legal danger in terms of the parties ousting the jurisdiction of Nigerian Courts to determine their disputes by the choice of a foreign law as governing law of their contract. Lord Denning, MR espoused a cardinal legal principle in the case of *The Fehmarn*[146] 'that no one by his private stipulation can oust these Courts of their jurisdiction in a matter that properly belongs to them'.[147] In adopting Lord Denning's reasoning, the Supreme Court held that

> as a matter of public policy, our Courts should not be too eager to divest themselves of jurisdiction conferred on them by the Constitution and by other laws, simply because parties in their private contracts chose a foreign forum and a foreign law. Courts guard, rather jealously, their jurisdiction and even where there is an ouster of that jurisdiction by Statute, it should be by clear and unequivocal words. If that is so, as indeed it is, how much less can parties by their private acts remove the jurisdiction properly and legally vested in our Courts? Our Courts should be in charge of their own proceedings. When it is said that parties make their own contracts and that the Courts will only give effect to their intention as expressed in and by the contract, that should generally be understood to mean and imply a contract which does not rob the Court of its jurisdiction in favour of another foreign forum.[148]

As enunciated in the *Sonnar* case, before assuming jurisdiction over the dispute and/or applying the foreign law as the governing law of the contract, the court, in applying the tests of genuineness, *bona fides*, legality and reasonableness, will have to determine the following questions:

(a) Which country is the evidence (*res*) located in?
(b) What implication does the location of the evidence have on the convenience and cost of holding the trial in either the domestic court or foreign court?
(c) Does the law of the foreign court apply to the contract and do its relevant provisions differ from the law of the domestic court?
(d) With what country is either party connected and how closely is such connection?
(e) Do the defendants genuinely desire trial in the foreign country or are they only seeking procedural advantages?
(f) Would the plaintiffs be prejudiced by having to sue in the foreign Court because (i) they would be deprived of security for that claim; (ii) they would be unable to enforce any judgment obtained; (iii) they would be faced with a time-bar in the foreign court which is not applicable in the domestic court; (iv) they would be unlikely get a fair trial for political, racial, religious or other reasons; or (v)

144 *Ibid.*
145 *Ibid.*
146 *The Fehmarn* (1958) 1 All ER 333.
147 *The Fehmarn* (1958) 1 All ER 333,335.
148 *Sonnar (Nig) Limited & Anor v Partnenreedri M.S Nordwind & Anor* (1987) LPELR-3494 (SC), 38. See also the following cases: *Fugro Subsea LLC v Petrolog Limited* (2021) LPELR-53133 (CA), 67–74; *Ahmadu Bello University v VTLS Inc.* (2020) LPELR-52142 (CA), 12–18; *Hull Blyth (Nig) Limited v Jetmove Publishing Limited* (2018) LPELR-44115 (CA), 8–25; *Lignes Aeriennes Congolaises v Air Atlantic (Nig.) Limited* (2005) LPELR-5808 (CA), 29–37.

> the granting of a stay of proceedings and referral to the foreign court would spell injustice to the plaintiff as where the action is already time-barred in the foreign court and the grant of stay would amount to permanently denying the plaintiffs any redress?[149]

It is worth noting that the *Admiralty Jurisdiction Act* and the *Civil Aviation Act* mandate that the Federal High Court shall have exclusive jurisdiction to try matters related to admiralty and aviation,[150] especially where relevant public bodies are one of the contracting parties (Employers), and drawing from the aforementioned cases, it is very likely that this court will apply Nigerian law as the governing law of admiralty and aviation-related contracts where the Site/Country is Nigeria. Thus, it is arguable that these mandatory jurisdictional requirements are applicable to contracts for the construction of aerodromes (airports) and sea ports.

There are two points to note from the foregoing analysis. The first point is that Nigerian courts may decide to assume jurisdiction over a dispute despite the fact that the choice of forum and governing law are those of a foreign jurisdiction, in a departure from the doctrine of *forum non conveniens*. Secondly, on compelling reasons of fraud, misrepresentation, illegality or public policy, the courts may even decide not to also apply the choice of foreign law (as could be seen with admiralty and aviation-related transactions) in determining the dispute and enforcing the contract.[151] The implication of both points is that the adherence to the doctrine of *forum non conveniens* by Nigerian courts is not strict. Thus, the invocation or otherwise of *forum non conveniens* and the application of a choice of foreign law as the governing law by Nigerian courts is discretionary.[152]

Consequently, from the cited cases, one point of view is that decisions in Nigerian cases on the invocation of *forum non conveniens* and application of foreign law as the governing law are somewhat contradictory and uncertain. Another point of view is that Nigerian courts will not invoke *forum non conveniens* or apply foreign law as the governing law of a contract unless there are compelling circumstances as enunciated in the *Sonnar* case. The invocation or otherwise of *forum non conveniens* all depends on the *situs* of the *res* and the general nature of the contract. Depending on which prism one looks at the issue through, both points of view appear to be tenable as Nigeria is not a signatory to *The Hague Convention of 30 June 2005 on Choice of Court Agreements*, which empowers courts of signatory countries to enforce the choice of a foreign law of another signatory country by parties in their contract. Until Nigeria becomes a signatory,

---

149 *Sonnar (Nig) Limited & Anor v Partnenreedri M.S Nordwind & Anor* (1987) LPELR-3494 (SC), 32–34.

150 *Admiralty Jurisdiction Act 1991*, Cap A5, LFN 2004, ss 1, 2, 3, 4, 19, 20, 21, 22 and 25; *Civil Aviation Act*, Cap C13, LFN 2004, s 63. But note that the referral of a contractual dispute to arbitration in a foreign jurisdiction and the governing of such dispute by a foreign arbitration law or the rules of an international arbitral institution by virtue of the arbitration clause is not generally viewed by Nigerian courts as an ouster of their jurisdiction; rather it is viewed as the postponement of the right of parties to litigate the dispute in the court pending arbitration. See: *Bill & Brothers Ltd & Ors v Dantata & Sawoe Construction Co. (Nig) Ltd & Ors* (2015) LPELR-24770(CA), 10–12; *R.C. Omeaku & Sons Ltd v Rainbownet Ltd* (pt. 2014) 6 NWLR (1401) 516, 534 and 535; *Lagos State Water Corporation v Sakamort Construction (Nig) Ltd* (2011) 12 NWLR (pt. 1262) 569, 599.

151 www.afronomicslaw.org/2020/12/17/the-practicality-of-the-enforcement-of-jurisdiction-agreements-in-nigeria (accessed on 29 September 2021).

152 www.templars-law.com/wp-content/uploads/2019/03/Templars-Thought-Leadership-Article-choice-of-law-clauses.pdf 6 (accessed on 29 September 2021).

this jurisprudential uncertainty may well continue, leaving jurisprudential development in this regard to judicial activism.

9.4.2 Formal requirements for a construction contract

Nigeria is a common law jurisdiction. Consequently, the formal requirements for the formation of a contract are similar to other common law jurisdictions. Generally, contractual transactions are regulated by the *Law Reform (Contracts) Act*,[153] although many of the 36 States in the country have enacted their respective contract laws.[154] Basically, for a contract to be deemed valid, there must be an offer, an acceptance, a consideration, an intention to create legal relations and the legal capacity of parties to create legal relations (enter into contracts).

Oral and written contracts, devoid of duress, fraud and misrepresentation, are deemed validly made and enforceable. However, contracts for the disposition of land in any manner and any other transaction involving the use of land – the definition of land under the *Act* includes buildings – must be in writing.[155] The *Act* expressly provides that

> [n]o contract to which this section applies shall be enforceable by action unless the contract or some memorandum or note in respect therefor[e] must be in writing and signed by the party to be charged therewith or by some other person lawfully authorized by him.[156]

This statutory provision implies – and it is rather logical – that contracts for construction works on land must be in writing, especially considering the technicalities and high capital intensity involved in construction contracts.[157] Written contracts could take the form of simple contracts or deeds (i.e. under seal). One advantage of a contract executed as a deed over simple contracts is that for instituting actions and arbitral proceedings, the former has a limitation period of 12 years[158] while the latter has a limitation period of six years.[159]

It is pertinent to note that in Nigeria's construction industry, depending on the circumstances, the mere exchange of letters by the parties may be deemed a validly made and enforceable contract.[160] We also add here that a letter from a party to another party may constitute a binding contract where the receiving party acts upon the provisions of the letter.[161] However, contracts may not be deemed validly made and enforceable via the exchange of letters where such letter(s) contain caveats such as 'without prejudice' or 'provisional offer/acceptance' or 'in principle' or 'subject to contract', as the intention to create legal relations as a formal requirement of a valid contract cannot be inferred in such

---

153 See generally: *Law Reform (Contracts) Act 1961.*

154 For example: *Lagos State Law Reform (Contracts) Law 2015*, *Delta State Contracts Law 2006*, etc.

155 *Law Reform (Contracts) Act*, s 5(1)(b) and (2). See also *Statute of Frauds 1677*, s 4.

156 *Law Reform (Contracts) Act*, s 5(2).

157 https://iclg.com/practice-areas/construction-and-engineering-law-laws-and-regulations/nigeria (accessed on 22 October 2021).

158 *Limitation Act No 88 of 1966*, s 11.

159 *Ibid.* s 7.

160 *Arfo Construction Co. Ltd. v Minister of Works & Anor* (2018) LPELR-46711(CA).

161 *Majekodunmi & Anor v National Bank of Nigeria Ltd.* (1978) LPELR-1825(SC), 11; *FGN & Ors v Zebra Energy Ltd.* (2002) LPELR-3172(SC), 18; *Aribisala Properties Ltd. v Adepoju* (2015) LPELR-25589(CA), 33. Vide these cases, it is settled that acceptance of an offer can be demonstrated by the conduct of the offeree.

circumstances.[162] Thus, any obligation or liability under such contracts is inadmissible in evidence and unenforceable by law.[163]

9.5 What Special Provisions in the Particular Conditions are necessary for consistency with applicable laws in Nigeria?

9.5.1 FIDIC General Conditions are incompatible or inconsistent with Nigeria's governing law of the contract

The following are examples of potential issues in the jurisdiction where the 2017 FIDIC General Conditions may be incompatible with the Nigerian governing law of the contract.

9.5.1.1 Illegality/unenforceability of certain contractual terms

9.5.1.1.1 Specified periods for payments upon issuance of IPC/FPC

Sub-clauses 14.6, 14.7(b), 14.8 and 14.13 of the General Conditions in the 2017 Red and Yellow Books are inconsistent with the provisions of s 37 of the *Public Procurement Act*, which states that:

> (1) Payment for the procurement of goods, works, and services shall be settled promptly and diligently.
> (2) Any payment due after more than sixty days from the date of the submission of the invoice, valuation certificate and confirmation or authentication by the Ministry, Extra-Ministerial Office, Government Agency, Parastatal or Corporation shall be deemed a delayed payment.

The implications of the interpretation of s 37 of the *Public Procurement Act* presuppose that:

(a) The decision of the Engineer in issuing valuation certificates is not final. The Engineer's decision is subject to the approval of the Employer.
(b) The issuance of an Interim Payment Certificate (**IPC**) under sub-clause 14.6 and a Final Payment Certificate (**FPC**) under sub-clause 14.13 of the 2017 FIDIC General Conditions by the Engineer may be a mere draft which would be subject to the verification of the Employer. After verification, the Employer may require the Engineer to submit a final IPC/FPC for payment. This may affect the right of the Contractor to challenge the valuation of works under sub-clause 12.3 of the 2017 FIDIC General Conditions because it is only a draft.
(c) The interest on delayed payment is determined only 60 days after the Contractor submits a statement/invoice.
(d) The 60-day period applies to both the IPC and FPC.

Thus, with respect to IPCs under sub-clause 14.6, payment under sub-clause 14.7, delayed payment under sub-clause 14.8 and FPCs under sub-clause 14.13, amendments may be

162 https://iclg.com/practice-areas/construction-and-engineering-law-laws-and-regulations/nigeria [1.6] (accessed on 22 October 2021).

163 *Acmel Nigeria Limited v FBN Plc* (2014) LPELR-22444 (CA), 14–15 and 26.

required in the Particular Conditions to align with the provisions of s 37 of the *Public Procurement Act*. Furthermore, the provisions of s 155 of the *Public Procurement Regulations for Goods and Works 2007* are instructive:

> Procuring Entities should endeavour to make payments promptly and in accordance with the terms and conditions of the contract. Any payment due for more than sixty days following submission and verification of an invoice shall be deemed a delayed payment. **The contract document shall state the period of sixty days.** [emphasis added]

In order to align FIDIC requirements with the position of the law, the Particular Conditions should include limiting the Engineer's authority (sub-clause 3.2) in the valuation of Works (sub-clause 12.3), delayed payment (sub-clause 14.8) and the issuance of IPCs (sub-clause 14.6) and FPCs (sub-clause 14.13) by incorporating alongside other parties' obligations, the action of the Employer to 'verify and confirm' the IPC/FPC within the maximum period of 60 days (i.e. 28 days + 28 days + *4 days*) after the Engineer receives the Contractor's statement.

9.5.1.1.2 Conflict of interest and related matters

Sub-clause 5.2.1 of the 2017 FIDIC Red Book defines a Nominated Subcontractor:

> In this sub-clause, 'nominated Subcontractor' means a Subcontractor named as such in the Specification or whom the Engineer, under sub-clause 13.4 [*Provisional Sums*], instructs the Contractor to employ as a Subcontractor.

Similar provisions exist in sub-clause 4.5 of the Yellow Book and the Silver Book. Relevant to this point, s 16(25) of the *Public Procurement Act* provides that

> A procuring entity shall not request or stipulate that a bidder should engage a particular sub-contractor as a requirement for participating in any procurement proceedings.

The foregoing provision of the law clearly prohibits the possibility of the Employer (either directly in the contract or through the Employer's Personnel such as the Engineer by virtue of sub-clauses 1.1.33 and 1.1.35 of the 2017 FIDIC Red Book) nominating a Subcontractor under the contract. The *raison d'etre* is to forestall corrupt tendencies and any occurrence of a conflict of interest in the procurement process. While sub-clause 5.2.2 (Objection to Nomination) of the 2017 FIDIC Red Book allows the Contractor to object to the Engineer's instruction to engage a Subcontractor under stipulated reasonable grounds in sub-clause 5.2.2(a)–(c), the Contractor's objection does not preclude the Engineer from nominating another Subcontractor. Thus, to the extent that the contract specifies a particular Subcontractor or the Engineer nominates a Subcontractor, sub-clauses 5.2.1 and 5.2.2 of the 2017 FIDIC Red Book, as well as sub-clause 4.5 of the Yellow and Silver Books, are inoperative and should be amended accordingly in the Particular Conditions to align with the provisions of the *Act*.

9.5.1.1.3 Specified period for delivery of performance security

Sub-clause 4.2.1 of the 2017 FIDIC General Conditions requires the Contractor to deliver the Performance Security within 28 days of receiving the Letter of Acceptance. Nigerian law has proposed a different time for delivery of the Contractor's Performance Security and this provision has to be considered in the Particular Conditions. Thus, on this point, s 36 of the *Public Procurement Act* requires:

> The provision of a Performance Guarantee shall be a *precondition for the award of any procurement contract* upon which any mobilization fee is to be paid, provided however it shall not be less than 10% of the contract value in any case or an amount equivalent to the mobilization fee requested by the supplier or contractor whichever is higher.

In essence, the law stipulates that the Contractor shall deliver the Performance Security to the Employer prior to receiving the Letter of Acceptance (award). This provision is unusual and problematic because the basis for the performance guarantee prior to contractual commitment is unclear. However, s 6(117) of the *Public Procurement Regulations for Goods and Works 2007* attempts to correct this problematic provision of the *Act* by requiring the delivery of the Performance Security before the signing of the contract:

> Security for the guarantee of performance by the Bidders shall be provided by the selected Bidders prior to contract signature.

This regulatory provision cannot correct the problem created by the *Act*. Under Nigerian law, the *Regulation* is subsidiary legislation which only supplements the *Act* and cannot supersede or amend the provisions of the parent *Act* (in this case, the *Public Procurement Act*). In *Famfa Oil Ltd v AG Federation & Anor*,[164] the Court of Appeal held that '[i]t is the law that subsidiary legislation must conform with the principal law which provided the source of their existence'.[165] The Court of Appeal recently upheld its decision in *Famfa Oil* in the case of *African Natural Resources & Mines Ltd v SS Minerals Resources Ltd*[166] as follows:

> The Regulations referred to by the 1st and 2nd Respondents, are subject to Section 141 of the Act and are not contrary to it at all. Even if they are in conflict, it is the Act that supersedes, not the Regulations. This is because the Act is the principal law and it is the statute that makes provision for the Regulations to be made. The Act is the pillar against which the Regulations lean upon and so can never override or supercede the Act. If there is any inconsistency, it is the regulations that will give way to the Act.[167]

Thus, the position of Nigerian law on the delivery of performance security in procurement proceedings is that for every federal public contract, the Contractor (the preferred bidder) delivers the performance security prior to the award of the contract. In order to solve this contractual and regulatory challenge and ensure an alignment with the provisions of the *Act*, it is strongly recommended that the 2017 FIDIC General Conditions be amended to stipulate that the Procuring Entity (the Employer under FIDIC General Conditions) may be required to issue 'an intention to award contract', so that this may justify the issuance of Performance Securities by the Contractor's bankers to the Contractor for onward delivery to the Employer. This amendment will most likely satisfy the statutory requirement under s 36 of the *Public Procurement Act* to deliver a Performance Security prior to the award of the contract.

164 (2007) LPELR-9023(CA).
165 (2007) LPELR-9023(CA), 29.
166 (2021) LPELR-55151(CA).
167 (2021) LPELR-55151(CA), 10–11.

9.5.1.2 Employer's sale of Contractors' Equipment, surplus material, wreckage and Temporary Works

Sub-clause 11.11 [*Clearance of Site*] of the 2017 FIDIC General Conditions provides that promptly after the issuance of the Performance Certificate by the Contractor, the Contractor shall remove any remaining Contractor's Equipment, surplus material, wreckage, rubbish and Temporary Works from the Site within 28 days, failing which the Employer may sell (to the extent permitted by applicable Laws) or otherwise dispose of any remaining items and/or may reinstate and clean the Site (as may be necessary) at the Contractor's cost.[168]

Where the applicable law is that of Nigeria, the Employer may not enjoy the automatic right of sale of Contractor's equipment. The legal doctrine of *nemo dat quod non habet* ('no one can give what he does not have') is relevant to the analysis. It is only the owner of a property or his/her agent that can validly transfer title in that property by way of assignment. The Employer is clearly not the owner of the Contractor's equipment, surplus material, wreckage and Temporary Works and therefore cannot validly pass title in the Contractor's equipment etc., despite the words of the contract allowing the Employer to do so. In addition, the said sub-clause does not clearly appoint the Employer as an agent of the Contractor for the purposes of selling the Contractor's equipment on its behalf. More so, the title in the equipment may not even belong to the Contractor as s/he may have obtained them for construction works by way of a hire-purchase or another form of bailment. In the construction industry, the hire-purchase of equipment by Contractors is a usual occurrence because they cannot afford to purchase all the equipment that they would need for the construction works.

The contractual power of sale of the Contractor's equipment under the sub-clause, it could be counter-argued, implies an agency by necessity to sell on the Contractor's behalf on one hand or an implied pledge of the Contractor's equipment on the other hand. For failure to remove his/her equipment from the Site within 28 days after the issuance of a Performance Certificate, it becomes necessary for the Employer to sell the equipment on behalf of the Contractor. Also, by virtue of entering into the construction contract, the Contractor has impliedly pledged his/her equipment in exchange for fulfilling a promise – completing the construction work according to specification and within specified timelines. However, the law of agency presupposes the prerequisites that there must be a fiduciary relationship between the principal (Contractor) and the agent (Employer), of which the principal either expressly, impliedly or constructively delegated to the agent the authority to sell on its behalf,[169] and there must be an element of control by the principal over the agent.

Thus, a critical analysis shows that no principal–agent arrangement has been created by this sub-clause; the entire 2017 FIDIC General Conditions rather envisages between the Employer and the Contractor an independent contractor relationship at best, thus the element of control in the 2017 FIDIC General Conditions (if any) does not necessarily amount to that of a principal–agent relationship. Furthermore, with respect to the notion

168 Similarly, Clause 53(2) of the Contract Agreement and Standard Conditions of Contract (Road Works), created by the Federal Ministry of Works and Housing, vests ownership of all construction plants, temporary works and materials owned by the Contractor on the Employer immediately when the Employer brings them on site, implying that the Employer can sell the plants, equipment and materials where the Contractor fails to remove them from the site within the stipulated period.

169 *Asaka v Raminkura* (2015) All FWLR (pt. 787) 774 (CA).

that an implied pledge has been created by virtue of the sub-clause, the Contractor may have mainly obtained the equipment via a hire-purchase from a third party. Section 28 of the *Pawnbrokers Act*[170] prohibits the pawning of goods by a person who does not exercise title over the goods in any manner. Thus, interpreting the sub-clause as an implied pledge would amount to an offence punishable by payment of a fine or penalty.[171]

While there is a dearth of case law on the pledge/pawn of goods, it remains to be seen how the courts or arbitral tribunals will interpret this sub-clause and resolve the legal problem caused by it. But the law is clear that a pledge by a non-owner of an item renders the transaction void for lack of proprietary title to sell. Perhaps, one recommendation for addressing this challenge is for sub-clause 11.11 of the 2017 FIDIC General Conditions to be amended according to Clause 53(3) of the Contract Agreement and Standard Conditions of Contract (Road Works) which states that

> [T]he Contractor shall not bring on to the site any essential hired plant unless the agreement for hire thereof contains a provision that the owner thereof will on request in writing made by the Employer within seven days after the date on which any such forfeiture has become effective and the Employer undertaking to pay all hire charges in respect thereof from such date hire such essential hired plant to the Employer on the same terms in all respects as the same was hired to the Contractor save that the Employer shall be entitled to permit the use thereof by any other Contractor employed by him for the purpose of completing the works under the terms of the said clause 63.

By virtue of the foregoing, in the case where the Contractor sourced construction equipment from hire-purchases, sub-clause 11.11 can be amended to mandate the Contractor (hirer) to include the Employer as a potential successor-in-title of the Contractor's hire-purchase agreement so that the Employer can validly step in the Contractor's position in the hire-purchase agreement upon the default of the Contractor to the third party hiree/owner under the hire-purchase agreement. Even with this recommended amendment, the Employer will not have the automatic right to sell the hired equipment. The Employer must return the hired equipment back to the owner after the payment of the hire charges has been completed. It is only where the Employer pays a sum of money upon which the owner will pass title to the Employer as stipulated by the hire-purchase agreement that the Employer can validly sell the materials/equipment under the law. But where the Contractor is the owner of the equipment or other material, it is very likely that the courts will not enforce the sale of the equipment and materials by the Employer where there is no valid instrument evidencing a passage of title from the Contractor to the Employer.

9.5.2 FIDIC General Conditions are incompatible or inconsistent with the law of the Site/Country

No Special Provisions in the Particular Conditions are necessary for consistency with the applicable laws of Nigeria.

170 *Pawnbrokers Act 1964*, Cap 531 Laws of FCT Nigeria 2007. Many provisions of this Act, including those that pertain to fines upon conviction, are obsolete and unrealistic in contemporary economics and would require urgent legislative amendment.

171 *Pawnbrokers Act*, ss 27(g), 28 and 29(1).

9.5.3 FIDIC General Conditions are incompatible or inconsistent with the relevant laws on dispute determination in Nigeria

The following are examples of potential issues in Nigeria where 2017 FIDIC General Conditions may be incompatible or inconsistent with the law of the seat of the arbitration or relevant laws on dispute resolution, additional explanation of the relevant law is appropriate and/or a court or arbitrator may construe the issues differently than expected from the words of the contract because of local law or custom.

9.5.3.1 Disputes relating to non-contractual claims may not be arbitrable

The general principle of the law of arbitration in Nigeria is that parties are at liberty to agree to submit any dispute arising out of or connected with their agreement to arbitration. Generally, according to Hoellering, any dispute capable of settlement by the regular courts could be arbitrable.[172] Nevertheless, when disputes arise, the question as to whether such disputes fall within the scope of arbitration under the applicable governing laws of the 'seat' of arbitration comes up for consideration.[173] This is usually referred to as the principle of arbitrability of disputes, the purpose of which is to preserve the jurisdiction of the courts in specific matters for reasons of public policy and overriding national interest.[174] The determination of the arbitrability of disputes curtails the right of parties to refer certain disputes to arbitration on public policy considerations by either conferring exclusive jurisdiction on a court or preferring a uniform method of settlement for those types of disputes.[175] On the scope of arbitrability of disputes, s 65 of the *Arbitration and Mediation Act* provides that

> This Act does not affect any other law by virtue of which certain disputes may –
>
> (a) not be submitted to arbitration; or
> (b) be submitted to arbitration only in accordance with the provisions of that or another law.

By virtue of the foregoing provision, some subject matters have been taken away from the competence of arbitral proceedings/tribunals in favour of the courts. Thus, where a contractual dealing between parties has a law regulating it, and for public policy reasons and/or national interest, such law confers exclusive jurisdiction on a court to entertain matters related to such contractual dealing, then such a dispute is no longer arbitrable.[176] In some instances, arbitrability could be subject to prerequisites set out in the law governing the field of the subject matter of the dispute.[177]

In *KSUDB v Fanz Construction Ltd*[178] and *United World Ltd Inc. v Mobile Telecommunications Services Ltd*,[179] the test for determining whether a dispute or differ-

172 MF Hoellering, 'Arbitrability of Disputes' [1985–1986] 41 *Business Law* 125, 127.
173 *Ibid.*
174 MM Akanbi, 'Contending Without Being Contentious: Arbitration, Arbitrators and Arbitrability' (Paper delivered at the 152nd Inaugural Lecture of the University of Ilorin, Ilorin, 2014) 17.
175 *Ibid.* 18.
176 *Arbitration and Mediation Act*, s 65(a).
177 *Ibid.*, s 65(b).
178 (1990) 4 NWLR (pt. 142) 1, 32–33 (SC)
179 (1998) 10 NWLR (pt. 568) 106, 116 (CA).

ence can be referred to arbitration (arbitrability) was discussed. It was held in both cases that the following causes are all non-arbitrable issues: (i) an indictment for an offence of a public nature; (ii) disputes arising out of illegal contracts and void agreements; (iii) disputes leading to a change of status; (iv) disputes that may result in the arbitral tribunal giving awards/decisions *in rem*; (v) rights exercisable against the world; (vi) disputes where a party already admits liability but only fails to comply/act; and (vii) disputes where the cause of action no longer exists.

There are a number of laws which confer sole jurisdiction on the courts, thereby divesting the power of arbitral tribunals to entertain such disputes, as disputes relating to these laws are considered matters of public policy and national interest. Those which are relevant to the 2017 FIDIC General Conditions include the following.

9.5.3.1.1 Intellectual property laws

By the provisions of s 46 of the *Copyright Act*,[180] any person who infringes on the performer's rights as set out under s 25 of the *Act* commits an offence triable only by the Federal High Court. Likewise, by virtue of s 26 of the *Patents and Designs Act 1971*,[181] the exclusive power to entertain infringements of patents/inventions and designs under the *Act* is vested in the Federal High Court. The Court may however aid itself by sitting with intellectual property experts acting as assessors during proceedings.[182]

With respect to trademarks, the *Trademarks Act*[183] is not very clear on which particular court has sole jurisdiction over trademark disputes. However, the *Act* provides for some form of adjudication by the Registrar of Trademarks over disputes relating to registration of identical trademarks by separate parties, and the decision of the Registrar is subject to appeal at the Federal High Court.[184] Nevertheless, s 251(1)(f) of the *Constitution of the Federal Republic of Nigeria 1999* vests the Federal High Court with the exclusive jurisdiction to entertain claims relating to trademarks and all other intellectual property to the exclusion of every other court.[185] This position of law has been confirmed in several cases including *Dyson Tech. Ltd. v Nulec Ind. Plc. & Registrar General of Trademarks*,[186] *Barde v Honourable Minister of Health & Ors*,[187] *Shell Nigeria Exploration and Production Nigeria Ltd v Federal Inland Revenue Service*[188] and *Esso Petroleum and Production Nigeria Ltd & SNEPCO v NNPC*.[189] In fact, in the *Dyson* case, the Court of Appeal held that the only other body outside the Federal High Court empowered to exercise quasi-judicial powers with respect to trademark infringement is the Registrar of Trademarks.[190]

180 Cap C28, LFN 2004.

181 Cap P2, LFN 2004.

182 *Patents and Designs Act*, s 26(2).

183 Cap T13, LFN 2004.

184 *Trademarks Act*, s 13(3). See also the *Merchandise Marks Act*, Cap M10, LFN 2004.

185 The Registrar of Trademarks in exercising his power over trademark registration disputes constitutes an adjudication tribunal.

186 (2017) LPELR-50572(CA), 10–11.

187 (2017) LPELR-42998(CA), 17–18.

188 (Unreported) Appeal No CA/A/208/2012, delivered on 31 August 2016, cited in www.ibanet.org/ip-july-2021-ip-property-disputes-nigeria#_edn2 (accessed on 15 November 2021).

189 (Unreported) Appeal No CA/A/507/2012, delivered on 22 July 2016, cited in www.ibanet.org/ip-july-2021-ip-property-disputes-nigeria#_edn2 (accessed on 15 November 2021).

190 (2017) LPELR-50572(CA) 11. Note that the Registrar General of the Corporate Affairs Commission and the Director General of the Federal Competition and Consumer Protection Commission also play very limited

It is important to note that while the previously cited judicial authorities border on the infringement of intellectual property *simpliciter*, sub-clause 17.3 of the FIDIC General Conditions borders on a contracting party's indemnity of an infringement by another contracting party of the intellectual property of a third party who is not a party to the construction contract. One view is that because the matter or claim borders on indemnity for infringement of intellectual property, the matter or claim is not about infringement of intellectual property in the strict sense but merely a fallout or consequence of an infringement by a contracting party of the intellectual property of a non-contracting third party and therefore falls under the competence of the Engineer or the DAAB or arbitration by the International Chamber of Commerce (**ICC**) to entertain and resolve. This is strengthened by the vesture of jurisdiction on the Federal High Court to the exclusion of any other court (which does not expressly include an ADR tribunal such as the Engineer, DAAB or ICC). Another view is that because the matter or claim is for a contracting party's indemnity of an infringement by another contracting party of the intellectual property of a non-contracting third party, it is still in connection with or arising out of an infringement of intellectual property howsoever, hence by virtue of the *Dyson, Barde, Shell* and *Esso Petroleum* cases as well as s 251(1)(f) of the *Constitution of the Federal Republic of Nigeria 1999 (as amended)*, the Federal High Court has sole jurisdiction to entertain matters or claims related to infringement of intellectual property.

Given that the issue of the judicial determination of indemnity claims for intellectual property infringement is novel in the context of Nigeria's jurisprudence *vis-à-vis* the 2017 FIDIC General Conditions, it will be interesting to see which argument or interpretation the courts will uphold in determining the question whether a claim of indemnity for a contracting party's infringement of intellectual property belonging to a non-contracting third party is determinable by the Engineer, the DAAB or arbitration. The continuous evaluation of the implications of either arguments or interpretations leads to extended legal analysis beyond the scope of this chapter.

Nevertheless, it is clear that to the extent that the determination of claims involving the infringement of intellectual and industrial property rights is concerned, the Federal High Court has exclusive jurisdiction over every other court by virtue of the *Constitution*, the *Copyrights Act*, the *Patents and Designs Act* and the *Trademarks Act*. The courts will likely exercise jurisdiction over indemnity claims for intellectual property infringement belonging to a non-contracting third party, thus the Engineer's determination, the DAAB's adjudication and ICC's arbitration of such claims under sub-clauses 17.3, 20.1, 21.6 and 3.7.2 of the 2017 FIDIC General Conditions are inconsistent with extant Nigerian law.

9.5.3.1.2 Fraud

Section 14 of the *Advance Fee Fraud and Other Fraud Related Offences Act*[191] confers jurisdiction on the High Courts of the States, the High Court of the Federal Capital Territory and the Federal High Court to entertain fraud-related matters which are usually determined at criminal trials and not civil proceedings. The State (Federal Government

administrative roles in resolving trademark infringements: https://iclg.com/practice-areas/trade-marks-laws-and-regulations/nigeria (accessed on 4 March 2022).

191 Cap A6, LFN 2004.

or State Government) or its appropriate agency have the sole power to prosecute criminal cases in Nigerian courts. Thus, any fraud-related claims arising from sub-clause 1.15 [*Limitation of Liability*], sub-clause 2.3 [*Employer's Personnel or Other Contractors*], sub-clause 6.9(e) [*Contractor's Personnel*], sub-clause 8.8 [*Delay Damages*], sub-clause 11.10 [*Unfulfilled Obligations*], sub-clause 14.14 [*Cessation of Employer's Liability*], sub-clause 15.2.1(h) [*Termination for Contractor's Default*] and sub-clause 16.2.1(j) [*Termination by Contractor*] cannot be submitted to the Engineer's determination, adjudication or arbitration by virtue of the *Act*.

9.5.3.1.3 BANKRUPTCY ACT 1979[192]

Where a party to a contract becomes bankrupt and cannot perform their obligations due to such bankruptcy, the resolution of any dispute or matter arising therefrom lies within the exclusive jurisdiction of the Federal High Court sitting in its bankruptcy jurisdiction.[193] Thus, bankruptcy-related matters arising out of sub-clause 15.2.1(j) [*Termination for Contractor's Default*] and sub-clause 16.2.1(i) [*Termination by Contractor*] are generally not arbitrable under Nigerian law.

9.6 What Special Provisions in the Particular Conditions are desirable for consistency with applicable laws in Nigeria?

9.6.1 Limitation periods for 'Claims', 'claims' and Disputes

A 'Claim', as defined in sub-clause 1.1.6, 'means a request or assertion by one Party to the other Party for an entitlement or relief under any Clause of these Conditions or otherwise in connection with, or arising out of, the Contract or the execution of the Works'. From this definition, a 'Claim' is made for the purposes of determination by the Engineer. Under sub-clause 1.1.29, a Dispute arises where a party makes a 'claim' against another party which may entail a matter to be determined by the Engineer under these Conditions, or otherwise, and the respondent party or the Engineer rejects the 'claim', and the claiming party issues a Notice of Dissatisfaction (**NOD**) with the Engineer's determination.

The *Limitation Act* does not provide a specific definition for the words 'Claim' or 'claim' but merely prescribes a limitation period of six years for bringing an action arising out of a contract under s 7(1)(a) of the *Act*.[194] It is also worthy of note that the *Act* uses the words 'claim' and 'claiming' interchangeably or in the same sentence with the words 'cause of action' or 'action' to the extent that these words carry similar statutory meaning and effect.[195]

The word 'action' under the Interpretation Section of the *Act* 'includes any proceedings (other than criminal proceedings) in a court of law'.[196] The operative word here is

192 Cap B2, LFN 2004.

193 *Bankruptcy Act*, s 142. See also the *Constitution of the Federal Republic of Nigeria 1999 (as amended)*, s 251(j).

194 The limitation period for actions under a contract executed as a deed (instrument under seal) is 12 years: *Limitation Act*, s 11.

195 For example, see *Limitation Act*, s 3: 'For the purposes of this Act, a claim by way of set-off or counter-claim shall be deemed to be a separate action and to have been commenced on the same date as the action in which the set-off or counter-claim is pleaded'.

196 *Limitation Act*, s 68. Furthermore, '"Action" in the sense of a judicial proceeding ... includes recoupment, counterclaim, set-off, suit in equity, and *any other proceeding in which rights are determined*': Black's

'includes' (note the non-use of the word 'means'), which can be interpreted to mean that other kinds of proceedings, except criminal proceedings, fall within the definition of action for the purposes of applying the statutory limitation periods. Adjudication has been defined as a quasi-judicial proceeding where a neutral third party gives a decision, which is binding on the parties in dispute unless or until revised in arbitration or litigation.[197] This definition aids the categorisation of the DAAB's adjudication among 'any other proceedings in which rights are determined',[198] and justifies the application of the *Limitation Act* to the proceedings in an adjudication by the DAAB.

Thus, with respect to the determination of a Dispute, the DAAB's adjudication falls under the definition of action and is therefore subject to limitation periods as prescribed by the *Act*. In other words, the statutory limitation period for an action founded on contract as per the FIDIC General Conditions is applicable to Disputes. It is not in contention that the long title and other relevant sections of the *Act* provide for the application of the *Act* to arbitral proceedings.

It can also be deduced from the foregoing definitions that the limitation period for actions founded on contract under the *Limitation Act* is not applicable to 'Claims' or 'claims' to be determined by the Engineer, and therefore, except where such 'Claims' or 'claims' metamorphose into Disputes to be determined by the DAAB's adjudication, the limitation periods for bringing a 'Claim' or 'claim' to be determined by the Engineer is governed by the contract (FIDIC General Conditions) and not the *Act*.

Sub-clause 21.4.1 of the 2017 FIDIC General Conditions provides a time limit (a limitation period) of 42 days between the issuance of a NOD and the referral to adjudication by the DAAB, failure of which renders the NOD invalid and inoperative. This sub-clause, as far as the Nigerian statute of limitations is concerned, has abridged the limitation period for bringing actions for a contractual entitlement or relief. While it is certain that parties cannot extend the statutory limitation period for actions via their contract,[199] the *Act* is silent on whether parties can agree to abridge the limitation period for bringing actions. In addition, there is no judicial authority in Nigeria which directly decided on the issue of abridgment of limitation periods by parties via their contract.[200] On the one hand, it is arguable that the limitation period of 42 days is inconsistent with the provisions of the *Act* which limits actions (in this case DAAB's adjudication) for contractual claims to be instituted within six years (or 12 years in the case of a contract executed as a deed/under seal), hence sub-clause 21.4.1 is unenforceable. The Supreme Court of Nigeria has generally held that a question bordering on the issue of 'limitation of action ... is not a matter of *practice or procedure*, but rather *a question of law as contained in relevant statutes*'.[201]

Law Dictionary, 10th ed, 35 (citing *Uniform Commercial Code* (*UCC*) § 1 – 201[b][1]).

197 www.fenwickelliott.com/sites/default/files/nick_gould_-_adjudication_and_adr_-_an_overview_matrics_paper.indd_.pdf 7 and 22 (accessed on 16 November 2021).

198 Black's Law Dictionary, *above* n196.

199 It is only a court in limited circumstances that can extend a limitation period. See *Limitation Act*, s 63. The *Act* is silent on whether a court can abridge the limitation period.

200 There is an abundance of judicial authorities where the courts held that actions instituted after the expiration of the limitation periods are statute-barred. See the following cases: *Adetula v Akinyosoye* (2017) 16 NWLR (pt. 1592) 492, 515, [A]–[C], 520, [G]–[H], CA; *Nasir v Civil Service Commission, Kano* (2007) 5 NWLR (pt. 1190) 253, 266–270, [F]–[D], SC; *Atolagbe v Awuni* (1997) 9 NWLR (pt. 522) 536, 591–592, [H]–[C], SC; *Egbe v Adefarasin* (1985) 1 NWLR (pt. 3) 549, 551.

201 *Owners of the MV 'Arabella' v Nigerian Agricultural Insurance Cooperation* (2008) 11 NWLR (pt. 1097) 182 at 210, paras D–E, SC. See also *Corona Schiffah R. MBH & Co. v Emespo J. Continental Ltd* (2002)

By implication, there is a chance that the courts may not uphold the limitation period of 42 days for referring a Dispute to the DAAB because the Supreme Court has also held that 'limitation statutes are laws that fix certain periods within which actions must be brought or proceedings taken'.[202] On the other hand, it leaves to conjecture whether Nigerian courts might be open to enforcing the abridged limitation period for the DAAB's adjudication of Disputes given the peculiarities of the construction industry and the advanced technicalities involved in operating highly specialised construction contracts such as the FIDIC rainbow suite. This is because there is no direct judicial pronouncement that upholds the parties' freedom to contract to abridge the limitation period of an action despite the provisions of the *Limitation Act* prescribing a longer limitation period.

This uncertainty surrounding the judicial enforceability of the 42-day limitation period for the DAAB's adjudication is of particular concern as it creates potential landmines for the operation of the FIDIC General Conditions in the event of major contractual disputes between the parties in Nigeria. So far, there is no known dispute on the applicability of the 42-day limitation period and it is unsure how Nigerian courts will treat this conflict in the light of the doctrine of parties' freedom of contract as it applies in other common law jurisdictions.[203]

Drafters of FIDIC contracts for use in Nigeria need to be aware of this issue of limitation periods as it may have implications for actions founded on contractual claims under s 7(1)(a) of the *Limitation Act*.

9.6.2 The law of the seat of arbitration under sub-clause 21.6

The FIDIC Guidance for the Preparation of Particular Conditions recommends that '[f]or major projects tendered internationally, it is desirable that the place of arbitration be situated in a country other than that of the Employer or Contractor'.[204] It further recommends that such country should have a modern and liberal arbitration law and be a signatory to the *New York Convention* for easy enforcement of the award. This provision implies that despite the governing law of the contract being the Laws of the Federation of Nigeria, the applicable arbitration law should be that of a neutral country, that is, neither the country of the Employer nor the Contractor. This provision appears to be in conformity with Section 32(1)(a) of the new *Arbitration and Mediation Act* which allows parties to an arbitration agreement to designate the seat of the arbitration. Also, Section 32(1)(b) of the new *Act* empowers an arbitral or other institution (e.g. the court) or other person to designate a place as the seat of the arbitration where mandated for that purpose by the parties to the arbitration agreement. However, Sections 32(1)(c) and 32(2) of the new *Act* mandate the

---

3 NWLR (pt. 753) 205 at 209, CA.

202 *Atolagbe v Awuni* (1997) 9 NWLR (pt. 522) 536,590, paras G–H, SC.

203 For example, the limitation laws of the Canadian jurisdictions of Alberta, Ontario and Saskatchewan allow parties to extend statutory limitation periods via their contracts. While Ontario law allows parties to abridge the statutory limitation periods, Albertan law prohibits parties to contract to abridge statutory limitation periods. Furthermore, while British Columbia and Manitoba laws are unclear as to whether parties could extend limitation periods, it is unsettled in British Columbia, Manitoba and Saskatchewan whether parties can agree to abridge statutory limitation periods: www.mondaq.com/canada/contracts-and-commercial-law/1011726/can-a-statutory-limitation-period-be-varied-by-agreement (accessed on 22 March 2022).

204 See Notes on the Preparation of Special Provisions, FIDIC Guidance for the Preparation of Special Provisions, 52.

arbitral tribunal to designate any place in Nigeria as the seat of the arbitration where the parties failed to designate the seat in their arbitration agreement. Furthermore, where the parties failed to designate the seat of the arbitration in their arbitration agreement, Section 32(2) of the new *Act* specifically allows the arbitral tribunal to designate a place in another country as the seat of the arbitration, having regard to the country with the closest connection to the parties and their transaction, the governing law of the contract and the governing law of the arbitration. This is an improvement in Nigeria's arbitration law as no such provisions were contained in the old *Arbitration and Conciliation Act*.

It has been noted earlier that the referral of a contractual dispute to arbitration in a foreign jurisdiction and, perhaps, the governing of such dispute by a foreign arbitration law or the rules of an international arbitral institution by virtue of the arbitration clause are not generally viewed by Nigerian courts as an ouster of their jurisdiction.[205] Although the general judicial attitude is supportive of the development of arbitration, the cases cited in section 9.4.1 of this chapter suggest that Nigerian courts are loath to allow the application of a foreign law where doing so will be inimical to public policy or ultimately enforce an absurdity, fraud or illegality. Thus, based on the foregoing, it is open to conjecture as to whether Nigerian courts will allow the application of a foreign arbitration law in a contract for the procurement of critical infrastructure in Nigeria such as airports or seaports and the procuring entity (Employer) is a public entity, considering that the arbitration was agreed by the parties to take place in a foreign forum. But it is likely that Nigerian courts will not readily enforce an award delivered under a foreign arbitration law with respect to a contract for the construction of a federal airport or seaport because the application of a foreign arbitration law for such public infrastructure may be regarded as inimical to public policy. Possible public policy considerations in this context include the nature of the Parties (whether a public entity is a Party) and the nature of the contract (whether it is a public contract). Note that the *Arbitration and Mediation Act* is a new law which the courts have not yet had the opportunity to interprete Section 32 of the new *Act* vis-à-vis the court's inclination towards protecting public policy.

Thus, in the light of this issue and the attitude of the courts to protect public policy, it is difficult to take a firm position because Nigeria's jurisdiction on this point is uncertain, coupled with the fact that Nigeria is not yet a signatory to the *Hague Convention of 30 June 2005 on the Choice of Court Agreement*. This is despite the fact that Nigeria is a signatory to the *New York Convention*. A possible solution to avoid a challenge on grounds of repugnance to public policy in the courts of the respondent country may be to apply to enforce the monetary award at the courts of the foreign forum of the arbitration against the assets of the respondent country hosted by the country of the forum of arbitration. Even this solution will be difficult to achieve as challenges regarding economic sovereignty, especially for counties regarded as the Global South, may begin to arise. Aside from this proposed solution, based on the cases discussed in section 9.4.1, there is a likelihood that Nigerian courts will not enforce the arbitral award for a dispute arising out of a contract for the provision of public infrastructure in Nigeria on grounds that it is inimical to public policy.

205 *Bill & Brothers Ltd & Ors v Dantata & Sawoe Construction Co. (Nig) Ltd & Ors* (2015) LPELR-24770(CA), 10–12; *R.C. Omeaku & Sons Ltd v Rainbownet Ltd* (2014) 6 NWLR (pt. 1401) 516, 534 and 535; *Lagos State Water Corporation v Sakamort Construction (Nig) Ltd* (2011) 12 NWLR (pt. 1262) 569, 599.

9.7 Summary of applicable legislation for Nigerian governing law of the contract

Except where otherwise stated, the following statutes are federal legislation.

9.7.1 Entry into a construction contract

Contracts generally	*Law Reform (Contracts) Act* *Statute of Frauds 1677*, s 4 (this 'received' English Law is applicable in Nigeria as a Statute of General Application which is a law that was operational in England on 1 January 1900) Contracts Laws of the various 36 States may also be applicable ((e.g. *Lagos State Law Reform (Contracts) Law 2015; Delta State Contracts Law*)) *Federal Competition and Consumer Protection Act 2018*, s 124 (right to fair dealing); s 125 (false, misleading or deceptive representation); s 127 (unfair, unreasonable or unjust contract terms); s 129 (prohibition of certain restrictive transactions/terms/ conditions;[1] ss 130–131 (rights to good quality and safe goods and services); s 132 (implied warranty of quality)
Construction contracts	*Public Procurement Act 2007* *Public Procurement Regulations for Goods and Works 2007* *Public Procurement Regulations for Consultants' Services 2007*[2] Some States have also enacted public procurement laws to govern public contracts within their respective jurisdictions where the Employer (Procuring Entity) is the State Government (e.g. *Delta State Public Procurement Law 2020* (applicable in Delta State); *Lagos State Public Procurement Law 2021* (applicable in Lagos State); *Rivers State Public Procurement Law 2008* (applicable in Rivers State), etc. See footnote 34)

9.7.2 Operation of a construction contract

Force majeure	*Public Procurement Regulations for Goods and Works 2007*, s 158 *Law Reform (Contracts) Act*, ss 2, 3 and 4 which provide for frustrated contracts may also be applicable
Hardship	While there is no specific law on hardship in contracts, the *Law Reform (Contracts) Act*, ss 2, 3 and 4 which provide for frustrated contracts may also be applicable
Guarantees under forms of Security (Tender Security, Demand Guarantee, Surety Bond, Advance Payment Guarantee, Retention Money Guarantee, Payment Guarantee by Employer)	*Public Procurement Act*, ss 19(g) and 36 (Contract Performance Guarantee) and ss 26 and 35 (Bank Guarantees) *Asset Management Corporation of Nigeria Act 2010*, s 6(1)(i), (k), (o) and (r)

9.7.3 Termination of a construction contract

Frustration	*Law Reform (Contracts) Act*, ss 2, 3 and 4 On applicable contract laws on frustration in some States, see also the *Lagos State Law Reform (Contracts) Law 2015*, ss 7 and 8 (applicable in Lagos State) and the *Delta State Contracts Law*, s 8 (applicable in Delta State)
Bankruptcy, insolvency, liquidation	*Bankruptcy Act 1992, LFN 2004*, particularly s 5 (bankruptcy of a firm carrying on business in Nigeria) *Bankruptcy Rules – 1st Schedule to the Bankruptcy Act* *Companies and Allied Matters Act (CAMA) No. 3 of 2020*, particularly ss 704–709 (insolvency of companies), ss 585–595 (liquidators), s 679 (notification of liquidation) and s 683 (information on pending liquidation and disposal of unclaimed assets) *Asset Management Corporation of Nigeria Act 2010* *Nigerian Deposit Insurance Corporation Act 2006* (particularly applicable where the Employer is a bank or other deposit-taking financial institution)

9.7.4 Dispute resolution

Limitation periods	*Limitation Act No. 88 of 1966* The *Limitation Act* once applied throughout the Federation until many States started enacting their own limitation statutes (e.g. *Lagos State Limitation Law, Cross River State Limitation Law, Bayelsa State Limitation Law*, etc.). The *Limitation Act* is still applicable to the Federal Capital Territory, Abuja (which was created by military decree in 1975) as well as a contract in any State that prescribes Nigerian Law as the governing law of the contract
Liability	*Law Reform (Contracts) Act*, s 4 See also the *Lagos State Law Reform (Contracts) Act*, ss 6 and 8 applicable in Lagos State
Arbitration	*Arbitration and Mediation Act 2023* *Arbitration Rules – First Schedule to the Arbitration and Mediation Act 2023* *Convention on the Recognition and Enforcement of Foreign Arbitral Awards ('New York Convention') – Second Schedule to the Arbitration and Mediation Act 2023* *Arbitration Proceedings Rules 2020 – Third Schedule to the Arbitration and Mediation Act 2023* Some States have enacted their own arbitration laws (e.g. *Lagos State Arbitration Law 2009, Rivers State Arbitration Law 2019, Kano State Arbitration Law, Kaduna State Arbitration Law*, etc.)

1 Waiver of right to return defective goods, avoidance of an Undertaking's statutory obligations, authorization to execute unlawful contractual provisions, exemption/limitation of an Undertaking's liability for losses attributable its gross negligence, assumption of risk or liability by a Consumer for a loss, imposition of obligations on Consumer to pay damages for or assume the risk of handling of goods displayed by a Supplier, acknowledgement of absence of pre-contractual representations/warranties, and deposition of certain documents/property with an Undertaking including identity documents, bank cards, bank account numbers and identification numbers).

2 These *Regulations* may be relevant to the regulation of the Engineer because FIDIC treats the Engineer as a Consultant vide the recommendation in the FIDIC Guidance for the Preparation of Particular Conditions

(Clause 3) that the Employer and the Engineer use the form of agreement known as FIDIC Clients/Consultants Model Services Agreement, Fifth Edition, 2017.

9.8 Summary of applicable legislation if the Site/Country is in Nigeria

9.8.1 Operation of a construction contract

Registration and administration of professionals – Engineers, Architects, Quantity Surveyors, Building Surveyors, Surveyors	*Engineers (Registration, etc.) (Amendment) Act, Cap E11, LFN 2004* *Architects (Registration, etc.) Act, Cap A19, LFN 2004* *Builders (Registration, etc.) Act, Cap B13, LFN 2004* *Surveyors Registration Council of Nigeria Act, No. 44 of 1989, LFN 2004* *Estate Surveyors and Valuers (Registration, etc.) Act 1975, LFN 2004* *Quantity Surveyors (Registration, etc.) (Amendment) Act 2016*
Registration/licensing of Contractors and subcontractors	*Public Procurement Act 2007*, s 6(1)(f) *Public Procurement Regulations for Goods and Works 2007*
Subcontractors	*Public Procurement Act 2007*, s 16(24) and (25) *Public Procurement Regulations for Goods and Works 2007*
Use of liens/assignment of debts	*Bankruptcy Act*, ss 43, 45, 46, 47, 48, 49, 55 and 56 *Asset Management Corporation of Nigeria*, ss 33(1), 32(2), 33(3)–(4) and 34(2) *Judicature Act*, s 25(6) (this 'received' English Law is applicable in Nigeria as a Statute of General Application which is a law that was operational in England on 1 January 1900)
Labour	*Labour Act 1971, LFN 2004* *Employees' Compensation Act, Cap E7A, LFN 2004* *Factories Act, No. 16 of 1987, Cap F1, LFN 2004* *Child Rights Act 2003* *Lagos State Construction Workers Safety Law 2015* (applicable in Lagos State, Nigeria)
Design/moral rights	*Patents and Designs Act 1971, Cap P2, LFN 2004*
Copyright	*Copyrights Act, Cap. C28, LFN 2004*
The product being produced from the Works	*Patents and Designs Act 1971, Cap P2, LFN 2004*
First Nation people's land rights	*Constitution of the Federal Republic of Nigeria 1999 (as amended)* *Land Use Act 1978* *African Charter on Human and Peoples' Rights (Ratification and Enforcement) Act Cap A9, LFN 2004* *Fundamental Rights (Enforcement Procedure) Rules 2009* Some Nigerian States have enacted subsidiary laws that govern indigenous peoples' land rights within their respective jurisdictions (e.g. *Delta State Land Use Law*; *Delta State Native Lands Acquisition Law*; *Lagos State Acquisition of Land by Aliens Law*; *Land Use Act and Subsidiary Legislation made by the Government of Lagos State*, etc.)
Planning	*Nigerian Urban and Regional Planning Act* Nigerian States have enacted subsidiary laws, substantially adapted from the foregoing federal *Act*, that govern urban and physical planning within their respective jurisdictions (e.g. *Delta State Urban and Regional Planning Law*; *Lagos State Urban and Regional Planning (Amendment) Act 2019*, etc.)

Work affecting adjacent property to the Site	*Land Use Act*, ss 5(b) and 51, which empowers the Governor of a State to grant a right of occupancy and appurtenant easements for land may be a basis for the holder of a certificate of occupancy to challenge construction works that negatively impact on his/her land and his/her right to an easement
Heritage	*National Commission for Museums and Monuments Act, Cap N19, LFN 2004*
Environment	*National Environmental Standards, Regulation and Enforcement Agency (Establishment) Act 2007* *Environmental Impact Assessment Act, Cap E12, LFN 2004* *Harmful Waste (Special Criminal Provisions, etc) Act, Cap H1, LFN 2004* *National Environmental (Construction Sector) Regulations, SI No. 19, 2011* *National Environmental (Permitting and Licensing System) Regulations, SI No. 19, 2009* *National Environmental (Electrical/Electronic Sector) Regulations, SI No. 23, 2011* *National Environmental (Standards for Telecommunications and Broadcast Facilities) Regulations, SI No. 11, 2011* *The Environmental Guidelines and Standards for the Petroleum Industry in Nigeria (EGASPIN) 2020*
Local procurement	*Nigerian Oil and Gas Industry Content Development Act 2010* *Public Procurement Act 2007*, s 34 *Public Procurement Regulations for Goods and Works 2007*, 2nd Schedule *Regulations on National Content Development for the Nigerian Electricity Supply Industry 2013* *Guidelines for the Development of Local Content in the Nigerian Electricity Supply Industry 2013*
Public procurement	*Public Procurement Act 2007* *States Public Procurement Laws* (e.g. Lagos, Delta, Kaduna, Kano, Anambra, Rivers, Ondo, etc. See footnote 34) *Finance Act 2020* *Federal Competition and Consumer Protection Act*, s 107 (prohibition of price-fixing); s 108 (prohibition of conspiracy to undermine the integrity of the bidding process); s 109 (prohibition of bid-rigging) *Public Procurement Regulations for Goods and Works 2007* *Public Procurement Regulations for Consultants' Services 2007* (see 'Construction contracts' above) *Executive Order 001 of 2017 on the Promotion of Transparency and Efficiency in the Business Environment*
Building and construction permits, execution of construction work, standard of construction work	*Standards Organization of Nigeria Act, Cap S9, LFN 2004* *Nigerian Standards for Construction Materials and Building Manufacturing Engineering* (made pursuant to the *Standards Organization of Nigeria Act*) *National Building Code 2006*

Health and safety	*Labour Act 1971, LFN 2004* *Employees' Compensation Act, Cap E7A, LFN 2004* *Factories Act, Cap F1, LFN 2004* *National Environmental Standards, Regulation and Enforcement Agency (Establishment) Act 2007* *Nuclear Safety and Radiation Protection Act, Cap N142, LFN 2004* *The Nigerian Minerals and Mining Act 2011,* Part VIII (makes provision for inquiries into occupational accidents at mine project sites) *Petroleum Industry Act 2020* *First Aid Boxes (Prescribed Standards) Order 1959* *Factories (Notification of Dangerous Occurrences) Regulations 1961* *Factories (Woodworking Machinery) Regulations 1958* *Factories (Registration, etc., Fees) Regulations 2007* *Declaration of Industrial Diseases Notice 1956* *Lifting and Allied Work Equipment (Safety) Regulations 2018* *Nigerian Electricity Health and Safety Code 2014* *Nigerian Electricity Health and Safety Standards Manual 2008* *Mineral Oils (Safety) Regulations 2020* *Nigerian Basic Ionizing Radiation Regulations 2003* *Nigerian Safety and Security of Radioactive Sources Regulations 2006* *Nigerian Transportation of Radioactive Sources Regulations 2006* *Nigerian Naturally Occurring Radioactive Materials (NORM) Regulations 2008* *Nigerian Radiation Safety in Industrial Irradiator Regulations 2008* *Guide for Maintenance Engineers and Technicians* *Guide for the Provision of Dosimetry Service in Nigeria* *Guide for Licensing of Nuclear Research Reactor Operators in Nigeria* *Guide for Licensing of Gamma Irradiation Facility in Nigeria* *National Building Code 2006* (see 'Building and construction permits, execution of construction work, standard of construction work') *Lagos State Construction Workers Safety Law* (applicable in Lagos State, Nigeria) *Lagos State Safety Commission Law 2011* (applicable in Lagos State, Nigeria) International Labour Organization ISO Standards and Codes adopted by extant laws of Nigeria and applicable to the construction sector (e.g. *C155 – Occupational Safety and Health 1981; C019 – Equality of Treatment (Accident Compensation) 1925; C081 – Labour Inspection Convention 1947; C045 – Underground Work (Women) Convention 1935; Occupational Health and Safety Management – General Guidelines for Safe Working During the COVID-19 Pandemic*)
Calibration of testing apparatus, equipment and instruments	*Weights and Measures Act, Cap W3, LFN 2004* *Lifting and Allied Work Equipment (Safety) Regulation 2018* *Weights and Measures (Legal Metrology and Related Services) Regulations 2012* *National Building Code 2006* (see 'Building and construction permits, execution of construction work, standard of construction work')

Ownership of Plant and Materials	*Sale of Goods Act 1893* (this 'received' English Law is applicable in Nigeria as a Statute of General Application which is a law that was operational in England on 1 January 1900. A number of states have enacted their own similar laws, including Abia State, Bayelsa State, Benue State, Lagos State, Ogun State, Ondo State and the Federal Capital Territory, Abuja. However, the *Act* remains applicable in some eastern and northern States)
Employer's sale of Contractor's Equipment, surplus material, wreckage and Temporary Works	*Sale of Goods Act 1893* (see 'Ownership of Plant and Materials') *Pawnbrokers Act 1964*, Cap 531 Laws of FCT Nigeria 2007 (a federal Act applicable in the FCT Abuja and such States that have not enacted a similar law. Some States have enacted their own laws governing pawning within their jurisdictions, e.g. *Lagos State Pawnbrokers Law, Cross River State Pawnbrokers Law*, etc.)
Insurance	*Insurance Act, Cap I17 LFN 2004*, s 65 *Pension Reform Act 2014* *Motor Vehicle (Third Party Insurance) Act, Cap M22* *Motor Vehicles (Third Party Liability Insurance) (ECOWAS Brown Card Scheme) Act, Cap M23, LFN 2004* *National Health Insurance Scheme Act, Cap N42, LFN 2004* *Employees' Compensation Act, Cap E7A, LFN 2004* *Lagos State Construction Workers Safety Law 2015* (applicable in Lagos State, Nigeria)
Statutory rights that coexist with contractual rights	*Constitution of the Federal Republic of Nigeria 1999 (as amended)* *Public Procurement Act 2007* *Public Procurement Regulations for Goods and Works 2007* *Public Procurement Regulations for Consultants' Services 2007* (see 'Construction contracts') *Law Reform (Torts) Act*, s 10 (implied terms in a contract)
Liability for defective work	*National Building Code 2006* (see 'Building and construction permits, execution of construction work, standard of construction work')
Liability for nuisance	*Penal Code,* ss 192 and 194 (applicable in the states in Northern Nigeria) *Criminal Code,* s 234 (applicable in the states in Southern Nigeria) *Explosives Act, Cap E18, LFN 2004* *National Environmental Standards, Regulation and Enforcement Agency (Establishment) Act 2007,* s 22 *National Environmental (Noise Standards and Control) Regulations 2009*

9.8.2 Termination of a construction contract

Bankruptcy, insolvency, liquidation	*Bankruptcy Act 1992, LFN 2004,* particularly s 5 (bankruptcy of a firm carrying on business in Nigeria) *Bankruptcy Rules – 1st Schedule to the Bankruptcy Act* *Companies and Allied Matters Act (CAMA) No. 3 of 2020*, particularly ss 704–709 (insolvency of companies), ss 585–595 (liquidators), s 679 (notification of liquidation) and s 683 (information on pending liquidation and disposal of unclaimed assets) *Asset Management Corporation of Nigeria Act 2010* *Nigerian Deposit Insurance Corporation Act 2006* (particularly applicable where the Employer is a bank or other deposit-taking financial institution in Nigeria)

Liability generally for the total or partial collapse of structures	*Law Reform (Torts) Act*, s 10 (duty of care/liability arising from implied terms of a contractual obligation) *National Building Code 2006*, s 7.34 (see 'Building and construction permits, execution of construction work, standard of construction work')

9.8.3 Dispute resolution

Limitation periods	*Limitation Act No 88 of 1966* See 'Limitation periods' in section 9.7.4

9.9 Summary of applicable legislation if the 'seat' of the dispute determination is Nigeria

Dispute resolution	*Constitution of the Federal Republic of Nigeria 1999 (as amended)*, ss 6(6)(b), 251, 257 and 272 (with respect to litigation and/or referral to arbitration via traditional courts) *Admiralty Jurisdiction Act* (for maritime construction-related contracts) *Civil Aviation Act* (for aviation construction-related contracts)
Limitation periods	*Limitation Act No 88 of 1966* See 'Limitation periods' in section 9.7.4
Arbitration	*Arbitration and Mediation Act 2023* *Arbitration Rules – First Schedule to the Arbitration and Mediation Act 2023* *Convention on the Recognition and Enforcement of Foreign Arbitral Awards ('New York Convention') – Second Schedule to the Arbitration and Mediation Act 2023* *Arbitration Proceedings Rules 2020 – Third Schedule to the Arbitration and Mediation Act 2023* Some States have enacted their own arbitration laws (e.g. *Lagos State Arbitration Law 2009*; *Rivers State Arbitration Law 2019*; *Kano State Arbitration Law*; *Kaduna State Arbitration Law*, etc.)

9.10 Issues that a court or arbitrator may construe differently than expected from the words of the Contract because of local law or custom

9.10.1 Limitation period for liability

As highlighted in section 9.6.1, the limitation period for actions (such as the DAAB's adjudication) and arbitrations in Nigeria is governed by the *Limitation Act.* The submissions made in respect of limitation periods for adjudication and arbitration in section 9.6.1 also apply to the limitation period for an action for liability. The abridgement of the limitation period for liability by parties in their contract is a novel issue and it will be interesting to see which way the courts will determine, bearing in mind the general pronouncements of the Supreme Court on the issue of limitation of actions in cases of the *MV 'Arabella'* and *Atolagbe v Awuni* cited in section 9.6.1.

9.10.2 Appeal to a court may mean that the right to arbitration is lost

Sub-clause 21.4 of the 2017 FIDIC General Conditions provides for the settlement of disputes via arbitration. Generally, Nigerian courts are increasingly disposed to supporting the development of domestic and international arbitration and are statutorily required to seldom intervene in arbitral processes and proceedings except where allowed by law.[206] Thus, under the new *Arbitration and Mediation Act*, where a party to an arbitration agreement commences an action in court in any matter which is the subject of the arbitration agreement, any party to the said arbitration agreement may, at any time after appearance, apply to the court to stay the proceedings pending arbitration.[207] However, this application must be brought before any of the parties *submit* their first statement on the substance of the dispute.[208]

The meaning of a party *submitting* its first statement on the substantive dispute is somewhat unclear. Is it a mere filing of the party's statement on the substantive dispute or the party's actual giving of testimony/evidence on the substantive case? In practice, where a claimant institutes an action in court on an arbitrable dispute arising out of an agreement containing an arbitration clause, the claimant is required to file originating court processes, namely a writ of summons, statement of claim, witness statement on oath and documents or other evidence that such party intends to rely upon in proving his/her case. The witness statement on oath of the claimant can be regarded as the first statement on the substantive dispute which the claimant will naturally move to be adopted as the claimant's evidence/testimony in the case. In other words, the adoption of the witness statement on oath by the claimant is the submission of first statements on the substance of the dispute. From a procedural and technical standpoint, the jurisdiction of the court to stay proceedings pending arbitration cannot be legally activated without the claimant first filing these originating processes which ensure that the court is seised of the case to dispense justice.

Prior to and around the period when the old *Arbitration and Conciliation Act* came into force, the only originating process necessary for instituting a suit on a contentious dispute was a writ of summons and statement of claim. It was later during the proper hearing of suit that the claimant gives his first statements on the substance of the dispute via oral testimony as evidence in support of his case. In contemporary times, most Rules of Courts require that the claimant's witness statement on oath are filed alongside the writ of summons and statement of claim to institute the suit pursuant to the practice known as frontloading. If Section 5(1) of the new *Arbitration and Mediation* Act is to be strictly interpreted, there are risks of a *fait accompli* in the sense that the right of arbitration could be extinguished because the witness statement on oath (the first statement on the substantive suit) has already been filed prior to commencement of hearing.

To have a full grasp of the intricacies of this delicate legal issue, it is pertinent to understand the provisions and judicial interpretations of Sections 4(1) and 5(1) of the old *Act* vis-à-vis the implications of Section 5(1) of the new *Act*. Section 4(1) of the old Act contains a similar provision to Section 5(1) of the new *Act* regarding parties submitting their first statements and therefore needs no repetition. However, Section 5(1) of the old *Act* provides that an application seeking the court to refer the dispute to arbitration must be brought before the delivery of any pleadings or `taking any other steps in the proceedings'. Under the old *Act*, the consequence of 'taking any other steps' in the proceedings, other than applying for a stay of proceedings pending arbitration, could lead to the extinguishment of

206 *Arbitration and Mediation Act*, s 64; *Adamen Publishers (Nig.) Ltd v Abhulimen* (2016) 6 NWLR (pt. 1509) 431, 454 (CA).

207 *Arbitration and Mediation Act*, s 5(1).

208 *Ibid.*

the right of the parties to arbitration and the substantive case would have to be determined by the court despite the arbitration clause/agreement. In the celebrated case of *Obembe v Wemabod Estates Ltd.*,[209] the Supreme Court held that

> No stay was asked for by the defendants/respondents after they were served with the writ of summons. On the contrary, they accepted service of the statement of claim, filed their own statement of defence, testified in their defence, and took part in the proceedings until judgment was delivered. In order to get a stay, a party to a submission must have taken NO step in the proceedings. A party who makes any application whatsoever to the Court, even though it be merely an application for extension of time, takes a step in the proceedings. Delivery of a statement of defence is also a step in the proceedings (see *West London Diary Society Ltd. v Abbot* (1881) 44 L.T. 376). Moreover, if the Court has refused to stay an action, or if the defendant has abstained, as in the case in hand, from asking it to do so, the Court has seising of the dispute, and it is by its decision, and by its decision alone, that the rights of the parties are settled. (See *Doleman & Sons v Ossett Corporation* (1912) 3 K.B. (C.A.) 257 as per Fletcher-Moulton, L.J. at p.269; also *Hasting v Nigerian Railway Corporation* (1964) Lagos High Court Reports 135 at pp.136–137).[210]

Thirteen years later, the Supreme Court reiterated its position on this issue in *Kano State Urban Development Board (K.S.U.D.B.) v Fanz Construction Ltd.*[211]

In *Onward Enterprises Ltd v MV 'Matrix'*,[212] while the plaintiff/appellant filed a writ of summons, the defendant/respondent filed three separate applications asking the court (i) to release the defendants/respondents' vessel, (ii) to shift the vessel to anchorage and (iii) to stay proceedings pending arbitration in London. Relying on the *Wemabod* case, the Court of Appeal enumerated several scenarios constituting 'taking steps' in a proceeding:

> In order to get a stay [of proceedings pending arbitration], a party to a submission must have taken no step in the proceedings. A party who makes any application for extension of time takes a step in the proceedings. Delivery of a statement of defence is also a step in the proceedings. However, mere entering an appearance, be it conditional or unconditional, is not controlling or relevant to the party's right to rely on the arbitration clause inserted in the parties' agreement. On the contrary, it is in fact what happens after a party has entered an appearance that matters in determining whether or not such a party can still take advantage of the aforesaid arbitration clause. Steps in the proceedings have been held to include:
>
> (a) the filing of an affidavit in opposition to a summons for summary judgment;
> (b) service of a defence; and
> (c) an application to the court for leave to serve interrogatories, or for a stay pending the giving of security or costs, or for an order for discovery, or for an order for further and better particulars.
>
> In the instant case, the respondents had not done anything before the trial court to make them lose their right to apply for stay of proceedings under section 5 of the *Arbitration and Conciliation Act*.[213]

Thus, pursuant to the above judicial decisions based on the old *Act*, in order to avoid taking other steps that may extinguish the right to arbitration and enable the court to be seised

209 (1977) LPELR-2161(SC).

210 (1977) LPELR-2161(SC), 19–20.

211 (1990) LPELR-1659(SC).

212 (2010) 2 NWLR (pt. 1179) 530 (CA).

213 (2010) 2 NWLR (pt. 1179) 530, 551. See also *Confidence Insurance Ltd v Trustees of O.S.C.E* (1999) 2 NWLR (pt. 591) 373 (CA); *Niger Progress Ltd v North East Line Corporation* (1989) 3 NWLR (pt. 107) 68, 91–92 (SC).

of the substantive case, the aforementioned cases are instructive that a party would need to bring an application before the court seeking an order to refer the case to arbitration in accordance with the agreement and stay the proceedings in court pending arbitration. However, the aspect of 'taking other steps in the proceedings' has been omitted from the new *Act*, leaving only the aspect of parties `submitting their first statements on the substance of the dispute' under Section 5(1) of the new *Act*. This new provision is important because there are some interim/interlocutory applications to the court that are contentious and somewhat touch on the substance of the dispute, such as applications to preserve the *res* pending the substantive suit, that could influence a court to make a ruling with the effect that may extinguish the parties' right to arbitration and assume substantive jurisdiction over the dispute. This provision helps to limit such occurrences only to circumstances where either parties' submit their first statements on the substantive dispute.

Notwithstanding, the new *Act* – just like the old *Act* – did not expressly specify the fate of the parties' right to arbitration where they submit their first statements/testimonies before applying for stay of proceedings pending arbitration. One viewpoint is that the applicability of the above cases of *Obembe* and *MV 'Matrix'* still suffices only to the extent where the parties submit their first statements before applying for a stay of proceedings pending arbitration. By implication, the parties submitting their first statements before an applying for stay of proceedings pending arbitration can be regarded as the only statutorily recognized, procedural and practical step that parties could take which could extinguish their right to arbitration. Another viewpoint is that the failure to apply for stay of proceedings pending arbitration before submitting first statements is a mere technicality which should not extinguish on right to arbitration. This is because the validity, bindingness and enforceability of the arbitration agreement is statutorily guaranteed.[214]

Thus, the courts should refer the dispute to arbitration regardless since the issue somewhat borders on the court's substantive jurisdiction over the dispute where there is an arbitration agreement. More so, the new *Act* enjoins the courts to do all that is necessary to ensure the proper conduct of the arbitration.[215]

As at the time of writing, the courts have not had the opportunity to interprete Section 5(1) of the new *Act* and it would be interesting to see what the courts will hold in this circumstance. However, it is more practicable to argue in this new dispensation that the claimant will have to make an application seeking a stay of proceedings pending arbitration and avoid moving to adopt the statement on oath in evidence. On the other hand, if the claimant fails to make such application, the defendant can equally make such application seeking referral to arbitration in order to preclude the claimant from the earliest opportunity to give evidence in the substantive case.

9.11 Additional references for Nigeria

9.11.1 Internet

Laws of Nigeria (Policy and Legal Advocacy Centre [PLAC]). https://lawsofnigeria.placng.org/
Laws of the Federation (Law Pavilion). https://primsol.lawpavilion.com/laws-of-federation
Law Pavilion Electronic Law Reports (LPELR). https://primsol.lawpavilion.com/i-d

214 *Arbitration and Conciliation Act*, s 5(1).
215 *Ibid.*, s 1(4).

CHAPTER 10

Applying FIDIC Contracts in South Africa

Johan Beyers

CONTENTS

DOI: 10.4324/9781003206910-10

10.1 Outline of South Africa's legal environment

10.1.1 The constitutional structure of South Africa

South Africa is a constitutional democracy. The *Constitution of the Republic of South Africa*, 108 of 1996, which was promulgated on 18 December 1996 and took effect on 4 February 1997, establishes South Africa as a sovereign, democratic state[1] founded on the core values of human dignity and equality,[2] non-racialism and non-sexism,[3] the supremacy of the *Constitution* and the rule of law[4] and universal adult suffrage.[5]

The *Constitution* expressly provides that it is the supreme law of the country and that any law or conduct inconsistent with it is invalid.[6]

Legislative authority in the national sphere of government is vested in Parliament, whilst the provincial and local spheres are vested in provincial legislatures and municipal councils,[7] respectively. The Republic has nine Provinces.[8]

Executive authority vests in the presidency, with the President as the Head of State and head of the National Executive,[9] whilst judicial authority vests in the courts, as set out in section 10.1.3.

The *Bill of Rights*, contained in Chapter 2 of the *Constitution*, affirms the democratic values of human dignity, equality and freedom.[10] It applies to all law and binds the legislature, the executive, the judiciary and all organs of the State,[11] as well as natural and juristic persons.[12] It expressly protects a broad range of fundamental rights, including economic, administrative and environmental rights.

Section 36(1) of the *Constitution* provides that the rights in the *Bill of Rights* may be limited only in terms of law of general application to the extent that the limitation is reasonable and justifiable in an open and democratic society based on human dignity, equality and freedom, taking into account all relevant factors. Chapter 2 further provides[13] that, when applying a provision of the *Bill of Rights* to a natural or juristic person, a court, in order to give effect to a right in the *Bill*, must apply or, if necessary, develop the common law to the extent that legislation does not give effect to such right. Courts may also develop rules of the common law to limit such right, provided that the limitation is in accordance with section 36(1).

---

1 Section 1 of the *Constitution of the Republic of South Africa*, 108 of 1996.
2 Section 1(a) of the *Constitution*.
3 Section 1(b) of the *Constitution*.
4 Section 1(c) of the *Constitution*.
5 Section 1(d) of the *Constitution*.
6 Section 2 of the *Constitution*.
7 Section 43 of the *Constitution*.
8 Section 103 of the *Constitution*. The nine provinces of the republic are the Eastern Cape, the Free State, Gauteng, KwaZulu-Natal, Limpopo, Mpumalanga, Northern Cape, North West and the Western Cape.
9 Section 83 of the *Constitution*.
10 Section 7(1) of the *Constitution*.
11 Section 8(1) of the *Constitution*.
12 Section 8(2) of the *Constitution*.
13 Section 8(3) of the *Constitution*.

10.1.2 The legal system in South Africa

The South African legal system is a hybrid of civil and common-law principles which reflects the country's colonial past.[14]

The Cape of Good Hope was initially settled by the Dutch East India Company in 1652, resulting in the introduction of the law of Holland to the Cape. The substantive law of Holland at the time consisted of uncodified Germanic custom, substantially modified and supplemented by Roman law, mainly the compilations of Justinian.[15] Dutch commentators and the courts of Holland, together with influences of other continental jurists during the 16th and 17th centuries, contributed to the development of this system of Roman-Dutch common law.[16]

During 1795, pursuant to a war between France and England, England undertook to protect the Cape from the French and took control of the colony. A peace treaty between Britain and France in 1802 re-established Dutch rule of the colony. However, this was short-lived, and in 1806 the British took control of the Cape Colony and maintained its colonial rule until 1910. During the course of the South African War between 1899 and 1902, Britain extended its colonial reach to the remainder of South Africa. The South African Union was established in 1910 and the Republic of South Africa in 1961.

During the course of British occupation of South Africa, the English did not attempt to replace the existing Roman-Dutch legal system with English common law, but rather incrementally introduced certain portions of English common law, mainly through a system of binding precedent and the requirement that judges be members of the English bar.[17] Through legal precedent, English common law was gradually introduced and grafted onto the original Roman-Dutch rootstock, resulting in the development of a uniquely South African hybrid common-law system.

As a result of the historic influence of English law in the development of South African law, English court decisions, whilst not representing binding precedent, still have strong persuasive value provided that they do not offend fundamental principles of South African law.

The introduction of the *Constitution of the Republic of South Africa* in 1996 represented a further fundamental development of the South African legal system, in that it established a baseline of values against which all principles of the South African common law are to be measured and further developed by the South African courts.

The principal sources of South African law are thus represented by national, provincial and municipal legislation, including the *Constitution*; the decisions of the Constitutional Court, the Supreme Court of Appeal and the various divisions of the High Court of South Africa; and the South African common law. Provincial and municipal legislation is relevant to procurement, planning and the execution of works (permits, etc.).

---

14 See, with respect to what is set out in this section, Schreiner, 'The Contribution of English Law to South African Law; and the Rule of Law in South Africa', The Hamlyn Lectures, 19th Series (Juta & Co Ltd 1967), https://socialsciences.exeter.ac.uk/media/universityofexeter/schoolofhumanitiesandsocialsciences/law/pdfs/The_Contribution_of_English_Law_to_South_African_Law.pdf (accessed 4 April 2019).

15 *Ibid.*, 5.

16 *Ibid.*, 5.

17 See Brand, 'The Role of Good Faith, Equity and Fairness in the South African Law of Contract: The Influence of the Common Law and the Constitution' (2016) V27(2) *Stellenbosch Law Review* 238–253.

10.1.3 The court system in South Africa

The judicial authority of the Republic is constitutionally vested in the courts.[18] These courts are:[19]

- a The Constitutional Court
- b The Supreme Court of Appeal
- c The High Court of South Africa, and any High Court of Appeal that may be established by an Act of Parliament to hear appeals from any court of a status similar to the High Court of South Africa
- d The Magistrates' Courts, and
- e Any other court established or recognised in terms of an Act of Parliament, including any court of a status similar to either the High Court of South Africa or the Magistrates' Courts.

The Constitutional Court[20] is the highest court of the Republic and may decide constitutional matters and any other matter in respect whereof the Constitutional Court has granted leave to appeal on the grounds that the matter raises an arguable point of law of general public importance which ought to be considered by that court. This court consists of the Chief Justice of South Africa, the Deputy Chief Justice, and nine other judges[21] and has its seat in Johannesburg.[22] Any matter before the Constitutional Court must be heard by at least eight judges.[23]

The Supreme Court of Appeal may decide appeals in any matter arising from the High Court of South Africa or a court of a status similar to the High Court of South Africa[24] and is seated in Bloemfontein.[25] Proceedings in the Supreme Court of Appeal must ordinarily be presided over by five judges, but the President of the Supreme Court of Appeal may direct that a court be constituted by three judges.[26]

The relationship between the Constitutional Court and the Supreme Court of Appeal has been described by Mr Justice Brand as follows:[27]

> The Constitution also created a so-called 'twin apex' court system; that is, the Constitutional Court, which has the final say in constitutional matters, and the Supreme Court of Appeal, which is the highest court in non-constitutional matters. In accordance with the principles of stare decisis, these two courts thus bind all courts – including each other – in their respective fields of final jurisdiction.

18 Section 165(1) of the *Constitution*.
19 Section 166 of the *Constitution*.
20 Section 167(3) of the *Constitution*.
21 Section 167(1) of the *Constitution*.
22 *Superior Courts Act*, 10 of 2013, section 4(1)(b).
23 *Superior Courts Act*, 10 of 2013, section 12(1).
24 Section 168(3)(a) of the *Constitution*, except with respect to labour or competition matters to such an extent as may be determined by an Act of Parliament.
25 *Superior Courts Act*, 10 of 2013, section 5(1)(b).
26 *Superior Courts Act*, 10 of 2013, section 13(1).
27 Brand, 'The Role of Good Faith, Equity and Fairness in the South African Law of Contract: The Influence of the Common Law and the Constitution' (2016) V27(2) *Stellenbosch Law Review* 238–253.

The High Court of South Africa may decide any constitutional matter[28] and any other matter not assigned to another court by an Act of Parliament.[29] Since the jurisdictions of the Magistrate's Courts are constrained, relating both to the value and permissible subject matter of claims, the High Court usually operates as the court of first instance for the determination of disputes which arise within the context of an engineering or construction project, including as it relates to the supervision of arbitral proceedings and the review or enforcement of arbitral awards.

The High Court of South Africa consists of nine divisions, each situated in one of South Africa's nine Provinces.[30] A court of a division must be constituted before a single judge when sitting as a court of first instance for the hearing of any civil matter, but the Judge President may direct that up to three judges (the full court) hear a matter.[31]

An appeal against any decision of a division of the High Court as a court of first instance is subject to leave having been granted by such court.[32] Where such leave is granted, an appeal against a decision of a single judge lies either to the full court of that division or to the Supreme Court of Appeal. An appeal against any decision where the court consisted of more than one judge lies to the Supreme Court of Appeal.[33] Leave to appeal may, *inter alia*, only be given where the judge or judges concerned are of the opinion that the appeal would have a reasonable prospect of success or there is some other compelling reason why the appeal should be heard.[34]

10.2 The construction industry in South Africa

10.2.1 Overview

South Africa has a strong, well-developed construction industry with proven technical competence and large resourceful contractors capable of delivering complex mega projects. The industry is supported by a large body of competent construction professionals. South Africa self-produces all of its required strategic construction materials but relies on imported plants and equipment.[35]

The South African construction industry is a principal driver of socio-economic development and a key employment multiplier. During 2019, the value added by the construction sector accounted for around 4% of South Africa's GDP and the sector employed well over 1.3 million people.[36]

28 Except a matter that the Constitutional Court has agreed to hear directly in terms of section 167(6)(a) or that has been assigned by an Act of Parliament to another court of a status similar to the High Court of South Africa.

29 Section 169(1) of the *Constitution*.

30 *Superior Courts Act*, 10 of 2013, section 6(1).

31 *Superior Courts Act*, 10 of 2013, section 14(1).

32 *Superior Courts Act*, 10 of 2013, section 16(1).

33 *Superior Courts Act*, 10 of 2013, section 16(1).

34 *Superior Courts Act*, 10 of 2013, section 17(1).

35 Abimbola Olukemi Windapo and Keith Cattell, 'Perceptions of Key Construction and Development Challenges Facing the Construction Industry in South Africa', Proceedings of the 5th Built Environment Conference, 18–20 July 2010, 249; www.irbnet.de/daten/iconda/CIB_DC22754.pdf (accessed 30 November 2021).

36 C Veitch, 'The Construction Industry in South Africa', a report published by Who Owns Whom, 29 September 2020, www.whoownswhom.co.za/store/info/4877?segment=The+Construction+Industry+in+South+Africa) (accessed 30 November 2021).

However, despite its strategic importance, the construction industry has been suffering diminishing output and profitability since 2010 and was in distress prior to the onset of the COVID-19 pandemic. Its declining performance has been exacerbated by a reduction in government and private sector investment. Some local construction companies have diversified into other sectors, while others have gone out of business or sold their local construction business to focus on other markets. Construction companies under business rescue include Basil Read, Esor Construction and Group Five.[37]

10.2.2 Structure e.g. size of contractors, extent of subcontracting, international contractors

The total income of the South African construction industry in 2017 amounted to ZAR495.459 billion (US$ 31.9 billion).[38] This compares to a total income of ZAR169.249 billion (US$10.9 billion) in 2007.[39] Of the total income in 2017, 64.1% was comprised of two activities, namely 'construction of civil engineering structures' (40.0%) and 'construction of buildings' (23.8%).[40]

In 2017, the top 100 enterprises in the construction industry contributed 36.3% of the total income, the top 20 contributed 21.7% of the total income and the top five contributed 10.7% of the total income.

Total turnover of construction firms in 2017 was ZAR477.35 billion (US$30.7 billion), generating a net profit of R13.606 billion (US$0.9 billion) and an aggregate profit margin across all activities of 2.9%.[41] This margin compares to an achieved margin of 4% in 2007.[42]

The total number of persons formally employed in the construction industry at the end of June 2017 was 597,006.[43] 'Construction of civil engineering structures' employed the largest number of persons (210,808 or 35.3%), followed by 'construction of buildings' (124,176 or 20.8%), 'other building completion' (72,535 or 12.1%) and 'electrical contractors' (43,060 or 7.2%).[44] However, when informal employment is included, the construction industry is responsible for the employment of more than one million persons.[45]

As of October 2016, the market capitalisation of the top nine construction companies were reported as follows:[46] WBHO ZAR9.6 billion (US$620 million); Murray & Roberts ZAR4.1 billion (US$260 million); Raubex ZAR4.6 billion (US$300 million); Calgro M3 ZAR2.4 billion (US$150 million); Group Five ZAR2.6 billion (US$170 million); Aveng

37 *Ibid.*

38 R Maluleke, 'Construction Industry, 2017', a report published by Statistics South Africa, 2019, www.statssa.gov.za/publications/Report-50-02-01/Report-50-02-012017.pdf (accessed 30 November 2021).

39 *Ibid.*

40 *Ibid.*

41 Above, n38.

42 *Ibid.*

43 *Ibid.*

44 *Ibid.*

45 Nandi Mokoena and Precious Mathibe (eds), *Competition Challenges in African Construction Markets*, (African Competition Forum, November 2019), 45; www.compcom.co.za/wp-content/uploads/2020/02/African-Competition-Forum-Competition-challenges-in-African-construction-markets-A-study-across-East-and-Southern-Africa.pdf (accessed 30 November 2021).

46 Deveshnee Naidoo, Alwina Brand, Bianca Raghuber, Fiona Suburaman, Sarah Beukes and Tebogo Serepong, *SA Construction 4th Edition, Highlighting Trends in the South African Construction Industry*, a report published by PWC, November 2016, 5; www.pwc.co.za/en/assets/pdf/sa-construction-2016.pdf (accessed 30 November 2021).

ZAR2.9 billion (US$190 million); Stefanutti Stocks ZAR 0.9 billion (US$58 million); Basil Read ZAR0.3 billion (US$19 million); and Esor ZAR0.2 billion (US$13 million).

However, by 2021, of these nine top companies, three – Group Five, Basil Read and Esor – had been placed in business rescue, and Murray & Roberts was significantly restructured.

The largest South African construction firms are international contractors with operations throughout the world. WBHO, for example, operates offices throughout South Africa and in Botswana, Ghana and Mozambique, and has subsidiaries in Australia and the United Kingdom.[47]

Subcontracting in the South African construction industry is commonplace for both infrastructure and building projects, with up to 70% of building and 30% of civil construction projects being subcontracted out.[48] The most prevalent types of subcontracting are labour-only, trade contracting in the building sector and specialist subcontracting in the building and civil sectors.[49] The duration of typical subcontracts in the building industry is between three and six months, with the civil sector industry having longer duration subcontracts of about 12 months on average.[50]

Historically the public sector has accounted for the major part of the construction spend in the country. However, due to the faltering growth in the public sector, the private sector became the biggest investor in the civil construction industry for the first time ever in 2018, surpassing the investment of the government and parastatals.[51] In 2018, out of a total spend of ZAR430.206 billion (US$27.7 billion), the private sector accounted for ZAR225.238 billion (US$14.5 billion), whereas the combined spend of the government and state-owned enterprises amounted to only R204.878 billion (US$12.2 billion).[52]

10.2.3 Licensing/registration

Subject to the exceptions set out below, there is no general requirement that a contractor has to be licenced or registered in order to be permitted to conduct a construction business in South Africa.

The first exception is proffered by the *Housing Consumers Protection Measures Act*, 95 of 1998 (the *NHBRC Act*).

Section 10(1)(a) of the *NHBRC Act* provides that

> no person shall –
>
> (a) carry on the business of a home builder; or

47 See WBHO 'About Us' webpage, www.wbho.co.za/about-us/ (accessed 30 November 2021).

48 Construction Industry Development Board Report, 'Subcontracting in the South African Construction Industry; Opportunities for Development' (2013) i; https://pdf4pro.com/view/subcontracting-in-the-south-african-construction-2b5536.html (accessed 30 November 2021).

49 *Ibid.*

50 *Ibid.*

51 R Waterneyer and S Phillips, 'Public infrastructure delivery and construction sector dynamism in the South African economy', Policy paper for the National Planning Commission of the Department of Planning, Monitoring and Evaluation, 4 March 2020, 16; www.cesa.co.za/sites/default/files/Public%20Infrastructure%20delivery%20and%20Construction%20Sector%20Dynamism%20in%20RSA%20economy_giz%20npc%20initiative_Watermeyer%20Phillips%204%20March%202020.pdf (accessed 30 November 2021).

52 *Ibid.*, 17.

(b) receive any consideration in terms of any agreement with a housing consumer in respect of the sale or construction of a home,

unless that person is a registered home builder.

The purpose of the *Act* was described as follows by the Supreme Court of Appeal in *National Home Builders Registration Council and Another v Xantha Properties 18 (Pty) Ltd*:[53]

> The Act was designed to afford adequate housing for residents by ensuring that their homes were constructed by competent builders to approved standards. These objectives were sought to be achieved, first by s 10 (to ensure that homes are constructed by persons having the necessary competence); and secondly by s 14 (to enrol such homes and ensure that they are built to a prescribed level of structural and technical quality).

Where a contractor renders construction services in respect of the construction of any building which is intended, wholly or partially, for residential purposes, it is required to obtain the required registration with the National Home Builders Registration Council in advance of the commencement of construction works. Where a contractor fails to do so, section 10(1)(b) of the *NHBRC Act* disentitles it from recovering any payment in respect of construction work effected.

The commitment of the South African Courts to protect consumers within this context is illustrated by the decision of the Constitutional Court in *Cool Ideas 1186 CC v Hubbard and Another*.[54] This case concerned the attempted enforcement of an arbitral award by an unregistered contractor against a housing consumer for payment in respect of construction services performed. In refusing to enforce the arbitral award at the contractor's instance, the Court held that the enforcement of the award would disregard a clear statutory prohibition, would undermine the purpose of the legislation, and would be contrary to public policy.[55]

The second exception concerns contractors tendering for contracts in the public sector.

The *Construction Industry Development Board Act*, 38 of 2000 (*CIDB Act*), established the Construction Industry Development Board (**CIDB**). One of the objects of the CIDB is to promote, establish or endorse uniform standards and ethical standards that regulate the actions, practices and procedures of parties engaged in construction contracts.[56]

Section 16 of the *CIDB Act inter alia* provides that the CIDB is obliged to establish a national register of contractors, which categorises contractors in a manner that facilitates public sector procurement and promotes contractor development. This register of contractors must:

(a) Indicate the size and distribution of contractors operating within the construction industry
(b) Indicate the volume, nature and performance of contractors and target groups, and
(c) Enable access by the private sector and thus facilitate private sector procurement.

53 2019 (5) SA 424 (SCA).
54 2014 (4) SA 474 (CC).
55 Paragraphs 55 to 60 at 492–494 of the judgment.
56 Section 10(f) of the *CIDB Act*.

Section 16 further provides that the Minister must prescribe the manner in which public sector construction contracts may be invited, awarded and managed within the framework of the register and the policy on procurement[57] and that every organ of state must, subject to the policy on procurement, apply the register of contractors to its procurement process.

The *Construction Industry Development Regulations*, 2004, promulgated under section 33 of the *CIDB Act*, confirm that public sector clients may only award construction contracts to contractors that are registered with the CIDB.

The CIDB's Register of Contractors categorises and grades contractors from levels 1 to 9, according to financial and works capability. A grade is represented by one digit and two letters. These reflect the maximum level at which the contractor is permitted to execute projects and the class of works it is certified capable of executing projects in.[58]

Regulation 4 exempts certain contractors from the requirement to register, namely:

(a) Any contractor who is registered as a homebuilder in terms of section 10 of the *Housing Consumer Protection Measures Act*, 95 of 1998 for the purposes of construction works in relation to the provision of a home
(b) A contractor who undertakes a construction works contract substantially consisting of the provision of labour, and
(c) A contractor who undertakes a construction works contract substantially consisting of the provision of supplies.

10.2.4 Labour relations

Labour relations in South Africa are extensively regulated by statute, regulations and industry-specific collective agreements, the scope and complexity of which fall outside of the ambit of this chapter. The applicable legislative enactments include the *Labour Relations Act*, 66 of 1995, the *Basic Conditions of Employment Act*, 75 of 1997, the *Employment Equity Act*, 55 of 1998, the *Occupational Health and Safety Act*, 85 of 1993, and regulations issued under these statutes.

Construction workers are well-organised in established trade unions. Labour unrest, often of a violent and destructive nature, strikes and lockouts are recurring risks on South African construction projects and often last many months at a time.

Public projects often contain a requirement for the employment of local labour. Since there is a finite number of persons that can be so employed on a project, and since the level of unemployment in South Africa is extremely high, civil unrest instigated by those persons that were not fortunate enough to obtain employment on the project is a regular occurrence and is usually accompanied by violence and damage to or the destruction of the project works. In general, the South African Police Service has been incapable of restoring law and order at project sites and specialised private security services are usually procured by contractors to do so.

57 Section 16(3) of the *CIDB Act*.

58 See CIDB website for details of grades, classes of work, and registration fees and requirements at www.cidb.org.za/contractors/register-of-contractors/overview/ (accessed on 1 December 2021).

10.2.5 Safety culture

Construction safety in South Africa is extensively regulated by the *Occupational Health and Safety Act* 85 of 1993 and, in particular, the Guidelines for Construction Regulations, 2014.

Despite these legislative attempts to improve safety on construction projects, a CIDB report published in 2009 indicated that, whilst construction health and safety had long been the focus of attention of many industry stakeholders and role players in South Africa and contracting organisations and others had made significant efforts to improve health and safety within the construction industry, overall construction health and safety had not improved commensurately.[59] Notably, construction continues to contribute a disproportionate number of fatalities and injuries relative to other industrial sectors and there continues to be high levels of non-compliance with health and safety legislation generally, and specifically the construction and other health and safety regulations in South Africa.[60]

During 1999 South African construction projects evidenced a fatality rate of 19.2 per 100,000 workers and an accident rate of 14,626 per 100,000 workers.[61] This compared favourably with equivalent statistics of other countries in Sub-Saharan Africa, with an average fatality rate of 21 per 100,000 workers and an accident rate of 16,012 per 100,000 workers. South Africa's health and safety statistics nevertheless compare poorly with those in developed countries, which experience only 4.2 fatalities per 100,000 workers and an accident rate of 3,240 per 100,000 workers per annum.[62] A South African construction worker is thus 4.5 times more likely to suffer a work-related accident or fatality, compared to construction workers in developed countries.

10.2.6 Modular construction using factory fabricated components

Although there are specialist contractors in South Africa that use modular construction systems, a research report published in 2017[63] suggested that modular construction systems are not widely utilised in the building sector of the South African construction industry. The report indicated that clients incorporated these systems in 12% of residential, 60% of commercial, 20% of industrial, 8% of institutional and 24% of mining projects, whereas construction industry professionals incorporated modular construction systems in 11% of residential, 39% of commercial, 28% of industrial, 22% of institutional and 4% of mining projects.[64]

59 CIDB Report, 'Construction Health & Safety in South Africa', 2009, ii, available at www.cidb.org.za/resource-centre/downloads-1/#45-59-wpfd-health-and-safety (accessed on 1 December 2021).

60 *Ibid.*

61 *Ibid.*, 6.

62 *Ibid.*

63 Rufaro Patience Dupwa, 'Investigation of the Utilisation of Modular Construction in South Africa', A research report submitted to the Faculty of Engineering and the Built Environment, University of the Witwatersrand, in partial fulfilment of the requirements for the degree of Master of Science Building, November 2017, 86 available at https://wiredspace.wits.ac.za/bitstream/handle/10539/25495/Rufaro%20Patience%20Dupwa_702743_Msc%20in%20Project%20Management%20in%20Co.pdf?sequence=1 (accessed on 1 December 2021).

64 *Ibid.*, ii.

Challenges that reduced the more widespread adoption of these systems were reported as including local building regulations restrictions, an inability to make changes onsite, transportation restraints, increased construction cost and limited design options.[65]

10.2.7 Technology/innovation/BIM

A research report published in 2018[66] suggests that the South African construction industry has not seen a marked increase in the implementation and use of Building Information Modelling (BIM) compared to other countries such as the USA, the UK and Hong Kong. Whilst 90% of the respondents in the study were familiar with BIM, only some 70% had implemented BIM on local construction projects, and only 13% had done so on five or more projects.[67] Reasons for the limited implementation of BIM were reported by respondents to include the costs thereof and a lack of skills.[68]

10.2.8 Government/private sector procurement

The process of procurement in the government sector in South Africa differs fundamentally from private sector procurement. Government sector procurement is extensively regulated by statute, whereas, in the case of the private sector, there are no specific legal requirements that have to be met, other than meeting the basic requirements for a valid contract.

Private sector procurement may involve a tender process, but more usually involves a negotiated contract with a preferred contractor.

Government sector procurement requires compliance with an extensive number of legislative enactments. In South Africa, public procurement is constitutionally regulated by section 217 of the *Constitution*, which provides that when organs of state contract for goods or services, they should do so in accordance with a system that is fair, equitable, transparent, competitive and cost-effective.[69]

Public procurement is further regulated by various statutes, including:

(a) The Public Finance Management Act, 10 of 1999
(b) The Preferential Procurement Policy Framework Act, 5 of 2000
(c) The Promotion of Administrative Justice Act, 3 of 2000

65 *Ibid.*; CIDB, 'Construction Procurement Best Practice', published under BN 63 in GG 26427 of 9 June 2004; CIDB Best Practice Guideline #C2, 'Choosing an appropriate form of contract for engineering and construction works', September 2005, Second edition of CIDB document 1010, 85–86, available at http://toolkit.cidb.org.za/Shared%20Documents/DP2-S22%20CIDB%20BPG%20C2%20-%20Choosing%20an%20appropriate%20Form%20of%20Contract%20for%20Eng%20and%20Constr%20Works%20Ed%202-0.pdf (accessed on 1 December 2021)

66 Mduduzi Mlungisi Beryldon Ndhlela, *The Use and Effectiveness of Building Information Modelling (BIM) in the South African Construction Industry*, A research report submitted to the Faculty of Engineering and the Built Environment, University of the Witwatersrand, Johannesburg, in partial fulfilment of the requirements for the degree of Master of Science in Building, School of Construction Economics and Management University of the Witwatersrand Johannesburg, 2018, v, available at https://wiredspace.wits.ac.za/bitstream/handle/10539/26933/ResearchReport_MNdhlela_0009258E_Final_Nov2018.pdf?sequence=2&isAllowed=y (accessed on 1 December 2018).

67 *Ibid.*, 40.

68 *Ibid.*, 52.

69 *Constitution of the Republic of South Africa*, 1996.

(d) The Local Government: Municipal Finance Management Act, 56 of 2003
(e) The Local Government: Municipal Systems Act, 32 of 2000
(f) The Broad-Based Black Economic Empowerment Act, 53 of 2003, and
(g) The Promotion of Access to Information Act, 2 of 2000.

These statutes regulate public procurement throughout South Africa, irrespective of the type of procurement or the industry in which it takes place.

Within the construction industry, public procurement is further regulated by the *Construction Industry Development Board Act*, 38 of 2000 which empowers the CIDB to issue best practice guidelines and standards that have to be followed by government and parastatals in procuring goods and services in the construction sector.

In addition, section 76 of the *Public Finance Management Act*, 10 of 1999, allows the National Treasury the authority to publish further rules for the regulation of public procurement. This includes the new Framework for Infrastructure Delivery and procurement management that came into operation on 1 October 2019.

The public procurement regime in South Africa is accordingly complex and is regulated through a highly fragmented legal framework.[70] In practice, review applications in the High Court which seek to challenge public tender awards are commonplace.

10.2.9 Insurance requirements

All of the construction standard forms in use in South Africa regulate the extent to which the parties are required to procure insurance coverage in respect of the insurable risks identified in the particular standard form.

The *Short-Term Insurance Act*, 53 of 1998, governs insurance coverage provided in respect of the insurable risks identified in construction standard forms.

A Contractor is usually required to obtain coverage for the risk of loss or damage to the Works as well as public indemnity coverage for the risk of personal injury and damage that may be suffered by third parties during the course of construction.

Since loss and damage resulting from civil unrest is a perennial risk in South Africa, Contractors are usually also required to obtain coverage for this risk from the South African Special Risk Insurance Association (**SASRIA**), the only insurer in South Africa that covers such risk events.[71]

In addition, Contractors and Subcontractors are also required to take out insurance in terms of the *Compensation for Occupational Injuries and Diseases Act*, 130 of 1993, to obtain indemnification in respect of claims made by employees who sustain injuries or disease as a result of their employment on the Works.[72]

Professional service providers are as a matter of course required to take out and maintain professional indemnity insurance coverage. Professional service contracts often stipulate

70 Allison Anthony, 'Regulating construction procurement law in South Africa – does the new framework for infrastructure delivery and procurement management undermine the rule of law?' (2021) 42 *Obiter* 1, available at http://www.scielo.org.za/scielo.php?script=sci_arttext&pid=S1682-58532021000100009 (accessed on 1 December 2021).

71 See *Reinsurance of Material Damage and Losses Act* No. 56 of 1989, read in conjunction with the *Conversion of SASRIA Act* No. 134 of 1998.

72 E Finsen, *The Building Contract – A commentary on the JBCC Agreements* (2nd ed, Juta Cape Town, 2005) 92–96.

the value of the coverage that is to be obtained and limit the extent of recovery by the Employer against the service provider with reference to the available value of coverage.

10.2.10 Common forms of contract

There are a number of construction standard form suites that are in common use in South Africa. The popularity of these forms is due, on the one hand, to their longstanding use by the industry, and, on the other, by the fact that these forms have been recommended for use in public procurement in South Africa by the CIDB.

For the execution of construction works, the CIDB identified the recommended forms of contract as those contained in the following series of documents:

(a) The FIDIC suite of standard forms, published by the International Federation of Consulting Engineers
(b) The General Conditions of Contract for Construction Works, published by the South African Institution of Civil Engineering (**SAICE**)
(c) The JBCC Series 2000 forms, published by the Joint Building Contracts Committee, and
(d) The NEC3 family of standard contracts.[73]

In addition, the CIDB publishes a Standard Professional Services Contract, a standard form intended for use for professional service provision on all construction projects, which is in widespread use in South Africa.

Prior to the CIDB's recommendations in 2004 for the standardisation of public procurement in South Africa, large infrastructure projects were in practice procured under a diverse arrangement of in-house standard forms that had been developed over many years by various government departments and parastatals. Transnet, the South African parastatal responsible for rail, pipelines and ports and harbours, for example, used to employ their Transnet E5 in-house standard form for many years. These in-house standard forms have, subsequent to the CIDB's recommendations, fallen into disuse.

The FIDIC suite, particularly the Red, Yellow and Silver Books, is widely used in South Africa for large infrastructure projects. This is particularly the case for projects financed by the World Bank. The 1999 edition is the most prevalent, but this is expected to change as the newer editions obtain traction in the market.

The General Conditions of Contract for Construction Works (**GCC 2015**), published by the South African Institution of Civil Engineering, is a popular choice for civil engineering projects where the Works are designed by the Employer. It is frequently used for road, pipeline, water infrastructure, housing and general civil engineering, mechanical and electrical projects and, as such, represents an alternative to the FIDIC Red Book. The GCC 2015 is currently in its third edition.[74] SAICE also publishes a back-to-back subcontract standard form as a companion to the GCC 2015, namely the GCSC 2018:

73 CIDB, 'Construction Procurement Best Practice', published under BN 63 in GG 26427 of 9 June 2004; CIDB Best Practice Guideline #C2, 'Choosing an appropriate form of contract for engineering and construction works', September 2005, second edition of CIDB document 1010, available at http://toolkit.cidb.org.za/Shared%20Documents/DP2-S22%20CIDB%20BPG%20C2%20-%20Choosing%20an%20appropriate%20Form%20of%20Contract%20for%20Eng%20and%20Constr%20Works%20Ed%202-0.pdf (accessed on 1 December 2021).

74 See SAICE website for further details, available at https://saice.org.za/saice-publications/ (accessed on 2 December 2021).

General Conditions of Subcontract.[75] In addition, SAICE publishes a short form of the GCC 2018, namely the SGCC 2018: General Conditions of Contract for Construction Works (Simplified Form), for works of small value and short duration.[76]

The NEC suite, mainly the NEC3, is occasionally used in South Africa. The NEC suite places significant emphasis on strong project management and timeous decision-making, also on the side of the Employer's representatives. In practice, public employers in South Africa suffer from an immense shortage of competent in-house project managers. In addition, the financial approval processes required to obtain additional project funding are often laborious and protracted in the public sector. This creates serious difficulties in the case of the NEC suite since timeous decision-making on the Employer's side is often absent. The FIDIC and GCC forms are more forgiving in this respect and, perhaps as a consequence thereof, appear to be more prevalent in practice.

The Joint Building Contracts Committee publishes the JBCC Series 2000 suite of standard forms which are intended for use in building projects where the Works are designed by the Employer. This standard form is, by a large margin, the most prevalent standard form in South Africa. The suite consists of a number of forms,[77] including:

(a) The JBCC Principal Building Agreement (Edition 6.2, May 2018)
(b) The JBCC Nominated/Selected Subcontract Agreement (Edition 6.2, May 2018)
(c) The JBCC Minor Works Agreement (Edition 5.2, May 2018)
(d) The JBCC Small and Simple Works Contract (Edition 1.0, May 2020), and
(e) The JBCC Direct Contractors' Contract (Edition 1.0, May 2020).

The JBCC suite is not only popular in South Africa, but is also used on building projects in other southern African countries.

10.2.11 Dispute resolution

The contractual dispute resolution regimes employed by standard forms in use in South Africa typically provide for a tiered process, which commences with a contract administrator's decision, followed by adjudication and, finally, by either litigation or arbitration.

Adjudication in South Africa is a creature of contract since there is no statutory adjudication scheme as yet. The Construction Industry Development Board expressed strong support for the inclusion of adjudication provisions in construction contracts in its Best Practice Guideline issued in September 2005.[78] As a consequence, all standard construction forms used in South Africa, whether in the public or private sector, include adjudication as a default position, and it is unusual for this provision to be removed from the standard forms by the parties in practice. The only exception is in the case of the Standard Professional Services Contract, which provides for a choice between mediation and adjudication, and where Employers in practice appear to prefer mediation rather than adjudication.

75 *Ibid.*

76 *Ibid.*

77 See the JBCC website for details on these forms, available at http://jbcc.co.za/documents/quick-guide/, (accessed on 2 December 2021).

78 Construction Industry Development Board, 'Construction Procurement Best Practice Guideline #C3 – Adjudication', September 2005, Second edition of CIDB document 1011, available at www.cidb.org.za/wp-content/uploads/2021/04/Adjudication.pdf (accessed 2 September 2021).

Except where the FIDIC suite is adopted in large infrastructure projects, adjudication appointments in South Africa are usually made on an *ad hoc* basis once a referral to adjudication has been notified, rather than in the form of the appointment of a standing Dispute Board at the outset of the project.

Arbitration represents the most usual final dispute resolution mechanism in practice, although there remain some governmental Employers who seem to prefer their disputes to be finally determined through litigation in the High Court of South Africa. In practice, arbitrations are usually finally resolved in a period of 12 months or less, whilst proceedings in the High Court may take upwards of two years. As a consequence of the widespread adoption by the construction industry of arbitration, there is a relative paucity of local judicial precedent in respect of construction disputes. The preference of some governmental Employers for litigation appears to be motivated by the fact that a High Court judgment establishes a precedent, which allows for legal certainty in respect of the interpretation of certain contract provisions that often form the subject matter of disputes.

There are a number of adjudication and arbitration bodies that are often nominated as appointing bodies under the Contract. These include the Arbitration Foundation of Southern Africa, the Association of Arbitrators, the Construction Adjudication Association of South Africa, the various Bar Councils, Consulting Engineers South Africa and the South African Institute of Civil Engineers, all of whom maintain panels of suitable adjudicators and arbitrators for appointment in construction disputes.

10.2.12 Current challenges

The South African construction industry has been under considerable economic pressure for a number of years, which has led to the demise of a number of top-tier contractors. These pressures have been exacerbated by rampant and wide-scale corruption in the public sector and continued decreasing investment, in real terms, by the government in infrastructure projects in South Africa since 2010.

The continued economic downturn during the past decade has caused a significant emigration of skilled construction workers who are unlikely to return even if conditions improve. Decades of governmental corruption and state capture have significantly increased South Africa's fiscal debt, have resulted in credit-rating downgrades by international rating agencies and have reduced the government's borrowing capacity for large infrastructure projects.

South Africa, as a result of its political past, remains one of the most unequal societies in the world. Public construction projects represent a unique opportunity for the government to effect transformation by creating jobs, upskilling workers and opening up the formal economy to previously disadvantaged contractors. However, achieving these critical goals whilst still succeeding in delivering projects within their budgeted time and cost remains extremely challenging. [79]

This is amply demonstrated by the disastrous implementation by the South African power utility, ESKOM, of the Medupi and Kusile projects. By 2007, after many years of neglect and a lack of planning, South Africa had developed a critical energy shortage.

79 See F Tshidavhu and N Khatleli, 'An assessment of the causes of schedule and cost overruns in South African megaprojects: A case of the critical energy sector projects of Medupi and Kusile' (2020) V27(1) *Acta Structilia* (Online), available at www.scielo.org.za/scielo.php?script=sci_arttext&pid=S2415-04872020000100005, (accessed on 2 December 2021).

In order to avoid a total collapse of the national energy grid, ESKOM had to commence the implementation of rolling electricity blackouts or load shedding. This precipitated a botched and over-hasty roll-out of the Medupi and Kusile projects that has and continues to haunt the country. [80]

Medupi and Kusile are two 4,800 MW coal-fired dry-cooled power stations presently under construction in South Africa. In the case of Medupi, construction activities commenced in 2007 with an estimated price of ZAR79 billion (US$5.1 billion) and a planned completion date in 2014. This was not met, and the cost has ballooned to ZAR122 billion (US$7.9 billion) so far, with an estimate of ZAR135 billion (US$8.7 billion) at eventual completion. Kusile was to be constructed over a similar timeline, with an original cost estimate of ZAR70 billion (US$4.5 billion). It is now only expected to be complete by 2025, at an estimated cost of ZAR161 billion (US$10.4 billion). Both of these projects are already overrunning on time and cost by more than 200%. It is widely believed that the presently estimated cost and timeframes are over-optimistic and that these power stations, even if completed, might never be fully operational.

As a consequence of these project failures, South Africa is presently experiencing consistent and varying degrees of load shedding, whereby planned power cuts are implemented across the country on a daily basis to avert a total failure of the power grid. If a total failure does occur, it will plunge the country into a nationwide blackout for a period of 14 days or more.

The time and cost overruns on the Kusile and Medupi powerplants provide an indication of the degree to which mismanaged mega-projects can damage the economy in that those projects have failed to resolve the energy shortfall that they were planned to address, caused severe damage to the economy and economic growth, put the sovereign balance sheet at risk and been a major contributor to the downgrades of South Africa's investment gradings by international grading agencies.[81]

Not only is economic growth and social development critically hampered by the lack of consistent power, but a national grid failure may have national security consequences which could endanger the future of the South African democracy.

The reasons for the failure of the Medupi and Kusile projects have been reported as including slow client decision-making, shortages of skilled labour, inaccurate material estimation and poor material planning, unforeseen ground conditions, scope changes on site and poor site management.[82]

---

80 *Ibid.*

81 R Watermeyer and S Phillips, 'Public Infrastructure delivery and construction sector dynamism in the South African economy', a report to the National Planning Commission, 4 March 2020, available at www.nationalplanningcommission.org.za/assets/Documents/Public%20infrastructure%20delivery%20and%20construction%20sector%20dynamism%20in%20the%20South%20African%20economy.pdf (accessed on 3 December 2021).

82 F Tshidavhu and N Khatleli, 'An assessment of the causes of schedule and cost overruns in South African megaprojects: A case of the critical energy sector projects of Medupi and Kusile' (2020) 2(1)7 *Acta Structilia* (Online), available at www.scielo.org.za/scielo.php?script=sci_arttext&pid=S2415-04872020000100005 (accessed on 2 December 2021).

10.3 The impact of COVID-19 in South Africa

10.3.1 The impact of COVID-19 on the execution of construction projects in South Africa

The direct impact of COVID-19 on the execution of construction projects in South Africa was initiated by the Declaration of a National State of Disaster and the promulgation of COVID-19 *Regulations* under the *Disaster Management Act*, 57 of 2002, during March 2020.

However, even prior to the introduction of these measures, governments across the world had introduced responses which involved, *inter alia*, social distancing measures, travel bans and lockdowns, which, in turn, placed restrictions on the movement of labour and materials to and from South Africa.

In South Africa, the response by the South African government has involved, *inter alia*, the Declaration of a National State of Disaster in terms of the *Disaster Management Act*, 57 of 2002 and the promulgation of various sets of *Regulations* in terms of the *Act*.

Regulation 11B(1)(b), which was introduced on 26 March 2020, provided that:

> During the lockdown, all businesses and other entities shall cease operations, except for any business or entity involved in the manufacturing, supply, or provision of an essential good or service, save where operations are provided from outside of the Republic or can be provided remotely by a person from their normal place of residence.

'Lockdown' was defined as:

> the restriction of movement of persons during the period for which this regulation is in force and effect namely from 23h59 on Thursday, 26 March 2020, until 23h59 on Thursday, 16 April 2020, and during which time the movement of persons is restricted.

'Movement', in this context, meant 'entering or leaving a place of residence or, in the case of people not ordinarily resident in the Republic, their place of temporary residence within the Republic'.

The period of the lockdown was extended until 30 April 2020 at 23h59 by the promulgation of further *Regulations*.

In practice, these *Regulations* prohibited the continued execution of all construction work in the country from 26 March 2020 onwards. On 29 April 2020 *Regulations* were issued which allowed for the resumption of public works civil engineering and construction projects.

The Level 4 lockdown was subsequently eased to Level 3 from 1 June 2020 onwards which permitted the resumption of construction activities in general, subject to, *inter alia*, strict compliance with health protocols and social distancing measures. The *Regulations* have been periodically adjusted since, with reference to the level of infections and available hospital beds, but have not again involved a closure of construction sites.

The impact of COVID-19 on the execution of construction projects has manifested in a number of ways. The responses of governments elsewhere resulted in the reduced availability of materials, including imported, specialist work elements the procurement of which are typically subject to long lead times, as well as the reduced availability of imported labour. The lockdown regulations restricted the movement of materials and labour and prohibited the execution of any construction activities from 26 March 2020 to 29 April 2020. Not only were construction activities prohibited, but so was every other section of the economy that did not qualify as essential services. The import of manufactured materials and the local manufacture and supply of materials and goods were similarly prohibited.

Despite the easing of the lockdown after 30 April 2020, construction activities could not continue unaffected as before. Construction firms were required to maintain health protocols and social distancing measures, and sector-specific health protocols such as work rotation, staggered working hours, shift systems and remote working arrangements had to be implemented. Both international and inter-provincial travel bans placed limitations on the availability of skilled workers and the availability of materials and supplies. In particular, the requirement for infected workers to isolate for ten days caused significant absenteeism and disruption on construction sites.

These events resulted in a proliferation of claims for extensions of time and additional financial compensation throughout the construction industry.

A number of measures were implemented by the government in an attempt to support the economy. These economic relief measures included:

(a) A soft-loan facility to small businesses
(b) A Debt Restructuring Facility to debtors who had received financing from the Small Enterprise Financing Agency (**SEFA**)
(c) Making available working capital to local manufacturers of hygiene, medical and food products necessary to curb the spread of the virus
(d) Economic relief measures for small food outlets, small-holders and communal farmers
(e) The establishment of a Tourism Relief Fund, and
(f) Tax relief measures.

10.3.2 The impact of COVID-19 on the operation of construction contracts in South Africa

The effects of COVID-19 and in particular the responses of international governments and the South African government to the virus caused delays, disruption and significantly increased costs on South African construction projects.

From a contractual perspective, a number of avenues arose through which Contractors could obtain redress.

In terms of the common law, where performance of a contractual obligation by the debtor becomes impossible, either physically or legally, after the contract was made, the debtor is discharged from liability if it was prevented from performing its obligation by *vis major* or *casus fortuitus*, but not if the impossibility was due to its own fault,[83] or if the event was actually foreseen or was reasonably foreseeable.[84] This means that the contract is brought to an end by the supervening impossibility of performance, as if the performance was impossible from the outset. ***Vis major***, or superior force, is some force, power or agency which cannot be resisted or controlled by the ordinary individual. It includes

83 *Wilma Petru Kooij v Middleground Trading 251 CC and Another* (1249/18) [2020] ZASCA 45 (23 April 2020), par 33.

84 F Du Bois (ed), *Wille's Principles of South African Law* (9th ed, Juta Cape Town 2007) 849.

not only the acts of nature, *vis divina*, or an 'act of God', but also the acts of man.[85] ***Casus fortuitus***, or inevitable accident, is a species of *vis major*, and imports something exceptional, extraordinary or unforeseen, and which human foresight cannot be expected to anticipate, or which, if it can be foreseen, cannot be avoided by the exercise of reasonable care or caution. The outbreak of a serious plague is recognised in our common law as an example of *casus fortuitus*.[86] On this basis, the COVID-19 pandemic represents an incidence of *casus fortuitous*.

In addition, the COVID-19 pandemic resulted in lockdown *Regulations* which prohibited the performance by service providers of their contractual obligations for the duration of the period of the lockdown. The lockdown *Regulations* represent an incidence of *vis major*.[87]

In order to result in a discharge of the parties of their obligations, the supervening events must have rendered the performance absolutely (i.e. permanently) or objectively impossible. The mere fact that the events have made it uneconomical for a party to carry out its obligations does not mean that performance has become impossible.[88] A temporary impossibility which merely delays performance by the debtor does therefore not bring the contract to an end but merely excuses the debtor in respect of its dilatory performance.[89] In addition, parties are not prevented by the common law from regulating the consequences of *vis major* or *casus fortuitous* in their agreement[90] by providing for consequences which differ from those dictated by the common law. By expressly providing for such circumstances the parties have removed the unforeseeability and unavoidability which are requirements for supervening impossibility in terms of the common law.[91]

Within the context of a construction contract, the application of these common-law principles to the events surrounding the COVID-19 pandemic and the lockdown may be summarised as follows:

(a) The consequences dictated by the common law in the case of supervening impossibility of performance will not find application where the construction contracts contain provisions which regulate these risks, and
(b) To the extent that the common law does find application, neither the COVID-19 pandemic nor the lockdown rendered performance by Contractors in terms of the construction contracts absolutely or permanently impossible. At best,

85 *Ibid.*, 849–850.

86 *Ibid.*, 850, and footnote 1091 citing Voet 19.2.23.

87 *Ibid.*, 850; *Peters, Flamman & Co v Kokstad Municipality* 1919 AD 427. In this case the contractor was discharged from its obligations in terms of a construction contract concluded with a municipality after the contractor was interned during wartime thus preventing performance by it of its contractual obligations; *Wilma Petru Kooij v Middleground Trading 251 CC and Another* (1249/18) [2020] ZASCA 45 (23 April 2020) at par 33; GB Bradfield, *Christie's Law of Contract in South Africa*, (7th ed, LexisNexis Durban, 2016) 549 and the authorities cited in footnote 452.

88 GB Bradfield, *Christie's Law of Contract in South Africa* (7th ed, LexisNexis Durban, 2016) 550 and the authorities cited in footnote 458.

89 Du Bois, above, n84, 860, on the effect of temporary impossibility, which absolves the debtor from *mora debitoris*.

90 Thus, even if the impossibility of performance is not due to the debtor's fault, it will nevertheless not be discharged where it expressly or impliedly took upon itself the risk of such impossibility supervening. See Du Bois, above, n84, 851, and the authorities cited in footnote 1099.

91 Bradfield, above, n88, 548; *Totalquip (Pty) Ltd t/a Total Tech c Connec Joint Venture* [2007] 3 All SA 200 (SE) 206.

performance by the Contractors has been rendered more onerous and costly. This is a risk that the common law devolves upon the Contractor. To the extent that the events have resulted in delays that will cause the Contractors to perform after their due date for performance, such dilatory performance will not represent a breach of contract. It may, however, set time at large by precluding reliance by the Employer on the originally agreed completion date.

However, the scope of application of these common law principles within the operation of construction standard forms in South African common law is very narrow, if it exists at all, since all of the standard forms in use in South Africa provide for the effects of the pandemic and the lockdown in one way or another.

Under the FIDIC forms,[92] the COVID-19 pandemic would arguably qualify as an incidence of *force majeure* and allow for a Party to be excused from performing obligations that it is prevented from performing as a consequence of the *force majeure* event.

In addition, the Contractor may also become entitled under sub-clause 8.5 and clauses 18 and 20 of the 2017 Red Book to an extension of time. Since COVID-19 does not appear to qualify as one of the *force majeure* events in clause 18 that qualify for additional cost, it would appear that the Contractor does not enjoy entitlement to recovery of additional costs attributable to the *force majeure* event.

However, the imposition of the lockdown regulations may allow the Contractor a recovery of both an extension of time and additional cost under sub-clauses 13.6, 8.5 and 20.1 of the 2017 Red Book.

Thus, whereas the broad consequences of COVID-19 *per se* only entitle a Contractor to an extension of time, but not to additional compensation, the more immediate consequences suffered as a result of the lockdown regulations arguably allow for recovery of both time and cost.

Under the GCC 2015 standard form, there are a number of provisions which afford a Contractor an entitlement to an extension of time and the recovery of additional cost on account of the COVID-19 pandemic, the lockdown and the consequences of these events.

As a point of departure, the GCC identifies a number of extraordinary events as 'excepted risks', which devolves the risk of these events upon the Employer, including an 'epidemic … or plague'.[93] The occurrence of an excepted risk renders the Employer liable in terms of clause 8.3.1 for 'risks of damage or physical loss caused by or arising directly or indirectly as a result or consequence of' the said risk. In addition, clause 8.3.2 further provides that:

> if, in carrying out the Works, any of the excepted risks, other than pertaining to the damage or physical loss referred to in Clause 8.2.2.2, causes the Contractor to suffer delay to Practical Completion and/or brings about proven additional costs, the Contractor shall be entitled to make a claim in accordance with Clause 10.1.

The GCC 2015 thus allows the Contractor to claim for an extension of the date for practical completion, which automatically results in a recovery by the Contractor of its time-related costs for the period of delay under clause 5.12.3 of the contract.

92 For example Clause 18 of the 2017 Red Book.
93 Clause 8.3.1.7 of the GCC 2015.

Clause 5.12 of the GCC 2015 also affords the Contractor an entitlement to an extension of time on account of any disruption which is entirely beyond the Contractor's control.

Furthermore, clause 6.8.4 of the GCC affords the Contractor an entitlement to a rate-based adjustment where there is change in legislation that occurs during the course of the Works which results in additional cost to the Contractor in carrying out the Contract. The response by the South African government to the COVID-19 pandemic included the introduction of a number of *Regulations* which would almost axiomatically burden the Contractor with increased costs in executing the work, and which would entitle the Contractor to additional compensation under clause 6.8.4.

The JBCC Principal Building Agreement contains a *force majeure* provision which is very similarly worded to that in the FIDIC Suite and which arguably is sufficiently wide to include the COVID-19 pandemic. Once an event of circumstance qualifies as *force majeure*, the risk is distributed upon the parties as follows:

(a) In terms of clause 8.5.7, the Contractor is not liable for the cost of making good physical loss and repairing damage to the works caused by or arising from *force majeure*, and
(b) The Contractor is entitled to a revision of the date for practical completion in terms of clause 23.1 on account of *force majeure*. However, such revision does not entitle the Contractor to an adjustment of the contract value in respect of any additional time-related costs suffered during the delay.

The JBCC applies a similar dispensation where the extension of time is sought on account of clause 23.1.5, i.e. an extension of time on account of the delays attributable to the lock-down *Regulations*. Also, in this case, an extension of time is cost-neutral.

10.4 South African governing law of the contract

10.4.1 Constraints on the governing law of a construction contract

South African law applies no constraint on the freedom of contracting parties to select the governing law of a construction contract. It is submitted, however, that where such a contract is to be enforced in South Africa, the South African courts will not enforce obligations imposed by a different governing law which offend fundamental constitutional values, which are illegal or which are otherwise considered to be ***contra bonos mores***, i.e. against good morals, the public interest or public policy.

The essential requirements for a valid contract in South Africa may be summarised as follows:

i There must be *consensus* between the parties as to the identity of the parties and the contractual obligations they wish to create[94]
ii The agreement must be one for performance or non-performance in the future by one or more of the parties; that is, one or more of them undertakes to give something, to do something or not to do something[95]

94 Van Huyssteen, Lubbe and Reinecke, *Contract General Principles* (5th ed, Juta & Co Ltd 2016) 23.
95 Du Bois (ed.), *Wille's Principles of South African Law* (9th ed, Juta & Co Ltd 2007) 736.

iii The parties must be of full legal capacity to contract[96]
iv The content of the agreement must be certain or ascertainable[97]
v Performance of the stipulated obligations must be objectively possible as of the date of conclusion of the agreement
vi The agreement must, in exceptional cases, meet party-imposed or statutory formalities,[98] and
vii The agreement must not suffer from illegality in respect of its formation, performance or purpose.[99] Illegality may arise as a result of a conflict with statutory law, including the *Constitution*.[100] Illegality may also arise from a conflict with the common law, in the sense that the agreement is considered to be *contra bonos mores* in that it offends public policy, the public interest or good morals.[101]

Party autonomy and the principle of *pacta sunt servanda* are cornerstones of the South African legal system. In principle, therefore, agreements that meet the foregoing requirements will be enforced by the South African courts.[102]

10.4.2 Formal requirements for a construction contract

The South African common law does not impose any formal requirements that have to be met for a binding contract to be concluded.[103] As noted earlier, contracts are enforceable where there exists consensus between the parties and the contractual terms are certain, objectively possible and not illegal or otherwise against public policy.

South African law recognises, however, that parties may themselves elect to require certain formal requirements to be met before contractual liability ensues. Such party-imposed formalities may, for example, stipulate writing as a condition precedent for the conclusion or amendment of a binding contract, and are enforceable. It is a factual question in every case whether parties required writing to operate as a formal requirement for contractual liability, or whether writing was intended merely as an evidentiary tool, there being a factual presumption in favour of the latter.[104]

Exceptionally, certain statutes impose formal requirements for the conclusion of a binding contract.[105] Within the construction context, government procurement processes are

96 Du Bois (ed.), *Wille's Principles of South African Law* (9th ed, Juta & Co Ltd 2007) 736; Van Huyssteen, Lubbe and Reinecke, *Contract General Principles* (5th ed, Juta & Co Ltd 2016) 8.

97 Van Huyssteen, Lubbe and Reinecke, *Contract General Principles* (5th ed, Juta & Co Ltd 2016) 217.

98 *Ibid.*, 146.

99 Van Huyssteen, Lubbe and Reinecke, *Contract General Principles* (5th ed, Juta & Co Ltd 2016) 188; Du Bois (ed.), *Wille's Principles of South African Law* (9th ed, Juta & Co Ltd 2007) 736; *Conradie v Rossouw* (1919) AD 279.

100 Van Huyssteen, Lubbe and Reinecke, *Contract General Principles* (5th ed, Juta & Co Ltd 2016) 188; *Barkhuizen v Napier* (2007) (5) SA 323 (CC).

101 Van Huyssteen, Lubbe and Reinecke, *Contract General Principles* (5th ed, Juta & Co Ltd 2016) 188.

102 *Ibid.*, 310.

103 *Conradie v Rossouw* (1919) AD 279; Bradfield, *Christie's Law of Contract in South Africa* (7th ed, LexisNexis 2016) 123; Van Huyssteen, Lubbe and Reinecke, *Contract General Principles* (5th ed, Juta & Co Ltd 2016) 146; *Goldblatt v Freemantle* (1920) AD 123; *Novartis SA (Pty) Ltd and Another v Maphil Trading (Pty) Ltd* (2016) (1) SA 518 (SCA).

104 *Goldblatt v Freemantle* (1920) AD 123.

105 For example, section 2(1) of the *Alienation of Land Act*, 68 of 1981 and consumer protection legislation.

heavily regulated at national, provincial and local government levels through a complex set of inter-related legislative enactments.[106]

Where a governmental or parastatal entity is a party to a construction contract, these procurement provisions are activated. As a result, the formal requirements for the validity and enforceability of such a construction contract usually include not only that the construction contract must be evidenced in writing but also that the entire tender-driven procurement process be conducted in accordance with the provisions of the relevant applicable procurement legislation and fair administrative process. The complexity of the prevailing procurement legislation in South Africa is such that it cannot be appropriately addressed within the context of this book.

10.5 What Special Provisions in the Particular Conditions are necessary for consistency with applicable laws in South Africa?

10.5.1 FIDIC General Conditions are incompatible or inconsistent with South African governing law of the contract

This section considers the extent to which certain FIDIC General Conditions may be considered to be incompatible or inconsistent with the governing law of the contract, where such governing law is South African law.

10.5.1.1 Good faith

In keeping with its Roman-Dutch roots, good faith has always been recognised as a cornerstone of the South African law of contract.[107] Good faith is considered to be constituted by the concepts of justice, reasonableness and fairness.[108]

In *Brisley v Drotsky*[109] the Supreme Court of Appeal held that, whilst the values of good faith, reasonableness and fairness were fundamental to the South African law of contract and performed creative, informative and controlling functions through established rules of contract law, these did not constitute independent, substantive hard rules of law that courts could employ to intervene in contractual relationships as this would lead to unacceptable legal and commercial uncertainty.[110]

In the Constitutional Court judgment in *Barkhuizen v Napier*,[111] Mr Justice Ngcobo indicated, within the context of a time-limitation clause in an insurance contract, that public policy tolerates time-limitation clauses subject to considerations of reasonableness and fairness. He went on to indicate:[112]

---

106 See Bolton, *The Law of Government Procurement in South Africa* (Lexis Nexus Butterworths 2007); section 217 of the *Constitution of South Africa*, 108 of 1996; *Public Finance Management Act*, 1 of 1999; *Local Government: Municipal Systems Act*, 32 of 2000; *Local Government: Municipal Finance Management Act*, 56 of 2003; *Preferential Procurement Policy Framework Act*, 5 of 2000; *Promotion of Administrative Justice Act*, 3 of 2000; *Construction Industry Development Board Act*, 38 of 2000, and *Regulations* published in terms thereof.

107 See, for example, *Bank v Grusd* (1939) TPD 286; *Barkhuizen v Napier* (2007) (5) SA 323 (CC) [80] 346.

108 *Barkhuizen v Napier* (2007) (5) SA 323 (CC), [80] 347.

109 2002(4) SA 1 (SCA).

110 Brand, 'The Role of Good Faith, Equity and Fairness in the South African Law of Contract: The Influence of the Common Law and the Constitution' (2016) V27(2) *Stellenbosch Law Review* 81.

111 [2007] (5) SA 323 (CC), [48], 338.

112 [56] 431.

56 There are two questions to be asked in determining fairness. The first is whether the clause itself is unreasonable. Secondly, if the clause is reasonable, whether it should be enforced in the light of the circumstances which prevented compliance with the time-limitation clause.

57 The first question involves the weighting-up of two considerations. On the one hand public policy, as informed by the Constitution, requires in general that parties should comply with contractual obligations that have been freely and voluntarily undertaken. This consideration is expressed in the maxim pacta sunt servanda, which, as the Supreme Court of Appeal has repeatedly noted, gives effect to the central constitutional values of freedom and dignity. Self-autonomy, or the ability to regulate one's own affairs, even to one's own detriment, is the very essence of freedom and a vital part of dignity. The extent to which the contract was freely and voluntarily concluded is clearly a vital factor as it will determine the weight that should be afforded to the values of freedom and dignity. The other consideration is that all persons have a right to seek judicial redress. These considerations express the constitutional values that must now inform all laws, including the common-law principles of contract.

58 The second question involves an inquiry into the circumstances that prevented compliance with the clause. It was unreasonable to insist on compliance with the clause or impossible for the person to comply with the time limitation clause. Naturally, the onus is upon the party seeking to avoid the enforcement of the time-limitation clause. What this means in practical terms is that once it is accepted that the clause does not violate public policy and non-compliance with it is established, the claimant is required to show that in the circumstances of the case there was a good reason why there was a failure to comply.

In *Beadica 231 CC and Others v Trustees, Oregon Trust and Others* 2020 (5) SA 247 (CC), the Constitutional Court clarified the role of equity in contract, as part of public policy considerations. The Court held that:

(a) *Barkhuizen* remained the leading authority in South African law on the role of equity in contract by recognising that good faith was not a self-standing rule, but an underlying value that was given expression through rules of law. Abstract values did not provide a freestanding basis upon which a court may interfere in contractual relationships, but instead performed creative, informative and controlling functions.[113]

(b) The impact of the *Constitution* on the enforcement of contractual terms through the determination of public policy was profound. It required that courts employ constitutional values to achieve a balance that strikes down the unacceptable excesses of freedom of contract, while seeking to permit individuals the dignity and autonomy of regulating their own lives. Public policy impacted values of fairness, reasonableness and justice, and *ubuntu*.[114]

113 See paragraphs [38] and [58] of the judgment.
114 See paragraphs [71] to [73] of the judgment.

(c) In developing the common law courts must develop clear and ascertainable rules and doctrines to ensure that our law of contract is substantively fair, whilst at the same time providing predictable outcomes for contracting parties.[115]
(d) A court may, however, not refuse to enforce contractual terms on the basis that the enforcement would, in its subjective view, be unfair, unreasonable or unduly harsh. It was only where a contractual term, or its enforcement, was so unfair, unreasonable or unjust that it was contrary to public policy that a court may refuse to enforce it.[116]

As a general proposition, therefore, parties should bear in mind that the inclusion of unreasonable or unfair Particular Conditions may place these provisions at risk of ultimately being declared unenforceable where these offend underlying constitutional values. If such unenforceable provisions are not severable from the remainder of the agreement, it may vitiate the contract as a whole. In addition, even if a particular clause is not *per se* unreasonable or unfair from a public policy perspective, reliance by a party on such a clause in the circumstances of a particular case may be found to be unreasonable and unfair and thus impermissible.

10.5.1.2 Sub-clause 1.4 (Law and Language)
Although the *Constitution* recognises 11 official languages,[117] English is, in practice, the language used by government, the courts and the business community. As such, no amendment of sub-clause 1.4 of the General Conditions is required.[118]

10.5.1.3 Sub-clause 2.1 [Right of Access to the Site]
Sub-clause 2.1 imposes a duty upon the Employer to provide the Contractor with access to, and possession of, all parts of the Site within the time (or times) stated in the Contract Data. It further provides that the right of access and possession may not be exclusive to the Contractor.

It is important to recognise that a Contractor's possession of the Site implies legal consequences in South African law that are not purely defined by the terms of the Contract.

As a point of departure, a Contractor is protected against an unlawful[119] disturbance of its possession of the Site, whether or not it has a contractual right to possess the Site, through the operation of the ***mandament van spolie***, a possessory remedy.[120]

Furthermore, in terms of the South African common law, a Contractor who is placed in possession of land upon which the Contractor thereafter effects improvements will obtain a builder's or enrichment lien over the land as security for payment with respect to the improvements.[121] Such a lien affords the Contractor a right of retention over the

115 See paragraphs [76], [78] and [81].

116 See paragraph [80] of the judgment.

117 Section 6(1) of the *Constitution*.

118 All reference to sub-clause numbers in this chapter refer to the 2017 editions of the FIDIC rainbow suite.

119 Unlawful in the sense that proper legal process was not followed in disturbing the Contractor's possession, not in the sense that the disturbance was contrary to the terms of the Contract.

120 *Nino Bonino v De Lange* (1906) TS 120; *Bon Quelle (Edms) Bpk v Munisipaliteit van Otavi* (1989) (1) SA 508 (A) at 514; *Jigger Properties CC v Maynard NO and others* (2017) (4) SA 569 (KZP).

121 *United Building Society v Smookler's Trustees and Golambick's Trustee* (1906) TS 623; *McCarthy Retail Ltd v Shortdistance Carriers CC* (2010) (3) SA 482 (SCA).

Site as security for payment with respect to the improvements effected and may allow the Contractor to retain possession even if the Contract has been cancelled.

Where such a lien has thus accrued in favour of a Contractor, the ability to disturb the Contractor's possession of the Site in the absence of payment of any amounts due to the Contractor in respect of the improvements made to the Site may be limited.

The Parties can exclude the accrual of such a lien in favour of the Contractor with appropriate provisions in the Particular Conditions.

10.5.1.4 Sub-clause 2.5 [Site Data and Items of Reference]

Sub-clause 2.5 provides that thc 'Employer shall have made available to the Contractor, for information, before the Base Date, all relevant data in the Employer's possession on the topography of the Site and on sub-surface, hydrological, climatic and environmental conditions at the Site'.

This clause places an obligation upon the Employer which may, if the Employer fails to meet this obligation, allow the Contractor to pursue contractual remedies for breach.

It is important to bear in mind, however, that a Contractor may, in addition to its contractual remedies pursuant to a breach of sub-clause 2.5, in terms of South African law, become entitled to extra-contractual remedies where the information provided by the Employer was materially incorrect or where the Employer in breach of the legal duty failed to disclose such information. Such duty to disclose exists where the information is within a party's exclusive knowledge (so that, in a practical business sense, the other party has it as its only source), and the information, moreover, is such that the right to have it communicated to the other party would be mutually recognised by honest men in the circumstances.[122]

A misrepresentation within this context, may, depending on the facts, render the contract void, as a result of an absence of consensus, or voidable (even if the misrepresentation was innocent). A misrepresentation, whether by positive conduct or omission, which was made negligently or fraudulently, may also afford the innocent party a delictual claim for damages.[123]

Parties may, through the inclusion of appropriate provisions in the Particular Conditions, exclude responsibility for innocent or negligent misrepresentation.[124] However, responsibility for fraudulent conduct can never be contractually excluded.[125]

10.5.1.5 Sub-clause 7.7 [Ownership of Plant and Materials]

Sub-clause 7.7 provides that each 'item of Plant and Materials shall, to the extent consistent with the mandatory requirements of the Laws of the Country become the property of the Employer'.

The South African law of property follows an abstract theory for transfer of ownership in property, in terms whereof the real agreement to pass ownership is abstracted from the

122 *ABSA Bank Ltd v Fouche* 2003(1) SA 176 (SCA), [5] 181; *Pretorius and Another v Natal South Sea Investment Trust Ltd (under Judicial Management)* 1965(3) SA 410 (W) 418E–F.

123 *ABSA Bank Ltd v Fouche* 2003(1) SA 176 (SCA).

124 Van Huyssteen, Lubbe and Reinecke, *Contract General Principles* (5th ed, Juta & Co Ltd 2016) 143; *Trollip v Jordaan* 1961(1) SA 238 (A).

125 Van Huyssteen, Lubbe and Reinecke, *Contract General Principles* (5th ed Juta & Co Ltd 2016) 143; *Wells v South African Aluminite Company* 1927 AD 69.

contractual agreement providing the cause for the transfer.[126] Thus, whilst sub-clause 7.7 creates enforceable personal rights *vis-à-vis* the Employer and the Contractor, the breach of which may entitle the Employer to claim specific performance or damages from the Contractor, the actual real right of ownership would only vest in the Employer and be enforceable against the world at large if the requirements of the law of property for the transfer of ownership have been met.

10.5.1.6 Sub-clause 8.7 [Rate of Progress] and sub-clause 8.8 [Delay Damages]

Sub-clause 8.8 provides for the payment by the Contractor of Delay Damages in the amount stated in the Contract Data where the Contractor failed to comply with sub-clause 8.2 as it relates to meeting the Time for Completion.

Penalty and liquidated damages provisions are regulated in South Africa by the *Conventional Penalties Act*, 15 of 1962:

- i A provision which provides for the payment of a sum of money by any person on account of an act or omission in conflict with a contractual obligation, either by way of a penalty or as liquidated damages, is considered to be a 'penalty stipulation'[127]
- ii A penalty stipulation is, subject to the provisions of this *Act*, capable of being enforced in any competent court[128]
- iii However, if it appears to the court that such penalty is out of proportion to the prejudice suffered by the creditor by reason of the act or omission in respect of which the penalty was stipulated, the court may reduce the penalty to such extent as it may consider equitable in the circumstances – provided that in determining the extent of such prejudice the court shall take into account not only the creditor's proprietary interest but every other rightful interest which may be affected by the act or omission in question[129]
- iv In addition, section 2(1) of the *Act* provides that a creditor shall not be entitled to recover, in respect of an act or omission which is the subject of a penalty stipulation, both the penalty and damages or, except where the relevant contract expressly so provides, to recover damages in lieu of the penalty.

Against this legislative background, sub-clause 8.8 qualifies as a penalty stipulation, the enforcement of which is regulated by the *Act*. Whilst a claim for Delay Damages is, therefore, enforceable in principle, a court may reduce the extent of the penalty claimed on equitable grounds in accordance with section 3 of the *Act*.

In addition, where a penalty has been stipulated, the Employer may not, in addition to the penalty, seek to recover damages for the breach that activated the penalty provision. In this regard, clause 8.7 of the General Conditions, which affords the Employer an entitlement to the recovery of damages if the rate of progress is insufficient, may offend the provisions of the *Conventional Penalties Act* where the Contractor's dilatory conduct results in damages both on account of an insufficient rate of progress and a consequent failure to meet the Time for Completion. It is submitted that, in such circumstances, a court may

126 Du Bois (ed.), *Wille's Principles of South African Law* (9th ed, Juta & Co Ltd 2007) 411–412.
127 Section 1(2) of the *Conventional Penalties Act.*
128 Section 1(1) of the *Conventional Penalties Act.*
129 Section 3 of the *Conventional Penalties Act.*

find that only the stipulated Delay Damages are recoverable and that the Employer is limited to this recovery, irrespective of the extent of its actual loss.

It may thus be advisable for an Employer to include, in the Particular Conditions, a right of election in the case of a breach of clauses 8.7 and 8.8, between claiming the Delay Damages stipulated or the full extent of the actual loss suffered on account of the Contractor's breach. Where the Employer elects to enforce the latter, it would, in principle, be able to claim the full extent of the loss suffered in terms of clauses 8.7 and 8.8 but would then be disentitled from relying on the stipulated penalty.

10.5.1.7 Sub-clause 15.2 [Termination for Contractor's Default]

Sub-clause 15.2.1(g) entitles the Employer to terminate the Contract upon notice where the Contractor 'becomes bankrupt or insolvent; goes into liquidation, administration, reorganisation, winding-up or dissolution; becomes subject to the appointment of a liquidator, receiver, administrator, manager or trustee; enters into a composition ... under applicable laws'.

The application of this provision in a particular case should be considered against applicable statutory provisions relating to insolvency and business rescue proceedings in South Africa.[130] In principle, the creation of the ***concursus creditorum***[131] in insolvency or winding up neither alters nor suspends the rights and obligations of the parties in terms of an agreement, and the Liquidator steps into the shoes of the insolvent and does not acquire any rights greater than the insolvent. The other party can, nevertheless, not exact specific performance against the Liquidator, and the Liquidator has a right of election whether or not to abide by the Contract. This does not, however, disentitle the other party from cancelling the Contract on account of a breach by the insolvent, even if the right to cancel only accrues after the commencement of the *concursus creditorum*.[132]

10.5.2 FIDIC General Conditions are incompatible or inconsistent with the law of the Site/Country

Apart from the considerations addressed in section 10.5.1, there are no additional FIDIC General Conditions which are considered to be incompatible or inconsistent with the law of the Site/Country.

10.5.3 FIDIC General Conditions are incompatible or inconsistent with the relevant laws on dispute determination in South Africa

There are no FIDIC General Conditions which are considered to be incompatible or inconsistent with the laws of the seat of the arbitration or relevant laws on dispute resolution.

130 See: for business rescue, chapter 6 of the *Companies Act*, 71 of 2008; [67]; for insolvency and liquidation, chapter XIV of the *Companies Act* of 1973; the *Insolvency Act*, 24 of 1936; *Ellerine Brothers (Pty) Ltd v McCarthy Ltd* 2014(4) SA 22 (SCA).

131 This is the point upon which the hand of the law is laid upon the debtor's estate, from which point onwards the rights of the general body of creditors have to be taken into consideration. The claim of each creditor is dealt with as it existed at the issue of the order initiating insolvency proceedings. See *Walker v Syfront* NO 1911 AD 141 at 166; Meskin, *Insolvency Law and Its Operation in Winding-Up* (Lexis Nexis Butterworths 1990), Service Issue 22, June 2004 [5.20] 5–50.

132 *Ellerine Brothers (Pty) Ltd v McCarthy Ltd* 2014(4) SA 22 (SCA).

10.6 What Special Provisions in the Particular Conditions are desirable for consistency with applicable laws in South Africa?

There are no special provisions, other than those identified in section 10.5.1, that are considered desirable to achieve consistency with applicable laws.

10.7 Summary of applicable legislation for South African governing law of the contract

South Africa Capital Territory	
10.7.1 Entry into a construction contract	
Construction Contracts	Procurement legislation applying to government procurement processes at national, provincial and local government levels, including: *Constitution of South Africa*, 108 of 1996 *Public Finance Management Act*, 1 of 1999 *Local Government: Municipal Systems Act*, 32 of 2000 *Local Government: Municipal Finance Management Act*, 56 of2003 *Preferential Procurement Policy Framework Act*, 5 of 2000; *Promotion of Administrative Justice Act*, 3 of 2000 The *Construction Industry Development Board Act*, 38 of 2000, and *Regulations* published in terms thereof
10.7.2 Termination of a construction contract	
Bankruptcy, insolvency, liquidation	*Companies Act*, 71 of 2008 Chapter XIV of the *Companies Act*, 61 of 1973 *Insolvency Act*, 24 of 1936
10.7.3 Dispute resolution	
Limitation periods Liability Arbitration	*Prescription Act*, 68 of 1969 *Apportionment of Damages Act*, 34 of 1956 *Arbitration Act*, 42 of 1965 *International Arbitration Act*, 15 of 2017

10.8 Summary of applicable legislation if the Site/Country is in South Africa

South Africa Capital Territory	
10.8.1 Operation of a construction contract	
Registration and administration of professionals – engineers, architects, quantity surveyors	*Architectural Profession Act*, 44 of 2000 *Engineering Profession Act*, 46 of 2000

	Quantity Surveyors Profession Act, 49 of 2000
Registration/licensing of contractors and subcontractors	*Construction Industry Development Board Act*, 38 of 2000, and *Regulations* promulgated in terms thereof
Labour	*Labour Relations Act*, 66 of 1995
	Occupational Health and Safety Act, 85 of 1993, together with *Construction Regulations* of 7 February 2014
	Basic Conditions of Employment Act, 75 of 1997
Design/Moral Rights	*Designs Act*, 195 of 1993
	Trade Marks Act, 194 of 1993
	Patents Act, 57 of 1978
Copyright	*Copyright Act*, 98 of 1978
First Nation people's land rights	*Constitution of South Africa*, 108 of 1996
	Restitution of Land Rights Act, 1994 (Act No. 22 of 1994)
	Broad-Based Black Economic Empowerment Act, 53 of 2003
Planning	*Spatial Planning and Land Use Management Act*, 16 of 2013 and *Spatial Planning and Land Use Management Regulations*
Heritage	*National Heritage Resources Act*, 25 of 1999 and *National Heritage Resources Act Regulations* of 2 June 2000
Environment	*Constitution of the Republic of South Africa*, 108 of 1996
	Sea-Shore Amendment Act, 190 of 1993
	World Heritage Convention Act, 49 of 1999
	National Environmental Management Act, 70 of 1998
	National Water Act, 36 of 1998
	Marine Living Resources Act, 18 of 1998
	Environmental Laws Rationalisation Act, 51 of 1997
	National Environmental Management: Air Quality Act, 39 of 2004
	National Environmental Management: Protected Areas Act, 31 of 2004
	National Environmental Management: Protected Areas Act, 57 of 2003
	Broad-Based Black Economic Empowerment Act, 53 of 2003
	Mineral and Petroleum Resources Development Act, 49 of 2008
	National Environmental Management: Waste Act, 59 of 2008
	National Environmental Management Act, 62 of 2008
Local procurement	*Broad-Based Black Economic Empowerment Act*, 53 of 2003
	Construction Industry Development Board Act, 38 of 2000, and *Regulations* published in terms thereof
	Preferential Procurement Policy Framework Act, 5 of 2000
	Competition Act, 89 of 1998
	Prevention and Combating of Corrupt Activities Act, 12 of 2004
	Promotion of Access to Information Act, 2 of 2000
	Promotion of Administrative Justice Act, 3 of 2000
	Promotion of Equality and Prevention of Unfair Discrimination Act, 4 of 2000
	Public Finance Management Act, 1 of 1999

	Local Government: Municipal Systems Act, 32 of 2000 *Local Government: Municipal Finance Management Act*, 56 of 2003
Building and construction permits, execution of construction work, standard of construction work	*Housing Consumers Protection Measures Act*, 95 of 1998
	Construction Industry Development Board Act, 38 of 2000, and *Regulations* published in terms thereof *Spatial Planning and Land Use Management Act*, 16 of 2013 and *Spatial Planning and Land Use Management Regulations* *National Building Regulations and Building Standards Act*, 103 of 1977 and the *Regulations* promulgated in terms thereof South African National Building Regulations SANS 10400
Health and safety	*Occupational Health and Safety Act*, 85 of 1993, together with *Construction Regulations* of 7 February 2014
Calibration of testing apparatus, equipment and instruments	Accreditation for Conformity Assessment Calibration and *Good Laboratory Practice Act*, 19 of 2006 and South African National Accreditation System (SANAS) established in terms thereof
Insurance	*Insurance Act*, 18 of 2017 *Short-term Insurance Act*, 53 of 1998 *Long-term Insurance Act*, 52 of 1998
Liability for defective work	*Housing Consumers Protection Measures Act*, 95 of 1998 *Consumer Protection Act*, 68 of 2008

10.8.2 Termination of a construction contract

Bankruptcy, insolvency, liquidation	*Companies Act*, 71 of 2008
	Chapter XIV of the *Companies Act*, 61 of 1973 *Insolvency Act*, 24 of 1936
Decennial liability and liability generally for the total or partial collapse of structures	*Housing Consumers Protection Measures Act*, 95 of 1998
	Prescription Act, 68 of 1969

10.8.3 Dispute resolution

Dispute before a local board	*Promotion of Administrative Justice Act*, 3 of 2000
Limitation periods	*Prescription Act*, 68 of 1969

10.9 Applicable legislation if the 'seat' of the dispute determination is in South Africa

10.9.1 Sub-clause 21 [Disputes and Arbitration]

South Africa does not enjoy statutory provisions for adjudication, adjudication proceedings being regulated exclusively by contract. Despite the absence of statutory provisions, adjudication is the preferred pre-arbitration or pre-litigation dispute resolution process in all four standard-form construction contracts[133] approved by the Construction Industry Development Board for use in government procurement in South Africa. Adjudication decisions are robustly enforced by the High Court of South Africa.[134] As a result, consensual adjudication proceedings operate very effectively in practice despite, and arguably perhaps as a result of, the absence of statutory regulation.

Arbitration has developed into the preferred choice for the resolution of contractual disputes in commerce and the construction industry in South Africa during the past 25 years. This trend resulted in the development of reputable regional African arbitral institutions of long standing, such as the Arbitration Foundation of South Africa (AFSA), which is able to offer arbitral participants a selection of astute commercial and construction arbitrators, arbitration facilities and administrative service to an international standard.

Until recently, all arbitrations in South Africa were governed by the *Arbitration Act*, 42 of 1965. By modern standards, this *Act* represents a somewhat antiquated piece of legislation, originally derived from the English *Arbitration Act* of 1950, which allows courts a level of interference in arbitrations which is not in keeping with modern arbitral trends. Despite these deficiencies, the grounds upon which a court may refuse to enforce an arbitral award in terms of this *Act* are nevertheless very narrow. A court is only permitted to set aside an arbitral award in terms of section 33 of the *Act* where:

a Any member of an arbitration tribunal had misconducted himself/herself in relation to his/her duties as arbitrator
b An arbitration tribunal had committed any gross irregularity in the conduct of the arbitration proceedings or had exceeded its powers, or
c An award had been improperly obtained.

South African courts have, in keeping with the expectations of international arbitration practitioners, always been strongly supportive of arbitration and have not been prepared, within the context of section 33 of the *Arbitration Act*, to entertain a reconsideration of the merits of an arbitral award.[135]

In recognition of the shortcomings of the *Arbitration Act* of 1965 and pursuant to recommendations by the South African Law Commission, the *International Arbitration Act*, 15 of 2017 was promulgated and came into operation on 19 December 2017, intended to regulate international arbitrations. As a consequence, South Africa now has a dual arbitration regime: the *Arbitration Act*, 42 of 1965, which now only regulates domestic arbitrations, and the *International Arbitration Act*, 15 of 2017, which applies to international arbitrations.

133 The FIDIC suite of standard forms, the NEC, the JBCC form and the General Conditions of Contract (GCC) form.

134 *Stocks and Stocks (Cape) (Pty) Ltd v Gordon and others NNO* 1993(1) SA 156 (T): interim mediator's decision enforced; *Freeman NO and another v Eskom Holdings Ltd* [2010] JOL 25357 (GSJ): enforcement of adjudication decision under NEC form; *Basil Read (Pty) Ltd v Regent Devco (Pty) Ltd* (unreported): enforcement of adjudicator's decision under JBCC form; *Stefanutti Stocks (Pty) Ltd v S8 Property (Pty) Ltd* [2013] ZAGPJHC 388: enforcing Adjudicator's decision into JBCC form; *Tubular Holdings (Pty) Ltd v DBT Technologies (Pty) Ltd* 2014(1) SA 244 (GSJ): enforcing a FIDIC DAB decision under clause 20.4 of the 1999 edition.

135 *Telecordia Technologies Inc v Telkom SA Ltd* 2007(3) SA 266 (SCA).

The *International Arbitration Act* is a thoroughly modern piece of legislation and incorporates the *UNCITRAL Model Law on International Commercial Arbitration*,[136] in keeping with the expectations of international arbitration practitioners. The *Act* applies to any international commercial dispute that the parties have agreed to submit to arbitration under an arbitration agreement.[137] The *Act* also binds public bodies. An arbitration is, *inter alia*, considered international, as set out in Article 1(3) of the *Model Law*, if the parties have expressly agreed that the subject matter of the agreement relates to more than one country.

The provision in clause 21.8 of the General Conditions[138] to the effect that 'any Dispute … shall be finally settled by international arbitration' should thus be effective in ensuring that arbitration proceedings arising from the Contract are regulated by the new *International Arbitration Act*, rather than the domestic *Arbitration Act*. It is suggested, in any event, that parties expressly indicate this to be so in the Particular Conditions if the arbitration is to be seated in South Africa.

South Africa acceded to the *New York Convention* of 1958 on 3 May 1976. Chapter 3 of the *International Arbitration Act* contains appropriate provisions to ensure that foreign arbitral awards may be effectively recognised and enforced in South Africa, in accordance with the provisions of the *New York Convention*.

South Africa is not a signatory to the *Convention on the Settlement of Investment Disputes between States and Nationals of Other States* (***Washington Convention***). In addition, the *Protection of Investment Act*, 22 of 2015, together with the cancellation by South Africa of a number of international investment treaties since 2015, has unfortunately significantly curtailed the availability of treaty-based remedies to investors in the South African market.

10.10 Summary of applicable legislation if the 'seat' of the dispute determination is in South Africa

	South Africa Capital Territory
Dispute resolution	*Constitution of South Africa*, 108 of 1996
	Superior Courts Act, 10 of 2013
Limitation periods	*Prescription Act*, 68 of 1969
Arbitration	*Arbitration Act*, 42 of 1965
	International Arbitration Act, 15 of 2017

10.11 Issues that a court or arbitrator may construe differently than expected from the words of the Contract because of local law or custom

The following are issues that a court or arbitrator may construe differently than expected from the words of the Contract because of local law or custom.

136 As adopted by the United Nations Commission on International Trade on 21 June 1985, with amendments adopted by the Commission on 7 July 2006, subject to certain adaptations set out in the *Act*.

137 Section 7(1) of the *International Arbitration Act*, 15 of 2017.

138 In the Red Book.

10.11.1 The Constitution

As discussed in section 10.4.1, the South African courts will not enforce obligations imposed by a different governing law which offend fundamental constitutional values.

10.11.2 Good faith

The influence of the principle of good faith in the interpretation of contractual provisions is discussed in section 10.3.1.1.

10.11.3 Right of access to the Site

As noted in section 10.5.1.3, a Contractor's possession of the Site implies legal consequences in South African law that are not purely defined by the terms of the Contract.

10.11.4 Site data

A Contractor may, in addition to its contractual remedies pursuant to a breach of sub-clause 2.5, in terms of South African law become entitled to extra-contractual remedies where the information provided by the Employer was materially incorrect or where the Employer in breach of the legal duty failed to disclose such information. Refer to section 10.5.1.4.

10.11.5 Ownership of plant and materials

As discussed in section 10.5.1.5, whilst sub-clause 7.7 creates enforceable personal rights *vis-à-vis* the Employer and the Contractor, the breach of which may entitle the Employer to claim specific performance or damages from the Contractor, the actual real right of ownership would only vest in the Employer and be enforceable against the world at large if the requirements of the law of property for the transfer of ownership have been met.

*10.11.6 Sub-clause 1.15 [*Limitation of Liability*]*

Sub-clause 1.15 provides, *inter alia*, that neither Party shall be liable to the other for loss of use of any Works, loss of profit, loss of any contract, or for any indirect or consequential loss or damage which may be suffered by the other Party in connection with the Contract.

Whilst provisions of this nature are enforceable in South Africa, these are usually restrictively interpreted. In addition, these would not be enforced to exclude a claim for loss or damage attributable to the fraudulent conduct of the defendant.

10.11.7 Delay Damages

As discussed in section 10.5.1.6, whilst a claim for Delay Damages is, in principle, enforceable, a court may reduce the extent of the penalty claimed on equitable grounds in accordance with section 3 of the *Penalties Act*.

10.11.8 Proportionate liability

South African law affords a plaintiff who has suffered damage as a result of the wrongful, negligent conduct of a defendant with a remedy in terms of the law of **delict**.[139] Where the

139 This is a remedy similar to the tort of negligence in English law.

plaintiff's loss was caused partly by its own fault and partly by the fault of the defendant or where the plaintiff's loss was caused by more than one defendant, the *Apportionment of Damages Act*, 34 of 1956, *inter alia*, provides for the apportionment of this loss between the plaintiff and the defendant or amongst the defendants in proportion to their respective degrees of fault. It should be noted, however, that these provisions do not apply to contractual liability for damages.[140]

10.11.9 Limitations of action/prescription

The rights of parties to payment in terms of a construction contract, whether in terms of a payment certificate or otherwise, represents a 'debt', the prescription of which is regulated by the provisions of the *Prescription Act*, 68 of 1969.

In terms of the provisions of this *Act*, a debt shall be extinguished by prescription after the lapse of a period of three years from the date upon which the debt became due.[141]

A construction contract is, in terms of the common law, considered to be in the nature of a ***locatio conductio operis***,[142] in terms whereof a Contractor would, in principle, only become entitled to payment after completion of the Works as a whole.[143] Interim payment certificates are thus considered to represent a contractual mechanism through which the Contractor is able to obtain interim payment in advance of the accrual of entitlement to full payment of the contract price upon completion. A Payment Certificate issued by the duly authorised agent of the Employer in favour of the Contractor is considered a liquid document in South African law, which creates, in favour of the Contractor, a separate and independent cause of action subject to the terms of the Contract.[144]

From a prescription perspective, the three-year prescription period would not commence running in respect of a Contractor's claim for payment:

- a In terms of an interim Payment Certificate, until the certificate is issued and the amount certified has become due for payment by the Employer, and
- b In terms of payment of the Contract Price for the Works overall, prior to the completion of the Works in all respects by the Contractor and, where the Contractor's right to payment is additionally dependent upon the issuing of a final Payment Certificate in terms of a contractual mechanism, until the amount certified in terms of the final payment certificate has become due and payable.[145]

---

140 *Thoroughbred Breeders' Association v Price Waterhouse* 2001(4) SA 551 (A).

141 *Prescription Act*, 68 of 1969, sections 10(1), 11(d), and 12(1).

142 An agreement for the letting and hiring of work.

143 *Martin Harris & Seuns OVS (Edms) Bpk v QwaQwa Regeringsdiens; QwaQwa Regeringsdiens v Martin Harris & Seuns OVS (Edms) Bpk* 2000(3) SA 339 (SCA) 355; *Dalinga Beleggings (Pty) Ltd v Antina (Pty) Ltd* 1977(2) SA 56 (A); *Thomas Construction (Pty) Ltd (in liquidation) v Grafton Furniture Manufacturers (Pty) Ltd* 1988(2) SA 546 (A) 563 G.

144 *Group Five Construction (Pty) Ltd v Minister of Water Affairs and Forestry (3916/05)* [2010] ZAGPPHC36 (5 May 2010); *Martin Harris & Seuns OVS (Edms) Bpk v QwaQwa Regeringsdiens*; *QwaQwa Regeringsdiens v Martin Harris & Seuns OVS (Edms) Bpk* 2000(3) SA 339 (SCA) 355.

145 *Martin Harris & Seuns OVS (Edms) Bpk v QwaQwa Regeringsdiens*; *QwaQwa Regeringsdiens v Martin Harris & Seuns OVS (Edms) Bpk* 2000(3) SA 339 (SCA) 355; *Secure Electronics v The City of Cape Town* [2017] ZAWCHC 95, a decision by Mr Justice Kusevitsky in the Western Cape High Court under case number 24107/2012, referring to the Martin Harris case; *Evins v Shield Insurance Co Ltd* 1980(2) SA 814 (A), *Deloitte Haskins & Sells v Bowthorpe Hellerman Deutsch* 1991(1) SA 525 (A), and *Smith v Mouton* 1977(3) SA 9 (W).

With respect to the prescription of claims by the Employer against the Contractor, the prescription will begin to run as soon as the debt is due and not when the Contract is ultimately completed. However, where the entitlement of the Employer to make a Claim against the Contractor is subject to completion of a contractual mechanism (for example, an Engineer's decision in terms of clause 3.5 and subsequent certification), the three-year prescription period will only begin to run once the amount due by the Contractor has become due and payable.

10.12 Additional references for South Africa

10.12.1 Books

FE Finsen, *The Building Contract: A Commentary on the JBCC Agreements* (2nd edn, Juta & Co Ltd, 2005)

Francois Du Bois (ed), *Wille's Principles of South African Law* (9th edn, Juta & Co Ltd, 2007)

GB Bradfield, *Christie's Law of Contract in South Africa* (7th edn, LexisNexis, 2016)

Karl Marxen, *Demand Guarantees in the Construction Industry* (Juta & Co Ltd, 2018)

LF Van Huyssteen, GF Lubbe and MFB Reinecke, *Contract General Principles* (5th edn, Juta & Co Ltd, 2016)

Philip C Loots, *Construction Law and Related Issues* (Juta & Co Ltd, 1995)

Peter A Ramsden, *McKenzie's Law of Building and Engineering Contracts and Arbitration* (7th edn, Juta & Co Ltd, 2014)

10.12.2 Internet

Society of Construction Law for Africa. www.sclafrica.org (accessed 14 July 2019)

South African Legislation. www.gov.za (accessed 14 July 2019)

Southern and East African Court Decisions. www.saflii.org (accessed 14 July 2019)

CHAPTER 11

Applying FIDIC Contracts in Türkiye

S Aslı Budak and Levent Irmak

CONTENTS

DOI: 10.4324/9781003206910-11

11.1 Outline of the legal environment in Türkiye

11.1.1 The constitutional structure of Türkiye

The legal basis of the Turkish legal system was laid in the *Constitution of the Republic of Türkiye*, usually referred to as the *Constitution of 1982*. The *Constitution* has been amended several times, the last in 2017. The 2017 amendment ended the parliamentary government system in *Türkiye* and adopted a presidential system.

The *Constitution* is built around the principle of separation of powers. The legislative power is vested in the Grand National Assembly of Türkiye. This power cannot be delegated. Executive power and function are entrusted to the President of the Republic, to be exercised in conformity with the *Constitution* and laws. Judicial power rests with independent and impartial courts, to be exercised on behalf of the Turkish Nation.

The *Constitution* regulates the fundamental rights and duties, namely the rights and duties of individuals, social and economic rights and duties, political rights and duties, fundamental organs of the Republic and financial and economic provisions.

11.1.2 The legal system of Türkiye

The Republic of Türkiye has a civil law legal system. The Turkish civil judicial system mirrors the system of continental Europe.

Since its foundation, Türkiye has adapted its main bodies of laws, such as commercial law, civil law and criminal laws, from European countries. With a view towards eventually acceding to the European Union as a member state, Türkiye has reflected a wide range of European Union regulations in its domestic law through a selective adaptation process. There may be differences as to how these laws and regulations are implemented; however, relatively new areas of law such as antitrust and personal data protection, as well as the framework of certain regulated markets, resemble European Union law pertaining to the same field. As the most important trade partner of Türkiye, the European Union has influenced and is continuing to influence harmonisation of legislation affecting cross-border trade and investment. In addition, as per the *Turkish Constitution*, duly ratified international treaties are superior to national laws, and therefore, national laws must be in line with such treaties. Any contradictions with these treaties must be corrected through necessary amendments.

As for the hierarchy of laws, the *Constitution* is the supreme body of law. *Codes*, *Presidential Decrees* and international treaties come right after the *Constitution*, and *Regulations* follow them.

11.1.3 The court system of Türkiye

The Turkish court system can be divided into two main groups: (i) civil and criminal courts and (ii) administrative courts. Each group includes courts of first instance and high courts.

The judicial courts hear civil and criminal disputes. Basic judicial authorities for civil and criminal cases are civil courts and criminal courts. The civil courts have jurisdiction over general disputes or issues that are not specifically assigned to specialised courts. Specialised courts handle issues that require expertise. For example, commercial courts hear disputes with commercial elements (e.g. company law or commercial contract disputes). There are lLabour Courts, Family Courts, Cadastral Courts, Consumer Courts, Civil Courts of intellectual and industrial property rights, maritime courts, etc. The Criminal Courts deal with criminal issues. The regional Appellate Courts are the intermediary appeals courts in the Turkish judicial court system. Parties unsatisfied with the decision of the court of first instance must apply to regional Appellate Courts before applying to the Court of Appeals. The Court of Appeals examines appeal requests against decisions of the regional Appellate Courts.

The Administrative Courts are entitled to hear cases filed by individuals against the transactions and acts of the governmental or regulatory bodies wielding public administrative power. The regional Administrative Courts examine appeal requests against the decisions of the Administrative Courts. The supreme court of administrative law is the Council of State, which reviews the decisions of regional Administrative Courts.

There is also the Constitutional Court, which acts as the extraordinary high court that examines laws, decrees and the internal directive of the Grand National Assembly of Türkiye for compliance with the *Constitution*. The Constitutional Court also examines the constitutionality, in respect of both form and substance, of laws, *Presidential Decrees* and the rules of procedure of the Grand National Assembly of Türkiye and decides on individual applications.

11.2 The construction industry in Türkiye

11.2.1 Overview

The construction industry plays a crucial role in Türkiye's economic development, accounting for nearly 6% of GDP and employing almost 1.5 million people. With the direct and indirect impacts on other sectors, the share of the construction sector in the Turkish economy reaches 30%.[1] In the period of 1972–2021, Turkish contractors have undertaken 11,125 projects in 131 countries, with a total value of US$ 453 billion. In 2021, with the effect of the pandemic being brought under control to a certain extent and the increase in oil prices, a recovery was observed in the international construction market. In this context, the business volume of Turkish contracting companies has also increased and 413 projects worth US$ 30.7 billion have been undertaken in 69 countries. On the other hand, Türkiye is among the world's leading producers of construction materials. Türkiye's unique geographical location contributes a great deal to the global competitiveness of Turkish contracting services abroad. Türkiye's strength in the field is not only due to its location, but also the cost-effective services provided at international standards, high client satisfaction and credibility in partnerships, vast international experience in a wide variety of projects, familiarity with the business environments especially in the neighbouring regions, qualified manpower and a calculated risk-based approach to business. Rich experience in diverse markets, cost-effective service at international standards,

1 Turkish Contractors Association, Turkish International Contracting Services (1972–2021), www.tmb.org.tr/files/doc/1623914018902-ydmh-en.pdf (accessed 1 December 2022).

ability to take the initiative, willingness to take risks and extensive partnership experience are the key factors behind the success of the Turkish contractors.[2]

11.2.2 Licensing/registration

11.2.2.1 Requirement to obtain a contracting authorisation certificate

The *Regulation Relating to Classification and Recording of Building Contractors* requires, in principle, that all buildings that are subject to building permits must be constructed under the liability of an individual or legal entity building contractor or by a joint venture formed by them, and that each building contractor must obtain a contracting authorisation certificate issued by the provincial contracting authorisation commission contained within the Provincial Environment and Urban Planning Directorate. Construction works that (i) fall under the scope of the *Public Procurement Law No. 4734*; (ii) qualify for an exemption under the *Public Procurement Law No. 4734*; (iii) are carried out under the *State Tender Law No. 2886*; or (iv) are carried out by establishments subject to the *Capital Market Law No. 6362*, having at least one public institution or public establishment shareholder with at least 20% contribution to its capital, are exempt from the certification requirement.

11.2.2.2 Types of contracting authorisation certificates

Subject to the occupational, technical, economic and financial qualifications of building contractors, authorisation certificates are classified into the following groups: A, B, B1, C, C1, D, D1, E, E1, F, F1, G, G1, H and Temporary. The qualifications required for each group and the relevant thresholds[3] are as follows:

- **Group A**: Contractors with work experience amounts exceeding double the building threshold amount and with no fewer than 50 annual skilled Labourers and no fewer than eight technical personnel.
- **Group B**: Contractors with work experience amounts exceeding seven-fifths of the building threshold amount and with no fewer than 24 annual skilled Labourers and no fewer than six technical personnel minimum.
- **Group B1**: Contractors with work experience amounts exceeding six-fifths of the building threshold amount and with no fewer than 18 annual skilled Labourers and no fewer than four technical personnel.
- **Group C**: Contractors with work experience amounts exceeding the building threshold amount and with no fewer than 12 annual skilled Labourers and no fewer than three technical personnel.
- **Group C1**: Contractors with work experience amounts exceeding five-sixths of the building threshold amount and with no fewer than ten annual skilled Labourers and no fewer than three technical personnel.

2 Turkish Contractors Association, Turkish International Contracting Services (1972–2021), www.tmb.org.tr/files/doc/1623914018902-ydmh-en.pdf (accessed 1 December 2022).

3 The threshold amounts for 2022 are stated in https://webdosya.csb.gov.tr/db/izmir/menu/basvuru-klavuzu-18-subat-2022-son_20220221113420.pdf (accessed 2 December 2022).

- **Group D**: Contractors with work experience amounts exceeding two-thirds of the building threshold amount and with no fewer than nine annual skilled Labourers and no fewer than two technical personnel.
- **Group D1**: Contractors with work experience amounts exceeding one-half of the building threshold amount and with no fewer than eight annual skilled Labourers and no fewer than two technical personnel.
- **Group E**: Contractors with work experience amounts exceeding one-third of the building threshold amount and with no fewer than six annual skilled Labourers and no fewer than two technical personnel.
- **Group E1**: Contractors with work experience amounts exceeding one-fifth of the building threshold amount and with no fewer than five annual skilled Labourers and no fewer than two technical personnel.
- **Group F**: Contractors with work experience amounts exceeding one-tenth of the building threshold amount and with no fewer than three annual skilled Labourers and no fewer than one technical personnel.
- **Group F1**: Contractors with work experience amounts exceeding 17/200 of the building threshold amount and with no fewer than three annual skilled Labourers and no fewer than one technical personnel.
- **Group G**: Contractors with work experience amounts exceeding seven-hundredths of the building threshold amount and with no fewer than one annual skilled Labourer and no fewer than one technical personnel.
- **Group G1**: Contractors with work experience amounts exceeding one-twentieth of the building threshold amount and with no fewer than one annual skilled Labourer and no fewer than one technical personnel.
- **Group H**: Work experience and workforce conditions at the first application are not required. However, at the time of renewal, the conditions of having minimum one annual skilled Labourer and minimum one technical personnel are required.
- **Temporary Group**: Economical, financial, occupational and technical qualifications and work experience and workforce conditions are not required.

In determining the group of joint ventures, the partner holding the highest partnership share is accepted as the pilot partner. If all partners hold equal shares, the partner holding the higher group certificate is accepted as the pilot partner, unless otherwise stated. If the partnership percentage is not stated in the Joint Venture Statement, it is presumed that all partners hold equal shares. The certificate group for joint ventures is determined by taking into consideration the minimum work experience amounts of the pilot/coordinator partner and others. For this purpose, the pilot/coordinator partner needs to provide at least 60% of the minimum work experience amount required for the group of the joint venture and each of the other partners needs to provide at least 10%.

Group A contractors are not subject to any limitations in carrying out building works but there are certain limitations set forth for other contractors. Group B, B1, C, C1, D, D1 and E contractors can carry out building works with building approximate costs not exceeding the minimum work experience amount required for the respective group. Group G and G1 contractors can carry out building works with building approximate costs not exceeding 1.5 times the minimum work experience amount required for the respective group. The ratio for Group F is two times, for Group F1 it is 1.75 and for E1 it is four-thirds, whereas

Group H contractors can carry out building works with building approximate costs not exceeding five-sixths of the minimum work experience amount required for Group G1.

The validity period of the contracting authorisation license is equal to the validity period of the work experience certificate license, but it may not be shorter than three years or longer than five years.

11.2.2.3 Other consents, licenses and permits

There are permits, approvals, licenses and consents that must be obtained from relevant authorities in Türkiye in order to carry out a construction project. The following list is only for information purposes and of a non-exhaustive nature and may vary due to the characteristics of the project.

No.	Consent/license/permit	Issuing/approving authority	Relevant legislation
1.	**Approval of the Zoning Plan** (*İmar Planı'nın Onaylanması*)	**In municipal areas:** Municipality **Outside of municipal areas:** Governorship or the Ministry of Environment, Urbanisation and Climate Change	Articles 8 and 9 of the *Zoning Law*
2.	**Demolition Permit** (*Yıkım İzni*)	**In municipal areas:** Municipality **In metropolitan areas:** Relevant provincial municipality **Outside of municipal areas:** Highest local authority	Article 18 of the *Regulation on the Control of Excavation Soil, Construction and Wreckage Wastes*
3.	**Construction Permit** (*Yapı Ruhsatı*)	Municipality or Governorship	Articles 21 and 44 of the *Zoning Law* and Article 56 of the *Planned Areas Zoning Regulation*
4.	**Building Utilisation Permit** (*Yapı Kullanma İzni*)	Municipality or Governorship	Articles 30 and 44 of the *Zoning Law* and Article 56 of the *Planned Areas Zoning Regulation*
5.	**Forestry Permit** (*Orman İzni*)	Ministry of Forest and Hydraulic Works	Article 17 of the *Forestry Law*
6.	**Waste Transportation and Acceptance Permit** (*Atık Taşıma ve Kabul Belgesi*)	Relevant Province Municipality in Metropolitan Municipality Area	Article 16 of the *Regulation on the Control of Excavation Soil, Construction and Wreckage Wastes*

No.	Consent/license/permit	Issuing/approving authority	Relevant legislation
7.	**Permit for Purchase and Use of Explosive Materials** (*Patlayıcı Madde Satın Alma ve Kullanma İzni*)	Governorship	Article 118 of *Bylaw regarding the Purchase and Use of Explosive Materials* put into force by *Decree No. 87/12028 of the Council of Ministers*
8.	**Permit for Storage of Explosive Materials** (*Patlayıcı Madde Depolama İzin Belgesi*)	Governorship	Article 82 of *Bylaw regarding the Purchase and Use of Explosive Materials* put into force by *Decree No. 87/12028 of the Council of Ministers*
9.	**Notification for Commencement of Construction Works** (*Yapı İşlerine Başlama Bildirimi*)	Relevant Regional Directorate of the Ministry of Labour	Article 8 of the *Regulation on Health and Security in Construction Works*
10.	**Workplace Opening and Operation License** (*İşyeri Açma ve Çalışma Ruhsatı*)	Municipality	Article 6 of the *Regulation on Workplace Opening and Operation Licenses*
11.	**Health Security Belt** (*Sağlık Koruma Bandı*)	Municipality	Article 16 of the *Regulation on Workplace Opening and Operation Licenses*
12.	**Work Permit for Foreigners** (*Yabancılar için Çalışma İzni*)	Embassies of the Republic of Türkiye and Ministry of Labour and Social Security	*Law on International Work Force*
13.	**Health Report** (*Sağlık Raporu*)	Healthcare Institution	Article 75 of the *Labour Law*
14.	**Permission for Installation and Use of Radio** (*Telsiz Kurma ve Kullanma İzni*)	Information and Communication Technologies Authority	Articles 5 and 6 of the *Regulation on Procedures and Principles Regarding Radio Procedures*
15.	**Radio License** (*Telsiz Ruhsatı*)	Information and Communication Technologies Authority	Article 8 of the *Regulation on Procedures and Principles Regarding Radio Procedures*
16.	**Private Security Permit** (*Özel Güvenlik İzni*)	Governorship	Article 3 of the *Law on Private Security Services* and Article 8 of the *Regulation on Implementation of the Law on Private Security Services*
17.	**Fire Report** (*Yangın Yeterlilik Raporu*)	Municipality	Article 6 of the *Municipality Fire Department Regulation* and Article 5 of the *Regulation on Workplace Opening and Operation Licenses*

No.	Consent/license/permit	Issuing/approving authority	Relevant legislation
18.	**Place Selection and Facility Establishment Permit** (*Yer Seçimi ve Tesis Kurma İzni*)	Municipality	Article 18 of the *Regulation on Workplace Opening and Operation Licenses*
19.	**Trial Permit** (*Deneme İzni*)	Municipality	Article 20 of the *Regulation on Workplace Opening and Operation Licenses*
20.	**Provincial Local Environment Board Decision** (*Çevre Kurul Kararı*)	Provincial Local Environment Board	Article 23 of the *Environmental Noise Assessment and Control Regulation*
21.	**Waste Declaration Form** (*Atık Beyan Formu*)	Governorship	Article 9 of the *Regulation on Waste Management*
22.	**Transportation Form** (*Taşıma Formu*)	Governorship	Article 10 of the *Regulation on Waste Management*
23.	**Provisional Storage Permit** (*Geçici Depolama İzni*)	Governorship	Article 13 of the *Regulation on Waste Management*
24.	**Soil Protection Project** (*Toprak Koruma Projesi*)	Governorship	Article 12 of the *Soil Protection and Land Utilisation Law*
25.	**Permit regarding Utilisation of Agricultural Fields Outside of Their Purpose** (*Tarım Arazilerinin Amaç Dışı Kullanımına İlişkin İzin*)	Ministry of Agriculture and Regional Areas/ Governorship	Article 13 of the *Soil Protection and Land Utilisation Law*
26.	**Sewage Connection Permit** (*Kanalizasyon Bağlantı İzni*)	Water and Sewage Authority in Metropolitan Municipality	Article 5 of the *Regulation on Purification of Urban Waste Water*
27.	**Waste Water Connection Permit** (*Atık Su Bağlantı İzni*)	Waste Water Infrastructure Facilities Management	Article 44 of the *Regulation on Control of Water Pollution*
28.	**Connection Quality Control Permit Certificate** (*Bağlantı Kalite Kontrol İzin Belgesi*)	Waste Water Infrastructure Facilities Management	Article 44 of the *Regulation on Control of Water Pollution*
29.	**Environment Permit** (*Çevre İzni*)	Provincial Directorate of the Ministry of Environment, Urbanisation and Climate Change	Article 5 of the *Regulation on Environmental Permits and Licenses Required to be Obtained Under the Environmental Law*

11.2.3 Labour relations

Contractors have to adhere to the limitations introduced under the *Labour Law* and its secondary legislation, including, among others, those addressing employment contracts, working hours, trial periods, overtime work, working in shifts, work on holidays, termination of employment, notice periods, severance pay and notice pay liability, workplace practices, minimum wage, employment of handicapped personnel as well as annual paid leave periods. Some details of significant employment-related matters are listed here:

- **Average working hours**: The maximum working hours per week allowed under the *Labour Law* is 45 hours. The weekly actual working time of 45 hours may be evenly distributed between workdays, or, if agreed between the employee and the employer, may be distributed unevenly. According to the *Labour Law*, employees must be given at least a one-hour lunch break per day. This lunch break is not included in the actual working time of 45 hours.
- **Overtime work**: The term 'overtime' is generally defined as the amount of working time that exceeds the legally applicable weekly work limit of 45 hours under the *Labour Law*. There are limitations set forth for overtime work under the *Labour Law*. Total overtime work performed by a worker cannot exceed 270 hours per year and the length of working time, including overtime work, cannot exceed 11 hours per day. Employees that work overtime at workplaces are entitled to choose between an overtime salary compensation (which equals one and a half times their hourly salaries for each hour of overtime work) or use free time (which is one hour and thirty minutes for each hour worked overtime). Employees shall use the free time to which they are entitled within six months, within their working time and without any deduction in their wages. In order to have any given employee perform overtime work, their written consent to perform overtime work should be obtained at the beginning of each year, and such consent should be kept by the employer in the personal employment file of such employee.
- **Work on holidays**: The *Labour Law* states that parties to an employment agreement may agree that the employee will work on national and general public holidays. In the absence of such prior agreement, the written consent of the employee is required to be obtained on a case-by-case basis for performance of work on these holidays. Furthermore, employees who complete their contractual weekly working hours are entitled to take at least one day off that week. However, in cases where the nature of the work performed by an employee requires performance of work on Sundays, another day of the week must be granted to such employee as a weekend holiday. According to the *Labour Law*, upon the performance of work by an employee on the weekend holiday, an amount that equals double his/her daily salary is required to be paid for each day worked on the weekend holiday. If the work performed on a weekend holiday also qualifies as overtime work (i.e., in excess of 45 hours in the respective week), an amount equal to 2.5 times his/her hourly salary is required to be paid for each hour worked on the weekly holiday.
- **Working in shifts**: The *Labour Law* and the *Regulation on Working in Shifts* introduced a number of restrictions for working in shifts, which include the requirement to announce in the workplace: (i) the number of shifts; (ii) the start

and end times for each shift; (iii) the names of the employees who will work in shifts; (iv) the timing and duration of breaks; (v) weekly holidays; and (vi) any amendments to the foregoing items. Furthermore, if the nature of the business requires working around the clock, but may be carried out in shifts, the working hours should be divided into at least three shifts per day and the daily working hours should not exceed eleven hours. Employers are required to submit to the relevant district office of the Ministry of Labour, the names of employees who work in shifts as well as their periodical health reports evidencing that they are apt to be employed in shifts prior to the commencement of multiple shift business operations. Finally, work carried out between 8 pm and 6 am is defined as night work. Night shifts cannot exceed 7.5 hours and performance of overtime work by employees who work on night shift is prohibited.

- **Foreign employees**: Unless otherwise stated in bilateral or multilateral treaties or international conventions to which Türkiye is a party or other laws, all foreigners must obtain a work permit before starting to work in Türkiye. Work permit and work permit exemption granted in accordance with the *Law on International Workforce* substitute for a residence permit. Therefore, foreign employees who obtain work permits do not need to apply for residence permits to reside in Türkiye. The Ministry of Labour and Social Security is authorised to grant work permit exemptions to certain employees as per Article 16 of the *Law on International Workforce*. Accordingly, the exempted employees do not need to obtain residence permits, since the work permit exemption document also grants a residence permit. Different legal regimes apply to key personnel and other foreign staff.
- **Disabled employees**: From the perspective of the *Labour Law*, disabled persons are those who: (i) have difficulties in adapting to the social life and in meeting daily needs due to the loss of physical, mental, psychological, sensory and social capabilities at various levels by birth or by any reason thereafter, (ii) therefore need protection, care, rehabilitation, consultancy and support services and (iii) document their bodily function loss is minimum 40% with a medical board report. In private sector workplaces employing 50 or more employees within the boundaries of a province, an employer must ensure that no less than 3% of the workforce is made up of disabled persons. When calculating this percentage, fractions of more than one-half are rounded up, and fractions of less than half are rounded down. For employers with more than one establishment within the boundaries of a province, the number that the employer must employ must be computed according to the total number of employees regardless of their type of contract.

11.2.4 Safety culture

The *Regulation on Health and Security in Construction Works* regulates the minimum health and safety conditions for construction works. The obligations and liabilities of employers and other persons, the appointment of health and safety coordinators, health and safety plans and providing information to the employees on the health and safety precautions at the site are among the issues set forth in the *Regulation on Health and Security in Construction Works.*

11.2.5 Modular construction using factory fabricated components

Taking into consideration the many advantages it has over conventional construction methodologies, the most prominent benefit of modular construction is shorter production time, which thus enables shorter procurement periods. Modular construction also has various other benefits including lower costs compared to conventional construction, more environmentally friendly procedures such as the use of multiple recycling for the steel material used in modular elements, elimination of the need for foundational structures to be built which in turn allows for faster and more economic construction, and higher quality due to production taking place on off-site fabrication facilities where advanced quality control measures are taken.

The Turkish construction sector is well-developed in terms of modular construction and has been adapting itself in conjunction with new trends and developments. There are hundreds of companies in the modular construction sector in Türkiye, and according to the Turkish Precast Concrete Association,[4] there are 109[5] companies that are only involved in prefabricated concrete element production in addition to other modular construction types. According to the Turkish Precast Concrete Association, the total volume of prefabricated concrete production by member and non-member companies was approximately 1.43 million cubic metres and 0.46 million cubic metres, respectively, totalling nearly 1.9 million cubic metres. The prefabricated concrete production line is comprised of various elements, from structural beams and columns to railway sleepers, from bridge girders to tunnel segments and from wind turbine towers to sound barriers.

The modular construction types involve, among many others, site camps, military camps, refugee camps, off-shore camps, residential and commercial projects, mobile hospitals, hangars and other special-purpose structures and buildings. Turkish modular and prefabricated construction companies export their products worldwide as one of the main global suppliers in this sector.

11.2.6 Technology/innovation/BIM

Many construction companies in Türkiye use information technology (**IT**) not only within their corporate organisations but also at their project sites. Some large companies have their own technology development divisions to cater to their own needs. It is an indispensable need for large construction companies to adopt IT software programmes in order to remain competitive in the construction market by minimising costs, reducing inefficiencies and increasing productivity. Almost all construction projects use scheduling and cost control software, enterprise resource planning (**ERP**) systems, BIM programmes, and many others.

Although the use of BIM is not yet widely adopted in the Turkish construction sector, in recent years there has been an increasing awareness amongst both construction companies and engineering and consultancy companies; thus, the private sector can be said to be leading the efforts in terms of implementing BIM technologies in Türkiye. Most companies have started to realise that using BIM throughout the life cycle of a project,

---

4 *Türkiye Prefabrik Birliği*.

5 '2021 Yılı Sektör Raporu' (*Türkiye Prefabrik Birliği*, Temmuz 2022) www.prefab.org.tr/icerik.php?yayinlar/sektor-raporu&tr (accessed 29 August 2022).

from planning to design and throughout the construction, is a significant value-added process due to its many advantages and benefits, *inter alia*, ease of integration and coordination of different disciplines during the design process, fast and easy data and document sharing, increased foreseeability and minimised error (i.e., by way of clash analysis) and faster delivery of the project. Only a few Turkish firms specialised in BIM have started to provide consultancy services to help construction projects, so there is currently an insufficient number of skilled and experienced professionals in this area in the Turkish market.

Based on a survey[6] conducted among construction professionals, the majority of professionals experienced in BIM applications are employed in large companies, i.e., with 100 or more employees. The survey also suggests that construction professionals in commercial real estate, metro and railway systems projects in Türkiye have shown the highest interest in using BIM applications. Another interesting outcome of the survey is that amongst the survey population, the ratios of those who use BIM in their projects are in the vicinity of 22%, 16%, 13% and 8% in the architectural, construction, mechanical and electrical disciplines, respectively. The authors are of the view that the requirements to use BIM applications in construction projects in Türkiye have been on an increasing trend; therefore, the aforementioned ratios are very likely to increase exponentially in the near future.

In recent years, a few IT start-up companies have emerged in Türkiye, specialising in the production of airborne drones equipped with **AI** (artificial intelligence) that collect and process site data to be used for managing construction projects. This high-tech equipment helps increase productivity and efficiency with increased accuracy in data that would otherwise be collected by site staff and reduces time and costs within a wide range of site activities, including preparing monthly reports, measuring quantities for the purpose of monthly payment statements, health and safety and monitoring and inspecting the works performed, among others.

11.2.7 Government/private sector procurement

11.2.7.1 Private procurement

Under Turkish law, there is no legal requirement for private companies to conduct a tender before awarding a contract to a Contractor. In addition, there are no special requirements as to the form of contract unless otherwise set forth under the laws. It is at the discretion of the persons subject to private law whether or not to lay down any conditions in a contract. It should be noted that even in the case of private procurement, if there are any legislative requirements relating to the construction that may affect the social order, environment, historic fabric, etc., those requirements should be complied with.

In practice, Employers tend to have construction contracts in writing for at least medium-scale projects due to the burden of proof.

11.2.7.2 Public procurement

Construction works carried out by public institutions and establishments that are subject to public law or under the control of public authorities or using public resources are subject to laws relating to public procurement. The main pieces of legislation relating to

6 İbrahim Utku Başyazıcı, 'Türkiye BIM Raporu 2018–2019' (June 2020) www.bimgenius.org/yayinlar.html (accessed 11 December 2021)

public procurement are the *State Procurement Law*, the *Public Procurement Law*, the *Public Procurement Contracts Law* and secondary legislation.

11.2.7.3 Procurement for infrastructure investments
There are various infrastructure investment models actively used in Türkiye, including the public–private partnership model, the intra-governmental agreement model, the pure license-based investment model and the conventional procurement model. In addition, specific pieces of legislation governing infrastructure investments need to be taken into consideration for construction as well.

11.2.8 Insurance requirements

11.2.8.1 Compulsory insurance
It is mandatory to procure and maintain building completion insurance for prepaid house sales in accordance with the *Regulation Regarding Prepaid House Sales*. This requirement aims to protect consumers in case of bankruptcy, abandonment or death of the Contractor. Even though this insurance is mandatory, in practice it is rarely used.

11.2.8.2 Non-compulsory insurance
In practice, Contractors are often required in a contract to purchase and maintain all-risk insurance and employer's liability insurance. In addition, subject to the risks contained in the project, other insurance including (i) personal liability insurance; (ii) contractors' plant and machinery insurance; (iii) machinery breakdown insurance; (iv) kidnap and ransom insurance; (v) professional liability insurance; (vi) electronic equipment insurance; (vii) hazardous materials/wastes insurance; (viii) fire insurance and (ix) freight insurance may be required.

11.2.9 Common forms of contract

11.2.9.1 Public works
The principles and procedures that pertain to regulating and implementing public procurement contracts under the *Public Procurement Law* are established in the *Public Procurement Contracts Law*.

In contracts to be made pursuant to the *Public Procurement Law*, no provisions that contradict the tender documents may be included in a contract. Contract provisions cannot be amended, and no supplementary contracts can be made, other than the cases specified in the *Public Procurement Law*. The parties to public procurement contracts made under the *Public Procurement Law* have equal rights and obligations in implementing the contractual provisions. No articles that are contrary to this principle may be included in the provisions of either the tender documents or contracts.

Standard contracts in connection with the procurement of works are published in the Official Gazette in order to assure uniformity.

In the procurement of works consequent to tenders carried out in accordance with the *Public Procurement Law*, contracts may be made as:

1. Turnkey lump-sum contracts, where the total tender price for the entire work is proposed by the tenderer on the basis of application projects and site lists thereof.

2. Unit-price contracts, where the total price is calculated by multiplying the quantity for each item of work specified in the schedule prepared by the contracting entity with unit prices proposed by the tenderer for each corresponding work item, on the basis of preliminary or final projects and site lists, along with unit price definitions in the procurement of works, on the basis of detailed specifications of the work involved in procurement of goods or services.
3. Hybrid contracts made by using the turnkey lump-sum method for a certain part of the works and the unit-price method for other parts.
4. Individual contracts on the basis of a framework agreement.

11.2.9.2 Private works

In Türkiye, there are no common forms of contract used for private construction works. In practice, the Contractor often drafts a contract and negotiates with the Employer. As for subcontracts, usually the Contractor uses a standard contract it has drafted.

With the huge and complex investments in Türkiye in the energy, infrastructure and healthcare sectors carried out by both local and foreign investors, Turkish contractors have started to use standard forms of construction contracts. Foreign employers and international funding institutions prefer to use contracts they are familiar with, and in construction, in general, they require the use of the FIDIC Standard Forms of Contract. However, there should not be a misconception that the FIDIC Standard Forms of Contract can only be used for international projects. They are used for local projects as well.

Even though Türkiye has several projects where foreign investors have succeeded in providing for the application of their substantive law for construction contracts, recently, we have started to have construction contracts with Turkish law as the governing law. Under these circumstances, the interface between Turkish law and the FIDIC contracts has significant importance.

11.2.10 Dispute resolution

11.2.10.1 Litigation in court

Disputes arising from relations governed by private law are resolved by civil courts. A decision rendered by foreign courts can be recognised and enforced in Türkiye subject to certain requirements set out in the *International Private and Procedural Law*.

Turkish courts generally prefer written submissions. The parties are free to submit evidence and legal opinions of experts together with their submissions. The main stages of proceedings are (i) exchange of petitions; (ii) preliminary proceedings; (iii) review of the case by the court; (iv) hearings; (v) rendering of the decision; and (vi) appeal (at the discretion of the parties). An average time period for the first instance proceedings for civil law disputes is around two years and one year for the appeal, unless the parties amicably settle at an early stage. It may take longer in complex cases.

11.2.10.2 Mediation

Parties may request, or in some cases may be required, to apply for mediation before initiating proceedings.

Mandatory mediation is a legal prerequisite for some disputes, such as those arising from the *Labour Law*, commercial law and consumer law. In such cases, lawsuits filed before going to a mediator are rejected due to the absence of a cause of action.

Parties may apply for arbitrary mediation before filing a private lawsuit to resolve a dispute quickly and in a cost-effective way.

11.2.10.3 Arbitration

Arbitration is the most widely used alternative dispute resolution method in Türkiye. Other forms of alternative dispute resolution such as mediation, conciliation, mini-trial, referee and expert determination are not as popular as arbitration. While large firms tend to opt for arbitration, Turkish small and medium-sized enterprises do not usually use arbitration due to a lack of information with regard to out-of-court settlements and potentially high arbitration fees, which may vary depending on the size of the dispute. In construction, energy and infrastructure disputes, in particular, arbitration is an appealing dispute resolution method. As Türkiye has been one of the significant emergent markets in recent years and with the upward trend in global trade and the growth of transnational companies, the number of international disputes to be settled through international arbitration has considerably increased.

As for the legislative scope, the main piece of legislation governing domestic arbitration in Türkiye is the *Civil Procedural Code*. International arbitration is governed by the *International Arbitration Law*, which is modelled on the UNCITRAL *Model Law* and the international arbitration section of the *Swiss Federal Private International Law* of 1987.

Türkiye is a party to the *European Convention on International Commercial Arbitration* of 1961 and the *Washington Convention on the Settlement of Investment Disputes* of 1965. In addition, Türkiye is a party to various other bilateral agreements. Putting these aside, very importantly, Türkiye is a party to the *Convention on the Recognition and Enforcement of Foreign Arbitral Awards*, also known as the *New York Convention*. Provisions of the *New York Convention* have the same force as the other Turkish statutory provisions and are regarded as part of the domestic legal system. However, domestic arbitral awards as well as those relating to non-commercial matters are not governed by the *New York Convention*.

It should be noted that according to the recent precedents of the Court of Appeals, the arbitration clause or the arbitration agreement should be in the Turkish language. Therefore, even if the prevailing language in a FIDIC contract is a language other than Turkish language, it would be advisable to have the arbitration clause in dual languages.

11.2.10.4 Dispute Boards

Turkish construction companies entered the international arena in the early 1970s, and since then, they have undertaken thousands of construction projects where the majority are based on the FIDIC Conditions of Contract of various versions. This has enabled such companies to be exposed to the concept and mechanism of Dispute Boards earlier in international projects rather than domestic ones. Although there is no sufficient database or records available, based on the authors' best knowledge, Dispute Boards started to be used in Türkiye in the early 2000s after the inception of the 1999 Editions of the FIDIC Suite of Contracts in projects funded by the European Union and International Financing Institutions, mostly in large infrastructure projects. In the early years, contract parties tended to delete the provisions for Dispute Boards in their contracts, mostly due to lack of awareness and knowledge of the concept, in order to incorporate local courts as the dispute resolution mechanism. Nevertheless, over the past decade, the general knowledge and understanding of the benefits and advantages of Dispute Boards, particularly those which are standing, within the construction sector has dramatically increased thanks to numerous international and local conferences, seminars and training organised throughout Türkiye.

According to sub-clause 20.4[7] of the 1999 FIDIC Conditions of Contract, decisions rendered by the Dispute Adjudication Board (DAB)[8] are binding upon the Parties who shall promptly give effect to such decision unless and until it is revised in an amicable settlement or on an arbitral award. If either party is dissatisfied with the DAB's decision, such Party may give a Notice of Dissatisfaction (NOD), where such notice must be given within 28 days from the date of receipt of the DAB's decision.[9] If a NOD is not given within the stipulated time, the decision becomes final. As in many jurisdictions, the state of finality of a decision enables the contract parties to commence enforcement proceedings; however, unlike the enforcement of a court decision, a final DAB decision is not construed as, or equivalent to, a court decision in Türkiye because a Dispute Board is not recognised as a legal authority within the Turkish legal system. Therefore, the decision of a Dispute Board cannot be considered a judgment within Turkish jurisprudence for the purposes of enforcement. It is also stipulated in sub-clause 20.4 that the DAB shall not be deemed to act as an arbitrator, suggesting that the decision of the DAB cannot be treated as an arbitral award, and as a result, the parties to the contract cannot apply to the local courts to enforce a DAB decision relying on the provisions for enforcement and the enforcement mechanisms envisaged in the *1958 New York Convention.*

Aside from the foregoing, according to sub-clause 20.3 of the 1999 FIDIC Conditions of Contract, if the Parties fail to agree on the appointment of a member of the DAB, the appointing entity (or the official) named in the Particular Conditions shall appoint the member upon the request of either or both of the Parties after due consultation with both parties. It is the authors' experience that in the majority of FIDIC-based construction contracts in Türkiye, the appointing entity is named the Association of Turkish Consulting Engineers and Architects[10] (**ATCEA**).

11.2.11 Current challenges

Despite the fact that the construction sector in Türkiye is well developed, it still presents challenges, particularly in the international market, which must be addressed. Turkish construction companies are keen to take on new projects and, in their eagerness, tend to neglect to review the contracts in detail or seek assistance from their legal advisers. This is one of the biggest reasons for disputes arising on the grounds that contractors do not have full knowledge of the provisions contained in the contracts and their legal consequences.

Since the construction industry is at the forefront of Türkiye's economic growth, there should be standards in construction contracts in order to ensure a certain level of quality

7 Sub-clause 21.4.3 in the 2017 FIDIC 2nd Edition Conditions of Contract.

8 DAAB – Dispute Avoidance/Adjudication Board in the 2017 FIDIC 2nd Edition Conditions of Contract.

9 Sub-clause 21.4.4 in the 2017 FIDIC 2nd Edition Conditions of Contract.

10 ATCEA is a non-governmental organisation established in 1980 in Ankara, Türkiye and became a member of FIDIC in 1987 and of the EFCA (European Federation of Engineering Consultancy Associations) in 2001, as the only representative of these two federations in Türkiye. ATCEA has 101 members as of September 2022 and its website address is www.tmmmb.org.tr

and reliability in the works. Standard form contracts, including the FIDIC Standard Forms of Contract, should often be used.

11.2.12 Unique features of the construction industry in Türkiye

The main sector in the construction industry in Türkiye is residential construction since owning residential property is considered one of the most preferred investment options. The demand for real estate in Türkiye almost never stops although small fluctuations may occur from year to year. As seen in the table below, even during the global economic slowdown due to the COVID-19 pandemic in 2020, the number of sales in residential property even showed a moderate jump that year. It should also be noted that purchases of residential property made by foreign nationals in Türkiye have been gradually increasing in recent years, and in 2022, a record number of residential property sales to foreign nationals is likely to be realised based on the actual numbers of sales shown within the first nine months of 2022.[11]

Year	**2018**	**2019**	**2020**	**2021**	**2022 (nine months)**
Total no. of sales (residential)	1,375,398	1,348,729	1,499,316	1,491,856	1,057,193
Total no. of sales to foreign nationals	39,663	45,483	40,812	58,576	49,644

Sales of residential property also have a direct positive effect on other industries, such as furniture, appliances, textiles and many others.

Construction material production is well developed in Türkiye. The main line of construction materials produced in Türkiye includes, among others, iron and steel products, mineral, stone and soil products, electrical products and equipment, metal-based products, chemical-based products, wood products, insulation products and prefabricated structures. Turkish producers not only supply these products for the local market but also export them worldwide. According to the Construction Material Manufacturers Association of Türkiye (**IMSAD**),[12] Turkish manufacturers have achieved an annual export of 61.15 million tonnes of construction materials worldwide for an amount of US$ 34.6 billion in value between October 2021 and September 2022, which represented a 21% increase in export value compared to the previous period.[13]

In 2020, unlike the situation for residential property sales realised in Türkiye, due to the global impact of the COVID-19 pandemic, the total value of construction projects undertaken by Turkish construction companies in international markets was only around US$ 15 billion; however, this amount dramatically increased to over US$ 29 billion in

11 Based on the statistics published by TUİK (Turkish Statistical Institute), https://data.tuik.gov.tr/Bulten/Index?p=Konut-Satis-Istatistikleri-Eylul-2022-45681 (accessed 11 November 2022).

12 İMSAD was established in 1984 as an NGO (www.imsad.org).

13 Türkiye İMSAD (September 2022) *İnşaat Malzemeleri Sanayi Diş Ticaret Endeksleri* 62, www.imsad.org/endeks/insaat-malzemeleri-sanayi-dis-ticaret-endeksleri/endeksler (accessed 10 November 2022).

2021 because Turkish contractors can adapt themselves quickly to changing market conditions and are able to turn such changes to their advantage.

11.3 The impact of COVID-19 in Türkiye

11.3.1 The impact of COVID-19 on the execution of construction projects in Türkiye

11.3.1.1 Constraints on contractual relationships

On 11 March 2020, the first coronavirus case was recorded in Türkiye and the government started to take precautionary measures. The initial measures were face mask use with certain exemptions, social distancing and hygiene. The Ministry of Health created a COVID-19 website to track down all the developments in Türkiye related to the pandemic. There have been lockdowns for certain periods. During the lockdowns there were restrictions including (i) staying at home except for essential shopping trips and urgent medical treatment; (ii) official approval for travelling between cities; (iii) closure of schools; and (iv) limitation on alcohol sales. However, some businesses, including those in the construction sector, were kept exempt from those restrictions.

The measures and legal changes made following the spread of the COVID-19 pandemic in Türkiye have affected contractual relationships in terms of the performance obligations of parties. The changes to commercial life consequent to the various mandatory measures, government advisory decisions and general health measures implemented to prevent the spread of the outbreak have made the continuation of contractual relationships and the performance of obligations difficult for certain legal transactions and impossible for others.

11.3.1.2 Health and safety constraints on employees

The Ministry of Labour and Social Security issued a general letter to the Governors of all cities. The general letter advised that employers should inform all of their employees about the protective and preventive precautions against the health and safety risks that may be faced at workplaces and that employers should, in addition, inform their employees who have not completed their COVID-19 vaccinations in writing. As of 6 September 2021, employers are entitled to require PCR tests once a week from their employees refusing vaccination. The test results must be kept at the workplace.

The *Guideline on Measures to Combat against New Coronavirus (COVID-19) Outbreak at Workplaces*, issued by the Ministry of Family, Labour and Social Services on 20 March 2020, regulates risk assessment and emergency planning; cleaning and hygiene rules; personal protective equipment; and advice on travels and meetings. On the same date, the Ministry of Environment and Urban Planning General Directorate of Construction Works issued a circular setting forth the measures that employers must take in order to ensure that construction and audit services in the public and private sectors are carried out safely. The *Guideline on Measures to Be Taken by Occupational Health and Safety Professionals at Workplaces in Scope of the Novel Coronavirus Outbreak*, issued by the General Directorate of Occupational Health and Safety on 25 March 2020, set forth the minimum requirements regarding the use of personnel vehicles; travel; entry to and exit from the workplace; working environment; meetings and training; and cafeterias and recreational areas. It stated that employers must follow the announcements of governmental authorities and take additional appropriate measures corresponding to the field of activity being carried out at the workplace, the number of employees, the working environment and the methods used. On 26 May 2020, the Scientific Advisory Board issued a Guidance on Outbreak Management and Working Principles specifically stipulating the measures on a sectoral basis and promoting, among others, abiding by social distancing principles, proper use of medical masks and complying with hygiene rules with a view to minimising the transmission risk of COVID-19. In addition, several workplaces formed their own emergency action plans and site operating procedures relating to COVID-19.

11.3.1.3 Changes to regular employment law

The measures taken due to the COVID-19 pandemic intended in part to provide temporary employment security to employees. The *Law on the Mitigation of the Impacts of the Novel Coronavirus (COVID-19) Outbreak on Economic and Social Life and on Amendment of Certain Laws* introduced certain amendments to the *Labour Law*. It set forth a prohibition against terminations, with certain exceptions, for a duration of three months starting from 17 April 2020. It was further stipulated that employers could impose unpaid leave without the employees' consent, partially or in full, while the prohibition was in effect. Employees were not allowed to terminate the employment contract based on just cause due to the implementation of unilateral unpaid leave. The term of the unilateral unpaid leave was later extended until 30 June 2021. During that period, employers were prohibited from terminating employment contracts, except on just cause due to incompatibility with goodwill and morals and similar circumstances.

Up until the end of the probation of termination period, US$ 2.08 (TRY 39.24) was paid from the Unemployment Insurance Fund per each of the unemployed day(s) spent on unpaid leave.

11.3.1.4 Financial support

In order to mitigate the impact on the economy of the protective measures that were adopted against the coronavirus, the President held a meeting with wide participation from Ministers, directors of public institutions, organisations and non-governmental organisations. Soon afterwards, a package called the Economic Stability Shield was published. The package covered several measures to subsidise the impacts of COVID-19 on all sectors including tourism, real estate and exports.

11.3.2 The impact of COVID-19 on the operation of construction contracts in Türkiye

The outbreak's effect on delays in performance or the inability to discharge contractual undertakings is evaluated under the notions of excessive difficulty of performance, partial impossibility of performance and impossibility of performance, all of which are regulated under the *Turkish Code of Obligations*. These are also examined in light of the concepts of *force majeure* and unexpected circumstances (extraordinary circumstances) as discussed in both Court of Appeal precedents and legal scholarship.

On 1 April 2020, the Presidency published a circular for public procurement contracts, which established, with respect to contracts executed under the *Public Procurement Law* (including its exceptions), that an application should be made to the contracting administration documenting the impossibility of performance, if the performance of a contract is not possible due to the COVID-19 outbreak, temporarily or permanently, in part or in whole. The contracting administration was to review the application before rendering a decision, after obtaining an assessment from the Ministry of Treasury and Finance. If the administration determined that (i) the event was not caused by the Contractor's fault; (ii) the event prevented the Contractor from performing the contract; and (iii) the Contractor was unable to remove the effects of the event, the administration could grant an extension of time or decide to terminate the contract.

Several Contractors who have executed public procurement contracts applied to the contracting administrations under this circular and often got time extensions. It is notable that some of Türkiye's major infrastructure projects that were exempt from the *Public Procurement Law*, yet satisfied the necessary qualifications, benefited from the referenced circular as well.

11.4 Turkish governing law of the contract

11.4.1 Constraints on the governing law of a construction contract

In principle, the Turkish 'conflict of laws' rules recognise and give effect to the choice of foreign law as the governing law of agreements so long as the agreement in question has a foreign element, provided that such choice of law does not violate the rules of public order. The choice must be expressed or demonstrated with reasonable certainty by the terms of the contract or the circumstances of the case.

The parties can select the law applicable to the whole or only a part of the contract. Accordingly, the parties are free to choose a foreign law as the governing law of a construction contract and such choice will be legally valid. However, the *Turkish International Private and Procedural Law* can only be applied to transactions with foreign elements. If a construction contract is executed between Turkish parties and there is no foreign element, the governing law should be Turkish law. In addition, the legislation may dictate the application of Turkish law as the governing law. As an example, it is set forth in *Decree No. 2011/1807 of the Council of Ministers on Procedures and Principles of Implementation of the Law No. 3996 on the Procurement of Certain Investments and Services under the Build-Operate-Transfer Model* that the applicable law to the substance of disputes arising from implementation contracts should be Turkish law. In practice, in public procurement projects, the contracting administration often chooses Turkish law as the governing law.

11.4.2 Formal requirements for a construction contract

Under Turkish law, construction contracts are characterised as contracts for work and services and are regulated by the *Turkish Code of Obligations* (*TCO*). Contracts for work and services are defined as contracts whereby a Contractor undertakes to produce a result and the party ordering the same undertakes to pay therefor (*TCO* Article 470). The object of the contract is the work itself, not merely the performance of some service. The Contractor owes a result to the owner of the work.

Unless there is an explicit provision set forth in the laws, construction contracts are not required to be in a specific form to be legally binding and valid. As an example of the exception, construction contracts that impose on the Contractor an obligation to transfer the ownership of the constructed immovable (such as a construction contract in return for flat[s]) must be executed in writing before a Notary Public to be legally binding and valid. In practice, parties prefer to have the construction contracts in writing. It is always recommended to have construction contracts in writing for the purposes of evidence.

11.5 What Special Provisions in the Particular Conditions are necessary for consistency with applicable laws in Türkiye?

11.5.1 FIDIC General Conditions that are incompatible or inconsistent with Turkish governing law of the Contract

11.5.1.1 Overview

Turkish law is part of the European continental legal system. The legal norms are incorporated into codes and promulgated legislation. However, FIDIC Standard Forms of Contract, in principle, have the characteristics of common law contracts. In light of this, one may face problems in aligning FIDIC Standard Forms of Contract with Turkish law due to the differences between the civil law system and the common law system, and some concepts including liquidated damages used in common law are not known in civil law.

It should be noted that in principle, FIDIC Standard Forms of Contract are viable without major adjustments in the Particular Conditions. However, if there is a mandatory provision of Turkish law, a divergent provision of a construction contract may be considered null and void despite complying with the provisions of FIDIC Standard Forms of Contract.

Under Turkish law, there is the principle of the freedom of contract. The *Turkish Code of Obligations* contains that the content of a contract may, within the limits of the law, be established at the discretion of the parties. If some of the provisions of the contract are null and void, this will not affect the validity of the other provisions, except that if it is apparent that the contract would not have been concluded without the referred provisions, then the contract, as a whole, will be null and void. The limits of the law are also set forth by the *Turkish Code of Obligations*. Contacts are null and void if they are against the mandatory provisions of law, *bonos mores*,[14] public order or personal rights or if the subject of the contract is impossible.

In addition, when interpreting a construction contract governed by Turkish law, the true and common intention of the parties must be ascertained without dwelling on any expressions they may have used either in error or by way of disguising the true nature of their purpose. This is one of the most important differences between Turkish law and the common law system. Under Turkish law, the court must go beyond the provisions of the contract in order to ascertain the true and common intention of the parties. However, in the common law system, the court will, to a much greater extent, interpret the contract literally.

14 Latin for good manners.

11.5.1.2 Language

The official language of FIDIC Standard Forms of Contract is English. Even though the Association of Turkish Consulting Engineers and Architects has translated the Red Book (1999) and the Yellow Book (1999) into Turkish, it is highly likely to encounter terminological problems when certain legal terms are aligned with common law legal terms. Therefore, it would be advisable for the contracting parties and their legal advisers to review and comprehend the original English version in depth before using its Turkish translation.

Another significant issue with respect to the choice of language is that under *Law No. 805 on the Compulsory Use of Turkish in Economic Enterprises*, it is compulsory that Turkish companies execute their agreements in the Turkish language. Therefore, if the contracting parties are Turkish, then the contract should be in Turkish or in dual columns with Turkish being the prevailing language. In project finance, where foreign parties are involved, people need to take this requirement into consideration.

11.5.1.3 Delay Damages

Under the FIDIC Standard Forms of Contract, if the Contractor fails to comply with the Time for Completion, the Contractor is subject to pay Delay Damages to the Employer for its default. It is not explicit whether the Delay Damages referred to under the FIDIC Standard Forms of Contract should be considered liquidated damages or penalties.

Liquidated damages are an estimation of damages that the Employer may incur in case of delay and will be due only if the Contractor is liable for the delay and if the Employer proves the existence of damage.

The concept of liquidated damages does not exist under Turkish law, whereas the concept of penalty is regulated under the *Turkish Code of Obligations*.

Where a penalty is agreed to be paid in the case of a failure to perform the contract at the stipulated time or place, the creditor may demand both the fulfilment of the contract and the penalty, unless it has waived its rights clearly or accepted the performance without reservation. The creditor should claim the penalty either prior to the acceptance of performance or at the latest at the time of the performance, or state that it reserves its right to claim the penalty at the time of the performance; otherwise, the creditor would not be able to claim the penalty.

Even if the creditor does not suffer any damage or loss, the penalty must be paid. However, if the damage that the creditor suffers is higher than the amount of the penalty, only in this case, the creditor can demand this further compensation on the condition that the fault of the debtor is proved.

The parties are free to determine the amount of the penalty. Judges may reduce excessive penalties at their discretion.

In order to avoid any disputes that may arise between contracting parties as to the legal nature of Delay Damages, it would be to their benefit to set forth whether Delay Damages are claimed as liquidated damages or as a penalty.

11.5.1.4 Compound interest

Under the FIDIC Standard Forms of Contract, the Contractor is entitled to receive financing charges compounded monthly on any unpaid amounts during periods of delay. However, under the *Turkish Code of Obligations*, default interest is never payable on default interest and this is mandatory. The parties need to include a Special Provision in the Particular Conditions eliminating the application of compound interest.

11.5.2 FIDIC General Conditions that are incompatible or inconsistent with the law of the Site/Country

The governing law of the contract and the law of the Site are different concepts. Whereas the governing law regulates the contractual relationship of the parties, the parties need to abide by the law of the Site in respect of transactions with third persons. With respect to Turkish law being the law of the Site, there are no provisions of the FIDIC Standard Forms of Contract that are incompatible or inconsistent with Turkish law.

11.5.3 The FIDIC General Conditions are incompatible or inconsistent with the relevant laws on dispute determination in Türkiye

As mentioned earlier, a final DAB/DAAB decision is neither construed as nor equivalent to a court decision in Türkiye since a Dispute Board is not recognised as a legal authority within the Turkish legal system. As a result, a decision of a Dispute Board cannot be considered a judgment within Turkish jurisprudence for the purposes of enforcement. A Dispute Board decision also cannot be treated as an arbitral award, so the parties to the contract cannot apply to the local courts to enforce a DAB decision relying on the provisions for enforcement and enforcement mechanisms envisaged in the *1958 New York Convention*.

11.6 What Special Provisions in the Particular Conditions are desirable for consistency with applicable laws in Türkiye?

11.6.1 Summary

As explained in the preceding section, due to the differences between the common law and civil law, it would be in the interest of the parties to make sure that they fully comprehend the concepts to be addressed below and if their understanding varies from the provisions of the FIDIC Standard Forms of Contract, the parties need to include Special Provisions to the Particular Conditions for this purpose.

The following concepts are much debated in Turkish domestic practice.

11.6.1.1 Engineer

While under the FIDIC Standard Forms of Contract the Engineer is the person appointed by the Employer and is deemed to act for the Employer, it is also foreseen that the Engineer is to certify the payments and make a fair determination in case of a disagreement between the contracting parties.[15]

This role of the Engineer as an independent contract administrator is similar to the model developed under the common law contract practice. Because the civil law system

15 It is set forth in sub-clause 3.7 of the 2017 FIDIC Red Book and Yellow Book that the Engineer shall act neutrally and shall not be deemed to act for the Employer when carrying out his/her duties under the sub-clause [*Agreement or Determination*].

has only recently become acquainted with this concept, there may be difficulties in its application and interpretation under Turkish law.

Another issue that may be raised in relation to the powers of the Engineer is that there should be a separate contract between the Employer and the Engineer, and the powers granted to the Engineer under the referred contract may not be similar to the powers granted under the FIDIC Standard Forms of Contract to be signed between the Employer and the Contractor. The Engineer's contract with the Employer may grant it fewer powers than those under the FIDIC contract. If the Engineer goes beyond its powers under its contract with the Employer but stays within the scope granted under the FIDIC contract, under Turkish law, the Employer will be bound by the acts of the Engineer unless the Contractor has been previously informed of the limited powers of the Engineer.

11.6.1.2 Priority of documents

The FIDIC Standard Forms of Contract set out a hierarchy of contractual documents, but this cannot be accepted as a rule of interpretation. If there are conflicting provisions, a court applying Turkish law has to examine the contract as a whole. Furthermore, it is stated that if there is an ambiguity or a discrepancy found in the documents, the Engineer will clarify. It should be emphasised that the contracting parties are not bound by such clarification. In a dispute, the contract, as a whole, will have to be interpreted in accordance with Turkish law.

11.6.1.3 Force Majeure/Exceptional Event

It is set forth in the FIDIC Standard Forms of Contract that in case of an event of *Force Majeure* (or an Exceptional Event in the 2017 FIDIC Standard Forms of Contract), if the Contractor suffers delays and/or incurs costs, then it is entitled to an extension of time and/or payment of incurred cost.

Under Turkish law, if work perishes by reason of an unexpected event before delivery, the Contractor cannot claim the payment of the price and expenses, unless the Employer is in default on acceptance of the work. In this case, damage to the materials is discharged by the party who provided them. The Contractor may claim the price and extra expenses of the work done if the perishing has occurred because of a defect in the material or the land provided or the direction given by the Employer, and it notified the Employer about the possible adverse outcomes in time. If the Employer is at fault, the Contractor has the right to claim compensation for damages as well. Even though the perishing of the work is regulated under the *Turkish Code of Obligations*, it is not mandatory, and the provisions of the FIDIC Standard Forms of Contract relating to *Force Majeure*/Exceptional Event regulating temporary or partial impossibilities remain valid.

Even though the concept of *Force Majeure*/Exceptional Event is set forth in the FIDIC Standard Forms of Contract, its impact on the Contract Price and payment is not regulated. Under Turkish law, for lump-sum contracts, if any unforeseeable or foreseeable but unconsidered circumstances prevent the work from being performed or make it difficult to perform at the previously decided lump sum price, the Contractor has the right to ask a judge to adapt the agreement to the new circumstances. If this is not possible or cannot be expected from the counterparty, the Contractor has the right to rescind the contract. Only in the case of violation of the principle of honesty, may the Contractor exercise its right of termination. It may be advisable for parties to lump sum contracts to include a Special Provision in the Particular Conditions for this purpose.

11.6.1.4 Defects liability

Under Turkish law, the concepts of delivery and acceptance are different from each other. Where reference is made to the concept of acceptance, the intention is final acceptance, not temporary acceptance – the term temporary acceptance is meant to determine and remedy any defects. The liabilities of the Contractor will cease only with final acceptance.

The *Turkish Code of Obligations* sets forth that where the party ordering the work accepts it, either expressly or impliedly, the Contractor is discharged from liability, except in the case of defects which could not be noticed upon acceptance after duly examining the work or which were intentionally concealed by the Contractor. The work is approved by implication if the party that ordered it fails to examine it and to give notice according to law. Defects that do not become apparent until later must be notified immediately after their discovery, in the absence of which the work is considered accepted.

The provisions of the *Turkish Code of Obligations* are not mandatory as regards defects liability and the parties do not need to include Special Provisions to the Particular Conditions. However, to avoid any misunderstanding, it is recommended for the contracting parties to review and agree on the timing of the Contractor's discharge from liability prior to entering into the Contract.

It is governed under Turkish law that an action for defects of immovable structures may be brought against the Contractor within five years from the date of acceptance. In case of gross default of the Contractor, the time bar is 20 years without regard to the quality of the defective work. Whereas the time bar for gross default is mandatory, the five-year time bar for immovable structures can be reduced or extended by the contracting parties provided that the right of claim of the Employer should not become, in practice, onerous or impossible in violation of the principle of good faith. It would be in the interest of the contracting parties to include a Special Provision in the Particular Conditions for this purpose.

11.6.1.5 Suspension of Work

Under the FIDIC Standard Forms of Contract arbitration may be commenced prior to or after completion of the Works and the parties will continue to perform their obligations without regard to arbitration. It is also set forth that the Contractor is entitled to suspend the Works upon the occurrence of certain conditions and claim an extension of time and compensation, i.e., cost plus reasonable profit. In practice, these provisions often cause a Dispute between the Parties. Employers allege that the Contractor has suspended the Works in bad faith and claim compensation (i.e., Delay Damages and/or other damages incurred as the case may be), and such Disputes are often settled by arbitration or adjudication. The good faith of a Contractor in suspending the Works has a crucial impact on the decision of the DAB/DAAB or arbitral tribunal. If the Dispute has arisen due to suspension by the Contractor prior to the completion of the Works, there should be an interim mechanism such as payment for the agreed part of the Works, depositing the payments to an escrow account or submission of a performance bond by the Employer until the decision of the DAB/DAAB or award of the arbitral tribunal, and it is recommended to include a Special Provision in the Particular Conditions for this purpose.

11.6.1.6 Fitness for purpose

It is regulated by the FIDIC Standard Forms of Contract that the Works will be fit for the purpose when they are completed. However, there is no such concept under Turkish law. It is governed by the *Turkish Code of Obligations* that the Contractor has to perform the Works it has undertaken by taking the Employer's justified interests into consideration and with loyalty and care.

The obligation of completing the Works fit for the purpose is much more onerous than the obligation of performing the Works with loyalty and care. The Contractor guarantees a specific work product in case of the obligation of fitness for purpose and it is not required for the Employer to prove negligence. This may be problematic in the case of professional indemnity insurance as well, since professional indemnity insurance does not cover the obligation of fitness for the purpose, and the coverage has to be expanded.

It is of paramount importance that the parties understand the differences between the concepts referred to and, if necessary, include a Special Provision in the Particular Conditions for this purpose.

11.7 Applicable legislation for Turkish governing law of the contract

The main pieces of legislation applicable to a construction contract containing Turkish law as the governing law is the *Turkish Code of Obligations* and the *Civil Procedural Code.*

11.8 Summary of applicable legislation for Turkish governing law of the contract

11.8.1 Entry into and operation of a construction contract

The *Turkish Code of Obligations No. 6098* dated 11 January 2011 is applicable for construction contracts. The construction contracts are in the legal nature of contracts for work and services and the applicable provisions of the *Turkish Code of Obligations* are Articles 470 to 481 inclusive. The titles of the applicable Articles of the *Turkish Code of Obligations* are:

- Article 470: A. Definition
- Article 471: B. Effect I. Obligations of contractor 1. In general
- Article 472: 2. In regard to materials
- Article 473: 3. Commencement and execution of work
- Article 474: 4. Liability for defects a. Ascertainment of defects
- Article 475: b. Optional rights of employer
- Article 476: c. Liability of employer
- Article 477: d. Acceptance of work
- Article 478: e. Statute of limitations
- Article 479: II. Obligations of employer 1. Maturity of price
- Article 480: 2. Price a. lump sum price
- Article 481: b. Price on quantum meruit basis

11.8.2 Termination of a construction contract

The titles of the applicable Articles of the *Turkish Code of Obligations* are:

- Article 482: C. Termination of contract I. Exceeding the estimated price
- Article 483: II. Destruction of work
- Article 484: III. Termination against payment of indemnity
- Article 485: IV. Impossibility of performance imputable to employer
- Article 486: V. Death or inability of contractor

11.8.3 Dispute resolution

Disputes can be settled either before the courts of Türkiye or by arbitration. The main piece of applicable legislation is the *Civil Procedural Code No. 6100* dated 12 January 2011.

11.9 Applicable legislation if the Site/Country is in Türkiye

The provisions of the FIDIC Standard Forms of Contract regarding calibration of testing apparatus, equipment and instruments, bankruptcy, insolvency, liquidation, rights of set off, termination, limitation of liability and misrepresentation are compatible with and valid under Turkish law. The main piece of legislation applicable to the referred concepts is the *Turkish Code of Obligations*.

11.10 Applicable legislation if the 'seat' of the dispute determination is Türkiye

If there is a domestic arbitration, then the *Civil Procedural Code* will be applicable. If there is an arbitration involving a foreign element, then the *International Arbitration Law* will be applicable.

11.11 References

11.11.1 Books

Hakan Acar, *FIDIC International Construction Contracts Red Book (1999)* (Adalet Yayınevi, 2015).

Tunay Köksal and Müjde Müminoğlu Güneri, *Construction Contracts Under FIDIC and Turkish Law* (Yetkin Yayınları, 2019).

Yeşim M Atamer, Ece Baş Süzel and Elliott Geisinger, *International Construction Contracts and Dispute Settlement* (Oniki Levha Yayıncılık, 2016).

Zeynep Sözen, *Management of Construction Contracts with Examples from FIDIC General Conditions* (Legal Yayıncılık, 2015).

11.11.2 Internet

Association of Turkish Consulting Engineers and Architects. www.tmmmb.org.tr/

Turkish Contractors Association. www.tmb.org.tr/en

Turkish Precast Concrete Association. www.prefab.org.tr/index.html

Turkish Statistical Institute. www.tuik.gov.tr/

CHAPTER 12

Applying FIDIC Contracts in the United Arab Emirates

Erin Miller Rankin, Samantha Lord Hill and Jamie Calvy[1]

CONTENTS

1 The authors thank Noha Elgendy of Freshfields Bruckhaus Deringer LLP (Dubai) for her assistance in the preparation of this chapter.

 DOI: 10.4324/9781003206910-12

12.1 Outline of the United Arab Emirates legal environment

The official language of the United Arab Emirates (**UAE**) is Arabic. This chapter refers to provisions of UAE law using unofficial English translations. In the event of any dispute between the Arabic and English text of a UAE law or judgment, the Arabic text would prevail.

12.1.1 The constitutional structure of the UAE

The UAE is a constitutional federation established in 1971. The *UAE Constitution*,[2] which provides the political and legal framework for the State, declares the UAE to be an 'independent, sovereign, federal state'[3] (otherwise known as the **Union**) comprised of seven constituent Emirates: Dubai, Abu Dhabi, Ajman, Sharjah, Fujairah, Ras Al Khaimah and Umm Al Quwain. An absolute monarch known as a Ruler rules each Emirate.

The Union is governed by the following authorities:[4]

- The Supreme Council, which is comprised of the Rulers of all of the Emirates and is the highest authority in the Union.[5]
- The President and Vice President of the Union, who are each elected by and from the members of the Supreme Council.[6] The President and Vice President each serve in that role for a period of five years, following which they are each capable of re-election.[7]
- The Council of Ministers of the Union, which comprises the Prime Minister, the Deputy Prime Minister and no more than 14 other Ministers,[8] all of whom are appointed by the President.[9] The current (2022) ruler of Dubai and Vice President, Sheikh Mohammed Bin Rashid Al Maktoum, serves as the Prime Minister while the remaining Ministers are citizens of the UAE who have relevant experience and expertise.[10] The Council of Ministers serves as the executive organ of the Union.
- The Federal National Council, which comprises 40 members, with seats distributed between the seven member Emirates.[11] Each Emirate determines the method of selection of citizens in its territory who represent it in the Federal National Council.[12] The Federal National Council forms part of the legislative organ of the Union and is primarily responsible for reviewing and deliberating draft legislation.
- The Federal Judiciary, which is comprised of the Union Supreme Court and Courts of First Instance. The Union Supreme Court consists of a President and

2 *United Arab Emirates Constitution* of 1971 with amendments through 2004.
3 *UAE Constitution*, Article 1.
4 *UAE Constitution*, Article 45.
5 *UAE Constitution*, Article 46.
6 *UAE Constitution*, Article 51.
7 *UAE Constitution*, Article 52.
8 *UAE Constitution*, Article 55.
9 *UAE Constitution*, Article 54(5).
10 *UAE Constitution*, Article 56.
11 *UAE Constitution*, Article 68.
12 *UAE Constitution*, Article 69.

> no more than five judges, who are each appointed by *Presidential Decree* and approved by the Supreme Council.[13] Judges of the Union Supreme Court serve for an indefinite term, ending in the event of death, resignation, completion of term of contract for judges who are seconded, permanent incapacity to carry out the burdens of their duties by reason of ill health, disciplinary discharge or appointment to other offices.[14]

The division of powers between the Union and the Emirates is established in chapter 7 of the *UAE Constitution.*

12.1.2 The legal system in the UAE

The UAE is a civil law jurisdiction, with its core principles enshrined in its *Constitution*, several key laws and *Codes*. The UAE's laws are influenced by the general principles of Islamic Shari'a[15] and seek to achieve consistency with other civil law jurisdictions. For example, the *UAE Civil Code, Federal Law No. 5 of 1985*, as amended, is, as with many of its regional neighbours, modelled on the *Egyptian Civil Code.*

The Union operates a two-tiered legal structure. Emirates enjoy constitutional sovereignty over matters associated with each of their respective territories, save for matters explicitly falling within the exclusive legislative and executive jurisdiction of the Union, such as foreign affairs, defence and the armed forces.[16] Accordingly, Federal laws apply across the UAE's seven Emirates, whilst Emirate-specific laws apply in each Emirate. In the event of any conflict between a Federal law and an Emirate-specific law, the Federal law prevails, and the inconsistent Emirate-specific law is considered null and void.[17]

Consistent with its civil law principles, there is no system of binding precedent in the UAE. Whilst Court of Cassation judgments are often published and can be persuasive authority in onshore UAE court cases, judges are not bound by these and are typically granted wide discretion when interpreting and applying the law. Judges in the UAE do, however, look to principles established in Court of Cassation or Supreme Court decisions (these courts are described further in section 12.1.3), and these are frequently cited in submissions in an effort to encourage consistency between decisions.[18] In particular, the lower courts in each Emirate must abide by the principles laid down by the relevant Supreme Court when those principles are confirmed in a consistent line of authority.

The UAE has enacted several Federal laws applicable to the construction industry, but each Emirate, in particular Abu Dhabi and Dubai, has enacted Emirate-specific legislation

13 *UAE Constitution*, Article 96.

14 *Federal Law No. 10 of 1973*, Article 18. A disciplinary board composed of the Chief Justice of the Union Supreme Court and two senior judges have oversight of Union Supreme Court judges and may carry out investigations into their actions, the outcome of which could lead to the possible resignation or dismissal of the relevant judge (*Federal Law No. 10 of 1973*, Articles 23–32). This process is distinct from any civil or criminal claims against the relevant judge arising out of the same action, which can continue in parallel with disciplinary proceedings (*Federal Law No. 10 of 1973*, Article 28).

15 Article 7 of the *UAE Constitution* provides that 'Islam is the official religion of the Union. The Islamic Shari'ah shall be the main source of legislation in the Union'.

16 *UAE Constitution*, Article 3.

17 *UAE Constitution*, Article 151.

18 Grose, *Construction Law in the United Arab Emirates and the Gulf* (Wiley, 2016) 5.

to supplement Federal laws to accommodate and encourage the construction boom that the UAE has witnessed since its establishment.

Arbitration onshore in the UAE is also governed at the federal level. In particular, the UAE acceded to the United Nations *New York Convention for the Recognition and Enforcement of Foreign Arbitral Awards* by *Federal Decree No. 43 of 2006*, and issued an arbitration law, *Federal Law No. 6 of 2018* (***UAE Arbitration Law***), largely modelled on the *1985 UNCITRAL Model Law on International Commercial Arbitration* (as amended in 2006).

In 2004, the *UAE Constitution* was amended to allow for the enactment of the *Financial Free Zone Law*,[19] granting each Emirate the authority to establish 'financial free zones' by *Federal decree*. A financial free zone is defined as a 'free zone established in any of the Emirates of the [UAE] in which Financial Activities are carried on'.[20] A free zone is empowered to create its own legal and regulatory framework for all civil and commercial matters and is therefore exempt from Federal civil and commercial laws, though still subject to UAE criminal laws.

There are presently two pertinent financial free zones: the Dubai International Financial Centre (**DIFC**) established in 2004[21] and, more recently, the Abu Dhabi Global Market (**ADGM**) established in 2013.[22] Both have enacted wide-ranging commercial laws including contract,[23] arbitration[24] and employment[25] laws. The DIFC and the ADGM are common-law jurisdictions and operate court systems modelled on the English common-law courts.[26]

Financial free zones are unique and are an exception to the UAE legislative framework described earlier. In this chapter, we focus on UAE law (excluding DIFC and ADGM law), referred to colloquially as 'onshore' law, and any reference to the UAE or UAE law excludes the DIFC and the ADGM and their laws respectively.

12.1.3 The court system in the UAE

The UAE operates two court systems: the Federal judiciary and the local (i.e. Emirate-specific) judiciary. Emirates can opt to establish their own judicial systems or to participate in the Federal judiciary.[27] Certain matters are, however, subject to the exclusive

19 *Federal Law No. 8 of 2004*.

20 *Federal Law No. 8 of 2004*, Article 1.

21 The DIFC was created by *Federal Decree No. 35 of 2004*, which, *inter alia*, set out the geographic boundaries of the DIFC. *Dubai Law No. 9 of 2004* acknowledged the financial and administrative independence of the DIFC, and *Dubai Law No. 12 of 2004*, as amended, established the DIFC Courts of First Instance and Appeal and the jurisdiction of the DIFC courts.

22 The ADGM was created by *Federal Decree No. 15 of 2013* and Cabinet Resolution No, 4 of 2013, which, *inter alia*, set out the geographic boundaries of the ADGM. *Abu Dhabi Law No. 4 of 2013* sets out details of the governance, legislative and regulatory framework and the activities to be carried out with the ADGM.

23 *DIFC Law No. 6/2004*.

24 *DIFC Law No. 1/2008, ADGM Arbitration Regulations 2015*.

25 *DIFC Law No. 2/2019, ADGM Employment Regulations 2019*.

26 That said, the ADGM has incorporated English common law on an evergreen basis (with certain exceptions), as opposed to the DIFC's approach of codifying the principles of English common law.

27 *UAE Constitution*, Articles 104–105.

jurisdiction of the Federal 'Union' courts.[28] The Emirates of Abu Dhabi, Dubai and Ras Al Khaimah have retained their own court systems with independent courts and judges.

Both Federal and Emirate court systems comprise Courts of First Instance, Courts of Appeal and Courts of Cassation (Emirate) or the Union Supreme Court (Federal).[29] Cases are assigned to circuits within each court, with specialised circuits established to deal with civil, commercial, real estate, labour and other disputes.[30] The Court of First Instance and Court of Appeal are courts of merit, whereas the Court of Cassation is a court of law: that is, judgments can only be challenged before the Court of Cassation on points of law, whereas Court of First Instance judgments can be appealed to the Court of Appeal on points of fact. Court of First Instance judgments are typically appealed to the Court of Appeal as a matter of course.

Among its many functions, the Union Supreme Court serves as the Court of Cassation for the Federal judiciary. It also has exclusive jurisdiction over certain matters,[31] such as hearing constitutional challenges and resolving conflicts of jurisdiction between the Federal judiciary and Emirate courts.

UAE court proceedings are conducted in Arabic. Accordingly, any submissions must be drafted in Arabic, and any non-Arabic supporting documents or other evidence must be accompanied by certified legal translations into Arabic. Equally, all UAE laws and UAE court judgments are drafted in Arabic. Further, only advocates licenced with the UAE Ministry of Justice have the right of audience before the UAE courts.[32]

The typical course of proceedings before the UAE courts involves parties' advocates submitting memoranda to the court at each hearing and, particularly in construction disputes, the court usually appoints an expert or panel of experts to consider and produce a report on certain aspects of the dispute such as delay or quantum or technical matters. The parties usually meet with the expert(s) and have the opportunity to make presentations or submissions, as well as to comment on the expert report before a final judgment is rendered. The expert stage is critical in the proceedings as judges typically rely heavily on expert reports when issuing judgments, sometimes adopting a report's finding in full. The expert stage distinguishes the UAE court system from its common law counterparts, where parties usually each engage independent expert witnesses to provide evidence to the court.

The DIFC and ADGM each have their own court system, independent of the UAE courts, which in each case comprises a Court of First Instance and a Court of Appeal. The DIFC courts have also recently established a Technology and Construction Division to deal with complex cases, modelled on the English Technology and Construction Court. All proceedings are in English. Both the DIFC and ADGM have several memoranda in place with the Dubai and Abu Dhabi judicial bodies, respectively, to ensure the enforceability of their judgments 'onshore' and in other jurisdictions where the UAE judgments

28 *UAE Constitution*, Articles 99, 102, 120. For example, the Union Supreme Court shall be competent to render judgement in the case of a miscellaneous dispute between member Emirates in the Union or in the case of interpretation of the provisions of the *Constitution*, etc. The Union shall also have exclusive legislative and executive jurisdiction in matters concerning foreign affairs, protection of the Union's security against internal or external threat, etc.

29 *UAE Constitution*, Article 95.

30 *UAE Civil Procedures Code*, Article 30.

31 *UAE Constitution*, Article 99.

32 *UAE Federal Law No. 23 of 1991*, as amended.

are subject to reciprocal enforcement. Since the DIFC and ADGM are part of the UAE, they benefit from the protections and rights afforded under conventions and treaties to which the UAE is party (e.g. arbitral awards rendered in the DIFC and ADGM are recognisable and enforceable under the *New York Convention* to which the UAE is a contracting state).

12.2 The construction industry in the UAE

12.2.1 Overview

The UAE construction market was valued at US$ 101.5 billion in 2020, with forecast growth to US$ 133.5 billion by 2026. Despite certain projects being suspended due to COVID-19, several government initiatives are expected to drive growth in the tourism, residential, utilities and energy sectors. For example:

- The Dubai 2040 Urban Master Plan provides for (1) doubling the size of green and recreational spaces, (2) increasing rural natural areas to 60% of Dubai's land mass; (3) increasing the size of tourism and hotel zones by 134%; (4) increasing commercial zones to over 150 km^2; (5) increasing education and health zones by 25%; and (6) increasing the length of public beaches by 400%.
- The UAE Energy Strategy 2050 aims to increase clean energy to 50% by 2050 and reduce carbon emissions from power generation by 70%, with major hydrogen investments already announced in 2022.

Recent major project announcements include the Abu Dhabi National Oil Company's Al-Nouf seawater treatment plant, Dubai Municipality's strategic sewerage tunnel and other mega construction projects such as the redevelopment of Port Rashid in Dubai and the DIFC's expansion.

The UAE also has a significant project pipeline for transportation and road infrastructure, including the US$ 11 billion Etihad Rail project and the US$ 5.9 billion proposed hyperloop project between Dubai and Abu Dhabi.

12.2.2 Structure

The construction market in the UAE is dynamic and competitive, with a broad mix of local and international contractors and subcontractors.

For some projects, Employers often seek tenders from joint-venture partners (including a mix of local and international contractors) and stipulate requirements for the appointment of nominated subcontractors.

12.2.3 Licensing/registration

A detailed overview of company incorporation in the UAE is beyond the scope of this chapter.

The applicable registration and licensing regulations differ depending on whether a construction company will be newly incorporated in the UAE, or whether a branch of an existing company is to be established – the requirements for branches also depend on whether it is a local company branch, a GCC company branch, a foreign company branch or a free zone company branch.

Further, each Emirate has specific procedures and licensing requirements. These requirements are administered by the Department of Economic Development in Abu Dhabi, the Department of Economy and Tourism in Dubai, the Economic Development Department in Sharjah, the Department of Economic Development in Ajman, the Department of Economic Development in Umm Al Quwain, the Department of Economic Development in Ras Al Khaimah and the Municipality in Fujairah.

For example, in Dubai, construction companies must (1) obtain trade and commercial licenses from the Dubai Department of Economy and Tourism to operate a commercial entity,[33] and (2) obtain building permits for specific construction activities, which differ depending on the type of activities and location of the project in Dubai and ensure the safety of buildings and structures. Depending on the type of project and location, the following permits may also be required:

- Permits and no-objection certificates from utilities and telecommunication regulators[34]
- No-objection certificates from Civil Defence or the Dubai Airports Company, and other related government entities
- Environmental permits
- Road access permits from the Roads and Transport Authority, and/or
- Approval of hazardous waste disposal plans.

Additionally, the Dubai Municipality sets general qualification standards for the licensing of engineering, consultancy and construction companies operating in Dubai, including:

- Qualifications for license owners, managers and technical staff of local/branch offices in Dubai,[35] and
- Technical staff requirements for architects, civil engineers, electrical engineers, geological engineers, mechanical engineers and petroleum engineers.[36]

Obtaining a licence and/or permit for a specific project in Dubai depends upon the type of contracting activities carried out, such as general building contracting or ports and marine

33 E-services for obtaining new licenses, Dubai Economic Department, available here: https://eservices.dubaided.gov.ae/Pages/Anon/GstHme.aspx?dedqs=PM671p6QBb0lV1okx2JABgxoLLKXOgPx (accessed 24 May 2022).

34 Request for Building No Objection Certificate for Electricity and Water, Dubai Electricity and Water Authority, available at www.dewa.gov.ae/en/about-us/service-guide/builder-services/building-no-objection-certificate (accessed 24 May 2022).

35 Consulting Offices Qualification Standards, Dubai Municipality, 15 June 2021, available at https://www.dm.gov.ae/wp-content/uploads/2021/06/Consulting-Offices-qualification-standards2021.pdf (accessed 24 May 2022).

36 Engineering Consultancy Activities – Technical Staff Requirements, Dubai Municipality, 9 August 2021, available at https://www.dm.gov.ae/documents/engineering-consultancy-activities-technical-staff-requirements/(accessed 24 May 2022).

construction.[37] The licensing of each contracting activity also has specific qualification and experience requirements.[38] Specifically, there are minimum numbers of experienced engineers and labourers required for the licensing of structural steel construction activities[39] and demolition works.[40]

To register a branch office of a foreign engineering company in Dubai, the following criteria must be met:[41]

- The foreign engineering company must have been incorporated in its home country for not less than 15 years and specialised in one or more specific engineering fields.
- The resident general manager must be registered in the Record of Municipal Practice and have not less than 15 years of experience.
- Each licensed activity within the branch shall be managed by a qualified engineer with not less than 15 years of experience.
- The licensed activity's manager shall be assisted by engineers with not less than seven years of experience (the number of assistants depends on the licensed activity).
- The general manager must have a visa issued in Dubai, sponsored by the branch company, and be resident in Dubai for not less than nine months per year.
- The technical staff must be registered in the Record of Municipal Practice.

12.2.4 Labour relations

The new *Federal Decree Law No. 33 of 2021* on the Regulation of Labour Relations in the Private Sector came into force on 2 February 2022.[42] It governs the employer–employee relationship and applies to all businesses, employees and employers in the private sector in the UAE, including free zones, except for the DIFC and the ADGM which implement their own employment laws. By way of summary, the decree updates several employment laws:

- It prohibits discrimination on the grounds of race, colour, sex, religion, national origin, ethnic origin or disability.
- It prohibits harassment, bullying or any verbal, physical or mental violence against employees.

37 Contracting Activities Classification, Dubai Municipality, 15 June 2021, available at https://www.dm.gov.ae/wp-content/uploads/2021/06/Contracting-Activities-Classification-2021.pdf (accessed 24 May 2022).

38 Contracting Activities Technical Staff Requirements, Dubai Municipality, 15 June 2021, available at https://www.dm.gov.ae/wp-content/uploads/2021/06/Contracting-Activities-Technical-Staff-Requirements-2021.pdf(accessed 24 May 2022).

39 Criteria for Licensing Evaluating – Steel Constructions, Dubai Municipality, 15 June 2021, available at https://www.dm.gov.ae/wp-content/uploads/2021/06/Criteria-for-licensing-evaluating-Steel-Constructions-Contracting-Companies-2021.pdf (accessed 24 May 2022).

40 Criteria for Licensing Evaluating – Wrecking Demolition Contracting, Dubai Municipality, 15 June 2021, available at https://www.dm.gov.ae/documents/contracting-criteria-for-licensing-and-evaluating-wrecking-demolition-works/ (accessed 24 May 2022).

41 Dubai Municipality Local Order No. 89 of 1994, Article 34, Foreign Engineering Branch Office, Dubai Municipality, 15 June 2021, available at https://www.dm.gov.ae/wp-content/uploads/2021/06/Foreign-Engineering-Branch-Office.pdf(accessed 24 May 2022).

42 *Federal Decree Law No. 33 of 2021*, Regulation of Labour Relations in the Private Sector.

- It mandates equal pay for women.
- All employees must be employed on fixed-term employment contracts not exceeding three years, which may be extended for the same or shorter period. Employers will have 12 months from 2 February 2022 to transition all their employees onto new contracts.
- Employees may undertake full-time, part-time, temporary or flexible work.
- Either party may terminate the employment relationship for 'good cause' by giving written notice.
- Minimum notice periods are 30 days, with a cap of 90 days.
- Reasons for termination now include the permanent closure of the employer, the bankruptcy of the employer and the failure of the employee to satisfy immigration requirements.
- Summary dismissal requires a written investigation and two written warnings to be given to an employee before dismissing them for failing to perform their main duties.
- Employers cannot withhold an employee's end-of-service gratuity if they are summarily dismissed.
- Maternity pay is increased from 45 to 60 days (45 days full pay and 15 days half pay).
- Employees are entitled to five days paid parental leave, 30 days paid (and 30 days unpaid) leave following the birth of a child with disabilities and five days paid compassionate leave.
- Overtime is capped at 144 hours in every three-week period and will be calculated according to basic pay.

12.2.5 Safety culture

Safety in the construction sector has improved in recent years. *Federal Law No. 13 of 2020* on Public Health requires construction companies to take the following precautions:[43]

- Provide employees with suitable means of protection against injuries and danger, including occupational diseases.
- Permanently display on site detailed instructions regarding the means of fire prevention and preventative measures against specific site hazards. These instructions must be in Arabic and all applicable languages of employees.
- Keep first aid kits, containing medicines and first aid material, readily available on site.

The UAE experiences very high temperatures throughout the summer months. *Ministerial Decree No. 365 of 2018* concerning the Determination of Midday Working Hours provides that construction workers must be provided with appropriate shelter to rest out of direct sunlight between 12:30 pm and 3 pm during the summer months.[44] Employers will be

43 *Federal Law No. 13 of 2020*, Public Health.
44 *Ministerial Decree No. 365 of 2018*, Determination of Midday Working Hours.

fined AED 5,000 (US$ 1,360) per worker, up to a maximum of AED 50,000 (US$ 13,600), for failing to comply with these requirements.

Employers in the private sector in Abu Dhabi and Dubai are also required to provide medical insurance to all employees. Compensation for death at work should be equal to the employee's basic wage for 24 months, provided such compensation is not less than AED 18,000 (US$ 4,900) or more than AED 200,000 (US$ 54,450).

12.2.6 Modular construction using factory fabricated components

Modular construction has gained popularity in the UAE in recent years and is now common across the construction sector.[45]

12.2.7 Technology/innovation/BIM

Digital transformation is at the heart of the UAE Government's economic strategy – it is focused on building smart cities and plans to digitise up to 1,000 government services.

There is a growing demand for technology-led construction in the UAE, such as building information modelling (BIM), augmented reality and 3D printing, amongst others.

BIM was first mandated by the Dubai Municipality for its projects in 2013. For example, BIM was used on recent landmark projects across the UAE including Dubai's Museum of the Future, Dubai Metro, the Louvre Abu Dhabi and Expo 2020.

Dubai is also home to the largest 3D-printed building in the world – Dubai Municipality's new head office. The project is 6,900 ft^2 in size and required just three workers and a 3D printer for the whole construction, reducing construction costs by 50–70% and labour costs by 50–80%.

A further example of technology and innovation in construction is the collaboration between ALEC Engineering and Contracting, a local UAE construction company, and Hilti, a multinational construction manufacturing company, to develop the region's first semi-autonomous drilling robot, 'Jaibot', during the construction of one of ALEC's commercial building projects in Dubai, *One Za'abeel.*

12.2.8 Government/private sector procurement

Traditional procurement, where design and construction of a building are negotiated and contracted separately, remains the most common form of procurement in the UAE, with government entities and Employers favouring single-stage tenders for both design and construction. For mega projects, some developers opt for two-stage tendering: design development and then design and build.

Administrative contracts (i.e. those entered into by government entities for the purpose of managing a public utility, and which include exceptional conditions) are regulated by a set of principles that is different to those governing 'private' contracts under UAE law.

45 The Future of Project Delivery – Technology Trends Shaping Construction and Engineering in the Middle East, MEED and Oracle Construction and Engineering, November 2020 – https://innovation.meed.com/transition-point-for-construction-and-engineering/ (accessed 24 May 2022); The Future of Construction – Getting Ready for the Next Generation of Technology, MEED and Autodesk, June 2021 – https://design.meed.com/report-future-of-construction/ (accessed 24 May 2022).

Therefore, parties should exercise caution when using a FIDIC template for an administrative contract to ensure that risks are appropriately allocated.

Public–Private Partnerships (PPP) are increasing in the UAE:

- The *UAE Cabinet Resolution No. 1 of 2017* enacted a manual for partnerships between public entities and the private sector, which sets out a general framework for partnering with the private sector.[46]
- The Government of Dubai enacted *Law No. 22 of 2015* to regulate PPPs in Dubai and sets out specific terms for PPPs, including economic, social and technological project feasibility requirements and allocation of budgeted public funds.[47] The law also sets out funding methods and PPP contract periods, which cannot exceed 30 years.
- The Government of Abu Dhabi enacted *Law No. 1 of 2019* establishing the Abu Dhabi Investment Office (**ADIO**),[48] which is responsible for executing a comprehensive strategy to increase foreign direct investment to Abu Dhabi. *Law No. 2 of 2019* sets out a framework for regulating partnerships between the public and private sector in Abu Dhabi.[49] This was followed by the *Abu Dhabi PPP Procurement Regulations* issued by ADIO in 2020 which seek to support long-term private sector investment in the procurement and delivery of public infrastructure assets.

PPP tenders have recently been issued for new schools and street lighting upgrades in Abu Dhabi, as well as several urban developments, road and transport projects and health and safety initiatives in Dubai.

12.2.9 Insurance requirements

Construction contracts in the UAE typically require certain insurance policies to be in place, including contractors' all risks; third-party liability; workers' compensation; and professional indemnity.

UAE law does not limit a contractor's liability. However, it is common for parties to limit liability expressly by contract. Article 390(2) of the *UAE Civil Code* provides that the court has discretion to adjust the amount payable in damages to reflect the actual loss suffered.

Specifically for projects incorporating structural works, Article 880 of the *UAE Civil Code* provides that architects and contractors shall be jointly liable for a period of ten years for any total or partial collapse of a building, unless the contract provides for a longer period. Article 882 provides that it is not possible to exclude or limit this liability.

Further, Article 296 of the *UAE Civil Code* provides that negligence or tort cannot be excluded or limited.

---

46 *UAE Cabinet Resolution No. 1 of 2017*, Procedures Manual for Partnership Between Federal Entities and Private Sector.

47 *Law No. 22 of 2015*, Regulating Partnership between the Public Sector and the Private Sector.

48 *Law No. 1 of 2019*, The Establishment of the Abu Dhabi Investment Office.

49 *Law No.2 of 2019*, The Organisation of Public-Private Partnership.

12.2.10 Common forms of contract

The predominant standard form suite of contracts used in the private sector in the UAE is FIDIC – for traditional procurement, the FIDIC 1999 Red Book is favoured, whereas for design and build, the FIDIC 1999 Yellow Book is preferred. For infrastructure and engineering, procurement and construction projects, the FIDIC 1999 Silver Book is preferred; however, bespoke contracts are more common for these projects.

Despite the prominence of FIDIC terms in the private sector, caution should be exercised when contracting with government entities as, for example, Article 120(d) of *Dubai Law No. 12 of 2020* prohibits the incorporation of FIDIC terms in contracts with Dubai Government entities, unless exceptional circumstances exist, or consent is obtained from His Highness the Ruler of Dubai.

Further, *Abu Dhabi Executive Decision 1 of 2007* provides that where Abu Dhabi government departments are procuring construction and/or engineering services from the private sector, standard forms issued by the government, based on FIDIC contracts, are to be used.[50]

12.2.11 Dispute resolution

Arbitration is the most common dispute resolution method for construction industry disputes involving international parties in the UAE. Multi-tiered dispute resolution clauses are gaining popularity, in particular the use of expert determination prior to arbitration. The FIDIC suite provides for final determination of disputes by arbitration pursuant to the Arbitration Rules of the International Chamber of Commerce. In practice, parties to construction contracts in the UAE typically agree that the rules of either one of the UAE-based arbitration institutions apply, including the Dubai International Arbitration Centre (**DIAC**) or the Abu Dhabi Commercial Conciliation and Arbitration Centre (**ADCCAC**).

For certain contracts with government entities, mandatory steps must be taken before a party can commence arbitration. For example, and as discussed in further detail in section 12.5.3, claims brought against the Government of Dubai or any of its government-owned entities must be submitted to the Legal Affairs Department of the Government of Dubai which will seek to settle the dispute amicably before the claimant is permitted to commence arbitration.[51]

Arbitration agreements that stipulate the UAE as the place or seat of arbitration will be subject to the *UAE Arbitration Law*.[52] The default language for arbitrations conducted under the *UAE Arbitration Law* is Arabic unless the parties agree otherwise. Parties can also choose ‘offshore’ seats, including the DIFC or the ADGM.

The DIFC-LCIA Arbitration Rules were commonly used in arbitrations between parties to construction contracts in the UAE. However, on 14 September 2021, the Government of Dubai issued *Decree 34 of 2021* abolishing the DIFC Arbitration Institute, which administered arbitrations pursuant to the DIFC-LCIA Arbitration Rules, and the Emirates

50 *Abu Dhabi Executive Council Resolution No. 1 of 2007*, Issue of Forms of Contracting, Designs and Building Contracts and Agreements.

51 *Dubai Law No. 3 of 1996* concerning government claims (as amended), Article 3(d)(2).

52 *Federal Law No. 6 of 2018*, UAE Arbitration Law

Maritime Arbitration Centre.[53] The two centres ceased to exist with immediate effect, and their functions were taken over by the DIAC. Article 6(b) of *Decree 34* provides that existing proceedings will not be interrupted and that arbitral tribunals formed under the applicable rules and procedures of the abolished centres should continue to hear and decide disputes under these rules unless parties agree otherwise.[54] Although the *Decree* provided that the DIAC would take over the administration of ongoing arbitrations,[55] the London Court of International Arbitration (**LCIA**) and the DIAC agreed on 29 March 2022 that the LCIA would administer all existing DIFC-LCIA arbitrations commenced and registered on or before 20 March 2022.[56]

Article 8 of *Decree 34* provides that the new DIAC Arbitration Rules will be adopted as the rules governing existing arbitration agreements.[57] The new DIAC Arbitration Rules, which came into effect on 21 March 2022, apply to all requests for arbitration filed after this date, regardless of the date of the underlying arbitration agreement, unless the parties have agreed otherwise.

As a signatory to the United Nations *New York Convention for the Recognition and Enforcement of Foreign Arbitral Awards*, the UAE courts will enforce arbitral awards rendered in foreign-seated arbitration proceedings in other signatory jurisdictions. The requirements for enforcing awards in the UAE are set out in UAE *Cabinet Resolution No. 57 of 2018* concerning the *Executive Regulations of the Civil Procedure Code* and the *UAE Arbitration Law*.[58]

The UAE courts can also have jurisdiction to determine disputes under construction contracts, as set out in section 12.1.3.

12.2.12 Current challenges

Whilst there is a very optimistic growth outlook for the construction industry in the UAE, challenges are inevitable. As a result of COVID-19, numerous foreign nationals left the UAE during the pandemic and various international contractors also wound up their local operations.

With a strong growth outlook for the industry and the announcement of numerous government initiatives in the tourism, residential, utilities and energy sectors (particularly as oil and gas companies seek to maximise profits from the expected remaining few investment cycles), there is a skilled labour shortage in the UAE which could increase labour costs for construction projects. This is compounded by competition for talent with the Kingdom of Saudi Arabia which has announced aggressive growth and diversification plans. Challenges will also result from the increased cost of raw materials and services, with significant escalation for steel, wood and freight.

53 *Decree 34 of 2021*, Dubai International Arbitration Centre, Article 4.
54 *Decree 34 of 2021*, Dubai International Arbitration Centre, Article 6(b).
55 *Decree 34 of 2021*, Dubai International Arbitration Centre, Article 6(b).
56 Update: DIFC-LCIA, 29 March 2022, available here.
57 *Decree 34 of 2021*, Dubai International Arbitration Centre, Article 8(c).
58 *UAE Cabinet Resolution No. 57 of 2018*, Implementing *Regulation of Federal Law No. 11 of 1992* on the *Civil Procedure Law*.

Further, *Decree 34 of 2021* has created some uncertainty and the sudden change in policy may make arbitration in Dubai less attractive to foreign investors and foreign construction companies.

12.2.13 Unique features of the construction industry in the UAE

The construction industry is one of the largest contributors to the UAE's economy. With a mix of governmental, private, local and international contracting parties and investors, the construction industry in the UAE is susceptible to the impacts of economic cycles locally and abroad. This is exacerbated by the UAE's reliance on imported raw materials and labour, making reliable supply chains particularly important.

The ongoing development of legal frameworks and regulations in the UAE requires the construction industry to continually adapt and evolve. This is especially the case where new frameworks and regulations are enacted partway through a project (often with little or no notice), meaning that contracting methodologies and dispute strategies may differ from project to project. Similarly, while Federal legislation and regulations apply throughout the UAE, each Emirate has their own laws and regulations, so construction companies must also have regard to local frameworks and regulations in the different Emirates.

12.3 The impact of COVID-19 in the UAE

Since the World Health Organization (**WHO**) declared COVID-19 a global pandemic in March 2020, the UAE Government (and the Dubai Government and Abu Dhabi Government in particular) has implemented various measures to contain the virus and maintain business continuity. The measures include lockdowns, face mask mandates, free vaccinations and 'green pass' apps for entry into public areas. Economic support was also provided to various industries, at both Federal and Emirate levels.

Shortly after the WHO's announcement, the UAE Government temporarily suspended the issuance of new visas for all foreigners, with the exception of diplomatic passport holders, and temporarily suspended passenger flights to contain the spread of the virus. The UAE Government also launched a National Disinfection Programme which imposed curfew restrictions to allow sterilisation of public facilities across the UAE, which concluded in June 2020. The UAE has recorded some of the highest vaccination rates in the world with vaccines being provided early and free to all residents. Accordingly, at the start of 2022, COVID-19 measures began to ease.

12.3.1 The impact of COVID-19 on the execution of construction projects in the UAE

The prompt and steady efforts of the UAE Government (and the Dubai Government and Abu Dhabi Government in particular) in containing the spread of COVID-19 helped to sustain the construction industry throughout the pandemic. As a vital sector in the UAE, construction works were exempt from lockdowns during the National Disinfection Programme. However, construction projects were still subject to heightened health and safety requirements to contain the spread of COVID-19 and enable works to continue. For example, social distancing restrictions were important as most construction workers in the UAE live in dormitories provided by employers and are transported to and from construction sites on buses.

Certain initiatives by governmental departments also sought to mitigate the impact of COVID-19 on the construction sector. At a Federal level, the UAE's Ministry of Human Resources and Emiratisation issued *Decree 279 of 2020* concerning private sector foreign workers and the implementation of the COVID-19 precautionary measures.[59] This directly impacted the construction industry in the UAE, as most construction workers are foreign nationals. The *Decree* provided for companies to implement certain measures, upon reaching agreement with their foreign workers, including remote working systems, paid and unpaid leaves, and temporary and/or permanent wage reductions. Further, employers with surplus employees had to register their data on a virtual labour system enabling employees to be rotated to other companies.

In March 2020, the Dubai Municipality required construction companies based in Dubai to (1) increase the frequency of cleaning and disinfection at construction sites, (2) ensure staff frequently washed their hands with water and soap or sanitisers, (3) ensure availability of hand sanitisers throughout construction sites, (4) document all cleaning and disinfection operations and (5) clean and disinfect worker buses before and after each trip.[60]

The Dubai Development Authority (**DDA**), which is responsible for commercial and trade licensing in Dubai, also provided and facilitated electronic approvals and permits.[61] Since part of the DDA's responsibilities is to undertake building and fit-out site inspections, it also introduced virtual site inspections.[62] The DDA also issued a Construction Site Hygiene Measures Checklist to be implemented daily at construction sites,[63] including temperature monitoring, wearing protective masks and gloves on site, maintaining a 1.5 m social distance and the provision of adequate sanitisers. The checklist further requires the provision of full personal protective equipment for workers carrying out the delivery and receipt of materials. The DDA also introduced stimulus initiatives ranging from waivers, postponement and fee instalments.[64]

The Abu Dhabi Municipality (**ADM**) issued various circulars for the prevention of COVID-19 for transportation services, labour accommodations and construction sites. ADM Circular 004/2020, which was directed to all consultants, contractors and developers,

59 *UAE Ministerial Decree No. 279 of 2020*, the Stability of Employment in Private Sector During the Period of Applying Precautionary Measures to Contain the Spread of the Novel Coronavirus.

60 *Dubai Municipality, Health and Safety Department, External Circular No. 21* 'Intensification of Cleaning and Disinfection Process in Construction Contracting Companies' 17 March 2020, https://dda.gov.ae/mailer/21CircularHealthSafety.pdf (accessed 24 May 2022).

61 *Dubai Development Authority, Circular No. 344* 'Measures in View of the Outbreak of Coronavirus Disease 2019 (COVID-19)' 24 March 2020, https://dda.gov.ae/wp-content/uploads/2020/03/Circular-344-Measures-In-View-of-the-Outbreak-of-Coronavirus-Disease-2019-COVID-19.pdf (accessed 24 May 2022).

62 *Dubai Development Authority, Circular No. 349*, 'Applications for Video Inspection', 13 April 2020 https://dda.gov.ae/wp-content/uploads/2020/06/Circular-349-Applications-for-Video-Inspection.pdf (accessed 24 May 2022)..

63 *Dubai Development Authority, Circular No. 348*, 'Construction Site Hygiene Measures – Checklist', 7 April 2020, https://dda.gov.ae/wp-content/uploads/2020/06/Circular-348-Construction-Site-Hygiene-Measures-Checklist.pdf (accessed 25 May 2022).

64 *Dubai Development Authority, Circular No. 346*, 'Planning and Development Stimulus Initiatives', 5 April 2020, https://dda.gov.ae/wp-content/uploads/2020/04/Circular-346-Planning-and-Development-Stimulus-Initiatives.pdf (accessed 25 May 2022).

provided for the sanitisation of camps and offices, reporting of persons showing COVID-19 symptoms and putting in place emergency plans for outbreaks of the virus.[65]

ADM Circular 005/2020 on COVID-19 Prevention in Labour Accommodations specifically required (1) increased cleaning and disinfection processes of accommodation facilities, (2) cancellation of all events inside accommodation facilities, (3) allocation of a separate wing or building for quarantine purposes, (4) availability of hand sanitisers and washing facilities throughout accommodation and (5) documentation of all daily cleaning and disinfection processes, amongst others.[66] The circular also required (1) increased cleaning and disinfection of labour buses, (2) social distancing by passengers, (3) reduced number of passengers and (4) documentation of all daily cleaning and disinfection processes, amongst others.[67] Additionally, ADM requires the presence of a healthcare provider within accommodation facilities.

The ADM also increased its inspections of accommodation facilities to ensure compliance with COVID-19 restrictions.[68]

Nevertheless, construction projects in the UAE still suffered some disruption. As different countries suspended their business operations, the global supply chain faced shortages that impacted projects in the UAE. Those suspensions paired with global travel restrictions were the cause of shipment delays and price increases for different materials. Travel restrictions and lockdown restrictions in various countries also impacted the cross-border mobilisation of resources.

12.3.2 The impact of COVID-19 on the operation of construction contracts in the UAE

The *UAE Civil Code* provides for exceptional and unforeseen circumstances in contracts governed by UAE law. For example, Article 273 of the *Civil Code* provides that if a *force majeure* event renders the performance of a contract impossible, all contractual obligations will cease, and the contract will be cancelled. In such case, the parties shall be restored to their original position prior to entering into the contract.[69]

Article 249 of the *UAE Civil Code* also provides judges with discretion to alter a party's obligations should they become onerous as a result of exceptional circumstances. In doing so, the judge is required to weigh the interests of both parties.

Article 273 of the *UAE Civil Code* has been invoked before the Dubai and Abu Dhabi courts as a result of COVID-19. For example, in a case concerning a residential construction project, the Dubai Court of Cassation emphasised that a party's impossibility to

65 *Abu Dhabi City Municipality, Circular No. 004 of 2020*, 'COVID-19 Prevention', www.dmt.gov.ae/adm/-/media/Project/DMT/ADM/AboutUs/EHS/Circulars/COVID-19-Prevention-Circular.pdf (accessed 25 May 2022).

66 *Abu Dhabi City Municipality, Circular No. 005 of 2020*, 'COVID-19 Prevention in Labor Accommodations', www.dmt.gov.ae/adm/-/media/Project/DMT/ADM/AboutUs/EHS/Circulars/Circular-No-0052020.pdf (accessed 25 May 2022).

67 *Abu Dhabi City Municipality, Circular No. 006 of 2020*, 'COVID-19 Prevention in Transportation Services', www.dmt.gov.ae/adm/-/media/Project/DMT/ADM/AboutUs/EHS/Circulars/Circular-No-0062020.pdf (accessed 25 May 2022).

68 *Abu Dhabi City Municipality, Circular No. 001 of 2022*, 'In regards of precautionary measures in cities and worker Camps', www.dmt.gov.ae/adm/-/media/Project/DMT/ADM/AboutUs/EHS/Circulars/CircularNo0012022.pdf (accessed 25 May 2022).

69 *UAE Civil Code*, Article 274.

perform its obligations must be a direct result of COVID-19 in order to rely on the defence of *force majeure*. In this case, it was clear that the works were delayed before the outbreak of the virus. Therefore, the court held that the pandemic was not the reason for delay and rejected the *force majeure* defence.[70]

The *UAE Civil Code* also provides that a contractual right is extinguished if a debtor proves that it has become impossible for it to perform its obligations due to an external reason, in which the debtor played no part.[71] Article 893 of the *UAE Civil Code* also provides that if an event prevents the performance or completion of a contract, any of the parties may request its termination. Further, Article 894 also provides that, if a Contractor commences the performance of a contract and is later incapable of completion for reasons outside of its control, it is entitled to the value of the works completed and any expenses incurred for the execution of the works.

The UAE Council of Ministers issued a *Decree* classifying the outbreak of COVID-19 as an 'exceptional economic circumstance' between 1 April 2020 and 31 July 2021 for the purpose of the *Federal Law on Bankruptcy* (as amended).[72] Under this law, an event that has an impact on trade and investment in the UAE can be classified as an exceptional economic circumstance. Such classification provides for less rigid bankruptcy limitations for debtors who prove that the disruption in their financial position is caused by those circumstances. For example, the law allows debtors who have ceased to pay their dues and debts for more than 30 consecutive days, as a result of COVID-19, to submit a request for bankruptcy. In regular circumstances, this would not be permitted and a debtor who ceases to pay their dues and debts for more than 30 consecutive days would be denied the benefits of bankruptcy schemes.

12.4 UAE governing law of the contract

12.4.1 Constraints on the governing law of a construction contract

Article 19(1) of the *UAE Civil Code* grants parties the freedom to agree to a choice of substantive law such that UAE parties, or foreign parties to a contract concerning a project in the UAE, can agree to a governing foreign law, subject to:

- The proviso that rights over real property located in the UAE are to be governed by UAE law,[73] and
- The mandatory application of UAE law where contracts are entered into with a UAE government or quasi-governmental body.[74]

If it is established that a foreign law is to be applied, Article 26(1) of the *UAE Civil Code* provides that only the domestic provisions thereof shall be applied, to the exclusion of those provisions relating to private international law.[75] Moreover, it is not permissible to

70 Dubai Court of Cassation, Petition No. 479 of 2021.

71 *UAE Civil Code*, Article 472.

72 *Council of Ministerial Decree No. 5 of 2021.*

73 *UAE Civil Code*, Article 19(2).

74 *Ministerial Decision No. 20 of 2000*; *Cabinet Resolution No. 4 of 2019* (note also that, at the local level, each Emirate may have its own laws applicable to construction contracts).

75 *UAE Civil Code*, Article 26(1).

apply any provision of law if it offends Islamic Shari'a or the public policy or morality of the UAE.[76]

In practice, while the parties' choice of a foreign governing law is usually respected by an arbitral tribunal, the situation may be different before an onshore UAE court, which may apply UAE law instead of the choice of foreign law if it finds that the parties have failed to present satisfactory evidence as to the existence of an agreed foreign law or if they have failed to properly establish the effects of the choice of the foreign law.[77]

12.4.2 Formal requirements for a construction contract

The *UAE Civil Code* contains provisions relating to the formation of nominate and innominate contracts. A construction contract is treated as a nominate or special contract and so must meet the following requirements:

- Offer and acceptance[78]
- Agreement as to the essential elements of the contract[79]
- Mutual intention of the parties to contract[80]
- Lawful cause for the obligations arising out of the contract,[81] and
- Capacity.[82]

Further, a construction contract is classed as a ***Muqawala***[83] contract under the *UAE Civil Code*, to which specific provisions of the *Code* apply, as discussed further later in this chapter.

12.4.2.1 Offer and acceptance

A contract is formed upon the acceptance of an offer. There is no requirement as to the form of the offer or acceptance. In particular, there is no formal requirement for the offer and acceptance to be contained in a single document[84] or to be recorded in writing (except for certain types of contracts where writing is required).[85] Notably, there is also no requirement for consideration. Practically speaking, however, documentary evidence is the primary source of evidence in UAE court proceedings, the absence of which may carry challenges in asserting a party's claims.

12.4.2.2 Agreement as to the basic elements of the contract

For a contract to be valid in the UAE, the subject matter of the contract must be clearly identified. The Union Supreme Court has recognised the importance of this requirement in the following:

---

76 *UAE Civil Code*, Article 27.
77 *UAE Civil Code*, Article 28.
78 *UAE Civil Code*, Articles 125, 130.
79 *UAE Civil Code*, Articles 129, 141.
80 *UAE Civil Code*, Article 129.
81 *UAE Civil Code*, Article 129.
82 Grose, *Construction Law in the United Arab Emirates and the Gulf* (Wiley, 2016) 26.
83 A *Muqawala* contract is an agreement to make a thing or to perform a task.
84 Dubai Cassation No. 350/2004 dated 16 April 2005.
85 *UAE Civil Code*, Article 132.

> Articles 125, 129 and 141 of the UAE Civil Code indicate that, for a contract to be concluded, agreement has to be reached on all the essential elements of the contract and on all the other elements that the parties regard as essential.[86]

Further, a *Muqawala* must describe the subject matter, the scope of work, the method of performance, the period in which it will be performed and the contract price.[87]

Where a contract is silent on certain terms, the UAE courts have a wide discretion to 'adjudicate thereon … in accordance with the nature of the transaction and the provisions of the law'.[88] Accordingly, leading evidence on industry practice and custom is essential in UAE construction disputes.

12.4.2.3 Mutual intention of the parties

Court judgments have indicated that the most important element necessary to create a legally binding contract is mutual intentions.[89] This has been highlighted by the Union Supreme Court, which has stated:

> A contract will be deemed to be perfected and binding upon there being evidence that the two intentions have come together to create the subject matter of the contract, and to render it effective.[90]

12.4.2.4 Lawful cause for the obligations arising out of the contract

Article 129 of the *UAE Civil Code* mandates that there must be a lawful cause for the obligations arising out of the contract.[91] Further, Article 205 provides that if the subject matter of the contract is prohibited by law or conflicts with public order and morals, then the contract will be void.[92]

12.4.2.5 Capacity

UAE law recognises explicit, implicit and ostensible authority to contract. Certain agreements, such as arbitration agreements, however, are subject to more stringent requirements with respect to evidencing capacity.

It is not uncommon for entities resisting the recognition (and subsequent enforcement) of a foreign arbitral award in the UAE to plead the lack of capacity of the individual signing an arbitration agreement as a basis for the agreement to be deemed void. Whilst the new *UAE Arbitration Law* has somewhat relaxed these requirements by codifying the courts' approach to capacity,[93] prudent parties should closely consider the relevant provisions of UAE law when concluding contracts with a UAE-based counterparty.

86 Grose, *Construction Law in the United Arab Emirates and the Gulf* (Wiley, 2016) 29; Union Supreme Court No. 140/22 dated 26 March 2002.
87 *UAE Civil Code*, Article 874.
88 *UAE Civil Code*, Article 141(2).
89 Grose, *Construction Law in the United Arab Emirates and the Gulf* (Wiley, 2016) 27.
90 Union Supreme Court No. 771/23 dated 5 December 2004.
91 *UAE Civil Code*, Article 129(c).
92 *UAE Civil Code*, Article 205.
93 *UAE Arbitration Law*, article 4.

12.5 What Special Provisions in the Particular Conditions are necessary for consistency with applicable laws in the UAE?

12.5.1 FIDIC General Conditions are incompatible or inconsistent with UAE governing law of the contract

Whether any provisions of FIDIC General Conditions are incompatible or inconsistent with a governing law in the UAE depends, in part, upon the identity of the contracting parties and the laws applicable thereto. By way of example, the Abu Dhabi Government passed *Law No. 21 of 2006* and *Abu Dhabi Executive Chairman's Decision No. 1 of 2007*, which promulgated under licence two FIDIC-based contracts for mandatory use in contracts with the Abu Dhabi government for the construction of certain public works.[94] Although *Law No. 21 of 2006* was repealed by *Abu Dhabi Law No. 1 of 2017* on the Financial System of Abu Dhabi, the *Abu Dhabi Executive Chairman's Decision No. 1 of 2007* remains in force and provides that the two FIDIC-based contracts are mandatory.

Where FIDIC Conditions of Contract are used for private sector construction projects, UAE law generally recognises the parties' freedom to contract subject to certain mandatory provisions of UAE law such as the following.

12.5.1.1 Liquidated damages

While the Parties are free to agree to a fixed amount of damages in their Contract,[95] Article 390(2) of the *UAE Civil Code* permits a court (or arbitral tribunal) to adjust the agreed amount in order to reflect the actual loss suffered by the Party asserting the right to liquidated damages.[96] Either Party may apply for the amount to be adjusted, and the court (or arbitral tribunal) has the power to increase or decrease the agreed amount commensurate with the loss actually suffered. Accordingly, although the Parties remain free to agree to liquidated damages in their contract,[97] when such a contract is governed by UAE law, there is a risk that the provision may not be strictly enforced. Accordingly, the primary benefit of including a liquidated damages clause in a contract governed by UAE law is to relieve the creditor of the burden of proving its loss in the event of a breach and to shift that burden to the debtor.

12.5.1.2 Exclusions and limitations of liability for structural failure or defects

Pursuant to Article 880 of the *UAE Civil Code*, a Contractor and an architect are jointly liable for a period of ten years from the date of handover to compensate the Employer for any total or partial collapse of a building or installation and for any defect which threatens the stability or safety of the building (known as **decennial liability**).[98] If, however, the architect is only responsible for the design and not for supervision of the Works, they shall be liable only for defects in the design.[99] Any agreement to exclude or limit the liability of the Contractor or the architect for structural failures or defects is void.[100] This should

94 *Abu Dhabi Law No. 21 of 2006*; Abu Dhabi Executive Chairman's Decision No. 1 of 2007.
95 *UAE Civil Code*, Article 390(1).
96 *UAE Civil Code*, Article 390(2).
97 See, for example, clause 8.8 of the FIDIC Red Book 2017.
98 *UAE Civil Code*, Article 880.
99 *UAE Civil Code*, Article 881.
100 *UAE Civil Code*, Article 882.

therefore be borne in mind when the Parties are agreeing to a Defects Notification Period and the indemnities and the limitations on liability in FIDIC contracts.[101] Any claim with respect to such liability must be brought within three years from the occurrence of the collapse or the discovery of the defect.[102]

12.5.1.3 Exclusions of liability for harmful acts, fraud or gross mistake

It is not permissible under the *UAE Civil Code* for parties to contract out of liability for their own harmful or unlawful acts,[103] deliberate breach or gross negligence.[104] This appears to be consistent with, for example, sub-clauses 17.1 (*Indemnities*] and 17.6 [*Limitation of Liability*] in the FIDIC Red Book 2017, but it may be prudent to add an express reference to gross negligence.

12.5.1.4 Agreement to curtail the statutory limitation period

It is not permissible under Article 487(1) of the *UAE Civil Code* to contract out of statutory prescription periods.[105] Generally, the period applicable to construction claims is 15 years[106] (although claims in relation to professional services rendered by engineers and experts must be brought within five years).[107] A party might therefore face difficulties in relying on a failure to provide notice of a Claim under, for example, sub-clause 20.2 [*Claims for Payment and/or an EOT*) in the FIDIC Red Book 2017, to argue that the Contractor is not entitled to additional payment and the Employer is discharged from all liability in connection with a Claim not notified.

12.5.1.5 Oppressive conditions

If a contract is made by way of adhesion and contains oppressive conditions, it is permissible for the court (or arbitral tribunal) to vary those conditions or to exempt a party from adhering to them.[108] The Dubai Court of Cassation has indicated that a contract of adhesion is one which involves an actual monopoly for the goods and services in a way that limits competition.[109] There is, however, little guidance as to what constitutes an oppressive provision, and it may be open to interpretation on the facts of each case.

12.5.1.6 Exceptional circumstances

Where exceptional events of a public nature, which could not have been foreseen, occur, as a result of which performance of a contractual obligation becomes onerous, even if not impossible, such as to threaten the party obliged to perform the obligation with grave loss, the court (or arbitral tribunal) has the power, in accordance with the circumstances and after weighing up the interests of the parties, to reduce the onerous obligation to a reasonable level if justice so requires.[110] While there are similarities between this mandatory

101 See, for example, clauses 11.1, 11.3, 17.1 and 17.6 of the FIDIC Red Book 2017.
102 *UAE Civil Code*, Article 883.
103 *UAE Civil Code*, Article 296.
104 *UAE Civil Code*, Article 383.
105 *UAE Civil Code*, Article 487(1).
106 *UAE Civil Code*, Article 473(1).
107 *UAE Civil Code*, Article 475.
108 *UAE Civil Code*, Article 248.
109 Dubai Court of Cassation No. 6 of 1992.
110 *UAE Civil Code*, Article 249.

provision of the *UAE Civil Code* and the *force majeure* clause in the FIDIC Conditions of Contract, careful consideration should be given to such clause to ensure its compatibility. However, it is worth noting that the *UAE Civil Code* permits the allocation of the risk of *force majeure* events between the parties by agreement.[111]

12.5.1.7 Termination

Article 892 of the *UAE Civil Code* provides that a *Muqawala* contract shall terminate upon the completion of the agreed-upon work, upon termination by consent or by order of the court.[112] Further, it is permissible for the Parties to agree that the Contract shall be regarded as being terminated automatically, without the need for an order of the court, upon non-performance of obligations under the Contract, provided that notice is given and the termination right is expressed in very clear terms.[113] The termination provisions in each FIDIC Contract[114] should therefore be reviewed very carefully to ensure that they are sufficiently clear to bring the Contract to an end automatically upon notice in certain circumstances; otherwise, there may be arguments as to whether a court order is necessary.

12.5.2 FIDIC General Conditions are incompatible or inconsistent with the law of the Site/Country

No Special Provisions in the Particular Conditions are necessary for consistency with applicable laws in the UAE.

12.5.3 FIDIC General Conditions are incompatible or inconsistent with relevant laws on dispute determination in the UAE

Whether the seat of the arbitration is onshore in the UAE or in the DIFC or ADGM, the FIDIC General Conditions are not incompatible or inconsistent with the laws thereof. Therefore, no Special Provisions in the Particular Conditions are necessary for consistency with applicable laws in the UAE.

However, where a UAE government entity is a party to the Contract, it must have approval from the Ministry of Justice before entering into an arbitration agreement.[115] In addition, claims brought against the Government of Dubai or any of its State-owned entities, whether in the local courts or before UAE-seated tribunals, must follow a certain procedure.[116] The claim must be submitted to the Legal Affairs Department of the Government of Dubai (**LAD**) which, within one week of receiving the complaint, will refer it to the concerned Government entity for comment.[117] The Government entity must provide its response to the LAD within 15 days from the date of receipt.[118] Upon receiv-

111 *UAE Civil Code*, Article 287.

112 *UAE Civil Code*, Article 892.

113 *UAE Civil Code*, Articles 271–272.

114 See, for example, clause 15 and sub-clause 16.2 of the FIDIC Red Book 2017.

115 *Council of Ministers Decision No. 406/2 of 2003.*

116 *Dubai Law No. 3 of 1996* concerning government claims (as amended), Article 3. Pursuant to Article 9 of *Dubai Law No. 32/2008* establishing the LAD, the LAD has replaced the Prosecutor-General of Dubai as the representative of the government in all proceedings to which it is a party, whether as claimant or respondent.

117 *Dubai Law No. 3 of 1996* concerning government claims (as amended), Article 3(d)(2).

118 *Dubai Law No. 3 of 1996* concerning government claims (as amended), Article 3(d)(2).

ing the Government entity's response, the LAD will seek to settle the dispute amicably.[119] If an amicable settlement cannot be reached within two months of submitting the claim to the LAD, the claimant may commence proceedings against the Government entity.[120]

In respect of the Dispute Adjudication Board mechanism, it is not a recognised form of dispute resolution in the UAE. Therefore, even if the DAB decision becomes final and binding under the terms of the FIDIC contract, a party would still need to go through the arbitration process in order to have the DAB decision converted into an arbitral award that could then be recognised and enforced in the UAE.

12.6 What Special Provisions in the Particular Conditions are desirable for consistency with applicable laws in the UAE?

The following Special Provisions in the Particular Conditions may be desirable for consistency with applicable laws.

12.6.1 Definition of 'day' and 'year'

While it is quite clear that the reference to dates and periods of time under the FIDIC Contracts is to the Gregorian calendar, it would be helpful to expressly state in the Particular Conditions that all dates and periods of time referred to in the Contract (including all references to day, month and year) shall be ascertained in accordance with the Gregorian calendar, thereby avoiding any confusion as to whether the Hijri calendar is applicable. This would be consistent with commercial practice in the UAE.[121]

12.6.2 Liability of Contractor for acts of Subcontractor

Sub-clause 5.1 of the FIDIC Red Book 2017 is consistent with Article 890(2) of the *UAE Civil Code* in providing that the Contractor remains responsible to the Employer for Works that it subcontracts. However, there is an issue as to whether the UAE Courts consider nominated Subcontractors to fall within the provision; therefore, it would be prudent to expressly state that they do in the Particular Conditions.

12.6.3 Working Hours

The FIDIC General Conditions allow the Parties to state in the Particular Conditions the normal working hours for a project. In doing so, care must be taken to ensure compliance with local labour laws, which, in Dubai for example, may restrict working hours during the peak heat months of July and August, as well as during the holy month of Ramadan.

119 LAD, 'Complaints Against Government Entities', https://legal.dubai.gov.ae/en/Services/Pages/Services-Desc.aspx?ServiceID=10 (accessed 22 April 2022).

120 *Dubai Law No. 3 of 1996* concerning government claims (as amended), Article 3(d)(2).

121 See *UAE Code of Commercial Practice*, Article 2(2); *UAE Civil Code*, Article 9; *Implementing Regulations of UAE Civil Procedure Code*, Article 9(6).

12.6.4 Visas

All foreign workers are required to hold a valid visa to enter, reside and work in the UAE; therefore, it may be desirable to include in the Contract a clear provision identifying who will be responsible for obtaining such visas and any other required permits.

12.7 Summary of applicable legislation for UAE governing law of the contract

	Federal	Local Dubai	Local Abu Dhabi
12.7.1 Entry into a construction contract			
Contracts generally	*Federal Law No. 5 of 1985 on Civil Transactions*, as amended (*UAE Civil Code*), Articles 125–275 *Federal Law No. 18 of 1993 on Commercial Transactions* (*Commercial Code*)		
Construction contracts	*Federal Law No. 5 of 1985 on Civil Transactions*, as amended, Articles 872–923	*Law No. 12 of 2020 on Contracts and Warehouse Management in the Government of Dubai*	*Law No. 1 of 2017* and *Abu Dhabi Executive Chairman's Decision No. 1 of 2007*
12.7.2 Termination of a construction contract			
Frustration	*Federal Law No. 5 of 1985 on Civil Transactions (UAE Civil Code)*, as amended, Articles 249, 287, 273		
Bankruptcy, insolvency, liquidation	*Federal Law No. 9 of 2016 on Bankruptcy*, as amended		
Guarantees under forms of Security (Tender Security, Demand Guarantee, Surety Bond, Advance Payment Guarantee, Payment Guarantee by Employer)	*Federal Law No. 18 of 1993 on Commercial Transactions*	*Law No. 12 of 2020 on Contracts and Warehouse Management in the Government of Dubai*	

	Federal	Local Dubai	Local Abu Dhabi
12.7.3 Dispute resolution			
Limitation periods	*Federal Law No. 5 of 1985 on Civil Transactions*, as amended, Articles 473–488		
Liability	*Federal Law No. 5 of 1985 on Civil Transactions*, as amended		
Adjudication	There is no mandatory adjudication prescribed in UAE law		
Arbitration	*Federal Law No. 6 of 2018 on Arbitration* *Federal Decree No. 43 of 2006* on the United Arab Emirates joining the *New York Convention on the Recognition and Enforcement of Foreign Arbitral Awards*	Federal legislation applies to onshore arbitration. In the DIFC: *DIFC Law No. 1 of 2008 on Arbitration*, as amended by *Law No. 6 of 2013*	Federal legislation applies to onshore arbitration. In the ADGM: *ADGM Arbitration Regulations 2015*

12.8 Summary of applicable legislation if the Site/Country is in the UAE

	Federal	Local Dubai	Local Abu Dhabi
12.8.1 Operation of a construction contract			
Registration and administration of professionals – engineers, architects, surveyors	*Federal Law No. 5 of 1985 on Civil Transactions (UAE Civil Code)*, as amended	*Administrative Resolution No. 125 of 2001* concerning the adoption of Building Regulations and Standards, as amended by *Administrative Resolution No. 37 of 2021 Dubai Local Order no. 89 of 1994* concerning regulation of Practising Engineering Consultancy, as amended	*Abu Dhabi Law No. 4 of 1983* (as amended) Regulating Construction Works – Building Law *Abu Dhabi Municipality Resolution No. 119 of 2017* regarding the executive regulations for regulating survey work in the Emirate of Abu Dhabi
Registration/ licensing of contractors and subcontractors	*Federal Law No. 5 of 1985 on Civil Transactions (UAE Civil Code)*, as amended	*Administrative Resolution No. 125 of 2001* concerning the adoption of Building Regulations and Standards, as amended by *Administrative Resolution No. 37 of 2021*	*Abu Dhabi Law No. 4 of 1983* (as amended) Regulating Construction Works – Building Law

	Federal	Local Dubai	Local Abu Dhabi
Subcontractors	*Federal Law No. 5 of 1985 on Civil Transactions (UAE Civil Code)*, as amended, Articles 890–891	*Administrative Resolution No. 125 of 2001* concerning the adoption of Building Regulations and Standards, as amended by *Administrative Resolution No. 37 of 2021*	*Abu Dhabi Law No. 4 of 1983* (as amended) Regulating Construction Works – Building Law
Use of liens/ assignment of debts	*Federal Law No. 5 of 1985 on Civil Transactions (UAE Civil Code)*, as amended, Articles 879, 1109–1113, 1527		
Labour	*Federal Law No. 33 of 2021 on Labour* (*Labour Law*)		
Copyright	*Federal Law No. 38 of 2021* (*Copyright Law*)		
The product being produced from the Works	*Federal Law No. 5 of 1985 on Civil Transactions (UAE Civil Code)*, as amended, Articles 544, 871, 880, 881, 883		
Planning		*Dubai Municipality Local Order No. 2 of 1999*, as amended	*Law (5) of 2018* establishing the Abu Dhabi Council for Urban Planning
Work affecting adjacent property to the Site	*Federal Law No. 5 of 1985 on Civil Transactions (UAE Civil Code)*, as amended, Articles 1139, 1140, 1143, 1333–1348	*Dubai Municipality Local Order No. 61 of 1991* on the environment protection regulations in the Emirate of Dubai, as amended, and its implementing regulations *Administrative Order No. 211 of 1991*	

	Federal	**Local Dubai**	**Local Abu Dhabi**
Environment	*Federal Law No. 24 of 1999* *Federal Law No. 6 of 2009*	*Dubai Municipality Local Order No. 61 of 1991* on the environment protection regulations in the Emirate of Dubai, as amended, and its implementing regulations *Administrative Order No. 211 of 1991 Regulations* passed from time to time by the Dubai Municipality (Environmental Department)	*Regulations* passed from time to time by the Abu Dhabi Environmental Agency *Law (21) of 2005* for managing waste in Abu Dhabi *Law (23) of 2007* establishing the Abu Dhabi Council for Urban Planning *Resolution 42 of 2009* concerning the Environmental Health and Safety Management System
Building and construction permits, execution of construction work, standard of construction work Health and safety	*Federal Law No. 5 of 1985 on Civil Transactions (UAE Civil Code)*, as amended *Federal Law No. 33 of 2021 on Labour* (*Labour Law*) *Federal Law No. 3 of 1987*, as amended (*Penal Code*) *UAE Civil Defence Fire and Life Safety Code 2017*	*Administrative Resolution No. 125 of 2001* concerning the adoption of Building Regulations and Standards, as amended by *Administrative Resolution No. 37 of 2021 Code of Construction Safety Practice Dubai Municipality Local Order No. 61 of 1991* on the environment protection regulations in the Emirate of Dubai, as amended, and its implementing regulations *Administrative Order No. 211 of 1991*	*Abu Dhabi Law No. 4 of 1983* (as amended) Regulating Construction Works – Building Law *Resolution 42 of 2009* concerning the Environmental Health and Safety Management System
Employer's sale of Contractor's Equipment, surplus material, wreckage and Temporary Works Insurance	*Federal Law No. 5 of 1985 on Civil Transactions (UAE Civil Code)*, as amended, Articles 511, 875, 876, 887 *Federal Law No. 5 of 1985 on Civil Transactions (UAE Civil Code)*, as amended, Articles 1026–1055		

	Federal	Local Dubai	Local Abu Dhabi
Liability for defective work	*Federal Law No. 5 of 1985 on Civil Transactions (UAE Civil Code)*, as amended, Articles 875–883		
Liability for nuisance	*Federal Law No. 5 of 1985 on Civil Transactions (UAE Civil Code)*, as amended		

12.8.2 Termination of a construction contract

Bankruptcy, insolvency, liquidation	*Federal Law No. 9 of 2016 on Bankruptcy*, as amended		
Decennial liability and liability generally, for the total or partial collapse of structures	*Federal Law No. 5 of 1985 on Civil Transactions (UAE Civil Code)*, as amended, Articles 880–883		

12.8.3 Dispute resolution

Dispute before a local board/ Adjudication	There is no mandatory adjudication prescribed in UAE law		
Limitation periods	*Federal Law No. 5 of 1985 on Civil Transactions*, as amended, Articles 473–488 *Federal Law No. 18 of 1993*		

12.9 Summary of applicable legislation if the 'seat' of the dispute determination is in the UAE

	Federal	Dubai	Abu Dhabi
Dispute resolution limitation periods	*Federal Law No. 5 of 1985 on Civil Transactions*, as amended, Articles 473–488		

Adjudication	There is no mandatory adjudication prescribed in UAE law		
Arbitration	*Federal Law No. 6 of 2018 on Arbitration Federal Decree No. 43 of 2006* on the United Arab Emirates joining the *New York Convention on the Recognition and Enforcement of Foreign Arbitral Awards*	Federal legislation applies to onshore arbitration. In the DIFC: *DIFC Law No. 1 of 2008 on Arbitration*, as amended by *Law No. 6 of 2013*	Federal legislation applies to onshore arbitration. In the ADGM: *ADGM Arbitration Regulations 2015*

12.10 Issues that a court or arbitrator may construe differently than expected from the words of the Contract because of local law or custom

12.10.1 Notice provisions

While Parties are permitted to include Notice provisions in their Contracts, the UAE (like many other civil law jurisdictions) takes a more lenient approach to their enforcement, in particular where the consequences prescribed in the Contract for failure to provide notice are that the Party is no longer entitled to make its Claim and the guilty Party is discharged from liability. The maxim underpinning the more lenient approach is the view that 'a just claim never dies', but there are certain specific provisions of the *UAE Civil Code* that are commonly relied upon to argue against the strict application of a time-bar provision.

First, Article 487(1) of the *UAE Civil Code* provides that 'it shall not be permissible to waive a time-bar defence prior to the establishment of the right to raise such defence, nor shall it be permissible to agree that a claim may not be brought after a period differing from the period defined by law'.[122] Accordingly, a Party may rely on this provision to argue that the other Party cannot rely on a time-bar provision which provides for the extinguishment of a Claim as a result of non-compliance since such provision would be contrary to UAE law.

Second, the principle of good faith is enshrined in Article 246(1) of the *UAE Civil Code*, which provides that 'the contract must be performed in accordance with its contents, and in a manner consistent with the requirements of good faith'.[123] Where the Contractor can demonstrate that, notwithstanding the lack of notice, the Employer was aware of the circumstances giving rise to the Claim and/or of the Contractor's intention to make a Claim, then the Employer is arguably acting against the principle of good faith if it later seeks to rely on the formal time bar in the Contract. Similarly, it can be said that an Employer may be acting contrary to the principle of good faith if its own breach of contract or an Employer-risk event forms the basis of the Claim, yet the Employer seeks to rely on the time-bar provision to circumvent liability.

Third, Article 106 of the *UAE Civil Code* precludes a party from exercising a right where to do so would be unlawful since the interests that are sought to be protected by exercising the right are disproportionate to the harm that will be suffered by others as a result.[124] By way of example, a Contractor may seek to rely on this provision to argue that

122 *UAE Civil Code*, Article 487(1).
123 *UAE Civil Code*, Article 246(1).
124 *UAE Civil Code*, Article 106.

the Employer's right to rely on a technical breach of the Notice provision is far outweighed by the loss suffered by the Contractor if it is not permitted to advance an otherwise meritorious claim.

12.10.2 Liquidated damages

Article 390(2) of the *UAE Civil Code* permits a court (or arbitral tribunal) to adjust the agreed amount of liquidated damages to reflect the actual loss suffered by the Party asserting the right to liquidated damages.[125] Either Party may apply for the amount to be adjusted and the court (or arbitral tribunal) has the power to increase or decrease the agreed amount commensurate with the loss actually suffered. Accordingly, although the Parties remain free to agree to liquidated damages in their Contract,[126] when such a contract is governed by UAE law, there is a risk that the provision may not be strictly enforced, and a Party may be ordered to pay more or less than the agreed sum. Still, the liquidated damages clause shifts the burden of proof to the debtor, who will not escape liability for the agreed amount in the event of breach unless it shows that the creditor did not suffer harm as a result of the breach or suffered less than the amount fixed in the Contract.

12.10.3 Proportionate liability

Article 290 of the *UAE Civil Code* permits a court (or arbitral tribunal) to reduce the level of damages or not to order damages at all if it finds that the person suffering harm participated by their own act in bringing about or aggravating the harm.[127] Where a number of parties are responsible for the breach, each of them shall be responsible in their proportionate share, and the court (or arbitral tribunal) may make an order against them in equal shares or by way of joint or several liability.[128] Accordingly, notwithstanding that the Contract may identify certain Contractor-risk and Employer-risk events, to the extent that the court (or arbitral tribunal) finds that both Parties were responsible for bringing about the harm that occurred, it may decide to apportion liability as it sees fit.

12.10.4 Suspension

While the FIDIC General Conditions provide the Engineer with the right to instruct the Contractor to suspend the Works, the *UAE Civil Code* also conveys independent statutory rights for a Party to suspend performance of its obligations under the Contract if the other Party has failed to perform its corresponding obligations.[129] However, the Parties can contract out of this provision. In all cases, care must be taken in exercising any statutory right to suspend performance because any improper exercise of that right may lead to adverse consequences.

125 *UAE Civil Code*, Article 390(2).
126 See, for example, clause 8.7 of the FIDIC Red Book 2017.
127 *UAE Civil Code*, Article 290.
128 *UAE Civil Code*, Article 291.
129 *UAE Civil Code*, Article 247.

12.11 Additional references for the UAE

12.11.1 Books

Michael Grose, *Construction Law in the United Arab Emirates and the Gulf* (Wiley, 2016)
Omer Amin Eltom, *Dubai Process of Law* (Future Bookshop, 2014)
Omer Amin Eltom, *The Emirates Law in Practice* (Future Bookshop, 2009)
James Whelan, *The UAE Civil Code and Ministry of Justice Commentary* (Sweet & Maxwell, 2010)

12.11.2 Legislation and case law

Legislation and cases referred to in this chapter are found on Eastlaws in Arabic. www.eastlaws.com/. Unofficial translations to English have then been used for the purposes of drafting this chapter in English.

12.11.3 Internet

Celine Abi Habib Kanakri and Andrew Massey, 'Legal issues relating to construction contracts in the United Arab Emirates' (2017) *Practical Law*. https://uk.practicallaw.thomsonreuters.com/0–619-1946?transitionType=Default&contextData=(sc.Default)&firstPage=true&comp=pluk (accessed 22 April 2022).
Michael Kerr, Dean Ryburn, Beau McLaren and Zehra Or, 'Construction and projects in the United Arab Emirates' (2013–2014) *Practical Law, Construction and Projects Multi-Jurisdictional Guide 2013–2014*. www.practicallaw.com/1–519-3663 (accessed 14 July 2019) (last revised 1 December 2018). This article is updated regularly.
Mark Raymont, Angus Frean and Ahmed Bobat, 'Construction Arbitration in United Arab Emirates' (2019) *Global Arbitration Review*. https://globalarbitrationreview.com/jurisdiction/1006126/united-arab-emirates (accessed 14 July 2019) (last updated 28 June 2019).

CHAPTER 13

Applying FIDIC Contracts in Zambia

James Banda and Johan Beyers

CONTENTS

 DOI: 10.4324/9781003206910-13

13.1 Outline of Zambia's legal environment

13.1.1 The constitutional structure of Zambia

Zambia is a constitutional sovereign republic. Article 1(1) of the *Constitution of the Republic of Zambia*[1] (the *Constitution*) states as follows: 'This Constitution is the supreme law of the Republic of Zambia and any other written law, customary law and customary practice that is inconsistent with its provisions is void to the extent of the inconsistency'. This means that all persons (including juridical persons), State organs and State institutions in Zambia are bound by the *Constitution*. Zambia is a unitary, indivisible, multiethnic, multi-racial, multi-religious, multi-cultural and multi-party democratic State.[2]

The *Constitution* establishes the traditional three branches of government, namely, (1) the Executive led by the President who is jointly elected with a Vice President, (2) the Legislature headed by the Speaker and comprising 166 Members of Parliament and (3) the Judiciary headed by the Chief Justice. The Zambian Court system is elaborated in the following. The duties and powers of each branch of government and all other constitutional offices are stipulated in the *Constitution*.

Part 3 of the *Constitution* is the bill of rights which provides for the protection of civil and political rights. Economic, social and cultural rights are provided for under Part II of the *Constitution*. The bill of rights has its roots in the *European Convention for the Protection of Human Rights and Fundamental Freedoms of 1950*. It was reproduced, with minor amendments, in the *Independence Constitution of 1964*, the *One-Party Constitution of 1973* and the *1991 Constitution*.[3] When the *Constitution* was amended in 1996 and 2016, the bill of rights was left intact. In 2016, a referendum to replace the current bill of rights with a more progressive one that provided for economic, social and cultural rights in addition to civil and political rights failed. Therefore, the form and content of most of the provisions of the bill of rights have remained largely the same despite the significant changes in the political systems that have taken place since independence.[4]

13.1.2 The legal system in Zambia

Article 7 of the *Constitution* states that the Laws of Zambia consist of:

1. The *Constitution*
2. Laws enacted by Parliament
3. Statutory instruments
4. Zambian customary law which is consistent with the *Constitution*, and
5. The laws and statutes which apply or extend to Zambia as prescribed.

Thus, Zambia has a dual legal system made up of statutory law and tribe-specific customary laws.[5] Like most other countries formerly colonised by Britain, Zambia is recognised

1 *Act No. 2 of 2016*.
2 Article 4(3) of the *Constitution of Zambia*.
3 Alfred W Chanda, *Human Rights Law in Zambia: Cases and Materials* (University of Zambia Lusaka, 2011) 4.
4 *Ibid.*
5 Mulela Margaret Munalula, *Legal Process in Zambia: Cases, Legislation and Commentaries* (University of Zambia Press, 2004) 52.

as a common law jurisdiction. British statutes, English common law and the principles of equity were introduced during the process of colonisation and applied to British subjects and the colonial administration, while the locals were allowed to resolve disputes amongst themselves using their own customary laws.[6]

After independence in 1964, Zambia adopted the common law, principles of equity and certain British statutes into its legal system. Section 2 of the *English Law (Extent of Application) Act*[7] provides that:

> Subject to the provisions of the *Constitution of Zambia* and to any other written law: (a) The common law; and (b) The doctrines of equity; and (c) The statutes which were in force in England on the 17th August, 1911 (being the commencement of the Northern Rhodesia Order in Council, 1911); ... shall apply to Zambia.

Further, the *British Acts Extension Act*[8] lists a number of British statutes enacted after 17 August 1911 that remain law in Zambia. Thus, even though Zambia began to enact its own laws after independence, British law, like the *Limitation of Actions Act 1939*, still applies *mutatis mutandis* to fill any gaps.[9]

13.1.3 The court system in Zambia

Judicial authority vests in the courts and is exercised by the courts in accordance with the *Constitution* and other laws.[10] The structure of Zambia's court system is outlined in Article 120 (1) of the *Constitution* which stipulates that: '(1) The Judiciary shall consist of the superior courts and the following courts: (a) subordinate courts; (b) small claims courts; (c) local courts; and (d) courts, as prescribed'.

According to Article 266 of the *Constitution*, 'Superior Courts' means the Supreme Court, Constitutional Court, Court of Appeal and High Court established in accordance with the *Constitution*. Apart from the *Constitution*, the main pieces of legislation which provide for the composition and jurisdiction of the courts are the *Local Courts Act*,[11] the *Small Claims Court Act*,[12] the *Subordinate Court Act*,[13] the *Industrial and Labour Relations Act*,[14] *the High Court Act*,[15] the *Court of Appeal Act*,[16] the *Constitutional Court Act*[17] and the *Supreme Court Act*.[18]

---

6 William L Church. 'The common law in Zambia', Southern Africa Institute for Policy and Research http://saipar.org/wp-content/uploads/2013/10/CHP_01_Law_in_Zambia.pdf (accessed 17 March 2022).

7 Chapter 11 of the *Laws of Zambia*. www.parliament.gov.zm/acts/volumes (accessed 31 May 2022).

8 Chapter 10 of the *Laws of Zambia*. These include *The Limitation Act of 1939*.

9 Certain Zambian *Acts* have made amendments to the British *Act*, e.g. the *Law Reforms (Limitation of Actions, etc) Act, Chapter 72* of the *Laws of Zambia* reduces the original limitation periods in the *Limitation Act 1939*.

10 Article 119 of the *Constitution of Zambia*.

11 Chapter 29 of the *Laws of Zambia*.

12 Chapter 47 of the *Laws of Zambia*.

13 Chapter 28 of the *Laws of Zambia*.

14 Chapter 269 of the *Laws of Zambia*.

15 Chapter 27 of the *Laws of Zambia*.

16 *Act No. 7 of 2016*.

17 *Act No. 8 of 2016*.

18 Chapter 25 of the *Laws of Zambia*.

13.1.3.1 The Local Court

The Local Court is established under Article 120 of the *Constitution*. Additionally, the *Local Courts Act* details the jurisdiction and powers of the Local Court. The Presiding Officers are lay persons with no legal training. Section 12 of the said *Act* states that the Local Court can administer the following law: Customary Law, By-Laws and other laws that can be allowed under a Statutory Instrument. The Local Courts are mostly preoccupied with matrimonial proceedings whereby the parties are married under customary law.

Legal practitioners do not enjoy a right of audience in the Local Court (unless such lawyer is representing themself).[19] A party who is dissatisfied with a judgment rendered by the Local Court can appeal to the subordinate courts and the matter can be heard *de novo* in the Subordinate Courts or decided on the record.[20]

13.1.3.2 The Small Claims Court (**SCC**)

The SCC primarily deals with minor financial claims not exceeding ZMW 20,000 (US$1,130).[21] The SCC is not bound by the rules of evidence but can administer the law and equity concurrently.[22] Furthermore, legal practitioners do not have the right of audience in the SCC.[23] It is also noteworthy that juridical persons cannot be plaintiffs or claimants in this court but are amenable to being sued as defendants or respondents.[24] The presiding officers are called Commissioners and are qualified legal practitioners with a minimum of five years of experience.[25]

There are no appeals available against decisions of the SCC, save for appeals to the High Court on points of law only.[26] A party aggrieved by the decision of a single Commissioner, however, can apply for a review of that decision before a panel of three Commissioners of the same court, who have the power to uphold the decision or set it aside and rehear the matter *de novo*. The grounds for review are very limited and centre around the (mis) conduct of the Commissioner.[27]

13.1.3.3 Subordinate Courts

Section 3 of the *Subordinate Courts Act*[28] creates subordinate courts of three different classes in each district of Zambia. Section 4 of the same *Act* limits each Subordinate Court's power and jurisdiction to the particular district for which it was created. This means that Subordinate Courts have limited territorial jurisdiction and as such, as a general rule, a Subordinate Court can only hear and determine matters that relate to events occurring within the geographical territory of the particular district for which it was created.

19 Section 15 of the *Local Courts Act*.
20 Section 58 (2) of the *Local Courts Act*, Chapter 29 of the *Laws of Zambia*.
21 Section 5 of the *Small Claims Court Act*, Chapter 47 of the *Laws of Zambia* as read together with the *Small Claims Court (Limit of Jurisdiction) (Liquidated Claims) Rules 2009* (SI No. 30 of 2009).
22 Section 16 of the *Small Claims Court Act*, Chapter 47 of the *Laws of Zambia*.
23 Section 13 of the *Small Claims Court Act*, Chapter 47 of the *Laws of Zambia*.
24 Section 12A (2) of the *Small Claims Court Act*, Chapter 47 of the *Laws of Zambia*.
25 Section 7 of the *Small Claims Court Act*, Chapter 47 of the *Laws of Zambia*.
26 Section 22 of the *Small Claims Court Act*, Chapter 47 of the *Laws of Zambia*.
27 Section 22A of the *Small Claims Court* Act Chapter 47 of the *Laws of Zambia*.
28 Chapter 28 of the *Laws of Zambia*.

In addition to limited territorial jurisdiction, Subordinate Courts are also limited in terms of the nature of cases that they may hear. With regard to civil matters, the relevant statutory provisions are ss 18, 20, 23 and 28 of the *Subordinate Courts Act*[29] which provide that subordinate courts do not have jurisdiction:

(i) To preside over matters arising out of tort, contract or both, where the value of the property, debt or damage claimed is more than ZMK 100,000 (US$5,650)
(ii) To hear and determine any action for the recovery of land where the value of the land in question exceeds ZMK 200,000 (US$11,300), or
(iii) To hear matters where the title to any land is disputed or where the question of the ownership of the land arises without the consent of the parties.

Appeals from the Subordinate Courts lie to the High Court.

The Presiding Officers are called Magistrates, enjoying the following jurisdictions:

- Chief Resident Magistrate: the maximum of ZMK 100,000 (US$5,650)
- Principal Resident Magistrate: the maximum of ZMK 90,000 (US$5,100)
- Senior Resident Magistrate: the maximum of ZMK 70,000 (US$3,950)
- Resident Magistrate: the maximum of ZMK 50,000 (US$2,800)
- Magistrate Class I: the maximum of ZMK 30,000 (US$$1,700)
- Magistrate Class II: the maximum of ZMK 25,000 (US$1,400)
- Magistrate Class III: the maximum of ZMK 20,000 (US$1,150).

13.1.3.4 The High Court

The High Court is established under Article 133 of the *Constitution* and consists of the Chief Justice, who is an ex-officio member, and other judges appointed by the President of the Republic of Zambia on the recommendation of the Judicial Service Commission.[30] The High Court has the following divisions: the Industrial Relations Court Division; the Commercial Court Division; the Family Court Division; the Children's Court Division; the General List Division; and the Economic and Financial Crimes Division.[31]

The High Court has unlimited and original jurisdiction in civil and criminal matters.[32] This means that, unlike Subordinate Courts and other lower courts, the High Court is not limited either geographically or in the nature of the cases that it may hear.

Within the context of construction disputes, depending on the contract provisions, the High Court generally functions as the court of first instance for the determination of such disputes, including matters that relate to arbitration proceedings such as applications to

---

29 *Ibid.*

30 Article 140 of the *Constitution of Zambia.*

31 Article 133(2) of the *Constitution of Zambia.*

32 Article 134 of the *Constitution of Zambia.* In the case of *Zambia National Holdings Limited and United National Independence Party (UNIP) v The Attorney General* SCZ Judgment No. 3 of 1994 the Supreme Court explained the term 'unlimited jurisdiction' as follows:

> In order to place the word 'unlimited' in Article 94(1) in its proper perspective, the jurisdiction of the High Court should be contrasted with that of lesser tribunals and courts whose jurisdiction in a cumulative sense is limited in a variety of ways, for example … the Local Courts and Subordinate Courts are limited as to geographical area of operation, types and sizes of awards and penalties, nature of causes they can entertain, and so on. The jurisdiction of the High Court on the other hand is not so limited; it is unlimited but not limitless since the court must exercise its jurisdiction in accordance with the law.

refer matters to arbitration and the appointment of arbitral tribunals, applications to register/enforce arbitral awards and applications to set aside arbitral awards.

High Court Judges are all qualified lawyers with a minimum of ten years post-admission experience.[33]

As a general rule, appeals from the High Court lie to the Court of Appeal. An appeal is available as of right against final judgments, while for appeals against rulings on interlocutory applications, litigants must obtain leave from the Court.[34]

13.1.3.5 The Court of Appeal

The Court of Appeal is established under Article 130 of the *Constitution.* According to Article 131 (1) of the *Constitution*, the Court of Appeal has jurisdiction to hear appeals from:

(a) The High Court;
(b) Other courts, except for matters under the exclusive jurisdiction of the Constitutional Court; and
(c) Quasi-judicial bodies, except a local government elections tribunal.

The Court of Appeal does not have original jurisdiction (that is, a matter cannot be commenced for the first time in the Court of Appeal).[35] Instead, the Court of Appeal has appellate jurisdiction, as seen in Article 131(1) of the *Constitution.* The rules of procedure and powers of the Court of Appeal are further elaborated in the *Court of Appeal Act No. 7 of 2016.*[36]

Appeals are presided over by a minimum of three judges of the Court of Appeal.[37] The judges of the Court of Appeal are appointed by the President on the recommendation of the Judicial Service Committee and must have a minimum of 12 years post-admission experience.[38]

13.1.3.6 The Supreme Court

Since 2016, Zambia has had a twin-apex court system shared between the Supreme Court and the Constitutional Court. According to Article 125 of the *Constitution*, the Supreme Court has appellate jurisdiction to hear appeals from the Court of Appeal. The Supreme Court does not have original jurisdiction to hear any matter. Being a final Court in Zambia, the Supreme Court is bound by the principle of *stare decisis* (judicial precedent) and can only set aside its own decisions or judgments in the interest of justice and for the development of jurisprudence or where there was fraud or concealment.[39] The Supreme Court comprises the Chief Justice, Deputy Chief Justice and 11 other Justices. [40]

---

33 Article 141(1)(d) of the *Constitution of Zambia.*

34 *Stanbic Bank PLC v Savenda Management Services Limited (Appeal 16 of 2017)* (Ruling) [2017] ZMCA 112.

35 Article 131(1) of the *Constitution of Zambia.*

36 See also, the *Court of Appeal Rules, 2016.*

37 Article 132 of the *Constitution of Zambia.*

38 Article 141(1)(c) of the *Constitution of Zambia.*

39 Article 125(3) of the *Constitution of Zambia.* See the recent case of *Jonathan Van Blerk v The Attorney General and others* SCZ/8/03/2020 [2021] ZMSC 31.

40 The *Supreme Court Act*, Chapter 25 of the *Laws of Zambia.*

The Judges of the Supreme Court are appointed by the President on the recommendation of the Judicial Service Commission and must have a minimum of 15 years post-admission experience.[41]

13.1.3.7 The Constitutional Court

This Court is established under Article 128 of the *Constitution* and came into being for the first time in 2016. The Constitutional Court has the authority to hear all matters relating to the *Constitution* and is presided over by the Judge President, Deputy Judge President and 11 other Judges.[42] The Constitutional Court has original and final jurisdiction to hear:

(a) Matters relating to the interpretation of the *Constitution*
(b) Matters relating to a violation of the *Constitution*
(c) Matters relating to the election of the President and Vice-President of the Republic of Zambia, Appeals relating to the election of Members of Parliament and Councillors, and
(d) Matters that question whether the Constitutional Court has the jurisdiction to entertain them.[43]

The extent to which other courts can deal with constitutional matters was discussed in the case of *Richard Mandona v Total Energy* Appeal No. 82 of 2019 where the Supreme Court said the following:

> We are fully alive to the provisions of Article 128(2) of the *Amended Constitution* which states that: 'Subject to Article 28(2), where a question relating to this *Constitution* arises in a court, the person presiding in that court shall refer the question to the Constitutional Court.' Article 28(1) on the other hand provides that: 'Subject to clause (5), if any person alleges that any of the provisions of Articles 11 to 28 inclusive has been, is being or is likely to be contravened in relation to him, then, without prejudice to any other action with respect to the same matter which is lawfully available, that person may apply for redress to the High Court which shall hear and determine any such application; determine any question arising in the case of any person which is referred to in pursuance of clause (2); … Granted that matters dealing with the bill of rights are constitutionally still very much within the jurisdictional ambit of the High Court to determine at first instance, with appeals on any such matters determined by the High Court lying to the Supreme Court under Article 28(l)(b), we are in no doubt that this court has jurisdiction to determine any issue raised touching on the bill of rights in the *Constitution* provided, of course, it comes to us by way of appeal from the High Court. This is so, notwithstanding the provisions of article 28(1) of the *Amended Constitution*. Where, however, a matter arises whose substance is primarily interpretation of a provision of the *Constitution*, this court would be obliged to refer such matter to the Constitutional Court in terms of Article 28(1) to which we have alluded. This does not in any case mean that every time the *Constitution* is mentioned in arguments made before this court, we shall close our records of appeal and rise until the Constitutional Court determines any such arguments. Making observations on obvious constitutional provisions as we determine disputes of a non-constitutional nature, is not, in our view, necessarily averse to the letter and spirit of the *Constitution* nor would it encroach or usurp the jurisdiction of the Constitutional Court. This court, as any other superior court for that matter, is made up of judges of note, capable in their own way of understanding and interpreting the *Constitution*. However, even if we do have the jurisdiction to interpret the *Constitution* in regard to the bill of rights and generally

41 Article 141(1)(a) of the *Constitution of Zambia*.
42 See the *Superior Courts (Number of Judges) Act No. 9 of 2016* for more information.
43 Article 128 of the *Constitution of of Zambia*.

> to refer to the *Constitution* when dealing with matters of a non-constitutional nature, we do not have original jurisdiction to do so. An allegation that a provision of the bill of rights has been violated is redressable through a petition in the High Court. It is not in the province of this court to deal with issues arising from the bill of rights at first instance through motions such as the one before us.

The Judges of the Constitutional Court are appointed by the President on the recommendation of the Judicial Service Commission and must have a minimum of 15 years post-admission experience with specialised training or experience in Human Rights or constitutional law.[44]

13.1.3.8 Specialist Tribunals

Zambia also has several specialist statutory Tribunals empowered to deal with various specific matters at first instance, and these include the following.

- The Lands Tribunal
- The Tax Appeals Tribunal
- The Ratings Tribunal
- The Competition and Consumer Protection Tribunal, and
- The National Construction Council Tribunal.

13.2 The construction industry in Zambia

13.2.1 Overview

Zambia's construction industry, as with other sectors of the economy, is still developing. Between 2011 and 2019, the industry contributed an average of 10% to the country's GDP or an annual average of US$2.23 billion.[45]

Global economic activity was estimated to have contracted by 3.5% in 2020 on account of the devastating effects of COVID-19.[46] Global economic contractions did not spare the sub-Saharan region, including Zambia, whose economy contracted by 3.0% in 2020.[47]

In 2020, Zambia's currency depreciated by 41.7% against the US dollar to an annual average of ZMW18.31 from ZMW12.92 in 2019.[48] End-year inflation in 2020 rose to 19.2% from 11.7% in 2019.[49] The net result was increased cost of imported commodities.[50] These macro-economic woes were worsened by the continuing COVID-19 pandemic, which lead to travelling restrictions and closure of public spaces such as schools, airports and restaurants. There was a general reduction in copper exports, reduced imports of essential commodities and general disruption to the global supply chain.

44 Article 141(1)(b) of the *Constitution of Zambia.*

45 Report of the National Assembly of Zambia Committee on Transport, Works and Supply www.parliament.gov.zm/node/8896 (accessed 31 May 2022).

46 Republic of Zambia Ministry of Finance, Annual Economic Report 2020 www.mof.gov.zm/?wpfb_dl=358 (accessed 31 May 2022).

47 *Ibid.*

48 *Ibid.*

49 *Ibid.*

50 Bank of Zambia Annual Report 2020 www.boz.zm/BankofZambia2020AnualReport.pdf (accessed 31 May 2022).

Although the weaknesses in the Zambian construction industry predated the COVID-19 outbreak, the problems were exacerbated by the pandemic and containment measures in 2020. Owing to this, the country's construction industry contracted by 5.3% in real terms in 2020, which was preceded by a contraction of 5% in 2019.[51] Ultimately, the Zambian Government reduced procurement of construction projects and only approved expenditure on projects that were 80% complete or more.[52]

The election of a new political party into power on 12 August 2021 has brought with it a renewed vigour in economic activities and its impact on the construction industry is yet to be seen.

13.2.2 Structure

There has been a steady increase in contractor registrations in Zambia from 3,887 in 2012 to 10,097 in 2020. This increase is generally attributed to the robust investment in infrastructure development embarked on by the government in order to boost socio-economic development in the country.[53]

Between 2011 and 2019, construction grew at an average of 4.7%. Records show that 91.4% of firms in the industry are Zambian owned while 4.2% and 4.4% are foreign and jointly owned firms, respectively. Despite being the majority in number, the level of participation of local contractors in the construction industry remained very low, and it was mostly confined to low-value and small contracts. Zambian-owned firms are mostly in the lower grades (4–6[54]) where they are limited in respect of the value of contracts put to tender. A report published in 2020 showed that only 3.5% of all Zambian enterprises in the sector were in grades 1 and 2 (the highest grades), which projected a low level of participation by Zambian enterprises in the top two grades of contractors, with the vast majority of enterprises within these two grades originating from China.[55]

This report gives the following overview:

> In terms of the value of pledged investment in the sector, a total of US$ 6.4 billion had been recorded since 2007, of which US$ 77.2 million had been pledged by Zambian firms. This represented only 1.2 per cent of capital belonging to Zambian firms in the sector. Further, since 2007, a total pledged employment of 44,355 was recorded in the sector, of which 3,337 was attributed to Zambian enterprises representing 7.5 per cent of jobs in the sector. As of 2019, the main Foreign Direct Investment (FDI) in the sector was Chinese (US$ 1.2 billion) ... Chinese investors also had the highest recorded pledged employment in the sector with about 6,400 jobs since 2007. Furthermore, for the period 2012 to 2014, most of the firms bidding and winning tenders were reported to have been foreign owned. The proportion of foreign owned firms winning tenders increased from 50.0 per cent in 2012 to 62.5 per cent in 2013 and 90.0 per cent in 2014. On the contrary, the proportion of Zambian owned firms

51 www.reportlinker.com/p06129890/Construction-in-Zambia-Key-Trends-and-Opportunities-H1.html#:~:text=The%20weakness%20in%20the%20Zambian,contraction%20of%205%25%20in%202019 (accessed 17 March 2022).

52 www.lusakatimes.com/2019/02/12/government-has-prioritised-the-completion-of-projects-that-have-reached-80-percent-and-above-chitotela/ (accessed 17 March 2022).

53 National Council for Construction Annual Report 2020 www.ncc.org.zm/annual-reports/ (accessed 31 May 2022).

54 Contractors are ranked according to grades with 1 being the highest and 6 the lowest.

55 Report of the National Assembly Committee on Transport, Works and Supply www.parliament.gov.zm/node/8896 (accessed 31 May 2022).

winning tenders increased from a lower proportion of 4.1 per cent in 2012 to 17.3 per cent in 2013 and finally dropped to 3.8 per cent in 2014. According to the 2018 National Road Fund Agency Annual Report, local contractors in the road sub-sector had 82 per cent of projects and foreign contractors had 18 per cent, 15 per cent of which were Chinese contractors. Despite the large share of project count, the local contractors only got 34 per cent in monetary terms compared with 66 per cent for foreign contractors, 50 per cent of which were Chinese. The low participation was also exemplified by the comparison of award values on the Link 8000 road development project by nationality which showed that 77.3 per cent of the award value went to Chinese, 15.1 per cent to South African 5.1 per cent to Indian and only 2.6 per cent to Zambian contractors. The participation levels in the four lower grades of contractors comprised exclusively of Zambian enterprises.[56]

The biggest challenge for most local contractors in the construction industry is funding and lack of expertise. Commercial banks impose very high interest rates and require collateral, usually in the form of real estate. It is still not clear if the enactment of the *Moveable Property (Security Interest) Act No. 3 of 2016*, which allows for movables to be put up as security, has helped to expand the range of security that businesses could put forward to access credit from banks. However, even if it did, the value of most moveable property would not provide adequate collateral for construction projects.

13.2.3 Licensing/registration

The Ministry of Infrastructure, Housing and Urban Development (**MIHUD**) oversees infrastructure development in Zambia and superintends the design, procurement and construction of all public infrastructure. The Ministry is responsible for building and construction industry policy,[57] as well as functioning as the line ministry for some statutory bodies like the National Council for Construction (**NCC**), the National Housing Authority (**NHA**) and the Road Development Agency (**RDA**).

The NCC is a statutory body established and governed by the *National Council for Construction Act No. 10 of 2020* of the *Laws of Zambia*. The NCC is charged with the responsibility of providing for the promotion, development, training and regulation of the construction industry in Zambia. The NCC is responsible for the registration of contractors, projects and manufacturers and suppliers of construction materials. The NCC is also responsible for monitoring and collecting data on the performance of the construction industry.

Registration of contractors is undertaken based on a self-assessment criterion by grade and category. Registration is mandatory for contractors wishing to undertake public construction works. [58]

Table 13.1 presents a breakdown of contractor registrations by grade and category in 2020, with 1 being the highest grade for large-scale projects.

Although the NCC is the main regulator and 'keeper of information' for all sectors of the construction industry, there are other sector-specific bodies which perform other

56 *Ibid.*
57 www.mhid.gov.zm (accessed 31 May 2022).
58 NCC Annual Report 2020 www.ncc.org.zm/annual-reports/ (accessed 30 May 2022).

Table 13.1 Contractor registrations in Zambia by grade and category

Grade	18 December 2020 classification and categorisation							
	ZCO[a] vs foreign	**B**	**C**	**E**	**M**	**ME**	**R**	**Totals**
1	ZCO	29	15	4	4	0	32	84
	Foreign	66	47	25	32	5	47	222
2	ZCO	36	18	17	6	2	45	124
	Foreign	38	13	14	16	2	11	94
3		75	32	21	7	1	114	250
4		303	85	65	21	6	230	710
5		716	247	150	55	22	1,024	2,214
6		2,287	883	558	422	191	2,041	6,382
S-class								17
Totals		**3,550**	**1,340**	**854**	**563**	**229**	**3,544**	**10,097**

[a] Zambian Citizen Owned

Notes: **B** = General Building and Housing, **C** = General Civil Engineering Works, **E** = General Electrical and Telecommunications, **M** = Mining Services – Construction Works within the Mining Areas, **ME** = Mechanical Engineering Works, **R** = General Roads and Earthworks, **S** = Specialist.

regulatory and registration functions for contractors and concessionaires, namely the Road Development Agency[59] and National Road Fund Agency.[60]

Professionals in the industry are required to be registered or licensed with the various bodies representing their profession, namely, the Engineering Institute of Zambia (**EIZ**),[61] the Zambia Institute of Architects (**ZIA**),[62] the Quantity Surveyors Registration Board (**QSRB**),[63] the Valuation Surveyors Registration Board[64] and the Zambia Institute of Planners (**ZIP**).[65] There are similar registration requirements for all skilled labour/technicians in these categories to register with their respective regulatory bodies.

13.2.4 Labour relations

Zambia has put in place legislation to govern labour relations. These include the *Employment Code Act No. 3 of 2019*, the *Industrial Relations and Labour Act, Chapter 269* and the *Minimum Wages and Conditions of Employment Act, Chapter 276.*

Zambia is also a signatory to the *International Labour Organization Convention of 1992.*

Trade Unions are allowed to operate freely in Zambia and within the construction industry the following trade unions are active:

- Mine Workers Union of Zambia
- National Union of Commercial and Industrial Workers, and
- National Union of Building Engineering and General Workers.

59 Established through the *Public Roads Act No. 12 of 2002.*
60 Established through the *Public Roads Act No. 13 of 2002.*
61 Established through *Engineering Institute of Zambia Act. No.17 of 2010.*
62 Established through the *Zambia Institute of Architects Ac*t, Chapter 442 of the *Laws of Zambia.*
63 Established through the *Quantity Surveyors Act*, Chapter 438 of the *Laws of Zambia.*
64 Established through the *Valuation Surveyors Act*, Chapter 207 of the *Laws of Zambia.*
65 Established through the *Urban and Regional Planners Act No. 4 of 2011.*

13.2.5 Safety culture

As the construction industry grew, incidences of on-site accidents affecting workers and projects increased. This is despite the existence of one of the earliest laws to affect the construction industry, the *Factories Act*[66] and company safety and health regulations. The *Factories Act* requires Employers and Contractors alike to provide a safe working environment for persons employed on construction sites. Causes of accidents were identified to result from a poor attitude to safety, not providing safety equipment, deficient enforcement of safety and health regulations, lack of safety training and inclement weather. Common effects of accidents identified included unnecessary costs, disabilities, reduced production, reduced productivity, job schedule delays and fatalities.[67]

The *Occupational Health and Safety Act, No. 36 of 2010*, introduced sweeping provisions to uplift safety standards in the industry and in general, which for long periods were considered to have been below par. The *Act* provides for the establishment of health and safety committees at workplaces. Construction companies are required to adhere to all health and safety requirements including the provision of safety clothing and a safe working environment.

In addition, the *National Council for Construction (Contractors) (Code of Conduct) Regulations, 2008*[68] requires Contractors to comply with minimum safety standards as stipulated, such as the provision of safety clothing and ensuring a safe work environment. The heaviest penalty for breach of these safety standards is two years imprisonment.[69]

The mining industry further requires all contractors working on mining sites to comply with the stringent safety regulations contained in the *Mining Regulations Statutory Instrument No. 107 of 1971* and the *Mining (Amended) Regulations Statutory Instrument No. 95 of 1973*.[70] In addition, the *Explosives Act*[71] and the *Environmental Management Act, No. 12 of 2011* impose further obligations that Employers and Contractors are expected to adhere to in the execution of their projects.

All in all, the safety culture remains a concern as reports of preventable accidents in the industry keep on recurring. The lack of monitoring capacity on the part of the National Council for Construction has not helped matters. Professional bodies, such as the Engineering Institute of Zambia, have, however, continued to raise awareness of the need to adhere to safe working methods as stipulated by law.

13.2.6 Modular construction using factory-fabricated components

In the private sector, concrete modular construction has been used in the housing sector to a limited extent by international contractors. Within civil infrastructure projects, modular construction of drainage structures such as bridges using pre-fabricated steel structures and concrete portals has been widely deployed. Steel structures are manufactured outside

66 Chapter 441 of the *Laws of Zambia* which came into effect on 1 May 1967.

67 www.researchgate.net/publication/323453480_Construction_Accidents_in_Zambia_Causes_and_Remedial_Measures (accessed 17 March 2022).

68 *Statutory Instrument No. 8 of 2008.*

69 *Regulation* 9(11) of *National Council for Construction (Contractors) (Code of Conduct) Regulations, 2000.*

70 A guide of these two statutory instruments is available on www.mmmd.gov.zm (accessed 31 May 2022).

71 Chapter 115 of the *Laws of Zambia*.

Zambia, but have been installed by Zambian contractors. Both Zambian and international contractors have extensive experience with prefabricated concrete portal drainage structures.[72]

In addition, this type of construction method has been extensively employed by Chinese contractors engaged by the government to construct housing units for police and military personnel. There are no public records which show the numbers used and the quality due to the nature of the end users, although some engineers interviewed have expressed strong reservations as to the quality and durability of the materials and building methods so employed.

13.2.7 Technology/innovation/BIM

Professionals working in the building industry have been adopting BIM technology to various degrees. Zambian professionals with international collaboration have been using these technologies for at least a decade. The number of such firms is very small, as the majority of professionals operate in firms of a very limited size. BIM implementation has been successfully deployed at the design stage of projects but is yet to be applied at construction job sites in a significant way. There is currently no legislation mandating the application of BIM protocols in public-sector projects, as is the case in other jurisdictions.[73]

A promising development on the technology front is proffered by the Electronic Government Procurement System (**E-GP System**) used for the acquisition of goods, works and consultancy services in the public sector.[74] The system was designed to reduce any malpractice which is likely to occur during the tendering process, which could end up disadvantaging local contractors who had little or no financial or other influence.

13.2.8 Government procurement

Public procurement in Zambia is governed by the *Public Procurement Act, No. 8 of 2020* (the *PP Act*).[75] It is mandatory for a procurement entity to use the standard solicitation documents issued by the Zambia Public Procurement Authority (**ZPPA**),[76] which should also incorporate the type of contract and terms and conditions to be used.[77] An infringement of these regulations could render the contract null and void.

There are two standard conditions of contract for works which the ZPPA mandates parties to public procurement contracts to use: the Small Works Contract which is used for national open bidding and the Open International Bidding form of contract. The Open International Bidding form adopts the FIDIC Conditions of Contract for Construction MDB Harmonised Edition 2005 (Pink Book). As the Multilateral Development Banks and other international financial institutions have endorsed the FIDIC 2017 Editions, it is reasonable to expect that the Government of the Republic of Zambia will formally transition to the FIDIC 2017 Edition in due course.

72 Comments from Eng. Suzanne Rattray, Managing Partner Ranking Engineering.

73 *Ibid.*

74 https://eprocure.zppa.org.zm/epps/home.do (accessed 17 March 2022).

75 The *PP Act 2020* repealed and replaced the *PP Act of 2008* as amended by the *PP Act of 2011.*

76 Section 60 of the *PP Act.*

77 Section 73 of the *PP Act.*

Small Works Contracts relate to contracts whose value does not exceed ZMW 50 million (US$ 3.8 million).[78] The standard bidding documents[79] for procurement of small works are also known as the Standard Bidding Documents for Open National Bidding (**ONB**) of works and must be used by prospective bidders.

The standard bidding documents for procurement of works for open international bidding[80] are to be used when a contract has a value equivalent to or above the open international bidding threshold set by the ZPPA, i.e. ZMW 50 million (US$ 3.8 million) or more.[81] Further, such bidding documents are to be used for the procurement of admeasurement (unit price or rate re-measurable) type of works through Open International Bidding (**OIB**) for works that are financed in whole or in part by the Zambian Government.

Zambia's economic policies, which do not prohibit the externalisation of profits, have attracted both local and foreign investors, although the latter have had the biggest share of large projects. The Government of the Republic of Zambia has put in place legislation and policies to empower local contractors. These include the following.

13.2.8.1 Road Development Agency's 20% sub-contracting policy

This provides that a minimum of 20% of the works on all road contracts awarded should be implemented by Zambian citizen-owned companies. The directive is meant to enhance the capacities and participation of local contractors in public works undertaken by foreign contractors.[82]

13.2.8.2 National Council for Construction, Act No. 10 of 2020

The relevant provisions on the empowerment of local contractors are set out in ss 42, 43 and 44:

> 42. The Council may advise a procuring entity or private body on enhancing citizen participation in construction works.
>
> 43. (1) Subject to this Act, a foreign contractor shall participate in a tender for construction works, if the foreign contractor bids for, and undertakes, the construction works as a joint venture with a Zambian contractor in a manner and to the extent as may be prescribed.
> (2) A foreign contractor shall, in undertaking a joint venture under subsection (1) comply with the requirements of this Act, the Public Procurement Act, 2020 and any other relevant written law.
> (3) A person who contravenes subsection (1) commits an offence and is liable, on conviction, to a fine not exceeding five hundred thousand penalty units, or a term of imprisonment not exceeding five years, or to both.

78 Schedule 2 of the *Public Procurement Regulations, 2008* as read with Circular Nos. 1 and 3 of 2013 issued by the ZPPA.

79 The standard bidding documents can be downloaded from the following link: www.zppa.org.zm/documents/20182/21181/SBD_SMALL_WORKS_OPEN_NATIONAL_BIDDING.doc/5de00be9-3d3e-437b-a699-9a3c9ad7709e?version=1.0 (accessed 17 March 2022).

80 The standard Bidding Documents can be downloaded from the following link: www.zppa.org.zm/documents/20182/21181/SBD_WORKS_OPEN_INTERNATIONAL_BIDDING.doc/01a3f956-80fb-4c63-bbf4-5210d4a6e337?version=1.0 (accessed 17 March 2022).

81 Section 60 of the *PP Act*.

82 Report of the National Assembly Committee on Works, Supply and Transport, 2020.

44. (1) A registered foreign contractor or a large-scale contractor who is awarded a contract for construction works of a prescribed value, shall subcontract a percentage of the contract value to a small or medium contractor as prescribed.
(2) The Council may impose on a person who contravenes subsection (1) an administrative penalty.

13.2.8.3 The Citizen Economic Empowerment Act, No. 9 of 2006 (the CEE Act)

The relevant provisions in the *CEE Act* on the empowerment of local contractors are ss 19, 20 and 21 (1) and (2)(b). They are, however, couched in general terms, and provide:

19. (1) Notwithstanding the Zambia National Tender Board Act or any other law relating to procurement of public services and goods, the Commission shall, in consultation with the Tender Board, determine the thresholds to be prescribed by the Minister responsible for finance for the participation of targeted citizens, citizen empowered companies, citizen influenced companies and citizen owned companies in tenders for the procurement of services and goods for any State institution at national, provincial and district levels.
(2) The Commission shall develop, in consultation with the Tender Board, policy guidelines to ensure that targeted citizens and companies specified in sub-section (1) are given preferential treatment in accessing and being awarded tenders for the procurement of services and goods for any State institution.
20. Promotion of local and foreign investment
The Commission shall, in liaison and close consultation with State institutions responsible for investment, trade development, tariff imposition and rebates, pensions, securities and finance, promote and facilitate increased flow of local and foreign investment into the economy by, amongst other measures, fostering the creation of an enabling macro-economic and micro economic environment –
(a) which does not constrain the flow of local and foreign investment;
(b) that is conducive to the promotion of a savings culture amongst citizens;
(c) that ensures mandatory contributions to national pensions schemes and funds by employers and employees; and
(d) that ensures timely and priority payments to micro and small enterprises, in particular, to citizens, citizen empowered companies, citizen influenced companies and citizen owned companies.
21. Investment opportunities
(1) Notwithstanding any other law, after the commencement of this Act, the Ministry responsible for commerce, trade and industry shall reserve, as prescribed by the President, specific areas of commerce, trade and industry for targeted citizens, citizens empowered companies, citizen influenced companies and citizen owned companies.
(2) Notwithstanding any other law, after the commencement of this Act –
(a) where any business deals with technological developments, as prescribed by the President, targeted citizens and companies specified under sub-section (1) shall be granted concessionary licenses;
(b) licenses to foreign investors to engage in specific businesses, as prescribed by the President, shall be granted on the basis of joint ventures and partnerships with citizens and citizen empowered companies.

13.2.8.4 Zambia Development Agency Act No. 11 of 2006

The Zambia Development Agency (**ZDA**) was established under the *ZDA Act No. 11 of 2006*. The *Act* empowers the ZDA in key areas of trade development, investment promotion, enterprise restructuring, development of green field projects, small and medium size enterprise development, trade and industry fund management and contributing to skills training development. Through this, local contractors are able to access the services of the agency on how to benefit from incentives provided under the above legislation.

13.2.8.5 National Local Content Strategy (2018)

The National Local Content Strategy (2018) represents a framework aimed at fostering business connections in growth sectors, as well as promoting linkages between micro, small and medium enterprises (**MSMEs**) and large enterprises, both local and foreign. Among the main features of this strategy is that it ensures that at least 35% of inputs in growth sectors are to be locally procured.

13.2.9 Insurance requirements

The standard forms widely used in Zambia, including those adopted by the ZPPA for public projects, provide for various types of insurance which need to be in place for any project.

It is standard for parties to agree to arrange cover for various scenarios including professional indemnity for engineers or project managers.

Contractors are also expected to comply with third-party insurance requirements for vehicles as stipulated in s 133 of the *Road Traffic Act* Chapter 464 of the *Laws of Zambia*, which provides that:

> It shall not be lawful for any person to use or cause or permit any other person to use a motor vehicle or trailer on a road unless there is in force in relation to the use of such vehicle or trailer by that person or that other person, as the case may be, such a policy of insurance or such a security in respect of third-party risks as complies with the requirements of this Part.

It must be noted that both Employers and Contractors alike are required to be fully compliant with compulsory national health insurance policies in respect of their employees.[83]

13.2.10 Forms of Contract

Within the Zambian private sector, there are no mandatory prescribed standard form construction contracts. The FIDIC forms, especially the 1999 Editions, are widely used. The NEC form is also in use. Parties also use bespoke agreements which borrow from the standard forms. In addition, as there is significant South African influence on the Zambian economy, the JBCC suite of building contracts in their various editions have been used on projects in Zambia, including the construction of shopping malls which house many South African retail outlets.

However, for public procurement, the *Public Procurement Act, No. 8 of 2020*, and the applicable *Regulations* discussed in section 13.2.3 require the use of specified contract forms which are attached to the bidding documents. Hence, the use of any other form must be justified, and prior permission for such use be obtained from the ZPPA.[84]

The FIDIC Pink Book (2005 Edition) is widely used for donor-funded public infrastructure projects, but it is not uncommon to see FIDIC 1999 versions in use on private

83 Sections 12 and 13 of the *National Health Insurance Act No. 2 of 2018*.

84 Section 79 of the *Public Procurement Act No. 8 of 2020*.

projects. It is expected that parties will eventually transition to the FIDIC 2017 editions as these become more popular.

13.2.11 Dispute resolution

13.2.11.1 Litigation

The High Court is usually the first port of call for disputes arising from contracts which do not have an adjudication or arbitration clause. Usually, these would be disputes between private parties who have used a bespoke contract and excluded an adjudication or arbitration clause or found the clause defective.

For publicly procured contracts, it is very rare to find construction disputes in the High Court as the applicable standard contracts provide for adjudication and arbitration. An action wrongly commenced in the High Court is routinely referred to adjudication or arbitration by the High Court judges either on the application of the parties or on the Court's own motion.

13.2.11.2 Adjudication and arbitration

The bulk of construction disputes are usually resolved via adjudication or arbitration. Disputes which arise on projects employing standard forms such as the FIDIC, NEC or JBCC forms, will usually be dealt with in a tiered manner by, firstly the contract administrator, thereafter adjudication and finally arbitration.

There is no statutory adjudication scheme in Zambia at present. Adjudication is contractual and in widespread use. The few qualified adjudicators are usually engineers and lawyers are on occasion called upon to sit on three-member panels. The adjudication process is contractually regulated and is expected to be expedient. There is no provision in any court rules for the direct enforcement of an adjudication decision in the same way as an arbitral award. Therefore, a Contractor with an adjudication decision in its favour will have to commence a new action (complete with all requisite pleadings and documents) in a competent court claiming for the enforcement of a binding contract (the adjudication decision). Although summary judgment might be obtained since the decision at this stage is probably final and binding, a trial is a possibility should the defendant delay the matter further and insist on a trial. The once common summary judgments under the *High Court Rules* are no longer available following an amendment of them.[85] Although recourse can be had to the *Rules of the Supreme Court* 1999 Edition of the United Kingdom, Zambian courts hardly encourage the summary judgment procedure preferring to hear the parties fully.

In the event that the Employer has taken the dispute to arbitration before the adjudication decision has become final and binding, the Contractor is in an even more perilous position as an interim enforcement order cannot be obtained from any court.

Arbitration is usually adopted as the final dispute resolution mechanism. It is not uncommon for parties to elect to forego adjudication and to progress immediately to arbitration, especially if the dispute concerns issues relating to the termination of the contract. It is submitted that this approach is unlawful under public procurement legislation, as any

85 Justice Dr Patrick Matibini, *Zambia Civil Procedure: Commentary and Cases* (LexisNexis, 2015) 459.

amendments to a contract (including the dispute resolution clause) without following the prescribed procedures require the approval of the Attorney General.

The *Arbitration Act No. 19 of 2000*, governs both domestic and international arbitrations in Zambia. Arbitration proceedings are usually expeditiously concluded within one year of commencement. In comparison, litigation in the High Court usually endures for three years or more depending on the judge, the parties or both.[86]

The Engineering Institute of Zambia is usually selected as the nominating body for the appointment of adjudicators, whilst the Chartered Institute of Arbitrators Zambia Branch usually performs this function for arbitrators.

The *UNCITRAL Model Law* has been adopted in Zambia with modifications. Schedule 1 of the *Arbitration Act No. 19 of 2000* is the *UNCITRAL Model Law* and the main *Act* are the amendments or modifications.

Zambia is a signatory to both the *New York Convention* and the *Washington Convention*. Accordingly, foreign awards are recognisable and enforceable in Zambia, and Zambian awards are recognised elsewhere within the regions covered by these *Conventions*.

The courts have in this regard been very supportive and do not interfere with arbitration proceedings. Courts have not and are not expected to reassess a decision on the merits and their role is limited to setting aside awards on the narrow grounds stipulated in s 17 of the *Arbitration Act No. 19 of 2000*. The grounds are:

(i) A party to the arbitration agreement was under some incapacity; or the said agreement is not valid under the law to which the parties have subjected it or, failing any indication thereon, under the laws of Zambia
(ii) The party making the application was not given proper notice of the appointment of an arbitrator or of the arbitral proceedings or was otherwise unable to present his case
(iii) The award deals with a dispute not contemplated by, or not falling within the terms of, the submission to arbitration, or contains decisions on matters beyond the scope of the submission to arbitration, provided that, if the decision on matters submitted to arbitration can be separated from those not so submitted, only that part of the award which contains decisions on matters not submitted to arbitration may be set aside
(iv) The composition of the arbitral tribunal or the arbitral procedure was not in accordance with the agreement of the parties or, failing such agreement, was not in accordance with this Act or the law of the country where the arbitration took place
(v) The award has not yet become binding on the parties or has been set aside or suspended by a court of the country in which, or under the law of which, that award was made
(vi) The subject matter of the dispute is not capable of settlement by arbitration under the law of Zambia
(vii) The award is in conflict with public policy, or

86 Recently, *Statutory Instrument No. 58 of 2020* was passed aimed at reducing the time it takes to conclude a matter in the High Court. Some notable changes include the requirement for parties to file their pleadings simultaneously with supporting lists of documents and list of witnesses and also that a judge should deliver judgment within 180 days of close of submissions.

(viii) The making of the award was induced or effected by fraud, corruption or misrepresentation.

Foreign practitioners are allowed to sit as arbitrators in Zambia subject to obtaining the requisite immigration permits if the venue is in Zambia.

There is debate, however, around whether a foreign practitioner can represent a party in arbitration held in Zambia. The debate arises from ss 41 and 42 of the *Legal Practitioners Act*[87] which, it is argued, preclude lawyers not admitted on the Zambian roll of practitioners from representing a party in Zambia. Some have argued that this prohibition is only in respect of representation in courts of law and not alternative dispute resolution processes like adjudication and arbitration.

It is submitted that ss 41 and 42 of the *Legal Practitioners Act* are expected to be interpreted broadly by the Courts and the Law Association of Zambia and thus foreign counsel would be precluded from representing parties in arbitrations 'seated' in Zambia. However, for arbitration to flourish in Zambia a broader interpretation to allow foreign practitioners to represent parties in Zambia is necessary. From experience, there is no doubt that local practitioners would benefit greatly from working with international practitioners.

13.2.12 Current challenges

COVID-19 and currency fluctuations have had a serious effect on the construction industry in Zambia resulting in a negative contribution to the country's GDP. The impact of the currency fluctuations has been discussed in a summary form in section 13.2.1. The effects of COVID-19 are discussed further in section 13.3.

In addition, the new government, which came into power following the August 2021 general elections, has embarked on an audit of all public projects, as it is believed there had been massive and rampant corruption in the sector resulting in a huge public construction debt. One report suggests that over ZMW 6 billion (US$ 340 million) was paid to contractors who were affiliated with the former ruling party but had no proper skillsets or equipment to undertake the projects awarded to them. Funds were thus diverted to other uses resulting in the abandonment of projects.[88]

13.3 The impact of COVID-19 in Zambia

13.3.1 The impact of COVID-19 on the execution of construction projects in Zambia

Zambia's first known cases of COVID-19 were reported in March 2020. By then, COVID-19 had been officially declared a worldwide pandemic. Several restrictions, including a ban on non-essential foreign travel, suspension of tourist visas, mandatory quarantine for travellers from high-risk countries, closure of learning institutions, wearing of masks, suspension of some cross-border transportation services and temporary closure of non-essential businesses such as bars, gyms, hotels, restaurants and cinemas, were put in place.

---

87 Chapter 30 of the *Laws of Zambia.*

88 *News Diggers Newspaper* 24 January 2022.

The *Public Health (Infected Areas) (Coronavirus Disease 2019) Regulations*[89] were then passed and these incorporated internationally accepted COVID-19 safety guidelines, such as social distancing and the wearing of face masks. The *Regulations* banned certain public gatherings and restricted the number of people attending funerals, weddings and similar events.

Further, in May 2020, *Regulations* aimed at easing employers' burdens as a result of the COVID-19 pandemic were passed.[90] The changes introduced by the *Regulations* included the exemption of expatriate employees and employees in management from entitlement to gratuity, severance pay and overtime. In addition, employers in financial dire straits were excluded from complying with the somewhat long-winded and strict procedures relating to employee redundancy. There was also an exemption from paying employees on forced leave.

Another welcome incentive involved the introduction of tax relief measures. There was a general waiver on penalties and interest imposed by the Zambia Revenue Authority[91] and a suspension of export duty on copper ores and concentrates,[92] precious metals[93] and crocodile skin.[94] Additionally, input VAT on imported spare parts was made deductible[95] and provision for a refund or remission of excise duty on ethyl alcohol was made.[96]

Businesses further benefited from the suspension of import duty on medical supplies such as COVID-19 testing equipment, protective garments, thermometers, disinfectants, sterilisation products and other medical equipment.[97]

The question of a complete shutdown arose early after the detection of the first COVID cases, but the Government never ordered one, perhaps in realisation that an already struggling economy would collapse. Thus, businesses were allowed to operate but had to adhere to the strict guidelines imposed. Accordingly, the construction industry, like many other sectors of the economy, did not receive any bailout payments from the government to cushion them against the losses suffered as a result of COVID-19. Businesses had to effect cost-saving measures to stay afloat and this led to many employees losing their jobs and, in some cases, companies completely shutting down operations.

The sharp increase in operational costs and disruption in the supply chain led to an increase in the time taken to complete projects. Contractors who were caught up in this crisis were mostly awarded extensions of time.

However, it was not uncommon for Employers to make additional payments to Contractors to cover mandatory items required by law to be on sites, such as masks and sanitisers.

89 *Statutory Instrument No. 22 of 2020.*

90 *Employment Code (Exemptions) Regulations, Statutory Instrument No. 48 of 2020.*

91 This wavier was applicable on all tax types applicable to any individual or businesses.

92 *Statutory Instrument No. 39 of 2020.*

93 *Statutory Instrument No. 40 of 2020.*

94 *Statutory Instrument No. 38 of 2020.*

95 Through a revocation of Regulation 9A of the *Value Added Tax Regulations of 2010, Statutory Instrument No. 36 of 2020* provides that input VAT on spare parts lubricants and stationery will be deductible.

96 *Statutory Instrument No. 41 of 2020* provides that excise duty paid or payable on imported ethanol for use in alcohol-based sanitisers and other medicine related activities qualifies for refund or remission, with effect from 1 March 2020.

97 *Statutory Instrument No. 42 of 2020* read together with *Statutory Instrument No. 37 of 2020.*

13.3.2 The impact of COVID-19 on the operation of construction contracts in Zambia

13.3.2.1 The application of force majeure clauses during the pandemic in Zambia

As a result of the COVID-19 pandemic, projects took longer than anticipated and cost much more than projected. This made it extremely difficult for Contractors to perform their contractual obligations. Contractors accordingly sought to employ the doctrines of frustration and *force majeure* in an attempt to excuse them from performing their contractual obligations.

The common law doctrine of frustration applies where an unforeseen event makes the performance of a contract impossible. If a contract is deemed by the courts to be frustrated it effectively comes to an end and the parties are released from their obligations. Thus, as a general rule, no party is liable for non-performance and a party cannot recover damages for loss suffered as a result of the non-performance by the other party. The *Law Reform (Frustrated Contracts) Act*[98] provides that sums paid before the frustrating event may be either partially or fully recoverable under certain circumstances.

It must be noted that in Zambia, as in most common law jurisdictions, the doctrine of frustration is so narrowly interpreted that it is difficult for parties to successfully rely on it. Recourse is thus more commonly made to *force majeure* clauses, rather than relying on the common law.

The term *force majeure* ('Exceptional Event' in the FIDIC 2017 rainbow suite) may be described as an event or situation beyond the control of the Parties that is not foreseeable, is unavoidable and the origin of which is not due to the negligence or lack of care on the part of either Party to the contract.[99] Zambian law does not imply the concept of *force majeure* in commercial contracts. It is up to the Parties to negotiate whether or not there would be a *force majeure* clause in the contract, including its scope and the circumstances in which it can be exercised. *Force majeure* clauses are, however, routinely included in the standard form contracts for construction in use in Zambia to protect parties from the consequences of events that are beyond their control and that adversely affect performance of the contract. *Force majeure* clauses operate to either suspend or terminate the rights and or obligations of the parties.

Within projects whose contracts incorporated a properly drafted *force majeure* clause, claims, mostly for extension of time, were granted. This was especially so for public contracts which use the FIDIC MDB Harmonised Version 2005 Edition. However, on projects where the contract did not have a *force majeure* clause, or had a deficient *force majeure* clause, Contractors could usually not rely on COVID-19 as a basis for making claims for extension of time. This was even more so as there had not been a complete or even partial lockdown ordered. Despite this, and thanks to the timely intervention from Engineers on projects, Employers recognised that COVID-19 was a new and real threat to businesses and the successful completion of their projects. Although the Government did not order a full lockdown in Zambia, the disruptions, especially in the supply chain (mostly of construction items from China),

98 Chapter 73 of the *Laws of Zambia*.

99 The World Bank Group. Sample Force Majeure Clauses, Public-Private Partnership Legal Resource Centre https://ppp.worldbank.org/public-private-partnership/ppp-overview/practical-tools/checklists-and-risk-matrices/force-majeure-checklist/sample-clauses (accessed 18 March 2022).

were obvious and Employers were agreeable to claims for EOT to avoid the application of delay damages. In some cases, costs were also granted.

By and large, disputes associated with the effects of COVID-19 were resolved by negotiation rather than litigation, adjudication or arbitration.

Going forward, some have suggested that the introduction of a so-called 'corona clause' should be considered to capture eventualities associated with the effects of the COVID-19 pandemic.

Practical experience with the operation of the FIDIC forms in Zambia, and in particular the positive manner in which contract administrators attempted to address the negative impact of COVID-19 on contracts, is testimony that the enhanced role of the Engineer in the FIDIC 2017 editions, especially with regard to dispute resolution, was a step in the right direction as it provides an inexpensive and immediate provision for the early resolution of Claims either through agreement or determination by the Engineer.

13.3.2.2 Dispute resolution during COVID-19 – litigation, arbitration, mediation and negotiation

As with all other sectors, dispute resolution processes were disrupted with court operations suspended for a few months.

In 2020, many arbitral tribunals held off convening virtual hearings in the hope that in-person hearings would become possible soon. However, as the pandemic evolved, it became clear that *sine die* adjournments of the hearing were an affront to a tribunal's duty to conduct the arbitration efficiently and expeditiously, and virtual hearings became the default position.

The pandemic has accelerated the widespread use of virtual hearings and digital tools. Before the pandemic, many practitioners had used these tools in their practice and, with the onset of the pandemic, it was much easier to transition to full virtual hearings. There are mixed views as to whether arbitration practice in Zambia will revert to in-person hearings, or whether virtual hearings will remain.

However, virtual hearings have come with their own challenges, such as:

(a) Concerns over due process
(b) Transparency
(c) Security
(d) Data protection and management
(e) Screen fatigue
(f) Arbitrators not in the same room to confer
(g) Difficulties with observing the demeanour of witnesses, and
(h) Arguments that virtual hearings unduly infringe upon the right to be heard.

A further question that arises is whether an arbitrator can order a virtual hearing against the wishes of a party. The risk, of course, is that the party who had objected to a virtual hearing may later apply to set aside the award on review. The argument is that virtual hearings disturb the flow of a hearing and thus hinder a party's right to be heard. In Zambia, a party to arbitral proceedings may apply to the High Court to set aside an award on the grounds that he/she was 'unable to present his case'.[100]

100 Section 17 of *Arbitration Act No.19 of 2000.*

It is submitted that electing not to participate in virtual hearings in the hope of challenging an award is unlikely to represent a good strategy, especially if the parties have been given every opportunity to participate. The need to give parties an opportunity to be heard must be balanced against the tribunal's duty to conduct hearings efficiently and expediently. Proceeding with a virtual hearing will not necessarily constitute a breach of due process, so long as parties are provided equal opportunities to present their respective cases. Arbitral tribunals should thus ensure that parties have reasonable access to the necessary technology, have had adequate time to prepare for the virtual hearing and are subjected to the same restrictions.

As virtual hearings have become popular, it is expected that modern international trends in the arbitration world will find widespread use in Zambia. Accordingly, the practice of deploying third-party neutrals in the same room as a witness, or the use of a camera with a 360-degree view to mitigate against possible allegations of witness-coaching during a virtual cross-examination, will inevitably be employed.

13.4 Zambian governing law of the contract

13.4.1 Constraints on the governing law of a construction contract

Zambian law does not proscribe the use of any law as the governing law of the contract on private projects. However, parties still have to comply with the local mandatory laws in implementing the contract or when a dispute arises. Courts or tribunals will generally not apply foreign law which conflicts with the *Constitution of Zambia* and any other local laws.

With regard to public projects, parties are only permitted to use the laws of the Republic of Zambia as the governing law of the construction contract.[101]

13.4.2 Formal requirements for a construction contract

Zambia follows English common law with regard to contract formation. Therefore, it must be clear that there was an offer which has been accepted. The consideration must be clearly identified, and it must be manifest that the parties intended to create a legally binding commercial relationship.

The practice by parties themselves to impose certain conditions for a contract to be valid is lawful under Zambian law. Thus, parties may agree that for a contract or any amendment thereto to be valid, it must be in writing. However, where disputes end up in the High Court, and in appropriate circumstances, courts have enforced contracts where the parties' conduct suggests an agreement and where it would be inequitable not to uphold a verbal agreement. This is possible because the law allows judges to administer principles of equity concurrently with the law.[102]

In arbitration, however, arbitral tribunals cannot employ equity unless the parties expressly authorise it. Article 28 (3) of the *UNCITRAL Model Law* as adopted in Schedule 1 of the Zambian *Arbitration Act No. 19 of 2000* provides that 'the arbitral tribunal shall

101 Section 73 of the *Public Procurement Act No. 8 of 2020* as read with *Regulation* 137 of the *Public Procurement Regulations Statutory Instrument No. 63 of 2008.*

102 Section 13 of the *High Court* Act, Chapter 27 of the *Laws of Zambia.*

decide *ex aequo et bono* or as *amiable compositeur* only if the parties have expressly authorised it to do so'.[103] Thus amendments to a contract which do not meet the standard agreed in writing by the parties cannot be upheld despite the conduct of the parties suggesting an amendment.

In addition, it is important for parties to comply with the *Authentication for Documents Act*[104] if execution is done outside Zambia. In as much as a contract fully or partially executed outside Zambia remains valid and binding between the parties, it might not be possible to enforce it in Zambia if it has not been properly authenticated. Thus, in agreements involving foreign entities, it is always important for parties to ensure that the last party to sign should be within the boundaries of Zambia as the authentication requirements are not applicable in such a case and the contract is enforceable.[105]

Further, publicly procured contracts need to be standard contracts issued by the ZPPA and must be in the approved format and ultimately approved by the Attorney General of the Republic of Zambia.[106]

13.5 What Special Provisions in the Particular Conditions are necessary for consistency with applicable laws in Zambia?

13.5.1 FIDIC General Conditions are incompatible or inconsistent with Zambian governing law of the contract

13.5.1.1 Sub-clause 1.4 (Law and Language]

With regard to privately funded projects, there is no prohibition under Zambian law on the applicable law and language of the Contract.

For public projects, however, Zambian law stipulates that English, which is the official language of Zambia, should be the language of the contract[107] and the governing law should be the laws of the Republic of Zambia.[108]

13.5.1.2 Sub-clause 1.7 [Assignment]

This sub-clause allows Parties to agree to assign the Contract or part thereof or the right to receive payment to a lending institution as security. For publicly procured contracts in

103 ***Ex aequo et bono*** and ***amiable compositeur*** both are Latin for 'according to the right and good' and refer to a tribunal's consideration of a dispute according to what is fair and just given the particular circumstances, rather than strictly according to the law.

104 Chapter 75 of the *Laws of Zambia*.

105 See leading case of *African Alliance Pioneer Master Fund v Vehicle* Appeal No. 21 of 2011 where the Supreme Court of Zambia stated as follows:

> In our view, what becomes a relevant question is that of *loci contractu*, that is to say, whether those documents were indeed executed outside Zambia so as to require authentication in accordance with the provisions of the *Authentication of Documents Act*, Chapter 75 of the *Laws of Zambia* bearing in mind that the Act only applies to contract executed outside Zambia. In determining, for legal purposes, where a written contract was executed, courts should consider (i) the place of execution as agreed to and specified in the contract, even if the contract was actually signed elsewhere, (ii) the place where the parties actually signed or sealed the contract, if all parties signed in one location; or (iii) *if the contract does not specify a place of execution and the parties did not sign or seal the contract in the same place, the place where the last signature was executed*.

106 See section 13.2.8.

107 Regulation 19 of the *Public Procurement Regulations Statutory Instrument No. 63 of 2011*.

108 Section 73 of the *Public Procurement Act No. 8 of 2020* as read with Regulation 137 of the *Public Procurement Regulations Statutory Instrument No. 63 of 2008*.

Zambia, however, the sub-clause will need to be amended in light of s 74 of the *Public Procurement Act*[109] which prohibits Contractors from assigning their rights and obligations under the contract and imposes a maximum of ten years imprisonment for breach. It can be argued that only obligations are unassignable. It is submitted, however, that the aforementioned law does not distinguish what can and cannot be assigned.

13.5.1.3 Sub Clause 2.4 [Employer's Financial Arrangements]

Section 77(4) of the *Public Procurement Act*[110] prohibits any Variations which will result in a cumulative additional payment of 25% or more of the original or Agreed Contract Sum. Any such Variation will lead to the automatic termination of the Contract. Sub-clause 2.4 will thus need to be amended to limit the cumulative value of variations to less than 25% of the Accepted Contract Amount.

13.5.1.4 Sub-clause 2.5 [Site Data and Items of Reference] and Sub-clause 4.10 [Use of Site Data] and 4.11 [Sufficiency of Accepted Contract Amount]

Sub-clause 2.5 provides that the

> Employer shall have made available to the Contractor, for information, before the Base Date, all relevant data in the Employer's possession on the topography of the site and on the sub-surface, hydrological, climatic and environmental conditions at the site. The Employer shall promptly make available to the Contractor all such data which comes into the Employer's possession after the Base Date.

Then sub-clause 4.10 provides that the 'Contractor shall be responsible for interpreting all data referred to under Sub-Clause 2.5'. Sub-clause 4.11 then deems a Contractor's tender to be adequate since it is expected to have undertaken its own investigations.

The sum total of these three sub-clauses is that even if the Employer has a duty to disclose all information of the Site in its possession, it is not responsible for any (mis) information therein since the Contractor has a duty to interpret that data and carry out its own investigations.

However, these three sub-clauses have to be considered carefully in light of s 4 of the *Misrepresentation Act*[111] which provides as follows:

> If any agreement (whether made before or after the commencement of this Act) contains a provision which would exclude or restrict –
>
> (a) Any liability to which a party to a contract may be subject by reason of any misrepresentation made by him before the contract was made; or
> (b) Any remedy available to another party to the contract by reason of such a misrepresentation;
>
> that provision shall be of no effect to the extent (if any) that in any proceedings arising out of the contract, the court or arbitrator may allow reliance on it being fair and reasonable in the circumstances of the case.

109 *Act No. 8 of 2020.*

110 *Act No. 8 of 2020.* It is submitted that this new law was not a proper inclusion on the statute books of Zambia as it has the potential of making projects even more costly in the event that after re-tendering a new Contractor is selected.

111 Chapter 69 of the *Laws of Zambia.*

It would seem that by virtue of this law, sub-clauses 4.10 and 4.11 cannot be relied on by an Employer guilty of misrepresentation, including innocent misrepresentation[112] to defeat claims for EOT or additional costs from a Contractor who, for instance in reliance on Employer data, suddenly meets unforeseen ground conditions. This is all the more so true considering that sub-clause 4.10 uses the phrase 'to the extent which was practicable (taking account of cost and time)' when placing investigatory obligations on the Contractor.

Further, a partial submission of facts can also be held to be a misrepresentation if the Employer, in carrying out its obligations under sub-clause 2.5 withholds vital site information.[113]

In practice, it will be an evidential issue as to what amounts to misrepresentation and to what extent an Employer's data could be deemed misrepresentation.

It would be appropriate to include a Special Provision to amend sub-clause 4.11 by beginning this sub-clause with 'To the extent allowed by law ...'.

13.5.1.5 Sub-clause 3.2 [Engineer's Duties and Authority]

Sub-clause 3.2 stipulates that the Engineer is not required to obtain the Employer's consent before the Engineer exercises his/her authority under sub-clause 3.7 to make a determination on a matter or a Claim. The Employer's consent is deemed to have been given. In public contracts in Zambia, this clause might not be tenable and will require amending for the reasons that follow.

Regulation 150 of the *Public Procurement Regulations No. 63 of 2011* provides for contract Variations and reads as follows:

> (1) A contract may, where appropriate, in order to facilitate adaptations to unanticipated events or changes in requirements, permit – (a) the contract manager, supervising engineer or other designated official to order variations to the statement of requirements for goods, works or services, the price or the completion date of the contract; or (b) defined compensation events to justify variations in the price or completion date of the contract.
> (2) Where a variation results in a change in price, any additional funds shall be committed before issue of the variation, unless such funds are already provided by any committed amount for contingencies or similar matters.
> (3) A contract shall include a maximum limit on the variations which may be issued without an amendment to the contract in accordance with regulation 149.
> (4) A contract shall state any approval requirements relating to contract variations.

The Zambian law thus places limits on the powers of the Engineer to order Variations only in circumstances where funds have already been committed if such Variation results in a change in price. Thus, an Engineer cannot make a determination on a Claim without prior confirmation from the Employer that such funds as are required for the Variation are available.

The law further stipulates that the Contract itself should place a limit on the Variations which may be issued without an amendment to the Contract. In addition, a recent

112 Compare with s 2 of the *Misrepresentation Act* which does not excuse innocent misrepresentation.
113 *Halsbury's Laws of England*, 4th Edition Reissue [750] 476.

amendment to the law[114] was passed limiting the accumulated value of Variations to 25% or less of the original contract price. Any Variations which will result in a cost of over 25% of the original contract price lead to automatic termination of the contract.

It is submitted that the unintended consequences of this law might be that the contract as a whole is undermined and project costs will greatly escalate especially if a new Contractor is chosen in the re-tendering process. It is thus further submitted that a possible amendment would be a termination arising under these circumstances would be deemed to be a termination for Employer's convenience under sub-clauses 15.5 to 15.7. Parties might also need to consider early warning provisions, perhaps when the 20% threshold is reached.

It should not be difficult to conclude that if an Engineer acts outside the law or the powers granted by the Employer, his/her actions, instructions or determinations will not be binding on the Employer. However, the question is: will the Engineer be liable for any loss incurred by the Contractor acting in reliance on the 'lawfulness' of the instruction or determination? This question could be a minefield for Engineers and might open a whole field of disputes and put Engineers at risk of potential suits from disgruntled Contractors.

13.5.1.6 Sub-clause 3.7.4 [Effect of the agreement or determination]

It is submitted that once an Engineer records the agreement of the Parties in any matter or Claim, this agreement becomes part of the Contract, and the obligations therein have to be performed by the respective parties. However, this sub-clause 3.7.4 allows the Engineer to apply the slip-rule[115] and make any corrections to the agreement of a typographical, clerical or mathematical error. The slip-rule is in essence an amendment mechanism. Although sub-clause 3.2 prohibits an Engineer from amending the Contract, it would appear that this is in contradiction to the slip-rule provision under sub-clause 3.7.4. Therefore, for publicly procured contracts, sub-clause 3.7.4, to the extent that it provides for the slip-rule, will have to be amended, as any amendment to a public contract must comply with the stipulated procedure including obtaining the consent of the Attorney General.[116]

13.5.1.7 Sub-clause 6.3 [Recruitment of Persons]

This sub-clause restrains both the Employer and the Contractor from recruiting or attempting to recruit personnel from each other. The restraints imposed under this sub-clause can be deemed unreasonable and thus unenforceable for failure to set time and geographical limits. In the case of *Patel v Patel*,[117] it was held that

> all covenants in restraint of trade are *prima facie* unenforceable unless they are reasonable with reference to the interests of the parties concerned and of the public. It is usual to find as reasonable covenants by employees leaving their master's employment not to practice or take employment in the same capacity within a reasonable period and within reasonable

114 This is provided for in s 77 (4) of the *Public Procurement Act, 2020* which states as follows:
The cumulative value of contract variation and amendment shall not result in an increment of the total contract price by more than twenty-five percent of the original contract price as prescribed, except that where the variation results in an increment exceeding twenty-five percent, the contract shall be cancelled and the procurement re-tendered.

115 The slip-rule allows for a Court order or judgment to be amended if it contains an accidental 'slip' such as a clerical error, mistake or omission.

116 Section 77 of the *Public Procurement Act No. 8 of 2020.*

117 [1985] Zambia Law Reports 220 (SC).

> geographical limitation. The purpose of this is to protect the employers' trade secrets and trade connections.

Parties will thus need to refine the restrictions in this sub-clause by only restricting either the Employer or Contractor from initiating the recruitment (as it seems a staff-initiated recruitment/move is also prohibited) and also stipulating reasonable periods of restraint and the geographical locations where such recruitment can or cannot be accepted for those periods.

13.5.1.8 Sub-Clause 6.5 [Working Hours]

The requirements in sub-clause 6.4 for a Contractor to comply with all local labour laws, including working hours, seem to be watered down in sub-clause 6.5, which provides that

> No work can be carried out on the Site on locally recognised days of rest or outside the normal working hours stated in the Contract Data, *unless*:
>
> (a) otherwise stated in the contract;
> (b) the Engineer gives consent; or
> (c) the work is unavoidable or necessary for the protection of life and property.

As such Parties can agree to carry out work on any day and for any number of hours. However, s 74 of the *Employment Code Act No. 3 of 2019* provides that the normal day's work of a full-time employee is eight hours of actual work. An employer and employee may agree that the employee works in excess of the stipulated hours without added remuneration on condition, however, that the number of hours covered in a week does not exceed 48 hours. This translates into a maximum of eight hours per day, 48 hours per week and 192 hours per month (28 days) of working hours. Accordingly, sub-clause 6.5 needs to be amended to bring it into harmony with Zambian law so that agreed work hours for personnel do not exceed 48 hours a week.

13.5.1.9 Sub-clause 11.9 [Performance Certificate] and sub-clause 14.7(c) [Payment]

Sub-clause 11.9 provides that if an Engineer fails to issue a Performance Certificate, he/she is deemed to have issued one on the date 28 days after the date on which it should have been issued. This then allows for the Contractor to receive its final payment (if it has satisfied all other conditions) in accordance with sub-clause 14.7(c).

However, for publicly procured contracts in Zambia, parties will have to consider the effect of s 78(1) of the *Public Procurement Act*[118] which states that 'a person shall not process final payment of a contract sum where a defects liability certificate or certificate of final completion has not been issued'.

Accordingly, it would appear that if an Engineer omits or fails to issue a performance certificate, a Contractor can only be paid its final payment after an adjudication, arbitration or litigation decision ordering or compelling such payment. The law envisages that an Engineer will issue a Performance Certificate and does not seem to allow for deeming. Therefore, the appropriate dispute resolution processes will inevitably have to be invoked if there is a failure by the Engineer to issue a Performance Certificate.

118 *Act No. 8 of 2020.*

For consistency with Zambian law, it would be appropriate to include a Special Provision amending sub-clause 11.9 for publicly procured contracts so that a Performance Certificate is deemed to have been given on the same date as the DAAB/DAB decision or arbitration award.

13.5.2 FIDIC General Conditions are incompatible or inconsistent with the law of the Site/Country

There are no other FIDIC General Conditions which are incompatible or inconsistent with Zambian law apart from those considered in section 13.5.1 and those discussed in section 13.5.3 regarding dispute resolution.

13.5.3 FIDIC General Conditions are incompatible or inconsistent with the relevant laws on dispute determination in Zambia

FIDIC 2017 provides for three different types of dispute resolution procedures, namely:

1. Dispute Avoidance/Adjudication Boards (DAABs)
2. Amicable settlement, and
3. Arbitration.

All the aforementioned processes are permitted in Zambia save for the limitations discussed in the following.

13.5.3.1 Clause 21 [Disputes and Arbitration]

13.5.3.1.1 Fees

The FIDIC 2017 rainbow suite provides for a DAAB to be appointed at the inception of the contract. However, it is anticipated that in Zambia this clause will always have to be amended to provide for *ad hoc* DAABs in light of the restrictions in the *Public Procurement Act*[119] regarding amounts payable under a contract. It will not be possible to know prior to execution of the contract the number of disputes which might arise and what the fees of the DAAB will be.

13.5.3.1.2 Procedural issues

A further difficulty with the DAAB provision under the FIDIC 2017 rainbow suite is the enforceability of DAAB decisions. In contrast to statutory adjudication, such as in the United Kingdom, decisions of a DAAB are not automatically enforceable in Zambia. Therefore, where a losing party refuses to comply with a DAAB decision, the matter has to be referred to arbitration as provided for in sub-clause 21.7 and then finally, if needs be, to courts of law for enforcement proceedings. This can be a long journey for a party to obtain a binding and enforceable decision. As such, Contractors, especially, might be disadvantaged as cash flow might be hindered until an award is delivered. It is thus expected that, as has been seen previously with the 1999 Editions, this clause will be

119 *Act No. 8 of 2020.*

amended, especially if the contract has been terminated to allow parties to go straight to arbitration.[120]

In addition, Zambian law requires that an arbitral award should review the merits of the dispute for the award to be valid and enforceable. The *Arbitration Act No. 19 of 2000* defines an award as 'a decision of an arbitral tribunal on the substance of a dispute and includes any interim interlocutory or partial award on any procedural or substantive issue'.[121] Since an 'enforcement award' under sub-clause 21.7 does not delve into the merits of the dispute per se, but only into the failure to comply with the decision, such an award might not be enforceable.[122] Therefore, an award which seeks to enforce a decision of a DAAB may not be enforceable, rendering the entire clause otiose. Viewed from this angle, it would thus potentially be an expensive and time-consuming exercise to have such a DAAB mechanism embedded in the contract in jurisdictions like Zambia. Amendments to deal with this scenario are thus advisable.

The complexity of the matter is increased when one considers that most governments in the world enjoy immunity against execution of judgments, and therefore, this clause which allows for enforcement via arbitration is redundant for projects where the government and certain statutory bodies like the University of Zambia and Local Authorities (which all enjoy immunity against execution) are the Employers. The payee Contractor is thus at the mercy of the recalcitrant Employer. Accordingly, this clause might not provide the security it was intended to provide and is thus not fit for purpose for all projects in Zambia.

Perhaps a solution would have been to make provision for Employers, especially governments or government-related entities, to provide funding in advance for projects and that such funds should be kept in 'escrow'-type accounts or Payment Bonds which a Contractor can cash if there is a failure to pay by the Employer. It is not uncommon for developing governments to divert project funds for use in election campaigns or other areas they consider politically expedient at that time. Projects have suffered as a result of this. Accordingly, if a contract requires that funds or a substantial percentage of the funds are secured separately then this would be helpful for project completion. It should be noted that Contractors are often required to take out performance or similar bonds. Similarly, it would not be unconscionable to contractually require Employers to put in place mechanisms which guarantee payment to Contractors at the conclusion of the dispute resolution process. The provisions of sub-clause 2.4 requiring an Employer to simply state how they will finance the project might not be enough.

However, in amending this clause, Parties must be aware that whilst you could simply remove the entire DAB clause in FIDIC 1999, this might not be so easy with FIDIC 2017 as the DAAB is embedded in the dispute resolution procedures. It will thus be imperative for Parties to carefully consider this clause before amending it to avoid creating absurd or confusing scenarios. Put differently, the specific references to a DAAB in clause 21 cannot be deleted without amending or deleting other references to the DAAB in other clauses such as clause 3.

120 For Public contracts this might come with its own challenges as any amendments to a contract, including the dispute resolution clauses have to go through a defined process which includes approval of the Attorney General.

121 Section 2.

122 Editor's note: this issue was litigated in the Singapore High Court and Court of Appeal in the long running saga of *PT Pedrusahaan Gas Negara (Persero) TBK v CRW Joint Operation*. See Donald Charrett, *Contracts for Construction and Engineering Projects* (Informa Law from Routledge, 2nd edn 2022) Chapter 27.

13.5.3.2 Sub-clause 21.5 [Amicable Settlement]

After a DAAB has made a decision and a Party is dissatisfied with that decision, sub-clause 21.5 requires the Parties to attempt amicable settlement discussions before proceeding to arbitration. The mandatory amicable settlement period has been reduced from 56 days (as provided for in FIDIC 1999) to 28 days.

Further, what is immediately obvious from sub-clause 21.5, is that no clear procedure is outlined which the Parties should follow in their effort to reach an amicable settlement, whether it is mediation or direct negotiations, for instance.

The foregoing two factors render this clause impossible to use in public contracts in Zambia which, first of all, require that the dispute resolution methods must be stated in the Contract itself.[123] Secondly, the 28 days required to reach settlement might not be achievable considering that various authorisations have to be obtained prior to settlement, including from the Attorney General of the Republic of Zambia.[124]

13.5.3.3 Sub-clause 21.6 [Arbitration]

The last stop in FIDIC 2017 dispute resolution procedures is arbitration and the procedure is provideD for in sub-clause 21.6. FIDIC has continued with the preference for the International Chamber of Commerce (ICC) International Arbitration with an option of a one or three-member tribunal. The Rules of the ICC are thus applicable.

The following are the issues to consider in Zambia.

13.5.3.3.1 Jurisdiction

Sub-clause 21.6 reads, *inter alia*, as follows:

> Unless settled amicably, and subject to Sub-Clause 3.7.5 [*Dissatisfaction with Engineer's Determination*], Sub-Clause 21.4.4 [*Dissatisfaction with DAAB's decision*], Sub Clause 21.7 [*Failure to comply with DAAB's decision*] and Sub- Clause 21.8 [*No DAAB in place*], any Dispute in respect of which the DAAB's decision (if any) has not become final and binding shall be finally settled by international arbitration. (emphasis added)

This sub-clause appears straightforward until one uses a 'magnifying glass'. Firstly, the arbitration clause in the FIDIC 2017 rainbow suite is not an all-encompassing clause which can deal with all disputes arising from or in connection with the Contract as one would usually see in many well-used arbitration agreements. The FIDIC 2017 clause limits itself to 'Disputes', a defined term. Sub-clause 1.1.29 of FIDIC 2017, in a nutshell, defines 'Dispute' as, *inter alia*, a Claim made by one Party and rejected by the other Party or the Engineer. FIDIC 2017 presupposes that the '**D**ispute' is one which must be referred to the Engineer for his/her consideration first, before it can be escalated to the DAAB and subsequently to arbitration. Any '**d**ispute' which has not been so referred to the Engineer (and the DAAB), even if it arises from and is connected to the Contract, cannot be the subject of a FIDIC 2017 arbitration. This clause can be exploited by a party who might argue that the '**d**ispute' is not a '**D**ispute' as defined, and therefore, that the arbitral tribunal has no jurisdiction and that such a matter should be referred to the conventional courts for determination. Thus, for the avoidance of doubt, it is submitted that the Particular Conditions

123 Regulation 137(3)(h) of *Public Procurement Regulations No. 63 of 2011.*

124 Sections 73 and 77 of the *Public Procurement Act No. 8 of 2020.*

should make it clear that all disputes arising from or connected with the Contract can be submitted to arbitration

13.5.3.3.2 Interim orders

Another issue concerns the binding nature of a DAAB decision and whether that restricts an arbitral tribunal from granting a stay of execution of such a DAAB decision. Arbitral tribunals generally have powers to grant interim relief, including stays of execution of judgments or orders. Section 14 of the *Arbitration Act No. 19 of 2000* gives an arbitral tribunal power to grant an injunction or other interim orders such as a stay of execution. Does it therefore mean that an arbitral tribunal in Zambia is proscribed from using this power since the parties have agreed under FIDIC 2017 to be bound by the decisions of the DAAB and to comply with it immediately? It certainly can be argued as such. However, it may be difficult to accept that a contract can be used to curtail the jurisdiction granted to an arbitral tribunal by statute. Parties thus need to consider this sub-clause carefully and make any necessary amendments in the Particular Conditions to avoid arguments which could have the potential of derailing or prolonging proceedings.

13.5.3.3.3 Enforcement awards

Where an Engineer's determination or DAAB decision becomes final and binding, and the losing party chooses not to comply, the winning party can seek an enforcement award under sub-clause 21.7.[125] However, such an award might be challenged as it is a decision not on the merits as is required of arbitral awards.

The *Arbitration Act No. 19 of 2000* defines an 'award' as 'the decision of an arbitral tribunal on the substance of a dispute and includes any interim, interlocutory or partial award and on any procedural or substantive issue'. Therefore, an 'enforcement' award which is not based on the merits or substance of the case is not an award as defined by law and can be set aside or its enforcement challenged. Accordingly, in Zambia, this clause will invariably have to be deleted altogether or amended to bring it in line with prevailing legislation where possible.

13.6 What Special Provisions in the Particular Conditions are desirable for consistency with applicable laws in Zambia?

13.6.1 Sub-clause 21.6 [Arbitration]

An important issue which has raised considerable debate, especially from Africa, is FIDIC's insistence on the International Chamber of Commerce (ICC) as the Arbitration centre. In this regard, sub-clause 21.6 further reads in part as follows:

> Unless otherwise agreed by both Parties:
>
> (a) the Dispute shall be finally settled under the Rules of Arbitration of the International Chamber of Commerce;
> (b) the Dispute shall be settled by one or three arbitrators appointed in accordance with these Rules.

125 See sub-clauses 3.7.5 and 21.4.4 for when an Engineer's decision and DAAB decision respectively become final and binding.

There is evidence, especially from African countries, of growing discontent with international arbitration centres.[126] Ramsay J[127] is of the view that FIDIC should have allowed for a range of options to allow parties to apply themselves to what arbitration forum is appropriate for their needs. Africa has competent international arbitration centres which would make the arbitration process more affordable. The top five arbitral centres in Africa as determined by an independent coding exercise are the Arbitration Foundation of Southern Africa (**AFSA**); the Cairo Regional Centre for International Commercial Arbitration (**CRCICA**); the Ouagadougou Arbitration and Mediation and Conciliation Centre (**OAMCC**); the OHADA Common Court of Justice and Arbitration Centre (**CCJA**); and the Kigali International Arbitration Centre (**KIAC**).[128]

Based on current experience, it is expected that this sub-clause will be amended by the parties to allow for local or regional arbitration bodies to appoint and manage the arbitrations. International funders have in the past resisted the use of local or regional arbitration centres in Africa, but this too is expected to change.

13.7 Summary of applicable legislation for Zambian governing law of contract

All legislation in the following table applies throughout the whole of Zambia.

13.7.1 Entry into a construction contract

Construction Contracts	Procurement legislation applying to government procurement processes at national, provincial, and local government levels, including: *Constitution of Zambia, Chapter 1 of the Laws of Zambia* *Public Procurement Act No. 8 of 2020* and supporting *Regulations* *Local Government Act No. 2 of 2019* *The National Council for Construction Act No. 10 of 2020* and supporting *Regulations* *Public Finance Management Act No. 1 of 2018* *Citizens' Economic Empowerment Act No. 9 of 2006* *Competition and Consumer Protection Act No. 24 of 2010*

13.7.2 Termination of a construction contract

Bankruptcy, insolvency, liquidation	*Companies Act No. 10 of 2017*
	Corporate Insolvency Act No. 9 of 2017

13.7.3 Dispute resolution

Limitation periods	*The Limitation Act, 1939*
Liability	*The Law Reform (Miscellaneous Provisions) Act, Chapter 74 of the Laws of Zambia*
Arbitration	*Arbitration Act No. 19 of 2000* and *Regulations* published in terms thereof

126 T Chidede, 'How African Countries Approach ISDS Arbitration: Any Effect on the AfCFTA Investment Protocol?' (2019) Lagos: Lagos Chamber of Commerce International Arbitration Centre.

127 V Ramsey, 'Fireside Chat with Guest Speaker: An Interview with FIDIC Chief Executive Officer' (FIDIC, 2019) FIDIC International Contract Users' Conference held on 3 and 4 December 2019, London.

128 https://eprints.soas.ac.uk/33162/1/2020%20Arbitration%20in%20Africa%20Survey%20Report%2030.06.2020.pdf (accessed 31 May 2022).

13.8 Summary of applicable legislation if the Site/Country is in Zambia

All legislation in the following table applies throughout the whole of Zambia.

13.8.1 Operation of a construction contract

Registration and administration of professionals – engineers, architects, quantity surveyors, surveyors	*Zambia Institute of Architects Act, Chapter 442 of the Laws of Zambia* *The Engineering Institution of Zambia Act No. 17 of 2010* *The Land Survey Act, Chapter 188 of the Laws of Zambia* *Valuation Surveyors Act, Chapter 207 of the Laws of Zambia* *Quantity Surveyors Act, Chapter 438 of the Laws of Zambia* *Urban and Regional Planners Act No. 4 of 2011*
Registration/licensing of contractors and subcontractors	*The National Council for Construction Act No. 10 of 2020* and supporting *Regulations*
Labour	*Employment Code Act No. 3 of 2019* and supporting *Regulations* *Industrial and Labour Relations Act, Chapter 269 of the Laws of Zambia* *Local Authorities Superannuation Fund Act, Chapter 284 of the Laws of Zambia* *National Pension Scheme Authority Act, Chapter 256 of the Laws of Zambia* *Workers' Compensation Act No. 10 of 1999*
Design/Moral Rights	*The Registered Designs Act, Chapter 402 of the Laws of Zambia* *Trade Marks Act, Chapter 401 of the Laws of Zambia* *Patents Act No. 40 of 2016*
Copyright	*Copyright and Performance Rights Act, Chapter 406 of the Laws of Zambia*
Human Rights	*Constitution of Zambia, Chapter 1 of the Laws of Zambia* *Gender Equity and Equality Act No. 22 of 2015* *Mental Health Act No. 6 of 2019* *Persons with Disabilities Act No. 6 of 2012* *Anti-Gender Based Violence Act No. 1 of 2011*
First Nation people's land rights	*Constitution of Zambia, Chapter 1 of the Laws of Zambia* *Lands Act, Chapter 84 of the Laws of Zambia* *Lands Acquisition Act, Chapter 189 of the Laws of Zambia* *Lands and Deeds Registry Act, Chapter 185 of the Laws of Zambia* *Lands Tribunal Act No. 39 of 2010*
Planning	*Urban and Regional Planning Act No. 3 of 2015* and the *Regulations* prescribed therein *Urban and Regional Planners Act No. 4 of 2011*

Heritage	*The National Heritage Conservation Commission Act Chapter 173 of the Laws of Zambia*
Environment	*Constitution of Zambia, Chapter 1 of the Laws of Zambia* *Environmental Management Act No. 12 of 2011* and the *Regulations* prescribed therein *Water Resources Management Act No. 21 of 2011* *Mines and Minerals Development Act No. 11 of 2015* *The Solid Waste Regulation and Management Act, No. 20 of 2018* *Forests Act No. 4 of 2015* *Zambia Wildlife Act No. 14 of 2015*
Local procurement	*Constitution of Zambia, Chapter 1 of the Laws of Zambia* *Citizens' Economic Empowerment Act No. 9 of 2006* *Cooperatives Societies Act, Chapter 197 of the Laws of Zambia* *Public Private Partnerships Act No. 14 of 2009* *The National Council for Construction Act No. 10 of 2020* *Public Procurement Act No. 8 of 2020* *Competition and Consumer Protection Act No. 24 of 2010* *The Anti-Corruption Act No. 3 of 2012* *Local Government Act No. 2 of 2019*
Building and construction, permits, execution of construction work	*The National Council for Construction Act No. 10 of 2020* *Local Government Act No. 2 of 2019* *Public Procurement Act No. 8 of 2020* *Public Health Act (Building Regulations) Act, Chapter 295 of the Laws of Zambia* *Urban and Regional Planning Act No. 3 of 2015* and *Regulations* prescribed therein *Public Roads Act No. 12 of 2002*
Standard of construction work	*Standards Act No. 4 of 2017* *Public Health Act (Building Regulations) Act, Chapter 295 of the Laws of Zambia* *The National Council for Construction Act No. 10 of 2020*
Health and safety	*Occupational Health and Safety Act, No. 36 of 2010* *Occupier's Liability Act, Chapter 70 of the Laws of Zambia* *Factories Act Chapter 441 of the Laws of Zambia*
Calibration of testing, apparatus, equipment and instruments	*The National Council for Construction Act No. 10 of 2020* *Standards Act No. 4 of 2017*

Insurance	*Insurance Act, No. 38 of 2021* and supporting *Regulations* *National Health Insurance Act No. 2 of 2018* *Road Traffic Act, Chapter 464 of the Laws of Zambia*
Liability for defective work	*Standards Act No. 4 of 2017* *Competition and Consumer Protection Act, No. 24 of 2010*
13.8.2 Termination of a construction contract	
Bankruptcy, insolvency, liquidation	*Companies Act, No. 10 of 2017* *Insolvency Act, No. 9 of 2017*
Decennial liability and liability generally for the total or partial collapse of structures	*The National Housing Authority Act, Chapter 195 of the Laws of Zambia*
13.8.3 Dispute resolution	
Dispute before a local board	*Zambia Institute of Architects Act, Chapter 442 of the Laws of Zambia* *The Engineering Institution of Zambia Act No. 17 of 2010* *The Land Survey Act, Chapter 188 of the Laws of Zambia* *Valuation Surveyors Act, Chapter 207 of the Laws of Zambia* *Quantity Surveyors Act, Chapter 438 of the Laws of Zambia*
Limitation periods	*Limitation Act, 1939*

13.9 Applicable legislation if the 'seat' of the dispute determination is in Zambia

13.9.1 Sub-clause 21 (Disputes and Arbitration)

Adjudication in Zambia is contractual and not based on statute. The adjudication field is mostly dominated by Engineers, with a few lawyers being involved in some matters, mostly requiring three-member panels. Adjudication decisions are not directly enforceable. The compliance of an adjudication decision can be escalated to arbitration for an enforcement award, which in turn, has to be registered at the High Court.

With regard to arbitration, the applicable legislation if Zambia is the seat is largely the *Arbitration Act No. 19 of 2000*. This act adopts the *UNCITRAL Model Law* with some modifications. The first schedule to the *Act* is the *Model Law* and the main *Act* is the amendments. The way the *Act* is formatted has been a source of confusion amongst practitioners, as was noted by one Supreme Court of Zambia Judge who stated:[129]

> Before we determine this ground, we feel that it is necessary for us to explain once again the relationship between the **Arbitration Act** and the **Model Law** which is the First Schedule to the Act.

129 *China Henan international Cooperation Group Company Limited V. G and G Nationwide (Z) Limited* Selected Judgment No. 8 of 2017.

> We are compelled to do because of the position taken by counsel for the Appellant that Articles 13 and 16 of the **Model Law** are subordinate to section 17 of the **Arbitration Act** because the **Model Law** is a Schedule to the Arbitration Act. The **Model Law** was adopted by the United Nations Commission on International Trade Law (UNCITRAL) in June 1985 and was introduced onto the international plane for purposes of harmonizing arbitration laws and thus providing a law consistent with the United Nations Convention on the Recognition and Enforcement of Foreign Arbitral Awards of 1958 (the New York Convention) … After the **Model Law** was introduced nations were given an opportunity to adopt it into their domestic legislation either in its entirety or with modifications … When the old Arbitration Act, Chapter 40 of our laws was repealed and replaced by the Arbitration Act No 19 of 2000, Zambia chose to adopt the **Model law** with modifications which are contained in the sections in the Arbitration Act. By this we mean that the sections in the **Arbitration Act** vary the application of the **Model Law** by substituting certain Articles in the **Model Law** with the sections in the **Arbitration Act**. The First Schedule to the **Arbitration Act** confirms this because the articles of the **Model Law** that are not applicable to Zambia are clearly indicated as 'modified by' specified sections of the Act … The effect of the foregoing, as we stated in the case of **Zambia Revenue Authority v Tiger Limited and Zambia Development Agency** is that our **Arbitration Law** is in effect the **Model Law** … From a practical point of view, in applying the **Arbitration Act** one must at all times look at the First Schedule, first, and only where a particular Article is not applicable, does one resort to the section in the Act that has modified the Article.

In addition, the *Arbitration (Court Proceedings) Rules*[130] are used for all arbitration-related applications in the High Court for Zambia. Arbitrators are also expected to comply with *Arbitration (Code of Conduct and Standards) Regulations*.[131]

A further piece of applicable legislation is the *Investment Disputes Convention Act*,[132] which domesticates the *Convention on the Settlement of Investment Disputes Between States and Nationals of Other States* (1965) (***ICSID Convention***).

The most active arbitral body currently is the Chartered Institute of Arbitrators Zambia Branch which plays the role of training and appointing adjudicators and arbitrators.

Courts in Zambia have largely been very supportive of arbitration[133] and will not interfere in arbitral proceedings. Courts play supportive roles of appointing arbitrators or granting interim measures of protection. The courts' role in setting aside an award is also restricted.[134]

13.10 Summary of applicable legislation if the 'seat' of the dispute determination is in Zambia

All legislation in the following table is applicable throughout the whole of Zambia.

Dispute resolution	*Constitution of Zambia* *Supreme Court Act, Chapter 25 of the Laws of Zambia* *Constitutional Court Act No. of 2016* *Court of Appeal Act No. 7 of 2016* *High Court Act, Chapter 27 of the Laws of Zambia*

130 *Statutory Instrument No. 75 of 2001.*

131 *Statutory Instrument No. 12 of 2007.*

132 Chapter 42 of the *Laws of Zambia*.

133 Section 10 of *Arbitration Act No. 19 of 2000* has been widely deployed by courts to compel parties to take their disputes which have been wrongly commenced in the High Court, to arbitration.

134 Section 17 of the *Arbitration Act No. 19 of 2000*.

Limitation periods	*Limitation Act, 1939* *Law Reforms (Limitation of Actions, etc.) Act, Chapter 72 of the Laws of Zambia*
Arbitration	*Arbitration Act No. 19 of 2000* *Arbitration (Court Proceedings) Rules, Statutory Instrument No. 75 of 2001* *Arbitrators (Code of Conduct and Standards) Regulations, Statutory Instrument No. 12 of 2007*

13.11 Issues that a court or arbitrator may construe differently than expected from the words of the Contract because of local law or custom

13.11.1 The Constitution

As discussed earlier, the *Constitution of Zambia* is the Supreme Law of the land. In as much as there is no restriction on the governing law of a contract, courts or arbitrators will not apply foreign or indeed local laws which offend the *Constitution.*

13.11.2 Good faith/misrepresentation/unfair terms

The law of contract in Zambia does not imply good faith in contracts. Thus, an unfair term in the contract cannot be struck down without evidence of fraud or misrepresentation.[135]

Therefore, parties should consider the effect of ss 2 and 4 of the *Misrepresentation Act*,[136] which could release a party from contractual obligations imposed by a clause which was introduced into the contract by misrepresentation.

It is submitted that the *Competition and Consumer Protection Act, No. 24 of 2010* (the *CCPC Act*) may also assist a Contractor faced with an unfair contract term. Section 53 of the *CCPC Act* provides as follows:

> (1) In a contract between an enterprise and a consumer, the contract or a term of the contract shall be regarded as unfair if it causes a significant imbalance in the parties' rights and obligations arising under the contract, to the detriment of the consumer.
> (2) An unfair contract or an unfair term of a contract between a consumer and an enterprise shall not be binding.

Then s 53(4)(f) of the *CCPC Act* reads as follows:

> Any person who alleges that any person or an enterprise has concluded or is enforcing an unfair contract or term of contract to the detriment of that person may lodge a complaint with the [Competition and Consumer Protection] Commission in the prescribed manner and for.

Although s 53 relating to unfair contract terms applies to consumers and enterprises as narrowly defined in the *CCPC Act*, it is submitted that the use of the phrase 'any person' in s 54 makes this latter provision wide enough for Contractors to utilise to lodge complaints.

135 See the case of *Kalusha Bwalya v Chadore Properties & Another* Appeal No. 222 of 2013 and the case of *Pre-Secure Limited v Union Bank Zambia Limited and Ikakumari Girishi Desai* – Appeal No. 13/2003.

136 Chapter 69 of the *Laws of Zambia*.

The *CCPC Act*, however, is not specific with regard to what the Competition and Consumer Protection Commission (**CCPC**) can do should it determine that the Contractor's complaint is valid. It is submitted that the wide powers of the CCPC, and perhaps an application to the CCP Tribunal, could lead to the offending clause being struck down.

Courts or arbitrators might be called upon to consider the effect of a report having been made to the Competition and Consumer Protection Commission pursuant to s 53(4)(f) of the *Competition and Consumer Protection Act No. 24 of 2010* which provides as follows:

> Any person who alleges that any person or an enterprise has concluded or is enforcing an unfair contract or term of contract to the detriment of that person may lodge a complaint with the [Competition and Consumer Protection] Commission in the prescribed manner and form'

It is submitted that if the CCPC upholds such a complaint an arbitrator or court might be expected to reach the same conclusion with the effect that an unfair clause in a contract might be struck down

13.11.3 Sub-clause 1.4 (Law and Language)

Courts or arbitrators will not uphold a clause in a public contract which stipulates a language other than English as the law of the contract and also a law other than Zambian law as the governing law of the contract.

13.11.4 Sub-clause 1.7 (Assignment)

It is common practice for Contractors on public projects to borrow from banks using the receivables under the contract as security. A court or arbitrator might rule that this form of security is null and void or at best lacks precedent in light of s 74 of the *Public Procurement Act No. 8 of 2020.* Lenders would thus be wary to extend credit to Contractors on public projects using the expected payments under the contract as security.

13.11.5 Sub-clause 2.4 (Employer's Financial Arrangements)

By virtue of s 77(4) of the *Public Procurement Act*,[137] any Variations which will result in a cumulative additional payment of 25% or more of the original or Agreed Contract Sum cannot be upheld by a court or arbitrator and may lead to an order or award to the effect that such Variation automatically terminated the contract.

13.11.6 Sub-clause 2.5 (Site Data and Items of Reference), sub-clause 4.10 (Use of Site Data) and sub-clause 4.11 (Sufficiency of Accepted Contract Amount)

The defences afforded to an Employer by the above sub-clauses might be defeated by virtue of s 4 of the *Misrepresentation Act*.[138] An Employer guilty of misrepresentation, including innocent misrepresentation,[139] can be precluded from relying on the aforesaid sub-clauses

137 *Act No. 8 of 2020.*
138 Chapter 69 of the *Laws of Zambia.*
139 Compare with s 2 of the *Misrepresentation Act* which does not excuse innocent misrepresentation.

to defeat claims for EOT or additional costs from a Contractor who, for instance, in full reliance on Employer data suddenly meets unforeseen ground conditions. Considering that sub-clause 4.10 uses the phrase 'to the extent which was practicable (taking account of cost and time)' when placing investigatory obligations on the Contractor, a Contractor who totally relies on Employer data might succeed in its Claim if the evidence proves that there was misrepresentation by the Employer.

13.11.7 Sub-clause 3.7.4 (Effect of the agreement or determination)

Arbitrators cannot apply the slip-rule freely as provided for under sub-clause 3.7.4. A full discussion on this topic is in section 13.5.1.7.

13.11.8 Sub-clause 6.3 (Recruitment of Persons)

The principles discussed in section 13.5.1.8 will have to be applied by courts or arbitrators faced with claims that the restraints in sub-clause 6.3 are unreasonable.

13.11.9 Sub-clause 6.5 (Working Hours)

An agreement which compels the Contractor's staff to work beyond the statutory 48 hours per week will not be upheld as it is in violation of s 74 of the *Employment Code Act No. 3 of 2019.*

13.11.10 Sub-clause 8.7 (Rate of Progress) and sub-clause 8.8 (Delay Damages)

Where a Contractor delays the completion of the Works, the Employer is entitled to Delay Damages as stipulated in the Contract Data. Zambia adopts the common law position on liquidated damages and will only restrict their applicability in limited circumstances. For instance, if they are deemed unconscionable, or the sum payable is disproportionate to the loss suffered by the claiming party they will not be upheld.

13.11.11 Sub-clause 8.8 (Delay Damages)

This sub-clause provides for Delay Damages in instances where a Contractor has delayed completing the project. Court and arbitrators will generally uphold this sub-clause unless they violate the principles of the common law discussed in section 13.5.1.10.

13.11.12 Sub-clause 11.9 (Performance Certificate) and sub-clause 14.7(c) (Payment)

As discussed in section 13.5.1.9, if an Engineer omits or fails to issue a Performance Certificate, a Contractor can only be paid its final payment after an adjudication, arbitration or litigation decision ordering or compelling such payment. Therefore, the appropriate dispute resolution processes will inevitably have to be invoked if there is failure by the Engineer to issue a Performance Certificate.

13.11.13 Sub-clause 15.2 (Termination for Contractor's Default)

Sub-clause 1.16 provides for contract termination. This clause states as follows:

> *Subject to any mandatory requirements under the governing law of the Contract*, termination of the Contract under any Sub-Clause of these Conditions shall require no action of whatsoever kind by either Party other than as stated in the Sub-Clause.

Thus, where a Contractor becomes insolvent an Employer has an automatic right of termination as provided for in sub-clause 15.2.1(g). It has been argued that careful consideration should be had to this clause in light of the provisions of the *Companies Act*[140] as read with the *Corporate Insolvency Act*[141] which allows an insolvent company the option of continuing with a contract previously executed before the insolvency event.

13.11.14 Proportionate liability

In terms of s 10(1) of the *Law Reform (Miscellaneous Provisions) Act*,[142] where any person suffers damage as the result partly of his own fault and partly of the fault of any other person or persons, a claim in respect of that damage shall not be defeated by reason of the fault of the person suffering the damage, but the damages recoverable in respect thereof shall be reduced to such extent as the court thinks just and equitable having regard to the claimant's share in the responsibility for the damage.

The proviso to this s 10 however, upholds contractual provisions on limitation of liability such that the amount of damages recoverable by the claimant by virtue of this section shall not exceed the maximum limit so applicable under the contract.

13.11.15 Limitations of action/prescription

The law of contracts in Zambia recognises a six-year limitation period for contracts.[143] The timelines stipulated in sub-clause 20 (and previously sub-clause 19) have thus posed a challenge for many a practitioner with some arguing that the sub-clause is unlawful. There is no reported case from the Superior courts of Zambia on this point. However, it is expected that the courts and arbitrators will uphold the timelines in clause 20 following the principles in English cases like *Bremer Handelgesellschaft mbH v Vanden Avenne Izegem nv*[144] where the House of Lords held that a notice provision should be construed as a condition precedent, and so would be binding if:

(i) It states the precise time within which the notice is to be served, and
(ii) It makes plain by express language that unless the notice is served within that time the party making the claim will lose its rights under the clause.

140 *Act No. 10 of 2017.*
141 *Act No. 9 of 2017.*
142 Chapter 74 of the *Laws of Zambia.*
143 Section 2 of the *Limitation Act, 1939.*
144 [1978] 2 Lloyd's Rep. 113.

13.12 Additional references for Zambia

13.12.1 Books

Joseph Chirwa and Cross Silwamba, *The Law Relating to Construction in Zambia* (Joseph Chirwa, 2021)

Joseph Chirwa and Cross Silwamba, *Construction Law in Zambiua* (Diamond Books, 2022)

13.12.2 Internet

Laws of Zambia. www.parliament.gov.zm/acts/volumes

GLOSSARY

Term	Meaning	Defined in section
1977 Red Book	**FIDIC**[1] Conditions of Contract for Works of Civil Engineering Construction – Third Edition 1977.	**1.3.1**
1987 Red Book	**FIDIC** Conditions of Contract for Works of Civil Engineering Construction – Fourth Edition 1987.	**1.3.1**
1987 Yellow Book	**FIDIC** Conditions of Contract for Electrical and Mechanical Works – Third Edition 1987.	**1.3.1**
1995 Orange Book	**FIDIC** Conditions of Contract for Design-Build and Turnkey – First Edition 1995.	**1.3.1**
1999 Red Book	**FIDIC** Conditions of Contract for Construction – First Edition 1999.	**1.3.1**
1999 Silver Book	**FIDIC** Conditions of Contract for EPC/ Turnkey Projects – First Edition 1999.	**1.3.1**
1999 Yellow Book	**FIDIC** Conditions of Contract for Plant and Design-Build – First Edition 1999.	**1.3.1**
2017 Red Book	**FIDIC** Conditions of Contract for Construction – Second Edition 2017.	**1.3.1**
2017 Silver Book	**FIDIC** Conditions of Contract for EPC/ Turnkey Projects – Second Edition 2017.	**1.3.1**
2017 Yellow Book	**FIDIC** Conditions of Contract for Plant and Design-Build – Second Edition 2017.	**1.3.1**
AAK	Architectural Association of Kenya.	**8.2.10**
Abrahamson Principles	Principles of fair and balanced risk allocation, articulated in Max W Abrahamson, 'Risk Management' (1983) *International Construction Law Review* 241, 244.	**2.4**
Accepted Contract Amount	**FIDIC** definition (Red,[2] Pink, Yellow,[3] Gold and Emerald Books).	**FIDIC GCs**
ADCCAC	Abu Dhabi Commercial Conciliation and Arbitration Centre.	**12.2.11**
ADGM	Abu Dhabi Global Market.	**12.1.2**

(Continued)

(Continued)

Term	Meaning	Defined in section
adhesion contract	A contract in which its essential clauses are imposed or are drafted by one party, by a third person especially for a party or as a result of its instructions, the other party having only the possibility to accept the contract as such.	
ADIO	Abu Dhabi Investment Office.	**12.2.8**
ADM	Abu Dhabi Municipality.	**12.3.1**
ADR	Alternative dispute resolution – alternative to resolution by litigation in court.	
Advance Payment Certificate	**FIDIC** definition (2017 Red, 2017 Yellow and Emerald Books).	**FIDIC GCs**
Advance Payment Guarantee	**FIDIC** definition (2017 Red, 2017 Yellow, 2017 Silver[4] and Emerald Books).	**FIDIC GCs**
AEC	Architecture, engineering and construction.	**8.2.6**
AfDB	African Development Bank.	**9.2.1**
AFSA	Arbitration Foundation of Southern Africa.	**13.6.1**
AI	Artificial intelligence.	**11.2.6**
AIPEX	Foreign Investment Regulator (Angola).	**4.2.3**
amiable compositeur	An arbitrator acting as *amiable compositeur* is not bound by strict rules of law but is entitled to decide according to their subjective sense of what is fair and just (equitably) without strict regard to the rules of law that would otherwise apply. See also ***ex aequo et bono***.	**13.4.2**
ANPG	National Concessionaire Angolan Agency for Petroleum, Gas and Biofuels.	**4.2.8**
AOA	The symbol for Kwanza, the currency of Angola.	**4.2.1**
APIL	*Angolan Private Investment Law.*	**4.1.2**
Appendix to Tender	**FIDIC** definition (1987 Red, 1999 Red and 1999 Yellow Books).	**FIDIC GCs**
ARCON	Architects Registration Council of Nigeria.	**9.2.3**
ATCEA	Association of Turkish Consulting Engineers and Architects.	**11.2.10.4**
Bank	**FIDIC** definition (Pink Book).	**FIDIC GCs**
Base Date	**FIDIC** definition (Red, Pink, Yellow, Silver, Gold and Emerald Books).	**FIDIC GCs**
BaTCoDA	Building and Transport Construction Design Authority (Ethiopia)	**6.2.9**
BDS	Bid Data Sheet.	**6.4.2**
Bill of Quantities	**FIDIC** definition (1987 Red, Red, Pink and Emerald Books).	**FIDIC GCs**
BIM	Building information modelling or building information management.	**5.8**

Term	Meaning	Defined in section
Blue-Green Book	**FIDIC** Form of Contract for Dredging and Reclamation Works – First Edition 2006, Second Edition 2016.	**1.3.1**
bonos mores	Good manners (Latin).	**11.5.1.1**
BoQ	Bill of quantities.	
BORAQS	Board of Registration of Architects and Quantity Surveyors (Kenya).	**8.2.3.3**
Borrower	**FIDIC** definition (Pink Book).	**FIDIC GCs**
BOT	Build-Operate-Transfer.	**8.2.10**
BPP	Bureau of Public Procurement (Nigeria).	**9.2.3**
CAGR	Compound annual growth rate.	**5.2.1**
CAR insurance	Construction All Risks insurance or Contractor's All Risk insurance.	**7.2.9** **9.2.8**
casus fortuitus	A happening so exceptional or extraordinary as not to be foreseeable (South Africa).	**10.3.2**
causa	A lawful cause required for the existence of a contract in a civil law system.	
CBE	Central Bank of Egypt.	**5.2.12**
CCPC	Competition and Consumer Protection Commission (Zambia).	**13.4.2**
CIArb	Chartered Institute of Arbitrators.	**9.2.10**
CIDB	Construction Industry Development Board (South Africa).	**10.2.3**
civil law	A system of law in which the laws are codified in a large number of general rules and principles.	**1.1.2**
CJA	OHADA Common Court of Justice and Arbitration Centre (Ivory Coast).	**13.6.1**
Claim	**FIDIC** definition (2017 Red, 2017 Yellow, 2017 Silver and Emerald Books).	**FIDIC GCs**
COMESA	Common Market for Eastern and Southern Africa – a free trade area.	**6.2.8**
Commencement Date	**FIDIC** definition (1987 Red, Red, Pink, Yellow, Silver, Gold and Emerald Books).	**FIDIC GCs**
Commercial Law	*Egyptian Commercial Law No. 17 for 1999.*	**5.1.2**
common law	The body of law developed by judges from around the 11th century in England and later exported to its various colonies such as Canada, the USA, Australia, Fiji, Hong Kong, India, Malaysia and Singapore.	**1.1.2**
Completion Schedule	**FIDIC** definition (Emerald Book).	**FIDIC GCs**
Conditions of Contract	**FIDIC** definition (2017 Red, 2017 Yellow, 2017 Silver and Emerald Books).	**FIDIC GCs**
Contract	The construction contract being referred to.	**1.1.1**
Contract	**FIDIC** definition (1987 Red, Red, Pink, Yellow, Silver, Gold and Emerald Books).	**FIDIC GCs**
Contract Agreement	**FIDIC** definition (1987 Red, Red, Pink, Yellow, Silver, Gold and Emerald Books).	**FIDIC GCs**

(Continued)

(Continued)

Term	Meaning	Defined in section
Contract Data	**FIDIC** definition (2017 Red, Pink, 2017 Yellow, 2017 Silver, Gold and Emerald Books).	**FIDIC GCs**
contract of adhesion	See **adhesion contract**.	
Contract Participants	All the persons referred to in a **FIDIC Contract**.	**2.4**
Contract Price	**FIDIC** definition (1987 Red, Red, Pink, Yellow, Silver, Gold and Emerald Books).	**FIDIC GCs**
Contract Risk Management Plan	**FIDIC** definition (Emerald Book).	**FIDIC GCs**
Contract Risk Register	**FIDIC** definition (Emerald Book).	**FIDIC GCs**
Contractor	The party to a construction contract (the **Contract**) who carries out the work.	**1.1.1**
Contractor	**FIDIC** definition (1987 Red, Red, Pink, Yellow, Silver, Gold and Emerald Books).	**FIDIC GCs**
Contractor's Documents	**FIDIC** definition (Red, Pink, Yellow, Silver, Gold and Emerald Books).	**FIDIC GCs**
Contractor's Equipment	**FIDIC** definition (1987 Red, Red, Pink, Yellow, Silver, Gold and Emerald Books).	**FIDIC GCs**
Contractor's Key Equipment	**FIDIC** definition (Emerald Book).	**FIDIC GCs**
Contractor's Key Personnel	**FIDIC** definition (Emerald Book).	**FIDIC GCs**
Contractor's Personnel	**FIDIC** definition (Red, Pink, Yellow, Silver, Gold and Emerald Books).	**FIDIC GCs**
Contractor's Proposal	**FIDIC** definition (Yellow, Gold and Emerald Books).	**FIDIC GCs**
Contractor's Representative	**FIDIC** definition (Red, Pink, Yellow, Silver, Gold and Emerald Books).	**FIDIC GCs**
CORBON	Council of Registered Builders of Nigeria.	**9.2.3**
COREN	Council for the Regulation of Engineering in Nigeria.	**9.2.3**
Cost	**FIDIC** definition (1987 Red, Red, Pink, Yellow, Silver, Gold and Emerald Books).	**FIDIC GCs**
Cost Plus Profit	**FIDIC** definition (2017 Red, 2017 Yellow, 2017 Silver, Gold and Emerald Books).	**FIDIC GCs**
Country	**FIDIC** definition (Red, Pink, Yellow, Silver, Gold and Emerald Books).	**FIDIC GCs**
CRA	*Constitution of the Republic of Angola.*	**4.1.1**
CREL	*Centro de Resolução Extrajudicial de Litígios* – an Angolan arbitration centre established by *Executive Decree.*	**4.2.10**
CRICA	Cairo Regional Centre for International Commercial Arbitration.	**5.2.10** **13.6.1**
curial law	The law governing the existence and operation of the arbitral tribunal, generally the law of the 'seat' of arbitration. Also known as the ***lex arbitrii***.	**1.5.5**
DAAB	**Dispute Avoidance/Adjudication Board.**	**FIDIC GCs**

Term	Meaning	Defined in section
DAAB Agreement	**FIDIC** definition (2017 Red, 2017 Yellow, 2017 Silver and Emerald Books).	**FIDIC GCs**
DAB	**FIDIC** definition (1999 Red, 1999 Yellow, 1999 Silver and Gold Books).	**FIDIC GCs**
Date of Completion	**FIDIC** definition (Red, Yellow, Silver and Emerald Books).	**FIDIC GCs**
day	**FIDIC** definition (1987 Red, Red, Pink, Yellow, Silver, Gold and Emerald Books).	**FIDIC GCs**
Daywork Schedule	**FIDIC** definition (Red, Pink, 2017 Yellow, 2017 Silver and Emerald Books).	**FIDIC GCs**
DB	**FIDIC** definition (Pink Book).	**FIDIC GCs**
DBO	Design-Build-Operate.	**8.2.10**
DDA	Dubai Development Authority.	**12.3.1**
decennial liability	The joint liability of a **Contractor** and an architect for a period of ten years from the date of handover to compensate the **Employer** for any total or partial collapse of a building or installation, and for any defect which threatens the stability or safety of the building.	**12.5.1.2**
Defects Notification Period	**FIDIC** definition (Red, Pink, Yellow, Silver and Emerald Books).	**FIDIC GCs**
Delay Damages	**FIDIC** definition (2017 Red, 2017 Yellow, 2017 Silver and Emerald Books).	**FIDIC GCs**
dépeçage	Different issues within a particular case may be governed by the laws of different states (French).	**5.4.6**
design	All plans, drawings, sketches, instructions, and descriptions that determine the way the **Works** (or parts of them) are to be constructed. Design includes the writing or selection of specifications as well as the production of plans and drawings and any element of choice on the part of the designer, such as requirements as to materials or working methods.	
design contract	A contract for the preparation of a **design** to be constructed under a construction contract.	
DIAC	Dubai International Arbitration Centre.	**12.2.11**
DIFC	Dubai International Financial Centre,	**12.1.2**
Dispute	**FIDIC** definition (2017 Red, 2017 Yellow, 2017 Silver, Gold and Emerald Books).	**FIDIC GCs**
Dispute Avoidance/ Adjudication Board	**FIDIC** definition (2017 Red, 2017 Yellow, 2017 Silver and Emerald Books).	**FIDIC GCs**
Dispute Adjudication Board	A **Dispute Board** that provides a provisionally binding decision on a dispute referred to it; if neither party issues a notice of dissatisfaction within a defined time, the decision becomes final and binding.	

(Continued)

(Continued)

Term	Meaning	Defined in section
Dispute Board	A panel of one or three suitably qualified and experienced independent persons appointed under the **Contract** to provide a determination of a dispute referred to it. A Dispute Board may be a **Dispute Avoidance/Adjudication Board (DAAB)**, a **Dispute Adjudication Board (DAB)**, a **Dispute Review Board (DRB)** or a **Dispute Resolution Board (DRB)**.	
DNP	**Defects Notification Period.** FIDIC definition (2017 Red, 2017 Yellow, 2017 Silver and Emerald Books).	**FIDIC GCs**
doctrine of separability	The generally recognised principle of the law of international arbitration that an arbitration agreement incorporated in a contract is treated for legal purposes as a separate and independent agreement for the purpose of determining its validity or enforceability.	**1.5.6**
DOSHS	Directorate of Occupational Health and Safety (Kenya).	**8.2.5**
DPR	Department of Petroleum Resources (Nigeria).	**9.3.1.2**
Drawings	**FIDIC** definition (1987 Red, Red, Pink Books).	**FIDIC GCs**
E-GP System	Electronic – Government Procurement System (Zambia).	**13.2.7**
EBK	Engineers' Board of Kenya.	**8.2.3.2**
ECC	*Egyptian Civil Code of 1948.*	**5.1.2**
ECPN	Ethiopian Construction Practice Norm.	**6.2.13**
EIZ	Engineering Institute of Zambia.	**13.2.3**
ELRC	Employment and Labour Relations Court (Kenya).	**8.1.3**
Emerald Book	**FIDIC** Conditions of Contract for Underground Works, First Edition 2019.	**1.3.1**
Employer	The party to a construction contract for whom the work is done. Also referred to as the Principal or sometimes the Owner or Client.	**1.1.1**
Employer	**FIDIC** definition (1987 Red, Red, Pink, Yellow, Silver, Gold and Emerald Books).	**FIDIC GCs**
Employer's Equipment	**FIDIC** definition (Red, Pink, Yellow, Silver, Gold and Emerald Books).	**FIDIC GCs**
Employer's Personnel	**FIDIC** definition (Red, Pink, Yellow, Silver, Gold and Emerald Books).	**FIDIC GCs**
Employer's Representative	**FIDIC** definition (2017 Silver and Gold Books).	**FIDIC GCs**

Term	Meaning	Defined in section
Employer's Requirements	**FIDIC** definition (Yellow, Silver, Gold and Emerald Books).	**FIDIC GCs**
Employer-Supplied Materials	**FIDIC** definition (2017 Red, 2017 Yellow, 2017 Silver and Emerald Books).	**FIDIC GCs**
ENAA	Engineering Advancement Association of Japan.	**9.2.9**
Engineer	**FIDIC** definition (1987 Red, Red, Pink, Yellow and Emerald Books).	**FIDIC GCs**
Engineer's Representative	**FIDIC** definition (1987 Red, 2017 Red, 2017 Yellow and Emerald Books).	**FIDIC GCs**
EOC	Engineering Offices Commission (Jordan).	**7.2.1**
EOT	Extension of time.	
EPC contract	Engineer, procure and construct contract. A construction contract (also referred to as a turnkey contract) in which the **Contractor** takes total responsibility for the engineering (**design**), procurement and construction, and provides a fully equipped facility ready for operation (at the 'turn of the key').	**1.1.1**
EPCM contract	Engineer, Procure and Construction Management contract. A construction contract in which the **Contractor**, as Construction Manager, designs, procures and manages the construction as agent of the **Employer**.	**1.1.1**
EPS	Expanded polystyrene.	**8.2.6**
ERA	Ethiopian Road Authority.	**6.2.11**
ERP	Enterprise resource planning.	**11.2.6**
ESCONE	Egyptian Society for Consulting Engineers.	**5.2.10**
ex aequo et bono	Latin for 'according to the right and good' or 'from equity and conscience'. An arbitrator authorised to act *ex aqueo et bono* has the power to dispense with strict consideration of the law and consider solely what they consider to be fair and equitable in the circumstances.	**13.4.2**
exceptio non adempleti contractus	The exception of the unfulfilled contract (Latin).	**5.14**
exequatur	The ability to enforce an obligation through state authorities.	**5.5.3**
Excavation	**FIDIC** definition (Emerald Book).	**FIDIC GCs**
Exceptional Event	**FIDIC** definition (2017 Red, 2017 Yellow, 2017 Silver, Gold and Emerald Books).	**FIDIC GCs**
Extension of Time or **EOT**	**FIDIC** definition (2017 Red, 2017 Yellow, 2017 Silver and Emerald Books).	**FIDIC GCs**
fait du prince	Compliance with mandatory regulation (French).	**5.3.2**

(Continued)

(Continued)

Term	Meaning	Defined in section
FCCP	Federal Competition and Consumer Protection Commission (Nigeria).	**9.2.7.1**
FCCPA	*Federal Competition and Consumer Protection Act 2018* (Nigeria).	**9.2.7.1**
FCT	Federal Capital Territory (Nigeria).	**9.1.1**
FDRE	Federal Democratic Republic of Ethiopia.	**6.1.1**
FEC	Federal Executive Council (Nigeria).	**9.2.7**
Federation	The Egyptian Federation for Construction and Building Contractors.	**5.2.3**
FIDIC	International Federation of Consulting Engineers (Fédération Internationale des Ingénieurs-Conseils).	**1.3.1**
FIDIC	**FIDIC** definition (Red, Pink, Yellow, Silver, Gold and Emerald Books).	**FIDIC GCs**
FIDIC Golden Principles	The essential features of a FIDIC Contract that make the risk/reward allocation fair and balanced.	**2.1**
Final Payment Certificate or **FPC**	**FIDIC** definition (1987 Red, Red, Pink, Yellow and Emerald Books).	**FIDIC GCs**
Final Statement	**FIDIC** definition (Red, Pink, Yellow, Silver and Emerald Books).	**FIDIC GCs**
FOCI	Federation of Construction Industry (Nigeria).	**9.2.2**
force majeure	In civil law, *force majeure* applies to situations where the performance of a contract is substantially impossible, not merely something different from what was originally contemplated by the parties. In civil law systems, *force majeure* operates independently of party agreement, which means that it will protect an obligee even if the contract does not contain a *force majeure* clause. Since in civil law the liability is based on fault, the party will not be liable in case of *force majeure*.[5]	
Force Majeure	**FIDIC** definition (1999 Red, Pink, 1999 Yellow and 1999 Silver Books).	**FIDIC GCs**
Foreign Currency	**FIDIC** definition (1987 Red, Red, Pink, Yellow, Silver, Gold and Emerald Books).	**FIDIC GCs**
fraude à la loi	Fraudulent evasion of the law (French).	**5.4.6**
GCC 2015	General Conditions of Contract for Construction Works published by the South African Institution of Civil Engineering.	**10.2.10**
GCC	General Condition of Contract.	**6.5.1.3**

Term	Meaning	Defined in section
GCC	Gulf Cooperation Council – a political and economic union of Arab states bordering the Gulf. It was established in 1981 and its six members are the United Arab Emirates, Saudi Arabia, Qatar, Oman, Kuwait and Bahrain.	
GCs	**General Conditions**. **FIDIC** definition (Emerald Book).	**FIDIC GCs**
GDP	Gross domestic product.	
General Conditions	**FIDIC** definition (2017 Red, 2017 Yellow, 2017 Silver and Emerald Books).	**FIDIC GCs**
General Conditions	**FIDIC** definition (Red, Yellow, Silver and Emerald Books).	**FIDIC GCs**
GNP	Gross National Product.	
Gold Book	**FIDIC** Conditions of Contract for Design, Build and Operatre Projects – First Edition, 2008.	**1.3.1**
Goods	**FIDIC** definition (Red, Pink, Yellow, Silver, Gold and Emerald Books).	**FIDIC GCs**
governing law of the contract	The law that governs the Parties' contractual relations. Also known as the **proper law of the contract**.	**1.1.6**
GPs	**FIDIC Golden Principles**.	**2.1**
Green Book	**FIDIC** Short Form of Contract – First Edition, 1999.	**1.3.1**
Hague Principles	*Principles on Choice of Law in International Commercial Contracts* (2015) published by the Hague Conference on Private International Law.	**3.2.1**
Head Contract	A contract for construction of a facility between the owner or user of the facility (**Employer**) and a contractor (**Contractor**) who takes responsibility for construction of the complete **Works** in accordance with the requirements of the **Contract**. The **Contractor** generally employs one or more **Subcontractors** to execute some (but not all) of the **Works**.	**1.1.1**
HPR	House of People's Representatives (Ethiopia).	**6.1.3**
IAP	Infrastructure Action Plan proposed by **AfDB** in 2013 to guide Nigeria towards securing adequate financing for infrastructure development.	**9.2.1**
ICB	International competitive bidders (Ethiopia).	**6.2.10**
ICC	International Chamber of Commerce.	**7.2.11.2**
ICDR	International Centre for Dispute Resolution.	**7.2.11.2**

(Continued)

(Continued)

Term	Meaning	Defined in section
ICE	Institution of Civil Engineers.	**5.2.5**
ICRC	Infrastructure Concession and Regulatory Commission (Nigeria).	**9.2.1**
ICSID Convention	*Convention on the Settlement of Investment Disputes Between States and Nationals of Other States* (World Bank, 1965). Also known as the *Washington Convention.*	**13.9.1**
ICT	Information and communication technology.	**6.2.1**
IHI	Imperial Highway Authority (Ethiopia).	**6.2.11**
ILO	International Labour Organization.	**6.2.4, 9.3.1.3**
IMF	International Monetary Fund.	**5.2.12**
imprévision	The unexpected (it presumes the fulfilment of certain condition specifically imposed by the law).	**5.3.2**
IMSAD	Construction Material Manufacturers Association of Türkiye.	**11.2.12**
***in rem* claim**	A claim *in rem* literally means 'against the thing'. It is taken directly against property and it can be brought even though the owner has no personal liability.	**1.5.5**
INE	National Institute for Statistics (*Instituto Nacional de Estatística*) (Angola).	**4.2.11**
innominate contract	A contract that is not classifiable under any particular name (civil law).	
Interim Payment Certificate or **IPC**	**FIDIC** definition (1987 Red, Red, Pink, Yellow, Gold and Emerald Books).	**FIDIC GCs**
international construction contract	An international construction Contract is a contract for the provision of goods and services in which: (a) the parties to the Contract have, at the time of the conclusion of their agreement, their places of business in different legal jurisdictions; or (b) one of the following places is situated outside the legal jurisdiction in which the parties have their places of business: (i) the Site; or (ii) any place where a substantial part of the obligations for the Works is to be performed.	**1.1.7**
IP	Intellectual property.	
ipso facto	By the fact itself (Latin).	
ipso jure	By the operation of the law itself (Latin).	

Term	Meaning	Defined in section
IRCCOP	The Institute for the Regulation of Construction and Public Works (*Instituto Regulador da Construção Civil e Obras Públicas*) (Angola).	**4.2.1**
IT	Information technology.	**11.2.6**
JCCA	Jordanian Construction Contractors Association.	**7.2.1**
JCT	Joint Contracts Tribunal.	**9.2.9**
JICA	Japan International Cooperation Agency.	**1.3.2**
Joint Venture or **JV**	**FIDIC** definition (2017 Red, 2017 Yellow, 2017 Silver and Emerald Books).	**FIDIC GCs**
JV Undertaking	**FIDIC** definition (2017 Red, 2017 Yellow, 2017 Silver and Emerald Books)	**FIDIC GCs**
KIAC	Kigali International Arbitration Centre (Rwanda).	**13.6.1**
KCAA	Kenya Civil Aviation Authority.	**8.3.1.4**
LAD	Legal Affairs Department of the Government of Dubai (UAE).	**12.5.3**
LAV	*Law on Voluntary Arbitration* (Angola).	**4.1.2**
law of the forum	The law of the place in which court or arbitral proceedings are conducted.	**1.5.5**
Laws	**FIDIC** definition (2017 Red, Pink, 2017 Yellow, 2017 Silver, Gold and Emerald Books).	**FIDIC GCs**
LCIA	London Court of International Arbitration.	**7.2.11.2**
LCL	*Local Content Law* (Angola)	**4.2.8**
LDs	Liquidated damages.	
Letter of Acceptance	**FIDIC** definition (1987 Red, Red, Pink, Yellow, Gold and Emerald Books).	**FIDIC GCs**
Letter of Tender	**FIDIC** definition (Red, Pink, Yellow, Gold and Emerald Books).	**FIDIC GCs**
lex arbitrii	The law governing the existence and operation of the arbitral tribunal, generally the law of the 'seat' of arbitration. Also known as the **curial law**.	**1.5.6**
lex causae	Cause (for the) law (Latin) – the law or laws chosen by the forum court from amongst the relevant legal systems to arrive at its judgment of an international case.	
lex constructionis	The law relating to construction projects which is widely accepted internationally in legal jurisdictions subject to the rule of law and which recognises the parties' freedom of contract, irrespective of the specific impact of statute law (Latin).	**1.2**
lex fori	See **law of the forum**.	
lex loci contractus	The law of the place where a contract is made (Latin).	**5.4.2**

(Continued)

(Continued)

Term	Meaning	Defined in section
lex loci solutionis	The law of the place where relevant performance occurs (Latin).	**5.4.2**
lex loci rei sitae	A Latin phrase meaning law of the place where the property is situated.	**1.5.5**
lex situs	The law of the place where the property is situated.Inserted	**5.4.6**
Lining	**FIDIC** definition (Emerald Book).	**FIDIC GCs**
LLC	Limited liability company.	**8.2.3.1**
Local Currency	**FIDIC** definition (Red, Pink, Yellow, Silver, Gold and Emerald Books).	**FIDIC GCs**
lois de police	Overriding mandatory rules (French).	**5.4.6**
mandatory law or **mandatory rules of law**	Provisions of a statute which the parties to a contract may not derogate from.	**1.5**
Materials	**FIDIC** definition (Red, Pink, Yellow, Silver, Gold and Emerald Books).	**FIDIC GCs**
MDB	Multilateral Development Bank.	**1.3.2**
MIHUD	Ministry of Infrastructure, Housing and Urban Development (Zambia).	**13.2.3**
Milestone	**FIDIC** definition (Emerald Book).	**FIDIC GCs**
Milestone Certificate	**FIDIC** definition (Emerald Book).	**FIDIC GCs**
Model Law	*1985 UNCITRAL Model Law on International Commercial Arbitration.*	**Annexure to Chapter 1**
month	**FIDIC** definition (2017 Red, 2017 Yellow, 2017 Silver and Emerald Books).	**FIDIC GCs**
MoWUD	Ministry of Work and Urban Development (Ethiopia).	**6.2.11**
MoWUD 1994	Ministry of Work and Urban Development Standard Conditions of Contract for Construction of Civil Work Projects 1994 (Ethiopia).	**6.2.11**
MPWH	Ministry of Public Works and Housing (Jordan).	**7.2.10**
MSME	Micro, small, medium enterprise.	**13.2.8**
MUDHCo	Ministry of Urban Development, Housing and Construction (Ethiopia).	**6.2.13**
Muqawala	A *Muqawala* contract is an agreement to make a thing or to perform a task (UAE).	**12.4.2**
mutatis mutandis	Notwithstanding differences between two things being compared because of their different situations, the basic point remains the same.	
New York Convention	*United Nations 1958 New York Convention on the Recognition and Enforcement of Foreign Arbitral Awards.*	**1.8.1**
NCA	National Construction Authority (Kenya).	**8.2.1**
NCA Act	*National Construction Authority Act No. 41 of 2011* (Kenya).	**8.6.1.4**

Term	Meaning	Defined in section
NCB	National competitive bidding (Ethiopia).	**6.2.3**
NCC	National Council for Construction (Zambia).	**13.2.3**
NCPP	National Council of Public Procurement (Nigeria).	**9.2.7**
NHA	National Housing Authority (Zambia).	**13.2.3**
NHC	National Housing Corporation (Kenya).	**8.2.6**
NIA	Nigerian Institute of Architects.	**9.2.3**
NICON	National Insurance Commission (Nigeria).	**9.2.8**
NIOB	Nigerian Institute of Building.	**9.2.3**
NIQS	Nigerian Institute of Quantity Surveyors.	**9.2.3**
NMDPRA	Nigeria Midstream and Downstream Petroleum Regulatory Authority.	**9.3.1.2**
No-objection	**FIDIC** definition (2017 Red, 2017 Yellow, 2017 Silver and Emerald Books).	**FIDIC GCs**
NOD	**Notice of Dissatisfaction.**	**FIDIC GCs**
nominate contract	A contract with a particular name and defined rights and obligations prescribed by law (civil law).	
non-mandatory law or **non-mandatory rules of law**	Provisions of a statute which the parties can opt out of by appropriate agreement otherwise in their contract.	**1.5**
Notice	**FIDIC** definition (2017 Red, 2017 Yellow, 2017 Silver, Gold and Emerald Books).	**FIDIC GCs**
Notice of Dissatisfaction or **NOD**	**FIDIC** definition (2017 Red, Pink, 2017 Yellow, 2017 Silver and Emerald Books).	**FIDIC GCs**
NPCA	National Precast Concrete Association (USA).	**6.2.6**
NSE	Nigerian Society of Engineers.	**9.2.3**
NSIA	Nigeria Sovereign Investment Authority.	**9.2.1**
NUPRC	Nigeria Upstream Petroleum Regulatory Commission.	**9.3.1.2**
OAMCC	Ouagadougou Arbitration and Mediation and Conciliation Centre (Burkina Faso).	**13.6.1**
ONB	Open National Bidding (Zambia).	**13.2.8**
OIB	Open International Bidding (Zambia).	**13.2.8**
ordre public	Public policy (French).	**3.2.1**
OSH	Occupational safety and health.	**9.2.5**
pacta sunt servanda	A Latin phrase that means that agreements are to be kept.	**1.1.5**
Part	**FIDIC** definition (2017 Red, 2017 Yellow and Emerald Books).	**FIDIC GCs**
Particular Conditions	**FIDIC** definition (2017 Red, 2017 Yellow, 2017 Silver and Emerald Books).	**FIDIC GCs**
Party	**FIDIC** definition (Red, Pink, Yellow, Silver, Gold and Emerald Books).	**FIDIC GCs**
Payment Certificate	**FIDIC** definition (Red, Pink, Yellow and Emerald Books).	**FIDIC GCs**

(Continued)

(Continued)

Term	Meaning	Defined in section
PCL	*Public Contracts Law* (Angola).	**4.1.2**
PCs	**Particular Conditions**.	**2.3**
PDRE	People's Democratic Republic of Ethiopia.	**6.1.1**
Performance Certificate	**FIDIC** definition (Red, Pink, Yellow, Silver and Emerald Books).	**FIDIC GCs**
Performance Damages	**FIDIC** definition (2017 Yellow, 2017 Silver and Emerald Books).	**FIDIC GCs**
Performance Guarantees	**FIDIC** definition (1999 Silver Book).	**FIDIC GCs**
Performance Security	**FIDIC** definition (Red, Pink, Yellow, Silver, Gold and Emerald Books).	**FIDIC GCs**
Permanent Works	**FIDIC** definition (1987 Red, Red, Pink, Yellow, Silver, Gold and Emerald Books).	**FIDIC GCs**
PFI	Private Finance Initiative.	
PI insurance	Professional Indemnity insurance.	**7.2.9**
Pink Book	**FIDIC** Conditions of Contract for Construction MDB Harmonised Edition for Building and Engineering Works Designed by the Employer (MDB Harmonised Edition 2010).	**1.3.1**
PIP	Private Investment Project (Angola).	**4.2.3**
Plant	**FIDIC** definition (1987 Red, Red, Pink, Yellow, Silver, Gold and Emerald Books).	**FIDIC GCs**
PPA	Public Procurement Agency (Ethiopia).	**6.2.2**
PPA 2011	Public Procurement Agency Standard Conditions of Construction Contract 2011 (Ethiopia).	**6.2.2**
PPADA Act	*Public Procurement and Asset Disposal Act No 33* of 2015 (Kenya).	**8.2.8**
PBPPE	Prefabricated Building Parts Production Enterprise (Ethiopia).	**6.2.6**
PPE	Personal protective equipment.	**1.6.6**
PPOA	Public Procurement Oversight Authority (Kenya).	**8.2.8**
PPP	Public–Private Partnership.	**8.2.10** **9.2.1**
PPRA	Public Procurement Regulatory Authority (Kenya).	**8.2.8**
Programme	**FIDIC** definition (2017 Red, 2017 Yellow, 2017 Silver and Emerald Books).	**FIDIC GCs**
proper law of the contract	The law that governs the Parties' contractual relations. Also known as the **governing law of the contract**.	**1.1.6**
Provisional Sum	**FIDIC** definition (Red, Pink, Yellow, Silver, Gold and Emerald Books).	**FIDIC GCs**

Term	Meaning	Defined in section
public policy	Public policy is largely concerned with the potential for manifest unfairness or injustice within a given situation. Courts may disregard or refuse to give effect to contractual obligations which, whilst not directly contrary to any express or implied statutory prohibition, nevertheless contravene 'the policy of the law' as discerned from a consideration of the scope and purpose of the particular statute.	**1.1.4**
QM System	**FIDIC** definition (2017 Red, 2017 Yellow and 2017 Silver Books).	**FIDIC GCs**
QSRB	Quantity Surveyors Registration Board (Zambia).	**13.2.3**
QSRBN	Quantity Surveyors Registration Board of Nigeria.	**9.2.3**
Quality Management or **QM System**	**FIDIC** definition (Emerald Book).	**FIDIC GCs**
rainbow suite	The construction contracts published by **FIDIC**: Red Book Pink Book Yellow Book Silver Book	**1.3.1**
RDA	Road Development Agency (Zambia).	**13.2.3**
rebus sic stantibus	The civil law doctrine or rules relating to changed circumstances.	**1.2.3**
Red Book	**FIDIC** Conditions of Contract for Construction for Building and Engineering Works Designed by the Employer – First Edition 1999 and Second Edition 2017.	**1.3.1**
Retention Money	**FIDIC** definition (1987 Red, Red, Pink, Yellow, Silver, Gold and Emerald Books).	**FIDIC GCs**
Review	**FIDIC** definition (2017 Red, 2017 Yellow, 2017 Silver and Emerald Books).	**FIDIC GCs**
RFA	Request for approval.	
RFI	Request for information.	
Rome I	*Convention on the Law Applicable to Contractual Obligations. Regulation (EC) No 593/2008* of the European Parliament and of the Council of 17 June 2008 on the law applicable to contractual obligations.	**1.1.4**
SAICE	South African Institution of Civil Engineering.	**10.2.10**

(Continued)

(Continued)

Term	Meaning	Defined in section
SASRIA	South African Special Risk Insurance Association.	**10.2.9**
SBD	Standard Bidding Document.	**1.3.2**
SCC	Special Conditions of Contract.	**6.5.1.2**
SCC	Small Claims Court (Zambia).	**13.1.3.2**
Schedules	**FIDIC** definition (Red, Pink, Yellow, 2017 Silver, Gold and Emerald Books).	**FIDIC GCs**
Schedule of Guarantees	**FIDIC** definition (1999 Yellow Book).	**FIDIC GCs**
Schedule of Payments	**FIDIC** definition (Red, Yellow, Silver, Gold and Emerald Books).	**FIDIC GCs**
Schedule of Performance Guarantees	**FIDIC** definition (2017 Yellow, 2017 Silver and Emerald Books).	**FIDIC GCs**
Schedule of Rates and Prices	**FIDIC** definition (2017 Yellow, 2017 Silver and Emerald Books).	**FIDIC GCs**
Schedule, Payment Currencies	**FIDIC** definition (Pink Book).	**FIDIC GCs**
Section	**FIDIC** definition (1987 Red, Red, Pink, Yellow, Silver, Gold and Emerald Books).	**FIDIC GCs**
SEFA	Small Enterprise Financing Agency (South Africa).	**10.3.1**
Site	**FIDIC** definition (1987 Red, Red, Pink, Yellow, Silver, Gold and Emerald Books).	**FIDIC GCs**
Silver Book	**FIDIC** Conditions of Contract for EPC/Turnkey Projects – First Edition 1999, Second Edition 2017.	**1.3.1**
SME	Small and medium enterprise.	
SNCP	The National Service for Public Procurement (*Serviço Nacional de Contratação Pública*) (Angola).	**4.2.6.1**
Special Provisions	**FIDIC** definition (2017 Red, 2017 Yellow, 2017 Silver and Emerald Books).	**FIDIC GCs**
Specification	FIDIC definition (1987 Red, Red, Pink and Yellow Books).	**FIDIC GCs**
SRCN	Surveyors Registration Council of Nigeria.	**9.2.3**
stare decisis	'The decision stands' (Latin). The doctrine under which a common law court is required to follow previous decisions, unless they are inconsistent with a higher court's decision or determined to be wrong in law.	**1.1.2**
Statement	**FIDIC** definition (Red, Pink, Yellow, Silver, Gold and Emerald Books).	**FIDIC GCs**
STD	Standard tender documents.	**8.2.10**
Subcontractor	**FIDIC** definition (1987 Red, Red, Pink, Yellow, Silver, Gold and Emerald Books).	**FIDIC GCs**

Term	Meaning	Defined in section
sujétions imprévues	Technical difficulties of an unforeseeable nature and of sufficient magnitude to affect fundamentally the Contractor's performance (French).	**5.13**
Taking-Over Certificate	**FIDIC** definition (1987 Red, Red, Pink, Yellow, Silver and Emerald Books).	**FIDIC GCs**
Technical Committee	The specialised technical committee chaired by the Minister of Public Works and Housing that determines the specialised nature of projects requiring foreign expertise (Jordan).	**7.2.3**
Temporary Works	**FIDIC** definition (Red, Pink, Yellow, Silver and Emerald Books).	**FIDIC GCs**
Tender	**FIDIC** definition (1987 Red, Red, Pink, Yellow, Silver, Gold and Emerald Books).	**FIDIC GCs**
Tests after Completion	**FIDIC** definition (Red, Pink, Yellow, Silver and Emerald Books).	**FIDIC GCs**
Tests on Completion	**FIDIC** definition (1987 Red, Red, Pink, Yellow, Silver and Emerald Books).	**FIDIC GCs**
TG15	**FIDIC** Task Group 15, responsible for articulating the **FIDIC Golden Principles**.	**2.3**
Time for Completion	**FIDIC** definition (1987 Red, Red, Pink, Yellow, Silver and Emerald Books).	**FIDIC GCs**
tronc commun	Common core (French).	**5.4.1**
UAE	United Arab Emirates.	**12.1**
UAE Arbitration Law	*Federal Law No. 6 of 2018*, largely modelled on the *1985 UNCITRAL Model Law on International Commercial Arbitration* (as amended in 2006).	**12.1.2**
UNCITRAL	United Nations Commission on International Trade Law.	**1.5.6**
UNCITRAL Model Law	*UNCITRAL Model Law on International Commercial Arbitration 1985* with Amendments as adopted in 2006.	**1.8**
Underground Works	**FIDIC** definition (Emerald Book).	**FIDIC GCs**
Unforeseeable	**FIDIC** definition (Red, Pink, Yellow, Silver, Gold and Emerald Books).	**FIDIC GCs**
UNIDROIT	International Institute for the Unification of Private Law.	
Union	The 'independent, sovereign, federal state' of the **UAE**.	**12.1.1**
Variation	**FIDIC** definition (Red, Pink, Yellow, Silver, Gold and Emerald Books).	**FIDIC GCs**

(Continued)

Term	Meaning	Defined in section
vis major	A Latin term that means 'superior force' and describes an irresistible natural occurrence that causes damage or disruption that is neither caused by nor preventable by humans, even when exercising the utmost skill, care, diligence or prudence.	**10.3.2**
Washington Convention	The *ICSID Convention on the Settlement of Investment Disputes between States and Nationals of Other States*, a treaty formulated by the World Bank and ratified by 154 Contracting States.[6]	**13.2.11.2**
WHO	World Health Organization.	**4.3.1**
Works	**FIDIC** definition (1987 Red, Red, Pink, Yellow, Silver, Gold and Emerald Books).	**FIDIC GCs**
writing	**FIDIC** definition (1987 Red Book).	**FIDIC GCs**
WTO	World Trade Organization – the only global international organization dealing with the rules of trade between nations.[7]	**1.8.2**
WTO GPA	**WTO** Agreement on Government Procurement.	**1.8.2**
year	**FIDIC** definition (Red, Yellow, Silver, Gold and Emerald Books).	**FIDIC GCs**
Yellow Book	**FIDIC** Conditions of Contract for Plant and Design-Build for Electrical and Mechanical Plant and for Building and Engineering Works, designed by the Contractor – First Edition 1999, Second Edition 2017.	**1.3.1**
ZDA	Zambia Development Agency.	**13.2.8**
ZIA	Zambia Institute of Architects.	**13.2.3**
ZIP	Zambia Institute of Planners.	**13.2.3**
ZPPA	Zambia Public Procurement Authority.	**13.2.8**

1 Terms in bold are defined elsewhere in the Glossary.

2 Red Book refers to the 1999 Red Book and 2017 Red Book.

3 Yellow Book refers to the 1999 Yellow Book and 2017 Yellow Book.

4 Silver Book refers to the 1999 Silver Book and 2017 Silver Book.

5 Casalev Pepovic, 'Civil Law and Common Law: Two Different Paths Leading to the Same Goal' (2001) 32(3) *Victoria University of Wellington Law Review* 817. www.victoria.ac.nz/__data/assets/pdf_file/0008/830780/Pejovic.pdf (accessed 15 July 2018).

6 https://icsid.worldbank.org/sites/default/files/ICSID%20Convention%20English.pdf (accessed 24 July 2021).

7 www.wto.org/english/thewto_e/thewto_e.htm (accessed 9 November 2020).

INDEX